WINDOWS PROGRAMMING: AN INTRODUCTION

William H. Murray III and Chris H. Pappas

Osborne **McGraw-Hill**

Berkeley   New York   St. Louis   San Francisco
Auckland   Bogotá   Hamburg   London   Madrid
Mexico City   Milan   Montreal   New Delhi   Panama City
Paris   São Paulo   Singapore   Sydney
Tokyo   Toronto

Osborne **McGraw-Hill**
2600 Tenth Street
Berkeley, California 94710
U.S.A.

For information on translations and book distributors outside of the U.S.A.,
please write to Osborne **McGraw-Hill** at the above address.

A complete list of trademarks appears on page 633.

WINDOWS PROGRAMMING: AN INTRODUCTION

  3 4 5 6 7 8 9 0   DOC/DOC   9 9 8 7 6 5 4 3 2 1 0

ISBN 0-07-881536-3

WINDOWS PROGRAMMING: AN INTRODUCTION

William Murray —
To my cousin, Janet, who was doing windows before I was born.

Chris Pappas —
To my uncle Jim, who wouldn't buy a Lincoln till I did!

CONTENTS AT A GLANCE

CONTENTS

ACKNOWLEDGMENTS

Thanks must first go to the people at Osborne/McGraw-Hill for their help in the preparation of this manuscript. They bring a professional touch to every project. Additional recognition goes to Jeff Pepper, Senior Editor, for his special attention and professional guidance during this project.

Special thanks to the people at Microsoft Corporation for their help with software and technical questions. Windows 3.0 is "solid"—built upon a time-tested foundation. Congratulations on a superior operating environment and windows product.

This entire book was produced and edited on two IBM Model 80s running WordPerfect 5.0. Thanks to WordPerfect Corporation for a product that has made our writing so much easier. Additionally, the systems included 4MB of RAM, an 80387 math coprocessor, a 70MB hard drive, a VGA monitor, and a Microsoft mouse. All development work was completed with Microsoft's beta release of Windows 3.0 and tested with the final version. Additional software included the Microsoft Windows Software Development Kit, Microsoft C compiler, and Microsoft Assembler.

INTRODUCTION

What an exciting time for programmers. Windows 3.0 offers us a passageway into the next generation of graphical applications. Perhaps no other product has been more eagerly anticipated or needed than Windows 3.0. Windows 3.0 frees the programmer and software developer from the memory constraints of DOS. Windows 3.0 also offers the look and feel of its cousin, the OS/2 Presentation Manager. Together, these products will dominate both the DOS and OS/2 operating system environments. Now is the time to learn the programming techniques used in Windows.

You have declared, by purchasing this book, your interest in developing your programming capabilities in the Windows 3.0 environment.

We have assumed that you have Windows 3.0, the Windows Software Development Kit, the Microsoft C compiler, and the optional Macro Assembler packages correctly installed on your system. Some programming experience in C will be very helpful, but it is not absolutely necessary for you to use this book.

ABOUT THIS BOOK

There is a plan in the layout of this book. Early chapters get you off the ground by explaining and defining Windows terminology, the operating environment, and various functions. Simple programs illustrate these definitions and concepts. As you progress through later chapters, simple concepts are linked together to form more involved programs.

If you are a beginner to Windows programming, start with the first chapter of this book. Each chapter builds upon the knowledge gained in the previous chapter. Examples in early chapters are kept as short as possible. We want to teach programming concepts without burdening you with excessive program code. As you progress to later chapters, the programs become more involved, since we use earlier material as building blocks to more professional design. Stick with us—you will be absolutely amazed at what you can do by the end of this book.

If you are a seasoned C or Windows programmer you will be able to move at a more rapid pace through the book, learning about the new features of Windows 3.0. Our main programming language is C, but we will also show you some tricks with assembly language.

Many OS/2 Presentation Manager programming concepts are outgrowths of the DOS Windows environment. As you study the final chapters in this book, you will find that you have learned a lot about the Presentation Manager by learning Windows. Study the examples provided and with a little practice, you'll be able to write Presentation Manager applications in a minimum amount of time.

HOW THIS BOOK IS ORGANIZED

This book is arranged in a fashion that will introduce you to both Windows 3.0 programming theory and example programs on a graduated level. Chapters 1 and 2 teach the fundamental Windows concepts and terminology. Chapter 3 will help you develop your first Windows program, a platform from which many other applications can be launched. Chapters 4 and 5 show various methods and techniques for manipulating the Windows window.

Techniques and Skill Development

In Chapter 6 you will learn how to create your own icons, cursors, and bitmaps. These are the items that bring your screen alive. In Chapter 7 you will see how to incorporate menus and keyboard accelerators into your program code. Chapter 8 is a very important chapter. This chapter shows how to use dialog boxes for data entry. In this chapter you will learn how to input characters, integers, and real data types from the keyboard.

Chapter 9, "Fancy Fonts", will allow you to break out of the standard system font and use different fonts in your programs. But you say, "I came here for graphics." Well, Chapter 10 will teach you how to use the many Windows graphics primitives for drawing lines, boxes, circles, and arcs. The skills you learn in Chapter 10 will be put to good use in Chapter 11, for it's here that you will learn how to create presentation-quality graphics. The examples in this chapter include techniques for pie, bar, and line charts. In Chapter 12 the graphics concepts of the previous chapter will be further developed, and in 13 a Mouse-A-Sketch program will allow freehand drawing on the screen. Additionally, you will learn animation techniques and apply them to simple figures. The final chapter in this section, Chapter 14, is a power chapter. In this chapter assembly language is used to allow interfacing with external devices. The concepts are presented in a simple programming and hardware environment utilizing the parallel port as the I/O channel.

The remaining chapters are devoted to exploring the similarities and differences between Windows and the Presentation Manager. This section contains more than just a discussion. You will see and learn how to write and convert Windows programs to Presentation Manager programs. The skills developed here will prepare you for the challenges of DOS and OS/2 today and in the future.

CONVENTIONS

It was no easy task to settle on typographical and stylistic conventions for this book. We have attempted to mimic the style used in the Microsoft documentation. Ultimately, we settled on a minimum of typographical changes in text that we hope will make it easy on you, the reader.

The Microsoft Windows functions appear in roman text. They are easily distinguishable by their mixed-case spelling; for example, CreateWindow and WinMain. Boldface is used for **MAKE** because of the special place it holds in the C language. A boldface letter within a menu option indicates that letter is pressed to select the option.

C functions, statements, and keywords are italic, whereas Microsoft keywords (or reserved words) appear in all uppercase letters. File names and program names are also all uppercase. Variables and types are italic, and new terms appear in italic type when they are defined or explained.

ADDITIONAL HELP FROM OSBORNE/McGRAW-HILL

Osborne/McGraw-Hill provides top-quality books for computer users at every level of computing experience. To help you build your skills, we suggest that you look for the books in the following Osborne series that best address your needs.

The "Teach Yourself" Series is perfect for people who have never used a computer before or who want to gain confidence in using program basics. These books provide a simple, slow-paced introduction to the fundamental uses of popular software packages and programming languages. The "Mastery Skills Check" format ensures your understanding concepts thoroughly before you progress to new material. Plenty of examples and exercises (with answers at the back of the book) are used throughout the text.

The "Made Easy" Series is also for beginners or users who may need a refresher on the new features of an upgraded product. These in-depth introductions guide users step-by-step from the program basics to intermediate-level usage. Plenty of "hands-on" exercises and examples are used in every chapter.

The "Using" Series presents fast-paced guides that cover beginning concepts quickly and move on to intermediate-level techniques and some advanced topics. These books are written for users already familiar with computers and software who want to get up to speed fast with a certain product.

The "Advanced" Series assumes that the reader is a user who has reached at least an intermediate skill level and is ready to learn more sophisticated techniques and refinements.

"The Complete Reference" Series provides handy desktop references for popular software and programming languages that list every command, feature, and function of the product along with brief but detailed descriptions of how they are used. Books are fully indexed and often include tear-out command cards. "The Complete Reference" series is ideal for both beginners and pros.

"The Pocket Reference" Series is a pocket-sized, shorter version of "The Complete Reference" series. It provides the essential commands, features, and functions of software and programming languages for users of every level who need a quick reminder.

The "Secrets, Solutions, Shortcuts" Series is written for beginning users who are already somewhat familiar with the software and for experienced users at intermediate and advanced levels. This series provides clever tips, points out shortcuts for using the software to greater advantage, and indicates traps to avoid.

Osborne/McGraw-Hill also publishes many fine books that are not included in the series described here. If you have questions about which Osborne books are right for you, ask the salesperson at your local book or computer store, or call us toll-free at 1-800-262-4729.

OTHER OSBORNE/McGRAW-HILL BOOKS OF INTEREST TO YOU

We hope that *Windows Programming: An Introduction* will assist you in mastering this fine product, and will also pique your interest in learning more about other ways to better use your computer.

If you're interested in expanding your skills so you can be even more "computer efficient," be sure to take advantage of Osborne/McGraw-Hill's large selection of top-quality computer books that cover all varieties of popular hardware, software, programming languages, and operating systems. While we cannot list every title here that may relate to Windows and to your special computing needs, here are just a few books that complement *Windows Programming: An Introduction.*

If you're already programming with OS/2, see *OS/2 Presentation Manager Graphics: An Introduction* (ISBN: 0-07-881474-X) for a guide to unlocking the power of Presentation Manager graphics. The book starts with basic concepts and a discussion of individual Presentation Manager commands, and then builds to increasingly complex programs for line, bar, and pie charts.

OS/2 Programming: An Introduction (ISBN: 0-07-881427-8) is a fast-paced text that quickly gets you up to speed on OS/2 version 1.1 intermediate-level programming techniques. A background in assembly language programming is not a prerequisite although many sample C programs are used in the text. Applications are emphasized.

OS/2 Programmer's Guide, Second Edition, Volume 1 (ISBN: 0-07-881533-9), written by Ed Iacobucci, leader of the IBM OS/2 design team, offers an in-depth introduction to OS/2 through version 1.1, and presents a complete overview of the OS/2 operating system and Presentation Manager.

OS/2 Programmer's Guide, Second Edition, Volume 2 (ISBN: 0-07-881534-7), also by Ed Iacobucci, is written for experienced OS/2 programmers and provides comprehensive coverage of the OS/2 API structure of version 1.1 and advanced multitasking. It also includes thorough appendixes covering OS/2 function calls, the family API, OS/2 error codes, linker control statements, and sample programs.

DOS: The Complete Reference, Second Edition (ISBN: 0-07-881497-9) is a handy desktop resource to keep on hand for all your questions about MS-DOS and PC-DOS through version 3.3. Whether you're a beginner who

needs an overview of the disk operating system or an experienced programmer who needs a reference for advanced programming and disk
management techniques, you'll find it here. All DOS commands and features are clearly defined and presented in short applications.

WHY THIS BOOK IS FOR YOU

Are you a C programmer looking for the bold adventure of Windows 3.0 programming? If you are then this is the book for you!

Windows Programming: An Introduction is a fresh new look at Windows programming. Each chapter is carefully crafted to take you, the C programmer, on a journey that skillfully increases your Windows programming ability.

You'll learn Windows terminology, fundamentals, and tricks as programming examples illustrate all fundamental Windows concepts. Fonts, graphs, bitmaps, assembly language connections, hardware interfaces, menus, keyboard accelerators, and animation are covered in theory as well as by example.

LEARN MORE ABOUT WINDOWS

Here is another excellent Osborne/McGraw-Hill book on Microsoft Windows that will help you build your skills and maximize Windows' power.

Windows 3 Made Easy by Tom Sheldon is a quick-paced guide that briefly covers Windows fundamentals before focusing on Windows capabilities in customizing your system. You'll also find plenty of tips to help you experiment with Windows outside of your usual applications.

1

INTRODUCTION TO WINDOWS CONCEPTS

Microsoft Windows is the pinnacle of Microsoft's graphics-based operating environment. It brings together point-and-shoot control, pop-up menus, and the ability to run applications written specially for Windows, as well as standard applications that run under DOS.

WHAT IS WINDOWS?

Microsoft Windows is an operating environment that runs under MS-DOS. It is a graphics-based multitasking windowing environment. Programs written specifically for Windows all have a consistent appearance and command structure that makes new Windows applications easier to master.

For application development, Windows provides an abundance of built-in subroutines that allow easy implementation of pop-up menus, scroll bars, dialog boxes, icons, and many other features of a user-friendly graphical interface. Starting with Windows 3.0, applications can take advantage of new dialog controls, menu types, and "owner-draw controls." By using the extensive graphics programming language provided with Windows, an application can easily format and output text in a variety of fonts and pitches.

Windows also permits the applications developer to treat the video display, keyboard, mouse, printer, serial port, and system timers in a device-independent manner. This allows the same application program to run identically on a variety of hardware configurations.

Microsoft Windows is also an essential component of OS/2 (Operating System/2), developed jointly by Microsoft and IBM. Under this new protected-mode operating system, Windows is called "Presentation Manager." In the future, OS/2's Presentation Manager will be the primary development environment for graphics-based application programs.

While Windows and Presentation Manager share many design fundamentals, such as the user interface, the application program interface (API) is different—especially for graphics. The last portion of this book will address the conversions necessary to port a Windows application over to the API of OS/2 Presentation Manager.

A HISTORICAL PERSPECTIVE

To understand the historical development of graphics hardware and the foundation on which Windows is based, it is necessary to look back 40 years. Back in the 1940s, computers used hard-copy devices (antique by today's standards) that required users to sift through reams of printout. One of the first computers to use the cathode ray tube (CRT) was a 1950 system built at MIT (Massachusetts Institute of Technology) to investigate aircraft stability and control. The linking of this now-common display device and the computer was prompted by a need to shorten the time between user input and computer output. Aircraft also inspired the SAGE air-defense system of the 1950s, which converted radar blips into crude computer-generated images. This system was also the first to use a light pen to select symbols on a display screen.

Moving into the early 1960s, an MIT Ph.D. candidate developed the Sketchpad line-drawing system. This system enabled the user to sketch by directing a light pen at points on the screen. The graphics system could then draw lines or construct polygons between the points, thereby simplifying the creation of complex diagrams replicating simple objects.

Early CRTs could draw a straight line between any two points on the display screen. However, since the image faded away very quickly it had to be redrawn several times per second. Back in the 1960s, this required memory in which to store the line endpoints and hardware for rapidly redrawing the line—both of which were very expensive. For example, in 1965, IBM introduced the first mass-produced CRT for this type of graphics display. At a measly $100,000 for the display alone, you can easily see why more installations weren't made during this time.

Three years later, Tektronix developed the first storage-tube CRT. This type of CRT was capable of retaining a drawing until the user no longer needed it. Because of the display's architecture, expensive memory and redraw hardware could be eliminated, thereby bringing the cost of the display down to $15,000. At this price, the Tektronix display became an immediate success.

The graphics development environment was further encouraged in the 1970s by the dramatic reduction in the cost of both memory and hardware logic units. These developments led to a proliferation of memory-intensive raster-scan displays that could produce realistic looking shaded and colored images.

In the late 1980s, display monitors are no longer digital. The output from the IBM video graphics array (VGA) is analog, although to maintain compatibility with previous application environments, all previous video modes are supported. Monochrome, color graphics adapter (CGA), and enhanced graphics adapter (EGA) modes are reproduced through the VGA adapter. For example, if an analog monochrome display is connected to a VGA, colors will be converted to shades of gray. Additionally, several new modes are available with the VGA:

- 640 × 480 graphics (2 color and 16 color)

- 720 × 400 text (monochrome and color)

- 360 × 400 text (16 color)

- 320 × 200 graphics (256 color)

The future will bring monitors with increasing resolution and larger color palettes. And with a properly written Windows program, the source code will need no changes at all to take advantage of these imminent developments!

Software — (From BIOS 10H to Windows)

To understand the historical development of graphics software, let's take a moment to discuss BIOS (basic input/output subroutines). Built into every IBM PC, PS/2, and clone is a set of BIOS routines that are stored in ROM (read-only memory). These stored subroutines provide an interface to standard hardware features, including the time-of-day clock, the keyboard, floppy and fixed disks, and, of relevance for Windows, the video subsystem.

The video BIOS routines comprise a set of simple tools for performing basic video programming tasks, such as writing strings of characters to the screen, erasing the screen, changing colors, and so on.

Interrupt 10H

Historically, to perform any real-time graphics, a programmer had to write an assembly language program to access these BIOS routines that, coincidentally, were also written in assembly language. To access the video portion of BIOS, a programmer using the Intel family of 8086 processors must issue an Interrupt 10H.

The ROM BIOS supports several video input/output functions, each accessed by executing an Interrupt 10H. These functions are numbered; before executing an Interrupt 10H, the programmer must place the number of the desired function in the appropriate register, for example, ah.

When the interrupt is executed, other registers on the microprocessor may contain additional parameters to be passed to the BIOS routines. If the Interrupt 10H function called returns data to the program, it does so by leaving the data in one or more of the microprocessor registers. However, this register-based parameter-passing protocol is intended primarily for use in assembly language programs.

High-Level Languages

Regarding software, it is quite possible that your first experience with computer graphics was with BASIC commands: LINE, CIRCLE, COLOR, and so on. You may then have moved on to other languages, such as Pascal. This would have given your programs more structure, but not much more graphics capability.

With the introduction of Borland's Turbo Pascal, programmers were given a tremendously rich graphics environment. Starting with Turbo Pascal 4.0, sophisticated features such as viewports, clipping, user-definable fill patterns, three-dimensional bars, and many more, were available.

Another popular developmental language is C, which has been described as the best of both worlds—assembly language and a high-level language combined. C provides programmers with the hardware accessibility of assembly language and the powerful logical structures provided by a high-level language. C programmers can now include whole libraries of sophisticated graphics routines once reserved for dedicated graphics-intensive applications.

But what is missing from this brief historical journey is any discussion of concurrent graphics applications. Every program written up to this point in the continuum had exclusive use of the entire video subsystem, including all registers, memory, and display devices.

But as users' expectations for both hardware and software increased, demand grew for programs that could run concurrently. Users are no longer content to wait for a database to finish sorting before they edit a letter—they want to do both at the same time.

This demand helped usher in products such as Quarterdecks's DESQ-view and Microsoft Windows that gave the user multitasking capabilities. What is even more important are the graphic device interfaces provided by Windows.

With the Windows GDI (graphics device interface) functions, a programmer can write an application that will look familiar to the user (with menus, scroll bars, message boxes, and so on), and can be resized, moved, iconed, put into the background, and more, while other programs are

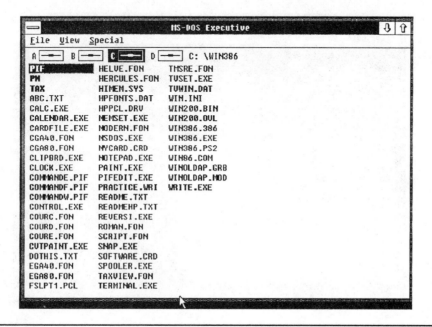

Figure 1-1.   MS-DOS Executive

working simultaneously. Even more important are the GDI functions that allow one application to communicate with another, although most applications still do not take full advantage of this powerful capability.

This brief historical survey of hardware and software developments illustrates how quickly both can change. What the user and applications developer wants today is a graphics-oriented user interface, multitasking capability, and hardware independence. Windows has come of age.

WHAT DOES WINDOWS DO?

The Windows operating environment offers considerable advantages to both users and programmers over the more conventional MS-DOS environment. Individually, the three primary capabilities (graphics-oriented user interface, multitasking, and hardware independence) are not new. What is innovative is attempting to combine all three of them into a single micro-computer operating environment.

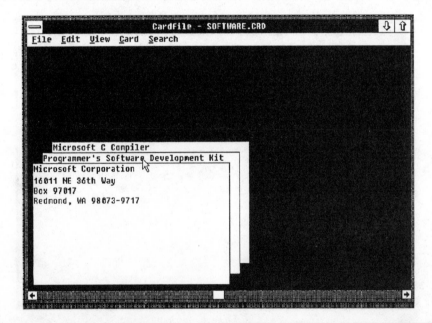

Figure 1-2.   Windows Cardfile

Standardized User Interface

Of the three primary capabilities provided by Windows, the standardized graphics-oriented user interface is the most noticeable, and certainly the most important for the user. The consistent user interface uses pictures, or *icons*, to represent drives, files, subdirectories, and many of the operating system commands and actions. Figure 1-1 shows what a typical MS-DOS Executive window looks like. Programs are identified by caption bars, and many of the basic file manipulation functions are accessed through menus by pointing and clicking with the mouse. Most Windows programs have both a keyboard interface and a mouse interface. Although most functions of Windows programs can be controlled through the keyboard, using the mouse is often easier for many tasks.

The user will no longer have to spend long hours learning to use a new application program since Windows programs all have the same "look." Figures 1-2 (Windows Cardfile) and 1-3 (Windows Write) illustrate this similarity; note the common File and Edit options and the scroll bars. For

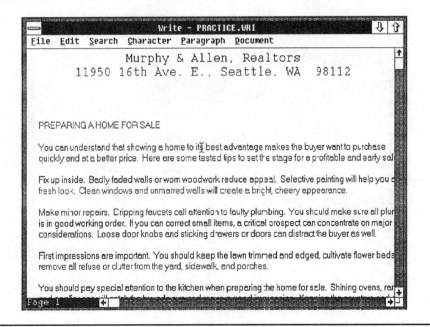

Figure 1-3.   Windows Write

the programmer, this consistent user interface is achieved by using the subroutines built directly into Windows to construct menus and dialog boxes. All menus have the same keyboard and mouse interface because Windows handles this job itself rather than the application program.

Multitasking

A multitasking operating system allows the user to have several applications, or several instances of the same application, running concurrently. Although some people still wonder whether multitasking is necessary on a microcomputer, the obvious success of such TSR (terminate-and-stay-resident) applications as SideKick and the Norton Guides, suggests that it is. Figure 1-4 shows several *tiled* Windows applications, each program occupying a rectangular window on the screen. At any time, the user can move the windows on the screen, change their size, switch between different applications, and exchange information among windows.

While the example (Figure 1-4) shows four concurrently running processes, only one of them can actually use the processor at any given time.

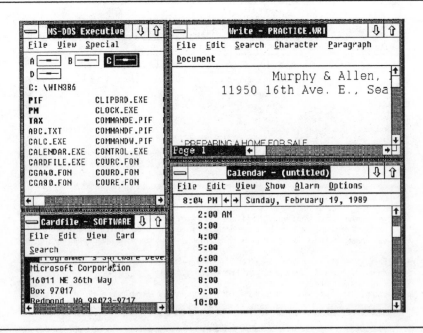

Figure 1-4.   Several tiled Windows applications

The distinction between a task that is processing and one that is merely running is important. There is also a third state that an application may be in, called the *active state*. An active application is the one receiving the user's attention. Just as only one application can be processing at any given instant, so there can be only one active application at a time. However, there can be any number of concurrently running tasks. Partitioning up the microprocessor's time is the responsibility of Windows. It controls the sharing of the microprocessor by using queued input and messages.

Prior to multitasking operating systems, application programs had exclusive control of all the computer's resources, including the input and output devices, memory, the video display, and even the CPU itself. Under Windows, however, all of these valuable resources must be shared. For example, a standard C program no longer has access to all the memory not used by the system, the program itself, or any TSR programs.

Memory Management

Memory is one of the important shared resources under Windows. With more than one application running at the same time, the applications must cooperate to share memory in order not to exhaust the resource. Additionally, as new programs are started up and old ones are terminated, memory can become fragmented. Windows is capable of consolidating free memory space by moving blocks of code and data in memory.

Windows permits applications to "over-commit" memory. That is, an application can contain more code than will actually fit into memory at one time. Windows can discard code from memory and later reload the code from the program's .EXE file.

Under other circumstances, a user may have several instances, or copies, of the same program running concurrently. To conserve space Windows shares the same code. Programs running in Windows can even share routines located in other .EXE files. The files that contain these shared routines are called *dynamic link libraries*. Windows includes the mechanism to link the program with the routines in the dynamic link library at run time. (Windows itself is a set of dynamic link libraries.) To facilitate all of this, Windows programs use a new format of .EXE file, called the "new executable" format. These files include the information Windows needs to manage the code and data segments and to perform the dynamic linking.

Queued Input

Just as memory is a shared resource under Windows, so too is keyboard and mouse input. No longer can a C program read directly from the keyboard by means of a *getchar* function call. Under Windows, an application does not make explicit calls to read from the keyboard or mouse input devices. Instead, Windows receives all input from the keyboard, mouse, and timer, in what is called the *system queue*. It is the queue's responsibility to redirect the input to the appropriate application by copying it from the system queue into the application queue. At this point, when the application is ready to process any input, it reads from its queue and dispatches a message to the appropriate window.

This input is provided in a uniform format called an *input message*. All input messages specify the system time, state of the keyboard, scan code of any depressed key, position of the mouse, which mouse button has been pressed (if any), as well as information specifying which device generated the message.

All keyboard, mouse, and timer messages have the identical format and are all processed in the same manner. Additionally, with each message, Windows provides a device-independent virtual key code that identifies the key (it doesn't matter which type of keyboard it is on), the device-dependent scan code generated by the keyboard, and the status of other keys on the keyboard, such as NUM LOCK, ALT, SHIFT, and CTRL.

With the keyboard and mouse being a shared resource, one keyboard and one mouse must supply all the input for each program running under Windows. With the keyboard, all input messages go directly to the currently active window. However, mouse messages are handled differently; they are sent to the window that is beneath the mouse cursor.

Timer messages are very similar to keyboard and mouse messages. Windows allows a program to set a timer so that one of its windows receives a message at periodic intervals. This message goes directly into the program's message queue. There are also other messages that get into a program's message queue as a result of the program calling certain Windows functions. (These will be discussed individually as they occur in example programs.)

Messages

Windows' message system is the underlying structure used to disseminate information in a multitasking environment. From your application's viewpoint, a message can be seen as a notification that some event of interest has occurred, which may or may not require a specific action. These events may be initiated by the user, such as clicking or moving the mouse, changing the size of a window, or making a menu selection. However, the signaled event could also be generated by the application. For example, a graphics-based spreadsheet could have finished a recalculation resulting in a need to update the displayed pie chart. Here the application would send itself an "update window" message.

It is also possible for Windows to generate messages, as in the case of a "close session" message. In this example, Windows must inform each application of the intent to shut down. One last major message source could be an instrument monitoring program, indicating that a critical chemical process has reached the specified temperature. Regardless of the source of the message, your program must take the appropriate action.

There are two major points to keep in mind when thinking about the role of messages in Windows. First, it is through the message system that Windows achieves its multitasking capabilities. The message system makes it possible for Windows to share the processor among different applications. Each time Windows sends a message to the application program it also grants processor time. (Actually, an application can only get access to the microprocessor when it receives a message.)

The second role of messages under Windows is to enable an application to respond to events in the environment, whether these events are generated by the application itself, by other concurrently running applications, by the user, or by Windows. Each time an event occurs, Windows makes a note of it and distributes an appropriate message to the interested applications. Therefore, at the simplest level, one could say that the major task of a Windows application is to process messages.

Device Independence

The third major capability provided by Windows is hardware device independence. Historically, you have seen how quickly the hardware devices an application program may have to interact with can change. In particular, you've seen the benefits of hardware independence as it relates to the video display. This section will focus on just how device independence is accomplished.

Windows frees the programmer from having to account for every possible variety of monitor, printer, and input device available. Currently, a non-Windows application must be written to include drivers for every possible device. Obviously, this is one of the major inefficiencies in software development.

Typically, to make an application capable of printing on any printer, the programmer furnishes a different driver for each one. This requires many software companies to write essentially the same device driver over and over, for instance, an IBM ProPrinter II driver for WordPerfect, one for WordStar, one for Ami, and so on.

In the Windows environment, each device driver—whether for a video display, printer, keyboard, or mouse—need only be written once. Instead of each software firm writing its own complete set, the hardware company writes one driver for the system. Microsoft includes many drivers with Windows, and others are available from the hardware manufacturer. One of the enhancements available with Windows version 3.0 and later is external support for font cartridges. This has been incorporated into the Hewlett-Packard LaserJet (HPPCL.DRV) driver. When Windows is installed, it includes one driver for each device in the current system. Whenever a command is sent from an application to print or draw, Windows feeds the output through the appropriate driver. Incorporating the necessary drivers directly into the system eliminates a great deal of redundant programming effort.

For the application developer, nothing could be easier. Your application interacts with Windows rather than with any specific device. It doesn't need to know what printer is hooked up. A command is sent from the application to draw a filled rectangle; Windows carries it out on the latest "3-D Surrealistic Animation Holographic SilkScreener." By the same token, each device driver works with every Windows application. Developers save time, and users no longer have to worry whether each new application will support their favorite generic brand light pen.

Windows accomplishes this device independence by specifying the capabilities the hardware must have. Used in conjunction with the Software Development Kit routines Windows provides your application, these are the minimum capabilities required to ensure the appropriate routines will function. Every Software Development Kit routine, regardless of its complexity, is capable of breaking itself down into the minimal set of operations required of a device. For example, not every plotter is capable of drawing an ellipse. As an application developer, however, you can still use the Kit routines to draw an ellipse, even if the plotter has no specific ellipse capabilities. Since every plotter connected to Windows must be minimally capable of drawing a line, Windows can break the ellipse routine down into a series of small lines.

Regarding input, Windows is able to specify a set of minimum capabilities to ensure your application will receive only valid, predefined input. Windows has predefined the set of legal keystrokes; in other words, Windows predefines all the keystrokes that a Windows application can possibly receive. The valid set is very similar to that produced by the IBM PC keyboard. Should a manufacturer produce a keyboard containing keys that do not exist in the Windows list of acceptable keys, the manufacturer would also have to supply additional software that would translate these "illegal" keystrokes into Windows' legal keystrokes. This predefined Windows input covers all the input devices, such as the mouse. Therefore, even if someone should develop a six-button mouse, you don't have to worry. The manufacturer would again have to supply the software necessary to convert all mouse input to Windows' predefined possibilities of mouse-button clicks.

Dynamic Link Libraries

Much of Windows' functionality is provided by new dynamic link libraries, called DLLs, which enhance the base operating system by providing a powerful and flexible graphics user interface. Dynamic link libraries contain predefined functions that are linked with an application program when it is loaded (dynamically), instead of when the .EXE file is generated (statically).

Windows did not originate the idea of dynamic libraries. For example, the C language depends heavily on libraries to implement standard functions for different systems. The linker copies run-time library functions, such as *getchar* and *printf*, into a program's executable file. Libraries of functions save each programmer from having to re-create a new procedure for a common operation such as reading in a character or formatting output. Programmers can easily build their own libraries to include additional capabilities such as changing a font and justifying text. Making the function available as a general tool eliminates redundant design.

As mentioned earlier, Windows libraries are dynamically linked. In other words, the linker does not copy the library functions into the program's executable file. Instead, while the program is executing, it makes calls to the function in the library. Naturally, this conserves memory. No matter how many applications are running, there is only one copy of the library in RAM at a time.

By changing the library format, Windows libraries are more versatile. While they have retained the same format as any other DOS executable file (although they cannot themselves be executed), they can hold anything programs hold. Besides functions, libraries can also encode data and even incorporate graphics resources such as cursor shapes and bitmaps. Windows libraries expand the range of shared resources and save programmers even more time.

Technically speaking, when a Windows application makes a call to a Windows function, the compiler must generate machine code for a far intersegment call to the function that is located in a code segment in one of the Windows libraries. This presents a problem, since until the program is actually running inside Windows, the address of the Windows function is unknown.

The solution to this problem is called *delayed binding* or *dynamic linking*. In Windows 3.0, or later versions, with only one minor change you can link a program using either the LINK provided in C version 6.0, or the linker that comes with Pascal. (The LINK4.EXE that is provided with the Windows Software Development Kit version 2.1 can also be used.) These linkers allow a program to have calls to functions that cannot be fully resolved at link time. Only when the program is loaded into memory to be run are the far function calls resolved.

Included in the Software Development Kit are special "import libraries" that are used to properly prepare a Windows program for dynamic linking. LIBW.LIB and SLIBW.LIB are the import libraries that will be used for many of the small-model Windows programs used in this text. The SLIBW.LIB library contains a record for each Windows function that your program can call. This record defines the Windows module that contains this function, and in many cases, an ordinal value that corresponds to the function in the module.

For example, a Windows application could make a call to the Windows' PostMessage function. When you link the program, the linker finds the PostMessage function listed in SLIBW.LIB. The linker obtains the ordinal number for the function and embeds this information in the program's .EXE file. When the program is run, Windows then links the call your program makes with the actual PostMessage function.

"New Executable" Format

The old MS-DOS executable-file header format had no place to embed all the additional dynamic link information. Instead, Windows programs use a format of .EXE file called the *new executable* format. This new format includes a "new-style" header.

Windows' library modules include KERNEL, USER, and GDI, which contain routines that help programs running under Windows to carry out various chores, such as sending and receiving messages. These library modules provide functions that can be called from the application program or from other library modules. To the module that contains the functions, the functions are known as *exports*. The new executable format identifies these exported functions with a name and an ordinal number. Included in the new executable format is an *entry table* section that indicates the address of each of these exported functions within the module.

Conversely, from the viewpoint of the application program, the library functions a program uses are known as *imports*. Using the various relocation tables, far calls the application makes to an imported function can be identified. Almost all Windows programs contain at least one exported function, or a function that is called from outside the program. This window function, generally from one of the library modules, is one that receives Windows messages. It is important that the application flag this function as exported so that Windows can allow the function to be properly called from an external module.

The new executable format also provides the additional information on each of the code and data segments in a program or library. Typically, code segments are flagged as "moveable" and "discardable," while data segments are flagged only as "moveable." This allows Windows to move code and data segments in memory, and even discard code segments if additional memory is needed. If Windows later decides it needs a discarded code segment, it can easily reload the code segment from the original .EXE file. Windows even has a third category called *load on call*. This defines a program or library code segment that will not be loaded into memory at all unless a function in the code segment is called from another code segment. This sophisticated memory management technique allows Windows to simultaneously run several programs in a memory space that would normally be sufficient for only one program.

MS-DOS Applications

Windows can easily run many existing MS-DOS programs, although its primary purpose is to run applications written specifically for it. The older or "standard" MS-DOS applications can be divided into two major categories: those that can run in a Windows window and those that cannot. A "well-behaved" application is one that uses the MS-DOS and PC BIOS software interrupts (described earlier) to read the keyboard and write to the display. Well-behaved applications can generally be run in a window.

An "ill-behaved" application is one that writes directly to the video display, uses graphics, or takes direct control of the hardware keyboard interrupts. Ill-behaved applications cannot run in a window. However, the latest version of Windows, which exploits the "virtual 86" mode of the 80386 microprocessor, provides a partial solution to this problem.

ENHANCEMENTS TO WINDOWS STARTING WITH VERSION 3.0

Along with the greatly improved performance, memory management, and multitasking capabilities starting with Windows version 3.0, there are many other major changes, including the following:

- Direct access to extended memory

- Up to 16 megabytes of virtual memory as a result of swapping memory pages to and from disk
- A Palette Manager that allows applications to take full advantage of the color capabilities of a device
- Device-independent color icons and bitmaps
- Device-independent cursors and icons that automatically select the appropriate device-specific image from a predefined set of images provided by the application
- An enhanced user interface that allows an application to use new dialog box controls, menu types, "owner-draw" controls, and a wider variety of font selections

The Windows Software Development Kit has also been enhanced to include

- A more adaptable installation procedure
- Three new tools: a color icon/bitmap and cursor editor, a CPU profiler, and a segment-swapping reporter
- Enhancements to the dialog editor, the font editor, the RC compiler, CodeView Windows, and the heap walker
- The Windows help compiler

WHAT YOU NEED TO GET STARTED

The intent of this book is to help moderately experienced C programmers make the transition to writing applications that use the Microsoft Windows application program interface. The text covers how to use all necessary Windows functions, messages, and data structures to carry out useful tasks common to all Windows applications. The book also introduces the reader to the OS/2 Presentation Manager, and addresses the issue of porting Windows applications over to Presentation Manager.

The C programming language is the preferred development language for Windows applications. Many of the programming features of Windows were designed with the C programmer in mind. Windows applications can also be developed in Pascal and assembly language, but these languages present additional challenges that are typically avoided when writing applications in C.

To build most Windows applications you will need the following development tools:

Development Tool	Windows Command
Microsoft C Optimizing Compiler	cl
Microsoft Resource Compiler	rc
Microsoft C 6.0, Pascal, or the Segmented_Executable Linker	link or link4
Microsoft Windows Icon Editor	sdkpaint
Microsoft Windows Dialog Editor	dialog
Microsoft Program Maintenance Utility	make
Microsoft CodeView Debug Utility	cvw
Microsoft Windows Software Development Kit	

The Software Development Kit is separate from Windows and must be ordered directly from Microsoft. The Kit includes several development utilities and libraries, as well as additional documentation from Microsoft (the *Programmer's Utility Guide, Programming Guide, Quick Reference Guide,* and *Application Style Guide*). The Microsoft documentation states that the minimal hardware requirements for Windows are a personal computer using an Intel 80286/80386 microprocessor (including IBM PS/2, PS/2 Model 80, COMPAQ 80386-based personal computers, and compatibles) or equipped with an Intel Inboard 386/AT. The faster processors are necessary for development work because of the time required to compile a Windows program. The following optimal development environment is suggested, although more elementary configurations may work:

- 2MB memory

- DOS 4.0 or later

- 1.2MB (5 1/4-inch) or 720K (3 1/2-inch) disk drive

- Hard disk

- Graphics adapter card (EGA, VGA, or compatible)

- Microsoft mouse

Note: The *Application Style Guide,* included in the Development Kit, is particularly useful because it makes specific recommendations regarding the appearance and behavior of the user interface you develop for your Windows applications. Since consistency between applications is one of the keys to satisfying users and making your program a success, it is recommended that you follow these guidelines.

Windows Software Development Kit

The Microsoft Windows Software Development Kit includes all the tools needed to develop graphical applications for Microsoft Windows 3.0. The Software Development Kit includes

- Enhanced application programming interface (API) that makes it easier to write Windows applications and increases execution speed of finished applications
- A user interface for applications that comply with IBM's systems application architecture (SAA) (visually consistent with the OS/2 Presentation Manager user interface)
- Support for Intel 80287/80387 math coprocessor
- Enhanced SDKPAINT for creating device-independent icons, cursors, and bitmaps
- Description of the dynamic data exchange (DDE). This allows your applications to communicate with other Windows applications without the user being aware of it
- Standardized TIFF (tagged image file format) for storing and transferring scanned and graphic images
- Revised *Programmer's Reference*

2

WINDOWS CONCEPTS
AND TERMINOLOGY

Windows concepts and terminology can be broken down into two major categories: those features of Windows that are visible, such as menus and icons; and the behind-the-scenes operations, such as messages and function access. In order for Windows application developers to communicate effectively with one another, all of the Windows features have been given a name and an associated usage. This chapter will introduce you to the basic vocabulary that will enable you to confidently discuss and develop Windows applications.

WHAT IS A WINDOW?

To the user, a window in Windows is a rectangular portion of the screen with an application-independent appearance. This is the visual interface between the user and the application generating the window. To the application, the window is a rectangular area of the screen that is under the control of the application. The application creates and controls everything about the window, including its size and shape. When the user starts a program, a window is created. Each time the user clicks on a window option, the program responds. Closing a window causes the program to terminate.

The role the window plays in representing the fundamental substructure of the Windows' system is just as important as this visual user-application information exchange. For example, while the window itself represents the graphics-oriented user interface, it is also the visible manifestation of both multitasking and hardware independence. The visible overlap of applications conveys to the user the true multitasking capabilities of Windows. By partitioning the screen into different windows, the user can direct input to a specific application within the multitasking environment by using the keyboard or mouse to select one of the concurrently running applications. Windows then intercepts the user's input and allocates any necessary resources (such as the processor) as needed.

The hardware-independent substructure of Windows is also highlighted by the window metaphor. To each application running under Windows, its window is the screen. However, since Windows does not permit applications direct access to the physical screen, all interaction must be performed through the window. Because of Windows' intervention, it doesn't matter to the application that the window may only be a portion of the entire display; to the application, the window *is* the entire display. Windows intervenes between applications and all I/O (input or output) devices, taking care of any differences.

THE VISUAL INTERFACE

All Windows applications have in common certain features and behaviors, such as borders, control boxes, and About boxes that give Windows a comforting predictability from application to application. Figure 2-1 shows the ten fundamental components of a window, explained in the following sections.

The Border

All Windows windows have a *border* around them. The border consists of the lines that frame a window. To the newcomer, the border may appear only to delineate one application window from another. However, a closer examination of several overlapped Windows applications will reveal something quite different. Not only does the border serve as a screen boundary, but it also indicates the active window. And by moving the mouse pointer over a border, the user can change the size of the window.

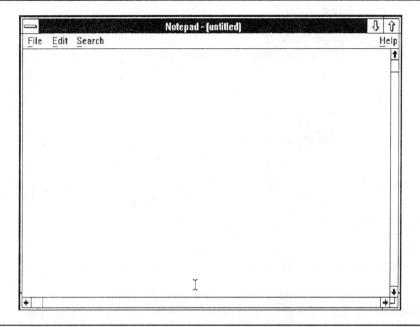

Figure 2-1.   Fundamental components of a Windows window

The Title Bar

To the application developer, one of the parameters passed to the Create-Window function is the *title bar* information. The title bar displays the name of the application program centered at the top of the associated window. They can be very useful for remembering which applications are concurrently running.

The Control Box

All Windows applications use a *control box*. The control box is a small white box with a flat, shadowed rectangle in the window's upper-left corner. Clicking the mouse pointer on the control box will cause Windows to display the system menu.

The System Menu

The *system menu* is activated by clicking the mouse pointer on the control box. It provides standard application options such as **Restore**, **Move**, **Size**, **Minimize**, **Maximize**, and **Close**.

The Minimize Box

The upper-right corner of each window displays two vertical arrows, one of which represents the *minimize box*. The minimize box contains a downward pointing arrow that causes the window to be shrunk down to a small picture, or icon.

The Maximize Box

The *maximize box*, in the upper-right corner of each window, displays an upward pointing arrow. The maximize box is used to make an application's window fill the entire screen, thereby covering any other concurrently running applications.

The Vertical Scroll Bar

Right below each window's maximize box is the *vertical scroll bar*. The vertical scroll bar has an arrow at either end, pointing in opposite directions, a colored band, and a transparent window block. The window block shows the position of the currently displayed contents in relation to the document as a whole, which is represented by the colored band. The vertical scroll bar is used to select which one of multiple pages of output you would like displayed. Clicking the mouse on either arrow shifts the display one line at a time. Clicking the mouse on the transparent window block below the upward arrow, and dragging it, causes screen output to be quickly changed to any portion of the application's screen output. One of the best uses for the vertical scroll bar is to move through a multiple-page word processing document.

The Horizontal Scroll Bar

The *horizontal scroll bar* is at the bottom of each window. It has arrows at its extremes that point in opposite directions, a colored band, and a transparent window block. The transparent window block shows the position of the currently displayed contents in relation to the document as a whole, which is represented by the colored band. The horizontal scroll bar is used to select which one of multiple columns of information you would like displayed. Clicking the mouse on either arrow causes the screen image to be shifted one column at a time. Clicking the mouse on the transparent window block, to the right of the left-pointing arrow, and dragging it, causes the screen output to be quickly shifted horizontally to any portion of the application's screen output. One of the best uses for the horizontal scroll bar is to move through multiple columns of a spreadsheet application in which all the columns of information cannot fit into one screen width.

The Menu Bar

Each Windows application has a *menu bar* below the title bar. The menu bar is used for making menu and submenu selections. These selections can be made by pointing and clicking on the menu command, or alternately, by using a "hot-key" combination. Hot-key combinations often use the ALT key in conjunction with a letter shown in bold and underlined, as the "F" is in the command File in Figure 2-1. Starting with Windows version 3.0, the menu bar also includes a Help option.

The Client Area

Although the *client area* description has been saved for last, it actually occupies the largest portion of each window. The client area is the primary output area for the application. Managing the client area is the responsibility of the application program, and only the application can output to the client area.

WINDOWS CLASSES

The ten fundamental components of a window discussed earlier help define the appearance of an application. There are going to be many occasions when an application program will need to create two windows with a similar appearance and behavior. An excellent example of this involves Windows' PAINT application. The way PAINT allows the user to clip or copy a portion of a graphics image is to run two instances (or copies) of PAINT and copy information from one instance to the other. It is only logical that each instance of PAINT looks and behaves like the other. This requires each instance to create its own window with an identical appearance and functionality.

Windows that look alike and behave in a similar fashion are said to be of the same *window class*. The windows that you create can take on a variety of characteristics. They may be of different sizes, placed on different areas of the display, have different text in the caption bars, have different display colors, or use different mouse cursors.

Every window that you create in a Windows program must be based on a window class. Five of these window classes have already been registered by Windows during its initialization phase and, in addition, your application may register its own classes. In order to allow several windows to be created based on the same window class, Windows specifies some of a window's characteristics as parameters to the CreateWindow function, while others are specified in a window class structure. When you register a window class, the class becomes available to all programs running under Windows.

Windows of similar appearance and behavior can be grouped into classes to reduce the amount of information that needs to be maintained. Each window class has its own shareable window class structure, so there is no needless replication of the window class parameters. And since two windows of the same class use the same function and any associated subroutines, classes save time and storage because there is no code duplication. Most importantly, however, windows of the same class perform the same way.

OBJECT-ORIENTED PROGRAMMING

The phrase *object-oriented* is becoming one of those buzzwords you hear from just about everyone. But what does object-oriented really mean?

The fundamental idea of the object-oriented approach is very simple. For example, people normally perceive the world as a variety of objects; when you look at an automobile, you see an automobile, not a mass of individual atoms. You can divide the automobile into tires, hood, doors, trunk, engine, and so on, but those are discrete units, or objects.

Even if you subdivide the bits and pieces of the automobile into molecules, they are still groupings of atoms, which are also single units. The last step in this analogy is to compare traditional procedural programming, which deals with "atoms," to object-oriented programming, which deals with the automobile as a whole.

Looking at it from the outside, object-oriented means the familiar — the way you normally look at the world around you. From the inside, however, it is a lot more complex than that.

You may have heard the terms "right-brain" and "left-brain." Right-brain individuals are supposed to be more artistic and intuitive, while left-brain people tend to be more logical and analytical. The historical standard computer languages and interfaces, which were more structured and used more detail, were better appreciated by those who were left-brain. Fortunately for right-brain types, there is the new world of object-oriented languages and interfaces.

At this point you may well be saying, "This is all fine and interesting, but what does it have to do with Windows?" When you are programming for Windows, you are actually using object-oriented programming. In object-oriented programming, an *object* is an abstract data type that consists of a data structure and various functions that act on the data structure. Additionally, objects receive messages that can cause them to change.

For example, a *graphics object* is a collection of data that can be manipulated as a single entity and is presented to the user as part of the visual interface. In particular, a graphics object represents both the data and the presentation of data. Some examples of graphics objects include menus, title bars, control boxes, and scroll bars. The next section describes several new graphics objects that affect the user's view of an application.

Icons

The *icon* graphic object is a small symbol used to remind the user of a particular operation, idea, or product. For example, when a spreadsheet application is minimized, it could display a very small histogram icon to remind the user the application is still running. Clicking the mouse on the histogram would cause Windows to bring the application to active status.

Because of the old proverb of one picture being worth a thousand words, icons can be very powerful. They attract the user's attention, for one thing, which proves useful for error warnings and new options, for example. Windows provides several stock icons, including a question mark, exclamation point, asterisk, and an upturned palm. Using Microsoft's SDKPAINT utility (version 3.0), supplied with the Software Development Kit, users can create their own device-independent color icon designs. Using the function DrawIcon allows an application to easily place an icon within the client area.

Cursors

Windows' cursors are quite different from the standard DOS variety. A Windows cursor is a graphic symbol, unlike the DOS blinking underscore. The graphic symbol changes according to the placement of the pointing device; this helps to show the operations currently available. The best example of this would be the change from the standard Windows arrow cursor to the small hourglass cursor that indicates a pause while a selected command is being executed. Incorporated into Windows are several stock cursors: the original diagonal arrow, a vertical arrow, an hourglass, cross hairs, I-beam, and several others. Using SDKPAINT, your application can also create its own cursors.

Carets

Carets are symbols applications usually place in a window to show the user where input will be received. Carets are easily distinguished from other screen markers because they blink. Most of the time mouse input is associated with a cursor and keyboard input with a caret. However, the mouse can move or change the input emphasis of a caret. To help clarify the difference between a cursor and a caret, remember that Windows' carets behave most like the standard DOS cursor. An example is the I-beam caret provided for you automatically in dialog boxes. Unlike icons and cursors, an application must create its own carets using the CreateCaret and ShowCaret functions. Except for the automatic I-beam dialog box caret, there are no stock carets.

Message Boxes

Another very common graphics object is the Windows *message box.* Message boxes are pop-up windows that contain a title, an icon, and a message. Figure 2-2 shows the standard message box presented when terminating a Windows session. A single function call to the MessageBox function creates, displays, and receives the user's response from the message box. The application needs to supply the message title, the message itself, instructions on which stock icon to use (if any), and the stock response to use, if applicable (such as OK). Additional stock user responses include Yes/No, Yes/No/Cancel, OK/Cancel, Retry/Cancel. Stock icons include IconHand, IconQuestion, IconExclamation, and IconAsterisk.

Dialog Boxes

Dialog boxes are similar to message boxes in that they are also pop-up windows. However, dialog boxes are primarily used to receive input from, rather than to present output to, the user. A dialog box allows an application to receive information, one field or box of information at a time, rather than one character at a time. Figure 2-3 illustrates the Windows dialog box that allows the user to change to another subdirectory. The graphic design

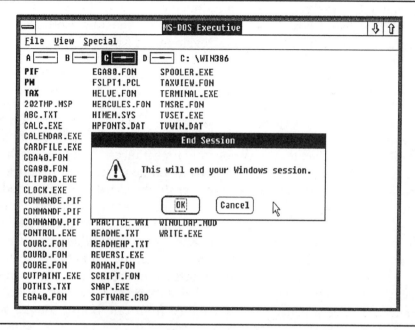

Figure 2-2.   End Session message box

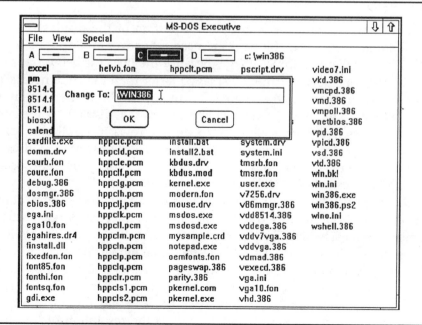

Figure 2-3.   Change To dialog box

of a dialog box is created for you automatically by Windows. The description of the dialog box is normally created by the Microsoft Dialog Box Editor provided with the Software Development Kit.

Fonts

A *font* is a graphics object, or resource, that defines a complete set of characters from one typeface, all with a certain size and style. Fonts can be manipulated to give text a variety of appearances. A *typeface* is a basic character design that has certain serifs and stroke widths. For instance, your application can use different fonts — either the standard fonts provided with Windows (such as, System, Courier, and Times Roman) or custom fonts that you define and include in the application program's executable file. Using built-in routines, Windows allows for the dynamic modification of a typeface including changing to boldface, italic, underline, and changing the font size. Windows provides all of the necessary functions for displaying text anywhere within the client area. And even better is that an application's output will have a consistent appearance from one output device to the next due to Windows' device independence.

Bitmaps

A *bitmap* can be seen as a snapshot of a portion of the display (in pixels) that is stored in memory. Bitmaps are used whenever an application wants to quickly display a graphics image. Because the object is being transferred directly from memory, it can be displayed faster than the code necessary to re-create the image can be executed. There are two basic uses for bitmaps. First, bitmaps are used to draw pictures on the display. For example, Windows uses many small bitmaps to draw arrows in scroll bars, display check marks when selecting pull-down menu options, and to draw the system menu box, the size box, and many others. Bitmaps are also used for creating brushes, which will be covered shortly.

There are also two major disadvantages to using bitmaps. First, depending on their size, bitmaps can occupy an unpredictably large portion of memory. For each pixel being displayed, there has to be an equivalent representation in memory. Displaying the same bitmap on a color versus a monochrome monitor would require more memory. On a monochrome monitor, one bit can define a pixel as on or off. However, on a color monitor that can display 16 colors, each pixel would require 4 bits, or a *nibble*, to represent its characteristics. And, as the resolution of the display device increases, so do the memory requirements.

Another disadvantage of bitmaps is that they only contain a picture. Going back to the automobile object example, if the automobile were represented by a bitmap there would be no way to access the image's various components, such as tires, hood, and windows. However, if the automobile had been constructed from a series of routines, an application would be able to change the data to these routines and modify the picture. For example, an application could modify the tire-drawing routine to include a hubcap with the tire.

Pens

Each time Windows draws a shape on the screen it uses information about the current pen and brush. *Pens* are used to draw lines and outline shapes. They have three basic characteristics: line width, style (dotted, dashed, solid), and color. Windows always has a pen for drawing black lines and one for drawing white lines available to each application. Of course, you can always create your own pens. You might want to create a thick light-gray line to outline a portion of the screen, or a dot-dash-dot line for spreadsheet data analysis.

Brushes

Brushes are used to paint colors and fill areas with predefined patterns. Brushes have a minimum size of 8 × 8 pixels and, like pens, have three basic characteristics: size, pattern, and color. With their 8 × 8 pixel minimum, brushes are said to have a *pattern*, not a style, as pens do. The pattern may be anything from a solid color to hatched to diagonal, or any other user-definable combination.

GETTING THE MESSAGE

Windows is started just like any normal application running under DOS. However, by the time you see the MS-DOS Executive window, Windows has just about become a full-fledged operating system. While Windows does share the managing of all hardware resources, it concedes its rights to managing the file system of the PC. Windows is therefore totally at home taking charge of the keyboard, video display, mouse, parallel and serial ports, memory, and program execution. It is important to realize that Windows accomplishes all that it does because of its hardware dominance. For example, it is only by taking control of the hardware that Windows can partition the display screen into separate windows. By managing the hardware, Windows can intercept all user input and distribute that input, as messages, to the appropriate applications. Finally, it is only through the total control of the hardware that Windows can ensure that an application can interface with a variety of output devices, thereby creating a "virtual machine."

Under Windows, an application does not write directly to the screen, process any hardware interrupts, or output directly to the printer. Instead, the application uses the appropriate Windows functions, or it waits for an appropriate message to be delivered. Applications development under Windows must now incorporate the processing of the application and the user's view of the application through Windows.

In Chapter 1 you saw how the Windows message system was the underlying structure used to disseminate information in a multitasking environment. From your application's viewpoint, a message is seen as a notification that some event of interest had occurred, which may or may not require a specific action. These events may have been initiated by the user, such as by clicking or moving the mouse, changing the size of a window, or by making a menu selection. However, the signaled event could also have been generated by the application.

The net effect of all this is that your application must now be totally oriented toward the processing of messages. It must be capable of awakening, determining the appropriate action based on the type of message received, taking that action to completion, and returning to sleep.

As a result of this new communication, Windows applications are significantly different from their DOS counterparts. Windows provides an application program with access to about 450 function calls. Generally, these function calls are handled by three main modules, called KERNEL, GDI (graphics device interface), and USER. The KERNEL module is roughly 50K and is responsible for memory management, loading and running an application, and scheduling. The GDI is roughly 100K and contains all of the routines to create and display graphics. The 150K USER module takes care of all other application requirements.

The next section will take a closer look at the message system, examining the format and sources of messages, several common message types, and the ways in which both Windows and your application go about processing messages.

Message Format

The purpose of a message is to notify your program that an event of interest has occurred. Technically, a message is not just of interest to the application, but to a specific window within that application. Therefore every message is addressed to a window.

Windows has only one system message queue, but each program currently running under Windows also has its own program message queue. Each message in the system message queue must eventually be transferred by the USER module to a program's message queue. The program's message queue stores all messages for all the windows in that program.

The following four parameters are associated with all messages, regardless of their type:

- A window handle (16-bit word)

- A message type (16-bit word)

- One WORD parameter (16-bit word)

- One LONG parameter (32-bit word)

The first parameter specified in a window message is the *handle* of the window to which the message is addressed. In an object-oriented programming environment, a handle is just the identifier of an object, which for the current syntax is the identifier of the particular window to which the message is addressed.

A handle is a 16-bit unsigned number. Frequently, this handle will reference an object (defined in the form of a data structure) that is located in a moveable portion of memory. It is important to realize that even though the portion of memory can be moved, the handle remains the same. This allows Windows to manage memory efficiently while leaving the relocation invisible to the application.

Because multiple windows can be created based on the same window class, a single window function could process messages for more than one window within a single program. Under these circumstances, the application would use the handle to determine which window was receiving the message.

The second parameter in a message is its *message type*. This is one of the identifiers specified in the WINDOWS.H header file, covered later in the chapter. Under Windows, each message type is represented by a two-character mnemonic followed by the underscore character, and finally, a descriptor to complete the message. The most common type of message an application will process is the window message. Some examples of window messages are: WM_CREATE, WM_PAINT, WM_CLOSE, WM_COPY, WM_PASTE. Other message types include control window messages (BM_), edit control messages (EM_), and list box messages (LB_). When necessary, an application can create and register its own message type, which allows the use of private message types.

The purpose for the last two parameters, WORD and LONG, is to provide any additional information necessary to interpret the message. The contents of these last two parameters will therefore vary depending on the message type. Examples of the types of information that would be passed include which key was just struck, the position of the mouse, the position of the vertical or horizontal scroll bar elevators, and the selected pop-up menu item.

Where Do Messages Come From?

It is through the underlying structure of messages that Windows is capable of multitasking. Therefore, all messages must be processed by Windows. Basically, there are four sources for a message. An application can receive a message from the user, from Windows itself, from the application program itself, or from another application.

Messages from the user include keystroke information, mouse movements, point-and-click coordinates, menu selections, the location of scroll bar elevators, and so on. Your application program will devote a great deal of time to processing user messages. User-originated messages indicate that the person running the program wishes to change the way the application is viewed.

Windows typically originates a message to an application whenever a state change is to take effect—for example, when the user clicks on an application's icon to make that the active application. In this case, Windows tells the application that its main window is being opened, that its size and location are being modified, and so forth. Depending on the current state of an application, Windows-originated messages can be either responded to or ignored.

In the next chapter, you will learn how to write a simple Windows application. There you will see that your program is broken down into specific procedures, each one processing a particular message type for a particular window. One procedure, for example, will deal with resizing the application's window. It is quite possible that the application may want to resize itself. In other words, the source of the message is the application itself.

Currently, most applications written for Windows do not take full advantage of the fourth type of message source, inter-task communication. However, this category will become increasingly important as more and more applications use this integration capability. To facilitate this type of message, Microsoft has developed the DDE (dynamic data exchange) protocol.

What to Do with a Message Once You Have It

A Windows application will have a procedure for processing each type of message that is of interest to any of its windows. However, different windows will want to respond differently to messages of the same type. For example, one application may have two windows that respond to a mouse-button click in different ways. The first window could respond to the click by changing the background color, while the second window may respond to the click by placing cross-hatching on a spreadsheet. Since the same message can be interpreted differently by different windows, you can see why Windows addresses each message to a specific window within an application.

Not only will the application have a different procedure to handle each message type, it will also need a procedure to handle each message type for each window. The window procedure is used to group together all the message type procedures for a Windows application.

Message Loop

A fundamental component of all Windows applications is the *message processing loop*. Each application will contain procedures to create and initialize windows, followed by the message processing loop, and finally some required closing code. The message loop is responsible for processing a message delivered by Windows to the main body of the program. Here the program acknowledges the message, and then requests Windows to send it to the appropriate window procedure for processing, at which point the window procedure executes the desired action.

The message queue and dispatching priority are two factors that can influence the sequence in which a message is processed. Messages can be sent from one of two queues, either the system queue or the application's message queue. Messages are first placed in the system queue. When a message reaches the front of the queue it is sent over to the appropriate application's message queue. This dual mode allows Windows to keep track of all messages while allowing each application to track only those messages that pertain to it.

Normally, Windows places most messages into the queues as you would expect, in first-in first-out order (FIFO). These are called *synchronous messages*. Most Windows applications use this type of dispatching method. However, there are occasions when Windows will push a message to the end of the queue, thereby preventing it from being dispatched. Messages of this type are called *asynchronous messages*. Care must be taken when sending an asynchronous message that overrides the application's normal sequence of processing.

There are three types of asynchronous messages: paint, timer, and quit. A timer message, for example, causes a certain action to take effect at a specified time, regardless of the messages to be processed at that moment. Therefore a timer message will cause all other messages in the queue to be pushed farther from the queue front.

Windows also has asynchronous messages that can be sent to other applications. This scenario is unique in that the receiving application doesn't put the message into its queue. Instead, the message immediately calls the receiving application's appropriate window procedure, where the message then executes.

You may be wondering how Windows dispatches messages that are pending for several applications at once. Windows settles this issue in one of two ways. One method of message processing is called *dispatching priority*. Each time Windows loads an application it sets the application's priority to zero. Once the application is running, however, the application can change its priority to anything from −15 to +15. All things being equal, Windows would then settle any dispatching contention by sending messages to the highest priority application.

A data communications application is an example of a program that might need to raise its priority level. If your system were connected to a distant host computer, you would want to process the information being sent long distance as soon as possible.

However, since tampering with an application's priority level is very uncommon, Windows must have another method for dispatching messages to concurrent applications with the same priority level. Besides processing the messages in the queue, whenever Windows sees that a particular application has a backlog of unprocessed messages, it hangs on to any new messages for that application, while continuing to dispatch other messages to other applications.

WHAT IS A RESOURCE?

The graphics objects described earlier, namely icons and cursors, along with carets, message boxes, dialog boxes, fonts, bitmaps, pens, and brushes, are examples of *resources*. A resource represents data that is included in a program's .EXE file, although technically speaking, it does not reside in a program's normal data segment. When Windows loads a program into memory for execution, very often it will leave all of the resources on the disk. One example of this is when the user first requests to see an application's About dialog box. Before Windows can display the About box, it must first access the disk to copy this information from the program's .EXE file into memory.

Usually an application defines its resources as read-only and discardable. This allows Windows to discard the resource whenever more memory is required. Should the resource be requested again, Windows simply reads the disk and reloads the data into memory. Finally, should the user choose to have multiple instances of the same application running concurrently, for instance, a word processor, Windows will not only share the application's program code, but its resource definitions as well.

ACCESSING WINDOWS FUNCTIONS

Windows provides the application developer with roughly 450 functions. Some examples of these functions include DispatchMessage, PostMessage, RegisterWindowMessage, and SetActiveWindow. The interface to these functions is through a far intersegment call. This is because Windows treats the function as if it were located in a code segment other than the one the program occupies. Officially called the CALL-based API (application program interface), parameters are passed via the stack to the various modules that make up Windows. Since all Windows modules have code and data segments separate from an application's, Windows functions must be accessed using 32-bit far addresses. This address can be broken down into two components, the 16-bit segment address and the 16-bit offset address.

PASCAL Calling Convention

As you become more and more familiar with Windows source code, you'll start noticing function declarations that include the PASCAL modifier. As just discussed, parameters to all Windows functions are passed via the stack. In a C program, for example, function parameters are first pushed onto the stack and then the function is called. Normally, the parameters are pushed starting from the right-most parameter, and going to the left-most parameter. Upon return from the function, the calling procedure must adjust the stack pointer to a value equal to the number of bytes originally pushed onto the stack.

In Pascal, however, things look slightly different. While function parameters are still pushed from right to left, it is the called function's responsibility to adjust the stack before the return. It is no longer the job of the calling procedure to adjust the stack. Windows uses this calling convention because it turns out to be more space efficient. Therefore the Microsoft C compiler understands that any function declared with the reserved word PASCAL is to use the more efficient calling convention. However, the efficiency of using the PASCAL calling convention comes with its own set of problems. This calling sequence makes coding functions with a variable number of parameters more difficult. For example, whenever the wrong number of parameters are passed, the program tends to crash.

WHAT IS WINDOWS.H?

WINDOWS.H is a large (approximately 88K) header file that is very important to Windows applications. This file is included with the Software Development Kit and contains over 1,200 constant declarations, the *typedef* declarations, and over 450 Windows function declarations. One of the main reasons a Windows application takes longer to compile than an MS-DOS C program is because of the size of WINDOWS.H.

Many of the Windows functions found in the KERNEL, USER, and GDI modules work with their own specified data types and variables, which your program can access. These variables and types are defined in *header files*. To use certain functions you must include the header file in which they are defined. This is accomplished by placing an *#include* statement in your source program.

Chapter 3 will discuss, in detail, the components of a Windows application. Many of the parameters used by the various Windows function calls will have been previously defined in WINDOWS.H. Due to the size and importance of WINDOWS.H, it is suggested that you print a hard copy as a convenient reference.

Technically, the *#define* statements found in WINDOWS.H associate a numeric constant with a text identifier, for example:

```
#define WM_CREATE 0x0001
```

The C compiler will use the hexadecimal constant 0x0001 as a replacement for WM_CREATE during preprocessing.

Other *#define* statements may appear a bit unusual, for example:

```
#define NEAR near
#define VOID void
```

In Microsoft C both *near* and *void* are reserved words. Your applications should use the uppercase NEAR and VOID for one very good reason: should you decide to port your application over to another C compiler, it would certainly be much easier to change the *#define* statements within the header file than to change all the occurrences of a particular identifier.

WINDOWS NOTATION

If most of your programming to date has been in assembly language, Ada, or Pascal, then hang on. Windows source code has a style and indentation scheme that will initially look quite peculiar. Officially, this "Hungarian" style of notation can be credited to the Microsoft programmer Charles Simonyi.

In Hungarian notation, variable names begin with a lowercase letter or letters that describe the data type of the variable. This variable name prefix is then followed by the name of the variable, which is represented by a meaningful use of upper- and lowercase letters. This approach allows each variable to have attached a mnemonic representing the variable's data type, for example:

```
WORD wParam1
LONG lParam2
```

By prefacing each variable name with a reminder of its data type, you can actually avoid some very common mistakes before compiling your program. The following statement looks harmless but is incorrect and may go unchecked.

```
Param1 = Param2
```

However, using Hungarian notation you would undoubtedly catch the following mistake:

```
wParam1 = lParam2
```

Use Table 2-1 to familiarize yourself with some of Windows' data types.

Table 2-1. Standard Windows Data Types

Prefix	Data Type Represented
b	BOOL/(integer)
by	BYTE/(unsigned character)
c	character
dw	DWORD/(unsigned long)
fn	function
h	HANDLE /(unsigned integer)
i	integer
l	LONG/(long)
lp	long/(far) pointer
n	short integer
np	near/(short)pointer
p	pointer
s	string
sz	NULL/(0) terminated string
w	WORD/(unsigned integer)
x	short/(when used as the X coordinate)
y	short/(when used as the Y coordinate)

COMPONENTS OF A WINDOWS APPLICATION

Building a Windows application can involve some or all of the following seven steps:

1. Create the WinMain and associated Windows functions in C or assembly language.

2. Create the menu, dialog box, and any additional resource descriptions and put them into a resource script file.

3. (Optional) Use the SDKPAINT, supplied with the Software Development Kit, to create unique cursors, icons, and bitmaps.

4. (Optional) Use the Dialog Editor, supplied with the Software Development Kit, to create dialog boxes.

5. Create any module definitions and place them in the module definition file.

6. Compile and link all C language sources.

7. Compile the resource script file and add it to the executable file.

Figure 2-4 shows the seven steps required to build a Windows application. The major portion of this book will revolve around the explanation and use of each of these stages.

Creating the actual Windows application will require the use of several new and exciting development tools, as well as some familiar ones. This next section will take a brief look at each.

The C Compiler

When writing a Windows application you can use many of the same options you would normally use for a standard C program — along with the

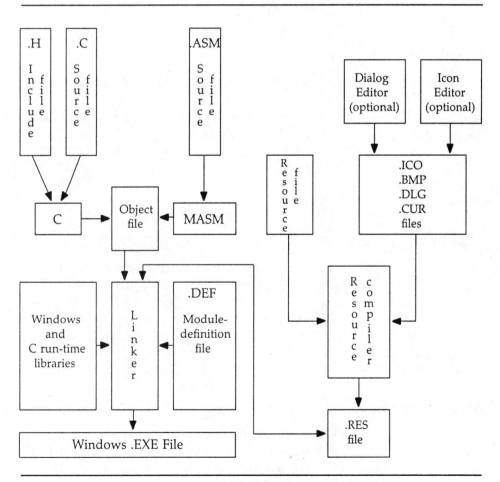

Figure 2-4.   Components of a Windows application

two mandatory Windows switches. These switches are **-Gw**, and **-Zp**. The first switch, **-Gw**, adds necessary Windows prolog and epilog code to each function; **-Zp** causes the C compiler to pack each structure. This will guarantee that the structures used within your application are the same size as the corresponding structure used by Windows.

Resource Editors

Included in the Software Development Kit are three resource editors: Icon Editor, Dialog Editor, and Font Editor. The Icon Editor allows for the quick definition of icons, cursors, and bitmaps. The Font Editor provides a convenient method for creating your own unique fonts. And the Dialog Editor makes it easy to create dialog box descriptions.

Resource Compiler

The resource compiler does pretty much what its name suggests. Frequently, a Windows application will use its own resources, such as dialog boxes, menus, and icons. Each of these resources must be predefined in a file called a *resource script file*. This file is then compiled by the resource compiler and the additional information is added to the application's final .EXE file. This allows Windows to load and use the resources from the executable file.

Linker

Starting with version 3.0, all Windows applications can be linked with either the C linker, the Pascal linker, or LINK4.EXE supplied with earlier Windows versions. When linking a Windows application, the linker requires a *module-definition file*. The module-definition file specifies the name of the application and contains the file names for all callback functions in the application.

MAKE/NMAKE

The MAKE.EXE program provides an efficient means of keeping the executable version of a program up to date. It accomplishes this by keeping track of the dates of source files. Because Windows applications can require the incorporation of so many files, **MAKE** is very important. In order for

MAKE to do its job, it needs its own file, called a *make file,* which contains a combination of commands and file names. **MAKE** will only execute a command if the file referenced in the command has changed.

For example, say you have created an IRS income tax preparation Windows application, and you later decide to create your own cursor. Instead of pointing with the system-supplied standard arrow, you want a cursor that looks like a judge's gavel. The remainder of the program stays the same; all you change is the cursor resource file, PROBITY.CUR. When you run the **MAKE** utility, only the information about the cursor will be updated. Starting with C 6.0, Microsoft has renamed the MAKE utility NMAKE. NMAKE offers extended features beyond those of MAKE. In this book only the features common to both utilities will be utilized. As a matter of convention, the name MAKE will be used to refer to both utilities.

3

WRITING SIMPLE
WINDOWS PROGRAMS

At this point, you are probably wondering what comes next. As you have read along you've learned new terms and concepts specific to multitasking window-oriented object programming! It sounds intriguing—applications having a common visual interface, device independence, and concurrent execution—but what does that mean in practice? It's time to find out.

GETTING STARTED

In this chapter you will develop a program called SWP.EXE (for "Simplified Windows Platform"). SWP will incorporate all of the Windows components necessary to create and display a window (main window with a border, title bar, system menu, and maximize and minimize boxes), print a text message to the monitor, and gracefully quit. You will also be shown how to use SWP and all of its related files as boilerplates for other Windows applications. This will save time and help you develop an understanding of how Windows applications are put together and how they work. However, before getting started, take a moment to look over the Windows data types and structures listed in Tables 3-1 and 3-2. This will help you understand what each Windows function call is passing.

Table 3-1.   Frequently Used Windows Data Types

Data Type	Meaning
HANDLE	Defines a 16-bit unsigned integer that is used as a handle
HWND	Specifies the 16-bit unsigned integer used as the handle to a window
LONG	Defines a 32-bit signed integer
LPSTR	Identifies a 32-bit pointer to a character data type
FARPROC	Identifies a 32-bit pointer to a function
WORD	Defines a 16-bit unsigned integer

More on Handles

Windows uses handles to identify many different types of objects, such as menus, icons, controls, memory allocation, output devices, pens and brushes, windows, and even *instances*. Windows allows you to run more than one copy of an application at a time, and keeps track of each of these instances by giving each one its own unique handle.

Under most circumstances a handle is used as an index into an internal table. By having a handle reference a table element, rather than contain an actual memory address, Windows can continue to dynamically rearrange all resources simply by inserting a resource's new address into the identical table position. If Windows associates a particular application's icon resource with table look-up position 10, then no matter where Windows moves the icon in memory, table position 10 contains the current location.

Table 3-2.   Frequently Used Windows Structures

Structure	Usage
MSG	Specifies the fields of an input message
PAINTSTRUCT	Specifies the paint structure to be used when drawing within a window
RECT	Specifies a rectangle
WNDCLASS	Specifies a window class

Windows is very efficient in its management of multiple instances. Some multitasking environments load each instance as if it were an entirely new application. Windows conserves system resources by using the same code for all instances of an application. Only the data segment for each instance is uniquely managed. Also, the first instance of an application has a very important role; it creates all of the objects necessary for the functioning of the application. This can include dialog boxes, menus, and so on, and also window classes. What is even more important than the reuse of these objects is the fact that under most circumstances the same resources are available to all other applications.

BASIC COMPONENTS OF A WINDOWS APPLICATION

At the highest level, a Windows application can be broken down into two essential components: the WinMain function and the window function. Microsoft requires that the main body of your program be named WinMain. This function acts as the entry point for the application and behaves in a similar manner to the main function in a standard C program. However, the window function has a unique role. Your Windows applications never directly access any window functions. Instead, your application makes a request to Windows to carry out the specified operation. In order to facilitate this communication, Windows requires a *call back* function. A call back function is registered with Windows and it is called back whenever Windows executes an operation on a window.

A Closer Look at the WinMain Function

All Windows applications must have a WinMain function. WinMain is responsible for

- Registering the application's window classes
- Performing necessary initializations
- Creating and starting the application's message processing loop (accessing the application's message queue)
- Upon receiving a WM_QUIT message, terminating the program

The WinMain procedure receives four parameters from Windows. For the SWP.C boilerplate, the function looks like the following.

```
int PASCAL WinMain(hInst,hPreInst,lpszCmdLine,nCmdShow)
HANDLE hInst,hPreInst;
LPSTR  lpszCmdLine;
int    nCmdShow;
```

Notice the use of the PASCAL calling convention discussed in the last chapter. The first parameter, *hInst,* is passed the instance handle of the application. *hPreInst* contains a NULL if no previous instance exists—otherwise it returns the handle to the previous instance of the program. *lpszCmdLine* is a long pointer to a null-terminated string that points to the application's parameter line (it contains NULL if the application was started using Windows' Executive). The parameter *nCmdShow* defines whether the application is to be displayed as a window (SW_SHOWNORMAL) or as an icon (SW_SHOWMINNOACTIVE).

Registering the Window Class

Every window you create for a Windows application must be based on a window class. The windows you create for Windows can have a variety of styles, colors, text fonts, placement, caption bars, icons, and so on. The window class serves as a template that defines these attributes. Once a window class has been registered, the class becomes available to all programs running under Windows. Because of this, care must be taken to avoid any conflicting names between application window classes.

The window class is a data structure. For example, the WINDOWS.H header file contains a *typedef* statement that defines the structure WND-CLASS, as shown here:

```
typedef struct tagWNDCLASS {
    WORD    style;
    long    (FAR PASCAL *lpfnWndProc)();
    int     cbClsExtra;
    int     cbWndExtra;
    HANDLE  hInstance;
    HICON   hIcon;
    HCURSOR hCursor;
    HBRUSH  hbrBackground;
    LPSTR   lpszMenuName;
    LPSTR   lpszClassName;
} WNDCLASS;
```

While Windows does provide several predefined window classes, most applications define their own window class. In order to accomplish this your application must define a structure variable of this type, for example:

```
WNDCLASS wcSwp;
```

and then fill the *wcSwp* structure with information about the window class. Table 3-3 explains the various fields within the WNDCLASS structure. Some of the fields may be assigned a NULL, directing Windows to use predefined values, while others must be given specific values.

The following code section shows how the WNDCLASS structure has been defined and initialized for SWP.C.

```
char    szProgName[]="ProgName";
        .
        .
        .
  WNDCLASS wcSwp;
        .
        .
        .
  if (!hPreInst)
  {
    wcSwp.lpszClassName=szProgName;
    wcSwp.hInstance    =hInst;
    wcSwp.lpfnWndProc  =WindowProc;
    wcSwp.hCursor      =LoadCursor(NULL,IDC_ARROW);
    wcSwp.hIcon        =NULL;
    wcSwp.lpszMenuName =NULL;
    wcSwp.hbrBackground=GetStockObject(WHITE_BRUSH);
    wcSwp.style        =CS_HREDRAW|CS_VREDRAW;
    wcSwp.cbClsExtra   =0;
    wcSwp.cbWndExtra   =0;
    if (!RegisterClass (&wcSwp))
      return FALSE;
  }
```

For the Simplified Windows Platform, *wcSwp.lpszClassName* is assigned the generic "ProgName." This should be changed for each new window class. When the WinMain function is called, it will return a value for *wcSwp.hInstance* indicating the current instance of the application. The *wcSwp.lpfnWndProc* field is given a pointer to the window function that will carry out all of the tasks for the window. Here, the function is called WindowProc and must be declared somewhere before the assignment statement.

The next field, *wcSwp.hCursor*, is assigned the handle to the instance's cursor (IDC_ARROW—the standard tilted arrow cursor). However, since there is no default icon, *wcSwp.hIcon* is assigned NULL. This is accomplished by calls to the LoadCursor and LoadIcon Windows functions. Assigning a NULL to *wcSwp.lpszMenuName* indicates that the current application does not have a menu. If it did, the menu would have a name and it would appear between quotation marks.

The GetStockObject function returns a handle to a brush used to paint the background color of the client area of windows created of this class. In this example, the function returns a handle to one of Windows' predefined brushes, WHITE_BRUSH.

Table 3-3.   WNDCLASS Structure Field Definitions

Field Name	Description
style	Defines the class style. Styles can be combined by using the bitwise logical OR operator. Values for the style field include

Value	Meaning
CS_BYTEALIGNCLIENT	Using byte boundaries in the X direction, aligns a window's client area
CS_BYTEALIGNWINDOW	Using byte boundaries in the X direction, aligns a window
CS_CLASSDC	Assigns a window class its own display context that can be shared by instances
CS_DBCLKS	Sends a double-click message to a window
CS_GLOBALCLASS	Defines a global window class
CS_HREDRAW	If the horizontal size of a window changes, will redraw the entire window
CS_NOCLOSE	Deactivates the close option on the system menu
CS_OWNDC	Assigns each window instance its own display context
CS_PARENTDC	Gives the parent window's display context to the window class
CS_SAVEBITS	Saves the portion of the screen image that is obscured by a window
CS_VREDRAW	If the vertical size of a window changes, will redraw the entire window

Field Name	Description
lpfnWndProc	Receives a pointer to the window function that will carry out all of the tasks for the window
cbClsExtra	Designates the number of extra bytes to allocate for the WNDCLASS structure (can be NULL)
cbWndExtra	Designates the number of extra bytes to allocate for all additional structures created using this window class (can be NULL)
hInstance	Defines the instance of the application registering the window class
hIcon	Defines the icon to be used whenever the window is minimized (can be NULL)

Table 3-3.   WNDCLASS Structure Field Definitions (*continued*)

Field Name	Description
hCursor	Similar to hIcon, defines the cursor to be used for the window (can be NULL)
hbrBackground	Specifies a brush to be used for painting the window's background. This can be the handle to a physical brush or it can be a color value. If a color value is specified it must be one of the following standard system colors listed, and a 1 must be added to the chosen color COLOR_ACTIVEBORDER COLOR_ACTIVECAPTION COLOR_APPWORKSPACE COLOR_BACKGROUND COLOR_CAPTIONTEXT COLOR_INACTIVEBORDER COLOR_INACTIVECAPTION COLOR_MENU COLOR_MENUTEXT COLOR_SCROLLBAR COLOR_WINDOW COLOR_WINDOWFRAME COLOR_WINDOWTEXT
lpszMenuName	A long pointer to a null-terminated string, indicating the resource name of a menu (can be NULL)
lpszClassName	A long pointer to a null-terminated string, indicating the name of the window class. This name must be unique in order to avoid confusion when sharing a window class among applications

The style of the window class has been set to CS_HREDRAW or CS_VREDRAW. All window class styles have identifiers in WINDOWS.H that begin with "CS_". Each identifier represents a bit value. The logical OR operation is used to combine these bit flags. The two parameters used instruct Windows to redraw the entire client area whenever the horizontal or vertical size of the window is changed.

The last two fields, *wcSwp.cbClsExtra*, and *wcSwp.cbWndExtra*, are frequently assigned 0. These fields are used to indicate the count of extra bytes that have been reserved at the end of the window class structure and the window data structure used for each window class.

If you treat code the way Agatha Christie's Hercule Poirot treats mysteries, then you've probably noticed a couple of lines of code from the example that have not been explained. They are as follows:

```
if (!hPreInst)
{
  if (!RegisterClass (&wcSwp))
    return FALSE;
}
```

From the previous discussion about instances you know that an application only needs to register a window class if it is the first instance. Windows can check the number of instances by examining the *hPreInst* parameter. If this value is NULL, then this is the application's first instance. Therefore the first *if* statement fills the WNDCLASS structure only for first instances. The last *if* statement takes care of registering a new window class. It does this by sending over a far pointer to the address of the window class structure. The actual parameter's near pointer (*&wcSwp*) is converted to a far pointer by the compiler, since the function RegisterClass is expecting a far pointer. If Windows cannot register the window class, possibly due to a lack of memory, the RegisterClass will return a 0, terminating the program.

Creating a Window

Regardless of whether this is the first instance of an application or subsequent instances, a window must be created. All windows are of a predefined class type. The preceding section illustrated how and when to initialize and register a window class. This section will describe the steps necessary to create the actual window.

A window is created by making a call to Windows' CreateWindow function. While the window class defines the general characteristics of a window, which allows the same window class to be used for many different windows, the parameters to CreateWindow specify more detailed information about the window. This additional information falls under the following categories: the window's class; its title; the style; the window's screen position; its parent handle, menu handle, instance handle; and 32 bits of additional information. For SWP.C, the sample boilerplate source file, this would look like:

```
hwnd=CreateWindow(szProgName,"Simplified Window Platform",
             WS_OVERLAPPEDWINDOW,CW_USEDEFAULT,
             CW_USEDEFAULT,CW_USEDEFAULT,
             CW_USEDEFAULT,NULL,NULL,
             hInst,NULL);
```

The first field, *szProgName* (assigned earlier), defines the window's class, followed by the title to be used for the window ("Simplified Window Platform"). The third parameter (WS_OVERLAPPEDWINDOW) is the style of the window. This standard Windows style represents a normal overlapped window with a caption bar, a system menu box, minimize and maximize icons, and a thick window frame.

The next six parameters (either CS_USEDEFAULT, or NULL) represent the initial X and Y positions and X and Y size of the window, along with the parent window handle and window menu handle. Each of these fields has been assigned a default value. The *hInst* field contains the instance of the program, followed by no additional parameters (NULL).

Displaying and Updating a Window

To display a window you need to do more than register a window class and create a window from that class. Displaying a window requires a call to the ShowWindow function in the form

```
ShowWindow(hwnd,nCmdShow);
```

The second parameter to ShowWindow, *nCmdShow*, determines how the window is initially displayed. The value of *nCmdShow* can specify that the window be displayed as a normal window (SW_SHOWNNORMAL), or several other possibilities. For example, substituting *nCmdShow* with the WINDOWS.H constant SW_SHOWMINNOACTIVE, causes the window to be drawn as an icon.

```
ShowWindow(hwnd,SW_SHOWMINNOACTIVE);
```

Other possibilities include SW_SHOWMAXIMIZED, causing the window to be active, and filling the entire display along with its counterpart SW_SHOWMINIMIZED.

The last step in displaying a window requires the following call to the UpdateWindow function:

```
UpdateWindow(hwnd);
```

When ShowWindow is called with a SW_SHOWNORMAL parameter, the function erases the window's client area with the background brush specified in the window's class. The call to UpdateWindow causes the client area to be painted by generating a WM_PAINT message.

The Message Loop

Once an application's window has been created and displayed, the program is ready to perform its main task—processing messages. Remember, Windows does not send input from the mouse or keyboard directly to an application. Instead, it places all input into the application's queue. The queue can also contain messages generated by Windows or other applications. Once the WinMain function has taken care of creating and displaying the window, it needs to create a program message loop. This is most frequently accomplished by using a *while* loop as shown here:

```
while (GetMessage(&msg,NULL,NULL,NULL))
{
  TranslateMessage(&msg);
  DispatchMessage(&msg);
}
```

GetMessage

The GetMessage function is responsible for retrieving the next message from the application's message queue, copying it into the *msg* structure, and sending it to the main body of the program. The three NULL parameters instruct the function to retrieve all of the messages.

Windows is a *nonpreemptive multitasking* system. This means Windows cannot take control from an application. The application must yield control before Windows can reassign control to another application. In a nonpreemptive multitasking environment, the GetMessage function can automatically release control of the processor to another application if the current application has no waiting messages. The current application will pick up execution following the GetMessage statement whenever a message finally does arrive in the application's message queue. Sometimes a program has a long job to do, and all other programs running under Windows seem to stop running during this time period. Normally, a Windows application does not care how long it is inactive. An exception might be a data communications application. In this case the application could be written to check the time and take appropriate actions.

An application can normally return control to Windows anytime before starting the message loop. For example, an application will normally check that all steps leading up to the message loop have executed properly. This can include making sure each window class is registered and has been created. However, once the message loop has been entered, only one message can terminate the loop. Whenever the message to be processed is

WM_QUIT, the value returned is FALSE. This causes the processing to proceed to the main loop's closing routine. The WM_QUIT message is the only way for an application to get out of the message loop.

TranslateMessage

The TranslateMessage function call is only required for applications that need to process character input from the keyboard. This can be very useful for allowing the user to make menu selections without using the mouse. Technically, the TranslateMessage function creates an ASCII character message (WM_CHAR) from a WM_KEYDOWN and WM_KEYUP message. As long as this function is included in the message loop, the keyboard interface will be in effect.

DispatchMessage

The DispatchMessage function is responsible for sending the message to the correct window procedure. Using this function makes it easy to add additional windows and dialog boxes to your application, allowing DispatchMessage to automatically route each message to the appropriate window procedure.

THE WINDOW FUNCTION

Every Windows application must have a WinMain function and a window function. Remember that Windows applications never directly access any window functions. Instead, each application makes a request to Windows to carry out any specified operations. In order to facilitate this communication, Windows requires a call back function. (Remember that a call back function is registered with Windows and it is called back whenever Windows executes an operation on a window.) The window function itself may be very small, processing only one or two messages, or it may be very complex. Advanced window functions will not only process many types of messages, but will also deal with a variety of application windows.

Initially, this concept of an operating system making a call to the application program, can be quite a surprise! For our simplified windows platform boilerplate (SWP.C) the call back window function looks like the following (minus application-specific statements).

```
long FAR PASCAL WindowProc(hwnd,messg,wParam,lParam)
HWND    hwnd;
unsigned messg;
WORD    wParam;
LONG    lParam;
{
  #define RED 0x0000FFL
  PAINTSTRUCT ps;
  HDC  hdc;
  HPEN hPen;
  switch (messg)
  {
  case WM_PAINT:
    hdc=BeginPaint(hwnd,&ps);

/*--------- your routines below ---------*/

/*--------- your routines above ---------*/

    ValidateRect(hwnd,NULL);
    EndPaint(hwnd,&ps);
    break;
  case WM_DESTROY:
    PostQuitMessage(0);
    break;
  default:
    return(DefWindowProc(hwnd,messg,wParam,lParam));
    break;
  }
  return(0L);
}
```

Before going any further, it is important to notice that the name of this required window function, for our example, WindowProc, must be referenced by name in the *wcSwp.lpfnWndProc* field of the window class structure. WindowProc will be the windows function for all windows created from this window class. The following listing reviews this initialization:

```
        .
        .
        .
  if (!hPreInst)
  {
    wcSwp.lpszClassName=szProgName;
    wcSwp.hInstance     =hInst;
    wcSwp.lpfnWndProc   =WindowProc;
      .
      .
      .
```

Windows has approximately 220 different messages it can send to the window function. All of them are identified with names that begin with "WM_". These messages are defined in WINDOWS.H and are constants that refer to numbered codes. Windows can call the window function for many reasons, including window creation, resizing, moving, or reduction to an icon, menu item selection, moving or changing a scroll bar by a mouse click, repainting a client area, and destroying the window.

Like many of the other functions used in Windows, the WindowProc function uses the PASCAL calling convention. The first parameter to the function, *hwnd*, contains the handle to the window that Windows will send the message. Recall that one window function can process messages for several windows created from the same window class. By using the window handle, WindowProc can determine which window is receiving the message.

The second function parameter, *messg*, specifies the actual message as defined in WINDOWS.H. The last two parameters, *wParam* and *lParam*, contain additional information related to each specific message. Sometimes the values returned are NULL and can be ignored; at other times they can contain two byte values and a far pointer, or two word values.

WM_PAINT Message

The first thing the window function has to do is examine the type of the message it is about to process. It then must select the appropriate action to be taken. In the C language, this selection process is performed by the *switch* statement. The first message the window function will process is WM_PAINT. The paint procedure prepares the application's client area for updating and obtains a display context for the window. The display context comes equipped with a default pen, brush, and font. The display context is very important because all of the display functions used by Windows' applications require a handle to the display context.

Since Windows is a multitasking environment, however, it becomes quite possible for one application to display its dialog box over another application's client area, thereby creating a display problem whenever the dialog box is closed. Windows takes care of this possible "black hole" by sending the application a WM_PAINT message, requesting that the application's client area be updated.

Except for the first WM_PAINT message, which is sent by the call to UpdateWindow in WinMain, additional WM_PAINT messages are sent under the following conditions:

- When resizing a window

- Whenever a portion of a client area has been hidden by a menu or dialog box that has just been closed

- When using the ScrollWindow function
- When forcing a WM_PAINT message with a call to the InvalidateRect or InvalidateRgn functions

Any portion of an application's client area that has been corrupted by the overlay of, for example, a dialog box, has that part of the client area marked as invalid. Windows makes the redrawing of a client area extremely efficient by keeping track of the diagonal coordinates of this invalid rectangle. The presence of an invalid rectangle prompts Windows to send the WM_PAINT message.

Should the execution of statements invalidate several portions of the client area, Windows will adjust the invalid rectangle coordinates to encapsulate all invalid regions. Windows does not send a WM_PAINT message for each invalid rectangle.

By making a call to InvalidateRect, Windows can require the client area to be marked invalid, thereby forcing a WM_PAINT message. By calling GetUpdateRect, an application can obtain the coordinates of the invalid rectangle. Calling the ValidateRect function validates any rectangular region in the client area and removes any pending WM_PAINT messages.

The processing of the WM_PAINT message ends with a call to the EndPaint function. This function is called whenever the application is finished outputting information to the client area. It tells Windows that your program has finished processing all paint messages and it is now okay to remove the display context.

Terminating an application by selecting the Close option from the system menu initiates a WM_DESTROY message that causes the PostQuitMessage function to place a WM_QUIT message in the message queue. The program terminates after retrieving this message. The DefWindowProc (default window function) is used to process any WM_PAINT messages not processed by the window function.

CREATING A MODULE DEFINITION FILE

The Simplified Windows Platform example consists of two files, the C source code and the module definition file. A module definition file contains definitions and descriptive information that tells the linker just how to assemble the application's executable file. This information becomes part of the header section of the new executable file format.

Table 3-4 contains a listing of the most frequently used module definition file statements and a brief explanation of their use.

Table 3-4.   Frequently Used Module Definition Statements

Statement	Usage
CODE	Gives the memory attributes for the program's code segments. The code can be marked MOVEABLE or DISCARDABLE. In the first case, Windows is given permission to relocate code segments within memory to satisfy dynamic memory allocation requests. In the second case, Windows discards any unneeded code segments
DATA	Defines the memory attributes for the application's data segment. The MOVEABLE option allows Windows to move the data segment to satisfy memory allocation requests
DESCRIPTION	Allows the description of the module
EXPORTS	A very important statement. Any routine in Windows that is to be called from outside its own program must be exported. As described earlier, the window procedure will be called back by Windows, therefore it must be exported. Technically, the EXPORTS statement identifies the application's dynamic link entry point. These entry points must also be declared FAR and PASCAL in your program code
HEAPSIZE	Defines the minimum size for the local heap. The heap is a section of memory at the end of an application's data segment where local memory allocation requests are placed
NAME	Specifies the name of the executable module to be created
STACKSIZE	Specifies the size of the application's stack. Note however, that unlike the heap, the stack size remains fixed. The stack is used to store automatic local variables, pass parameters to subroutines, and store the calling routine's return address
STUB	Specifies the name of a non-Windows application program that will be run under regular DOS if the Windows program is run from the command line. WINSTUB.EXE, which is supplied with the Windows Software Development Kit, is normally used

For the Simplified Windows Platform example, the module definition file looks like this:

```
NAME        SWP
DESCRIPTION 'Simplified Windows Platform'
STUB        'WINSTUB.EXE'
CODE        PRELOAD MOVEABLE DISCARDABLE
DATA        PRELOAD MOVEABLE MULTIPLE
HEAPSIZE    4096
STACKSIZE   9216
EXPORTS     WindowProc      @1
```

The NAME statement defines SWP as a Windows program (not a dynamic link library) and gives the module a name. This name should be the same as the program's .EXE file.

The DESCRIPTION line copies the text into the .EXE file. Very often this is used to imbed additional information, such as a release date, version number, or copyright notice.

The STUB statement specifies the name of a program that is to be inserted into the .EXE file whenever the application is to be run from the DOS command line. WINSTUB.EXE is the file supplied with the Windows Software Development Kit.

Both the CODE and DATA segments have been marked MOVEABLE, allowing Windows to relocate them for any dynamic memory allocation requests. The MULTIPLE statement also instructs Windows to create unique data segments for each instance of the application.

The HEAPSIZE statement allocates an amount of extra, expandable, local memory from within the application's data segment. The STACKSIZE has been set to 9216. Larger values may be necessary for applications with large nonstatic variables, or those applications using recursion.

Finally, the EXPORTS statement identifies the application's dynamic link entry point and specifies the name of the procedure, in this case, WindowProc.

CREATING A MAKE FILE

Microsoft provides a program maintenance utility named **NMAKE** as part of the C compiler and macro assembler packages. The **NMAKE** utility can update an executable file when changes are made to the program's source or object files. That feature alone is not really unique — after all, programmers have used batch files to compile and link programs for years.

The feature that sets the **NMAKE** utility apart from common batch files is its unique ability to selectively recompile only the source files that have changed since the last complete compilation. This is particularly important in programs where multiple source files are brought together to create a final program.

Up to this point, you have worked with single source code programs — hardly a challenge for a batch program. But now, with multiple source and data files, an efficient means is needed to bring everything together. This is the **NMAKE** utility's greatest moment!

But what you didn't want to hear is that the **NMAKE** utility requires the creation of another file. This file contains the information necessary to create the final executable version of an application. The **MAKE** file does not have an extension, and in this case will simply be called SWP.

The **NMAKE** utility is called by typing

NMAKE SWP

The utility performs its magic by comparing dates. For example, if the date of SWP.C is 12/18/89 and that of SWP.OBJ is 12/07/89, the utility will recompile and link the C program in order to update the .OBJ and .EXE files. If a program contains five separate C source code files, and only one of them has changed, the utility will only recompile that particular file and then link all of the .OBJ files together to produce a final .EXE file. All of this is accomplished automatically from within the **NMAKE** utility.

For the boilerplate program (SWP), the **MAKE** file looks like this:

```
ALL : swp.exe # ALL needed for C 6.0 up

swp.obj: swp.c
    cl -c -AS -Gsw -Oas -Zpe swp.c

swp.exe: swp.obj swp.def
    link /NOD swp,,,libw slibcew, swp.def
```

In a **MAKE** file, the file named to the left of each colon is the file the **NMAKE** utility updates if any of the files to the right of the colon have a later date. The second and third lines specify the action taken by the utility.

The first line of the **MAKE** file compares the dates of the SWP.OBJ file with SWP.C. If the C source code has a more recent date, the C compiler will be invoked (using the compiler directives specified on the second line) to update the SWP.OBJ file.

The second set of statements compares the final SWP.EXE date with all of those files necessary to create it, in this case SWP.OBJ and SWP.DEF. Should there be any discrepancies, the linker would then be invoked (using the directives specified in the fourth line). Notice that if SWP.OBJ had been updated by the compiler, this would necessarily force a new linking.

PUTTING IT ALL TOGETHER

This is the moment you've waited for. Your disk now contains the following files: SWP, SWP.DEF, and SWP.C. Execute the **NMAKE** utility, and if everything goes okay you'll end up with two additional files—SWP.OBJ

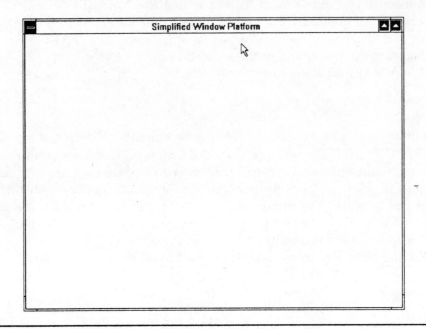

Figure 3-1. The Simplified Windows Platform

and SWP.EXE. If you execute SWP.EXE, you should end up with a screen similar to Figure 3-1.

HOW TO USE SWP.* TO CREATE OTHER WINDOWS APPLICATIONS

If at this point you are slightly dazed by all of the new terminology and concepts necessary for understanding and writing Windows applications, here is some good news. Most of the examples included in this text build upon the Simplified Windows Platform.

The following listing contains all of the files necessary to create a simple Windows application using the SWP.* files SWP **MAKE** file, SWP.DEF module definition file, and SWP.C C source code file.

```
THE SWP MAKE FILE:

ALL : swp.exe # ALL needed for C 6.0 up

swp.obj: swp.c
    cl -c -AS -Gsw -Oas -Zpe swp.c

swp.exe: swp.obj swp.def
    link/NOD swp,,,libw slibcew, swp.def
```

THE SWP.DEF MODULE DEFINITION FILE:

```
NAME        SWP
DESCRIPTION 'Simplified Windows Platform'
EXETYPE     WINDOWS
CODE        PRELOAD MOVEABLE DISCARDABLE
DATA        PRELOAD MOVEABLE MULTIPLE
HEAPSIZE    4096
STACKSIZE   9216
EXPORTS     WindowProc       @1
```

THE SWP.C APPLICATION FILE:

```c
/* Simplified Windows Platform (SWP)              */
/* (c) William H. Murray and Chris H. Pappas, 1989 */

#include <windows.h>

long FAR PASCAL WindowProc(HWND,unsigned,WORD,LONG);

char szProgName[]="ProgName";

int PASCAL WinMain(hInst,hPreInst,lpszCmdLine,nCmdShow)
HANDLE hInst,hPreInst;
LPSTR  lpszCmdLine;
int    nCmdShow;
{
  HWND hwnd;
  MSG  msg;
  WNDCLASS wcSwp;
  if (!hPreInst)
  {
    wcSwp.lpszClassName=szProgName;
    wcSwp.hInstance     =hInst;
    wcSwp.lpfnWndProc   =WindowProc;
    wcSwp.hCursor       =LoadCursor(NULL,IDC_ARROW);
    wcSwp.hIcon         =NULL;
    wcSwp.lpszMenuName  =NULL;
    wcSwp.hbrBackground=GetStockObject(WHITE_BRUSH);
    wcSwp.style         =CS_HREDRAW|CS_VREDRAW;
    wcSwp.cbClsExtra    =0;
    wcSwp.cbWndExtra    =0;
    if (!RegisterClass (&wcSwp))
      return FALSE;
  }
  hwnd=CreateWindow(szProgName,"Simplified Windows Platform",
                    WS_OVERLAPPEDWINDOW,CW_USEDEFAULT,
                    CW_USEDEFAULT,CW_USEDEFAULT,
                    CW_USEDEFAULT,NULL,NULL,
                    hInst,NULL);
  ShowWindow(hwnd,nCmdShow);
  UpdateWindow(hwnd);
  while (GetMessage(&msg,NULL,NULL,NULL))
  {
    TranslateMessage(&msg);
    DispatchMessage(&msg);
  }
```

```
    return(msg.wParam);
}


long FAR PASCAL WindowProc(hwnd,messg,wParam,lParam)
HWND    hwnd;
unsigned messg;
WORD    wParam;
LONG    lParam;
{
  #define RED 0x0000FFL
  PAINTSTRUCT ps;
  HDC  hdc;
  HPEN hPen;
  switch (messg)
  {
  case WM_PAINT:
    hdc=BeginPaint(hwnd,&ps);

/*--------- your routines below ---------*/

/*--------- your routines above ---------*/

    ValidateRect(hwnd,NULL);
    EndPaint(hwnd,&ps);
    break;
  case WM_DESTROY:
    PostQuitMessage(0);
    break;
  default:
    return(DefWindowProc(hwnd,messg,wParam,lParam));
    break;
  }
  return(0L);
}
```

Notice that within the body of the WindowProc procedure there are two comments.

```
/*--------- your routines below ---------*/
/*--------- your routines above ---------*/
```

If you want to experiment with writing your own Windows applications, simply place your C source code statements between these two comments. This will save you time and, while you are getting your feet wet on Windows fundamentals, prevent you from accidentally making code changes that could ripple throughout your application.

CREATING AN INCLUDE FILE

If you are familiar with C programming, then you have already encountered include or header files. For those of you who haven't, include files or header files are kept separate from the source file, but are merged into the source file during compilation. This separation makes include files easier to modify and share with several source files. Normally they contain definitions of certain values and serve to establish application-related constants. SWP.C includes this statement,

```
#include <windows.h>
```

which calls those definitions into the final compilation. WINDOWS.H is a huge file, over 88,000 bytes in size, that contains all of the Windows-specific definitions your application will need. You must include this file in your program or it will not successfully compile and execute. You can also create your own include files.

WHAT ABOUT RESOURCE FILES?

The latter part of this chapter has focused on the various files necessary to create a Windows application. One brief example of how the complexity of creating an application can grow was the second example **MAKE** file examined. To review briefly: an application has a .C source code file, a .DEF file, and a **MAKE** file. But a Windows application can also define its own header (.H), icon (.ICO), cursor (.CUR), bitmap (.BMP), and pointer (.PTR) files, and so on, all of which need to be incorporated into the executable version of the program.

Files, files everywhere—what's a programmer to do? First, don't panic. Those .DEF, .H, .C, .ICO, and .PTR files can all be spliced together to make a working program, but first (you guessed it) you need another file. You will also need to create a resource script file. For this you will use an example from Chapter 11, BAR11.RC (all resource script files have an .RC file extension). The following example defines the include files, cursor, menu, About box, and the dialog box text to be used in the BAR11.C application. The file is used by the Microsoft Resource Compiler.

```
#include "windows.h"
#include "bar11.h"

BarCursor CURSOR Bar11.cur

BarMenu    MENU
BEGIN
  POPUP "Bar_Chart_Input"
  BEGIN
    MENUITEM "About...",       IDM_ABOUT
    MENUITEM "Input...",       IDM_INPUT
    MENUITEM "Exit",           IDM_EXIT
```

```
      END
END

AboutDlgBox DIALOG LOADONCALL MOVEABLE DISCARDABLE
            50,300,180,80
            STYLE WS_DLGFRAME|WS_POPUP
  BEGIN
    CONTROL "Interactive Bar Chart Program",-1,"static",
            SS_CENTER|WS_CHILD,2,60,176,10
    CONTROL "by William H. Murray & Chris H. Pappas",-1,
            "static",SS_CENTER|WS_CHILD,2,45,176,10
    CONTROL "OK",IDOK,"button",
            BS_PUSHBUTTON|WS_TABSTOP|WS_CHILD,75,10,32,14
  END

BarDlgBox DIALOG LOADONCALL MOVEABLE DISCARDABLE
          42,-10,223,209
          CAPTION "Bar Chart Information"
          STYLE WS_BORDER|WS_CAPTION|WS_DLGFRAME|WS_POPUP
  BEGIN
    CONTROL "Bar Chart Title:",100,"button",
            BS_GROUPBOX|WS_TABSTOP|WS_CHILD,5,11,212,89
    CONTROL "Bar Chart Heights",101,"button",
            BS_GROUPBOX|WS_TABSTOP|WS_CHILD,5,105,212,90
    CONTROL "Title: ",-1,"static",SS_LEFT|WS_CHILD,
            43,35,28,8
    CONTROL "",DM_TITLE,"edit",ES_LEFT|WS_BORDER|WS_TABSTOP|
            WS_CHILD,75,30,137,12
    CONTROL "x-axis label:",-1,"static",SS_LEFT|
            WS_CHILD,15,55,55,8
    CONTROL "",DM_XLABEL,"edit",ES_LEFT|WS_BORDER|WS_TABSTOP|
            WS_CHILD,75,50,135,12
    CONTROL "y-axis label:",-1,"static",SS_LEFT|
            WS_CHILD,15,75,60,8
    CONTROL "",DM_YLABEL,"edit",ES_LEFT|WS_BORDER|WS_TABSTOP|
            WS_CHILD,75,70,135,12
    CONTROL "Bar #1: ",-1,"static",SS_LEFT|
            WS_CHILD,45,125,40,8
    CONTROL "Bar #2: ",-1,"static",SS_LEFT|
            WS_CHILD,45,140,40,8
    CONTROL "Bar #3: ",-1,"static",SS_LEFT|
            WS_CHILD,45,155,40,8
    CONTROL "Bar #4: ",-1,"static",SS_LEFT|
            WS_CHILD,45,170,40,8
    CONTROL "Bar #5: ",-1,"static",SS_LEFT|
            WS_CHILD,45,185,40,8
    CONTROL "Bar #6: ",-1,"static",SS_LEFT|
            WS_CHILD,130,125,40,8
    CONTROL "Bar #7: ",-1,"static",SS_LEFT|
            WS_CHILD,130,140,40,8
    CONTROL "Bar #8: ",-1,"static",SS_LEFT|
            WS_CHILD,130,155,40,8
    CONTROL "Bar #9: ",-1,"static",SS_LEFT|
            WS_CHILD,130,170,40,8
    CONTROL "Bar #10:",-1,"static",SS_LEFT|
            WS_CHILD,130,185,45,8
    CONTROL "10",DM_P1,"edit",ES_LEFT|WS_BORDER|WS_TABSTOP|
            WS_CHILD,90,120,30,12
    CONTROL "20",DM_P2,"edit",ES_LEFT|WS_BORDER|WS_TABSTOP|
            WS_CHILD,90,135,30,12
```

```
CONTROL "30",DM_P3,"edit",ES_LEFT|WS_BORDER|WS_TABSTOP|
    WS_CHILD,90,150,30,12
CONTROL "40",DM_P4,"edit",ES_LEFT|WS_BORDER|WS_TABSTOP|
    WS_CHILD,90,165,30,12
CONTROL "0",DM_P5,"edit",ES_LEFT|WS_BORDER|WS_TABSTOP|
    WS_CHILD,90,180,30,12
CONTROL "0",DM_P6,"edit",ES_LEFT|WS_BORDER|WS_TABSTOP|
    WS_CHILD,180,120,30,12
CONTROL "0",DM_P7,"edit",ES_LEFT|WS_BORDER|WS_TABSTOP|
    WS_CHILD,180,135,30,12
CONTROL "0",DM_P8,"edit",ES_LEFT|WS_BORDER|WS_TABSTOP|
    WS_CHILD,180,150,30,12
CONTROL "0",DM_P9,"edit",ES_LEFT|WS_BORDER|WS_TABSTOP|
    WS_CHILD,180,165,30,12
CONTROL "0",DM_P10,"edit",ES_LEFT|WS_BORDER|WS_TABSTOP|
    WS_CHILD,180,180,30,12
CONTROL "OK",IDOK,"button",BS_PUSHBUTTON|WS_TABSTOP|
    WS_CHILD,54,195,24,14
CONTROL "Cancel",IDCANCEL,"button",BS_PUSHBUTTON|
    WS_TABSTOP|WS_CHILD,124,195,34,14
END
```

The resource compiler is an application development tool that will let you add resources such as message strings, pointers, dialog boxes, and menus to the executable file of your program. All of these resources will be brought under your control with the use of the **MAKE** utility, although each operation could be carried out separately.

Understanding the Resource Compiler

The resource compiler's principal job is to prepare data for OS/2 applications that use the WinLoadString, WinLoadPointer, WinLoadMenu, WinLoadDlg (and so on) functions. The resource compiler and associated functions let you define and modify the resources in an executable file without changing the rest of the file.

There are several options available to the programmer in implementing the resource compiler. These options, and a complete description of the resource compiler, are contained in the Microsoft Quick Help program. For the purposes of this example, the resource compiler will be run with the **-r** option. The **-r** option directs the resource compiler to compile the resource definition file *without* adding it to the final executable file. In choosing this option a binary resource file is created that can be added to the executable file at a later date. The binary resource file will have an .RES file extension. Therefore, after compiling, your disk will also have a file named X.RES. Using the compiler in this manner with the BAR11.RC, you would type

RC -r BAR11

Applications can have any or all of the resources listed in Table 3-5.

MAKE REVISITED

As you have just seen, many files may be needed to create the final executable version of a Windows application. At any point in the maintenance phase of an application, any one, or several of these files could be modified. Keeping the executable version of the application up to date could be a painstaking task, were it not for the **NMAKE** utility. The following listing shows an example of the **MAKE** file used in Chapter 11 for the BAR11 program. It incorporates many of the files described earlier.

```
ALL : bar11.exe # ALL needed for C 6.0 up

bar11.obj : bar11.c bar11.h
    cl -c -AS -Gsw -Oas -Zpe bar11.c

bar11.res : bar11.rc bar.ico bar11.cur
    RC -r bar11.rc

bar11.exe : bar11.obj bar11.def bar11.res
    link/NOD bar11,,,libw slibcew, bar11.def
    rc bar11.res
```

Notice that there are three major blocks of code. The first block tells the utility that if BAR11.C or BAR11.H has been updated, then a recompile will be necessary to update the BAR11.OBJ file.

Table 3-5.   Predefined Windows Resources

Resource	Description
ACCELERATORS	Allow the user to select commands by means of keyboard input
BITMAPS	Represent graphics images
CURSORS	Track the movements of the mouse, allowing the user to select objects on the screen
DIALOG BOXES	Define the shape and contents of dialog box
FONTS	Represent character set descriptions
ICONS	Represent an application when it is reduced to an icon
MENUS	Permit the user to specify commands to a Windows application program

The second block of code states that if any of the resource script (.RC), icon (.ICO), or cursor (.CUR) files has been changed, then the resource compiler will have to update the BAR11.RES file.

Finally, if the .OBJ, .DEF, or .RES files have been updated, the linker will be run to produce a new .EXE file. **MAKE** files necessarily expand in complexity as the number of features a Windows application takes advantage of increases.

4

ACCESSING THE WINDOWS ENVIRONMENT

Remember back to your first programming course and the topic of subroutines in particular functions. You were probably told never to use the identifier for a function more than once within the body of the function. You probably accepted this as a compiler restriction. Then one day you learned about recursion.

The first time you encountered one-dimensional arrays you were probably awestruck. Then came multi-dimensional arrays. And who can forget their first encounter with dynamic variables!

This approach, presenting programming concepts using an incremental scale of complexity, worked to your advantage. As you solidified your programming fundamentals you moved into deeper water. Well, it's time to put on your wet suits and scuba equipment.

The software engineers that developed Windows have presented you with an almost limitless combination of application development tools. This chapter will begin to dive deeper into the richness of their capabilities. Many of the example programs throughout the text will use some or all of these features.

COORDINATE SYSTEMS

Windows encompasses a huge array of functions that allow an application to display text and graphics in whatever coordinate system most logically or physically maps the application's needs in the display context. Many times the default coordinate system will provide the most convenient object placement.

Eight Mapping Modes

Most of the GDI drawing functions specify coordinate values or sizes. For example, the frequently used TextOut function has X and Y specifications indicating where the beginning of the text is to be output. Specifically, the X parameter indicates the position on the horizontal axis and the Y parameter the position on the vertical axis. However, the parameters are specified in what are known as *logical units*. A logical unit or *logical coordinate* represents a virtual coordinate system that extends from +32K to −32K in the X and Y directions. GDI output routines then map the logical coordinates into the correct screen coordinates for output.

The translation of logical units to device units is governed by the current mapping mode, along with the window and viewport origins and extents. Regardless of the mapping mode, all coordinates you specify must be signed short integers in the range 32,767 to −32,768. The mapping mode also specifies an origin and orientation of the X and Y axes. Table 4-1 lists

Table 4-1.   Mapping Modes Defined in WINDOWS.H

Mapping Mode		X Axis	Y Axis	Logical Units
MM_TEXT	1	right	down	pixels
MM_LOMETRIC	2	right	up	0.1 mm
MM_HIMETRIC	3	right	up	0.01 mm
MM_LOENGLISH	4	right	up	0.01 inch
MM_HIENGLISH	5	right	up	0.001 inch
MM_TWIPS	6	right	up	1/1440 inch
MM_ISOTROPIC	7	either	either	arbitrary (x=y)
MM_ANISOTROPIC	8	either	either	arbitrary (x!=y)

the eight possible mapping modes using the WINDOW.H identifiers.

Setting the mapping mode requires a simple call to the SetMapMode-(hDC,nMapMode) function, with *nMapMode* being one of the eight mapping mode identifiers listed. While the default mapping mode is MM_TEXT, an application can obtain the current mapping mode by making a call to the GetMapMode(hDC) function, which would look something like this:

```
nMapMode = GetMapMode(hDC);
```

Using the TextOut(hDC,x,y,lpString,nCount) function as an example, let's see how the mapping modes affect the output. When the mapping mode is MM_TEXT (the default), logical units are mapped directly to physical units or pixels. If the TextOut function had been passed an *x* value of 10 and a *y* value of 20, the text output would begin 10 pixels from the left of the client area and 20 pixels from the top.

If the mapping mode had been set to MM_HIENGLISH with the TextOut function being passed an *x* value of 100 and a *y* value of −200, the text output would begin one inch from the left of the client area and two inches from the top. Did you notice the −200? When using the mapping modes MM_LOENGLISH, MM_HIENGLISH, MM_LOMETRIC, MM_HIMETRIC, or MM_TWIPS, all logical coordinates are expressed in physical measurements, with the origin at the upper-left corner of the selected area. Moving down the display requires a negative value.

To help clarify matters: all non-GDI functions use the device coordinate system, returning values in device units, which are pixels. Since the mapping mode is an attribute of a device context, the only time the mapping mode will come into play is when the application is using a GDI function that requires a handle to the device context.

Device Coordinates

All device coordinate systems that Windows uses are expressed in terms of pixels. The X axis increases in value going from left to right. The Y axis increases in value from the top of the display to the bottom.

Many Windows functions such as CreateWindow, MoveWindow, GetWindowRect (obtain whole window position and size in terms of screen coordinates), WindowFromPoint, GetMessagePos, GetCursorPos, SetCursorPos, and SetBrushOrg, use the *screen coordinate system* described in the preceding section.

The *whole window coordinate system* defines the application's entire window. The coordinates include access to the caption bar, main menu, any scroll bars, and the window frame itself. The GetWindowDC function will map logical coordinates in GDI functions into whole window coordinates.

Client area coordinates are the most frequently used of the three device coordinate systems. In this system the upper-left corner of the client area is (0,0). When using the GetDC or BeginPaint function, logical coordinates are translated into client area coordinates.

When necessary, converting from screen coordinates to client area coordinates is as easy as making the appropriate function call to either Screen-ToClient or ClientToScreen.

Viewports

To review, Windows maps logical coordinates to device coordinates based on two criteria: the mapping mode selected and the particular function used to obtain the device context. Actually, there's more to the story.

The mapping mode is used to define the mapping of the window's coordinates or logical units to the viewport or device coordinates. A *viewport* is defined in device coordinates or pixels and usually refers to the client area. However, if the application has made a call to GetWindowDC or CreateDC, the coordinates returned will refer to the whole window, or screen coordinates, respectively. Regardless, the point (0,0) is at the upper-left corner of the specified area, with X values increasing from left to right, and Y values increasing from top to bottom.

A "window" in this context refers to logical coordinates. These logical coordinates may be pixels, inches, millimeters, or user-defined. Logical window coordinates are passed to GDI functions.

A Word About MM_ISOTROPIC and MM_ANISOTROPIC

This set of mapping modes is the only one that will allow you to change the viewport and window extents. This allows an application-defined scaling factor for translating logical and device coordinates.

MM_ISOTROPIC provides a metric mapping mode where logical units on the X axis are identical to those of the Y axis. This mapping mode allows an application to display images with the correct aspect ratio, regardless of the aspect ratio of the display device itself.

MM_ANISOTROPIC allows an application to use arbitrary axes while providing equal logical units for both axes.

Changing Default Coordinates

The following example illustrates how to use the MM_ISOTROPIC mode to set the axes to equal physical distances. After the call is made to Set-MapMode, selecting MM_ISOTROPIC mode, the SetWindowExt function is called. Most of the time you will use parameters to SetWindowExt. For this example, the logical size of the logical window will be "hardwired" with fixed constants. The third statement makes a call to the SetViewport-Ext function passing parameters that define the actual height and width of the client area. When Windows adjusts these extents, it has to fit the logical window within the physical viewport. Therefore, Windows makes the best use of space whenever SetWindowExt is called before SetViewportExt. The last statement sets the logical point (*xClientView*/2,*yClientView*/2) to the device point (0,0).

```
SetMapMode(hdc,MM_ISOTROPIC);
SetWindowExt(hdc,500,500);
SetViewportExt(hdc,xClientView,-yClientView);
SetViewportOrg(hdc,xClientView/2,yClientView/2);
```

Earlier it was stated that if the mapping mode had been set to MM_HIENGLISH with the TextOut function being passed an *x* value of 100 and a *y* value of −200, the text output would begin one inch from the left of the client area and two inches from the top. The −200 was necessary because the default window and viewport origins were (0,0). Therefore, the only way to display anything in the client area is to use negative values for *y*. Since this can become quite disconcerting, why not just reset the logical origin? Assuming that *yClientView* is the height of the client area in pixels, you can accomplish this with the following statement:

```
SetViewportOrg(hdc,0,yClientView);
```

Now that the logical origin has been set to the lower-left corner of the client area, positive values can be used to move text up the display. This approach can be used for all five of the "metric" mapping modes.

SELECTING INITIAL WINDOW SIZE, POSITION, CURSORS, ICONS, AND STYLES

Of all of the Windows functions, CreateWindow is probably the most eclectic. In other words, if you can't do it with CreateWindow you don't need to do it. The following material is designed to explain the syntax and meaning behind all of the function's parameters.

```
HWND CreateWindow(lpClassName,lpWindowName,dwStyle,x,y,nWidth,
                nHeight,hWndParent,hMenu,hInstance,lpParam)
```

This frequently invoked Windows function creates either an overlapped, pop-up, or a child window, specifying the window's class, title, and style. It can even set the window's initial position and size. If the window being created has an owning parent or menu, this also is defined.

The function then sends the necessary messages (WM_CREATE, WM_GETMINMAXINFO, and WM_NCCREATE) to the window. If the WS_VISIBLE style option has been selected, all necessary window messages are sent to activate and display the window. The following explains each individual parameter:

Parameters   *lpClassName* (LPSTR) points to a null-terminated character string naming the window's class

lpWindowName (LPSTR) points to a null-terminated character string identifying the window by name

x (int) defines the initial X coordinate position for the window

Overlapped or Pop-up	X coordinate of the window's upper-left corner is given in screen coordinates. If the value is CW_USE-DEFAULT, Windows selects the default upper-left X coordinate
Child Window	X coordinate of the upper-left corner of the window in the client area of its parent window

y (int) defines the initial Y coordinate position for the window

Overlapped or Pop-up	Y coordinate of the window's upper-left corner is given in screen coordinates. If the value is CW_USE-DEFAULT, Windows selects the default upper-left Y coordinate
Child Window	Y coordinate of the upper-left corner of the window in the client area of its parent window

nWidth (int), using device units, defines width of the window

Overlapped	either the window's width in screen coordinates or CW_USEDEFAULT. If the latter, Windows selects the width and height for the window

nHeight (int), using device units, defines height of the window

Overlapped	either the window's height in screen coordinates or CW_USEDEFAULT, is given. If the latter, Windows ignores *nHeight*

hWndParent (HWND) specifies the parent window for the window that is about to be created. Overlapped windows must *not* have a parent (*hWndParent* must be NULL). A valid parent handle must be passed when creating a child window

hMenu (HMENU) is dependent on the window's style and specifies a menu or a child window identifier.

Overlapped or Pop-up	identifies the menu to be used with the window. A NULL value specifies the use of the class's menu
Child	contains a child window identifier. This is determined by the application and is to be unique for all child windows of the same parent

hInstance (HANDLE) specifies the instance of the module to be identified with the window

lpParam (LPSTR) is a pointer to a value passed to the window through the lParam parameter of the WM_CREATE message

The value returned is either a valid new window identifier if successful, or a NULL if not.

Tables 4-2 through 4-9 provide an alphabetical listing of window control classes (Table 4-2), window styles (Table 4-3), and control styles (Tables 4-4 through 4-9). Many of these styles will be used throughout the text. The tables can be used for reference when designing your own Windows applications.

THE SHOWWINDOW FUNCTION

The ShowWindow function must be called only once per program with the *nCmdShow* parameter from the WinMain function. This function displays the window on the screen.

```
ShowWindow(hWnd,nCmdShow)
```

However, subsequent calls to ShowWindow must use one of the constants shown in Table 4-10, instead of one specified by the *nCmdShow* parameter from the WinMain function.

Note: The primary difference between SW_MINNOACTIVATE and SW_SHOWMINIMIZED (see Table 4-10) is that the former does not make the window the active window, but the latter does.

Table 4-2.   Possible Control Classes

Class	Description
BUTTON	This identifies a small rectangular child window displaying a button the user can turn on or off with a mouse click. Buttons usually change display appearance when selected and deselected
	BUTTON Control Styles
	BS_AUTOCHECKBOX BS_AUTORADIOBUTTON BS_AUTO3STATE BS_CHECKBOX BS_DEFPUSHBUTTON BS_GROUPBOX BS_LEFTTEXT BS_PUSHBUTTON BS_RADIOBUTTON BS_3STATE BS_USERBUTTON
EDIT	This identifies a small, rectangular child window in which the user can enter text from the keyboard. Input focus can be changed by clicking the mouse button or using TAB. Edit control classes allow the user to repeatedly select the input focus, make entries, backspace over mistakes, and reenter information. The user inserts text whenever the control display exhibits a flashing caret
	EDIT Control Styles
	ES_AUTOHSCROLL ES_AUTOVSCROLL ES_CENTER

Table 4-2.   Possible Control Classes (*continued*)

Class	Description
EDIT (*continued*)	ES_LEFT ES_MULTILINE ES_NOHIDESEL ES_RIGHT
LISTBOX	This identifies a list of character strings. Most frequently used when an application needs to present a list of names, such as available file names, from which the user can select. Options are selected by moving the mouse and clicking on the selected item. This causes the item to be highlighted and a notification of the choice to be passed to the parent window. Whenever the list is long, LISTBOX controls can be used in conjunction with SCROLLBAR controls LISTBOX Control Styles LBS_MULTIPLESEL LBS_NOREDRAW LBS_NOTIFY LBS_SORT LBS_STANDARD
COMBOBOX	This designates a control consisting of a selection field similar to an EDIT control plus a list box. The list box may be displayed at all times or may be dropped down when the user selects a "pop box" next to the selection field
SCROLLBAR	The SCROLLBAR control displays a stretched rectangular box containing a page position reference, sometimes called a "thumb," along with direction arrows at both ends. The user selects a position within the list by sliding the thumb up or down the bar. SCROLLBAR controls are identical in appearance to scroll bars used in ordinary windows; however, they may appear anywhere within a window. Automatically associated with the SCROLLBAR controls is a SIZEBOX control. This small rectangle allows the user to change the size of the window SCROLLBAR Control Styles SBS_BOTTOMALIGN

Table 4-2.   Possible Control Classes (*continued*)

Class	Description
SCROLLBAR (*continued*)	SBS_HORZ SBS_LEFTALIGN SBS_RIGHTALIGN SBS_SIZEBOX SBS_SIZEBOXBOTTOMRIGHTALIGN SBS_SIZEBOXTOPLEFTALIGN SBS_TOPALIGN SBS_VERT
STATIC	The STATIC control class defines a simple text field, box, or rectangle, which is most frequently used to identify, box, or separate other controls. It therefore outputs or inputs information STATIC Control Styles SS_BLACKFRAME SS_BLACKRECT SS_CENTER SS_GRAYFRAME SS_GRAYRECT SS_ICON SS_LEFT SS_RIGHT SS_SIMPLE SS_USERITEM SS_WHITEFRAME SS_WHITERECT

Table 4-3.   Possible Window Styles

Style	Description
WS_BORDER	Creates a bordered window
WS_CAPTION	Adds a title bar to the bordered window
WS_CHILD	Creates a child window. Not to be used with WS_POPUP style windows

Table 4-3.   Possible Window Styles (*continued*)

Style	Description
WS_CHILDWINDOW	Creates a child window of the WS_CHILD style
WS_CLIPCHILDREN	Used when creating the parent window. The WS_CLIPCHILDREN window style prohibits drawing of the parent window within the area occupied by any child window
WS_CLIPSIBLINGS	Used with the WS_CHILD style only. This style clips all other child windows whenever a particular child window receives a paint message. Without this, it would be possible to draw within the client area of another child window
WS_DISABLED	Creates an initially disabled window
WS_DLGFRAME	Creates a double-bordered window without a title
WS_EX_DLGMODALFRAME	Creates a window with a double border that, optionally, may be created with a title bar. This style can only be used in the *dwExStyle* parameter of the CreateWindowEx function
WS_GROUP	Used only by dialog boxes. This window style defines the first control of a group of controls. The user can move from one control to another by using the direction keys
WS_HSCROLL	Creates a window with a horizontal scroll bar
WS_ICONIC	Used with the WS_OVERLAPPED style. WS_ICONIC creates a window that is initially displayed in its iconic form
WS_MAXIMIZE	Creates a window of maximum size
WS_MAXIMIXEBOX	Creates a window that includes a maximize box
WS_MINIMIZE	Creates a window of minimum size
WS_MINIMIZEBOX	Creates a window that includes a minimize box
WS_OVERLAPPED	Creates an overlapped window
WS_OVERLAPPEDWINDOW	Uses the WS_CAPTION, WS_OVERLAPPED, WS_THICKFRAME, and WS_SYSMENU styles to create an overlapped window
WS_POPUP	Not to be used with WS_CHILD style. Creates a pop-up window
WS_POPUPWINDOW	Uses the WS_BORDER, WS_POPUP, and WS_SYSMENU styles to create a pop-up window

Table 4-3.   Possible Window Styles (*continued*)

Style	Description
WS_SYSMENU	Used only with windows including title bars. Creates a window with a system-menu box displayed in its title bar. When used with a child window, this style creates only a close box instead of the standard system-menu box
WS_TABSTOP	Used only by dialog boxes. Indicates any number of controls the user can move by using TAB. Successive presses of TAB move through the controls specified by the WS_TABSTOP style
WS_THICKFRAME	Creates a thick-framed window that can be used to size the window
WS_VISIBLE	Creates a window that is automatically displayed. Can be used with overlapped and pop-up windows
WS_VSCROLL	Creates a window with a vertical scroll bar

Table 4-4.   BUTTON Class Control Styles

Style	Description
BS_AUTOCHECKBOX	Identical in usage to BS_CHECKBOX, except that the button automatically toggles its state when the user selects it by clicking the mouse button
BS_AUTORADIOBUTTON	Identical in usage to BS_RADIOBUTTON, except that when the button is selected, a BN_CLICKED message is sent to the application, removing check marks from any other radio buttons in the group
BS_AUTO3STATE	Identical to BS_3STATE, except that the button automatically toggles its state when the user selects it by clicking the mouse button

Table 4-4.   BUTTON Class Control Styles *(continued)*

Style	Description
BS_CHECKBOX	Defines a small rectangular button that can be checked. The check box is shown in bold when it is selected. Any associated text is printed to the right of the button
BS_DEFPUSHBUTTON	Defines a small elliptical bold-bordered button. Usually used to identify a user default response. Any associated text is displayed within the button
BS_GROUPBOX	Defines a rectangular region bounding a button group. Text is displayed within the rectangle's upper-left corner
BS_LEFTTEXT	Forces text to be displayed on the left side of the radio or check box button. Can be used with the control styles BS_3STATE, BS_CHECKBOX, or BS_RADIOBUTTON
BS_OWNERDRAW	Designates an owner-draw button. Here the parent window is notified whenever a button is clicked. This notification includes a request to paint, invert, and then disable the button
BS_PUSHBUTTON	Defines a small elliptical button containing the specified text. This control sends a message to the parent window whenever the user clicks the button
BS_RADIOBUTTON	Defines a small circular button with a border that is shown in bold when it has been selected with a mouse button click. The parent window is also notified via a message. A subsequent click produces a normal border, and another message is sent to the parent window indicating the change
BS_3STATE	Identical to BS_CHECKBOX, but the button can be grayed as well as checked. The grayed state is a visual reminder that the current check box has been disabled

Table 4-5.   EDIT Class Control Styles

Style	Description
ES_AUTOHSCROLL	Automatically scrolls text to the right ten characters whenever the user enters data at the end of a line. When the user presses ENTER the text scrolls back to the left edge border
ES_AUTOVSCROLL	Automatically scrolls text up one page when the user presses ENTER at the last line
ES_CENTER	Centers text
ES_LEFT	Uses flush-left text alignment
ES_MULTILINE	Provides multiple-line editing control. When used in conjunction with the ES_AUTOVSCROLL style, scrolls text vertically when the user presses ENTER. If ES_AUTOVSCROLL style is not specified, it beeps when the user presses ENTER, and no more lines can be displayed. A similar condition exists when used with the ES_AUTOHSCROLL style. If selected, the style will allow the user to remain on the same line, shifting text to the left. When deactivated, text not fitting on the same line within the window causes a new line to be created. ES_MULTILINE styles can include scroll bars
ES_NOHIDESEL	Overrides the default action, preventing the edit control from hiding the selection whenever the control loses the input focus, and does not invert the selection when the control receives the input focus
ES_RIGHT	Uses flush-right text alignment

THE SETCLASSWORD FUNCTION

The SetClassWord function is used to replace the specified word in the WNDCLASS data structure of the designated window. Any change made to the structure will cause Windows to make the selected change the next time the window is repainted. Here is the WNDCLASS data structure, for reference:

```
typedef struct tagWNDCLASS {
    WORD    style;
    long    (FAR PASCAL *lpfnWndProc)();
    int     cbClsExtra;
    int     cbWndExtra;
    HANDLE  hInstance;
    HICON   hIcon;
```

```
    HCURSOR hCursor;
    HBRUSH  hbrBackground;
    LPSTR   lpszMenuName;
    LPSTR   lpszClassName;
} WNDCLASS;
```

Table 4-6.   LISTBOX Class Control Styles

Style	Description
LBS_HASSTRINGS	Owner-draw list boxes contain items consisting of strings. The list box maintains the memory and pointers for these strings so the application can use the LB_GETTEXT message to retrieve the text for a particular string
LBS_MULTIPLESEL	Allows for the selection of any number of strings, with the string selection toggling each time the user clicks or double-clicks on the string
LBS_NOREDRAW	The LISTBOX display is not updated when changes are made
LBS_NOTIFY	Whenever the user clicks or double-clicks on a string, the parent window receives an input message
LBS_OWNERDRAWFIXED	Indicates that the owner of the list box is responsible for drawing its contents; the items in the list box are the same height
LBS_OWNERDRAWVARIABLE	Indicates that the owner of the list box is responsible for drawing its contents; however, unlike LBS_OWNERDRAWFIXED, the strings are of variable height
LBS_SORT	Sorts the strings in the LISTBOX alphabetically
LBS_STANDARD	Sorts the strings within the LISTBOX alphabetically, sending a message to the parent window whenever the user clicks or double-clicks on a string. The LISTBOX contains a vertical scroll bar and borders on all sides
LBS_USETABSTOPS	Permits a list box to recognize and expand all tab characters when drawing strings. The default tab positions are 32 dialog units. Using the GetDialogBaseUnits function, an application can obtain the current dialog base units in pixels. One horizontal dialog unit is equal to 1/4 of the current dialog base width unit. Dialog base units are calculated based on the height and width of the current system font

Table 4-7.   COMBOBOX Class Control Styles

Style	Description
CBS_AUTOHSCROLL	Automatically scrolls the text in the edit control to the right whenever the user types a character at the end of the line
CBS_DROPDOWN	Causes the list box not to be displayed unless the user selects an icon next to the selection field
CBS_DROPDOWNLIST	Replaces the EDIT control with a static text item that displays the current selection in the list box
CBS_HASSTRINGS	Indicates the owner-draw combo box contains items consisting of strings. LB_GETTEXT can be used to return the text for a particular item
CBS_OWNERDRAWFIXED	Indicates that the owner of the list box is responsible for drawing its contents; the items in the list box are the same height
CBS_OWNERDRAWVARIABLE	Indicates that the owner of the list box is responsible for drawing its contents; however, unlike LBS_OWNER-DRAWFIXED, the strings are of variable height
CBS_SIMPLE	Displays the list box at all times. The current selection in the list box is displayed in the EDIT control
CBS_SHORT	Will sort strings automatically that are entered into the list box. However, this style does not apply to owner-draw combo boxes

The syntax for the function looks like this:

```
SetClassWord(hWnd,nIndex,wNewWord)
```

hWnd identifies the handle to the window. *nIndex* designates which word in the WNDCLASS data structure is to be changed and the *wNew-Word* parameter specifies the replacement value (WORD).

Table 4-8.   SCROLLBAR Class Control Styles

Style	Description
SBS_BOTTOMALIGN	Used in conjunction with SBS_HORZ style. Scroll bar alignment is along the bottom edge of the rectangle defined by *x*, *y*, *nWidth*, and *nHeight*, using the system default scroll bar height
SBS_HORZ	Defines a horizontal scroll bar. The height, width, and position of the scroll bar will be determined by the CreateWindow function if neither SBS_BOTTOMALIGN nor SBS_TOPALIGN style is requested
SBS_LEFTALIGN	Used in conjunction with SBS_VERT style. Here the left edge of the scroll bar is aligned with the left edge of a rectangle defined by *x*, *y*, *nWidth*, and *nHeight*, using the system default scroll bar height
SBS_RIGHTALIGN	Used in conjunction with SBS_VERT style. Here the right edge of the scroll bar is aligned with the right edge of a rectangle defined by *x*, *y*, *nWidth*, and *nHeight*, using the system default scroll bar height
SBS_SIZEBOX	Defines a size box. The size box will have the height, width, and position given by the CreateWindow function if neither the SBS_SIZEBOXBOTTOM-RIGHTALIGN nor the SBS_SIZEBOX-TOPLEFTALIGN style is selected
SBS_SIZEBOXBOTTOMRIGHTALIGN	Used in conjunction with the SBS_SIZEBOX style. Here the lower-right corner of the scroll bar is aligned with the lower-right corner of a rectangle defined by *x*, *y*, *nWidth*, and *nHeight*, using the system default scroll bar height
SBS_SIZEBOXTOPLEFTALIGN	Used in conjunction with the SBS_SIZEBOX style. Here the upper-left corner of the scroll bar is aligned with the upper-left corner of a rectangle defined by *x*, *y*, *nWidth*, and *nHeight*, using the system default scroll bar height

Table 4-8.   SCROLLBAR Class Control Styles (*continued*)

Style	Description
SBS_TOPALIGN	Used in conjunction with SBS_HORZ style. Scroll bar alignment is along the top edge of the rectangle defined by *x, y, nWidth*, and *nHeight*, using the system default scroll bar height
SBS_VERT	Defines a vertical scroll bar. The height, width, and position of the scroll bar will be determined by the CreateWindow function if neither the SBS_RIGHT-ALIGN nor the SBS_LEFTALIGN style is requested

Table 4-9.   STATIC Class Control Styles

Style	Description
SS_BLACKFRAME	Defines a box with a black frame
SS_BLACKRECT	Defines a black-filled rectangle
SS_CENTER	Takes the given text and centers it within a simple rectangle. All text is formatted. Any text not fitting on one line is automatically wrapped to the next line, with the next line also being automatically centered
SS_GRAYFRAME	Defines a gray-framed box
SS_GRAYRECT	Defines a gray-filled rectangle
SS_ICON	Automatically sizes and displays an icon within the dialog box
SS_LEFT	Similar to SS_CENTER except the text displayed within the rectangle is aligned flush left. This includes auto word-wrap and next line flush-left alignment
SS_NOPREFIX	Normally, Windows interprets any "&" symbols in the control's text as accelerator prefix characters, which causes the next character to be underlined. If a static control is to contain text and this feature is not wanted, SS_NOPREFIX can be used with other styles, using the bitwise logical OR operator
SS_RIGHT	Similar to SS_CENTER except the text displayed within the rectangle is aligned flush right. This includes auto word-wrap and next line flush-right alignment
SS_SIMPLE	Defines a rectangle that will display a single line of flush-left aligned text
SS_USERITEM	Defines a user-defined item
SS_WHITEFRAME	Defines a white-framed box
SS_WHITERECT	Defines a white-filled rectangle

Table 4-10.   Window States

State	Description
SW_HIDE	Hides the window and passes activation to another window
SW_MINIMIZE	Minimizes the window and activates the top-level window in the window-manager's list
SW_RESTORE	Same as SW_SHOWNORMAL
SW_SHOW	Activates the window and displays it using its current position and size
SW_SHOWMAXIMIZED	Activates the window and displays it fully maximized
SW_SHOWMINIMIZED	Activates the window and displays it as an icon
SW_SHOWMINNOACTIVATE	Displays the window as an icon, with the window that is currently active remaining active
SW_SHOWNA	Displays the window in its current state; whichever window is currently active remains active
SW_SHOWNOACTIVATE	Displays the window in its most recent position and size; whichever window is currently active remains active
SW_SHOWNORMAL	Activates and displays the window. If the window had been an icon or was zoomed, Windows will restore the window to its original position and size

The following code sequence shows how to change the background color of a window using a color array table:

```
/* Delete the old brush. GCW_HBRBACKGROUND is the handle to the
   background brush.      */
DeleteObject(GetClassWord(hWnd,GCW_HBRBACKGROUND));
/* Create and insert the new brush's handle into the window
   class structure.     */
SetClassWord(hwnd,GCW_HBRBACKGROUND,
          CreateSolidBrush(RGB
          (wColorValue[wColor-IDM_BLACK][0],
          wColorValue[wColor-IDM_BLACK][1],
          wColorValue[wColor-IDM_BLACK][2])));
```

The following code sequence illustrates how easy it is to change a program's icon:

```
SetClassWord(hWnd,GCW_HICON,LoadIcon(hInstance,"NewIcon"));
```

This example assumes that the resource script included a line similar to this:

```
NewIcon ICON newicon.ico
```

VIRTUAL KEYS

The Windows virtual keyboard is the set of all possible keystrokes that can occur in the Windows environment. This set of keystrokes is defined in WINDOWS.H and constitutes the only keystrokes a Windows application can receive. The virtual key code identifies the key that was either pressed or released. Because the developers of Windows defined virtual keys for many different hardware configurations, IBM PC, compatibles, and so on, some virtual key codes cannot be generated on an IBM PC.

Table 4-11 shows the identifiers along with the numeric key codes and the IBM PC key that corresponds to the virtual key.

CONTROLS AND DIALOG BOXES

Controls and dialog boxes are predefined child windows that have features and capabilities other windows do not. Their purpose is to provide an easy method by which the user can interact with the application. Windows provides several ready-made control classes. Controls have their characteristics and functions defined by their window class, just as any other window would. The window function determines how the window will appear to the user and what actions are to be taken based on the responses. Even better is the fact that control window functions are predefined by Windows, thereby sidestepping any need to create additional code.

Static Controls

Static controls are generally used in conjunction with other controls. They typically produce small windows containing text or graphics elements, such as icons, and can be used to separate a group of controls. Static controls do not accept user input.

Table 4-11.   Virtual Key Codes

Required Windows Virtual Key	WINDOWS.H Identifier	IBM PC Key	Hex Value
	VK_LBUTTON		01
	VK_RBUTTON		02
Yes	VK_CANCEL	CTRL-BREAK	03
	VK_MBUTTON		04
Yes	VK_BACK	BACKSPACE	08
Yes	VK_TAB	TAB	09
	VK_CLEAR	Keypad 5#	0C
Yes	VK_RETURN	ENTER	0D
Yes	VK_SHIFT	SHIFT	10
Yes	VK_CONTROL	CTRL	11
Yes	VK_MENU	ALT	12
	VK_PAUSE		13
Yes	VK_CAPITAL	CAPSLOCK	14
Yes	VK_ESCAPE	ESC	1B
Yes	VK_SPACE	SPACEBAR	20
Yes	VK_PRIOR	PGUP	21
Yes	VK_NEXT	PGDN	22
	VK_END	END	23
Yes	VK_HOME	HOME	24
Yes	VK_LEFT	←	25
Yes	VK_UP	↑	26
Yes	VK_RIGHT	→	27
Yes	VK_DOWN	↓	28
	VK_SELECT		29
	VK_PRINT		2A
	VK_EXECUTE		2B
Yes	VK_INSERT	INS	2D
Yes	VK_DELETE	DEL	2E
	VK_HELP		2F
Yes		Keyboard 0 to 9	30-39
Yes		A to Z	41-5A
	VK_NUMPAD0	Keypad 0*	60
	VK_NUMPAD1	Keypad 1*	61
	VK_NUMPAD2	Keypad 2*	62
	VK_NUMPAD3	Keypad 3*	63
	VK_NUMPAD4	Keypad 4*	64
	VK_NUMPAD5	Keypad 5*	65

Table 4-11.   Virtual Key Codes (*continued*)

Required Windows Virtual Key	WINDOWS.H Identifier	IBM PC Key	Hex Value
	VK_NUMPAD6	Keypad 6*	66
	VK_NUMPAD7	Keypad 7*	67
	VK_NUMPAD8	Keypad 8*	68
	VK_NUMPAD9	Keypad 9*	69
	VK_MULTIPLY	Keypad *	6A
	VK_ADD	Keypad +	6B
	VK_SEPARATOR		6C
	VK_SUBTRACT	Keypad −	6D
	VK_DECIMAL	Keypad .	6E
	VK_DIVIDE	Keypad /	6F
Yes	VK_F1	F1	70
Yes	VK_F2	F2	71
Yes	VK_F3	F3	72
Yes	VK_F4	F4	73
Yes	VK_F5	F5	74
Yes	VK_F6	F6	75
Yes	VK_F7	F7	76
Yes	VK_F8	F8	77
Yes	VK_F9	F9	78
Yes	VK_F10	F10	79
	VK_F11	F11	7A
	VK_F12	F12	7B
	VK_F13		7C
	VK_F14		7D
	VK_F15		7E
	VK_F16		7F
	VK_NUMLOCK	NUMLOCK	90

Push Button Controls

The *push button control* style specifies a small rectangle with rounded corners, containing text. Examples of push buttons are the "OK" and "CANCEL" choices provided by many Windows applications. Clicking on the push button causes the application to take some form of immediate action.

Radio Button Controls

A *radio button control* is an open circle with text to its right. The user can select a circle to turn the particular control off or on. When the control is on, the circle will be filled in. A good analogy for radio buttons is the radio in your car. Just like the buttons on your automobile radio, you can only select one at a time. (Ever tried to play two stations at once?) Control radio buttons work the same way.

Radio button controls are usually grouped together logically, with the user able to select only one of the choices. When the user selects a second radio button control, the previously selected item is deselected. You could use radio button controls to give the user a list of disk drives to select from. Naturally, you can only read from one drive at a time. Selecting both Drive C and Drive A has no meaning. If used properly, radio buttons can prevent the user from making a mistake.

Check Box Controls

A *check box control* is a small square with text to the right. Unlike radio buttons, this control can appear in multiples, not logically related, and permits concurrent selections. For example, a desktop publishing application could present the user with several text format options: bold, underline, italics, subscript, and so on, that could be combined in numerous ways: bold italic, for instance, or underlined subscript.

Edit Boxes

An *edit box* is a window in which the user can enter and edit text. The application can define an edit control with multiple-line editing and scrolling if you select the appropriate control style (ES_MULTILINE, ES_AUTOHSCROLL, or ES_AUTOVSCROLL). If none of the three styles are specified, text entered by the user that does not fit on one line will be wrapped to the beginning of the next line.

List Boxes

List boxes respond to both mouse and keyboard input. They list character strings—for example, file names. The user can select one or several items. Control styles include list boxes that have their contents automatically sorted (LBS_SORT), automatically notify the parent window of a selection (LBS_NOTIFY), and can include scroll bar styles (WS_VSCROLL). When an LBS_STANDARD style is chosen, all three of these styles are selected.

A list box item can be selected by pressing the space bar or by double-clicking with the mouse. Either response will cause Windows to invert the selected character string text. Messages returned include LBN_SEL-CHANGE and LBN_DBLCLK (if the mouse was clicked).

Retrieving the index of the selected character string is as easy as making a call to LB_GETCURSEL (the selected item's index) and LB_GETTEXT (containing a copy of the selected text).

Scroll Bars

The scroll bar is a very common feature of Windows applications that need to move through lists, text, columns of information, or graphics displays that do not fit on a single screen (see Chapter 2, "The Vertical Scroll Bar" and "The Horizontal Scroll Bar" sections). Combined, the vertical and horizontal scroll bars allow the user to view a larger surface than can be displayed at one time, by shifting the displayed image up and down, left or right.

Windows provides two types of scroll bars: window scroll bars and scroll bar controls. As you've already seen, the CreateWindow function does a lot. It is also responsible for adding horizontal window scroll bars (WS_HSCROLL) or vertical window scroll bars (WS_VSCROLL). Vertical scroll bars are always displayed along the right side of the window and extend the full height of the client area. Horizontal scroll bars are always positioned at the bottom of the window and extend the full width of the client area. The following highlights how to add scroll bars to a window:

```
hWnd = CreateWindow("ScrollBar"          /* Window class name   */
                    "Sample Scroll Bar"  /* Window title        */
                    WS_VSCROLL |
                    WS_HSCROLL,          /* Window with scrolls */
                    CW_USEDEFAULT,       /* x - default location */
                    0,                   /* y - location        */
                    CW_USEDEFAULT,       /* cx - default size   */
                    0,                   /* cy - default size   */
                    NULL,                /* Window has no parent */
                    NULL,                /* Use the class menu  */
                    hInstance            /* Who created window  */
                    NULL                 /* No parameter to pass */
                    );
```

Scroll bar controls, on the other hand, are technically child windows. They can be any size and dimension, and can be placed anywhere within the client area of the window. They are created by making a call to (you guessed it) CreateWindow, requesting the creation of a child window with a scroll bar style.

SYSTEM TIMER

The *system timer* is an input device provided by Windows. Basically the application instructs Windows how often to give it a "buzz," and Windows sends the application recurrent WM_TIMER messages at that time interval.

The main purpose of a timer in a nonpreemptive multitasking environment, such as Windows, is to provide a method whereby a normally large, time-consuming process can be subdivided into smaller, interruptable tasks. Each subtask is activated whenever it receives a WM_TIMER message. This prevents any one application from monopolizing the CPU.

Additionally, a Windows timer can be used to activate a preset alarm used in a scheduling program, generate an auto save for a word processor at predefined intervals, control the speed of a graphics display, control the update for a clock display, and many other meaningful uses.

What Makes the Timer Tick?

The *wElapse* parameter to the SetTimer function defines the elapsed time (in milliseconds) between timer events. The interval can range from 1 to 65,535 msec, or up to 65.5 seconds. For example, if *wElapse* were 3,000 msec, Windows would send the application program a WM_TIMER message about every three seconds. The *lpTimerFunc* parameter to SetTimer points to the procedure-instance address of the callback function.

Windows accomplishes this feat by creating its own Interrupt 08H, which intercepts the normal PC BIOS Interrupt 08H. In conjunction with the USER module, when the SYSTEM.DRV receives an Interrupt 08H, it sends a message to the USER module instructing it to decrement each of the system timer counters set by Windows. Whenever the count reaches zero, the USER module sends a WM_TIMER message to the application's message queue. After this, the USER module resets the counter back to its original starting value.

With all Windows applications receiving WM_TIMER messages from the normal message queue, the application won't suddenly be interrupted in the middle of an important process. When writing an application that uses system timers, however, care must be taken to enable the application to continue proper execution if there are no timers available. There are roughly 16 timers available at any one time. Therefore, applications should stop any timer messages no longer needed by making a call to the KillTimer function.

Using the Timer

There are two common approaches to using timers. The first, and the easiest method to use with error checking, is to call the SetTimer function from the WinMain function or while processing the WM_CREATE message. This allows the application the earliest means of dealing with an unavailable timer. This method is ended by terminating the timer with a call to KillTimer in response to a WM_DESTROY message. With this method, all WM_TIMER messages are sent directly to the normal window function.

The second method of using timers causes Windows to send the WM_TIMER message to a function within the application program (callback function), instead of the WinMain function.

MEMORY

One of the major factors influencing the speed of your Windows applications is the amount of available memory. When you want to execute multiple programs, Windows will attempt to place as many of these programs into memory as possible. However, it seems no matter how much memory you purchase, you never have enough just when you want it! If you attempt to load several large programs under Windows, the majority of your system memory may be allocated. At this point, any additional programs you invoke will cause Windows to make space for the program in memory by temporarily swapping a current application out of memory and onto the fixed disk. One can quickly see that as the number of programs executing becomes very large, the amount of memory and disk swapping Windows must perform increases proportionately.

No matter how fast the access time is on your fixed disk, it is still a snail's pace compared to the speed of the electronic circuits making up the CPU. Because of this access time limitation, disk input and output operations are one of the major causes of computer processing delays. Performance is also degraded by the additional overhead required by all disk I/O operations generated by the frequent swapping.

Since a computer can only work on information when it is in memory, everything must eventually get into memory. For example, before Windows can draw a menu or icon, the description of the menu and the contents of the icon must be loaded into memory. The picture becomes even more complex since Windows also requires the display context, code segments, data segments, the window itself, and on and on, to reside in memory before they can execute.

When you consider the tremendous amount of memory required by Windows' graphics-oriented environment, as well as the fact that Windows accomplishes its multitasking in a finite amount of memory, you begin to appreciate why memory management is such an important issue in Windows programming.

Memory Allocation

The following example will give you an idea of just how quickly a Windows application can gobble up memory. As soon as the user selects a program to run by double-clicking on the application's name in MS-DOS Executive, the first instance of the application begins to execute. For a minimal application, this would require Windows to load at least one code segment and data segment, for a total of two objects loaded into memory.

On top of this, each Windows application must register a window class and create a window of that class. Most Windows applications use at least one menu and an icon. Total objects in memory—six.

To highlight some of Windows' memory management capabilities: suppose the user chooses to start a second instance of the application. The second instance shares the same code segment as its predecessor, along with the application's icon. However, the second instance has its own data segment. While the second instance has a window of the same class as the first instance, it is still a new window object. The menu of the first instance cannot be shared with the second instance because of the modifications (selection, activation, and deactivation of options) each instance can make. This brings the memory-object total to nine.

Keeping the example as basic as possible: almost all Windows applications create a font, pen, and brush, total objects—12. A poorly written Windows application (one not sharing objects) would cause the second instance to create its own font, pen, and brush, bringing the memory object tally to 15, and the application hasn't even done anything yet! As you can see, memory gets consumed at a startling rate in the Windows environment since graphics objects are an integral part of an application's basic functioning and multiple instances can be invoked at any moment. You can, however, minimize the amount of space an application requires by using special memory management techniques.

Memory Management

When developing a Windows application, you should consider that the application may run under several memory configurations. Windows supports the following three major memory configurations:

- The standard 640K memory configuration
- Beginning with Windows version 3.0, expanded memory specification (EMS) version 4.0 memory is supported
- A protected memory configuration

When the user selects an application, Windows automatically checks these four categories to determine which memory configuration it will use:

- The type of processor being used (Intel 8086, 80286, or 80386)
- Amount of basic 640K memory available
- Amount of EMS 4.0 expanded memory available
- Amount of extended memory available

Since there is no way Windows can know just how much memory an application will need at any particular moment, it is up to the application to manage this limited resource. While Windows does provide several memory management routines for your application to use, memory itself is a different type of resource since Windows is unable to abstract or separate it from the application. Therefore, Windows cannot mediate its use as it could the use of the display or printer. Windows cannot arbitrate an application's need for memory. Each Windows application controls how much memory it requires, while at the same time specifying how much memory is unavailable for other applications to use. This last point highlights the need for each Windows application to efficiently manage memory.

Enhancing the overall performance of Windows applications can be accomplished by remembering the following four basic memory management principles:

- Limit the number of objects used
- Minimize the size of each object
- Share objects whenever possible
- Define objects as relocatable

Limiting the Number of Objects

There are two ways to limit the number of objects in memory. The first is to share objects as much as possible, rather than forcing each task to create its own copy of the object. The second is to make certain that unused objects are not accidentally left in memory.

An object can be considered shareable whenever the object is not likely to be modified during program execution. Under these conditions the object can not only be shared by multiple instances of an application, but also between different applications. Icons, standard cursors, user-created brushes, pens, and objects are all examples of shareable objects.

Minimizing Object Size

There are basically three approaches to minimizing the size of an object. The first method involves making sure you segment your code. Limiting the size of your code segments to Microsoft's recommended 4K will also minimize the amount of code you have lying around in memory at one time. (The segment size restriction maps directly to the Intel 80386's 4K memory paging architecture.)

The final size of an object can also be reduced by only allocating the minimum amount of memory required to represent the object. One example of this approach would involve a disk file containing both graphics and text information. At one point in the application only the text information is required. Rather than dynamically allocating a portion of memory large enough to contain the entire text, a better approach would be to allocate enough memory for a small number of records, read more records, reallocate memory, and so on. With this last approach the amount of memory used most closely represents the actual size of the object.

It may be true that one picture is worth a thousand words, but when it comes to memory utilization, it might be better to use the thousand words. The last method in reducing the size of memory objects involves the conservative use of bitmaps. The problem with bitmaps is the tremendous amounts of memory they can require. Additionally, due to varying display resolutions, the size of a bitmap is somewhat unpredictable. On one monitor a bitmap may occupy 100×100 bits, while on another device $200 \times 200 \times 4$. A high-resolution graphics full-screen bitmap would require $1024 \times 768 \times 4$, or a whopping 393K of memory!

Relocatable Objects

When Windows loads an object into memory it always uses tangential pieces of memory. Each time an application is started, new memory objects are created. When the application terminates the memory objects are removed. This dynamic memory allocation-deallocation process is most efficient whenever Windows can move or relocate an object.

If each application that is run creates and then subsequently destroys fixed memory objects, memory can become fragmented. Since Windows will only allocate contiguous memory for each subsequent object, it is quite possible that a memory fragment will not be large enough for the new object. If the fragmentation is severe enough an out-of-memory error can be generated, even though sufficient total memory is actually available.

Most non-object-oriented programmers would flinch at the thought of moveable memory objects. Frequently, memory objects are kept track of with pointers. Moving memory objects would then require acquiring new pointers—a dynamic variable nightmare!

Fortunately, in an object-oriented programming environment, objects are kept track of by their handles. Technically, a handle is a pointer, but not to the memory object. Instead, handles are pointers to pointers. A program only needs to know where to look (the handle) for the object, while Windows supplies the address of the object (the pointer pointed to by the handle).

When creating Windows objects, a programmer has the option of defining the object as relocatable or nonrelocatable. By choosing the former, you allow Windows to move memory objects in order to maximize memory "real estate." About the only time an application will need to lock or mark a memory object as nonrelocatable is when it needs to write or read data in an object or when it is subscript indexing through the object.

Applications can create objects as relocatable. They can then subsequently lock the objects and eventually return them to their original relocatable state. It is best to keep locked objects to an absolute minimum between messages. Leaving a memory object locked while waiting for new messages can create additional problems if the new message is not addressed to the nonrelocatable memory object.

The following summary explains how to avoid protect-mode violations and other possible run-time errors under all versions of Windows 2.0 and later:

- The application should not load a segment register with a value other than the one provided by Windows or DOS.

- The application should not perform segment arithmetic.

- The application should not compare segment addresses.

- The application should not read or write past the ends of memory objects.

- The application should not use code segment variables.

- The application should not assume that the GlobalReAlloc function returns the same handle it was passed.

5

CONTROLLING THE WINDOWS WINDOW

In the first four chapters a great deal of time was devoted to explaining the details necessary to understanding and constructing a simple Windows application. The remainder of the book gives explicit examples showing how to take advantage of Windows' various capabilities. This chapter will show how to implement scroll bars and how to write a program using the system timer to create a dynamic ticker-tape message.

WHAT IS A SCROLL BAR?

It is often necessary for a Windows application to display large amounts of text—big spreadsheets, graphics, video-captured images—that cannot be fully displayed due to the limited size of the client area of a window. Scroll bars can be an easy solution to this dilemma.

Scroll bars are one of the best features of a graphics and mouse interface. Windows applications can have a vertical scroll bar that moves the display contents up and down, and/or a horizontal scroll bar that shifts the display contents left and right. At either end of the scroll bars are two arrows. Clicking the mouse on an arrow causes the display to shift a single line in the direction of the arrow. Scroll bars also incorporate a *thumb*, or *scroll box,* that visually represents the portion of the overall image that is being displayed. Thumbs can also be dragged along the scroll bar with the mouse to change the area displayed, usually in increments of a page or more.

When Down Means Up

Getting some Windows terminology straight at this point will make it much easier to understand applications that use scroll bars. Let's say that the user is running a word processing application and has loaded a 20-page document. After viewing the first screen of the document, he or she wants to scroll down a few lines. While the user wants to move *down* the document, in reality, the application must move the displayed text *up!* However, the developers of Windows have approached declarations from the user's perspective. WINDOWS.H identifiers, such as SB_LINEDOWN and SB_PAGEDOWN, correspond to the user's desire to move down the document.

Scroll Bar Range

All scroll bars have what is called a *range.* The scroll bar range is defined in terms of integer values that express the scroll bar's maximum and minimum extent. The minimum value for a vertical scroll bar occurs when the thumb is at the top of the scroll bar; when the thumb is positioned at the bottom, the scroll bar is in its maximum position. For horizontal scroll bars the minimum is to the extreme left, and the maximum to the scroll bar's extreme right. The default scroll bar range is from 0 (top or left) to 100 (bottom or right).

Scroll Bar Position

The scroll bar *position* is also determined by the location of the thumb, and is represented by an integer value. For example, if the range for a scroll bar is from 0 to 10, there would be 11 actual thumb positions.

Types of Scroll Bars

Technically, there are two types of scroll bars. Windows has defined scroll bars for windows, and a separate scroll bar control that is a child window.

The first example in this chapter uses window scroll bars. Unlike scroll bar controls, which can be positioned anywhere within the client area, vertical window scroll bars are automatically positioned along the right side of the client area. Horizontal window scroll bars are always placed along the bottom of the client area. Note that the client area does not include the space occupied by the scroll bar. The height and width of window scroll bars are dependent on the particular display driver.

Scroll bar controls are actually child windows that can be any size, height, and width. They are created by making a call to the CreateWindow function and requesting a child window with a scroll bar style.

HOW TO WRITE AN APPLICATION USING SCROLL BARS

The first example application, SCROLL5, will show you how to create and use both a vertical and horizontal scroll bar. For easy reference, the following listing includes all of the files necessary to create a working application. **Note:**   Although this listing and many of the others in the book have been organized in this manner, they *cannot* be entered as one single text file. Each code section must be broken down into its respective components.

THE SCROLL5 MAKE FILE:

```
all : scroll5.exe

scroll5.obj: scroll5.c
    cl -c -AS -Gsw -Oas -Zpe scroll5.c

scroll5.res : scroll5.rc
    rc -r scroll5.rc

scroll5.exe: scroll5.obj scroll5.def scroll5.res
    link /NOD scroll5,,,libw slibcew, scroll5.def
    rc scroll5.res
```

THE SCROLL5.H DEF DEFINITION FILE:

```
NAME           SCROLL5
DESCRIPTION    'Scroll Bar Example'
EXETYPE        WINDOWS
STUB           'WINSTUB.EXE'
CODE           PRELOAD MOVEABLE DISCARDABLE
DATA           PRELOAD MOVEABLE MULTIPLE
HEAPSIZE       4096
STACKSIZE      9216
EXPORTS        WindowProc      @1
```

THE SCROLL5.C APPLICATION FILE:

```
/* Simplified Windows Platform (SWP)               */
/* (c) William H. Murray and Chris H. Pappas, 1989 */
```

```c
#include <windows.h>
#include <stdio.h>
#include <string.h>

#define SCROLLLINES 100
#define SCROLLWIDTH 100

long FAR PASCAL WindowProc(HWND,unsigned,WORD,LONG);

char szProgName[]="ProgName";

int PASCAL WinMain(hInst,hPreInst,lpszCmdLine,nCmdShow)
HANDLE hInst,hPreInst;
LPSTR  lpszCmdLine;
int    nCmdShow;
{
  HWND hwnd;
  MSG  msg;
  WNDCLASS wcSwp;
  if (!hPreInst)
  {
    wcSwp.lpszClassName=szProgName;
    wcSwp.hInstance     =hInst;
    wcSwp.lpfnWndProc   =WindowProc;
    wcSwp.hCursor       =LoadCursor(NULL,IDC_ARROW);
    wcSwp.hIcon         =NULL;
    wcSwp.lpszMenuName  =NULL;
    wcSwp.hbrBackground=GetStockObject(WHITE_BRUSH);
    wcSwp.style         =CS_HREDRAW|CS_VREDRAW;
    wcSwp.cbClsExtra    =0;
    wcSwp.cbWndExtra    =0;
    if (!RegisterClass (&wcSwp))
       return FALSE;
  }
  hwnd=CreateWindow(szProgName,"Using Scroll Bars",
                    WS_OVERLAPPEDWINDOW|WS_VSCROLL|
                    WS_HSCROLL,CW_USEDEFAULT,
                    CW_USEDEFAULT,CW_USEDEFAULT,
                    CW_USEDEFAULT,NULL,NULL,hInst,NULL);
  ShowWindow(hwnd,nCmdShow);
  UpdateWindow(hwnd);
  while (GetMessage(&msg,NULL,NULL,NULL))
  {
    TranslateMessage(&msg);
    DispatchMessage(&msg);
  }
  return(msg.wParam);
}

long FAR PASCAL WindowProc(hwnd,messg,wParam,lParam)
HWND    hwnd;
unsigned messg;
WORD    wParam;
LONG    lParam;
{
  HDC hdc;
  PAINTSTRUCT ps;
  TEXTMETRIC tm;
  static short charwt,charht,xClientView,yClientView,
               poshorzscroll,posvertscroll;
```

```
FILE *fp;
short i,t,ch,sLength;
static char szBuffer[150]=" ";

switch (messg)
{
  case WM_CREATE:
    hdc=GetDC(hwnd);
    GetTextMetrics(hdc,&tm);
    charwt=tm.tmAveCharWidth;
    charht=tm.tmHeight+tm.tmExternalLeading;
    ReleaseDC(hwnd,hdc);

    SetScrollPos(hwnd,SB_HORZ,poshorzscroll,TRUE);
    SetScrollPos(hwnd,SB_VERT,posvertscroll,TRUE);
    SetScrollRange(hwnd,SB_HORZ,0,SCROLLWIDTH,FALSE);
    SetScrollRange(hwnd,SB_VERT,0,SCROLLLINES,FALSE);
    break;

  case WM_SIZE:
    xClientView=LOWORD(lParam);
    yClientView=HIWORD(lParam);
    break;

  case WM_HSCROLL:
    switch (wParam)
    {
      case SB_LINEDOWN:
        poshorzscroll+=1;
        break;
      case SB_LINEUP:
        poshorzscroll-=1;
        break;
      case SB_PAGEDOWN:
        poshorzscroll+=xClientView/charwt;
        break;
      case SB_PAGEUP:
        poshorzscroll-=xClientView/charwt;
        break;
      case SB_THUMBPOSITION:
        poshorzscroll=LOWORD(lParam);
        break;
      default:
        break;
    }
    if (poshorzscroll>SCROLLWIDTH)
      poshorzscroll=SCROLLWIDTH;
    if (poshorzscroll<0)
      poshorzscroll=0;
    if (poshorzscroll!=GetScrollPos(hwnd,SB_HORZ))
    {
      SetScrollPos(hwnd,SB_HORZ,poshorzscroll,TRUE);
      InvalidateRect(hwnd,NULL,TRUE);
    }
    break;

  case WM_VSCROLL:
    switch (wParam)
    {
      case SB_LINEDOWN:
        posvertscroll+=1;
        break;
```

```
              case SB_LINEUP:
                posvertscroll-=1;
                break;
              case SB_PAGEDOWN:
                posvertscroll+=yClientView/charht;
                break;
              case SB_PAGEUP:
                posvertscroll-=yClientView/charht;
              case SB_THUMBPOSITION:
                posvertscroll=LOWORD(lParam);
                break;
              default:
                break;
          }
          if (posvertscroll>SCROLLLINES)
            posvertscroll=SCROLLLINES;
          if (posvertscroll<0)
            posvertscroll=0;
          if (posvertscroll!=GetScrollPos(hwnd,SB_VERT))
          {
            SetScrollPos(hwnd,SB_VERT,posvertscroll,TRUE);
            InvalidateRect(hwnd,NULL,TRUE);
          }
          break;

      case WM_PAINT:
        hdc=BeginPaint(hwnd,&ps);

/*--------- your routines below ---------*/

        t=0;
        if ((fp=fopen("scroll5.doc","r"))!=NULL)
        {
          while(!feof(fp))
          {
            ch=fgetc(fp);
            i=0;
          while((ch!='\n') && (ch!=EOF))
            {
              szBuffer[i]=(char)ch;
              ch=fgetc(fp);
              i++;
            }
          TextOut(hdc,-charwt*(poshorzscroll),
              charht*(t-posvertscroll),szBuffer,i);
          t++;
        }
        }
        fclose(fp);

/*--------- your routines above ---------*/

        ValidateRect(hwnd,NULL);
        EndPaint(hwnd,&ps);
        break;

      case WM_DESTROY:
        PostQuitMessage(0);
        break;
```

```
    default:
        return(DefWindowProc(hwnd,messg,wParam,lParam));
    }
    return(0L);
}
```

One additional file, SCROLL5.DOC, is necessary. This is the text file used by the application to scroll up, down, left, and right, demonstrating how scroll bars function. You can use any text file you choose. However, to take full advantage of the horizontal scroll bar's ability to shift text left and right, your original document should be wider than 80 characters. Text that is significantly narrower than this will not emphasize horizontal displacement.

Assuming you have entered the four files, SCROLL5, SCROLL5.DEF, SCROLL5.C, and SCROLL5.DOC (the text file must have a .DOC file extension), and have compiled and linked them, you should see something similar to Figure 5-1.

The MAKE File (SCROLL5)

As discussed in earlier chapters, the **MAKE** file is responsible for splicing all of the code pieces together during the compile and link process. This

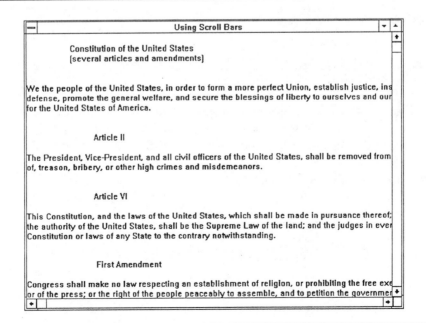

Figure 5-1.   Output from SCROLL5

MAKE file is very similar to earlier examples in which the SCROLL5.C file was used to generate the SCROLL5.OBJ file, and then this file was used along with SCROLL5.DEF to create SCROLL5.EXE.

The Definition File (SCROLL5.DEF)

This definition file is identical to the SWP.DEF file discussed in Chapter 3, except that the NAME (SCROLL5) and DESCRIPTION ('Scroll Bar Example') have been changed.

The Document File (SCROLL5.DOC)

This can be any ASCII text file of your choosing. This example uses the U.S. Constitution. For best results the file should be wider than 80 characters and longer than 25 lines. Each line must be terminated with a carriage return.

The Application File (SCROLL5.C)

Studying the listing you will find several changes to the Simplified Windows Platform.

```
#include <windows.h>
#include <stdio.h>
#include <string.h>

#define SCROLLLINES 100
#define SCROLLWIDTH 100
```

The two *#include* statements are responsible for pulling in the standard I/O and string-handling C header files, along with defining two constants specifying the maximum number of lines and their maximum width.

Reading down, everything in the source code is standard fare until you reach the CreateWindow call.

```
hwnd=CreateWindow(szProgName,"Using Scroll Bars",
            WS_OVERLAPPEDWINDOW|WS_VSCROLL|
            WS_HSCROLL,CW_USEDEFAULT,
            CW_USEDEFAULT,CW_USEDEFAULT,
            CW_USEDEFAULT,NULL,NULL,hInst,NULL);
```

The application has been given the "Using Scroll Bars" title, and creates a window with the following style:

WS_OVERLAPPEDWINDOW | WS_VSCROLL | WS_HSCROLL

The last two options add the vertical and horizontal scroll bars, respectively. Not only is adding scroll bars to a window this easy, but Windows takes care of all mouse logic for the scroll bars.

The WindowProc window function has four additional lines added to it that set the range and position of the horizontal and vertical scroll bars during processing of the WM_CREATE message.

```
SetScrollPos(hwnd,SB_HORZ,poshorzscroll,TRUE);
SetScrollPos(hwnd,SB_VERT,posvertscroll,TRUE);
SetScrollRange(hwnd,SB_HORZ,0,SCROLLWIDTH,FALSE);
SetScrollRange(hwnd,SB_VERT,0,SCROLLLINES,FALSE);
```

To make the processing of the WM_VSCROLL messages possible, two static variables called *poshorzscroll* and *posvertscroll* have been defined within the WindowProc window function. These variables are used as the current positions of the scroll bar thumbs. The calls to SetScrollRange set the scroll bar ranges from 0 to SCROLLWIDTH and 0 to SCROLLLINES, respectively. Each position of the scroll bars corresponds to a single character and line of text. As you increase the position of the scroll bars the text scrolls down and to the right (from the user's perspective).

Windows will send the window application function WM_HSCROLL and WM_VSCROLL messages whenever the scroll bar is clicked with a mouse or the thumb is moved (see Figures 5-2 and 5-3). For every mouse action on the scroll bar there are at least two messages sent: one when the mouse button is depressed and another message when the mouse button is released. The value contained in the *wParam* of the WM_HSCROLL and WM_VSCROLL messages indicates what the mouse is doing to the scroll bar. These values have WINDOWS.H identifiers that begin with the letters "SB" (scroll bar).

Note: The identifiers that use the words "UP" and "DOWN" are used for both vertical and horizontal scroll bars.

The following discussion centers around the WM_HSCROLL message and source code, which is similar in action to the WM_VSCROLL message except that the actions are horizontal instead of vertical.

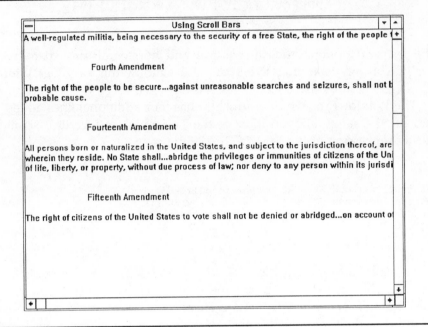

Figure 5-2.   Using SCROLL5 to scroll down

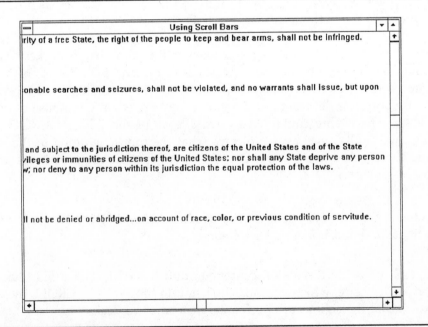

Figure 5-3.   Using SCROLL5 to shift right

```
case WM_HSCROLL:
  switch (wParam)
  {
    case SB_LINEDOWN:
      poshorzscroll+=1;
      break;
    case SB_LINEUP:
      poshorzscroll-=1;
      break;
    case SB_PAGEDOWN:
      poshorzscroll+=xClientView/charwt;
      break;
    case SB_PAGEUP:
      poshorzscroll-=xClientView/charwt;
      break;
    case SB_THUMBPOSITION:
      poshorzscroll=LOWORD(lParam);
      break;
    default:
      break;
```

Whenever the mouse is clicked on one of the vertical scroll bar arrows either an SB_LINEUP or SB_LINEDOWN message is sent. Adjusting the *poshorzscroll* position is simply a matter of either incrementing or decrementing the value.

If the mouse is clicked anywhere *between* an arrow and the thumb, either an SB_PAGEDOWN or SB_PAGEUP message is generated. This indicates that the user wants to jump an entire screen down or up or, for this section of code, that the user wants to move the display one character width left or right. (Remember, the words "UP" and "DOWN" are used to describe both vertical and horizontal messages.) In this case *poshorzscroll* is adjusted one character width left or right. *xClientView* was given the client window's width when the WM_SIZE message was processed. Adding the displacement of the client window's width, divided by the width of a single character, makes the necessary incremental adjustment.

When SB_THUMBPOSITION is the message WM_HSCROLL is processing, the low word of *lParam* contains the current position of the dragged scroll bar thumb. This position is within the minimum and maximum values of the scroll bar range.

Since it is possible that a request will be made to position the display too far to the left or right, the following code adjusts these requests to predefined maximums and minimums:

```
if (poshorzscroll>SCROLLWIDTH)
  poshorzscroll=SCROLLWIDTH;
if (poshorzscroll<0)
  poshorzscroll=0;
```

The first test condition takes care of reducing a request to shift the display too far right (user's view), by setting *poshorzscroll* to the predefined SCROLL-

WIDTH maximum. The second test condition handles requests for a too dramatic leftward shift by setting *poshorzscroll* to 0.

The last statement processed determines if there has been a change requested for the position of display contents by comparing the adjusted *poshorzscroll* value with the current position. If so, the position is changed and the area is redrawn.

```
if (poshorzscroll!=GetScrollPos(hwnd,SB_HORZ))
{
  SetScrollPos(hwnd,SB_HORZ,poshorzscroll,TRUE);
  InvalidateRect(hwnd,NULL,TRUE);
}
```

Reading in the text file is accomplished with the following standard echo print code segment:

```
t=0;
if ((fp=fopen("scroll5.doc","r"))!=NULL)
{
  while(!feof(fp))
  {
    ch=fgetc(fp);
    i=0;
    while((ch!='\n') && (ch!=EOF))
    {
      szBuffer[i]=(char)ch;
      ch=fgetc(fp);
      i++;
    }
    TextOut(hdc,-charwt*(poshorzscroll),
            charht*(t-posvertscroll),szBuffer,i);
    t++;
  }
}
fclose(fp);
```

The algorithm first checks to see if the SCROLL5.DOC file exists. If so, while there is data in the file it builds a line character by character. Once the line is built it is displayed with TextOut. Remember, if the user wants to shift right, the text must move to the left. This is why the horizontal scroll position is negated (*-charwt*(poshorzscroll)*). The process repeats until the entire file is read in, at which point the file is closed.

USING SYSTEM TIMERS

The next example program demonstrates how to use the system timer to produce a scrolling ticker-tape message across the client window. Actually, the program combines the use of a system timer with the use of scroll bar controls. Scroll bar controls were the second type of scroll bars discussed earlier.

Remember the discussion on system timers from the last chapter? A system timer is an input device provided by Windows that an application can use to instruct Windows on how often to give it a "buzz." Whenever the specified interval elapses, Windows sends the application a WM_ TIMER message. TICKER5 uses this message to update the ticker-tape message one character per interval. Here is the complete file listing:

THE TICKER5 MAKE FILE:

```
all : ticker5.exe

ticker5.obj: ticker5.c
    cl -c -AS -Gsw -Oas -Zpe ticker5.c

ticker5.res: ticker5.rc
    rc -r ticker5.rc

ticker5.exe: ticker5.obj ticker5.def ticker5.res
    link /NOD ticker5,,,libw slibcew ticker5.def
    rc ticker5.res
```

THE TICKER5 DEFINITION FILE:

```
NAME        TICKER5
DESCRIPTION 'Ticker Tape Example'
EXETYPE     WINDOWS
STUB        'WINSTUB.EXE'
CODE        PRELOAD MOVEABLE DISCARDABLE
DATA        PRELOAD MOVEABLE MULTIPLE
HEAPSIZE    4096
STACKSIZE   9216
EXPORTS     WindowProc      @1
```

THE TICKER5 MESSAGE FILE:

```
This is a ticker-tape program that will continuously display a
message.  The message is entered and saved as an ASCII file.  The
system timer paces how fast the message is displayed to the
window. Scrolling occurs by incrementing the horizontal scroll
position by 1 for each timer message. The ticker tape length is
400 characters.
```

THE TICKER5 APPLICATION FILE:

```
/* Simplified Windows Platform (SWP)              */
/* (c) William H. Murray and Chris H. Pappas, 1989 */

#include <windows.h>
#include <stdio.h>
#include <string.h>

#define SCROLLWIDTH 480        /* ticker length + 80 */
#define TIMERDELAY  150        /* delay in milliseconds */

long FAR PASCAL WindowProc(HWND,unsigned,WORD,LONG);
```

```
char szProgName[]="ProgName";

int PASCAL WinMain(hInst,hPreInst,lpszCmdLine,nCmdShow)
HANDLE hInst,hPreInst;
LPSTR  lpszCmdLine;
int    nCmdShow;
{
  HWND hwnd;
  MSG  msg;
  WNDCLASS wcSwp;
  if (!hPreInst)
  {
    wcSwp.lpszClassName=szProgName;
    wcSwp.hInstance    =hInst;
    wcSwp.lpfnWndProc  =WindowProc;
    wcSwp.hCursor      =LoadCursor(NULL,IDC_ARROW);
    wcSwp.hIcon        =NULL;
    wcSwp.lpszMenuName =NULL;
    wcSwp.hbrBackground=GetStockObject(GRAY_BRUSH);
    wcSwp.style        =CS_HREDRAW|CS_VREDRAW;
    wcSwp.cbClsExtra   =0;
    wcSwp.cbWndExtra   =0;
    if (!RegisterClass (&wcSwp))
      return FALSE;
  }
  hwnd=CreateWindow(szProgName,"Ticker Tape",
                    WS_POPUPWINDOW,
                    0,400,
                    640,60,
                    NULL,NULL,hInst,NULL);

  if (!SetTimer(hwnd,1,TIMERDELAY,NULL))
     {
     MessageBox(hwnd,"Too many timers started!",
                szProgName,MB_OK);
     return FALSE;
     }

  ShowWindow(hwnd,nCmdShow);
  UpdateWindow(hwnd);
  while (GetMessage(&msg,NULL,NULL,NULL))
  {
    TranslateMessage(&msg);
    DispatchMessage(&msg);
  }
  return(msg.wParam);
}

long FAR PASCAL WindowProc(hwnd,messg,wParam,lParam)
HWND    hwnd;
unsigned messg;
WORD    wParam;
LONG    lParam;
{
  HDC hdc;
  PAINTSTRUCT ps;
  TEXTMETRIC tm;
  static short charwt,charht,xClientView,
               poshorzscroll;
  FILE *fp;
```

```
   short i,ch,sLength;
   static char szBuffer[400]=" ";
   static char szPMessg1[35]="The above ticker message is located";
   static char szPMessg2[14]="in TICKER5.DOC";

   switch (messg)
   {
     case WM_CREATE:
       hdc=GetDC(hwnd);
       GetTextMetrics(hdc,&tm);
       charwt=tm.tmAveCharWidth;
       ReleaseDC(hwnd,hdc);
       SetScrollPos(hwnd,SB_HORZ,poshorzscroll,TRUE);
       SetScrollRange(hwnd,SB_HORZ,0,SCROLLWIDTH,FALSE);
       break;

     case WM_SIZE:
       xClientView=LOWORD(lParam);
       break;

     case WM_TIMER:
       poshorzscroll+=1;
       if (poshorzscroll>SCROLLWIDTH)
         poshorzscroll=0;
       if (poshorzscroll<0)
         poshorzscroll=0;
       if (poshorzscroll!=GetScrollPos(hwnd,SB_HORZ))
       {
         SetScrollPos(hwnd,SB_HORZ,poshorzscroll,TRUE);
         InvalidateRect(hwnd,NULL,FALSE);
       }
       break;

     case WM_PAINT:
       hdc=BeginPaint(hwnd,&ps);

/*--------- your routines below ---------*/

       if ((fp=fopen("ticker5.doc","r"))!=NULL)
       {
         i=0;
         while(!feof(fp))
           {
             ch=fgetc(fp);
             if(ch=='\n') ch=' ';
               szBuffer[i]=(char)ch;
             i++;
           }
         szBuffer[i-1]=' ';
         TextOut(hdc,xClientView-charwt*(poshorzscroll),
                 10,szBuffer,i);
       }
       fclose(fp);
       TextOut(hdc,170,150,szPMessg1,35);
       TextOut(hdc,240,165,szPMessg2,14);

/*--------- your routines above ---------*/

       ValidateRect(hwnd,NULL);
       EndPaint(hwnd,&ps);
       break;
```

```
case WM_DESTROY:
    PostQuitMessage(0);
    break;

default:
    return(DefWindowProc(hwnd,messg,wParam,lParam));
}
return(0L);
}
```

The preceding four files must be entered, compiled, and linked to produce a working program. Figure 5-4 shows the output generated by the ticker-tape program.

The MAKE File (TICKER5)

The TICKER5 **MAKE** file is identical to the previous application, except for the file name, and therefore needs no additional explanation.

The Definition File (TICKER5.DEF)

The TICKER5 definition file is also similar to the previous definition file and needs no further explanation.

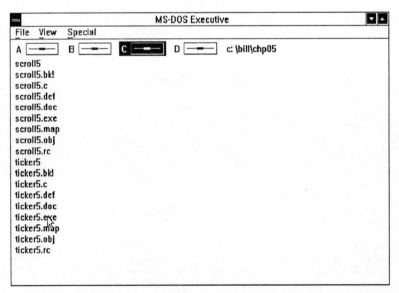

Figure 5-4.   Output from TICKER5

The Message File (TICKER5.DOC)

The message file, TICKER5.DOC, is an ASCII text file containing the text of ticker-tape banner messages that will be scrolled horizontally across the bottom of the display.

The Application File (TICKER5.C)

In the application file, TICKER5.C, if you examine the source code you will note that two constants have been identified.

```
#define SCROLLWIDTH 480      /* ticker length + 80 */
#define TIMERDELAY  150      /* delay in milliseconds */
```

SCROLLWIDTH is used to define the width of the ticker-tape message plus an additional 80 characters to allow the message to smoothly exit the left side of the display. TIMERDELAY is set to the timing interval (in milliseconds) Windows is to use for the WM_TIMER message.

To paint the background of the ticker-tape message a light gray, the *wcSwp.hbrBackground* field is set to GRAY_BRUSH using the next code segment.

```
if (!hPreInst)
{
  wcSwp.lpszClassName=szProgName;
  wcSwp.hInstance    =hInst;
  wcSwp.lpfnWndProc  =WindowProc;
  wcSwp.hCursor      =LoadCursor(NULL,IDC_ARROW);
  wcSwp.hIcon        =NULL;
  wcSwp.lpszMenuName =NULL;
  wcSwp.hbrBackground=GetStockObject(GRAY_BRUSH);
  wcSwp.style        =CS_HREDRAW|CS_VREDRAW;
  wcSwp.cbClsExtra   =0;
  wcSwp.cbWndExtra   =0;
  if (!RegisterClass (&wcSwp))
    return FALSE;
}
```

Setting the applications title, "Ticker Tape", is accomplished by making a call to the CreateWindow function.

```
hwnd=CreateWindow(szProgName,"Ticker Tape",
             WS_POPUPWINDOW,
             0,400,
             640,60,
             NULL,NULL,hInst,NULL);
```

Did you notice anything different about this CreateWindow call as opposed to the SCROLL5.C CreateWindow call? Where's the scroll bar parameter? Read on.

At this point the application is ready to set the timer. Actually, this application is slightly more sophisticated. It will try to set a timer and if all of the 16 timers are already active, the program will print a warning message.

```
if (!SetTimer(hwnd,1,TIMERDELAY,NULL))
  {
  MessageBox(hwnd,"Too many timers started!",
           szProgName,MB_OK);
  return FALSE;
  }
```

The first parameter to the SetTimer function is a handle to the window whose window function will receive the WM_TIMER messages. The second parameter is the timer ID, which should always be a non-zero value. This is arbitrarily set to 1. The third parameter specifies the delay interval in milliseconds (the largest possible value is 65535, or about once per minute). The fourth parameter (unused in this example) can be used to call a specified timer function. Here it is left NULL.

Much of the code, although abbreviated since the ticker message need only concern itself with horizontal scrolling, is similar to the SCROLL5.C example.

```
case WM_CREATE:
  hdc=GetDC(hwnd);
  GetTextMetrics(hdc,&tm);
  charwt=tm.tmAveCharWidth;
  ReleaseDC(hwnd,hdc);
  SetScrollPos(hwnd,SB_HORZ,poshorzscroll,TRUE);
  SetScrollRange(hwnd,SB_HORZ,0,SCROLLWIDTH,FALSE);
  break;

case WM_SIZE:
  xClientView=LOWORD(lParam);
  break;

case WM_TIMER:
  poshorzscroll+=1;
  if (poshorzscroll>SCROLLWIDTH)
    poshorzscroll=0;
  if (poshorzscroll<0)
    poshorzscroll=0;
  if (poshorzscroll!=GetScrollPos(hwnd,SB_HORZ))
    {
    SetScrollPos(hwnd,SB_HORZ,poshorzscroll,TRUE);
    InvalidateRect(hwnd,NULL,FALSE);
    }
  break;
```

The WM_CREATE message gets the handle to the device context and the text metrics for the selected font—in particular the character width (*charwt* = *tmAveCharWidth;*). It also sets the original scroll bar position and range. The ticker-tape message will be scrolled horizontally through the scroll bar control. Notice that this is where the scroll bar control is defined.

The remainder of the code segment positions the text within the scroll bar itself. This is very similar to SCROLL5.C. The meat of the ticker-tape display, or for vegetarians, the "protein" portion of the code looks like this:

```
if ((fp=fopen("ticker5.doc","r"))!=NULL)
{
  i=0;
  while(!feof(fp))
    {
      ch=fgetc(fp);
      if(ch=='\n') ch=' ';
        szBuffer[i]=(char)ch;
        i++;
    }
  szBuffer[i-1]=' ';
  TextOut(hdc,xClientView-charwt*(poshorzscroll),
          10,szBuffer,i);
}
fclose(fp);
TextOut(hdc,170,150,szPMessg1,35);
TextOut(hdc,240,165,szPMessg2,14);
```

This is also very similar to the SCROLL5.C code. First, the existence of the file TICKER5.DOC is checked. Next, while there is data in the file, characters are read one by one into the buffer. Notice that if a carriage return is processed (\n) the application turns this into a blank space, since carriage returns would be disastrous to a single-line horizontal text scroll. Setting *szBuffer[i-1]* equal to a blank space is necessary to eliminate the EOF marker. The code segment continues by printing the text using the TextOut function, calculating the horizontal position but "hard wiring" the vertical position on the screen to 10. The segment ends by closing the file and printing *szpMessg1* and *szPMessg2*, which were declared earlier in the program.

6

MAKING YOUR OWN ICONS, CURSORS, AND BITMAPS

Customizing a Windows application with your own icons, cursors, and bitmaps is a breeze when you use the SDKPAINT utility supplied with the Microsoft Windows Software Development toolkit. This chapter will show you how to create your own icons, cursors, and bitmaps and then teach you how to pull them into your application.

USING SDKPAINT TO CREATE ICONS, CURSORS, AND BITMAPS

SDKPAINT is just one of the useful application development tools provided in the Microsoft Windows Software Development Kit. Starting with Windows 3.0, this development tool permits the design of device-independent color icons. Icons and cursors created with SDKPAINT are functionally device-independent with respect to resolution.

This new file format allows you to tailor a bitmap so that it looks good on each type of display. For example, one icon might consist of four definitions (called DIBs): one designed for monochrome displays, one for CGAs, one for EGAs, and one for VGAs. Whenever the application displays the icon, it simply refers to it by name; Windows then automatically selects the icon image best suited to the current display.

Starting SDKPAINT

SDKPAINT is a Windows application. To run the editor you need to open the MS-DOS Executive window and double click the mouse on the SDKPAINT.EXE file. Figure 6-1 shows what the initial SDKPAINT window looks like. Table 6-1 explains each main menu option with its associated submenu.

Creating Your First Icon or Cursor

Creating your first icon or cursor is as simple as choosing the File option followed by New (Figure 6-2). This will clear the display box and drawing box if any previous design is present. Next you will see the Resource Type child window presenting the three types of files available. This example will use Icon (Figure 6-3). When creating an icon you simply click on the Icon option.

At this point SDKPAINT will provide an icon-sizing dialog box. By default, SDKPAINT displays icon image information appropriate for the display on which SDKPAINT is running. However, if you want to create an

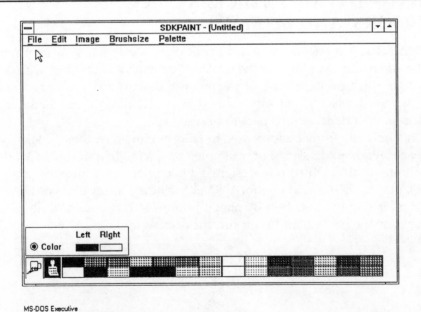

Figure 6-1. Initial SKDPAINT window

Table 6-1.   SKDPAINT Main Menu Options

Option		Description
File	New	Starts a new icon, cursor, or bitmap file
	Open	Opens an existing icon, cursor, or bitmap file for editing
	Save	Saves current screen to the open file. If this is the first save for a file, Windows prompts for the name of the file. Otherwise, you can accept the default file name, which is that of the file currently being edited
	Save As	A very important file option when creating icons, cursors, and bitmaps. Creating an appealing image can take several attempts; use this option to save potential final drafts to separate files
	Exit	Exits the editor
Edit	Undo	Restores the image to its state before the last editing change
	Copy	Moves the image to the clipboard
	Paste	Moves an image from the clipboard into SDKPAINT
Image	New	Initializes the workspace with an icon or cursor image
	Open	Opens images in a bitmap, icon, or cursor file
	Save	Retains an icon or cursor in the workspace
	Restore	Restores the image to its state when initially loaded into the editor or when last saved
	Clear	Clears an image from the workspace area of the SDKPAINT window
	Delete	Deletes the image from the work area and clears the image from the SDKPAINT window
Brushsize		Selects a drawing brush size from small, medium, or large
Palette	Edit Colors	Changes the currently selected color to the hue you specify or restores the color to its default value
	Get Colors	Loads a color palette (.PAL) file into the editor
	Save Colors	Saves newly created colors in a .PAL file
Hotspot		Indicates which portion of the screen image is to be used as a *hotspot*. The hotspot is the pixel Windows uses to determine where to place a window that has been dragged into the work area. Hotspots are only used for icons and cursors. If used in a cursor, Windows will use the hotspot to return the cursor's current screen coordinates

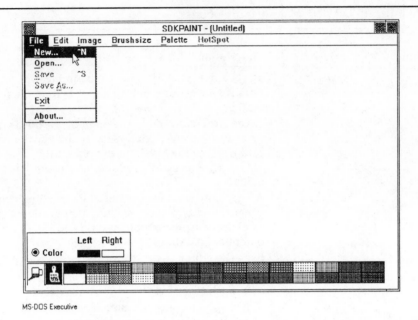

Figure 6-2.   Using the New option to start a new icon, cursor, or bitmap file description

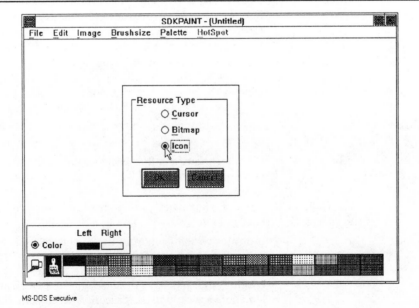

Figure 6-3.   Choosing the Icon resource type

icon image for a different type of device, open the pop-up combo box and choose the kind of device you want to target (Figure 6-4).

After selecting an icon size, you will need to pick a brush size (small, medium, or large) and brush color. Selecting a brush size is simply a matter of clicking on the **Brushsize** main menu option, and then choosing the width.

Beginning with Windows 3.0, SDKPAINT has provided a broad spectrum of painting colors. The SDKPAINT palette, at the bottom of the display, defines available and currently selected colors for drawing and display. By clicking the mouse on the Left color selection box, and then choosing a color, you can define the mouse's left button color. Clicking on the Right color selection box and repeating the process will select the color to be used when the mouse's right button is pressed. Making one of the mouse button colors the background color is an easy way to erase unsuccessful ideas.

The oilcan icon at the bottom left of the color selection box is used to indicate the color chosen to fill all bordered areas. The paint brush to its right identifies the color selected to paint with, using the preselected brush width.

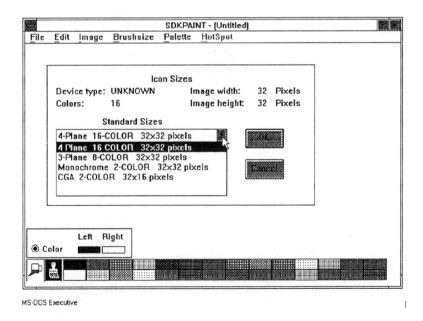

Figure 6-4.   Selecting the icon size

SDKPAINT displays two types of colors in the palette: true colors and what are called *dithered* colors. When you are creating a bitmap or icon, the 16 colors that SDKPAINT displays in the left-most eight columns of the palette are true colors. The remaining colors are dithered. When you are creating a cursor, all colors of the palette are true colors. The 16 true colors are red, green, and blue (RGB) values guaranteed to be distinct on any device that displays 16 or more colors.

When working with icons or cursors, you can get information about the RGB values of a color on the palette by first selecting the color and then choosing the EDIT COLORS command from the Palette menu (Figure 6-5). When editing a bitmap image, you can also get the information by double clicking the color. The palette differs with the type of resource you are editing.

Figure 6-6 shows an SDKPAINT window with a completed icon design. Notice that the image size specified is 64 × 64 pixels. Figure 6-7 illustrates the design of a bold cursor that an application could use to highlight important selections. When looking at the completed designs you will note that there are actually two renditions of the design. The larger one to the left, within the drawing box, allows the eye to easily create an exploded image. The smaller image to the right represents the actual size of the design as it would appear in the application.

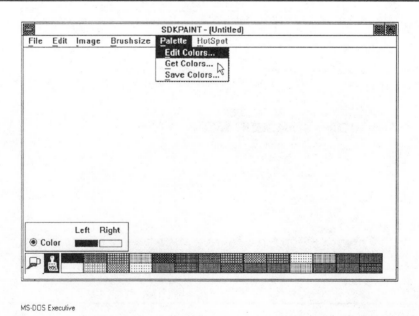

Figure 6-5.   Choosing the Edit Colors option

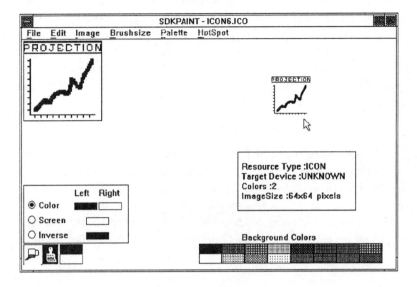

Figure 6-6.   Completed icon design

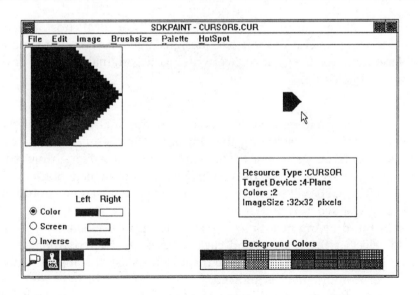

Figure 6-7.   Completed bold cursor design

A very important feature of SDKPAINT is its file conversion capability. Under most circumstances, all icons, cursors, and bitmaps created with SDKPAINT's predecessor, ICON EDIT, can be converted to version 3.0 and later format. The conversion process takes place automatically upon opening the file for editing. However, previously defined version 2.0 and later bitmaps with a 99 × 99 pixel resolution are in trouble. The maximum allowed with Windows 3.0 is 72 × 72.

Note: It takes a great deal of patience and experience to create a meaningful icon, cursor, or bitmap because a lot of trial and error is involved. Whenever you come up with a design that has possibilities, *stop* and *save* a copy of it. It is all too easy to get your design to a point where you really like it, and then make one additional change, only to ruin it. It may be impossible to reverse the change, and so an hour of design time has been lost.

The first time you select the **Save** option from the File main menu, Windows will prompt you for a file name. If you are creating an icon, the file system will automatically append an .ICO file extension. The .CUR file extension is used for cursors.

Note: The file extensions must be .ICO, .CUR, or .BMP (for bitmaps). If you are creating several possible icon designs, make certain you choose the Save **As** option *not* **S**ave. **S**ave overwrites your original file, and Save **As** creates multiple copies.

When creating either icons or cursors an optional hotspot can be selected. This is done by selecting the Hotspot main menu option. For icons the hotspot determines where to place the item that is being dragged into the work area. The hotspot on cursors determines which portion of the cursor (which pixel) will be used to return the current screen coordinates.

Once you have selected the hotspot option, a very small grid will appear in the drawing box. Simply place the grid on whichever pixel you want to select as the hotspot and click the mouse. The coordinates of the selected hotspot will be added to the display box's list of statistics. Only one hotspot per icon or cursor is allowed.

Figure 6-8 demonstrates this definition process. If you look closely at the tip of the cursor within the drawing box, you will see four small white blocks. The pixel in the center of the four blocks represents the coordinates

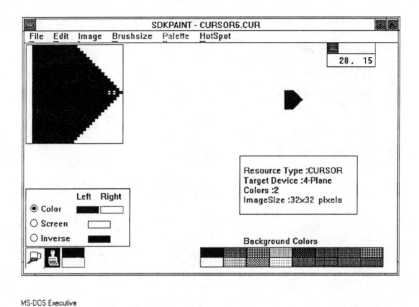

MS-DOS Executive

Figure 6-8.   Selecting a cursor hotspot

displayed in the upper-right corner of the SDKPAINT window (28, 15). Clicking the mouse on this point will lock in this definition.

Creating Your First Bitmap

To create a bitmap follow the same steps used in creating an icon or cursor, except choose the Bitmap option from the Resource Type dialog box. You must also select the bitmap's width and height. The drawing box can be sized from 1 × 1 to 72 × 72 pixels. Figure 6-9 shows a completed bitmap design. In Chapters 12 and 13, you will be shown another way to create bitmaps, and how to incorporate bitmaps into your applications.

USING ICONS

In this section you will learn how to incorporate custom icons into your Windows applications. The pattern of this discussion will be used for all of the examples in the text. Many of the books written about Windows illustrate a concept with "sniglets," bits of code that leave the reader uncertain how to generate an entire program. For all of the major examples

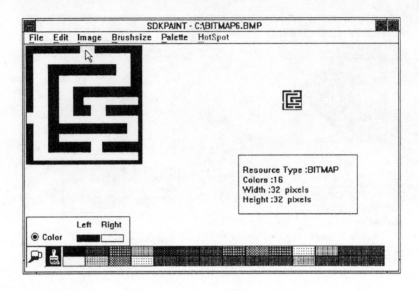

Figure 6-9.   Completed bitmap design

in this text, you will be given a complete listing of all of the files necessary to generate an executable program.

For each application, the complete listing will include (as appropriate) the **MAKE** file (no file extension), the definition file (.DEF file extension), the resource script (.RC file extension), and the C source code (with .C file extension). After compiling the application, three additional files (as appropriate) will be created. These include the binary resource file generated by the resource compiler (.RES), the object file (.OBJ), and the final executable program (.EXE). Following each complete listing, the various unique features of the application will be discussed in detail.

Using this format, the following listing contains all of the files necessary to add a custom icon to your Windows application:

```
THE MAKE FILE FOR ICON6:

ALL : icon6.exe # ALL needed for C 6.0 up

icon6.obj: icon6.c
    cl -c -AS -Gsw -Oas -Zpe icon6.c

icon6.res : icon6.rc icon6.ico
    RC -r icon6.rc
```

```
icon6.exe : icon6.obj icon6.def icon6.res
    link /NOD icon6,,,libw slibcew, icon6
    rc icon6.res
```

THE DEFINITION FILE FOR ICON6:

```
;ICON6.DEF for C Compiling

NAME            ICON6
DESCRIPTION     'Illustrate an Icon'
EXETYPE         WINDOWS
STUB            'WINSTUB.EXE'
CODE            PRELOAD MOVEABLE DISCARDABLE
DATA            PRELOAD MOVEABLE MULTIPLE
HEAPSIZE        4096
STACKSIZE       9216
EXPORTS         WindowProc      @1
```

THE RESOURCE FILE FOR ICON6:

```
#include "windows.h"

NewIcon ICON icon6.ico
```

THE APPLICATION FILE FOR ICON6:

```
/* Simplified Windows Platform (SWP)              */
/* (c) William H. Murray and Chris H. Pappas, 1989 */

#include <windows.h>
#include <string.h>

long FAR PASCAL WindowProc(HWND,unsigned,WORD,LONG);

char szProgName[]="ProgName";
char szIconName[]="NewIcon";

int PASCAL WinMain(hInst,hPreInst,lpszCmdLine,nCmdShow)
HANDLE hInst,hPreInst;
LPSTR  lpszCmdLine;
int    nCmdShow;
{
  HWND hwnd;
  MSG  msg;
  WNDCLASS wcSwp;
  if (!hPreInst)
  {
    wcSwp.lpszClassName=szProgName;
    wcSwp.hInstance     =hInst;
    wcSwp.lpfnWndProc   =WindowProc;
    wcSwp.hCursor       =LoadCursor(hInst,IDC_ARROW);
    wcSwp.hIcon         =LoadIcon(hInst,szIconName);
    wcSwp.lpszMenuName  =szProgName;
    wcSwp.hbrBackground=GetStockObject(WHITE_BRUSH);
    wcSwp.style         =CS_HREDRAW|CS_VREDRAW;
    wcSwp.cbClsExtra    =0;
    wcSwp.cbWndExtra    =0;
    if (!RegisterClass (&wcSwp))
```

```
      return FALSE;
   }
   hwnd=CreateWindow(szProgName,"A New Icon",
                     WS_OVERLAPPEDWINDOW,CW_USEDEFAULT,
                     CW_USEDEFAULT,CW_USEDEFAULT,
                     CW_USEDEFAULT,NULL,NULL,
                     hInst,NULL);
   ShowWindow(hwnd,nCmdShow);
   UpdateWindow(hwnd);
   while (GetMessage(&msg,NULL,NULL,NULL))
   {
      TranslateMessage(&msg);
      DispatchMessage(&msg);
   }
   return(msg.wParam);
}

long FAR PASCAL WindowProc(hwnd,messg,wParam,lParam)
HWND hwnd;
unsigned messg;
WORD wParam;
LONG lParam;
{
   HDC hdc;
   PAINTSTRUCT ps;
   static char szTString[80]="Minimize Window to see new Icon";

   switch (messg)
   {
      case WM_PAINT:
        hdc=BeginPaint(hwnd,&ps);

/*--------- your routines below ---------*/

        TextOut(hdc,200,200,szTString,strlen(szTString));

/*--------- your routines above ---------*/

        ValidateRect(hwnd,NULL);
        EndPaint(hwnd,&ps);
        break;

      case WM_DESTROY:
        PostQuitMessage(0);
        break;

      default:
        return(DefWindowProc(hwnd,messg,wParam,lParam));
   }
   return(0L);
}
```

The MAKE File (ICON6)

The **MAKE** files for both applications ICON6 and CURSOR6 are identical,
with the exception of the file names. These files will be discussed later in
the chapter in conjunction with a detailed discussion of the **MAKE** utility.

The Definition File (ICON6.DEF)

The standard definition files for both of the examples in this chapter are similar except for the file names and need no further discussion.

The Resource File (ICON6.RC)

The resource file contains the declaration for the icon designed earlier.

```
NewIcon ICON icon6.ico
```

NewIcon is the name the application will use to identify the icon defined by ICON6.ICO. Since both ICON6.RC and CURSOR6.RC are so similar, they will be used in the discussion later in this chapter, "Using the Resource Compiler."

The Application File (ICON6.C)

Pulling a custom icon into an application only involves two steps. First, *szIconName* is assigned the name of the icon defined in ICON6.DEF.

```
szIconName[]="NewIcon";
```

Next, the window class is assigned this new icon with the following line of code:

```
wcSwp.hIcon          =LoadIcon(hInst,szIconName);
```

When the window is created it will now have the custom icon.

USING CURSORS

Adding a customized cursor to a Windows application is just as easy as adding your own icon. The complete listing that follows has very few changes from the previous example.

```
THE MAKE FILE FOR CURSOR6:

ALL : cursor6.exe # ALL needed for C 6.0 up

cursor6.obj : cursor6.c
    cl -c -AS -Gsw -Oas -Zpe cursor6.c

cursor6.res : cursor6.rc cursor6.cur
```

```
    RC -r cursor6.rc

cursor6.exe : cursor6.obj cursor6.def cursor6.res
    link /NOD cursor6,,,libw slibcew, cursor6
    rc cursor6.res

THE DEFINITION FILE FOR CURSOR6:

;CURSOR6.DEF for C Compiling

NAME            cursor6
DESCRIPTION     'Illustrate a new Cursor'
EXETYPE         WINDOWS
STUB            'WINSTUB.EXE'
CODE            PRELOAD MOVEABLE DISCARDABLE
DATA            PRELOAD MOVEABLE MULTIPLE
HEAPSIZE        4096
STACKSIZE       9216
EXPORTS         WindowProc      @1

THE RESOURCE FILE FOR CURSOR6:

#include "windows.h"

NewCursor CURSOR cursor6.cur

THE APPLICATION FILE FOR CURSOR6:

/* Simplified Windows Platform (SWP)              */
/* (c) William H. Murray and Chris H. Pappas, 1989 */

#include <windows.h>
#include <string.h>

long FAR PASCAL WindowProc(HWND,unsigned,WORD,LONG);

char szProgName[]="ProgName";
char szCursorName[]="NewCursor";

int PASCAL WinMain(hInst,hPreInst,lpszCmdLine,nCmdShow)
HANDLE hInst,hPreInst;
LPSTR  lpszCmdLine;
int    nCmdShow;
{
  HWND hwnd;
  MSG  msg;
  WNDCLASS wcSwp;
  if (!hPreInst)
  {
    wcSwp.lpszClassName=szProgName;
    wcSwp.hInstance     =hInst;
    wcSwp.lpfnWndProc   =WindowProc;
    wcSwp.hCursor       =LoadCursor(hInst,szCursorName);
    wcSwp.hIcon         =0;
    wcSwp.lpszMenuName  =szProgName;
    wcSwp.hbrBackground=GetStockObject(WHITE_BRUSH);
    wcSwp.style         =CS_HREDRAW|CS_VREDRAW;
    wcSwp.cbClsExtra    =0;
    wcSwp.cbWndExtra    =0;
    if (!RegisterClass (&wcSwp))
```

```
            return FALSE;
      }
   hwnd=CreateWindow(szProgName,"A New Cursor",
                     WS_OVERLAPPEDWINDOW,CW_USEDEFAULT,
                     CW_USEDEFAULT,CW_USEDEFAULT,
                     CW_USEDEFAULT,NULL,NULL,
                     hInst,NULL);
   ShowWindow(hwnd,nCmdShow);
   UpdateWindow(hwnd);
   while (GetMessage(&msg,NULL,NULL,NULL))
   {
      TranslateMessage(&msg);
      DispatchMessage(&msg);
   }
   return(msg.wParam);
}

long FAR PASCAL WindowProc(hwnd,messg,wParam,lParam)
HWND hwnd;
unsigned messg;
WORD wParam;
LONG lParam;
{
   HDC hdc;
   PAINTSTRUCT ps;
   static char szTString[80]="BOLD cursors can draw attention!";

   switch (messg)
   {
     case WM_PAINT:
       hdc=BeginPaint(hwnd,&ps);

/*--------- your routines below ---------*/

       TextOut(hdc,200,200,szTString,strlen(szTString));

/*--------- your routines above ---------*/

       ValidateRect(hwnd,NULL);
       EndPaint(hwnd,&ps);
       break;

     case WM_DESTROY:
       PostQuitMessage(0);
       break;

     default:
       return(DefWindowProc(hwnd,messg,wParam,lParam));
   }
   return(0L);
}
```

The MAKE and .DEF Files (CURSOR6 and CURSOR6.DEF)

The **MAKE** and definition files remain identical to the previous example; the only change is the file names.

The Resource File (CURSOR6.RC)

Both resource files ICON6.RC and CURSOR6.RC are discussed in detail later in the chapter. They will be used to explain the workings of the resource compiler.

The Application File (CURSOR6.C)

Adding a custom cursor to an application is as easy as one, two. First, the *szIconName* is assigned the name of the icon defined in ICON6.DEF.

```
szCursorName[]="NewCursor";
```

Second, the window class is assigned this new cursor using the following line of code:

```
wcSwp.hCursor      =LoadCursor(hInst,szCursorName);
```

When the window is created the custom cursor will automatically be associated with the mouse position.

MAKE, THE PROGRAM MAINTAINER

As the number and complexity of the files necessary to create a Windows application grows, your appreciation of the **MAKE** utility will also increase. To review, **MAKE** intelligently inspects the dates of all files used in an application, checking .RES (resource files), .OBJ (object files), .EXE (executable files), and so on, and assembles, compiles, or links only those files that disagree by date. The entire process saves time when creating Windows applications that use many source files or take numerous steps to complete.

Creating a MAKE Description File

The **MAKE** source file is an ASCII text file using a command structure and syntax specific to the utility's abilities. The basic command structure for the **MAKE** description file involves a *TargetFile* and *DependentFile* instruction pair, using the following form:

```
TargetFile:DependentFiles command [[optional command]]. . .
```

The *TargetFile* is created from the *DependentFiles* using the command options specified. Any file that is not in the same subdirectory as the application's description file must be defined using a complete path name. The backslash (\) can be used to separate dependent file names that do not all fit on one line. Commands can be any valid DOS command. All commands must begin on a new line and be preceded by at least one space or a tab. Only commands that involve dependent files that have been modified since the target file was created will be executed.

You can make the **MAKE** description more readable by including comments. **MAKE** will ignore any character strings on a line that follows a number sign (#). If a comment is the only information on a line, then the # must be the first character on the line *without* any leading white space.

Last of all, the order of the commands in the **MAKE** description is important. **MAKE** will examine each *TargetFile:DependentFile* combination, checking the creation dates. Should a later **MAKE** description command modify a previous *TargetFile*'s *DependentFile*, **MAKE** has no facility to go back and update the previous *TargetFile*.

Let's take a look at the ICON6 **MAKE** file.

```
THE MAKE FILE FOR ICON6:
ALL : icon6.exe # ALL needed for C 6.0 up
icon6.obj : icon6.c
    cl -c -AS -Gsw -Oas -Zpe icon6.c
icon6.res : icon6.rc icon6.ico
    RC -r icon6.rc
icon6.exe : icon6.obj icon6.def icon6.res
    link /NOD icon6,,,libw slibcew, icon6
    rc icon6.res
```

The first line instructs the C compiler to create ICON6.OBJ using ICON6.RC as the source file. All of the command switches necessary to generate the .OBJ file follow on the second line. The third and fourth lines are used to create the ICON6.RES resource file by invoking the resource compiler and passing it the ICON6.RC resource script (the resource compiler is described later in this chapter) and the icon definition ICON6.ICO. All of the resource compiler's command switches are on the fourth line. The process of creating the ICON6.EXE file terminates with the invocation of "link." All of the *DependentFiles* (ICON6.OBJ, ICON6.DEF, ICON6.RES) are listed, along with the linkers' command options.

MAKE Options

MAKE file descriptions have no file extension and may contain the following four switches.

Switch	Description
/d	Instructs the **MAKE** utility to output the last modification date of each file as it is scanned
/i	Instructs **MAKE** to ignore exit codes returned by programs that are invoked by the **MAKE** description file
/n	Instructs **MAKE** to display all of the commands that would be executed by a description file; however, it does *not* actually execute the commands
/s	Instructs **MAKE** to execute all of its commands without outputting any information to the display

Invoking MAKE

MAKE is invoked simply by typing the name of the utility, followed by any switches, and then the name of the **MAKE** description file. For example, you would invoke **MAKE** on the previous description file this way:

```
make /s icon6
```

Notice in this example that the **/s MAKE** option was included, which suppresses the **MAKE** utility's current status output.

USING THE RESOURCE COMPILER

Windows applications often use their own resources. Remember, a resource can be a menu, dialog box, font, or, as we have seen in this chapter, icons, cursors, and bitmaps. To review, the resource compiler is used to create the binary resource file format of the resource, in order for the Windows application to load and use the object. This section describes how to create the resource script file used by the resource compiler and discusses some of the compiler's options.

As you've seen, the resource script file is nothing more than a syntactically correct ASCII text file that has an .RC file extension. The script uses resource description statements defining the resource's name, type, and other details.

The resource script may also contain compiler directives specifying certain actions to be taken before compiling the script file. The good news is that the resource compiler directives are identical to those used by the C programming language.

Resource Compiler Statements

Table 6-2 describes all ot the resource statements available.

Defining additional resources for an application is as simple as naming the *resourceID*, followed by a resource compiler keyword, and then the actual file name. Let's suppose you've created a resource script file called EXAMPLE.RC

```
myicon ICON myicon.ico
mycursor CURSOR mycursor.cur
mybitmap BITMAP mybitmap.bmp
```

that defines three new resources. The name of the three resources are "myicon," "mycursor," and "mybitmap." ICON, CURSOR, and BITMAP are reserved keywords defining the type of the resource. These are followed by the actual file names containing the resource information. Both of the resource script files ICON6.RC and CURSOR6.RC define only one resource, an icon and a cursor, respectively.

There are five additional options that can be included with each single-line statement. These options follow the resource type keyword and include PRELOAD, LOADONCALL, FIXED, MOVEABLE, and DISCARD-ABLE. The first two options define load options, the latter ones define memory options. The following is the syntax of the single-line statement:

```
resourceID resource-type [[load-option]] [[memory-option]] filename
```

The PRELOAD option automatically loads the resource whenever the application is run. LOADONCALL only loads the resource when it is called.

Table 6-2.   Resource Compiler Statements

Directive	Single-line	Multiple-line	User-defined
#include	BITMAP	ACCELERATORS	Supplied by user
#define	CURSOR	DIALOG	
#undef	FONT	MENU	
#ifdef	ICON	RCDATA	
#ifndef		STRINGTABLE	
#if			
#elif			
#else			
#endif			

If a FIXED memory option is selected, the resource remains at a fixed memory address. Selecting MOVEABLE allows Windows to move the resource to compress and conserve memory. The last choice, DISCARDABLE, allows Windows to discard the resource if it is no longer needed. However, it can be reloaded should a call be made requesting that particular resource. For example, selecting LOADONCALL and DISCARDABLE for *mybitmap* is as simple as entering the following modified single-line statement into the resource-script:

```
myicon ICON myicon.ico
mycursor CURSOR mycursor.cur
mybitmap BITMAP LOADONCALL DISCARDABLE mybitmap.bmp
```

Compiling Resources

The command to run the resource compiler includes the name of the resource script file, the name of the executable file that will receive the compiler's binary format output, and any optional instructions as shown in Table 6-3.

The resource compiler syntax is as follows:

```
rc [[compiler options]] filename.rc [[executable filename]]
```

For example, invoking the resource compiler with the sample resource script described earlier would look like this:

```
rc example
rc example.rc
rc -r example.rc
```

The first two examples read the EXAMPLE.RC resource script file, create the compiled resource file EXAMPLE.RES, and copy the resources into the executable file EXAMPLE.EXE. The third command performs the same actions, except that it does *not* put the resource into EXAMPLE.EXE. If the third command was executed, the EXAMPLE.RES binary file could be added to the EXAMPLE.EXE file at a later date, using the following command structure:

```
rc example.res
```

This causes the resource compiler to search for the .RES compiled file and places it into the .EXE file with the same file name.

Table 6-3.   Resource Compiler Options

Option	Description
-R	Instructs the resource compiler to place its output into a file with an .RES extension instead of putting it into the executable file
-D	Defines a symbol for the preprocessor that you can test with the *#ifdef* directive
-FO	Renames the .RES file
-FE	Renames the .EXE file
-I	Searches the specified directory before searching the directories specified by the INCLUDE environment variable
-V	Displays messages that report on the progress of the compiler
-X	Prevents the resource compiler from checking the INCLUDE environment variable when searching for include files or resource files
-L or LIM32	Causes the resource compiler to compile an application that will use the expanded memory supported by the Lotus Intel Microsoft Expanded Memory Specification, version 3.2
-M	Causes the resource compiler to compile an application using EMS, so that multiple instances of the application will use different EMS memory banks
-E	For a dynamic link library, changes the default location of global memory from below the EMS bank line to above the EMS bank line
-P	Creates a private dynamic link library that can be called by only one application. This lets Windows load the library above the EMS bank line
-? or -H	Displays a list of the resource compiler's command line options

7

DEVELOPING MENUS AND KEYBOARD ACCELERATORS

Menus are one of Windows' most important tools for creating interactive programs. They also form the gateway for easy, consistent interfacing among applications. In their simplest form, menus allow the user to point and click on selections that have been predefined. These selections can be screen color choices, sizing options, file operations, and so on. More advanced menu options allow the user to select a dialog box from the menu list, which permits data entry from the keyboard. Dialog boxes allow the user to enter strings, integers, and even real numbers. This is such a large and important topic that the next chapter has been reserved for its discussion. This chapter will introduce menu basics before going on to the more complex subject of dialog boxes.

During the course of this chapter, four programs will be developed to teach you the most important aspects of creating menus for your applications. These programs will show you how to use menus to change the size of objects, alter the background color, retrieve information about your system, and produce directory listings for various drives.

MENU MECHANICS

The following sections will describe what a menu is, what it looks like, how it is created in the resource file, and the various menu options available to the programmer. Menus are very easy to create and implement.

What Is a Menu?

A menu is a list of items or names that represent actions an application can take. In some cases, the items in a menu can even be bitmaps. The user selects an option with either the mouse or keyboard, moving to the desired item, and pressing the left mouse button or entering a combination of keystrokes. Windows, in turn, responds by sending a message to the application stating which command was selected.

Menus and the Resource Compiler

By following a set of simple rules, you can have Windows draw and manage menus for you. This way Windows will produce consistent menus from one application to another. Menus are usually defined in the resource script file, although they can be defined in the source file. (Resource script files and the resource compiler were described in Chapter 3.) The menu information will be combined with your program application at link time forming the final executable (.EXE) file. The structure of a simple menu is quite easy to understand.

```
#include "windows.h"
#include "menu3.h"
SystemInfo MENU
{
  POPUP "&Disk_Information"
    {
      MENUITEM "&Total Disk Space",   IDM_TDS
      MENUITEM "&Free Disk Space",    IDM_FDS
      MENUITEM "D&efault Drive",      IDM_DD
      MENUITEM "D&OS Version",        IDM_DV, MENUBARBREAK
      MENUITEM "&Windows Version",    IDM_WV
    }

  POPUP "&Time/Date_Information"
    {
      MENUITEM "&Time",               IDM_TIME
      MENUITEM "&Date",               IDM_DATE
    }
}
```

By studying this listing, you can identify a number of menu keywords such as MENU, POPUP, MENUITEM, and MENUBARBREAK. Braces ({ }) can be replaced with keywords BEGIN and END, if desired. It is also easy to identify the menu items in each of the two pop-up menus. The most important menu keywords will be discussed in the next section.

Menu Keywords and Options

The name of this program's menu definition is "SystemInfo." The menu definition name is followed by the keyword MENU. This particular example describes two pop-up menus, Disk_Information and Time/Date_Information, which will appear on the menu bar, as shown in Figure 7-1. Pop-up menus are arranged from left to right on the menu bar. If a large number of pop-up items are used, an additional bar will be provided automatically. Only one pop-up menu can be displayed at a time. The ampersand (&) produces an underscore beneath the character that follows it, which allows the menu item to be selected from the keyboard. To select the first pop-up, press ALT-D, or position the mouse and click the left button.

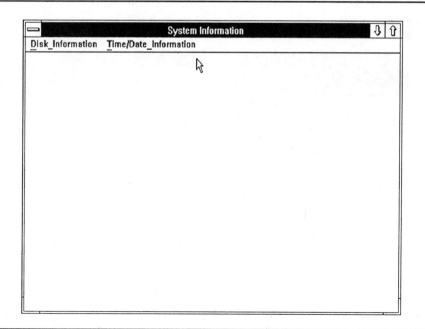

Figure 7-1.   Menu bar pop-up menus: Disk_Information and Time/Date_Information

When a pop-up is selected, Windows pops the menu to the screen immediately under the selected item on the menu bar.

Each use of MENUITEM describes one menu item or name; for example, "Total Disk Space" as shown in Figure 7-2. Again, the ampersand is used to permit keyboard selection of menu items. Obviously, a letter can only be used once in a particular pop-up for keyboard selection. This means that instead of the first letter of an item, another letter might have to be used.

The menu identification values are defined in the appropriate header file. IDM stands for the identification number of a menu item. This form of ID has become very popular, but is not required. Each menu item must have a unique identification number associated with it.

MENUBARBREAK is one of several menu design options shown in Table 7-1. This option will split the menu into two columns, separating the entries with a horizontal bar. MENUBREAK and MENUBARBREAK are useful when the number of items becomes too long for one vertical window column.

Keyboard Accelerators

Keyboard accelerators are most often used by menu designers as "hot-key" combinations for selecting menu items. For example, a menu may have 12

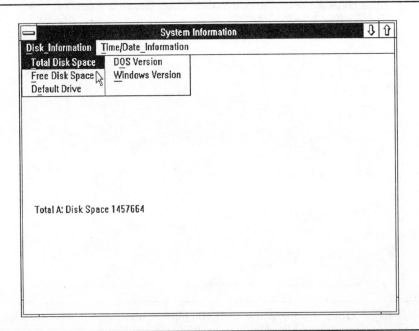

Figure 7-2.   Disk_Information menu

Table 7-1.   Menu Design Options

Option	Use
CHECKED	Menu item has a check mark next to it
END	Menu item is the last item in a pop-up or static menu
GRAYED	Menu item is set inactive and appears as a faded option on the menu list
HELP	Menu item is a right-justified static menu, selectable with the keyboard
INACTIVE	Menu item is displayed, but cannot be selected under the current set of circumstances
MENUBREAK	Menu item is placed in a new column
MENUBARBREAK	Menu item is placed in a new column Items are also separated by a horizontal bar
OWNERDRAW (version 3.0 and later)	The owner of the menu is responsible for drawing all visual aspects of the menu item, including highlighted, inactive, and checked states
POPUP	A sublist of items is displayed when this option is selected

color items for selecting a background color. The user could point and click the menu for each color, or keyboard accelerators could be used. If a keyboard accelerator were used, the 12 function keys, for instance, could be used for color selection, without having to show the menu at all!

```
#include "windows.h"
#include "menu2.h"

Alteration MENU
{
  POPUP "&Ellipse_Size"
    {
      MENUITEM "&small",          IDM_SMALL
      MENUITEM "&Medium",         IDM_MEDIUM
      MENUITEM "&LARGE",          IDM_LARGE
    }

  POPUP "Ba&ckground_Colors"
    {
      MENUITEM "BLAC&K\tF1",      IDM_BLACK
      MENUITEM "&WHITE\tF2",      IDM_WHITE
```

```
        MENUITEM "&RED\tF3",           IDM_RED
        MENUITEM "&ORANGE\tF4",        IDM_ORANGE
        MENUITEM "&YELLOW\tF5",        IDM_YELLOW
        MENUITEM "GREE&N\tF6",         IDM_GREEN
        MENUITEM "&BLUE\tF7",          IDM_BLUE
        MENUITEM "&MAGENTA\tF8",       IDM_MAGENTA
        MENUITEM SEPARATOR
        MENUITEM "Lt GR&EEN\tF9",      IDM_LTGREEN
        MENUITEM "Lt BL&UE\tF10",      IDM_LTBLUE
        MENUITEM "Lt RE&D\tF11",       IDM_LTRED
        MENUITEM "Lt GR&AY\tF12",      IDM_LTGRAY
    }
}


Alteration ACCELERATORS
{
  VK_F1,   IDM_BLACK,    VIRTKEY
  VK_F2,   IDM_WHITE,    VIRTKEY
  VK_F3,   IDM_RED,      VIRTKEY
  VK_F4,   IDM_ORANGE,   VIRTKEY
  VK_F5,   IDM_YELLOW,   VIRTKEY
  VK_F6,   IDM_GREEN,    VIRTKEY
  VK_F7,   IDM_BLUE,     VIRTKEY
  VK_F8,   IDM_MAGENTA,  VIRTKEY
  VK_F9,   IDM_LTGREEN,  VIRTKEY
  VK_F10,  IDM_LTBLUE,   VIRTKEY
  VK_F11,  IDM_LTRED,    VIRTKEY
  VK_F12,  IDM_LTGRAY,   VIRTKEY
}
```

You will note in the listing the addition of several items. First, under the Background _ Colors pop-up, each item is followed by a backslash and the letter "t" (\t) and a function key name, which separates the menu item from the keyboard accelerator text by a tab stop. This action simply places the keyboard accelerator text in the pop-up menu—it does not define an accelerator key. In this example, the function keys F1 to F12 have been identified as accelerator keys for selecting background colors. Figure 7-3 shows the appearance of a menu with the keyboard accelerators listed.

Keyboard accelerators are also defined in the resource script file. In the current example, "Alteration" is the name of the accelerator table. The name is followed by the keyword ACCELERATORS. The structure of each accelerator event line takes on the following form:

event, id, [type] [NOINVERT] [SHIFT] [CONTROL]

The *event* value is the keystroke to be used as an accelerator. This character can be a single character enclosed in double quotes, an integer representing an ASCII character (in which case the *type* field must be ASCII), or an integer representing a virtual key (in which case the *type* field must be VIRTKEY). The *id* value usually matches the menu identification values given for the pop-up in which the keyboard accelerators are used. The *type*

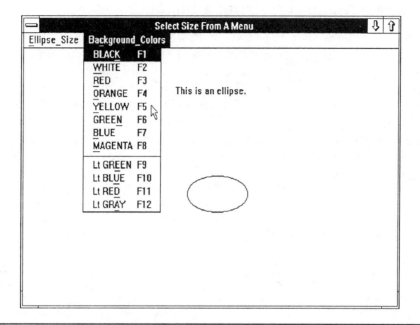

Figure 7-3.   Menu with listed keyboard accelerators

field contains ASCII or VIRTKEY as explained earlier. If the NOINVERT option is specified, no top-level menu item will be highlighted when the accelerator key is selected. The SHIFT or CONTROL options will activate the accelerator key only when the SHIFT or CTRL key is also depressed. Various accelerator key options were listed in Chapter 4 (see Table 4-10, Virtual Key Codes).

CREATING MENUS FOR EVERY OCCASION

The following section of text will guide you through the creation of the four examples mentioned at the beginning of this chapter. Each example will have a **MAKE** file, a header file, a definition file, a resource file, and a source file. For example, before compiling and linking, your disk might contain MENU1, MENU1.H, MENU1.DEF, MENU1.RC, and MENU1.C. After compiling and linking, your disk will also include the files, MENU1.RES, MENU1.OBJ, and MENU1.EXE. Please be extremely careful as you enter each example — as the listing size increases so does the likelihood of data entry mistakes.

Creating a Menu for Sizing a Shape

The first example is simple. MENU1 will produce one pop-up menu with three sizing options: Small, Medium, and Large. By selecting one of these items, an ellipse will be drawn on the screen in the appropriate size.

This and all remaining examples in this chapter will use a single listing containing all of the necessary files required to successfully compile and link the example. As the various files are discussed, pieces of code will be pulled out of this main listing for special explanations. The aim is to help you locate all the example code for any particular application in one central location.

```
THE MENU1 MAKE FILE:

ALL : menu1.exe # ALL needed for C 6.0 up

menu1.obj: menu1.c
    cl -c -AS -Gsw -Oas -Zpe menu1.c

menu1.res : menu1.rc
    rc -r menu1.rc

menu1.exe: menu1.obj menu1.def menu1.res
    link /NOD menu1,,,libw slibcew, menu1.def
    rc menu1.res


THE MENU1.H HEADER FILE:

/* MENU1.H header file */

/* size information */

#define IDM_SMALL     201
#define IDM_MEDIUM    202
#define IDM_LARGE     203


THE MENU1.DEF DEFINITION FILE:

NAME         menu1
DESCRIPTION  'Menu Example'
EXETYPE      WINDOWS
STUB         'WINSTUB.EXE'
CODE         PRELOAD MOVEABLE DISCARDABLE
DATA         PRELOAD MOVEABLE MULTIPLE
HEAPSIZE     4096
STACKSIZE    9216
EXPORTS      WindowProc        @1


THE MENU1.RC RESOURCE FILE:

#include "windows.h"
#include "menu1.h"
```

```
ShapeMenu MENU
{
  POPUP "&Ellipse_Size"
    {
      MENUITEM "&Small",      IDM_SMALL
      MENUITEM "&Medium",     IDM_MEDIUM
      MENUITEM "&Large",      IDM_LARGE
    }
}
```

THE MENU1.C APPLICATION FILE:

```
/* Simplified Windows Platform (SWP)              */
/* (c) William H. Murray and Chris H. Pappas, 1989 */

#include <windows.h>
#include "menu1.h"

long FAR PASCAL WindowProc(HWND,unsigned,WORD,LONG);

char szProgName[]="ProgName";
char szApplName[]="ShapeMenu";
static WORD wSize=25;

int PASCAL WinMain(hInst,hPreInst,lpszCmdLine,nCmdShow)
HANDLE hInst,hPreInst;
LPSTR  lpszCmdLine;
int    nCmdShow;
{
  HWND hwnd;
  MSG  msg;
  WNDCLASS wcSwp;
  if (!hPreInst)
  {
    wcSwp.lpszClassName=szProgName;
    wcSwp.hInstance    =hInst;
    wcSwp.lpfnWndProc  =WindowProc;
    wcSwp.hCursor      =LoadCursor(NULL,IDC_ARROW);
    wcSwp.hIcon        =LoadIcon(hInst,szProgName);
    wcSwp.lpszMenuName =szApplName;
    wcSwp.hbrBackground=GetStockObject(WHITE_BRUSH);
    wcSwp.style        =CS_HREDRAW|CS_VREDRAW;
    wcSwp.cbClsExtra   =0;
    wcSwp.cbWndExtra   =0;
    if (!RegisterClass (&wcSwp))
      return FALSE;
  }
  hwnd=CreateWindow(szProgName,"Select Size from a Menu",
                    WS_OVERLAPPEDWINDOW,CW_USEDEFAULT,
                    CW_USEDEFAULT,CW_USEDEFAULT,
                    CW_USEDEFAULT,NULL,NULL,
                    hInst,NULL);
  ShowWindow(hwnd,nCmdShow);
  UpdateWindow(hwnd);
  while (GetMessage(&msg,NULL,NULL,NULL))
  {
    TranslateMessage(&msg);
    DispatchMessage(&msg);
  }
```

```
    return(msg.wParam);
}


long FAR PASCAL WindowProc(hwnd,messg,wParam,lParam)
HWND hwnd;
unsigned messg;
WORD wParam;
LONG lParam;
{
  HDC hdc;
  PAINTSTRUCT ps;

  switch (messg)
  {
    case WM_COMMAND:
      switch (wParam)
      {
        case IDM_SMALL:
          wSize=25;
          break;
        case IDM_MEDIUM:
          wSize=50;
          break;
        case IDM_LARGE:
          wSize=100;
          break;
        default:
          break;
      }
      InvalidateRect(hwnd,NULL,TRUE);
    break;

    case WM_PAINT:
      hdc=BeginPaint(hwnd,&ps);

/*--------- your routines below ---------*/

      Ellipse(hdc,320-(wSize*2),200-wSize,
              320+(wSize*2),200+wSize);
      TextOut(hdc,250,50,"This is an ellipse.",19);

/*--------- your routines above ---------*/

      ValidateRect(hwnd,NULL);
      EndPaint(hwnd,&ps);
      break;

    case WM_DESTROY:
      PostQuitMessage(0);
      break;

    default:
      return(DefWindowProc(hwnd,messg,wParam,lParam));
  }
  return(0L);
}
```

The five files in the previous listing must be entered, compiled, and linked to produce a working program. This program will create the simple menu shown in Figure 7-4.

The MAKE File (MENU1)

The **MAKE** file is responsible for splicing all the pieces of code together during the compile and link process. The **MAKE** file shown here is similar to that of previous chapters and so warrants no further discussion.

The Header File (MENU1.H)

The header file for this example contains the definitions for several unique ID numbers. The IDs for menu items start with "IDM." The selection of the ID numbers is a programming choice. Sequential numbers are good for grouping related menu items together. The disadvantage of sequential IDs becomes apparent if a new ID value needs to be inserted in a previously

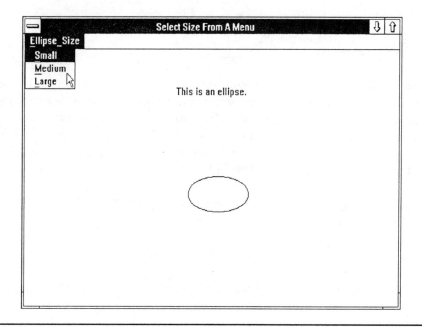

Figure 7-4.   Simple sizing pop-up menu

developed list. Careful planning is necessary when developing menus. This header file is used by both the resource file and the application file.

The Definition File (MENU1.DEF)

The definition file is similar to previous definition files. The use of menus does not require an additional procedure, as do the dialog boxes discussed in the next chapter. Thus, no additional EXPORT statements are necessary.

The Resource File (MENU1.RC)

The resource file was created by entering a text editor and typing in the menu information. Notice that the ID information from MENU1.H is available to this file. For this application, the menu will contain only three sizing options.

The Application File (MENU1.C)

As you study the MENU1.C listing, note the inclusion of two lines of code near the top of the listing.

```
char szApplName[]="ShapeMenu";
static WORD wSize=25;
```

The string held in *szApplName* identifies the name of the menu. The first use is in the WinMain procedure when the window class is defined. Here *wcSwp.lpszMenuName* is set equal to the string. This is the most common method of referencing a menu resource and will be used exclusively throughout this book. The variable, *wSize*, is declared as a global static WORD and is initialized to 25. This value will form the default value for the ellipse size.

When the menu is selected, Windows sends a WM_COMMAND message to the corresponding window function.

```
case WM_COMMAND:
  switch (wParam)
  {
  case IDM_SMALL:
    wSize=25;
    break;
  case IDM_MEDIUM:
    wSize=50;
    break;
  case IDM_LARGE:
    wSize=100;
```

```
   break;
default:
   break;
}
   InvalidateRect(hwnd,NULL,TRUE);
break;
```

The value of *wParam* is checked with three case statements. If **S**mall is selected from the menu, *wSize* is set to 25. Medium returns a 50, and Large returns 100. Regardless of which value is selected, the InvalidateRect function will send a message to WM_PAINT to update the entire window and draw the ellipse to the size specified by *wSize*. The global variable, *wSize*, is used to size the ellipse under WM_PAINT. The InvalidateRect, Ellipse, and TextOut functions are discussed in Chapter 10.

Changing the Background Color with a Menu

In this particular example, two pop-up menus are used. The first menu is similar to the menu of the previous example. Items selected from the first menu will size an ellipse on the screen. The second menu allows the user to select a new background color from a list of 12 predefined shades, as shown in Figure 7-5.

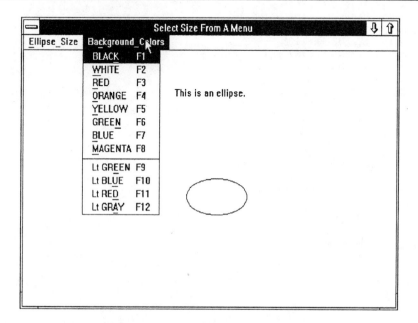

Figure 7-5.   Background color menu options

THE MENU2 MAKE FILE:

```
ALL : menu2.exe # ALL needed for C 6.0 up

menu2.obj: menu2.c
    cl -c -Gsw -Os -Zp -W2 menu2.c

menu2.res : menu2.rc
    rc -r menu2.rc

menu2.exe: menu2.obj menu2.def menu2.res
    link menu2, /align:16,, slibw, menu2.def
    rc menu2.res
```

THE MENU2.H HEADER FILE:

```
/* MENU2.H header file */

/* size information */

#define IDM_SMALL      201
#define IDM_MEDIUM     202
#define IDM_LARGE      203

/* background color information */

#define IDM_BLACK      101
#define IDM_WHITE      102
#define IDM_RED        103
#define IDM_ORANGE     104
#define IDM_YELLOW     105
#define IDM_GREEN      106
#define IDM_BLUE       107
#define IDM_MAGENTA    108
#define IDM_LTGREEN    109
#define IDM_LTBLUE     110
#define IDM_LTRED      111
#define IDM_LTGRAY     112
```

THE MENU2.DEF DEFINITION FILE:

```
NAME       menu2
DESCRIPTION 'Menu Example'
EXETYPE    WINDOWS
STUB       'WINSTUB.EXE'
CODE       MOVEABLE
DATA       MOVEABLE MULTIPLE
HEAPSIZE   4096
STACKSIZE  9216
EXPORTS    WindowProc       @1
```

THE MENU2.RC RESOURCE FILE:

```
#include "windows.h"
#include "menu2.h"

Alteration MENU
{
  POPUP "&Ellipse_Size"
    {
```

```
       MENUITEM "&small",              IDM_SMALL
       MENUITEM "&Medium",             IDM_MEDIUM
       MENUITEM "&LARGE",              IDM_LARGE
     }

  POPUP "Ba&ckground_Colors"
     {
       MENUITEM "BLAC&K\tF1",          IDM_BLACK
       MENUITEM "&WHITE\tF2",          IDM_WHITE
       MENUITEM "&RED\tF3",            IDM_RED
       MENUITEM "&ORANGE\tF4",         IDM_ORANGE
       MENUITEM "&YELLOW\tF5",         IDM_YELLOW
       MENUITEM "GREE&N\tF6",          IDM_GREEN
       MENUITEM "&BLUE\tF7",           IDM_BLUE
       MENUITEM "&MAGENTA\tF8",        IDM_MAGENTA
       MENUITEM SEPARATOR
       MENUITEM "Lt GR&EEN\tF9",       IDM_LTGREEN
       MENUITEM "Lt BL&UE\tF10",       IDM_LTBLUE
       MENUITEM "Lt RE&D\tF11",        IDM_LTRED
       MENUITEM "Lt GR&AY\tF12",       IDM_LTGRAY
     }
}


Alteration ACCELERATORS
{
  VK_F1,   IDM_BLACK,    VIRTKEY
  VK_F2,   IDM_WHITE,    VIRTKEY
  VK_F3,   IDM_RED,      VIRTKEY
  VK_F4,   IDM_ORANGE,   VIRTKEY
  VK_F5,   IDM_YELLOW,   VIRTKEY
  VK_F6,   IDM_GREEN,    VIRTKEY
  VK_F7,   IDM_BLUE,     VIRTKEY
  VK_F8,   IDM_MAGENTA,  VIRTKEY
  VK_F9,   IDM_LTGREEN,  VIRTKEY
  VK_F10,  IDM_LTBLUE,   VIRTKEY
  VK_F11,  IDM_LTRED,    VIRTKEY
  VK_F12,  IDM_LTGRAY,   VIRTKEY
}
```

THE MENU2.C APPLICATION FILE:

```
/* Simplified Windows Platform (SWP)              */
/* (c) William H. Murray and Chris H. Pappas, 1989 */

#include <windows.h>
#include "menu2.h"

long FAR PASCAL WindowProc(HWND,unsigned,WORD,LONG);

char szProgName[]="ProgName";
char szApplName[]="Alteration";
static WORD wSize=25;
static WORD wColor;

int PASCAL WinMain(hInst,hPreInst,lpszCmdLine,nCmdShow)
HANDLE hInst,hPreInst;
LPSTR  lpszCmdLine;
int    nCmdShow;
```

```
{
  HANDLE hAccel;
  HWND hwnd;
  MSG  msg;
  WNDCLASS wcSwp;
  if (!hPreInst)
  {
    wcSwp.lpszClassName=szProgName;
    wcSwp.hInstance    =hInst;
    wcSwp.lpfnWndProc  =WindowProc;
    wcSwp.hCursor      =LoadCursor(NULL,IDC_ARROW);
    wcSwp.hIcon        =LoadIcon(hInst,szProgName);
    wcSwp.lpszMenuName =szApplName;
    wcSwp.hbrBackground=GetStockObject(WHITE_BRUSH);
    wcSwp.style        =CS_HREDRAW|CS_VREDRAW;
    wcSwp.cbClsExtra   =0;
    wcSwp.cbWndExtra   =0;
    if (!RegisterClass (&wcSwp))
      return FALSE;
  }
  hwnd=CreateWindow(szProgName,"Select Size from a Menu",
                    WS_OVERLAPPEDWINDOW,CW_USEDEFAULT,
                    CW_USEDEFAULT,CW_USEDEFAULT,
                    CW_USEDEFAULT,NULL,NULL,
                    hInst,NULL);
  ShowWindow(hwnd,nCmdShow);
  UpdateWindow(hwnd);

  hAccel=LoadAccelerators(hInst,szApplName);

  while (GetMessage(&msg,NULL,NULL,NULL))
    {
    if (!TranslateAccelerator(hwnd,hAccel,&msg))
      {
      TranslateMessage(&msg);
      DispatchMessage(&msg);
      }
    }
  return(msg.wParam);
}

long FAR PASCAL WindowProc(hwnd,messg,wParam,lParam)
HWND    hwnd;
unsigned messg;
WORD    wParam;
LONG    lParam;
{
  HDC  hdc;
  PAINTSTRUCT ps;
  HMENU hmenu;
  static int wColorValue[12][3]={0,0,0,        /*BLACK*/
                                 255,255,255,  /*WHITE*/
                                 255,0,0,      /*RED*/
                                 255,96,0,     /*ORANGE*/
                                 255,255,0,    /*YELLOW*/
                                 0,255,0,      /*GREEN*/
                                 0,0,255,      /*BLUE*/
                                 255,0,255,    /*MAGENTA*/
                                 128,255,0,    /*LT GREEN*/
                                 0,255,255,    /*LT BLUE*/
                                 255,0,159,    /*LT RED*/
```

```
                                180,180,180}; /*LT GRAY*/

    switch (messg)
    {
      case WM_COMMAND:
        switch (wParam)
        {
          case IDM_SMALL:
            wSize=25;
            break;
          case IDM_MEDIUM:
            wSize=50;
            break;
          case IDM_LARGE:
            wSize=100;
            break;
          case IDM_BLACK:
          case IDM_WHITE:
          case IDM_RED:
          case IDM_ORANGE:
          case IDM_YELLOW:
          case IDM_GREEN:
          case IDM_BLUE:
          case IDM_MAGENTA:
          case IDM_LTGREEN:
          case IDM_LTBLUE:
          case IDM_LTRED:
          case IDM_LTGRAY:
            hmenu=GetMenu(hwnd);
            CheckMenuItem(hmenu,wColor,MF_UNCHECKED);
            wColor=wParam;
            CheckMenuItem(hmenu,wColor,MF_CHECKED);
            SetClassWord(hwnd,GCW_HBRBACKGROUND,
                         CreateSolidBrush(RGB
                         (wColorValue[wColor-IDM_BLACK][0],
                          wColorValue[wColor-IDM_BLACK][1],
                          wColorValue[wColor-IDM_BLACK][2])));
            break;
          default:
            break;
        }
        InvalidateRect(hwnd,NULL,TRUE);
      break;

      case WM_PAINT:
        hdc=BeginPaint(hwnd,&ps);

/*--------- your routines below ---------*/

        Ellipse(hdc,320-(wSize*2),200-wSize,
                320+(wSize*2),200+wSize);
        TextOut(hdc,250,50,"This is an Ellipse.",19);

/*--------- your routines above ---------*/

        ValidateRect(hwnd,NULL);
        EndPaint(hwnd,&ps);
        break;

      case WM_DESTROY:
        PostQuitMessage(0);
```

```
        break;

    default:
        return(DefWindowProc(hwnd,messg,wParam,lParam));
    }
    return(0L);
}
```

The MAKE and Definition Files (MENU2 and MENU2.DEF)

The **MAKE** and definition files remain identical to previous examples except for the file names.

The Header File (MENU2.H)

The header file values for this program have been separated into two groups. One group holds menu IDs for sizing and one holds the IDs for the color options. You can see from studying this listing that 3 sizes and 12 colors are available.

The Resource File (MENU2.RC)

The resource file contains the menu and accelerator key information discussed earlier in this chapter. For this example, the 12 function keys are used as accelerator keys for color selection. When the application is run, background colors can be selected from the menu or by simply pressing a function key; for example, F3 will change the background color to red.

The Application File (MENU2.C)

As you study this listing, note the addition of another global variable at the start of the listing, *wColor*. This variable will hold the color selection value in an indirect manner.

```
HMENU hmenu;
static int wColorValue[12][3]={0,0,0,          /*BLACK*/
                          255,255,255,    /*WHITE*/
                          255,0,0,        /*RED*/
                          255,96,0,       /*ORANGE*/
                          255,255,0,      /*YELLOW*/
                          0,255,0,        /*GREEN*/
                          0,0,255,        /*BLUE*/
                          255,0,255,      /*MAGENTA*/
                          128,255,0,      /*LT GREEN*/
                          0,255,255,      /*LT BLUE*/
                          255,0,159,      /*LT RED*/
                          180,180,180};   /*LT GRAY*/
```

This program will require a handle. The handle *hmenu* is of type *HMENU*. You'll see how this value is used shortly. A simple look-up table of RGB color values will be used to create a brush in order to paint the background. Chapter 11 will discuss how to use the new Windows 3.0 Palette Manager to accomplish a similar task. The look-up table, *wColorValue*, is a two-dimensional array. There are 12 colors specified by 3 integer values. The integer values specify the amount of each of the primary colors (red, green, blue) that are to be mixed. These range from 0 to 255 for each primary color.

The portion of WM_COMMAND that is of interest here contains the case statements for the color selection.

```
case IDM_BLACK:
case IDM_WHITE:
case IDM_RED:
case IDM_ORANGE:
case IDM_YELLOW:
case IDM_GREEN:
case IDM_BLUE:
case IDM_MAGENTA:
case IDM_LTGREEN:
case IDM_LTBLUE:
case IDM_LTRED:
case IDM_LTGRAY:
hmenu=GetMenu(hwnd);
CheckMenuItem(hmenu,wColor,MF_UNCHECKED);
wColor=wParam;
CheckMenuItem(hmenu,wColor,MF_CHECKED);
SetClassWord(hwnd,GCW_HBRBACKGROUND,
             CreateSolidBrush(RGB
             (wColorValue[wColor-IDM_BLACK][0],
             wColorValue[wColor-IDM_BLACK][1],
             wColorValue[wColor-IDM_BLACK][2])));
```

You can see that, regardless of which color is selected via the case statement, the GetMenu function will be called to return the menu handle. The structure of this code is typical for related menu items, but requires that the items have sequential identification numbers. Menus permit listed items to be checked or unchecked. The function CheckMenuItem has the ability to place or remove a check mark next to the specified menu item. It is customary to remove a previously placed check (MF_UNCHECKED) before placing a new check mark (MF_CHECKED). Thus the technique is to remove the old value, retrieve the new *wColor* value, and place the new check mark.

The function SetClassWord is used to change the background color. The handle for this function is the menu handle, *hmenu*. The second value, called the index, is selected from seven possible options:

GCW_CBCLSEXTRA
GCW_CBWNDEXTRA
GCW_HBRBACKGROUND

GCW_HCURSOR
GCW_HICON
GCW_HMODULE
GCW_STYLE

These options permit the replacement of the given parameter in the WND-CLASS structure at the beginning of each program. The option GCW_HBRBACKGROUND sets a new handle to a background brush. The third value in the function specifies the replacement value. For this example, the replacement value is derived from the color value, *wColor*. Suppose a red background was selected by the user. In that case, *wColor* will be passed the ID value of 103. Also notice that the color black has an ID value of 101. The black ID number is subtracted from the red ID number, giving a result of 2. The value of 2 is used as an index into the *wColorValue* array. The red values in the array correspond to [2][0], [2][1], and [2][2]. Now you know why the values must be sequential.

The only unfinished business is the explanation of how the accelerator keys are loaded into the application code. This is done under the WinMain procedure.

```
hAccel=LoadAccelerators(hInst,szApplName);

while (GetMessage(&msg,NULL,NULL,NULL))
   {
   if (!TranslateAccelerator(hwnd,hAccel,&msg))
      {
      TranslateMessage(&msg);
      DispatchMessage(&msg);
      }
   }
return(msg.wParam);
}
```

The function LoadAccelerators is used to load or return the handle of the specified accelerator table. The TranslateAccelerator function translates keyboard accelerators to WM_COMMAND messages. These messages are sent directly to the window and are not posted in the message queue.

Determining System Information with a Menu

In many applications it is necessary to know something about the system on which the program is running. For example, before saving a file you might have to poll the particular diskette for the amount of disk space available. Another case where sampling system information is important is when your program is dependent upon the DOS or Windows version number. All of this information is typically available through DOS or BIOS interrupts. Information on available DOS and BIOS interrupts can be found in many assembly language and C books. We recommend *80386/80286 Assembly Language Programming* (Murray and Pappas 1986) or *C: The Complete Reference* (Schildt 1987) both published by Osborne/McGraw-Hill.

THE MENU3 MAKE FILE:

```
all : menu3.exe

menu3.obj: menu3.c
    cl -c -AS -Gsw -Oas -Zpe menu3.c

menu3.res : menu3.rc
    rc -r menu3.rc

menu3.exe: menu3.obj menu3.def menu3.res
    link /NOD menu3,,,libw slibcew, menu3.def
    rc menu3.res
```

THE MENU3.H HEADER FILE:

```
/* MENU3.H header file */

/* system information */

#define IDM_TDS      201
#define IDM_FDS      202
#define IDM_DD       203
#define IDM_DV       204
#define IDM_WV       205
#define IDM_DATE     206
#define IDM_TIME     207
```

THE MENU3.DEF DEFINITION FILE:

```
NAME        menu3
DESCRIPTION 'Menu Example'
EXETYPE     WINDOWS
STUB        'WINSTUB.EXE'
CODE        PRELOAD MOVEABLE DISCARDABLE
DATA        PRELOAD MOVEABLE MULTIPLE
HEAPSIZE    4096
STACKSIZE   9216
EXPORTS     WindowProc       @1
```

THE MENU3.RC RESOURCE FILE:

```
#include "windows.h"
#include "menu3.h"

SystemInfo MENU
{
  POPUP "&Disk_Information"
    {
      MENUITEM "&Total Disk Space",   IDM_TDS
      MENUITEM "&Free Disk Space",    IDM_FDS
      MENUITEM "D&efault Drive",      IDM_DD
```

```
      MENUITEM "D&OS Version",        IDM_DV, MENUBARBREAK
      MENUITEM "&Windows Version",    IDM_WV
    }

  POPUP "&Time/Date_Information"
    {
      MENUITEM "T&ime",               IDM_TIME
      MENUITEM "&Date",               IDM_DATE
    }
}
```

THE MENU3.C APPLICATION FILE:

```
/* Simplified Windows Platform (SWP)              */
/* (c) William H. Murray and Chris H. Pappas, 1989 */

#include <windows.h>
#include <dos.h>
#include <stdio.h>
#include "menu3.h"

long FAR PASCAL WindowProc(HWND,unsigned,WORD,LONG);

char szProgName[]="ProgName";
char szApplName[]="SystemInfo";
char szMessage[40];
short sLength;

int PASCAL WinMain(hInst,hPreInst,lpszCmdLine,nCmdShow)
HANDLE hInst,hPreInst;
LPSTR  lpszCmdLine;
int    nCmdShow;
{
  HWND hwnd;
  MSG  msg;
  WNDCLASS wcSwp;
  if (!hPreInst)
    {
    wcSwp.lpszClassName=szProgName;
    wcSwp.hInstance     =hInst;
    wcSwp.lpfnWndProc   =WindowProc;
    wcSwp.hCursor       =LoadCursor(NULL,IDC_ARROW);
    wcSwp.hIcon         =LoadIcon(hInst,szProgName);
    wcSwp.lpszMenuName  =szApplName;
    wcSwp.hbrBackground=GetStockObject(WHITE_BRUSH);
    wcSwp.style         =CS_HREDRAW|CS_VREDRAW;
    wcSwp.cbClsExtra    =0;
    wcSwp.cbWndExtra    =0;
    if (!RegisterClass (&wcSwp))
      return FALSE;
    }
  hwnd=CreateWindow(szProgName,"System Information",
                    WS_OVERLAPPEDWINDOW,CW_USEDEFAULT,
                    CW_USEDEFAULT,CW_USEDEFAULT,
                    CW_USEDEFAULT,NULL,NULL,
                    hInst,NULL);
  ShowWindow(hwnd,nCmdShow);
  UpdateWindow(hwnd);
  while (GetMessage(&msg,NULL,NULL,NULL))
    {
```

```
      TranslateMessage(&msg);
      DispatchMessage(&msg);
   }
   return(msg.wParam);
}

long FAR PASCAL WindowProc(hwnd,messg,wParam,lParam)
HWND hwnd;
unsigned messg;
WORD wParam;
LONG lParam;
{
   HDC hdc;
   PAINTSTRUCT ps;
   union REGS inregs;
   union REGS outregs;
   char drvletter;
   short month,day,year,hrs,mins,secs,
         defdrv,intver,fracver;
   unsigned long secperclu,numfreeclu,
                 bytespersec,numclu;

   switch (messg)
   {
     case WM_COMMAND:
       switch (wParam)
       {
         case IDM_TDS:
           inregs.h.ah=0x36;
           inregs.h.dl=1;           /* A Drive */
           intdos(&inregs,&outregs);
           bytespersec=outregs.x.cx;
           numclu=outregs.x.dx;
           sLength=sprintf(szMessage,
                        "Total A: Disk Space %ld",
                        numclu*bytespersec);
           break;
         case IDM_FDS:
           inregs.h.ah=0x36;
           inregs.h.dl=1;           /* A Drive */
           intdos(&inregs,&outregs);
           numfreeclu=outregs.x.bx;
           bytespersec=outregs.x.cx;
           sLength=sprintf(szMessage,"Free A: Disk Space %ld",
                        numfreeclu*bytespersec);
           break;
         case IDM_DD:
           inregs.h.ah=0x19;
           intdos(&inregs,&outregs);
           defdrv=outregs.h.al;
           switch (defdrv)
           {
             case 0:
               drvletter=(char)"A";
               break;
             case 1:
               drvletter=(char)"B";
               break;
             case 2:
               drvletter=(char)"C";
               break;
```

```
              case 3:
                drvletter=(char)"D";
                break;
              default:
                sLength=sprintf(szMessage,
                              "No Drive within Range");
            }
            sLength=sprintf(szMessage,
                          "The Default Drive Is %s",
                          drvletter);
            break;
          case IDM_DV:
            inregs.h.ah=0x30;
            intdos(&inregs,&outregs);
            intver=outregs.h.al;
            fracver=outregs.h.ah;
            sLength=sprintf(szMessage,
                          "Current DOS Version %d.%d",
                          intver,fracver);
            break;
          case IDM_WV:
            intver=GetVersion();
            fracver=intver >> 8;
            intver= intver & 255;
            sLength=sprintf(szMessage,
                          "Current Windows Version %d.%d",
                          intver,fracver);
            break;
          case IDM_DATE:
            inregs.h.ah=0x2A;
            intdos(&inregs,&outregs);
            year=outregs.x.cx;
            month=outregs.h.dh;
            day=outregs.h.dl;
            sLength=sprintf(szMessage,
                          "Current Date %d/%d/%d",
                          month,day,year);
            break;
          case IDM_TIME:
            inregs.h.ah=0x2C;
            intdos(&inregs,&outregs);
            hrs=outregs.h.ch;
            mins=outregs.h.cl;
            secs=outregs.h.dh;
            sLength=sprintf(szMessage,
                          "Current Time %d:%d:%d",
                          hrs,mins,secs);
            break;
          default:
            break;
        }
        InvalidateRect(hwnd,NULL,TRUE);
      break;

    case WM_PAINT:
      hdc=BeginPaint(hwnd,&ps);

/*--------- your routines below ---------*/

      TextOut(hdc,20,200,szMessage,sLength);
```

```
/*--------- your routines above ---------*/

    ValidateRect(hwnd,NULL);
    EndPaint(hwnd,&ps);
    break;

  case WM_DESTROY:
    PostQuitMessage(0);
    break;

  default:
    return(DefWindowProc(hwnd,messg,wParam,lParam));
  }
  return(0L);
}
```

The MAKE and Definition Files (MENU3 and MENU3.DEF)

The **MAKE** and definition files remain identical to previous examples. Only file names have changed.

The Header File (MENU3.H)

The header file contains ID information for menu items. The ID numbers are assigned in the following manner:

IDM_TDS	total disk space
IDM_FDS	free disk space
IDM_DD	default drive
IDM_DV	current DOS version
IDM_WV	current Windows version
IDM_DATE	current date
IDM_TIME	current military time

The Resource File (MENU3.RC)

The resource file will produce two pop-up menus. The first menu, Disk_Information, allows the user to select information pertaining to disk and version numbers. The second menu, Time/Date_Information, will display time or date options. Note that the first pop-up menu contains a MENUBARBREAK after IDM_DV. The results of this option are shown in Figure 7-6.

The Application File (MENU3.C)

In this program all screen information, regardless of the menu item selected, will be returned to the *szMessage* array. The array is initialized to

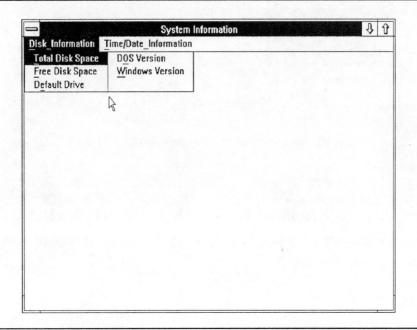

Figure 7-6. Using MENUBARBREAK to create menu columns

hold 40 characters, but the actual length of any string is held in *sLength*. Both of these variables are declared at the start of the program and are global in nature.

There are some unique features to be found in the variable declaration section of the WindowProc procedure.

```
union REGS inregs;
union REGS outregs;
char drvletter;
short month,day,year,hrs,mins,secs,
      defdrv,intver,fracver;
unsigned long secperclu,numfreeclu,
              bytespersec,numclu;
```

Microsoft provides several interrupt functions for C. The one used exclusively in this program is *intdos*. The values *inregs* and *outregs* represent unions that contain register values to be passed to and from the interrupt specified. The union type, *REGS*, is supplied by the header DOS.H. The remaining variables are an assortment of *char*, *short*, and *unsigned longs* used to hold the retrieved data.

WM_COMMAND messages are used to process selected menu items with case statements. Notice IDM_TDS, IDM_FDS, IDM_DD, IDM_DV,

IDM_WV, IDM_DATE, and IDM_TIME. Let us study the IDM_DATE case statement as an example.

```
case IDM_DATE:
  inregs.h.ah=0x2A;
  intdos(&inregs,&outregs);
  year=outregs.x.cx;
  month=outregs.h.dh;
  day=outregs.h.dl;
  sLength=sprintf(szMessage,
                  "Current Date %d/%d/%d",
                  month,day,year);
  break;
```

The *intdos* function calls a system 21H interrupt automatically. In order to request date information, the ah register must be set to the hexadecimal value 2A. Once the interrupt is serviced, the cx register will return the year, the dh register the month, and the dl register the day. The *sprintf* function then converts the date information into a string and saves it in *szMessage*. The length of this string is returned to *sLength*. All menu choices are handled in basically the same manner.

The information is printed to the screen with the WM_PAINT message. The information is updated each time a new menu selection is processed because of the InvalidateRect function at the end of WM_COMMAND. Figure 7-7 shows a typical date output to the window.

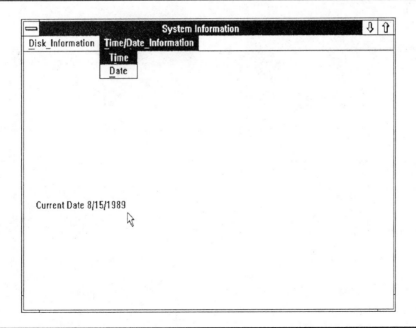

Figure 7-7. MENU3 date output

Viewing Directory Listings with a Menu

The last example in this chapter uses a pop-up menu that allows the user to select a directory listing from drive A, B, C, or D. This listing will then be displayed to the screen. In order to display long listings, a vertical scroll bar will also be used. Menus do not allow the user to retrieve data from the keyboard, so the program will be restricted to the four drives mentioned. One major drawback of this program is that only the main directory can be listed. No provision is made for listing subdirectories. This problem could be overcome and the program greatly enhanced with the use of a dialog box for data entry. Dialog boxes are explained in the next chapter.

THE MENU4 MAKE FILE:

```
all : menu4.exe

menu4.obj: menu4.c
    cl -c -AS -Gsw -Oas -Zpe menu4.c

menu4.res : menu4.rc
    rc -r menu4.rc

menu4.exe: menu4.obj menu4.def menu4.res
    link / NOD menu4,,,libw slibcew, menu4.def
    rc menu4.res
```

THE MENU4.H HEADER FILE:

```
/* MENU4.H header file */

/* system information */

#define IDM_AFILES    201
#define IDM_BFILES    202
#define IDM_CFILES    203
#define IDM_DFILES    204
```

THE MENU4.DEF DEFINITION FILE:

```
NAME        menu4
DESCRIPTION 'Menu Example'
EXETYPE     WINDOWS
STUB        'WINSTUB.EXE'
CODE        PRELOAD MOVEABLE DISCARDABLE
DATA        PRELOAD MOVEABLE MULTIPLE
HEAPSIZE    4096
STACKSIZE   9216
EXPORTS     WindowProc       @1
```

THE MENU4.RC RESOURCE FILE:

```
#include "windows.h"
```

```
#include "menu4.h"

Directory MENU
{
  POPUP "&Directory_Information"
    {
       MENUITEM "Directory A:",          IDM_AFILES
       MENUITEM "Directory B:",          IDM_BFILES
       MENUITEM "Directory C:",          IDM_CFILES
       MENUITEM "Directory D:",          IDM_DFILES
    }
}


THE MENU4.C APPLICATION FILE:

/* Simplified Windows Platform (SWP)                 */
/* (c) William H. Murray and Chris H. Pappas, 1989 */

#include <windows.h>
#include <dos.h>
#include <string.h>
#include <stdio.h>
#include "menu4.h"

#define SCROLLLINES 200
#define OFFSET 30

long FAR PASCAL WindowProc(HWND,unsigned,WORD,LONG);

char szProgName[]="ProgName";
char szApplName[]="Directory";
char szMessage[44];
char szBuffer[44];
char szMyfile[44];
short sLength;

int PASCAL WinMain(hInst,hPreInst,lpszCmdLine,nCmdShow)
HANDLE hInst,hPreInst;
LPSTR  lpszCmdLine;
int    nCmdShow;
{
  HWND hwnd;
  MSG  msg;
  WNDCLASS wcSwp;
  if (!hPreInst)
  {
    wcSwp.lpszClassName=szProgName;
    wcSwp.hInstance     =hInst;
    wcSwp.lpfnWndProc   =WindowProc;
    wcSwp.hCursor       =LoadCursor(NULL,IDC_ARROW);
    wcSwp.hIcon         =LoadIcon(hInst,szProgName);
    wcSwp.lpszMenuName  =szApplName;
    wcSwp.hbrBackground=GetStockObject(WHITE_BRUSH);
    wcSwp.style         =CS_HREDRAW|CS_VREDRAW;
    wcSwp.cbClsExtra    =0;
    wcSwp.cbWndExtra    =0;
    if (!RegisterClass (&wcSwp))
```

```
          return FALSE;
      }
  hwnd=CreateWindow(szProgName,"System Information",
                    WS_OVERLAPPEDWINDOW|WS_VSCROLL,
                    CW_USEDEFAULT,CW_USEDEFAULT,
                    CW_USEDEFAULT,CW_USEDEFAULT,
                    NULL,NULL,hInst,NULL);
  ShowWindow(hwnd,nCmdShow);
  UpdateWindow(hwnd);
  while (GetMessage(&msg,NULL,NULL,NULL))
  {
     TranslateMessage(&msg);
     DispatchMessage(&msg);
  }
  return(msg.wParam);
}

long FAR PASCAL WindowProc(hwnd,messg,wParam,lParam)
HWND    hwnd;
unsigned messg;
WORD    wParam;
LONG    lParam;
{
  HDC hdc;
  PAINTSTRUCT ps;
  TEXTMETRIC  tm;
  union REGS  inregs;
  union REGS  outregs;
  short  i;
  static short charht,yClientView,
               posvertscroll;

  switch (messg)
  {
    case WM_CREATE:
      hdc=GetDC(hwnd);
      GetTextMetrics(hdc,&tm);
      charht=tm.tmHeight+tm.tmExternalLeading;
      ReleaseDC(hwnd,hdc);

      SetScrollPos(hwnd,SB_VERT,posvertscroll,TRUE);
      SetScrollRange(hwnd,SB_VERT,0,SCROLLLINES,FALSE);
      break;

    case WM_SIZE:
      yClientView=HIWORD(lParam);
      break;

    case WM_VSCROLL:
      switch (wParam)
      {
        case SB_LINEDOWN:
          posvertscroll+=1;
          break;
        case SB_LINEUP:
          posvertscroll-=1;
          break;
        case SB_PAGEDOWN:
```

```
            posvertscroll+=yClientView/charht;
            break;
          case SB_PAGEUP:
            posvertscroll-=yClientView/charht;
            break;
          case SB_THUMBPOSITION:
            posvertscroll=LOWORD(lParam);
            break;
          default:
            break;
        }
        if (posvertscroll>SCROLLLINES)
          posvertscroll=SCROLLLINES;
        if (posvertscroll<0)
          posvertscroll=0;
        if (posvertscroll!=GetScrollPos(hwnd,SB_VERT))
        {
          SetScrollPos(hwnd,SB_VERT,posvertscroll,TRUE);
          InvalidateRect(hwnd,NULL,TRUE);
        }
        break;

      case WM_COMMAND:
        switch (wParam)
        {
          case IDM_AFILES:
            strcpy(szMyfile,"a:*.*");
            break;
          case IDM_BFILES:
            strcpy(szMyfile,"b:*.*");
            break;
          case IDM_CFILES:
            strcpy(szMyfile,"c:*.*");
            break;
          case IDM_DFILES:
            strcpy(szMyfile,"d:*.*");
            break;
          default:
            break;
        }
        InvalidateRect(hwnd,NULL,TRUE);
      break;

      case WM_PAINT:
        hdc=BeginPaint(hwnd,&ps);

/*--------- your routines below ---------*/

        i=0;
        bdos(0x1A,(short)szBuffer,0);
        bdos(0x4E,(short)szMyfile,0);
        sLength=sprintf(szMessage,"%s",&szBuffer[OFFSET]);
        TextOut(hdc,0,charht*(i-posvertscroll),
                szMessage,sLength);
        i++;
        for(;;)
        {
          if(18==bdos(0x4F,0,0))
```

```
        break;
      sLength=sprintf(szMessage,"%s",&szBuffer[OFFSET]);
      TextOut(hdc,0,charht*(i-posvertscroll),
              szMessage,sLength);
        i++;
    }

/*--------- your routines above ---------*/

      ValidateRect(hwnd,NULL);
      EndPaint(hwnd,&ps);
      break;

    case WM_DESTROY:
      PostQuitMessage(0);
      break;

    default:
      return(DefWindowProc(hwnd,messg,wParam,lParam));
  }
  return(0L);
}
```

The MAKE and Definition Files (MENU4 and MENU4.DEF)

The **MAKE** and definition files remain identical to previous examples except, as usual, for the file names.

The Header File (MENU4.H)

The header file uses four unique IDs and associated letters, one for each
drive's directory: IDM_AFILES, IDM_BFILES, IDM_CFILES, and
IDM_DFILES.

The Resource File (MENU4.RC)

The program utilizes a single pop-up menu named "Directory_Infor-
mation." Four menu items allow the user to select drive A, B, C, or D.

The Application File (MENU4.C)

This program will process five important messages: WM_CREATE,
WM_SIZE, WM_SCROLL, WM_COMMAND, and WM_PAINT.
    WM_CREATE gets information about the current text height using the
GetTextMetrics function. This information is returned in the *tm* structure.
Information concerning character height is necessary when flipping a page

of information up and down on the screen. The *tm* structure holds important information concerning current and available fonts; it will be discussed in detail in Chapter 9 along with numerous examples.

WM_SIZE returns information on the current window size (vertical only). This information is returned to *yClientView*. Window size information is also needed when scrolling a window one page at a time.

WM_VSCROLL processes five additional case statements. Table 7-2 lists the important scroll bar options.

```
case WM_VSCROLL:
  switch (wParam)
  {
    case SB_LINEDOWN:
      posvertscroll+=1;
      break;
    case SB_LINEUP:
      posvertscroll-=1;
      break;
    case SB_PAGEDOWN:
      posvertscroll+=yClientView/charht;
      break;
    case SB_PAGEUP:
      posvertscroll-=yClientView/charht;
    case SB_THUMBPOSITION:
      posvertscroll=LOWORD(lParam);
```

Table 7-2.　　Important Scroll Bar Options

Option	Use
SB_LINEUP	Top or left scroll arrow (single click moves one line up or left)
SB_LINEDOWN	Bottom or right scroll arrow (single click moves one line down or right)
SB_PAGEUP	Click above or left of thumb position to move one page up or left
SB_PAGEDOWN	Click below or right of thumb position to move one page down or right
SB_THUMBPOSITION	Position of dragged scroll bar
SB_THUMBTRACK	Tracks the thumb position as mouse moves
SB_TOP	Keyboard scroll information equivalent of HOME
SB_BOTTOM	Keyboard scroll information equivalent of END
SB_ENDSCROLL	End scroll

```
      break;
    default:
      break;
  }
  if (posvertscroll>SCROLLLINES)
    posvertscroll=SCROLLLINES;
  if (posvertscroll<0)
    posvertscroll=0;
  if (posvertscroll!=GetScrollPos(hwnd,SB_VERT))
    {
    SetScrollPos(hwnd,SB_VERT,posvertscroll,TRUE);
    InvalidateRect(hwnd,NULL,TRUE);
    }
  break;
```

SB_LINEDOWN and SB_LINEUP increment the variable *posvertscroll* by plus or minus 1, which represents one line of text in the window. The SB_PAGEDOWN and SB_PAGEUP must determine the number of lines contained on a page by dividing the *yClientView* size by the height of the text characters, *charht*. The remaining case statement determines the amount of scroll based on the position of the thumb in the scroll bar. SB_THUMBPOSITION passes the LOWORD of *lParam* to *posvertscroll*. You will also notice that two *if* statements limit *posvertscroll* to a range between 0 and SCROLLLINES. SCROLLLINES was defined as 200, which means that 200 lines can be scrolled. If this precaution isn't taken, scrolling will occur far beyond the beginning and end of the actual directory listing.

WM_COMMAND processes the directory selected from the menu. This program limits the choice to drives A, B, C, and D. Whatever the choice, the selection is saved in *szMyfile*. During a WM_PAINT message, this string information will be used in conjunction with an interrupt request. WM_COMMAND ends with a call to InvalidateRect. You'll recall from previous examples that this function posts a message to WM_PAINT for a screen update.

WM_PAINT uses three calls to the *bdos* function in order to print the directory listing. The *bdos* function is the speedy equivalent of the *intdos* function used in the previous example.

```
i=0;
bdos(0x1A,(short)szBuffer,0);
bdos(0x4E,(short)szMyfile,0);
sLength=sprintf(szMessage,"%s",&szBuffer[OFFSET]);
TextOut(hdc,0,charht*(i-posvertscroll),
        szMessage,sLength);
i++;
for(;;)
{
  if(18==bdos(0x4F,0,0))
    break;
  sLength=sprintf(szMessage,"%s",&szBuffer[OFFSET]);
  TextOut(hdc,0,charht*(i-posvertscroll),
```

```
            szMessage,sLength);
    i++;
}
```

This function is used when access to only the ah, dx, and al registers is needed. The first call to the *bdos* function is used to set the data transfer address (here, ah is specified as 1AH). The address for data transfer is given by *szBuffer* and is sent to the dx register. The al register is not needed, and is therefore set to 0 in this case. The second call requiring *bdos* is used to find the first file matching the specifications in *szMyfile*. This could be, for example, "a:*.*". In this case the ah register is set to 4EH before the call. Information is then transferred from the location pointed to by *&szBuffer[30]* to *szMessage* with the *sprintf* function. The length of the transfer, and hence the file name and extension, is saved in *sLength*.

You will notice that the information being returned to *szMessage* from *&szBuffer* is offset by 30. This is because this *bdos* interrupt returns additional information, such as attribute, time, and date, before the file name and extension. [Additional information on this function can be found in the various IBM technical reference manuals or books such as *The NEW Peter Norton Programmer's Guide to the IBM PC and PS/2*, by Peter Norton and Richard Wilton (Redmond, WA: Microsoft Press, 1988).] Remember that the second *bdos* call will only return information on the first file that matches the file specifications. The next line of code prints that information. The file name is printed in the current font, against the left border of the window (horizontal X in TextOut is set to 0). The vertical position is determined by the character height *(charht)* times the combination of the file number *(i)* minus the position of the vertical scroll *(posvertscroll)*.

vertical position = charht * (i - posvertscroll)

In order to print all remaining directory entries, another *bdos* function call is necessary. This time ah is set to 4FH. If *bdos* returns 18, this is an indication that no further files exist. Thus, a loop will be used to read and print each directory entry until the list is empty. With each pass through the loop, the file number *(i)* is incremented, forcing the next entry to be printed on the following line. Figure 7-8 shows a listing for the C drive.

LOOKING AHEAD

Menus have given us an important ability—the ability to interact with the application program. Menus are important in their own right, as a means of simple data entry. However, menus also form the gateway for a more

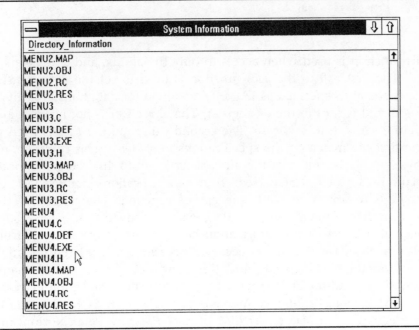

Figure 7-8.   MENU4 C drive listing

important form of data input device—the dialog box. The next chapter will investigate the additional data entry features of dialog boxes.

8

DATA ENTRY WITH DIALOG BOXES

The last chapter examined menus and keyboard accelerators as simple ways for users to enter data. This chapter will investigate a more significant means of data entry—the dialog box. While data can be entered directly into the application program's window, dialog boxes are preferable to maintain consistency among Windows programs.

Dialog boxes allow the user to check items in a window list, set push buttons for various choices, directly enter strings and integers from the keyboard, and indirectly enter real numbers (*floats*). Starting with Windows 3.0, dialog boxes can also contain *combo boxes,* which allow a combination of a single-line edit field and a list box. This will be explained in more detail later. The dialog box is the programmer's key to serious data entry in Windows programs. It is also the programmer's secret for ease of programming, since Windows handles all the necessary overhead.

Dialog boxes are called when selected as a choice from a menu; they appear as pop-up windows to the user. To distinguish a dialog box choice from ordinary selections in a menu, three dots (...) follow the dialog box option name. Figure 8-1 shows a menu with a dialog box option taken from an example developed later in this chapter. The specifications that make up a dialog box are typically produced with the DIALOG program, often called the "Dialog Box Editor," provided with the Microsoft Windows Software

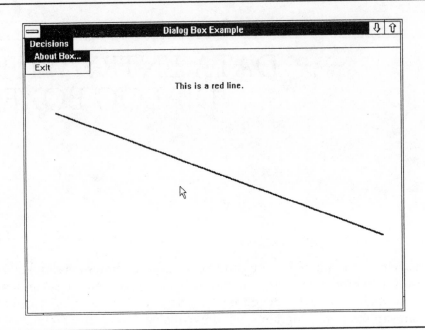

Figure 8-1.   A dialog box option provided in a menu

Development Kit. The resulting file, produced by the Dialog Box Editor, becomes part of the resource script file for the program, along with the specifications for program menus. Figures 8-2, 8-3, 8-4, 8-5, and 8-6 show a variety of dialog boxes that can be developed with the DIALOG program. If you study these dialog box figures, you will see the wide range of data types they allow the user to enter.

INTRODUCTION TO DIALOG BOXES

Dialog boxes are actually child windows that pop up when selected from the user's menu. When the various dialog box buttons, check boxes, and so on are selected, Windows provides the means necessary to process the message information. In all the applications here, messages produced by the dialog box window will be passed to a function or procedure in the actual program. This procedure will use an identifier name followed by "DlgProc," for example, AboutDlgProc, ShapeDlgProc, and TextDlgProc. The primary responsibility of each procedure is to initialize the various dialog box controls when the dialog box is created, evaluate the dialog box messages, and end the dialog box. A simple procedure can be quite short.

```
case WM_INITDIALOG:
  break;
case WM_COMMAND:
  switch (wParam)
  {
    case IDOK:
      EndDialog(hdlg,TRUE);
      break;
    default:
      return FALSE;
  }
  break;
  default:
    return FALSE;
}
```

Dialog boxes can be produced in two basic styles—*modal* and *modeless*. Modal dialog boxes are the most popular and are used for all of the examples in this chapter. When a modal dialog box is created no other options within the current program are available to the user until the dialog box is ended with a click to an Okay or Cancel button. The Okay button will process any new information selected by the user, while Cancel returns the user to the original window without processing new information. Windows expects the ID values for these push buttons to be 1 and 2, respectively. Modeless dialog boxes are more closely related to ordinary

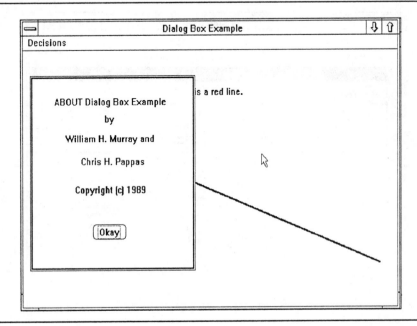

Figure 8-2.   A simple About dialog box

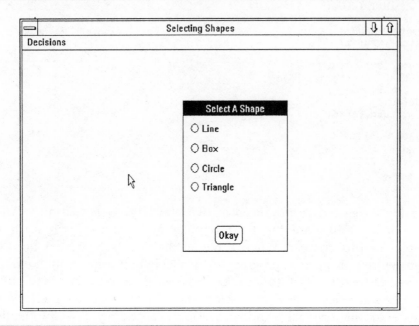

Figure 8-3.   A dialog box with radio buttons

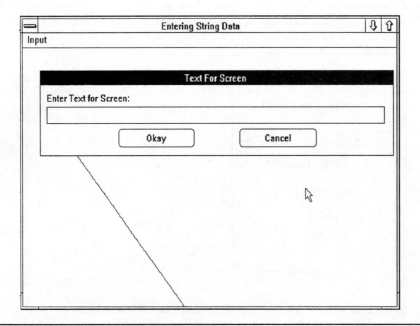

Figure 8-4.   A dialog box that allows text entry

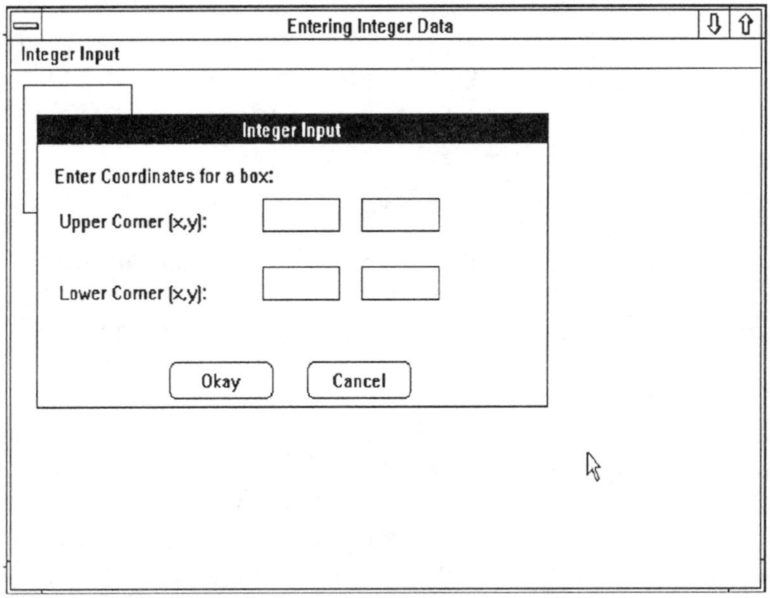

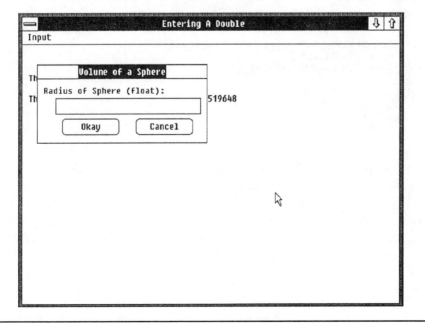

Figure 8-5.   A dialog box that allows integer input

Figure 8-6.   Entering real numbers (*float*) with a dialog box

windows. A pop-up window can be created from a parent window and allows the user to switch back and forth between the two. This is also permitted with a modeless dialog box. Modeless dialog boxes are preferred when a certain option must remain on the screen, such as a color select dialog box.

THE DIALOG BOX EDITOR

There are two ways to enter dialog box information into a resource script file. If you are entering information from a magazine or book listing, it will be easiest for you to use a text editor and simply copy the given menu and dialog box specifications into the resource file. This will be the case if you enter the code found in this chapter. However, if you are creating a dialog box from scratch, you should use the Dialog Box Editor provided with the development kit mentioned earlier. This section will discuss the fundamentals of using this editor and help you get started creating simple dialog boxes. The documentation provided with the toolkit will provide additional information for more advanced features and editing.

Why Use a Dialog Box Editor?

One look at a resource file containing dialog box information will convince you of the need for a Dialog Box Editor.

```
AboutDiaBox DIALOG LOADONCALL MOVEABLE DISCARDABLE
            9,20,131,133
            STYLE WS_DLGFRAME|WS_POPUP
{
  CONTROL "ABOUT Dialog Box Example",-1,"static",
          SS_CENTER|WS_CHILD,6,12,116,8
  CONTROL "Okay",IDOK,"button",
          BS_PUSHBUTTON|WS_TABSTOP|WS_CHILD,49,102,28,12
}
```

Where do all those terms come from? What do all those numbers mean? Without the Dialog Box Editor, it would be up to you to create, size, and place dialog boxes on the screen, experimentally. The editor, on the other hand, will do all this for you. Except for being able to say you created a dialog box without the editor, at least once in your life, there is no reason not to use this powerful development tool.

Using the Dialog Box Editor

One of the first things that must be mastered when using the Dialog Box Editor involves the use of files. Dialog box information will be returned from the editor with .RES and .DLG extensions. The .RES file is ready to be linked with the application's source file. The .DLG file is an ASCII version of the same information. Here is the problem: The Dialog Box Editor does not directly edit .DLG or ASCII files. This means that it will not edit menu files created with the .RC extension. However, the description for a dialog box should be included in the same ASCII file description (.RC) as the calling menu. You may be thinking, "How can this problem be solved?" The solution is to concatenate the .DLG file to the menu's .RC file with an editor capable of reading and saving ASCII files. It is recommended that you perform this operation manually. However, by using the *rcinclude* keyword, it can automatically be added before recompiling.

Therefore, the typical dialog box creation process will usually involve the creation of the menu description file (.RC) and the dialog box text file (.DLG) from the Dialog Box Editor. These files will be concatenated to form one file with the .RC extension. This file, which contains all needed information, will be attached to the application source file at link time.

There is one piece of bad news; if changes must be made to the dialog box, the Dialog Box Editor will only read the original .RES file information, not the .DLG or .RC files. This means the entire edit and concatenation process must be repeated. Usually, you must remove the old dialog box information and slip in the new specifications. Doing this manually will give you greater control over the appearance of the final files, even though it will certainly require more time. This is one of the reasons careful planning during the creation phase of dialog boxes will save a lot of editing time later.

The Dialog Box Editor can be entered by selecting the DIALOG.EXE file from the appropriate Windows subdirectory. Upon entering the Dialog Box Editor and selecting the File menu, a screen similar in appearance to Figure 8-7 should be seen. You must have a mouse attached to your computer in order to use the editor.

If you are creating a new dialog box, the File menu should be selected and the New option chosen. It is better not to allow the Dialog Box Editor to build the include file. Thus, when asked about a new include file, answer **No**. In order to start the editing process, the Edit menu is selected next. New Dialog...is probably the only option available for selection from this menu. Notice the three dots—a giveaway that this selection will call a dialog box within the editor. If you make this selection you will be asked to name the new dialog box. This will be the name attached to the dialog box description in the resource file and the name you will use to access the dialog box from the application program. Once the name is selected properly, the program will return you to the editor screen. The screen now contains the initial outline of the new dialog box. This can be moved around the screen and sized to fit your needs. An example is shown in Figure 8-8.

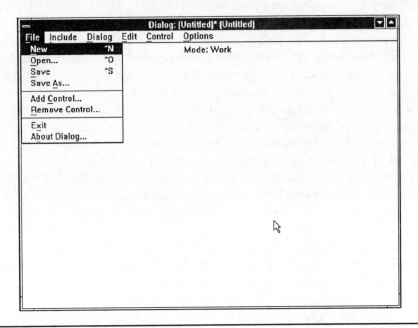

Figure 8-7.   Selecting the file option from the Dialog Box Editor

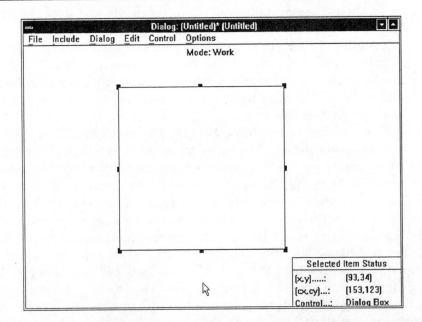

Figure 8-8.   Sizing an initial dialog box with the Dialog Box Editor

Editor Features

The main menu contains five menus that can be selected when working with a new dialog box. If you have gotten to this point, you have already used the File and Edit menus to name and initialize your new dialog box. The Include menu will not be used here, but additional information on its use is included with the Microsoft documentation. The two other menu selections are Control and Options.

The Control menu allows the selection of various controls, such as radio and push buttons, for inclusion in the final dialog box. The menu lists 14 items: Push Button, Radio Button, Check Box, Horizontal Scroll, Vertical Scroll, Edit, Static Text, Group Box, List Box, Combobox (new in 3.0), Frame, Icon, Rectangle, and Custom (new in 3.0). These controls provide the interface between the user and the Windows application program. Each of these controls will be explained in the next section.

The Option menu allows the selection of a test mode, a grid, and the ordering of groups. The test mode allows you to test the buttons, boxes, and so forth, placed on your dialog box while still in the editor. The grid feature eases placement of controls by forcing the alignment of these controls on predefined but invisible grid lines. Finally, the order groups selection allows you to define the order in which the controls are accessed.

The editor contains many built-in features that will make the editing process easier. In the lower-right corner of the editor's window is the Selected Item Status message box. The x and y values in this box give the coordinates of the upper-left corner dialog box or control that you have selected. The cx and cy values display the height and width of the dialog box being created. The control feature lists the type of control you are currently working with. This might be a push button or check box. If you are moving or sizing the dialog box, it will simply read "Dialog Box." Finally, if you selected a particular control, such as a push button, check box, or radio button, the ID value for that control will be shown. Keep your eye on the Selected Item Status message box during the creation of your complete dialog box. It will provide you with useful information.

Placing Controls

By far the most important aspect of using the Dialog Box Editor is understanding the various controls provided to the user. These are explained in the paragraphs that follow.

Controls can be placed in the current dialog box by selecting the appropriate control from the Control menu, positioning the mouse pointer in the dialog box, and clicking the mouse button. If the placement is not where you desired, the mouse can be used for repositioning.

Check Box   The Check Box control creates a small square box (a check box) with a label to its right. Check boxes are usually marked or checked by clicking with the mouse, but can also be selected with the keyboard. Several check boxes usually appear together in a dialog box and allow the user to check one or more features at the same time.

Radio Button   The Radio Button control creates a small circle (a radio button) with a label to its right. Radio buttons, like check boxes, typically appear in groups. However, unlike check boxes, only one radio button at a time can be selected in any given group.

Push Button   The Push Button control is a small, rounded rectangular button that can be sized. The push button contains a label within the button. Push buttons are used for an immediate choice such as accepting or canceling the dialog box selections made by the user. The dialog boxes in this chapter usually contain two push buttons—Okay and Cancel.

Group Box   The Group Box control creates a rectangular outline within a dialog box that encloses a group of controls that are to be used together. The group box has a label on its upper-left edge.

Horizontal and Vertical Scroll Bar   The Horizontal and Vertical Scroll Bar controls create the appropriate scroll bar for the dialog box. These are usually used in conjunction with another window or control that contains text or graphics information.

List Box   The List Box control creates a rectangular outline with a vertical scroll bar. List boxes are useful when scrolling is needed to allow the user to select a file from a long directory listing.

Edit Box   The Edit Box control creates a small interactive rectangle on the screen in which the user can enter string information. The edit box can be sized to accept short or long strings. This string information can be processed directly as character or numeric integer data, and indirectly as real number data in the program. The edit box is the most important control for data entry.

Text   The Text control allows the insertion of labels and strings within the dialog box. These can be used, for example, to label an edit box.

Frame   The Frame control can be used to frame a group of controls. It differs from the Group Box control in that the framed controls are not part of a specific group, other than in appearance.

Rectangle   The Rectangle control creates a filled rectangular shape. This control is useful in creating unique dialog windows.

Icon   The Icon control is used for the placement of a dialog box icon. It creates the rectangular space for the icon.

Combo Box   The Combo Box is made up of two elements. It is a combination of a single-line edit field (also called "static text") and a list box. With a combo box, the user has the ability to enter something into the edit box or scroll through the list box looking for an appropriate selection. Windows 3.0 provides several styles of combo boxes.

Custom   The Custom option allows you to create customized controls. Many such controls can be created and saved in a catalog recognized by the Dialog Box Editor. Custom controls are made up of dynamic link libraries that also contain the window procedure for the control. The catalog is contained in the Windows .INI file.

Editing with the Editor

Upon entering the dialog editor, the Edit menu allowed only one selection—the **N**ew Dialog. . . box feature. However, once a dialog box is established or modified, several additional editing features will become available. The most important options include Restore Dialog, Cut Dialog, Copy Dialog, Paste Dialog, Erase Dialog, and Styles.

The Restore Dialog feature allows you to restore a dialog box to a previously saved state. This is useful if an editing session goes astray and you find it necessary to start over. The Cut Dialog feature cuts the current dialog box and places it on the clipboard. The clipboard can be edited with the Windows PAINT program. The Copy Dialog feature makes a copy of the current dialog box to the clipboard. The Paste Dialog feature places the clipboard on the screen if the clipboard is in dialog box format. The Erase Dialog feature deletes the dialog box.

The Styles feature permits you to change the standard styles for a whole dialog box. Options include Title Bar, System Menu, Dialog Frame, Initially Visible, and so on.

In the next section, a simple About dialog box will be created with the Dialog Box Editor. The steps used to create this dialog box are common to all the dialog boxes created in this chapter.

Creating a Dialog Box

In this section, a simple About dialog box will be created. About dialog boxes are used to identify the program and the author, give a copyright date, and so forth. They usually contain only one push button—Okay!

Figure 8-9 shows a sized and positioned dialog box outline awaiting the placement of text and button controls. It also shows the Control menu. In this dialog box example only two types of controls will be used—text and push button. To enter text, just click that control option on the editor's menu. You will then be able to use the mouse to position the text in the dialog box window. Clicking the mouse button after positioning the text will allow editing of the text string with the Static Control Style dialog box, as shown in Figure 8-10. The Left Aligned Text option is the default. The string to be printed is entered in the text window. The ID value is automat-

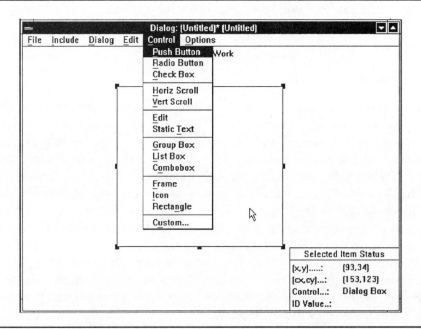

Figure 8-9.   Dialog control options available with the editor

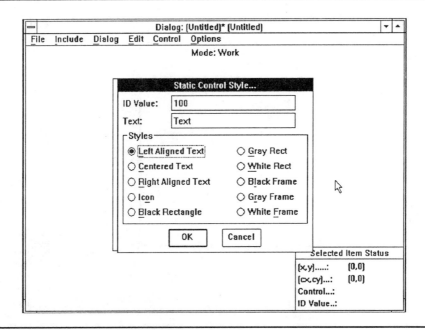

Figure 8-10.   Static style options for placing text within a dialog box

ically supplied. For static controls, this ID value is −1. When the Okay push button is selected, the string will be transferred to the dialog box window. Figure 8-11 shows the placement of the text for this example. Now suppose you want to place an Okay push button in the About dialog box. The Push-button option is selected from the Control menu and placed on the screen. The mouse is clicked to select the Button Control Styles dialog box, as shown in Figure 8-12. When the Okay push button is selected, the first simple dialog box design will be complete. As mentioned earlier, the Okay push button must have an ID value of 1. If the resource file uses IDOK, that value will be supplied. Figure 8-13 shows the placement of the push button and the final dialog box.

The dialog box information can now be saved by selecting Save from the File menu. Remember that the Dialog Box Editor will save this file in two forms, the .RES and .DLG forms. If this had been a serious example, the .DLG file could be brought into a text editor and combined with the necessary menu information. You'll see exactly how this is done in the first complete program in this chapter.

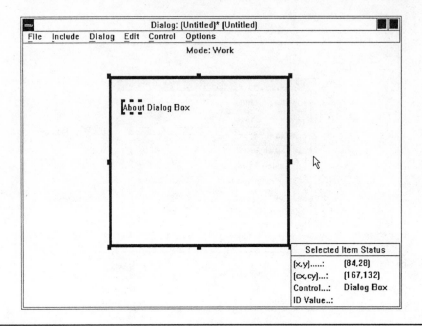

Figure 8-11.   Left-aligned text from the static style options

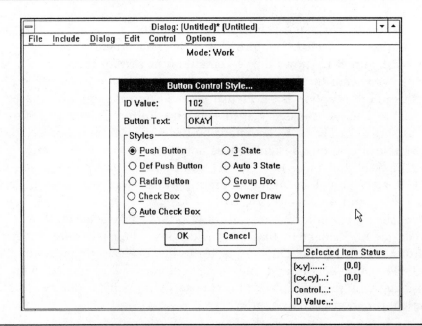

Figure 8-12.   Button control styles

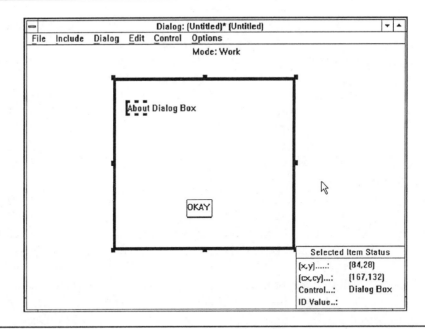

Figure 8-13.   A push button placed with the button control style options

Examining the .DLG File

The following listing shows a portion of a dialog box file for a complicated dialog box example:

```
INTEGERINPUTDLGBOX DIALOG LOADONCALL MOVEABLE DISCARDABLE
        9, 26, 210, 92
        CAPTION "Integer Input"
        STYLE WS_BORDER|WS_CAPTION|WS_DLGFRAME|WS_POPUP
{
  CONTROL "Enter Coordinates for a box:",-1,"static",
        SS_LEFT|WS_CHILD,7,7,145,8
  CONTROL "Upper Corner (x,y):",-1,"static",
        SS_LEFT|WS_CHILD,9,23,83,8
  CONTROL "",IDD_UPPERX,"edit",
        ES_LEFT|WS_BORDER|WS_TABSTOP|WS_CHILD,93,19,32,12
  CONTROL "",IDD_UPPERY,"edit",
        ES_LEFT|WS_BORDER|WS_TABSTOP|WS_CHILD,134,19,32,12
  CONTROL "Lower Corner (x,y):",-1,"static",
        SS_LEFT|WS_CHILD,9,48,81,8
  CONTROL "",IDD_LOWERX,"edit",
        ES_LEFT|WS_BORDER|WS_TABSTOP|WS_CHILD,93,43,32,12
  CONTROL "",IDD_LOWERY,"edit",
        ES_LEFT|WS_BORDER|WS_TABSTOP|WS_CHILD,134,43,32,12
  CONTROL "Okay",IDOK,"button",
        BS_PUSHBUTTON|WS_TABSTOP|WS_CHILD,54,76,44,14
  CONTROL "Cancel",IDCANCEL,"button",
        BS_PUSHBUTTON|WS_TABSTOP|WS_CHILD,111,76,44,14
}
```

The name of this dialog box is INTEGERINPUTDLGBOX. The editor has affixed various segment values along with size specifications for the box. The caption "Integer Input" will be at the top of the dialog box when called. The various style options further identify the dialog box as one with a border, caption, frame, and as a pop-up. Nine controls are listed.

The first control specification is for static text. The text string is "Enter Coordinates for a box:". The −1 is an ID value for static controls provided by the Dialog Box Editor. A list of other IDs is typically found in the header file (this will be covered in more detail later). The word "static" identifies the control as a static text box. The remaining specifications establish the text position and type.

The third control establishes an edit box. This edit box will hold the X value of an X,Y integer coordinate pair for drawing a figure. If a value is placed between the two double quotation marks, that will be the default value displayed in the edit box. Otherwise, the box will appear empty.

The final two controls specify Okay and Cancel push buttons. The text between the double quotation marks specifies what will appear within the push button. The labels for the ID values for both of these push buttons are system defaults.

As you can see, dialog box design without the editor would be a very unpleasant task.

CREATING DIALOG BOXES FOR EVERY NEED

This section will present five complete programming examples involving dialog boxes. The five examples will represent a fairly good cross section of data entry types and will expose you to the use of the major dialog box controls.

The first example creates a very simple About dialog box on the user's screen. The second example allows the user to select a graphics shape that will be drawn on the screen. The third will allow the user to input string information in an edit box and then print the string to the screen.

The fourth example will accept four integer values from an edit box. The four integers will specify the diagonally adjacent corners of a rectangle. Then, the rectangle will be drawn to the screen. The final example will allow the user to enter a real number (*float*) in an edit box and make a calculation. The results of the calculation will be printed to the screen.

One word of caution—the listings for each example are quite long. You must be very careful when entering each program listing so that all code is typed correctly. Also, Windows is a dynamic product. From time to time

Microsoft changes the name of such things as the Dialog Box Editor, for example. If you can't find a file under the name given here, just search around for something similar or resort to the Microsoft toolkit documentation for help.

Creating a Simple About Dialog Box

The About dialog box is as simple as it can be in terms of data entry and program size. In this and all remaining examples, a single listing is used that contains all of the files necessary to successfully compile and link the example. Then, as various files are discussed, pieces of code will be pulled out of this main listing for explanations. The aim is to help you locate all the example code in one central location for any particular example.

```
THE DIAG1 MAKE FILE:

all : diag1.exe

diag1.obj: diag1.c
    cl -c -AS -Gsw -Oas -Zpe diag1.c

diag1.res : diag1.rc
    rc -r diag1.rc

diag1.exe: diag1.obj diag1.def diag1.res
    link /NOD diag1,,,libw slibcew,diag1.def
    rc diag1.res

THE DIAG1.H HEADER FILE:

#define IDM_ABOUT    50
#define IDM_EXIT     51


THE DIAG1.DEF DEFINITION FILE:

NAME         Diag1
DESCRIPTION  'Dialog Box Example'
EXETYPE      WINDOWS
STUB         'WINSTUB.EXE'
CODE         PRELOAD MOVEABLE DISCARDABLE
DATA         PRELOAD MOVEABLE MULTIPLE
HEAPSIZE     4096
STACKSIZE    9216
EXPORTS      WindowProc       @1
             AboutDiaProc     @2


THE DIAG1.RC RESOURCE FILE:

#include "windows.h"
#include "diag1.h"

AboutMenu MENU
```

```
{
  POPUP "Decisions"
    {
      MENUITEM "About Box...",      IDM_ABOUT
      MENUITEM "Exit",              IDM_EXIT
    }
}


AboutDiaBox DIALOG LOADONCALL MOVEABLE DISCARDABLE
         9,20,131,133
         STYLE WS_DLGFRAME¦WS_POPUP
{
  CONTROL "ABOUT Dialog Box Example",-1,"static",
        SS_CENTER¦WS_CHILD,6,12,116,8
  CONTROL "by",-1,"static",
        SS_CENTER¦WS_CHILD,55,24,16,8
  CONTROL "William H. Murray and",-1,"static",
        SS_CENTER¦WS_CHILD,18,38,91,10
  CONTROL "Chris H. Pappas",-1,"static",
        SS_CENTER¦WS_CHILD,30,54,72,8
  CONTROL "Copyright (c) 1989",-1,"static",
        SS_CENTER¦WS_CHILD,10,74,108,8
  CONTROL "Okay",IDOK,"button",
        BS_PUSHBUTTON¦WS_TABSTOP¦WS_CHILD,49,102,28,12
}


THE DIAG1.C APPLICATION FILE:

/* Simplified Windows Platform (SWP)              */
/* (c) William H. Murray and Chris H. Pappas, 1989 */

#include <windows.h>
#include "diag1.h"

long FAR PASCAL WindowProc(HWND,unsigned,WORD,LONG);
BOOL FAR PASCAL AboutDiaProc(HWND,unsigned,WORD,LONG);

char szProgName[]="ProgName";
char szApplName[]="AboutMenu";

int PASCAL WinMain(hInst,hPreInst,lpszCmdLine,nCmdShow)
HANDLE hInst,hPreInst;
LPSTR  lpszCmdLine;
int    nCmdShow;
{
  HWND hwnd;
  MSG  msg;
  WNDCLASS wcSwp;
  if (!hPreInst)
    {
      wcSwp.lpszClassName=szProgName;
      wcSwp.hInstance     =hInst;
      wcSwp.lpfnWndProc   =WindowProc;
      wcSwp.hCursor       =LoadCursor(NULL,IDC_ARROW);
      wcSwp.hIcon         =NULL;
      wcSwp.lpszMenuName  =szApplName;
      wcSwp.hbrBackground =GetStockObject(WHITE_BRUSH);
      wcSwp.style         =CS_HREDRAW¦CS_VREDRAW;
      wcSwp.cbClsExtra    =0;
```

```
      wcSwp.cbWndExtra    =0;
      if (!RegisterClass (&wcSwp))
        return FALSE;
  }
  hwnd=CreateWindow(szProgName,"Dialog Box Example",
                    WS_OVERLAPPEDWINDOW,CW_USEDEFAULT,
                    CW_USEDEFAULT,CW_USEDEFAULT,
                    CW_USEDEFAULT,NULL,NULL,
                    hInst,NULL);
  ShowWindow(hwnd,nCmdShow);
  UpdateWindow(hwnd);
  while (GetMessage(&msg,NULL,NULL,NULL))
  {
    TranslateMessage(&msg);
    DispatchMessage(&msg);
  }
  return(msg.wParam);
}


BOOL FAR PASCAL AboutDiaProc(hdlg,messg,wParam,lParam)
HWND hdlg;
unsigned messg;
WORD wParam;
LONG lParam;
{
switch (messg)
  {
  case WM_INITDIALOG:
    break;
  case WM_COMMAND:
    switch (wParam)
    {
      case IDOK:
        EndDialog(hdlg,0);
        break;
      default:
        return FALSE;
    }
    break;
  default:
    return FALSE;
  }
return TRUE;
}


long FAR PASCAL WindowProc(hwnd,messg,wParam,lParam)
HWND    hwnd;
unsigned messg;
WORD    wParam;
LONG    lParam;
{
  HDC   hdc;
  HMENU hMenu;
  HPEN  hPen;
  PAINTSTRUCT ps;
  #define RED 0x0000FFL
  static FARPROC lpfnAboutDiaProc;
  static HWND hInst;
```

```
switch (messg)
{
  case WM_CREATE:
    hInst=((LPCREATESTRUCT) lParam)->hInstance;
    lpfnAboutDiaProc=MakeProcInstance(AboutDiaProc,hInst);
    break;
  case WM_COMMAND:
    switch (wParam)
    {
      case IDM_ABOUT:
        DialogBox(hInst,"AboutDiaBox", hwnd,lpfnAboutDiaProc);
        break;
      case IDM_EXIT:
        SendMessage(hwnd,WM_CLOSE,0,0L);
        break;
      default:
        break;
    }
  break;

  case WM_PAINT:
    hdc=BeginPaint(hwnd,&ps);

/*--------- your routines below ---------*/

    hPen=CreatePen(0,2,RED);
    SelectObject(hdc,hPen);
    MoveTo(hdc,50,100);
    LineTo(hdc,590,300);
    TextOut(hdc,250,50,"This is a red line.",19);
    SelectObject(hdc,GetStockObject(WHITE_PEN));
    DeleteObject(hPen);

/*--------- your routines above ---------*/

    ValidateRect(hwnd,NULL);
    EndPaint(hwnd,&ps);
    break;

  case WM_DESTROY:
    PostQuitMessage(0);
    break;

  default:
    return(DefWindowProc(hwnd,messg,wParam,lParam));
}
return(0L);
}
```

The five files in the previous listing must be entered, compiled, and linked to produce a working program. This program will create the About dialog box you saw in Figure 8-2 and will draw the diagonal line shown in Figure 8-1.

The MAKE File (DIAG1)

The **MAKE** file is responsible for splicing all the pieces of code together during the compile and link process. The **MAKE** file shown here is similar to that of previous chapters and warrants no further discussion.

The Header File (DIAG1.H)

The header file for this example contains the definitions for several unique ID numbers. The IDs for menu items start with "IDM" and those for dialog boxes with "IDD." Actually, this is just a programming choice; any designator would do. Likewise, the selection of the ID numbers is also a programming choice. Sequential numbers are nice for grouping box commands together. The disadvantage of sequential IDs becomes apparent if a new ID value needs to be inserted in a previously developed list. Careful planning is necessary when developing dialog boxes. This header file is used by both the resource file and the application file.

The Definition File (DIAG1.DEF)

The definition file is similar to previous definition files with the exception that an additional EXPORT procedure is identified. Most dialog boxes will utilize a separate procedure for processing the dialog box messages. Each procedure must be declared as an EXPORT in the definition file.

The Resource File (DIAG1.RC)

The resource file was created by entering a text editor and typing in the menu information. The AboutDiaBox dialog information was added to this file by concatenation of the DIAG1.DLG file. Recall that this text file is returned by the Dialog Box Editor. When the resource file is compiled, it will overwrite the DIAG1.RES file also created by the Dialog Box Editor. This file originally contained information for the dialog box only.

The Application File (DIAG1.C)

As you study the DIAG1.C listing given earlier, you will notice the additional AboutDiaProc. This code is responsible for processing the dialog box messages.

```
BOOL FAR PASCAL AboutDiaProc(hdlg,messg,wParam,lParam)
HWND hdlg;
unsigned messg;
WORD wParam;
LONG lParam;
{
switch (messg)
  {
  case WM_INITDIALOG:
    break;
  case WM_COMMAND:
    switch (wParam)
    {
      case IDOK:
        EndDialog(hdlg,0);
        break;
      default:
        return FALSE;
    }
    break;
  default:
    return FALSE;
  }
  return TRUE;
}
```

The procedure uses a handle, *hdlg*, as the handle for the dialog box window. This is in accordance with a style of notation among Windows programmers for making things as easy to read and identify as possible. You will also notice that the dialog procedure is of type *BOOL*, which sets it apart from regular Windows procedures, which are of type *LONG*. As such, all dialog box procedures return either a TRUE or FALSE. A TRUE is returned if the dialog box processes a message and FALSE if it does not.

The first of two messages that the procedure processes is sent to WM_INITDIALOG. If a TRUE is returned, the input will be channeled to the first control in the dialog box that has a WS_TABSTOP style. This is the focus. If you study the previous resource file, you will note that this is the Okay push button. The second message is WM_COMMAND. This message will be sent to the application program if the push button, Okay, is selected with the mouse or RETURN key. In order to remove the dialog box, the user must select the Push-button option. In the case where IDOK is TRUE, a call will be made to the EndDialog function—ending the dialog box. All other messages return FALSE. The *switch* and *case* statements used in this procedure follow normal C programming style.

The dialog box is called from the Decisions menu. This option is added during the processing of the normal WindowProc procedure. If you study this section of code you will notice the addition of two new *case* statements—WM_CREATE and WM_COMMAND.

```
switch (messg)
{
  case WM_CREATE:
    hInst=((LPCREATESTRUCT) lParam)->hInstance;
    lpfnAboutDiaProc=MakeProcInstance(AboutDiaProc,hInst);
    break;
  case WM_COMMAND:
    switch (wParam)
    {
      case IDM_ABOUT:
        DialogBox(hInst,"AboutDiaBox", hwnd,lpfnAboutDiaProc);
        break;
      case IDM_EXIT:
        SendMessage(hwnd,WM_CLOSE,0,0L);
        break;
      default:
        break;
    }
    break;
```

WM_CREATE is responsible for obtaining and storing the instance handle for the dialog box in the static variable *hInst*. MakeProcInstance obtains the correct segment address for AboutDiaProc.

The Decisions menu for this application allows one of two selections—the About dialog box or an Exit from the program. Both of these options are handled by WM_COMMAND. For the case of IDM_ABOUT, the Dialog-Box function establishes the predefined dialog box on the screen. This dialog box will not be erased until the EndDialog function, discussed earlier, receives the message formed by selecting the IDOK push button. An exit from the entire program can be achieved by selecting the IDM_EXIT case and utilizing the SendMessage function.

Many of the programs in this chapter draw simple graphics shapes to the screen in addition to processing the dialog box information. Chapter 10 is devoted to completely explaining the various Windows graphics primitives and functions. For this particular program, a red diagonal line is drawn to the screen when WM_PAINT is processed. This requires the creation of a drawing pen of a specified color, moving the pen to a particular spot on the screen, and using the LineTo function to actually draw the line. The TextOut function is used to print a text label to the screen.

Changing Graphics Shapes with a Dialog Box

In this particular example, the user will be permitted to select a predefined graphics shape from a dialog box. This graphics shape will be drawn to the screen when the dialog box information is processed. This example uses two dialog boxes: the ABOUTDLGBOX description is similar to the dialog box from the previous example; the new dialog box description, SHAPE-DLGBOX, contains radio buttons for selecting shapes. Users will now be able to request that programs take certain actions based on their direct input, interactively. The dialog box for this example was shown earlier, in Figure 8-3.

THE DIAG2 MAKE FILE:

```
all : diag2.exe

diag2.obj: diag2.c
    cl -c -AS -Gsw -Oas -Zpe diag2.c

diag2.res : diag2.rc
    rc -r diag2.rc

diag2.exe: diag2.obj diag2.def diag2.res
    link /NOD diag2,,,libw slibcew,diag2.def
    rc diag2.res
```

THE DIAG2.H HEADER FILE:

```
#define IDM_ABOUT       10
#define IDM_SHAPE       20
#define IDM_EXIT        30

#define IDD_LINE        200
#define IDD_BOX         201
#define IDD_CIRCLE      202
#define IDD_TRIANGLE    203
```

THE DIAG2.DEF DEFINITION FILE:

```
NAME        Diag2
DESCRIPTION 'Dialog Box Example'
EXETYPE     WINDOWS
STUB        'WINSTUB.EXE'
CODE        PRELOAD MOVEABLE DISCARDABLE
DATA        PRELOAD MOVEABLE MULTIPLE
HEAPSIZE    4096
STACKSIZE   9216
EXPORTS     WindowProc      @1
            AboutDlgProc    @2
            ShapeDlgProc    @3
```

THE DIAG2.RC RESOURCE FILE:

```
#include "windows.h"
#include "diag2.h"

AboutMenu MENU
{
  POPUP "Decisions"
    {
      MENUITEM "About Box...",        IDM_ABOUT
      MENUITEM "Select a Shape...",   IDM_SHAPE
      MENUITEM "Exit",                IDM_EXIT
```

```
      }
}


ABOUTDLGBOX DIALOG LOADONCALL MOVEABLE DISCARDABLE
          9,20,131,133
          STYLE WS_DLGFRAME|WS_POPUP
{
  CONTROL "ABOUT Dialog Box Example",-1,"static",
       SS_CENTER|WS_CHILD,6,12,116,8
  CONTROL "by",-1,"static",
       SS_CENTER|WS_CHILD,55,24,16,8
  CONTROL "William H. Murray and",-1,"static",
       SS_CENTER|WS_CHILD,18,38,91,10
  CONTROL "Chris H. Pappas",-1,"static",
       SS_CENTER|WS_CHILD,30,54,72,8
  CONTROL "Copyright (c) 1989",-1,"static",
       SS_CENTER|WS_CHILD,10,74,108,8
  CONTROL "Okay",IDOK,"button",
       BS_PUSHBUTTON|WS_TABSTOP|WS_CHILD,49,102,28,12
}

SHAPEDLGBOX DIALOG LOADONCALL MOVEABLE DISCARDABLE
          136, 46, 85, 95
          CAPTION "Select A Shape"
          STYLE WS_BORDER|WS_CAPTION|WS_DLGFRAME|WS_POPUP
{
  CONTROL "Line",IDD_LINE,"button",BS_RADIOBUTTON|
       WS_TABSTOP|WS_CHILD,6,3,28,12
  CONTROL "Box",IDD_BOX,"button",BS_RADIOBUTTON|
       WS_TABSTOP|WS_CHILD,6,17,28,12
  CONTROL "Circle",IDD_CIRCLE,"button",BS_RADIOBUTTON|
       WS_TABSTOP|WS_CHILD,6,31,36,12
  CONTROL "Triangle",IDD_TRIANGLE,"button",BS_RADIOBUTTON|
       WS_TABSTOP|WS_CHILD,6,44,45,12
  CONTROL "Okay",IDOK,"button",BS_PUSHBUTTON|
       WS_TABSTOP|WS_CHILD,25,77,24,14
}


THE DIAG2.C APPLICATION FILE:

/* Simplified Windows Platform (SWP)            */
/* (c) William H. Murray and Chris H. Pappas, 1989 */

#include <windows.h>
#include "diag2.h"

long FAR PASCAL WindowProc(HWND,unsigned,WORD,LONG);
BOOL FAR PASCAL ABOUTDLGPROC(HWND,unsigned,WORD,LONG);
BOOL FAR PASCAL SHAPEDLGPROC(HWND,unsigned,WORD,LONG);

char szProgName[]="ProgName";
char szApplName[]="AboutMenu";
short myshape;

int PASCAL WinMain(hInst,hPreInst,lpszCmdLine,nCmdShow)
HANDLE hInst,hPreInst;
LPSTR  lpszCmdLine;
int    nCmdShow;
{
  HWND hwnd;
```

```
MSG  msg;
WNDCLASS wcSwp;
if (!hPreInst)
{
   wcSwp.lpszClassName=szProgName;
   wcSwp.hInstance    =hInst;
   wcSwp.lpfnWndProc  =WindowProc;
   wcSwp.hCursor      =LoadCursor(NULL,IDC_ARROW);
   wcSwp.hIcon        =NULL;
   wcSwp.lpszMenuName =szApplName;
   wcSwp.hbrBackground=GetStockObject(WHITE_BRUSH);
   wcSwp.style        =CS_HREDRAW|CS_VREDRAW;
   wcSwp.cbClsExtra   =0;
   wcSwp.cbWndExtra   =0;
   if (!RegisterClass (&wcSwp))
      return FALSE;
}
hwnd=CreateWindow(szProgName,"Selecting Shapes",
                  WS_OVERLAPPEDWINDOW,CW_USEDEFAULT,
                  CW_USEDEFAULT,CW_USEDEFAULT,
                  CW_USEDEFAULT,NULL,NULL,
                  hInst,NULL);
ShowWindow(hwnd,nCmdShow);
UpdateWindow(hwnd);
while (GetMessage(&msg,NULL,NULL,NULL))
{
   TranslateMessage(&msg);
   DispatchMessage(&msg);
}
return(msg.wParam);
}


BOOL FAR PASCAL ABOUTDLGPROC(hdlg,messg,wParam,lParam)
HWND hdlg;
unsigned messg;
WORD wParam;
LONG lParam;
{
switch (messg)
   {
   case WM_INITDIALOG:
     break;
   case WM_COMMAND:
     switch (wParam)
     {
       case IDOK:
         EndDialog(hdlg,TRUE);
         break;
       default:
         return FALSE;
     }
     break;
   default:
     return FALSE;
   }
return TRUE;
}


BOOL FAR PASCAL SHAPEDLGPROC(hdlg,messg,wParam,lParam)
```

```
HWND hdlg;
unsigned messg;
WORD wParam;
LONG lParam;
{

switch (messg)
  {
  case WM_INITDIALOG:
    return FALSE;
  case WM_COMMAND:
    switch (wParam)
    {
      case IDOK:
        EndDialog(hdlg,TRUE);
        break;
      case IDD_LINE:
        myshape=1;
        CheckRadioButton(hdlg,IDD_LINE,
                         IDD_TRIANGLE,wParam);
        break;
      case IDD_BOX:
        myshape=2;
        CheckRadioButton(hdlg,IDD_LINE,
                         IDD_TRIANGLE,wParam);
        break;
      case IDD_CIRCLE:
        myshape=3;
        CheckRadioButton(hdlg,IDD_LINE,
                         IDD_TRIANGLE,wParam);
        break;
      case IDD_TRIANGLE:
        myshape=4;
        CheckRadioButton(hdlg,IDD_LINE,
                         IDD_TRIANGLE,wParam);
        break;
      default:
        return FALSE;
    }
    break;

  default:
    return FALSE;
  }
return TRUE;
}


long FAR PASCAL WindowProc(hwnd,messg,wParam,lParam)
HWND    hwnd;
unsigned messg;
WORD    wParam;
LONG    lParam;
{
  HDC hdc;
  HMENU hMenu;
  HPEN hPen;
  PAINTSTRUCT ps;
  #define RED 0x0000FFL
  static FARPROC lpfnABOUTDLGPROC;
  static FARPROC lpfmyshapeDLGPROC;
```

```
       static HWND hInst1,hInst2;

       switch (messg)
       {
         case WM_CREATE:
           hInst1=((LPCREATESTRUCT) lParam)->hInstance;
           hInst2=((LPCREATESTRUCT) lParam)->hInstance;
           lpfnABOUTDLGPROC=MakeProcInstance(ABOUTDLGPROC,
                                       hInst1);
           lpfmyshapeDLGPROC=MakeProcInstance(SHAPEDLGPROC,
                                       hInst2);

           break;
         case WM_COMMAND:
           switch (wParam)
           {
             case IDM_ABOUT:
               DialogBox(hInst1,"AboutDlgBox",hwnd,
                         lpfnABOUTDLGPROC);
               break;
             case IDM_SHAPE:
               DialogBox(hInst2,"ShapeDlgBox",hwnd,
                         lpfmyshapeDLGPROC);
               InvalidateRect(hwnd,NULL,TRUE);
               UpdateWindow(hwnd);
               break;
             case IDM_EXIT:
               SendMessage(hwnd,WM_CLOSE,0,0L);
               break;
             default:
               break;
           }
         break;

         case WM_PAINT:
           hdc=BeginPaint(hwnd,&ps);

/*--------- your routines below ---------*/

           hPen=CreatePen(0,1,RED);
           SelectObject(hdc,hPen);
           if (myshape==1)
           {
             MoveTo(hdc,50,100);
             LineTo(hdc,300,300);
           }
           else
             if (myshape==2)
             {
               Rectangle(hdc,50,100,300,300);
             }
             else
               if (myshape==3)
               {
                 Ellipse(hdc,50,50,400,400);
               }
               else
                 if (myshape==4)
                 {
                   MoveTo(hdc,50,100);
                   LineTo(hdc,300,300);
```

```
                LineTo(hdc,50,300);
                LineTo(hdc,50,100);
            }

        SelectObject(hdc,GetStockObject(WHITE_PEN));
        DeleteObject(hPen);

/*--------- your routines above ---------*/

        ValidateRect(hwnd,NULL);
        EndPaint(hwnd,&ps);
        break;

    case WM_DESTROY:
        PostQuitMessage(0);
        break;

    default:
        return(DefWindowProc(hwnd,messg,wParam,lParam));
    }
    return(0L);
}
```

The MAKE File (DIAG2)

The **MAKE** file remains identical to previous examples; the only change is in the file name.

The Header File (DIAG2.H)

The header file values for this program have been separated into two groups. One group holds menu IDs and the other holds the IDs for the second dialog box. You can see from studying this listing that four primitive shapes are available for drawing: a line, a box, a circle, and a triangle.

The Definition File (DIAG2.DEF)

The definition file for this example shows three EXPORTS. This means a separate procedure will be used to process the About and Shape dialog box messages.

The Resource File (DIAG2.RC)

The resource file contains the menu and information for two dialog boxes. This file was created by using the information in the resource file from the previous example and concatenating the .DLG file for the new dialog box to it. The DIAG2.DLG file was created with the Dialog Box Editor. You will notice that a new item has been added to the menu selection—"Select a Shape...".

The SHAPEDLGBOX description holds the information for the placement of four radio buttons and two push buttons.

```
SHAPEDLGBOX DIALOG LOADONCALL MOVEABLE DISCARDABLE
        136, 46, 85, 95
        CAPTION "Select A Shape"
        STYLE WS_BORDER¦WS_CAPTION¦WS_DLGFRAME¦WS_POPUP
{
  CONTROL "Line",IDD_LINE,"button",BS_RADIOBUTTON¦
        WS_TABSTOP¦WS_CHILD,6,3,28,12
  CONTROL "Box",IDD_BOX,"button",BS_RADIOBUTTON¦
        WS_TABSTOP¦WS_CHILD,6,17,28,12
  CONTROL "Circle",IDD_CIRCLE,"button",BS_RADIOBUTTON¦
        WS_TABSTOP¦WS_CHILD,6,31,36,12
  CONTROL "Triangle",IDD_TRIANGLE,"button",BS_RADIOBUTTON¦
        WS_TABSTOP¦WS_CHILD,6,44,45,12
  CONTROL "Okay",IDOK,"button",BS_PUSHBUTTON¦
        WS_TABSTOP¦WS_CHILD,25,77,24,14
}
```

Notice that each button contains WS_TABSTOP. The first control with WS_TABSTOP determines where the input focus for the box will be placed. Actually, the focus can be changed with the SetFocus function. By default, Windows will place the focus at the control with the first WS_TABSTOP.

The Application File (DIAG2.C)

You will notice in studying the application listing that the ABOUT-DLGPROC is processed exactly the same way it was in the last example. For this reason it is fairly easy to boilerplate ABOUT box code from application to application.

The SHAPEDLGPROC is used to process information from the shape dialog box.

```
switch (messg)
  {
  case WM_INITDIALOG:
    return FALSE;
  case WM_COMMAND:
    switch (wParam)
      {
      case IDOK:
        EndDialog(hdlg,TRUE);
        break;
      case IDD_LINE:
        myshape=1;
```

```
                CheckRadioButton(hdlg,IDD_LINE,
                              IDD_TRIANGLE,wParam);
            break;
        case IDD_BOX:
          myshape=2;
          CheckRadioButton(hdlg,IDD_LINE,
                          IDD_TRIANGLE,wParam);
            break;
        case IDD_CIRCLE:
          myshape=3;
          CheckRadioButton(hdlg,IDD_LINE,
                          IDD_TRIANGLE,wParam);
            break;
        case IDD_TRIANGLE:
          myshape=4;
          CheckRadioButton(hdlg,IDD_LINE,
                          IDD_TRIANGLE,wParam);
            break;
        default:
          return FALSE;
      }
    break;

  default:
    return FALSE;
  }
  return TRUE;
}
```

WM_COMMAND is responsible for five *case* statements. IDOK represents the dialog box push button for accepting input and removing the dialog box. The other four represent the radio buttons corresponding to the selected shapes. In a simplified, and somewhat primitive approach, each case is examined. If a case is TRUE, the global variable, *myshape*, is set to a particular integer value. This value will be examined in WM_PAINT by the WindowProc procedure to determine which shape is plotted. The CheckRadioButton function is used to "check" the button circle on the dialog box. This function is additionally responsible for sending the *wParam* part of the message sent to WM_COMMAND. The range of radio buttons must be sequential when using CheckRadioButton. The first is IDD_LINE and the last is IDD_TRIANGLE, as you can observe from the DIAG2.H header file.

What the SHAPEDLGPROC lacks is a method of canceling the dialog box when the user doesn't want to make a selection. Usually, dialog boxes will include another push button, called Cancel, that will return you to the application window without making any changes. The Cancel push button must have an ID value of 2. This value is supplied in the resource file by using IDCANCEL. You will see how this is done in the remaining examples in this chapter.

In order to draw the various figures, an *if-else* ladder is used in WM_PAINT.

```
    case WM_PAINT:
      hdc=BeginPaint(hwnd,&ps);

/*--------- your routines below ---------*/

      hPen=CreatePen(0,1,RED);
      SelectObject(hdc,hPen);
      if (myshape==1)
      {
        MoveTo(hdc,50,100);
        LineTo(hdc,300,300);
      }
      else
        if (myshape==2)
        {
          Rectangle(hdc,50,100,300,300);
        }
        else
          if (myshape==3)
          {
            Ellipse(hdc,50,50,400,400);
          }
          else
            if (myshape==4)
            {
              MoveTo(hdc,50,100);
              LineTo(hdc,300,300);
              LineTo(hdc,50,300);
              LineTo(hdc,50,100);
            }

      SelectObject(hdc,GetStockObject(WHITE_PEN));
      DeleteObject(hPen);

/*--------- your routines above ---------*/

      ValidateRect(hwnd,NULL);
      EndPaint(hwnd,&ps);
      break;
```

The global variable, *myshape,* is checked and used to determine which shape is plotted. The shapes are drawn with several graphics functions—MoveTo, LineTo, Rectangle, and Ellipse. Details on these and other graphics functions are contained in Chapter 10. Figure 8-14 shows the triangle that can be drawn with this program.

Entering Text with a Dialog Box

The ability to enter text or string information during the execution of an application program is of major interest. A dialog box can be used, for example, to allow the user to enter labels for a pie, line, or bar chart. Text information is entered with the dialog box's edit control. Text information is

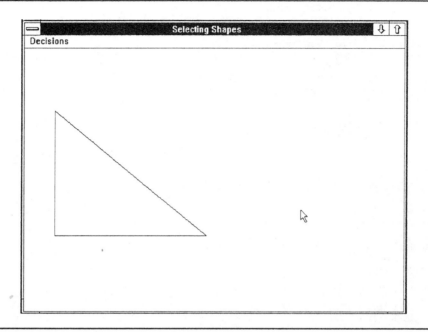

Figure 8-14.   A triangular figure selected from the Decisions dialog box

processed with the GetDlgItemText function within the application program. In the next example, the dialog box shown in Figure 8-4 will be used to accept user text. This dialog box contains two push buttons. Okay will accept the new text and print it to the screen. The Cancel push button will cancel the dialog box without changing the current message on the screen.

THE DIAG3 MAKE FILE:

```
ALL : diag3.exe # ALL needed for C 6.0 up

diag3.obj: diag3.c
    cl -c -AS -Gsw -Oas -Zpe diag3.c

diag3.res : diag3.rc
    rc -r diag3.rc

diag3.exe: diag3.obj diag3.def diag3.res
    link /NOD diag3,,,libw slibcew,diag3.def
    rc diag3.res
```

THE DIAG3.H HEADER FILE:

```
#define IDM_ABOUT       10
#define IDM_TEXT        20
#define IDM_EXIT        30

#define IDD_EDIT       201
```

THE DIAG3.DEF DEFINITION FILE:

```
NAME        Diag3
DESCRIPTION 'Dialog Box Example'
EXETYPE     WINDOWS
STUB        'WINSTUB.EXE'
CODE        PRELOAD MOVEABLE DISCARDABLE
DATA        PRELOAD MOVEABLE MULTIPLE
HEAPSIZE    4096
STACKSIZE   9216
EXPORTS     WindowProc      @1
            AboutDlgProc    @2
            TextDlgProc     @3
```

THE DIAG3.RC RESOURCE FILE:

```
#include "windows.h"
#include "diag3.h"

AboutMenu MENU
{
  POPUP "Input"
    {
      MENUITEM "About Box...",          IDM_ABOUT
      MENUITEM "Text Input...",         IDM_TEXT
      MENUITEM "Exit",                  IDM_EXIT
    }
}


ABOUTDLGBOX DIALOG LOADONCALL MOVEABLE DISCARDABLE
        9,20,131,133
        STYLE WS_DLGFRAME|WS_POPUP
{
  CONTROL "ABOUT Dialog Box Example",-1,"static",
        SS_CENTER|WS_CHILD,6,12,116,8
  CONTROL "by",-1,"static",
        SS_CENTER|WS_CHILD,55,24,16,8
  CONTROL "William H. Murray and",-1,"static",
        SS_CENTER|WS_CHILD,18,38,91,10
  CONTROL "Chris H. Pappas",-1,"static",
        SS_CENTER|WS_CHILD,30,54,72,8
  CONTROL "Copyright (c) 1989",-1,"static",
        SS_CENTER|WS_CHILD,10,74,108,8
  CONTROL "Okay",IDOK,"button",
        BS_PUSHBUTTON|WS_TABSTOP|WS_CHILD,49,102,28,12
}


TEXTINPUTDLGBOX DIALOG LOADONCALL MOVEABLE DISCARDABLE
        13, 26, 292, 49
        CAPTION "Text For Screen"
        STYLE WS_BORDER|WS_CAPTION|WS_DLGFRAME|WS_POPUP
{
  CONTROL "Enter Text for Screen:",-1,"static",
        SS_LEFT|WS_CHILD,5,5,145,8
  CONTROL  "",IDD_EDIT,"edit",
        ES_LEFT|WS_BORDER|WS_TABSTOP|WS_CHILD,5,15,280,12
  CONTROL "Okay",IDOK,"button",
        BS_PUSHBUTTON|WS_TABSTOP|WS_CHILD,65,30,64,14
```

```
      CONTROL "Cancel",IDCANCEL,"button",
            BS_PUSHBUTTON¦WS_TABSTOP¦WS_CHILD,165,30,65,14
}


THE DIAG3.C APPLICATIONS FILE:

/* Simplified Windows Platform (SWP)              */
/* (c) William H. Murray and Chris H. Pappas, 1989 */

#include <windows.h>
#include <string.h>
#include "diag3.h"

long FAR PASCAL WindowProc(HWND,unsigned,WORD,LONG);
BOOL FAR PASCAL ABOUTDLGPROC(HWND,unsigned,WORD,LONG);
BOOL FAR PASCAL TEXTDLGPROC(HWND,unsigned,WORD,LONG);

char szProgName[]="ProgName";
char szApplName[]="AboutMenu";
char myscreen[80]="Sample Text Line";

int PASCAL WinMain(hInst,hPreInst,lpszCmdLine,nCmdShow)
HANDLE hInst,hPreInst;
LPSTR  lpszCmdLine;
int    nCmdShow;
{
  HWND hwnd;
  MSG  msg;
  WNDCLASS wcSwp;
  if (!hPreInst)
  {
    wcSwp.lpszClassName=szProgName;
    wcSwp.hInstance     =hInst;
    wcSwp.lpfnWndProc   =WindowProc;
    wcSwp.hCursor       =LoadCursor(NULL,IDC_ARROW);
    wcSwp.hIcon         =NULL;
    wcSwp.lpszMenuName  =szApplName;
    wcSwp.hbrBackground=GetStockObject(WHITE_BRUSH);
    wcSwp.style          =CS_HREDRAW¦CS_VREDRAW;
    wcSwp.cbClsExtra    =0;
    wcSwp.cbWndExtra    =0;
    if (!RegisterClass (&wcSwp))
      return FALSE;
  }
  hwnd=CreateWindow(szProgName,"Entering String Data",
                    WS_OVERLAPPEDWINDOW,CW_USEDEFAULT,
                    CW_USEDEFAULT,CW_USEDEFAULT,
                    CW_USEDEFAULT,NULL,NULL,
                    hInst,NULL);
  ShowWindow(hwnd,nCmdShow);
  UpdateWindow(hwnd);
  while (GetMessage(&msg,NULL,NULL,NULL))
  {
    TranslateMessage(&msg);
    DispatchMessage(&msg);
  }
  return(msg.wParam);
}

BOOL FAR PASCAL ABOUTDLGPROC(hdlg,messg,wParam,lParam)
```

```
HWND hdlg;
unsigned messg;
WORD wParam;
LONG lParam;
{
switch (messg)
  {
  case WM_-INITDIALOG:
    break;
  case WM_COMMAND:
    switch (wParam)
    {
      case IDOK:
        EndDialog(hdlg,TRUE);
        break;
      default:
        return FALSE;
    }
    break;
  default:
    return FALSE;
  }
  return TRUE;
}


BOOL FAR PASCAL TEXTDLGPROC(hdlg,messg,wParam,lParam)
HWND hdlg;
unsigned messg;
WORD wParam;
LONG lParam;
{

switch (messg)
  {
  case WM_INITDIALOG:
    return FALSE;
  case WM_COMMAND:
    switch (wParam)
    {
      case IDOK:
        GetDlgItemText(hdlg,IDD_EDIT,myscreen,80);
        EndDialog(hdlg,TRUE);
        break;
      case IDCANCEL:
        EndDialog(hdlg,FALSE);
        break;
      default:
        return FALSE;
    }
    break;

  default:
    return FALSE;
  }
  return TRUE;
}


long FAR PASCAL WindowProc(hwnd,messg,wParam,lParam)
HWND    hwnd;
```

```
unsigned messg;
WORD    wParam;
LONG    lParam;
{
  HDC   hdc;
  HMENU hMenu;
  HPEN  hPen;
  PAINTSTRUCT ps;
  #define RED 0x0000FFL
  static FARPROC lpfnABOUTDLGPROC;
  static FARPROC lpfnTEXTDLGPROC;
  static HWND hInst1,hInst2;

  switch (messg)
  {
    case WM_CREATE:
      hInst1=((LPCREATESTRUCT) lParam)->hInstance;
      hInst2=((LPCREATESTRUCT) lParam)->hInstance;
      lpfnABOUTDLGPROC=MakeProcInstance(ABOUTDLGPROC,hInst1);
      lpfnTEXTDLGPROC=MakeProcInstance(TEXTDLGPROC,hInst2);
      break;
    case WM_COMMAND:
      switch (wParam)
      {
        case IDM_ABOUT:
          DialogBox(hInst1,"AboutDlgBox",hwnd,
                    lpfnABOUTDLGPROC);
          break;
        case IDM_TEXT:
          DialogBox(hInst2,"TextInputDlgBox",hwnd,
                    lpfnTEXTDLGPROC);
          InvalidateRect(hwnd,NULL,TRUE);
          UpdateWindow(hwnd);
          break;
        case IDM_EXIT:
          SendMessage(hwnd,WM_CLOSE,0,0L);
          break;
        default:
          break;
      }
      break;

    case WM_PAINT:
      hdc=BeginPaint(hwnd,&ps);

/*--------- your routines below ---------*/

      hPen=CreatePen(0,1,RED);
      SelectObject(hdc,hPen);
      MoveTo(hdc,50,100);
      LineTo(hdc,300,400);

      TextOut(hdc,40,40,myscreen,strlen(myscreen));

      SelectObject(hdc,GetStockObject(WHITE_PEN));
      DeleteObject(hPen);

/*--------- your routines above ---------*/

      ValidateRect(hwnd,NULL);
      EndPaint(hwnd,&ps);
```

```
    break;

  case WM_DESTROY:
    PostQuitMessage(0);
    break;

  default:
    return(DefWindowProc(hwnd,messg,wParam,lParam));
  }
  return(0L);
}
```

The MAKE File (DIAG3)

The MAKE file, again, uses a format common to previous examples.

The Header File (DIAG3.H)

The header file contains ID information for menu items and dialog boxes. The new dialog box will process text (string) information.

The Definition File (DIAG3.DEF)

The definition file for this example contains three EXPORTS: WindowProc, AboutDlgProc, and TextDlgProc. The first two are similar to procedures used in previous examples in this chapter. The TextDlgProc is responsible for capturing user input from the keyboard.

The Resource File (DIAG3.RC)

Only minor changes have occurred in the resource file, with the exception that a new dialog box procedure, TEXTINPUTDLGBOX, has been added. This dialog box will display "Enter Text for Screen:" with a static text control. Notice that the edit control contains a pair of double quotation marks with no text in between. That means when the edit box is created, it will initially be blank. Two push buttons, Okay and Cancel, allow users to accept and process the text they have typed or completely cancel the dialog box without updating the screen.

The Application File (DIAG3.C)

The first major change in the application program code appears in the TEXTDLGPROC procedure.

```
switch (messg)
  {
  case WM_INITDIALOG:
    return FALSE;
  case WM_COMMAND:
    switch (wParam)
    {
      case IDOK:
        GetDlgItemText(hdlg,IDD_EDIT,myscreen,80);
        EndDialog(hdlg,TRUE);
        break;
      case IDCANCEL:
        EndDialog(hdlg,FALSE);
        break;
      default:
        return FALSE;
    }
    break;

  default:
    return FALSE;
  }
  return TRUE;
}
```

If the dialog box is selected and the user enters a text string, that information can be processed by the GetDlgItemText function. This function will return the text string to the global variable, *myscreen*, when the IDOK push button is selected by the user. In this case the function is passed the handle, the ID value, the location for the string (*myscreen*), and the maximum length of the string. If the user selects the Cancel push button, the dialog box is erased without further window updating.

The text string is finally printed to the screen under the control of WM_PAINT. This program also draws a diagonal line. The TextOut function is used to print the information returned by the TEXTDLGPROC to the global character array, *myscreen*. Figure 8-15 shows a sample screen and text entered from the dialog box.

You might consider modifying the dialog box in this example to accept a drive letter and directory entry, which could then be applied to the directory listing example of the previous chapter. This would allow the user to specify the drive and subdirectory, rather than just clicking a predefined choice as that example did.

Entering Integers with a Dialog Box

In addition to entering text information, many programs rely on the user's ability to enter numeric data. Windows can accept integer data directly in a dialog box's edit control statement. (Well, actually it is string information that is eventually converted and processed as integer data.) This is done

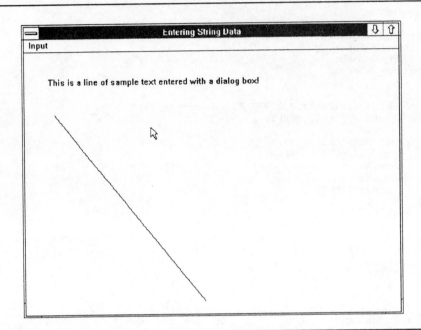

Figure 8-15.   Sending text to the window with the help of the Input dialog box

with a GetDlgItemInt function call. The dialog box for this program was shown in Figure 8-5. The coordinates for diagonally adjacent corners of a rectangle will be entered by the user in four separate edit controls. The information, if it is in the form of numeric digits, will be converted to integer values and used by the Rectangle graphics function.

```
THE DIAG4 MAKE FILE:

all : diag4.exe

diag4.obj: diag4.c
    cl -c -AS -Gsw -Oas -Zpe diag4.c

diag4.res : diag4.rc
    rc -r diag4.rc

diag4.exe: diag4.obj diag4.def diag4.res
    link /NOD diag4,,,libw slibcew,diag4.def
    rc diag4.res

THE DIAG4.H HEADER FILE:

#define IDM_ABOUT     10
#define IDM_SHAPE     20
#define IDM_EXIT      30

#define IDD_LINE      200
#define IDD_BOX       201
```

```
#define IDD_CIRCLE    202
#define IDD_TRIANGLE  203
```

THE DIAG4.DEF DEFINITION FILE:

```
NAME        Diag4
DESCRIPTION 'Dialog Box Example'
EXETYPE     WINDOWS
STUB        'WINSTUB.EXE'
CODE        PRELOAD MOVEABLE DISCARDABLE
DATA        PRELOAD MOVEABLE MULTIPLE
HEAPSIZE    4096
STACKSIZE   9216
EXPORTS     WindowProc      @1
            AboutDlgProc    @2
            IntegerDlgProc  @3
```

THE DIAG4.RC RESOURCE FILE:

```
#include "windows.h"
#include "diag4.h"

AboutMenu MENU
{
  POPUP "Integer Input"
    {
      MENUITEM "About Box...",         IDM_ABOUT
      MENUITEM "Integer Input...",     IDM_INTEGER
      MENUITEM "Exit",                 IDM_EXIT
    }
}

ABOUTDLGBOX DIALOG LOADONCALL MOVEABLE DISCARDABLE
        9,20,131,133
        STYLE WS_DLGFRAME¦WS_POPUP
{
  CONTROL "ABOUT Dialog Box Example",-1,"static",
        SS_CENTER¦WS_CHILD,6,12,116,8
  CONTROL "by",-1,"static",
        SS_CENTER¦WS_CHILD,55,24,16,8
  CONTROL "William H. Murray and",-1,"static",
        SS_CENTER¦WS_CHILD,18,38,91,10
  CONTROL "Chris H. Pappas",-1,"static",
        SS_CENTER¦WS_CHILD,30,54,72,8
  CONTROL "Copyright (c) 1989",-1,"static",
        SS_CENTER¦WS_CHILD,10,74,108,8
  CONTROL "Okay",IDOK,"button",
        BS_PUSHBUTTON¦WS_TABSTOP¦WS_CHILD,49,102,28,12
}

INTEGERINPUTDLGBOX DIALOG LOADONCALL MOVEABLE DISCARDABLE
        9, 26, 210, 92
        CAPTION "Integer Input"
        STYLE WS_BORDER¦WS_CAPTION¦WS_DLGFRAME¦WS_POPUP
{
  CONTROL "Enter Coordinates for a box:",-1,"static",
        SS_LEFT¦WS_CHILD,7,7,145,8
  CONTROL "Upper Corner (x,y):",-1,"static",
        SS_LEFT¦WS_CHILD,9,23,83,8
```

```
    CONTROL "",IDD_UPPERX,"edit",
        ES_LEFT|WS_BORDER|WS_TABSTOP|WS_CHILD,93,19,32,12
    CONTROL "",IDD_UPPERY,"edit",
        ES_LEFT|WS_BORDER|WS_TABSTOP|WS_CHILD,134,19,32,12
    CONTROL "Lower Corner (x,y):",-1,"static",
        SS_LEFT|WS_CHILD,9,48,81,8
    CONTROL "",IDD_LOWERX,"edit",
        ES_LEFT|WS_BORDER|WS_TABSTOP|WS_CHILD,93,43,32,12
    CONTROL "",IDD_LOWERY,"edit",
        ES_LEFT|WS_BORDER|WS_TABSTOP|WS_CHILD,134,43,32,12
    CONTROL "Okay",IDOK,"button",
        BS_PUSHBUTTON|WS_TABSTOP|WS_CHILD,54,76,44,14
    CONTROL "Cancel",IDCANCEL,"button",
        BS_PUSHBUTTON|WS_TABSTOP|WS_CHILD,111,76,44,14
}


THE DIAG4.C APPLICATION FILE:

/* Simplified Windows Platform (SWP)           */
/* (c) William H. Murray and Chris H. Pappas, 1989 */

#include <windows.h>
#include <string.h>
#include "diag4.h"

long FAR PASCAL WindowProc(HWND,unsigned,WORD,LONG);
BOOL FAR PASCAL ABOUTDLGPROC(HWND,unsigned,WORD,LONG);
BOOL FAR PASCAL INTEGERDLGPROC(HWND,unsigned,WORD,LONG);

char szProgName[]="ProgName";
char szApplName[]="AboutMenu";
int upperx=10;
int uppery=10;
int lowerx=100;
int lowery=100;

int PASCAL WinMain(hInst,hPreInst,lpszCmdLine,nCmdShow)
HANDLE hInst,hPreInst;
LPSTR  lpszCmdLine;
int    nCmdShow;
{
  HWND hwnd;
  MSG  msg;
  WNDCLASS wcSwp;
  if (!hPreInst)
  {
    wcSwp.lpszClassName=szProgName;
    wcSwp.hInstance     =hInst;
    wcSwp.lpfnWndProc   =WindowProc;
    wcSwp.hCursor       =LoadCursor(NULL,IDC_ARROW);
    wcSwp.hIcon         =NULL;
    wcSwp.lpszMenuName  =szApplName;
    wcSwp.hbrBackground=GetStockObject(WHITE_BRUSH);
    wcSwp.style         =CS_HREDRAW|CS_VREDRAW;
    wcSwp.cbClsExtra    =0;
    wcSwp.cbWndExtra    =0;
    if (!RegisterClass (&wcSwp))
      return FALSE;
  }
  hwnd=CreateWindow(szProgName,"Entering Integer Data",
```

```
                    WS_OVERLAPPEDWINDOW,CW_USEDEFAULT,
                    CW_USEDEFAULT,CW_USEDEFAULT,
                    CW_USEDEFAULT,NULL,NULL,
                    hInst,NULL);
  ShowWindow(hwnd,nCmdShow);
  UpdateWindow(hwnd);
  while (GetMessage(&msg,NULL,NULL,NULL))
  {
    TranslateMessage(&msg);
    DispatchMessage(&msg);
  }
  return(msg.wParam);
}


BOOL FAR PASCAL ABOUTDLGPROC(hdlg,messg,wParam,lParam)
HWND hdlg;
unsigned messg;
WORD wParam;
LONG lParam;
{
switch (messg)
  {
  case WM_INITDIALOG:
    break;
  case WM_COMMAND:
    switch (wParam)
    {
      case IDOK:
        EndDialog(hdlg,TRUE);
        break;
      default:
        return FALSE;
    }
    break;
  default:
    return FALSE;
  }
  return TRUE;
}


BOOL FAR PASCAL INTEGERDLGPROC(hdlg,messg,wParam,lParam)
HWND hdlg;
unsigned messg;
WORD wParam;
LONG lParam;
{

switch (messg)
  {
  case WM_INITDIALOG:
    return FALSE;
  case WM_COMMAND:
    switch (wParam)
    {
      case IDOK:
        upperx=GetDlgItemInt(hdlg,IDD_UPPERX,NULL,0);
        uppery=GetDlgItemInt(hdlg,IDD_UPPERY,NULL,0);
        lowerx=GetDlgItemInt(hdlg,IDD_LOWERX,NULL,0);
        lowery=GetDlgItemInt(hdlg,IDD_LOWERY,NULL,0);
```

```
          EndDialog(hdlg,TRUE);
          break;
        case IDCANCEL:
          EndDialog(hdlg,FALSE);
          break;
        default:
          return FALSE;
    }
    break;

  default:
    return FALSE;
  }
  return TRUE;
}


long FAR PASCAL WindowProc(hwnd,messg,wParam,lParam`
HWND    hwnd;
unsigned messg;
WORD    wParam;
LONG    lParam;
{
  HDC   hdc;
  HMENU hMenu;
  HPEN hPen;
  PAINTSTRUCT ps;
#define RED 0x0000FFL
  static FARPROC lpfnABOUTDLGPROC;
  static FARPROC lpfnINTEGERDLGPROC;
  static HWND hInst1,hInst2;

  switch (messg)
  {
    case WM_CREATE:
      hInst1=((LPCREATESTRUCT) lParam)->hInstance;
      hInst2=((LPCREATESTRUCT) lParam)->hInstance;
      lpfnABOUTDLGPROC=MakeProcInstance(ABOUTDLGPROC,
                                        hInst1);
      lpfnINTEGERDLGPROC=MakeProcInstance(INTEGERDLGPROC,
                                          hInst2);
      break;
    case WM_COMMAND:
      switch (wParam)
      {
        case IDM_ABOUT:
          DialogBox(hInst1,"AboutDlgBox",hwnd,lpfnABOUTDLGPROC);
          break;
        case IDM_INTEGER:
          DialogBox(hInst2,"IntegerInputDlgBox",
                    hwnd,lpfnINTEGERDLGPROC);
          InvalidateRect(hwnd,NULL,TRUE);
          UpdateWindow(hwnd);
          break;
        case IDM_EXIT:
          SendMessage(hwnd,WM_CLOSE,0,0L);
          break;
        default:
          break;
      }
```

```
          break;

     case WM_PAINT:
       hdc=BeginPaint(hwnd,&ps);
/*--------- your routines below ---------*/

       hPen=CreatePen(0,1,RED);
       SelectObject(hdc,hPen);

       Rectangle(hdc,upperx,uppery,lowerx,lowery);

       SelectObject(hdc,GetStockObject(WHITE_PEN));
       DeleteObject(hPen);

/*--------- your routines above ---------*/

       ValidateRect(hwnd,NULL);
       EndPaint(hwnd,&ps);
       break;

     case WM_DESTROY:
       PostQuitMessage(0);
       break;

     default:
       return(DefWindowProc(hwnd,messg,wParam,lParam));
   }
   return(0L);
}
```

The MAKE File (DIAG4)

Again, no changes have been made to the structure of the **MAKE** file. This file remains the same, except for name changes, as in all previous examples in this chapter.

The Header File (DIAG4.H)

The resource file will utilize a menu and two dialog boxes. The second dialog box utilizes the ID numbers from 200 to 206 as shown in the DIAG4.H header file. The values IDD_UPPERX and IDD_UPPERY will be identified with one corner of the rectangle, and IDD_LOWERX and IDD_LOWERY with the diagonally adjacent corner.

The Definition File (DIAG4.DEF)

The definition file contains a new EXPORT, named IntegerDlgProc. The IntegerDlgProc procedure is responsible for processing the four integer values that will be entered by the user.

The Resource File (DIAG4.RC)

The dialog box specification for INTEGERINPUTDLGBOX contains nine control statements. Several of these are simple static text controls, while others are edit controls for receiving the integer data (in the form of strings).

```
INTEGERINPUTDLGBOX DIALOG LOADONCALL MOVEABLE DISCARDABLE
        9, 26, 210, 92
        CAPTION "Integer Input"
        STYLE WS_BORDER|WS_CAPTION|WS_DLGFRAME|WS_POPUP
{
  CONTROL "Enter Coordinates for a box:",-1,"static",
        SS_LEFT|WS_CHILD,7,7,145,8
  CONTROL "Upper Corner (x,y):",-1,"static",
        SS_LEFT|WS_CHILD,9,23,83,8
  CONTROL "",IDD_UPPERX,"edit",
        ES_LEFT|WS_BORDER|WS_TABSTOP|WS_CHILD,93,19,32,12
  CONTROL "",IDD_UPPERY,"edit",
        ES_LEFT|WS_BORDER|WS_TABSTOP|WS_CHILD,134,19,32,12
  CONTROL "Lower Corner (x,y):",-1,"static",
        SS_LEFT|WS_CHILD,9,48,81,8
  CONTROL "",IDD_LOWERX,"edit",
        ES_LEFT|WS_BORDER|WS_TABSTOP|WS_CHILD,93,43,32,12
  CONTROL "",IDD_LOWERY,"edit",
        ES_LEFT|WS_BORDER|WS_TABSTOP|WS_CHILD,134,43,32,12
  CONTROL "Okay",IDOK,"button",
        BS_PUSHBUTTON|WS_TABSTOP|WS_CHILD,54,76,44,14
  CONTROL "Cancel",IDCANCEL,"button",
        BS_PUSHBUTTON|WS_TABSTOP|WS_CHILD,111,76,44,14
}
```

Since the edit controls have no values between the double quotation marks, there are no default values shown in the dialog box. In other words, no string information (and hence no integer data) is provided as a default in the dialog box.

Upon entering the program, however, a small rectangular box will be drawn to the screen because the four global variables that hold the coordinate information are initialized with integer data. If the dialog box is selected and no values are entered, the screen will be erased and no rectangle drawn since the values in these global variables will be set to 0 if left empty. This feature can be a blessing and a curse, as you'll see in later chapters.

Two push buttons, Okay and Cancel, are also provided for the user.

The Application File (DIAG4.C)

Information will be passed to the four global integer values with the help of the INTEGERDLGPROC procedure.

```
BOOL FAR PASCAL INTEGERDLGPROC(hdlg,messg,wParam,lParam)
HWND hdlg;
unsigned messg;
WORD wParam;
LONG lParam;
{

switch (messg)
    {
    case WM_INITDIALOG:
      return FALSE;
    case WM_COMMAND:
      switch (wParam)
      {
        case IDOK:
          upperx=GetDlgItemInt(hdlg,IDD_UPPERX,NULL,0);
          uppery=GetDlgItemInt(hdlg,IDD_UPPERY,NULL,0);
          lowerx=GetDlgItemInt(hdlg,IDD_LOWERX,NULL,0);
          lowery=GetDlgItemInt(hdlg,IDD_LOWERY,NULL,0);
          EndDialog(hdlg,TRUE);
          break;
        case IDCANCEL:
          EndDialog(hdlg,FALSE);
          break;
        default:
          return FALSE;
      }
      break;

    default:
      return FALSE;
    }
    return TRUE;
}
```

The four variables are named *upperx, uppery, lowerx,* and *lowery.* The GetDlgItemInt function returns an integer value to each of these functions. The function is passed a handle, an ID value, a NULL, and a 0 if the translation is to be an unsigned integer. A 1 would be used for signed numbers. Unsigned numbers can range from 0 to 65535, while signed numbers range from 0 to 32767. The *lpTranslated* parameter, which in this case receives a NULL, can be used to warn of errors in data entry. Only the numeric digits 0 to 9 are considered valid (for example, hexadecimal integers cannot be entered with this technique). As in the previous example, this information is processed with the selection of the IDOK push button.

The four variables containing the coordinate information are directly used by the Rectangle function under WM _ PAINT.

```
/*--------- your routines below ---------*/

     hPen=CreatePen(0,1,RED);
     SelectObject(hdc,hPen);
```

```
    Rectangle(hdc,upperx,uppery,lowerx,lowery);

    SelectObject(hdc,GetStockObject(WHITE_PEN));
    DeleteObject(hPen);

/*--------- your routines above ---------*/
```

Figure 8-16 shows a rectangle with coordinates specified using the dialog box.

Entering Real Numbers with a Dialog Box

It is a popular misconception that Windows will not allow real number arithmetic. If you give it some thought, you have certainly seen Windows programs that process real numbers. Why, then, do so many introductory Windows books deal only with integer numbers? This is probably because Windows parameters must be integer values. Consider the parameters *wParam* and *lParam,* used in so many procedures. The *wParam* value is a **WORD** that represents a 16-bit unsigned integer. The *lParam* value is a **LONG**, or 32-bit signed integer. Several messages have been passed throughout Windows programs with these parameters, but they cannot be used to pass real number information.

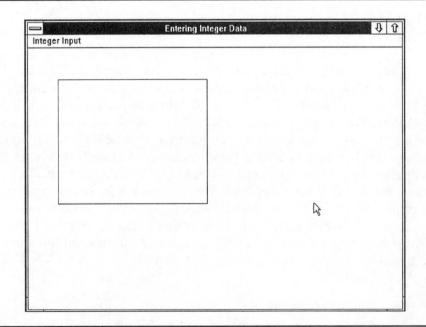

Figure 8-16.   The Integer Input dialog box controls the size of this figure

One trick that can be used is to obtain real number information and immediately store it in a global variable. The global variable will be available to all procedures. This example will show you how to enter a real number (*float*) using the edit control in a dialog box. The program will then use that number as the radius and calculate the volume of the corresponding sphere. The volume of a sphere is given by

Volume = (4/3) * pi * r^3

This program will accept a real number in the dialog box and, of course, return a real number for the sphere's volume. The dialog box used in this example was shown previously in Figure 8-6.

THE DIAG5 MAKE FILE:

```
all : diag5.exe

diag5.obj: diag5.c
    cl -c -AS -FPi -Gsw -Oas -Zpe diag5.c

diag5.res : diag5.rc
    rc -r diag5.rc

diag5.exe: diag5.obj diag5.def diag5.res
    link /NOD diag5,,,libw slibcew,diag5.def
    rc diag5.res
```

THE DIAG5.H HEADER FILE:

```
#define IDM_ABOUT      10
#define IDM_INPUT      20
#define IDM_EXIT       30

#define IDD_FLOAT      201
```

THE DIAG5.DEF DEFINITION FILE:

```
NAME        Diag5
DESCRIPTION 'Dialog Box Example'
EXETYPE     WINDOWS
STUB        'WINSTUB.EXE'
CODE        PRELOAD MOVEABLE DISCARDABLE
DATA        PRELOAD MOVEABLE MULTIPLE
HEAPSIZE    4096
STACKSIZE   9216
EXPORTS     WindowProc      @1
            AboutDlgProc    @2
            FloatDlgProc    @3
```

THE DIAG5.RC RESOURCE FILE:

```
#include "windows.h"
#include "diag5.h"
```

```
AboutMenu MENU
{
  POPUP "Input"
    {
       MENUITEM "About Box...",           IDM_ABOUT
       MENUITEM "Float Input...",         IDM_INPUT
       MENUITEM "Exit",                   IDM_EXIT
    }
}


ABOUTDLGBOX DIALOG LOADONCALL MOVEABLE DISCARDABLE
        9,20,131,133
        STYLE WS_DLGFRAME|WS_POPUP
{
  CONTROL "ABOUT Dialog Box Example",-1,"static",
        SS_CENTER|WS_CHILD,6,12,116,8
  CONTROL "by",-1,"static",
        SS_CENTER|WS_CHILD,55,24,16,8
  CONTROL "William H. Murray and",-1,"static",
        SS_CENTER|WS_CHILD,18,38,91,10
  CONTROL "Chris H. Pappas",-1,"static",
        SS_CENTER|WS_CHILD,30,54,72,8
  CONTROL "Copyright (c) 1989",-1,"static",
        SS_CENTER|WS_CHILD,10,74,108,8
  CONTROL "Okay",IDOK,"button",
        BS_PUSHBUTTON|WS_TABSTOP|WS_CHILD,49,102,28,12
}


FLOATINPUTDLGBOX DIALOG LOADONCALL MOVEABLE DISCARDABLE
        13, 26, 140, 49
        CAPTION "Volume of a Sphere"
        STYLE WS_BORDER|WS_CAPTION|WS_DLGFRAME|WS_POPUP
{
  CONTROL "Radius of Sphere (float):",-1,"static",
        SS_LEFT|WS_CHILD,5,5,145,8
  CONTROL "",IDD_FLOAT,"edit",ES_LEFT|WS_BORDER|WS_TABSTOP|
        WS_CHILD,15,15,120,12
  CONTROL "Okay",IDOK,"button",BS_PUSHBUTTON|WS_TABSTOP|
        WS_CHILD,20,30,48,14
  CONTROL "Cancel",IDCANCEL,"button",BS_PUSHBUTTON|WS_TABSTOP|
        WS_CHILD,81,30,48,14
}


THE DIAG5.C APPLICATION FILE:

/* Simplified Windows Platform (SWP)              */
/* (c) William H. Murray and Chris H. Pappas, 1989 */

#include <windows.h>
#include <stdlib.h>
#include <string.h>
#include <math.h>
#include "diag5.h"

long FAR PASCAL WindowProc(HWND,unsigned,WORD,LONG);
BOOL FAR PASCAL ABOUTDLGPROC(HWND,unsigned,WORD,LONG);
BOOL FAR PASCAL FLOATDLGPROC(HWND,unsigned,WORD,LONG);
```

```c
char szProgName[]="ProgName";
char szApplName[]="AboutMenu";
char numstringl[20]="45.5";
double sphereradius;

int PASCAL WinMain(hInst,hPreInst,lpszCmdLine,nCmdShow)
HANDLE hInst,hPreInst;
LPSTR  lpszCmdLine;
int    nCmdShow;
{
  HWND hwnd;
  MSG  msg;
  WNDCLASS wcSwp;
  if (!hPreInst)
  {
    wcSwp.lpszClassName=szProgName;
    wcSwp.hInstance    =hInst;
    wcSwp.lpfnWndProc  =WindowProc;
    wcSwp.hCursor      =LoadCursor(NULL,IDC_ARROW);
    wcSwp.hIcon        =NULL;
    wcSwp.lpszMenuName =szApplName;
    wcSwp.hbrBackground=GetStockObject(WHITE_BRUSH);
    wcSwp.style        =CS_HREDRAW|CS_VREDRAW;
    wcSwp.cbClsExtra   =0;
    wcSwp.cbWndExtra   =0;
    if (!RegisterClass (&wcSwp))
      return FALSE;
  }
  hwnd=CreateWindow(szProgName,"Entering A Double",
                    WS_OVERLAPPEDWINDOW,CW_USEDEFAULT,
                    CW_USEDEFAULT,CW_USEDEFAULT,
                    CW_USEDEFAULT,NULL,NULL,
                    hInst,NULL);
  ShowWindow(hwnd,nCmdShow);
  UpdateWindow(hwnd);
  while (GetMessage(&msg,NULL,NULL,NULL))
  {
    TranslateMessage(&msg);
    DispatchMessage(&msg);
  }
  return(msg.wParam);
}


BOOL FAR PASCAL ABOUTDLGPROC(hdlg,messg,wParam,lParam)
HWND hdlg;
unsigned messg;
WORD wParam;
LONG lParam;
{
switch (messg)
  {
  case WM_INITDIALOG:
    break;
  case WM_COMMAND:
    switch (wParam)
    {
      case IDOK:
        EndDialog(hdlg,TRUE);
        break;
```

```
              default:
                 return FALSE;
        }
        break;
      default:
        return FALSE;
    }
    return TRUE;
}


BOOL FAR PASCAL FLOATDLGPROC(hdlg,messg,wParam,lParam)
HWND hdlg;
unsigned messg;
WORD wParam;
LONG lParam;
{

switch (messg)
    {
    case WM_INITDIALOG:
        return FALSE;
    case WM_COMMAND:
      switch (wParam)
        {
          case IDOK:
            GetDlgItemText(hdlg,IDD_FLOAT,numstring1,15);
            EndDialog(hdlg,TRUE);
            break;
          case IDCANCEL:
            EndDialog(hdlg,FALSE);
            break;
          default:
            return FALSE;
        }
        break;

      default:
        return FALSE;
      }
      return TRUE;
}


long FAR PASCAL WindowProc(hwnd,messg,wParam,lParam)
HWND    hwnd;
unsigned messg;
WORD    wParam;
LONG    lParam;
{
    HDC   hdc;
    HMENU hMenu;
    PAINTSTRUCT ps;
    static FARPROC lpfnABOUTDLGPROC;
    static FARPROC lpfnFLOATDLGPROC;
    static HWND hInst1,hInst2;
    double spherevolume;
    char numstring2[15];

    switch (messg)
    {
```

```
    case WM_CREATE:
      hInst1=((LPCREATESTRUCT) lParam)->hInstance;
      hInst2=((LPCREATESTRUCT) lParam)->hInstance;
      lpfnABOUTDLGPROC=MakeProcInstance(ABOUTDLGPROC,
                                        hInst1);
      lpfnFLOATDLGPROC=MakeProcInstance(FLOATDLGPROC,
                                        hInst2);
      break;
    case WM_COMMAND:
      switch (wParam)
      {
        case IDM_ABOUT:
          DialogBox(hInst1,"AboutDlgBox",hwnd,lpfnABOUTDLGPROC);
          break;
        case IDM_INPUT:
          DialogBox(hInst2,"FloatInputDlgBox",hwnd,lpfnFLOATDLGPROC);
          InvalidateRect(hwnd,NULL,TRUE);
          UpdateWindow(hwnd);
          break;
        case IDM_EXIT:
          SendMessage(hwnd,WM_CLOSE,0,0L);
          break;
        default:
          break;
      }
      break;

    case WM_PAINT:
      hdc=BeginPaint(hwnd,&ps);

/*--------- your routines below ---------*/

      sphereradius=atof(numstring1);

      spherevolume=(4.0/3.0)*3.14159*
                  (sphereradius*sphereradius*sphereradius);
      gcvt(spherevolume,12,numstring2);
      TextOut(hdc,10,40,"The Radius of the Sphere is: ",29);
      TextOut(hdc,250,40,numstring1,strlen(numstring1));
      TextOut(hdc,10,70,"The Volume of the Sphere is: ",29);
      TextOut(hdc,250,70,numstring2,strlen(numstring2));

/*--------- your routines above ---------*/

      ValidateRect(hwnd,NULL);
      EndPaint(hwnd,&ps);
      break;

    case WM_DESTROY:
      PostQuitMessage(0);
      break;

    default:
      return(DefWindowProc(hwnd,messg,wParam,lParam));
  }
  return(0L);
}
```

The MAKE File (DIAG5)

Just when you were sure that the **MAKE** file for this example would be the same as for all the previous samples, a change occurs! If real numbers are to be utilized by the application program, several changes are required in the **MAKE** file.

```
cl -c -AS -FPi -Gsw -Oas -Zpe diag5.c
        .
        .
        .
link /NOD diag5,,,libw slibcew,diag5.def
```

The C compiler must be told how to handle floating point arithmetic for the C application. Various floating point options are contained in Microsoft's *C User's Guide*. For purposes of this example the compiler option, FPi, was chosen to generate in-line instructions and select the emulator math package.

The Header File (DIAG5.H)

The header file for this example is fairly simple; only one new identification number is needed for this program, IDD_FLOAT.

The Definition File (DIAG5.DEF)

The definition file contains three EXPORTS. FloatDlgProc will be used to process the real number returned from the dialog box. This real number will be returned in the form of a string that will have to be converted later.

The Resource File (DIAG5.RC)

The resource file is also fairly simple. The new dialog box information is contained in FLOATINPUTDLGBOX and contains four controls.

```
FLOATINPUTDLGBOX DIALOG LOADONCALL MOVEABLE DISCARDABLE
        13, 26, 140, 49
        CAPTION "Volume of a Sphere"
        STYLE WS_BORDER|WS_CAPTION|WS_DLGFRAME|WS_POPUP
{
  CONTROL "Radius of Sphere (float):",-1,"static",
        SS_LEFT|WS_CHILD,5,5,145,8
  CONTROL "",IDD_FLOAT,"edit",ES_LEFT|WS_BORDER|WS_TABSTOP|
        WS_CHILD,15,15,120,12
  CONTROL "Okay",IDOK,"button",BS_PUSHBUTTON|WS_TABSTOP|
```

```
        WS_CHILD,20,30,48,14
    CONTROL "Cancel",IDCANCEL,"button",BS_PUSHBUTTON│WS_TABSTOP│
        WS_CHILD,81,30,48,14
}
```

One control places static text control information in the dialog box, which identifies the purpose of the edit control that follows. Two push-button controls provide the Okay and Cancel options you have come to expect in each dialog box. Finally, the edit control is used to retrieve the real number information. Remember, this information will be retrieved as a string.

The Application File (DIAG5.C)

The application program uses the FLOATDLGPROC procedure to return the text string to a global string array, *numstring1[20]*.

```
BOOL FAR PASCAL FLOATDLGPROC(hdlg,messg,wParam,lParam)
HWND hdlg;
unsigned messg;
WORD wParam;
LONG lParam;
{

switch (messg)
  {
  case WM_INITDIALOG:
    return FALSE;
  case WM_COMMAND:
    switch (wParam)
    {
      case IDOK:
        GetDlgItemText(hdlg,IDD_FLOAT,numstring1,15);
        EndDialog(hdlg,TRUE);
        break;
      case IDCANCEL:
        EndDialog(hdlg,FALSE);
        break;
      default:
        return FALSE;
    }
    break;

  default:
    return FALSE;
  }
  return TRUE;
}
```

Actually, this is the same technique that was used when text informa-tion was being entered for the screen. The GetDlgItemText function returns a "numeric" character string of up to 15 characters to *numstring1*. The C language contains functions that allow the conversion of strings containing numeric digits into actual numbers.

```
/*--------- your routines below ---------*/

    sphereradius=atof(numstring1);

    spherevolume=(4.0/3.0)*3.14159*
                (sphereradius*sphereradius*sphereradius);
    gcvt(spherevolume,12,numstring2);
    TextOut(hdc,10,40,"The Radius of the Sphere is: ",29);
    TextOut(hdc,250,40,numstring1,strlen(numstring1));
    TextOut(hdc,10,70,"The Volume of the Sphere is: ",29);
    TextOut(hdc,250,70,numstring2,strlen(numstring2));

/*--------- your routines above ---------*/
```

The variable *sphereradius* is a *double* that will hold the numeric data returned by the *atof* function. To utilize this function, either MATH.H or STDLIB.H must be included in your application program. The *atof* expects a string containing numeric digits. It will stop the conversion process upon receiving the first non-numeric character. For correctly entered string data, this will be the null character that terminates the string. Once converted, *sphereradius* is immediately used to calculate the volume of the sphere, *spherevolume*.

Now, here's the hook; the sphere's volume must be printed to the screen, but only string information can be printed with the TextOut function. Since *spherevolume* holds numeric data, that data will have to be converted back to a string! The C language has a function that will make this conversion—*gcvt*. This function will convert a *double* into a string of the specified length and return it to the given character array.

The four remaining TextOut function calls print the required information to the screen, as shown in Figure 8-17.

CREATING MESSAGE BOXES

The *message box* is a special form of dialog box. Message boxes are often used to report system status, warning, caution, and stop messages to the user. Windows provides the MessageBox function for processing this special dialog box.

The last example in this chapter is a small program that will allow you to look at several message boxes and learn how to use the message box function.

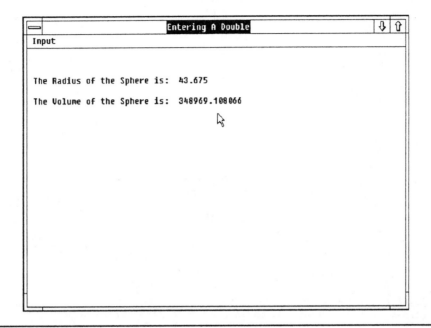

Figure 8-17.   Real numbers entered with the Input dialog box

THE DIAG6 MAKE FILE:

```
all : diag6.exe

diag6.obj: diag6.c
    cl -c -AS -Gsw -Oas -Zpe diag6.c

diag6.res : diag6.rc
    rc -r diag6.rc

diag6.exe: diag6.obj diag6.def diag6.res
    link /NOD diag6,,,libw slibcew,diag6.def
    rc diag6.res
```

THE DIAG6.H HEADER FILE:

```
#define IDM_STATUS    10
#define IDM_WARNING   20
#define IDM_CAUTION   30
#define IDM_STOP      40
#define IDM_EXIT      50
```

THE DIAG6.DEF DEFINITION FILE:

```
NAME        Diag6
DESCRIPTION 'Dialog Box Example'
EXETYPE     WINDOWS
STUB        'WINSTUB.EXE'
CODE        PRELOAD MOVEABLE DISCARDABLE
DATA        PRELOAD MOVEABLE MULTIPLE
```

```
HEAPSIZE     4096
STACKSIZE    9216
EXPORTS      WindowProc       @1
```

THE DIAG6.RC RESOURCE FILE:

```
#include "windows.h"
#include "diag6.h"

MessageMenu MENU
{
  POPUP "Message Box"
    {
      MENUITEM "Status...",    IDM_STATUS
      MENUITEM "Warning...",   IDM_WARNING
      MENUITEM "Caution...",   IDM_CAUTION
      MENUITEM "Stop...",      IDM_STOP
      MENUITEM "Exit",         IDM_EXIT
    }
}
```

THE DIAG6.C APPLICATION FILE:

```
/* Simplified Windows Platform (SWP)          */
/* (c) William H. Murray and Chris H. Pappas, 1989 */

#include <windows.h>
#include "diag6.h"

long FAR PASCAL WindowProc(HWND,unsigned,WORD,LONG);

char szProgName[]="ProgName";
char szApplName[]="MessageMenu";

int PASCAL WinMain(hInst,hPreInst,lpszCmdLine,nCmdShow)
HANDLE hInst,hPreInst;
LPSTR  lpszCmdLine;
int    nCmdShow;
{
  HWND hwnd;
  MSG  msg;
  WNDCLASS wcSwp;
  if (!hPreInst)
  {
    wcSwp.lpszClassName=szProgName;
    wcSwp.hInstance     =hInst;
    wcSwp.lpfnWndProc   =WindowProc;
    wcSwp.hCursor       =LoadCursor(NULL,IDC_ARROW);
    wcSwp.hIcon         =NULL;
    wcSwp.lpszMenuName  =szApplName;
    wcSwp.hbrBackground=GetStockObject(WHITE_BRUSH);
    wcSwp.style         =CS_HREDRAW|CS_VREDRAW;
    wcSwp.cbClsExtra    =0;
    wcSwp.cbWndExtra    =0;
    if (!RegisterClass (&wcSwp))
      return FALSE;
  }
  hwnd=CreateWindow(szProgName,"Message Box Information",
                WS_OVERLAPPEDWINDOW,CW_USEDEFAULT,
```

```
                        CW_USEDEFAULT,CW_USEDEFAULT,
                        CW_USEDEFAULT,NULL,NULL,
                        hInst,NULL);
    ShowWindow(hwnd,nCmdShow);
    UpdateWindow(hwnd);
    while (GetMessage(&msg,NULL,NULL,NULL))
    {
      TranslateMessage(&msg);
      DispatchMessage(&msg);
    }
    return(msg.wParam);
}

long FAR PASCAL WindowProc(hwnd,messg,wParam,lParam)
HWND    hwnd;
unsigned messg;
WORD    wParam;
LONG    lParam;
{
  HDC hdc;
  HMENU hMenu;
  PAINTSTRUCT ps;
  static FARPROC lpfnMESSAGEDLGPROC;
  static HWND hInst1,hInst2;

  switch (messg)
  {
    case WM_COMMAND:
      switch (wParam)
      {
        case IDM_STATUS:
          MessageBox(hwnd,"A Status Box with an Asterisk icon",
                     "Status",MB_ICONASTERISK|MB_OK);
          break;
        case IDM_WARNING:
          MessageBox(hwnd,"A Warning Box with Exclamation icon",
                     "Warning",MB_ICONEXCLAMATION|MB_OK);
          break;
        case IDM_CAUTION:
          MessageBox(hwnd,"A Caution Box with Question icon",
                     "Caution",MB_ICONQUESTION|MB_OK);
          break;
        case IDM_STOP:
          MessageBox(hwnd,"A Stop Box with Hand icon",
                     "Stop",MB_ICONHAND|MB_OK);
          break;
        case IDM_EXIT:
          SendMessage(hwnd,WM_CLOSE,0,0L);
          break;
        default:
          break;
      }
      break;

    case WM_PAINT:
      hdc=BeginPaint(hwnd,&ps);

/*--------- your routines below ---------*/

      TextOut(hdc,10,40,"The Program allows you to ",26);
      TextOut(hdc,20,60,"experiment with the ",20);
```

```
      TextOut(hdc,20,80,"MessageBox function.",20);

/*--------- your routines above ---------*/

      ValidateRect(hwnd,NULL);
      EndPaint(hwnd,&ps);
      break;

    case WM_DESTROY:
      PostQuitMessage(0);
      break;

    default:
      return(DefWindowProc(hwnd,messg,wParam,lParam));
  }
  return(0L);
}
```

The WindowProc procedure uses WM_COMMAND to examine several *case* statements. Four of these *case* statements contain MessageBox functions. The MessageBox function requires a handle, a string, a caption, and an assortment of types. The fourth parameter, types, can have several values coupled with ORs. Each of the message box types starts with "MB_" and includes:

ABORTRETRYIGNORE
APPLMODAL
DEFBUTTON1
DEFBUTTON2
DEFBUTTON3
ICONASTERISK
ICONEXCLAMATION
ICONHAND
ICONQUESTION
OK
OKCANCEL
RETRYCANCEL
SYSTEMMODAL
YESNO
YESNOCANCEL

Most of these types are self-explanatory, but additional information can be found in the Microsoft *Programmer's Reference*.

Figure 8-18 shows the screen output for one message box. A message

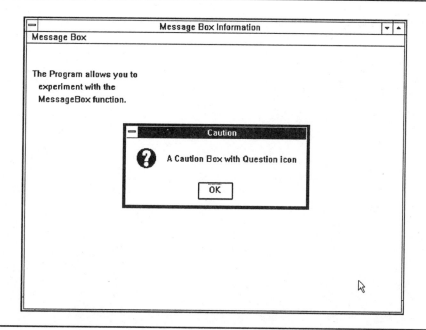

Figure 8-18.   The message box dialog box allows you to experiment with
different message boxes

box could also be used as sort of a poor person's About dialog box. For
simple applications, this could bypass the need for the Dialog Box Editor
altogether.

9

FANCY FONTS

You have heard it said many times that appearances count. If the most eloquent programming algorithm has apparently been coded with a random space generator it will leave the programmer seriously doubting the abilities of the software designer. Likewise, printer or video display output that looks as if the device driver has hiccuped leaves you wondering why you paid so much for a particular software package.

This chapter is dedicated to those software engineers who feel the visual appearance of an application is just as important as the amount of memory the application needs and the speed at which the application executes. Windows provides a profuse bouquet of font capabilities. When they are properly managed they will give applications a professional appearance that sets them apart from the pack.

If you are a person who has trouble using one brush and a set of eight colors to create a painting, you probably also have trouble just using the standard font supplied with Windows. How would you like to feel confident about using several brushes and a virtually unlimited palette of paints? How would you like to have a virtually unlimited number of custom fonts at your fingertips?

Before discussing GDI character functions, let's review some terminology. Recall from Chapter 2 that typeface is a basic character design, defined by stroke width and *serifs* (the smaller line used to finish off a main stroke of a letter, as at the top and bottom of the uppercase letter "M"). Some typefaces are *sans serif*—they have no serifs.

A font is a complete set of characters of the same typeface and size, including letters, punctuation marks, and other symbols. The size of a font is measured in points. For example, 12-point Times Roman is a different font from 12-point Times Roman italic, 14-point Times Roman, or 12-point Helvetica. A *point* is the smallest unit of measure used in typography. There are 72 points to the inch and 12 points in a pica. A *pica* is a unit of measure in typography equaling approximately 1/6 inch.

FONT STRUCTURE AND DEFINITIONS

Learning to master all of Windows' font capabilities often requires many hours of work. To make life easier, two of the most frequently referenced GDI character-function font structures (TEXTMETRIC and LOGFONT), and their associated constant declarations, have been included here. These can be found in the WINDOWS.H header file. Reading these declarations will give you a feeling for the richness of character-display possibilities.

Logical Font Constants

The following logical font constants are listed in the WINDOWS.H header file and are listed here for your convenience. You should print a hard copy of WINDOWS.H.

```
/* Logical font constants. */

OUT_DEFAULT_PRECIS
OUT_STRING_PRECIS
OUT_CHARACTER_PRECIS
OUT_STROKE_PRECIS

CLIP_DEFAULT_PRECIS
CLIP_CHARACTER_PRECIS
CLIP_STROKE_PRECIS

DEFAULT_QUALITY
DRAFT_QUALITY
PROOF_QUALITY

DEFAULT_PITCH
FIXED_PITCH
VARIABLE_PITCH
```

ANSI_CHARSET

OEM_CHARSET

/* GDI font families. */

```
FF_DONTCARE    /* Don't care or don't know. */
FF_ROMAN       /* Variable stroke width, serifed. */
               /* Times Roman, Century Schoolbook, etc. */
FF_SWISS       /* Variable stroke width, sans-serifed. */
               /* Helvetica, Swiss, etc. */
FF_MODERN      /* Fixed stroke width, serifed or sans-serifed. */
               /* Pica, Elite, Courier, etc. */
FF_SCRIPT      /* Cursive, etc. */
FF_DECORATIVE  /* Old English, etc. */
```


/* Font weights lightest to darkest. */

```
FW_DONTCARE
FW_THIN
FW_EXTRALIGHT
FW_LIGHT
FW_NORMAL
FW_MEDIUM
FW_SEMIBOLD
FW_BOLD
FW_EXTRABOLD
FW_HEAVY
```

```
FW_ULTRALIGHT   FW_EXTRALIGHT
FW_REGULAR      FW_NORMAL
FW_DEMIBOLD     FW_SEMIBOLD
FW_ULTRABOLD    FW_EXTRABOLD
FW_BLACK        FW_HEAVY
```


/* EnumFonts masks. */

```
RASTER_FONTTYPE
DEVICE_FONTTYPE
```


TEXTMETRIC Structure

The TEXTMETRIC data structure, also listed in WINDOWS.H, is the most important data structure used in font manipulations.

```
/* TextMetric data structure */
typedef struct tagTEXTMETRIC {
    short int tmHeight;
    short int tmAscent;
    short int tmDescent;
    short int tmInternalLeading;
    short int tmExternalLeading;
    short int tmAveCharWidth;
```

```
    short int tmMaxCharWidth;
    short int tmWeight;
    BYTE      tmItalic;
    BYTE      tmUnderlined;
    BYTE      tmStruckOut;
    BYTE      tmFirstChar;
    BYTE      tmLastChar;
    BYTE      tmDefaultChar;
    BYTE      tmBreakChar;
    BYTE      tmPitchAndFamily;
    BYTE      tmCharSet;
    short int tmOverhang;
    short int tmDigitizedAspectX;
    short int tmDigitizedAspectY3;
} TEXTMETRIC;
```

LOGFONT Structure

The LOGFONT data structure is shown here:

```
/* Logical Font Data Structure */

#define LF_FACESIZE 32

typedef struct tagLOGFONT {
    short int lfHeight;
    short int lfWidth;
    short int lfEscapement;
    short int lfOrientation;
    short int lfWeight;
    BYTE      lfItalic;
    BYTE      lfUnderline;
    BYTE      lfStrikeOut;
    BYTE      lfCharSet;
    BYTE      lfOutPrecision;
    BYTE      lfClipPrecision;
    BYTE      lfQuality;
    BYTE      lfPitchAndFamily;
    BYTE      lfFaceName[LF_FACESIZE];
} LOGFONT;
```

If you are reading this sentence, congratulations! You have obviously made it through the font declarations and *not* moved on to some other chapter! Fortunately, most applications only need six of the fields defined in the TEXTMETRIC structure: *tmHeight, tmAscent, tmDescent, tmInternal-Leading, tmExternalLeading,* and *tmAveCharWidth.* Figure 9-1 illustrates how the various fields are used to define a font.

Character Cells

Table 9-1 describes the basic elements of a font *character.* Font characters are much more complex than the symbols on the output device. The Windows

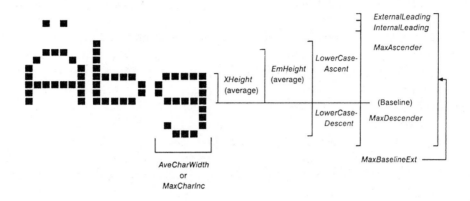

Figure 9-1.   Using various fields to define a font

GDI places each symbol within a rectangular region called a *character cell.* Each cell consists of a predefined number of rows and columns and is described by six specific measurement points: ascent, baseline, descent, height, origin, and width. While some of these terms are obvious in meaning, others are specific to the field of typography.

Table 9-1.   Basic Elements of a Font

Point of Measurement	Description
Ascent	The distance in character cell rows from the character cell baseline to the top of the character cell
Baseline	The base on which all of the characters stand Lowercase letters like "p" and "q" have descenders that extend below the baseline
Descent	The distance in character cell rows from the character cell baseline to the bottom of the character cell
Height	The height of a character cell row
Origin	The upper-left corner of the character cell. It is used as a point of reference when a character is output to a particular device or display
Width	The width of a character cell column

Within the TEXTMETRIC structure there are some obvious parameters, such as *lfitalic* and *lfunderline,* that are self-explanatory. Others need clarification.

The *tmInternalLeading* parameter defines how much space is to be inserted within the character cell for characters such as accents, umlauts, and tildes in foreign character sets. Similarly, *tmExternalLeading* defines how much white space is to be inserted between the top and bottom of a character cell in adjacent rows.

Using *lfPitchAndFamily* indicates the number of characters from a particular font that will fit in a single inch. In Windows this is either fixed pitch or variable pitch. (See "Font Widths" for further explanation.)

In combination, *tmDigitizedAspectX* and *tmDigitizedAspectY* are used whenever a *raster font* is created. A character font's aspect ratio is based on the ratio between the width and height of a device's pixel. Together *tmDigitizedAspectX* and *tmDigitizedAspectY* represent the ideal X- and Y-aspect ratio for each individual font as supplied by the GDI. (Both raster font and X- and Y-aspect ratio will be explained later.)

Of particular importance is the *tmOverhang* parameter. This parameter tells the GDI to synthesize a font. Whenever an application requests a font that is unavailable on a device, the GDI creates one. The difference in width (the amount of extra character cell columns) between a string created with the normal font and a string created with the synthesized font is called the *overhang.*

ADDITIONAL FONT ATTRIBUTES

Remember that a font represents a complete set of characters from one specific typeface, all with the same specific size and *style* (style could be italics or boldface). Usually the system owns all of the font resources and shares them with the application program. Fonts are not usually compiled into the final executable version of a program.

Application programs treat fonts like other drawing objects so they are therefore manipulated using handles. An application program will create a font, can repeatedly associate the font with different contexts, and will delete a font.

Font Widths

Fonts that display all characters using the same width are called *fixed fonts.* Fixed fonts make alignment easier since narrow characters, such as "i," occupy the same space as wide characters, such as "W."

Variable width, or *proportionally spaced, fonts,* on the other hand, allocate differing amounts of space to each character, much the same as if you were writing them by hand. With a proportionally spaced font, the "i" would occupy much less line space than the "W."

Figure 9-2 outputs the same text to the display screen using two different font widths. The first string is printed using a fixed font. One of the easiest ways to spot a fixed font is to locate the letters "i" and "W" or "M." In a fixed font the uppercase "W" or "M" will be just as wide as the lowercase "i."

Figure 9-3 shows a sentence printed in a variable pitch font. Many people think variable pitch fonts are easier to read than fixed fonts. Windows 3.0 and OS/2 Presentation Manager use variable width fonts.

Automatic Leading and Kerning

The term *leading* refers to the amount of vertical space, measured in points, between the baselines of two lines of text. Remember that the baseline of any line of text is the invisible line on which the letters sit. A descender is the part of a lowercase letter that extends below this invisible line, such as in the letter "p" or "y." *Kerning* is the subtraction of space between certain

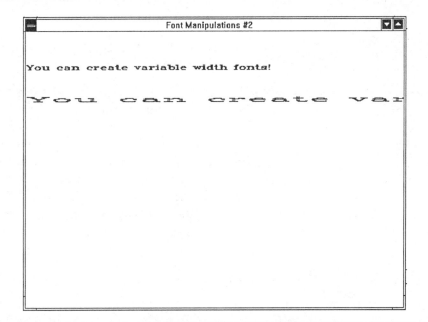

Figure 9-2.   Printing text in a window with two different font widths

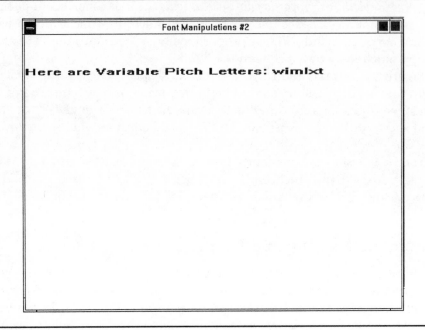

Figure 9-3.   Printing a sentence with a variable width font

letter combinations—for example, an uppercase "T" and lowercase "o"—to create a visually consistent image. Windows is capable of querying a font's metrics or characteristics and adjusting the output accordingly.

OEM Versus ANSI Character Sets

Various manufacturers have at times included their own definitions for character sets, called OEM for Original Equipment Manufacturer. These are different from the American National Standards Institute (ANSI) character set definitions, which in turn differ from IBM's extended character set definitions. This jumble of definitions can create a problem when mapping certain graphics symbols, mathematical symbols, and foreign letters. Although it is beyond the scope of this chapter, Windows 3.0 does provide for character set redefinition by means of the AnsiToOem and OemToAnsi functions.

Logical Versus Physical Fonts

In one respect, you could think of a *logical font* as satisfying your wildest dreams of font manipulation. A logical font can, for example, specify a character font using bold italics with the symbols spaced widely apart. A *physical font* is the actual device context translation of that specification. It is possible to specify a size of letter (in a logical font) that is not actually available on your printer (in the physical font). Many of the GDI character functions have been written to provide as close a match as possible between the two.

Vector Versus Raster Fonts

In addition to determining whether a font is supplied by Windows or by the device, whether it is in ANSI format, and so on, you will need to know whether it is a *vector* or a raster font.

Basically, a vector font (typically used by plotters) defines each character with a set of points connected by lines. Raster fonts, on the other hand, are created in much the same way a dot matrix printer prints. A raster font character is defined more like a bitmap image.

Naturally, each font has its own advantages and disadvantages. While a vector font can be easily scaled and rotated to any size, raster fonts are more easily designed and more quickly displayed. Vector fonts can be scaled continuously, providing a wide range of character sizes, while raster fonts are only generated in multiples of their original size.

Generated Fonts

Windows is also capable of generating variations on a physical font. For instance, given one 10-point Times Roman font, Windows can synthesize 10-point Times Roman italics, 20-point Times Roman bold, and so forth. However, most fonts generated by Windows will not be as clear as the original base font.

TYPES OF FONTS

There are several types of fonts your Windows applications can use. From the simplest fonts (default fonts) to the more difficult and complex (custom designed fonts) Windows provides a very rich type foundry.

Default Fonts

Windows 3.0 supplies several fonts: System, Terminal, Courier, Helvetica, Modern, Roman, Script, and Times Roman. These are called *GDI-supplied fonts.* These resources are installed from the Fonts disk and become part of the Windows system.

Printer and Display Fonts

A *printer font* is a device font supplied by the printer manufacturer. *Display fonts,* sometimes called *screen fonts,* are those that Windows can draw to the screen. Printer device fonts are never display fonts. This can create some confusion in certain types of applications. For example, a desktop publishing application might provide for WYSIWYG screen display—that is, What You See Is What You Get. The user selects a script font for writing an informal letter. However, when the application goes to print the letter, there is no matching script font available for the printer. Windows tries to make the best match possible based on the parameters specified. On the other hand, had the user chosen to write a business letter using a display screen Courier font, the hard copy would look identical. In this case the printer manufacturer supplied a Courier printer font and Windows made the correct type match.

Custom Fonts

When all else fails in obtaining the type you desire, you can design your own font. The Microsoft Windows Software Development Kit supplies a Font Editor. The Font Editor allows the creation of font files that can be used with your applications. Each font file contains a header defining the font and a collection of bitmaps representing the individual letters, digits, and punctuation characters that can be used to display text on a display surface. This will be discussed in more detail shortly.

FONT MAPPING SCHEME

Windows has a very powerful scheme that it uses to decide which fonts "match." Remember that it is quite possible for an application to select a video display font that isn't available for a particular printer. The process of selecting the physical font that bears the closest resemblance to the specified logical font is known as *font mapping.*

Basically, the font mapper assigns certain penalty values to physical fonts with characteristics that do not match the characteristics of the specified logical font. The physical font with the lowest penalty total is the one Windows selects. Table 9-2 lists the penalty values from the most to the least severe. The SelectObject function is used to select the physical font (applicant font) that most closely matches the logical font.

USING THE MICROSOFT FONT EDITOR

For most programming needs, the abundant font foundry supplied with Windows 3.0 will satisfy the most demanding of video display require-

Table 9-2.   Font Mapping Penalty Weights

Selector	Penalty Weight	Explanation
CharSets	4	When character sets do not match, the applicant font is penalized severely
Pitch	3	When a proportionally spaced font is requested, the applicant font with fixed-pitch is penalized very severely (or vice versa)
Family	3	When the font families do not match, the applicant font is severely penalized
FaceName	3	When typeface names do not match, the applicant font is severely penalized
Height	2	When the applicant font height is less than the requested font, Windows will multiply (up to a factor of 8) the applicant font height to produce a match. A penalty is assessed for any modifications made and for any additional height changes
Width	2	The same approach is used here as is applied to differences in height
Weight	1	When the applicant font weight is not what was requested, Windows assigns a penalty
Slant	1	When the applicant font is not italicized, the applicant font is penalized (or vice versa)
Underline	1	When the applicant font is not underlined, the applicant font is penalized (or vice versa)
StrikeOut	1	When the applicant font is not struck out, the applicant font is penalized (or vice versa)

ments. However, for those applications that require more visual panache, Microsoft has included a Font Editor with the Software Development Kit. This easy-to-use editor lets you create your own font files (raster fonts) to use with your applications.

Technically, a *font file* consists of a font header, which contains the information about the font, and a collection of character bitmaps representing the individual letters, digits, and punctuation characters that are used to display text.

Loading the Font Editor

Since the Font Editor is a Windows application, you must first open the MS-DOS Executive window. Once you have done that, load the Font Editor by simply double clicking on FONTEDIT.EXE. Figure 9-4 shows a dialog box for obtaining file information for the Font Editor. The Font Editor will not allow you to create a font totally from scratch. Instead, it has been designed to allow you to modify an existing font. Figure 9-5 shows a supplied font file named ATRM1111.FNT. This is the default font file used

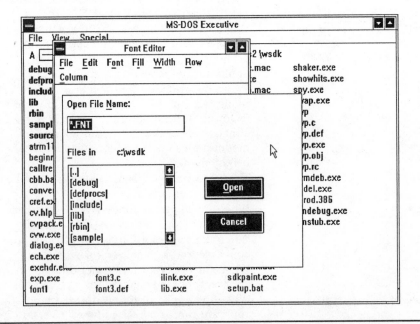

Figure 9-4.   The dialog box used to obtain information for the Font Editor

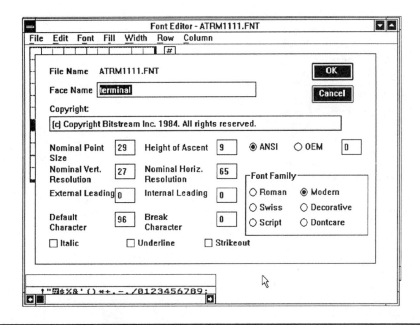

Figure 9-5.   A supplied font, ATRM1111.FNT, used for creating a custom font

to create an initial custom font. ATRM1111.FNT is loaded into the Font Editor by moving the pointer to the file name and double clicking the right mouse button.

Basic Font Editor Window

Figure 9-6 shows the basic Font Editor window. The largest portion of the window is occupied with an exploded view of the uppercase letter "A," called the *character window.*

Immediately below the character window is the *font window.* The font window contains a font viewing area and a scroll bar. It also contains a normal-scale copy of the font's character set. With the font window you can scroll through the entire font set and select a particular character or symbol for editing. An edit symbol is selected by double clicking on the item within the font window.

At the upper-right corner of the character window is a small two-character window called the *character-viewing window.* Here, you can see the

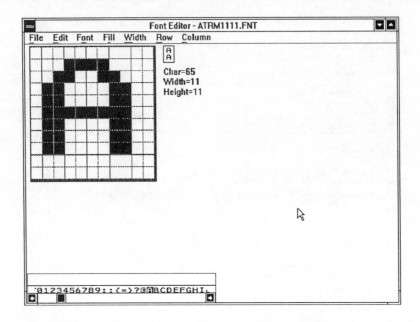

Figure 9-6.   The main Font Editor window

effects of changes made to the character. One common mistake when first designing a custom font is forgetting to account for the white space between characters and rows of characters. The character-viewing window can be used to make certain that two rows of the newly defined font don't collide.

Immediately below the character-viewing window are statistics about the character. They include the character's ANSI code value and the character's width and height in pixels.

Changing the Font Header

Figure 9-7 shows the dialog box displayed whenever the user selects the Font main menu item followed by the Header option. The font header contains all the information about the font except the bitmap. This is the information used to fill the TEXTMETRIC and LOGMETRIC data structures when requesting information about a particular font. See Table 9-3.

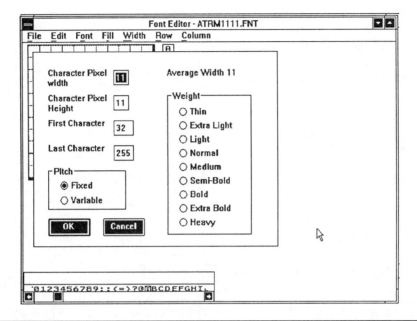

Figure 9-7.   The dialog box for the Font main menu item

Customizing Fonts

Once you have loaded a font into the Font Editor, creating a custom font only requires a little creativity. Figure 9-8 shows an uppercase letter "A" modified with a shadowing effect. The time-consuming part involves selecting each character, digit, and symbol within the font and then applying a little inventiveness to create the desired effect.

Actually modifying each symbol is very simple. Once the symbol to edit has been selected and displayed in the character window, the mouse is used to invert the selected cell. When the mouse button is clicked on a white cell, it turns black, and vice versa. Holding down the mouse button will continue the originally selected option; in other words, if the mouse button was clicked over a black cell, moving the pointer over any other black cells will cause them to invert to white, or vice versa.

Don't forget to save your changes after you redefine *each* character. Creating and verifying a single symbol's design can take several minutes. Designing an entire character set can take a couple of hours. You wouldn't want to have to invent the font a second time.

Table 9-3.   Font Header Information

Dialog Box Item	Description
Face Name	A 32-character string that names the font and distinguishes it from other fonts. It does not have to be the same as the font file name, although keeping them the same will help to easily manage a growing font library
File Name	The name of the font file being edited
Copyright	A maximum of 60 characters. This string can be used for a copyright notice or any additional information the user may need to know about the font
Nominal Point Size	One point = approximately 1/72 of an inch. It is used to define the point size of the characters in the font
Height of Ascent	In pixels, defines the distance from the top of an ascender to the baseline
Nominal Vertical Resolution	The vertical resolution at which the characters were digitized
Nominal Horizontal Resolution	The horizontal resolution at which the characters were digitized
External Leading	The amount of white space to be inserted between the top and bottom of a character cell in adjacent rows
Internal Leading	The amount of space to be inserted within the character cell for such characters as accents, umlauts, and tildes in foreign character sets
Default Character	Usually the ANSI value for the default character. This character is typically used when an attempt is made to display a character whose character value is less than or greater than that of the font's defined range
Break Character	The ANSI value for the break character (usually a space character). This character is used to pad lines that are justified
ANSI or OEM	Defines the character set. The valid range is from 0 to 255 (inclusive) with 0 reserved for a Windows understood ANSI character set, and 255 reserved for the machine-specific OEM character set

Table 9-3.   Font Header Information (*continued*)

Dialog Box Item	Description
Font Family	Defines the family to which the font belongs. Font families define the general characteristics of the font from this list:

Font Family	Definition
Roman	Proportionally spaced fonts using serifs
Modern	Fixed-pitch fonts
Swiss	Proportionally spaced fonts without serifs
Decorative	A novelty font
Script	Script or cursive fonts
Dontcare	Custom font

Dialog Box Item	Description
Italic	Defines an italic font
Underline	Defines an underlined font
Strikeout	Defines a font with characters that have a line through them

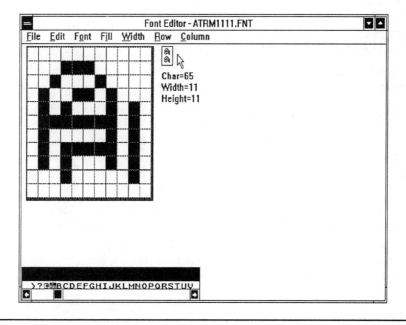

Figure 9-8.   Uppercase "A" modified with a shadow effect

Saving a Custom Font Design

The word to remember here is *caution!* Saving a character font is achieved by selecting the File item from the main menu, followed by Save. The editor then displays a dialog box requesting a file name. For your first character font redefinition, the default file name is the original file supplied to you by Windows. If you save your changes using this file name, you will have lost the base character set from which to build additional font descriptions. Try to make the file name meaningful so you can keep your custom fonts straight as your collection builds. All font files must have an .FNT file extension. For the custom font described earlier, the font description file was given the name SHADOW.FNT.

Making a Font Resource File

The Graphics Device Interface (GDI) stores all information about a physical font in a font file. This is the file you created using the font editor— SHADOW.FNT. A font resource is a collection of one or more of these physical font files. Application programmers who want to use fonts in their applications must add the new font file(s) to a font resource file.

FANCY FONT PROGRAMS

In the following section, four application programs are developed to illustrate various font manipulation techniques. Two of these applications will work directly with the CreateFont function, while the remaining two applications will use the CreateFontIndirect function. The first application will show you how to print text horizontally and vertically on the screen. This technique is very important for labeling graphs, as you will see later in Chapter 11. The second application changes the character set's height and width. The techniques, shown here, can add emphasis to any screen output. The third application uses a loop that prints the same message in script in several different font sizes. Finally, the fourth example will show you how to rotate an entire line of text around a starting point. The font height and angle are specified in the CreateFontIndirect function.

Before studying these programs, let us examine in detail the CreateFont and CreatFontIndirect functions.

The CreateFont Function

The CreateFont function is of type *HFONT* as defined in the WINDOWS.H header file. This function selects the logical font from the GDI's pool of physical fonts that most closely matches the characteristics specified by the developer in the function call. Once created, this logical font can be selected by any device. The syntax for CreateFont is

HFONT CreateFont(Height,Width,Escapement,Orientation,Weight
Italic,Underline,StrikeOut,CharSet,
OutputPrecision,ClipPrecision,Quality,
PitchAndFamily,Facename)

With 14 parameters, CreateFont requires quite a bit of baggage when used by the programmer.

(int) *Height*	Desired font height in logical units
(int) *Width*	Average font width in logical units
(int) *Escapement*	Angle (tenths of a degree) for each line written in the font
(int) *Orientation*	Angle (tenths of a degree) for each character's baseline
(int) *Weight*	Weight of font (0 to 1000); 400 is normal, 700 is bold
(byte) *Italic*	Italic font
(byte) *Underline*	Underline font
(byte) *StrikeOut*	Strike through fonts (redline)
(byte) *CharSet*	Character set (ANSI_CHARSET, OEM_CHARSET)
(byte) *OutputPrecision*	How closely output must match the requested specifications? (OUT_CHARACTER_PRECIS, OUT_DEFAULT_PRECIS, OUT_STRING_PRECIS, OUT_STROKE_PRECIS)
(byte) *ClipPrecision*	How to clip characters outside of clipping range (CLIP_CHARACTER_PRECIS, CLIP_DEFAULT_PRECIS, CLIP_STROKE_PRECIS)
(byte) *Quality*	How carefully the logical attributes are mapped to the physical font (DEFAULT_QUALITY, DRAFT_QUALITY, PROOF_QUALITY)

| (byte) *PitchAndFamily* | Pitch and family of font (DEFAULT_PITCH, FIXED_PITCH, PROOF_QUALITY, FF_DECORATIVE, FF_DONTCARE, FF_MODERN, FF_ROMAN, FF_SCRIPT, FF_SWISS) |
| (lpstr) *Facename* | A string pointing to the name of the desired font's typeface |

The CreateFontIndirect Function

The CreateFontIndirect function frees the programmer from the baggage of CreateFont. This function will create or modify a logical font with the characteristics given in the data structure specified by *lpLogFont*.

The syntax is

HFONT CreateFontIndirect(lpLogFont)

where *lpLogFont* points to a LOGFONT data structure specified in WINDOWS.H. The LOGFONT data structure was discussed earlier in the chapter.

The FONT1 Program

The program will illustrate how to use the CreateFont function to print two strings to the screen. One string will be printed horizontally, while the other will be printed vertically.

The FONT1 program initially consists of three files: the **MAKE** file, the definition file, and the application file. If you follow the complete development cycle, you will have five files on disk when the **MAKE** utility is finished: FONT1, FONT1.DEF, FONT1.C, FONT1.OBJ, and FONT1.EXE.

```
THE FONT1 MAKE FILE (FONT1):

all : font1.exe #

font1.obj: font1.c
    cl -c -AS -Gsw -Oas -Zpe font1.c

font1.exe: font1.obj font1.def font1.res
    link /NOD font1,,,libw slibcew, font1.def


THE FONT1 DEFINITION FILE (FONT1.DEF):

;FONT1.DEF for C Compiling

NAME            Font1
DESCRIPTION     'Font Manipulations'
EXETYPE         WINDOWS
```

```
STUB            'WINSTUB.EXE'
CODE            PRELOAD MOVEABLE DISCARDABLE
DATA            PRELOAD MOVEABLE MULTIPLE
HEAPSIZE        4096
STACKSIZE       9216
EXPORTS         WindowProc       @1
```

THE FONT1 APPLICATION FILE (FONT1.C):

```c
/* Simplified Windows Platform (SWP)              */
/* (c) William H. Murray and Chris H. Pappas, 1989 */

#include <string.h>
#include <windows.h>

LONG FAR PASCAL WindowProc(HWND,unsigned,WORD,LONG);

char szProgName[]="ProgName";

int PASCAL WinMain(hInst,hPreInst,lpszCmdLine,nCmdShow)
HANDLE hInst,hPreInst;
LPSTR  lpszCmdLine;
int    nCmdShow;
{
  HWND hwnd;
  MSG  msg;
  WNDCLASS wcSwp;
  if (!hPreInst)
  {
    wcSwp.lpszClassName=szProgName;
    wcSwp.hInstance     =hInst;
    wcSwp.lpfnWndProc  =WindowProc;
    wcSwp.hCursor       =LoadCursor(hInst,IDC_ARROW);
    wcSwp.hIcon         =NULL;
    wcSwp.lpszMenuName =NULL;
    wcSwp.hbrBackground=GetStockObject(WHITE_BRUSH);
    wcSwp.style         =CS_HREDRAW|CS_VREDRAW;
    wcSwp.cbClsExtra   =0;
    wcSwp.cbWndExtra   =0;
    if (!RegisterClass (&wcSwp))
      return FALSE;
  }
  hwnd=CreateWindow(szProgName,"Font Manipulations",
                    WS_OVERLAPPEDWINDOW,CW_USEDEFAULT,
                    CW_USEDEFAULT,CW_USEDEFAULT,
                    CW_USEDEFAULT,NULL,NULL,
                    hInst,NULL);
  ShowWindow(hwnd,nCmdShow);
  UpdateWindow(hwnd);
  while (GetMessage(&msg,NULL,NULL,NULL))
  {
    TranslateMessage(&msg);
    DispatchMessage(&msg);
  }
  return(msg.wParam);
}


long FAR PASCAL WindowProc(hwnd,messg,wParam,lParam)
HWND hwnd;
```

```
unsigned messg;
WORD wParam;
LONG lParam;
{
   HDC          hdc;
   PAINTSTRUCT ps;
   HFONT        hOFont,hNFont;
   static char szXString[]="This is the horizontal string.";
   static char szYString[]="This is the vertical string.";

   switch (messg)
   {

     case WM_PAINT:
        hdc=BeginPaint(hwnd,&ps);

/*--------- your routines below ---------*/

        /* Print Horizontal Text to Screen */
        hNFont=CreateFont(12,12,0,0,FW_BOLD,
                          FALSE,FALSE,FALSE,
                          OEM_CHARSET,
                          OUT_DEFAULT_PRECIS,
                          CLIP_DEFAULT_PRECIS,
                          DEFAULT_QUALITY,
                          VARIABLE_PITCH|FF_ROMAN,
                          "Roman");
        hOFont=SelectObject(hdc,hNFont);
        TextOut(hdc,180,360,szXString,strlen(szXString));

        /* Print Vertical Text to Screen */
        hNFont=CreateFont(12,12,900,900,FW_BOLD,
                          FALSE,FALSE,FALSE,
                          OEM_CHARSET,
                          OUT_DEFAULT_PRECIS,
                          CLIP_DEFAULT_PRECIS,
                          DEFAULT_QUALITY,
                          VARIABLE_PITCH|FF_ROMAN,
                          "Roman");
        hOFont=SelectObject(hdc,hNFont);
        TextOut(hdc,320,340,szYString,strlen(szYString));

        SelectObject(hdc,hOFont);
        DeleteObject(hNFont);

/*--------- your routines above ---------*/

        ValidateRect(hwnd,NULL);
        EndPaint(hwnd,&ps);
        break;

     case WM_DESTROY:
        PostQuitMessage(0);
        break;

     default:
        return(DefWindowProc(hwnd,messg,wParam,lParam));
   }
   return(0L);
}
```

The FONT1 File

As you can see from the FONT1 **MAKE** file listing, this program will be compiled in the normal manner.

The FONT1.DEF File

The FONT1.DEF file is similar to many previous listings. It contains only one export: EXPORTS: WindowProc.

The FONT1.C File

If you examine the application file you will notice that except for the declaration of *hOFont* and *hNFont,* the structure of the overhead code is identical to the Windows platform developed in Chapter 3. All font action takes place in WM_PAINT.

The first time CreateFont is called, the parameters are set to the following values:

> *Height* = 12
> *Width* = 12
> *Escapement* = 0
> *Orientation* = 0
> *Weight* = FW_BOLD
> *Italic* = FALSE
> *Underline* = FALSE
> *StrikeOut* = FALSE
> *CharSet* = OEM_CHARSET
> *OutputPrecision* = OUT_DEFAULT_PRECIS
> *ClipPrecision* = CLIP_DEFAULT_PRECIS
> *Quality* = DEFAULT_QUALITY
> *PitchAndFamily* = VARIABLE_PITCH | FF_ROMAN
> *Facename* = "Roman"

The function will attempt to find a font match to these specifications. This font is used to print the horizontal string of text to the window.

The second time CreateFont is called, the parameters are set to these values:

> *Height* = 12
> *Width* = 12
> *Escapement* = 900

Orientation = 900
Weight = FW_BOLD
Italic = FALSE
Underline = FALSE
StrikeOut = FALSE
CharSet = OEM_CHARSET
OutputPrecision = OUT_DEFAULT_PRECIS
ClipPrecision = CLIP_DEFAULT_PRECIS
Quality = DEFAULT_QUALITY
PitchAndFamily = VARIABLE_PITCH ¦ FF_ROMAN
Facename = "Roman"

As you can see, the only values that have changed are *Escapement* and *Orientation*. Both of these parameters have angles specified in tenths of a degree. In this case, then, the actual angle is 90 degrees. The *Escapement* parameter thus rotates the line of text from horizontal to vertical. *Orientation* rotates each character, in the string, 90 degrees. The results of this font manipulation are shown in Figure 9-9.

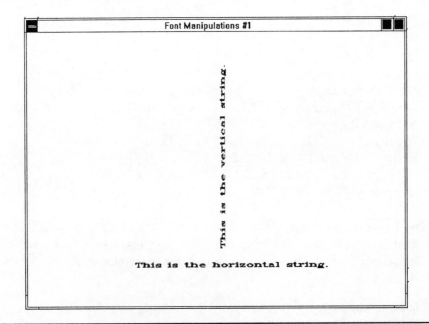

Figure 9-9.   The FONT1 program output, using the CreateFont function

The FONT2 Program

This program is identical to the last example, except this time the size of the text printed to the window will be changed. Changing the height or width of a font is a simple task.

If you follow the complete development cycle, you will have five files on disk when the **MAKE** utility is finished: FONT2, FONT2.DEF, FONT2.C, FONT2.OBJ, and FONT2.EXE.

THE FONT2 MAKE FILE (FONT2):

```
all : font2.exe

font2.obj: font2.c
    cl -c -AS -Gsw -Oas -Zpe font2.c

font2.exe: font2.obj font2.def font2.res
    link /NOD font2,,,libw slibcew, font2.def
```

THE FONT2 DEFINITION FILE (FONT2.DEF):

```
;FONT2.DEF for C Compiling

NAME            Font2
DESCRIPTION     'Font Manipulations'
EXETYPE         WINDOWS
STUB            'WINSTUB.EXE'
CODE            PRELOAD MOVEABLE DISCARDABLE
DATA            PRELOAD MOVEABLE MULTIPLE
HEAPSIZE        4096
STACKSIZE       9216
EXPORTS         WindowProc      @1
```

THE FONT2 APPLICATION FILE (FONT2.C):

```
/* Simplified Windows Platform (SWP)               */
/* (c) William H. Murray and Chris H. Pappas, 1989 */

#include <string.h>
#include <windows.h>

LONG FAR PASCAL WindowProc(HWND,unsigned,WORD,LONG);

char szProgName[]="ProgName";

int PASCAL WinMain(hInst,hPreInst,lpszCmdLine,nCmdShow)
HANDLE hInst,hPreInst;
LPSTR  lpszCmdLine;
int    nCmdShow;
{
  HWND hwnd;
  MSG  msg;
  WNDCLASS wcSwp;
  if (!hPreInst)
  {
    wcSwp.lpszClassName=szProgName;
    wcSwp.hInstance     =hInst;
```

```
    wcSwp.lpfnWndProc  =WindowProc;
    wcSwp.hCursor      =LoadCursor(hInst,IDC_ARROW);
    wcSwp.hIcon        =NULL;
    wcSwp.lpszMenuName =NULL;
    wcSwp.hbrBackground=GetStockObject(WHITE_BRUSH);
    wcSwp.style        =CS_HREDRAW¦CS_VREDRAW;
    wcSwp.cbClsExtra   =0;
    wcSwp.cbWndExtra   =0;
    if (!RegisterClass (&wcSwp))
      return FALSE;
  }
  hwnd=CreateWindow(szProgName,"Font Manipulations",
                    WS_OVERLAPPEDWINDOW,CW_USEDEFAULT,
                    CW_USEDEFAULT,CW_USEDEFAULT,
                    CW_USEDEFAULT,NULL,NULL,
                    hInst,NULL);
  ShowWindow(hwnd,nCmdShow);
  UpdateWindow(hwnd);
  while (GetMessage(&msg,NULL,NULL,NULL))
  {
    TranslateMessage(&msg);
    DispatchMessage(&msg);
  }
  return(msg.wParam);
}


long FAR PASCAL WindowProc(hwnd,messg,wParam,lParam)
HWND hwnd;
unsigned messg;
WORD wParam;
LONG lParam;
{
  HDC         hdc;
  PAINTSTRUCT ps;
  HFONT       hOFont,hNFont;
  static char szTextString[]="This is a text string.";
  short       nHeight,nWidth;

  switch (messg)
  {

    case WM_PAINT:
      hdc=BeginPaint(hwnd,&ps);

/*--------- your routines below ---------*/

      nHeight=10;
      nWidth=10;
      hNFont=CreateFont(nHeight,nWidth,0,0,FW_BOLD,
                        FALSE,FALSE,FALSE,
                        OEM_CHARSET,
                        OUT_DEFAULT_PRECIS,
                        CLIP_DEFAULT_PRECIS,
                        DEFAULT_QUALITY,
                        VARIABLE_PITCH¦FF_ROMAN,
                        "Roman");
      hOFont=SelectObject(hdc,hNFont);
      TextOut(hdc,0,50,szTextString,strlen(szTextString));
```

```
        nHeight=30;
        nWidth=30;
        hNFont=CreateFont(nHeight,nWidth,0,0,FW_BOLD,
                          FALSE,FALSE,FALSE,
                          OEM_CHARSET,
                          OUT_DEFAULT_PRECIS,
                          CLIP_DEFAULT_PRECIS,
                          DEFAULT_QUALITY,
                          VARIABLE_PITCH|FF_ROMAN,
                          "Roman");
        hOFont=SelectObject(hdc,hNFont);
        TextOut(hdc,0,100,szTextString,strlen(szTextString));

        nHeight=240;
        nWidth=60;
        hNFont=CreateFont(nHeight,nWidth,0,0,FW_BOLD,
                          FALSE,FALSE,FALSE,
                          OEM_CHARSET,
                          OUT_DEFAULT_PRECIS,
                          CLIP_DEFAULT_PRECIS,
                          DEFAULT_QUALITY,
                          VARIABLE_PITCH|FF_ROMAN,
                          "Roman");
        hOFont=SelectObject(hdc,hNFont);
        TextOut(hdc,0,200,szTextString,strlen(szTextString));

        SelectObject(hdc,hOFont);
        DeleteObject(hNFont);

/*--------- your routines above ---------*/

        ValidateRect(hwnd,NULL);
        EndPaint(hwnd,&ps);
        break;

      case WM_DESTROY:
        PostQuitMessage(0);
        break;

      default:
        return(DefWindowProc(hwnd,messg,wParam,lParam));
    }
    return(0L);
}
```

The FONT2 and FONT2.DEF Files

This program is compiled in the normal manner, as you can see from the FONT2 **MAKE** file listing. Again, the FONT2.DEF file is similar to previous listings. It contains one export statement: EXPORTS: WindowProc.

The FONT2.C File

In this program, three different type sizes are created by changing the height and width parameters in CreateFont. For the first string the height

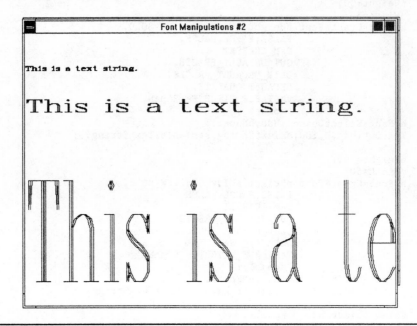

Figure 9-10.   Using CreateFont to change character heights and widths in the
FONT2 program

and width are both set to 10. For the second string they are both set to 30.
Finally, for the third string the height is set to 240 and the width to 60. The
output from this program is shown in Figure 9-10.

Having studied the last two examples, what would you say was the
greatest shortcoming of CreateFont? You would probably agree that it is
the parameter list itself, since it must be repeated for each font change.
Perhaps there is a better way of manipulating font parameters.

The FONT3 Program

This program will illustrate another approach to changing font parameters.
It will probably become a favorite method for applications that are "font
intensive." If you follow the complete development cycle, you will have
five files on disk when the **MAKE** utility is finished: FONT3, FONT3.DEF,
FONT3.C, FONT3.OBJ, and FONT3.EXE.

```
THE FONT3 MAKE FILE (FONT3):

ALL : font3.exe # ALL needed for C 6.0 up

font3.obj: font3.c
    cl -c -AS -Gsw -Oas -Zpe font3.c
```

```
font3.exe: font3.obj font3.def font3.res
    link /NOD font3,,,libw slibcew,font3.def
```

THE FONT3 DEFINITION FILE (FONT3.DEF):

```
;FONT3.DEF for C Compiling

NAME            Font3
DESCRIPTION     'Font Manipulations'
EXETYPE         WINDOWS
STUB            'WINSTUB.EXE'
CODE            PRELOAD MOVEABLE DISCARDABLE
DATA            PRELOAD MOVEABLE MULTIPLE
HEAPSIZE        4096
STACKSIZE       9216
EXPORTS         WindowProc      @1
```

THE FONT3 APPLICATION FILE (FONT3.C):

```
/* Simplified Windows Platform (SWP)            */
/* (c) William H. Murray and Chris H. Pappas, 1989 */

#include <string.h>
#include <windows.h>

LONG FAR PASCAL WindowProc(HWND,unsigned,WORD,LONG);

char szProgName[]="ProgName";

int PASCAL WinMain(hInst,hPreInst,lpszCmdLine,nCmdShow)
HANDLE hInst,hPreInst;
LPSTR  lpszCmdLine;
int    nCmdShow;
{
  HWND hwnd;
  MSG  msg;
  WNDCLASS wcSwp;
  if (!hPreInst)
  {
    wcSwp.lpszClassName=szProgName;
    wcSwp.hInstance    =hInst;
    wcSwp.lpfnWndProc  =WindowProc;
    wcSwp.hCursor      =LoadCursor(hInst,IDC_ARROW);
    wcSwp.hIcon        =NULL;
    wcSwp.lpszMenuName =NULL;
    wcSwp.hbrBackground=GetStockObject(WHITE_BRUSH);
    wcSwp.style        =CS_HREDRAW|CS_VREDRAW;
    wcSwp.cbClsExtra   =0;
    wcSwp.cbWndExtra   =0;
    if (!RegisterClass (&wcSwp))
      return FALSE;
  }
  hwnd=CreateWindow(szProgName,"Font Manipulations",
                    WS_OVERLAPPEDWINDOW,CW_USEDEFAULT,
                    CW_USEDEFAULT,CW_USEDEFAULT,
                    CW_USEDEFAULT,NULL,NULL,
                    hInst,NULL);
  ShowWindow(hwnd,nCmdShow);
  UpdateWindow(hwnd);
```

```
  while (GetMessage(&msg,NULL,NULL,NULL))
  {
    TranslateMessage(&msg);
    DispatchMessage(&msg);
  }
  return(msg.wParam);
}


long FAR PASCAL WindowProc(hwnd,messg,wParam,lParam)
HWND hwnd;
unsigned messg;
WORD wParam;
LONG lParam;
{
  HDC          hdc;
  static LOGFONT lf;
  PAINTSTRUCT ps;
  HFONT        hNFont;
  static char szTextString[]="This is a text string.";
  short        i,ypos;

  switch (messg)
  {

    case WM_PAINT:
      hdc=BeginPaint(hwnd,&ps);

/*--------- your routines below ---------*/

      lf.lfWeight=FW_HEAVY;
      lf.lfCharSet=OEM_CHARSET;
      lf.lfPitchAndFamily=FF_SCRIPT;
      ypos=0;

      for (i=1;i<10;i++)
      {
        lf.lfHeight=6+(6*i);
        hNFont=CreateFontIndirect(&lf);
        SelectObject(hdc,hNFont);
        TextOut(hdc,0,ypos,szTextString,
                strlen(szTextString));
        ypos+=10*i;
      }

/*--------- your routines above ---------*/

      ValidateRect(hwnd,NULL);
      EndPaint(hwnd,&ps);
      break;

    case WM_DESTROY:
      PostQuitMessage(0);
      break;

    default:
      return(DefWindowProc(hwnd,messg,wParam,lParam));
  }
  return(0L);
}
```

The FONT3 and FONT3.DEF Files

Once again, the FONT3 **MAKE** and definition files are identical to previous listings and warrant no additional explanation.

The FONT3.C File

As you examine the application portion of the listing, notice the declarations under WindowProc. First, a LOGFONT structure, *lf,* is declared. Additionally, *hNFont* is declared to be of type *HFONT,* as in the last two programs. The LOGFONT structure, described earlier in the chapter, can be accessed with normal C techniques. Notice which parameters are being changed in this example.

```
lf.lfWeight=FW_HEAVY;
lf.lfCharSet=OEM_CHARSET;
lf.lfPitchAndFamily=FF_SCRIPT;
```

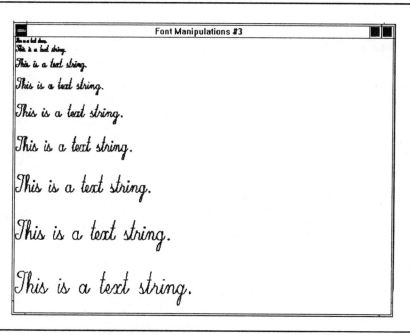

Figure 9-11.   Using CreateFontIndirect to create and manipulate a script font in the FONT3 program

In this example, several different sizes of Script font are created and placed on the screen. A simple *for* loop achieves the desired results. How many lines of code would have been required with CreateFont? Don't you like this technique better? Figure 9-11 shows the string in script as it appears in the window.

The FONT4 Program

In this last example, CreateFontIndirect is used to create a font that will print a string at a 45-degree angle on the screen.

If you follow the complete development cycle, you will have five files on disk when the **MAKE** utility is finished: FONT4, FONT4.DEF, FONT4.C, FONT4.OBJ, and FONT4.EXE.

```
THE FONT4 MAKE FILE (FONT4):

all : font4.exe

font4.obj: font4.c
    cl -c -AS -Gsw -Oas -Zpe font4.c

font4.exe: font4.obj font4.def font4.res
    link /NOD font4,,,libw slibcew, font4.def


THE FONT4 DEFINITION FILE (FONT4.DEF):

;FONT4.DEF for C Compiling

NAME            Font4
DESCRIPTION     'Font Manipulations'
EXETYPE         WINDOWS
STUB            'WINSTUB.EXE'
CODE            PRELOAD MOVEABLE DISCARDABLE
DATA            PRELOAD MOVEABLE MULTIPLE
HEAPSIZE        4096
STACKSIZE       9216
EXPORTS         WindowProc      @1


THE FONT4 APPLICATION FILE (FONT4.C):

/* Simplified Windows Platform (SWP)              */
/* (c) William H. Murray and Chris H. Pappas, 1989 */

#include <string.h>
#include <windows.h>

LONG FAR PASCAL WindowProc(HWND,unsigned,WORD,LONG);

char szProgName[]="ProgName";

int PASCAL WinMain(hInst,hPreInst,lpszCmdLine,nCmdShow)
HANDLE hInst,hPreInst;
LPSTR  lpszCmdLine;
int    nCmdShow;
{
```

```
       HWND hwnd;
       MSG  msg;
       WNDCLASS wcSwp;
       if (!hPreInst)
       {
         wcSwp.lpszClassName=szProgName;
         wcSwp.hInstance    =hInst;
         wcSwp.lpfnWndProc  =WindowProc;
         wcSwp.hCursor      =LoadCursor(hInst,IDC_ARROW);
         wcSwp.hIcon        =NULL;
         wcSwp.lpszMenuName =NULL;
         wcSwp.hbrBackground=GetStockObject(WHITE_BRUSH);
         wcSwp.style        =CS_HREDRAW|CS_VREDRAW;
         wcSwp.cbClsExtra   =0;
         wcSwp.cbWndExtra   =0;
         if (!RegisterClass (&wcSwp))
            return FALSE;
       }
       hwnd=CreateWindow(szProgName,"Font Manipulations",
                         WS_OVERLAPPEDWINDOW,CW_USEDEFAULT,
                         CW_USEDEFAULT,CW_USEDEFAULT,
                         CW_USEDEFAULT,NULL,NULL,
                         hInst,NULL);
       ShowWindow(hwnd,nCmdShow);
       UpdateWindow(hwnd);
       while (GetMessage(&msg,NULL,NULL,NULL))
       {
         TranslateMessage(&msg);
         DispatchMessage(&msg);
       }
       return(msg.wParam);
     }
     long FAR PASCAL WindowProc(hwnd,messg,wParam,lParam)
     HWND hwnd;
     unsigned messg;
     WORD wParam;
     LONG lParam;
     {
       HDC          hdc;
       static LOGFONT lf;
       PAINTSTRUCT ps;
       HFONT        hNFont;
       static char szTextString[]="This is a text string.";

       switch (messg)
       {

         case WM_PAINT:
           hdc=BeginPaint(hwnd,&ps);

/*--------- your routines below ---------*/

           lf.lfWeight=FW_HEAVY;
           lf.lfCharSet=OEM_CHARSET;
           lf.lfPitchAndFamily=FF_SCRIPT;
           lf.lfEscapement=450;
           lf.lfHeight=100;
           hNFont=CreateFontIndirect(&lf);
           SelectObject(hdc,hNFont);
           TextOut(hdc,10,380,szTextString,
                   strlen(szTextString));
```

```
/*--------- your routines above ---------*/

     ValidateRect(hwnd,NULL);
     EndPaint(hwnd,&ps);
     break;

   case WM_DESTROY:
     PostQuitMessage(0);
     break;

   default:
     return(DefWindowProc(hwnd,messg,wParam,lParam));
 }
 return(0L);
}
```

The FONT4 and FONT4.DEF Files

Enter the FONT4 **MAKE** and definition files as they are shown in the listing.

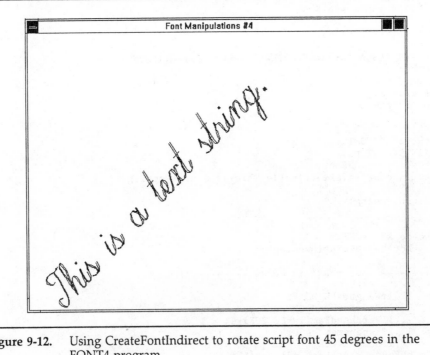

Figure 9-12.   Using CreateFontIndirect to rotate script font 45 degrees in the FONT4 program

The FONT4.C File

In this example, five parameters are changed in the LOGFONT data structure, *lf*.

```
lf.lfWeight=FW_HEAVY;
lf.lfCharSet=OEM_CHARSET;
lf.lfPitchAndFamily=FF_SCRIPT;
lf.lfEscapement=450;
lf.lfHeight=100;
```

Figure 9-12 shows the 45-degree angle text string.

MORE FANCY FONTS

The four programs in this chapter are only a preview of what can be done with custom fonts under Windows 3.0. Start with simple programs, like the previous examples, and change one or two parameters at a time. You will be amazed at how easy it is to create professional looking results with just a little effort. Many of the techniques developed in this chapter will be used in future chapters for printing labels on graphs and charts.

10

GRAPHICS CONCEPTS AND PRIMITIVES

In this chapter you will learn how to use the various graphics primitives for drawing basic shapes such as lines, circles, and arcs. The graphics primitives will then be utilized in more sophisticated programs to create various combinations of shapes on the user's screen.

THE GRAPHICS DEVICE INTERFACE (GDI)

The graphics device interface (GDI) is the Windows code module that manages graphics instructions. This interface contains a large number of graphics functions, capable of drawing dots, lines, rectangles, arcs, ellipses, circles, and so on. The GDI is also responsible for translating these graphics commands for all output device drivers, including monitors, printers, and plotters. As such, the GDI is a device-independent interface. Thus, graphics programs that adhere to the Windows standards will run on any installed printer, plotter, or graphics display.

This chapter will introduce you to the basic concepts of using the GDI. You will learn much of the basic terminology used in association with the GDI environment. Graphics primitives will be introduced for drawing basic shapes, along with many pieces of example code. As the chapter progresses, you will learn how to tie these building blocks together to create simple graphics screens.

The Purpose of the GDI

The GDI determines from the list of installed drivers how to interface with the various hardware items installed with the computer system. For example, raster devices, such as monochrome and color monitors, must be handled differently than vector devices, such as plotters. Even among display monitors, further differentiation must be considered because of resolution, color, and aspect ratios. This device-independent environment gives Windows (3.0 and later versions) the portability that many programming languages cannot offer, along with the ability to perform powerful pixel manipulations.

The GDI environment is limited in some areas. For example, the GDI lacks the built-in ability to directly produce three-dimensional images, rotate objects, and animate screens. If these effects are desired they will have to be programmed manually. Rotations, for instance, are possible by applying mathematical transformations. Simple animation is possible with a technique that involves erasing and redrawing the figure.

One of the GDI's most important features is its close parallel to the OS/2 Presentation Manager environment. Concepts learned under Windows 3.0 will be very easy to extend into this powerful operating system.

Operating with Pixels

The GDI operates, by default, in a pixel coordinate mode (text mode). It obtains information about the device driver and adjusts its graphics output to produce a figure in the correct aspect ratio and in the correct resolution for the hardware device. Seven other *mapping modes* are available for mapping in metric, English, and user-defined units. These will be discussed shortly. Many of the programs in this chapter and in later chapters have been developed for the VGA screen using the default pixel mode, MM_TEXT. As such, the pixel ranges used to define various shapes will be from 0 to 639 pixels horizontally, and from 0 to 479 pixels vertically. However, these programs are still portable and the GDI will make the necessary adjustments when using other installed hardware devices.

Device Information

Information regarding the installed hardware that the GDI must contend with can be obtained by using the GetDeviceCaps function. This function returns information on 24 hardware device attributes, including horizontal and vertical resolutions, aspect ratios, color planes, and so forth.

```
GetDeviceCaps(hdc,nIndex);
```

The index value, *nIndex,* is a *short* that specifies the item to return. GetDeviceCaps returns a type *short.* Table 10-1 gives a description of these attributes.

Also included in this arsenal of information are details on built-in hardware capabilities, such as a device's ability to draw ellipses, pie wedges, circles, and so on, without the help of the GDI. If the hardware device does not have these abilities Windows will provide an equivalent software routine through the GDI.

The IBM VGA display, for example, has a horizontal size of 240 millimeters, and a vertical size of 180 millimeters. This produces a horizontal and vertical aspect of 36, which means that ten dots drawn in either direction will produce lines of the same length.

In the default mapping mode, the GDI has its origin in the upper-left part of the window. The X axis increases positively to the right and the Y axis positively downward, as shown in Figure 10-1.

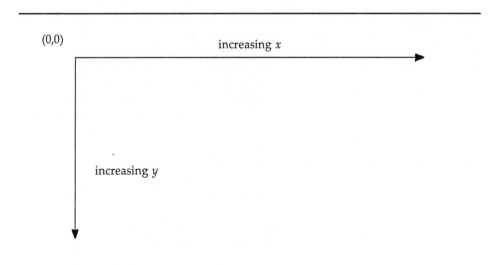

Figure 10-1.   The default Windows 3.0 coordinate system

Table 10-1. Device-Specific Information Returned by GetDeviceCaps

Index	Meaning
DRIVERVERSION	Version Number
TECHNOLOGY	0 — vector plotter
	1 — raster display
	2 — raster printer
	3 — raster camera
	4 — character stream
	5 — metafile
	6 — display file
HORSIZE	Width of display in millimeters
VERTSIZE	Height of display in millimeters
HORZRES	Width of display in pixels
VERTRES	Height of display in pixels
BITSPIXEL	Number of adjacent color bits per pixel
PLANES	Number of color planes
NUMBRUSHES	Number of brushes
NUMPENS	Number of pens
NUMMARKERS	Number of markers
NUMFONTS	Number of fonts
NUMCOLORS	Number of entries in color table
ASPECTX	Relative width of pixel
ASPECTY	Relative height of pixel
ASPECTXY	Relative diagonal width of pixel
PDEVICESIZE	Size of PDEVICE data structure
CLIPCAPS	1 — can clip to a rectangle
	0 — cannot clip to a rectangle
RASTERCAPS	RC _ BANDING — requires banding support
	RC _ BITBLT — bitmap support
	RC _ BITMAP64 — bitmap support > 64K
	RC _ GDI20 _ OUTPUT — support for Windows 2.0
	RC _ SCALING — can scale
CURVECAPS	0 — able to draw circles
	1 — able to draw pie wedges
	2 — able to draw chord arcs
	3 — able to draw ellipses
	4 — able to draw wide borders
	5 — able to draw styled borders

Table 10-1.   Device-Specific Information Returned by GetDeviceCaps (*continued*)

Index	Meaning
	6 — able to draw wide and styled borders
	7 — able to do interiors
LINECAPS	0 — not used
	1 — able to draw a polyline
	2 — not used
	3 — not used
	4 — able to draw wide lines
	5 — able to draw styled lines
	6 — able to draw wide styled lines
	7 — able to do interiors
POLYGONALCAPS	0 — able to create alternate fill polygon
	1 — able to draw a rectangle
	2 — able to create winding fill polygon
	3 — able to draw scanline
	4 — able to draw wide borders
	5 — able to draw styled borders
	6 — able to draw wide styled borders
	7 — able to draw interiors
TEXTCAPS	0 — able to do character output precision
	1 — able to do stroke output precision
	2 — able to do stroke clip precision
	3 — able to rotate characters 90 degrees
	4 — able to do any character rotation
	5 — able to do independent scaling
	6 — able to do double character scaling
	7 — able to do integer multiple scaling
	8 — able to do any multiple scaling
	9 — able to do double-weight characters
	10 — able to italicize
	11 — able to underline
	12 — able to strike out
	13 — able to use raster fonts
	14 — able to use vector fonts
	15 — not used (0)
LOGPIXELSX	Pixels/inch in X direction
LOGPIXELSY	Pixels/inch in Y direction

Obtaining the Device Context Handle

All GDI graphics functions require a handle to a device context. The technique used most frequently in this book is to obtain the handle from the BeginPaint function.

```
hdc=BeginPaint(hwnd,&ps);
```

In this case, *hwnd* is the handle of the current window and *&ps* is a structure of type PAINTSTRUCT, as described in the WINDOWS.H header file.

```
typedef struct tagPAINTSTRUCT {
    HDC  hdc;
    BOOL fErase;
    RECT rcPaint;
    BOOL fRestore;
    BOOL fIncUpdate;
    BYTE rgbReserved[16];
} PAINTSTRUCT;
```

The device context handle, *hdc*, is actually returned from the PAINT-STRUCT structure. PAINTSTRUCT allows drawing only on a valid region of the screen. The invalid region is described by the *rcPaint* structure, which is of type *RECT*.

```
typedef struct tagRECT {
    int left;
    int top;
    int right;
    int bottom;
} RECT;
```

Painting is completed in a window with a call to the EndPaint function.

```
EndPaint(hwnd,&ps);
```

For every BeginPaint function call there should be a corresponding call to the EndPaint function.

Mapping Modes

All the GDI graphics functions are dependent on the selected mapping mode. As mentioned earlier, the default mapping mode, MM_TEXT, measures point values in pixels. Table 10-2 shows the mapping modes.

If you want to change the default mapping mode, it can be done with the SetMapMode function.

```
SetMapMode(hdc,nMapMode);
```

The parameter, *nMapMode,* is of type *short* and is specified by one of the eight value types shown in Table 10-2. The function returns a type *short.*

Regardless of the mapping mode selected, it is Windows' responsibility to map the given logical coordinates to device coordinates.

GDI DRAWING PRIMITIVES

Starting with Windows 3.0, Microsoft has provided an environment rich in graphical functions. The world outside this operating environment is not always so friendly. Assembly language programmers, for example, only have two basic graphics primitives—draw dot and read dot. From there

Table 10-2.   Mapping Modes

Value	Meaning
MM_ANISOTROPIC	Arbitrary units with arbitrarily scaled axes
MM_HIENGLISH	Logical unit mapped to 0.001 inch; positive X is to the right, positive Y is up
MM_HIMETRIC	Logical unit mapped to 0.01 millimeter; positive X is to the right, positive Y is up
MM_ISOTROPIC	Arbitrary units with equally scaled axes
MM_LOMETRIC	Logical unit mapped to 0.1 millimeter; positive X is to the right, positive Y is up
MM_LOENGLISH	Logical unit mapped to 0.01 inch; positive X is to the right, positive Y is up
MM_TEXT	Logical unit mapped to device pixel; positive X is to the right, positive Y is down
MM_TWIPS	Logical unit mapped to 1/20 of printer's point; positive X is to the right, positive Y is up

they must write their own line, box, and circle functions. Programmers specializing in high-level languages have had it a little easier. BASIC, C, and Pascal, for example, contain many powerful graphics functions. Unfortunately, these functions do not necessarily extend from language to language. Thus, BASIC's rectangle function syntax is not necessarily the same as that of Pascal.

Windows provides a consistent and complete graphics environment. Program developers must adhere to the programming constraints and guidelines of this environment. As a result, once you learn how to use the various GDI functions they will always work the same way for you and all other programmers.

Graphics primitives are the building blocks of all other graphics drawing functions. They are not "cake mixes" of graphics, but the raw materials: flour, sugar, and eggs. These primitives are the foundation on which all graphics programs, small and great, rise.

Graphics Primitives

There are numerous primitive categories. Most of these categories are composed of only one function. The most often-used categories include routines for drawing arcs, chords, ellipses, lines, pie wedges, polygons, polylines, rectangles, rectangles with rounded corners and single pixels, and for setting cursor positions. Many of these same functions have been extended into the OS/2 Presentation Manager environment, making their mastery even more of a prize. All functions are drawn with the current pen and, where applicable, filled with the current brush. Additional details on pen and brush selections are included in the next section.

The Arc Function

Arc is used to draw an elliptical arc. The center of the arc is also the center of an imaginary rectangle described by the points $x1,y1$ and $x2,y2$, as shown in Figure 10-2. The actual length of the arc is described as lying between points $x3,y3$ and $x4,y4$, with the drawing performed in a counterclockwise direction. An arc is not filled since it is not a closed figure. The handle for the device context is given by *hdc*. All other parameters are of type *short*. This function returns a type *bool*.

The syntax for the command is

Arc(hdc,x1,y1,x2,y2,x3,y3,x4,y4)

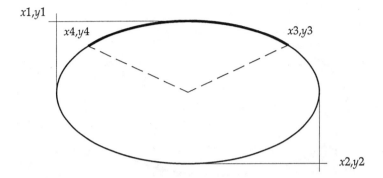

Figure 10-2.   Variables used by the Arc function

For example, the following line of code will draw a small arc in the user's window:

```
Arc(hdc,100,100,200,200,150,175,175,150);
```

The Chord Function

Chord is identical to the Arc function, with the added feature that the figure is closed by a line between the two arc points $x3,y3$ and $x4,y4$. Figure 10-3 shows these points. A chord is filled with the current brush since it is a closed figure. The handle for the device context is given by *hdc*. All other parameters are of type *short*. This function returns a type *bool*.

The syntax for the command is

Chord(hdc,x1,y1,x2,y2,x3,y3,x4,y4)

For example, the following line of code will draw a small chord in the user's window:

```
Chord(hdc,550,20,630,80,555,25,625,70);
```

The Ellipse (and Circle) Function

Ellipse is used to draw an ellipse. The center of the ellipse is also the center of an imaginary rectangle described by the points $x1,y1$ and $x2,y2$, as

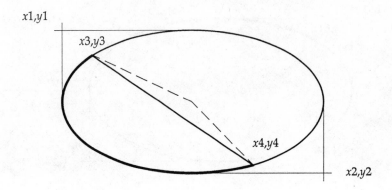

Figure 10-3.   Variables used by the Chord function

shown in Figure 10-4. An ellipse is filled since it is a closed figure. The handle for the device context is given by *hdc*. All other parameters are of type *short*. This function returns a type *bool*.

The syntax for the command is

Ellipse(hdc,x1,y1,x2,y2)

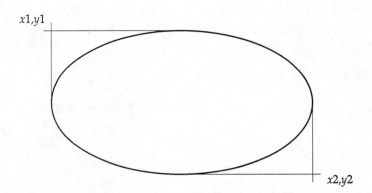

Figure 10-4.   Variables used by the Ellipse function

For example, the following line of code will draw a small ellipse in the user's window:

```
Ellipse(hdc,200,200,275,250);
```

A special case of the ellipse specifies a circle when the boundary rectangle is a square. The following code will draw a circle:

```
Ellipse(hdc,400,200,550,350);
```

The LineTo Function

LineTo draws a line from the current point up to, but not including, the specified point. The current point can be set with the MoveTo function. The current point will be *x,y* when the function is successful. The handle for the device context is given by *hdc*. All other parameters are of type *short*. This function returns a type *bool*.

The syntax for the command is

LineTo(hdc,x,y)

The following lines of code will draw a diagonal line in the user's window:

```
MoveTo(hdc,300,300);
LineTo(hdc,640,430);
```

The MoveTo Function

MoveTo moves the current point to the specified point. The handle for the device context is given by *hdc*. All other parameters are of type *short*. This function returns a type *dword*. The Y coordinate is returned in the high-order word of the double word, while the X coordinate is returned in the low-order word.

The syntax for the command is

MoveTo(hdc,x,y)

The following line of code illustrates the use of this function:

```
MoveTo(hdc,10,50);
```

The Pie Function

Pie is used to draw pie-shaped wedges. The center of the elliptical arc is also the center of an imaginary rectangle described by the points $x1,y1$ and $x2,y2$, as shown in Figure 10-5. The starting and ending points of the arc are points $x3,y3$ and $x4,y4$. Two lines are drawn from each end point to the center of the rectangle in a counterclockwise direction. The pie wedge is filled since it is a closed figure. The handle for the device context is given by *hdc*. All other parameters are of type *short*. This function returns a type *bool*.

The syntax for the command is

Pie(hdc,x1,y1,x2,y2,x3,y3,x4,y4)

For example, the following line of code will draw a small pie-shaped wedge in the user's window:

```
Pie(hdc,300,50,400,150,300,50,300,100);
```

The Polygon Function

Polygon draws a polygon that consists of points connected by lines. How the lines are drawn is dependent on the filling mode. In *alternate* mode

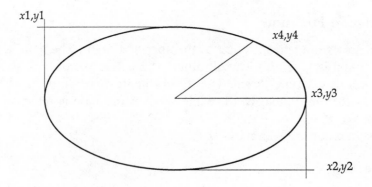

Figure 10-5.   Variables used by the Pie function

lines are drawn from the first point to the last. In *winding* mode the points are used to calculate a border; then the border is drawn. Both modes use the current pen for drawing and the current brush for filling. The polygon is filled since it is a closed figure, as shown in Figure 10-6. The handle for the device context is given by *hdc*. The location of the data points is held in an array of type *POINT* in the example that follows. The number of points in the array is a *short*. This function returns a type *bool*.

The syntax for the command is

Polygon(hdc,pointarray,#points)

As an example, the following lines of code will draw a polygon in the user's window:

```
polygpts[0].x=40;
polygpts[0].y=200;
polygpts[1].x=100;
polygpts[1].y=270;
polygpts[2].x=80;
polygpts[2].y=290;
polygpts[3].x=20;
polygpts[3].y=220;
polygpts[4].x=40;
polygpts[4].y=200;
Polygon(hdc,polygpts,5);
```

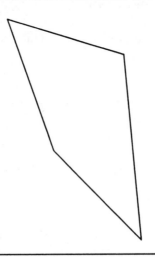

Figure 10-6.   An example of a closed polygon

The Polyline Function

Polyline draws a group of connected line segments given in a type *POINT* array. This function behaves like multiple MoveTo and LineTo calls, except that the position of the starting point is not changed. The polyline shape is not filled. The handle for the device context is given by *hdc*. The location of the data points is held in an array of type *POINT* in the example that follows. The number of points in the array is a *short*. This function returns a type *bool*.

The syntax for the command is

Polyline(hdc,pointarray,#points)

As an example, the following lines of code will draw a polyline figure in the user's window:

```
polylpts[0].x=10;
polylpts[0].y=30;
polylpts[1].x=10;
polylpts[1].y=100;
polylpts[2].x=50;
polylpts[2].y=100;
polylpts[3].x=10;
polylpts[3].y=30;
Polyline(hdc,polylpts,4);
```

The Rectangle Function

Rectangle draws a rectangle or box described by *x1,y1* and *x2,y2*. The rectangle is filled since it is a closed figure. The values for the parameters cannot exceed 32,767 (7FFFH). The handle for the device context is given by *hdc*. All other parameters are of type *short*. This function returns a type *bool*.

The syntax for the command is

Rectangle(hdc,x1,y1,x2,y2)

As an example, the following line of code will draw a rectangular figure in the user's window:

```
Rectangle(hdc,50,300,150,400);
```

The RoundRect Function

RoundRect draws a rectangle or box, with rounded corners, described by *x1,y1* and *x2,y2*. The parameters *x3* and *y3* specify the width and height of the ellipse used to round the corners. The rounded rectangle is filled since it is a closed figure. The values for the parameters cannot exceed 32,767 (7FFFH). The handle for the device context is given by *hdc*. All other parameters are of type *short*. This function returns a type *bool*.

The syntax for the function is

RoundRect(hdc,x1,y1,x2,y2,x3,y3)

As an example, the following line of code will draw a rectangular figure in the user's window:

```
RoundRect(hdc,60,310,110,350,20,20);
```

The SetPixel and GetPixel Functions

SetPixel is used to light a pixel at the location specified by x and y. It will select the RGB color closest to that requested. The handle for the device context is given by *hdc*. The x and y parameters are of type *short*. Color is of type *dword*. This function returns a type *dword*.

The syntax for the function is

SetPixel(hdc,x,y,Color)

As an example, the following line of code will light one pixel in the user's window:

```
SetPixel(hdc,40,150,240L);
```

GetPixel retrieves the RGB color value at the specified point and returns it as a *dword*.

The syntax for GetPixel is

GetPixel(hdc,x,y)

Drawing with GDI Primitives

The following program illustrates the various graphics primitives just discussed. Study the program listing and identify the values used for each figure.

```
THE GDI1 MAKE FILE:

all : gdi1.exe

gdi1.obj: gdi1.c
    cl -c -AS -Gsw -Oas -Zpe gdi1.c

gdi1.exe: gdi1.obj gdi1.def gdi1.res
    link /NOD gdi1,,,libw slibcew, gdi1.def
```

THE GDI1.DEF DEFINITION FILE:

```
NAME        GDI1
DESCRIPTION 'Simplified Windows Platform'
EXETYPE     WINDOWS
STUB        'WINSTUB.EXE'
CODE        PRELOAD MOVEABLE DISCARDABLE
DATA        PRELOAD MOVEABLE MULTIPLE
HEAPSIZE    4096
STACKSIZE   9216
EXPORTS     WindowProc        @1
```

THE GDI1.C APPLICATION FILE:

```c
/* Simplified Windows Platform (SWP)          */
/* (c) William H. Murray and Chris H. Pappas, 1989 */

#include <windows.h>

long FAR PASCAL WindowProc(HWND,unsigned,WORD,LONG);

char    szProgName[]="ProgName";

int PASCAL WinMain(hInst,hPreInst,lpszCmdLine,nCmdShow)
HANDLE hInst,hPreInst;
LPSTR  lpszCmdLine;
int    nCmdShow;
{
  HWND hwnd;
  MSG  msg;
  WNDCLASS wcSwp;
  if (!hPreInst)
  {
    wcSwp.lpszClassName=szProgName;
    wcSwp.hInstance     =hInst;
    wcSwp.lpfnWndProc   =WindowProc;
    wcSwp.hCursor       =LoadCursor(NULL,IDC_ARROW);
    wcSwp.hIcon         =LoadIcon(hInst,szProgName);
    wcSwp.lpszMenuName  =NULL;
    wcSwp.hbrBackground =GetStockObject(WHITE_BRUSH);
    wcSwp.style         =CS_HREDRAW|CS_VREDRAW;
    wcSwp.cbClsExtra    =0;
    wcSwp.cbWndExtra    =0;
    if (!RegisterClass (&wcSwp))
      return FALSE;
  }
  hwnd=CreateWindow(szProgName,"GDI Graphics Primitives",
                    WS_OVERLAPPEDWINDOW,CW_USEDEFAULT,
                    CW_USEDEFAULT,CW_USEDEFAULT,
                    CW_USEDEFAULT,NULL,NULL,
                    hInst,NULL);
  ShowWindow(hwnd,nCmdShow);
  UpdateWindow(hwnd);
  while (GetMessage(&msg,NULL,NULL,NULL))
  {
    TranslateMessage(&msg);
    DispatchMessage(&msg);
  }
  return(msg.wParam);
}
```

```
long FAR PASCAL WindowProc(hwnd,messg,wParam,lParam)
HWND    hwnd;
unsigned messg;
WORD    wParam;
LONG    lParam;
{
  PAINTSTRUCT ps;
  HDC    hdc;
  short xcoord;
  POINT polylpts[4],polygpts[5];

  switch (messg)
  {
    case WM_PAINT:
      hdc=BeginPaint(hwnd,&ps);

/*--------- your routines below ---------*/

      /* draw a diagonal line */
      MoveTo(hdc,0,0);
      LineTo(hdc,640,430);
      TextOut(hdc,55,20,"<-diagonal line",15);

      /* draws an arc */
      Arc(hdc,100,100,200,200,150,175,175,150);
      TextOut(hdc,80,180,"small arc->",11);

      /* draw a chord */
      Chord(hdc,550,20,630,80,555,25,625,70);
      TextOut(hdc,485,30,"chord->",7);

      /* draw an ellipse */
      Ellipse(hdc,200,200,275,250);
      TextOut(hdc,210,215,"ellipse",7);

      /* draw a circle with ellipse function */
      Ellipse(hdc,400,200,550,350);
      TextOut(hdc,450,265,"circle",6);

      /* draw a pie wedge */
      Pie(hdc,300,50,400,150,300,50,300,100);
      TextOut(hdc,350,80,"<-pie wedge",11);

      /* draw a rectangle */
      Rectangle(hdc,50,300,150,400);
      TextOut(hdc,160,350,"<-rectangle",11);

      /* draw rounded rectangle */
      RoundRect(hdc,60,310,110,350,20,20);
      TextOut (hdc,120,310,"<------rounded rectangle",24);

      /* set several pixels on screen to red */
      for(xcoord=400;xcoord<450;xcoord+=5)
        SetPixel(hdc,xcoord,150,0L);
      TextOut(hdc,455,145,"<-pixels",8);

      /* drawing several lines with polyline */
      polylpts[0].x=10;
      polylpts[0].y=30;
```

```
        polylpts[1].x=10;
        polylpts[1].y=100;
        polylpts[2].x=50;
        polylpts[2].y=100;
        polylpts[3].x=10;
        polylpts[3].y=30;
        Polyline(hdc,polylpts,4);
        TextOut(hdc,10,110,"polyline",8);

        /* drawing with polygon */
        polygpts[0].x=40;
        polygpts[0].y=200;
        polygpts[1].x=100;
        polygpts[1].y=270;
        polygpts[2].x=80;
        polygpts[2].y=290;
        polygpts[3].x=20;
        polygpts[3].y=220;
        polygpts[4].x=40;
        polygpts[4].y=200;
        Polygon(hdc,polygpts,5);
        TextOut(hdc,70,210,"<-polygon",9);

/*--------- your routines above ---------*/

        ValidateRect(hwnd,NULL);
        EndPaint(hwnd,&ps);
        break;
    case WM_DESTROY:
        PostQuitMessage(0);
        break;
    default:
        return(DefWindowProc(hwnd,messg,wParam,lParam));
        break;
    }
    return(0L);
}
```

The various shapes are shown and labeled in Figure 10-7.

A Simple Bar Chart

A more practical use of graphics primitives can be found in the development of business and scientific graphs. In this section a very simple bar graph will be drawn with the MoveTo, LineTo, and Rectangle functions. Study the listing and observe how each bar was created.

```
THE GDI2 MAKE FILE:

all : gdi2.exe

gdi2.obj: gdi2.c
    cl -c -AS -Gsw -Oas -Zpe gdi2.c

gdi2.exe: gdi2.obj gdi2.def gdi2.res
    link /NOD gdi2,,,libw slibcew, gdi2.def

THE GDI2.DEF DEFINITION FILE:
```

```
NAME        GDI2
DESCRIPTION 'Simplified Windows Platform'
EXETYPE     WINDOWS
STUB        'WINSTUB.EXE'
CODE        PRELOAD MOVEABLE DISCARDABLE
DATA        PRELOAD MOVEABLE MULTIPLE
HEAPSIZE    4096
STACKSIZE   9216
EXPORTS     WindowProc       @1
```

THE GDI2.C APPLICATION FILE:

```c
/* Simplified Windows Platform (SWP)            */
/* (c) William H. Murray and Chris H. Pappas, 1989 */

#include <windows.h>

long FAR PASCAL WindowProc(HWND,unsigned,WORD,LONG);

char    szProgName[]="ProgName";

int PASCAL WinMain(hInst,hPreInst,lpszCmdLine,nCmdShow)
HANDLE hInst,hPreInst;
LPSTR  lpszCmdLine;
int    nCmdShow;
{
  HWND hwnd;
  MSG  msg;
  WNDCLASS wcSwp;
  if (!hPreInst)
  {
    wcSwp.lpszClassName=szProgName;
    wcSwp.hInstance     =hInst;
    wcSwp.lpfnWndProc   =WindowProc;
    wcSwp.hCursor       =LoadCursor(NULL,IDC_ARROW);
    wcSwp.hIcon         =LoadIcon(hInst,szProgName);
    wcSwp.lpszMenuName  =NULL;
    wcSwp.hbrBackground=GetStockObject(WHITE_BRUSH);
    wcSwp.style         =CS_HREDRAW|CS_VREDRAW;
    wcSwp.cbClsExtra    =0;
    wcSwp.cbWndExtra    =0;
    if (!RegisterClass (&wcSwp))
      return FALSE;
  }
  hwnd=CreateWindow(szProgName,"GDI Graphics Primitives",
                    WS_OVERLAPPEDWINDOW,CW_USEDEFAULT,
                    CW_USEDEFAULT,CW_USEDEFAULT,
                    CW_USEDEFAULT,NULL,NULL,
                    hInst,NULL);
  ShowWindow(hwnd,nCmdShow);
  UpdateWindow(hwnd);
  while (GetMessage(&msg,NULL,NULL,NULL))
  {
    TranslateMessage(&msg);
    DispatchMessage(&msg);
  }
  return(msg.wParam);
}

long FAR PASCAL WindowProc(hwnd,messg,wParam,lParam)
HWND    hwnd;
```

```
unsigned messg;
WORD    wParam;
LONG    lParam;
{
   PAINTSTRUCT ps;
   HDC  hdc;

   switch (messg)
   {
     case WM_PAINT:
       hdc=BeginPaint(hwnd,&ps);

/*--------- your routines below ---------*/

        /* draw x & y coordinate axes */
        MoveTo(hdc,99,49);
        LineTo(hdc,99,350);
        LineTo(hdc,500,350);

        /* draw four bars on graph */
        Rectangle(hdc,100,350,200,200);
        Rectangle(hdc,200,350,300,150);
        Rectangle(hdc,300,350,400,250);
        Rectangle(hdc,400,350,500,75);

/*--------- your routines above ---------*/

        ValidateRect(hwnd,NULL);
        EndPaint(hwnd,&ps);
        break;
     case WM_DESTROY:
       PostQuitMessage(0);
       break;
     default:
       return(DefWindowProc(hwnd,messg,wParam,lParam));
       break;
   }
   return(0L);
}
```

Figure 10-8 shows the basic bar chart. In the next section you will learn how this "vanilla" bar chart can be individualized by filling the bars with different colors and crosshatched patterns.

GDI TOOLS

Windows provides an environment rich in graphical tools. Stock tools can be chosen, or special tools can be designed for a particular application. Stock brushes and pens are described in the WINDOWS.H header file

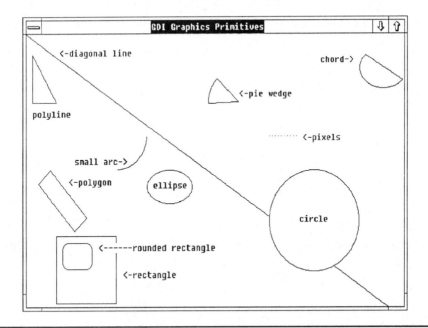

Figure 10-7.   Several primitive shapes

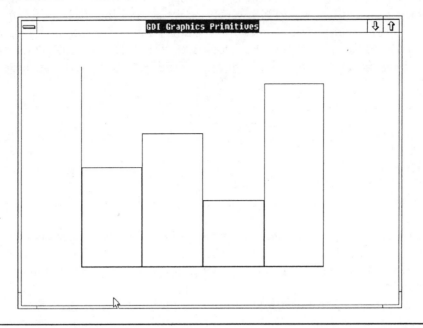

Figure 10-8.   A very simple bar chart

supplied with the Microsoft Windows Software Development Kit. If you have not printed a copy of this file for your own use, you should do so now. Stock brushes and pens include

WHITE_BRUSH
LTGRAY_BRUSH
GRAY_BRUSH
DKGRAY_BRUSH
BLACK_BRUSH
HOLLOW_BRUSH (or NULL_BRUSH)
WHITE_PEN
BLACK_PEN
NULL_PEN

In the next sections you will learn how to select stock pens and brushes and how to create custom pens and brushes with dazzling colors.

Using Pens

Pens are used to draw the outlines for all GDI graphics functions. Pens can be specified with three attributes—color, style, and width. The default pen is a black pen (BLACK_PEN), which draws a solid line (PS_SOLID), one device pixel wide. Other stock pen color choices include a white pen (WHITE_PEN) and a pen that does not draw (NULL_PEN), which is useful for drawing figures without an outline. Stock line styles include the following:

PS_SOLID   _____
PS_DASH   ---------
PS_DOT   . . . .
PS_DASHDOT   _._._._._
PS_DASHDOTDOT   _.._.._..
PS_NULL

Line widths are specified in logical units as integer numbers. Thus, a width of 10 in the default mode, MM_TEXT, will draw a line ten pixels wide. All pens greater than one logical unit default to either a null or solid line style.

Pens are referenced with the use of a handle of type *HPEN*. Stock pens can be obtained with the GetStockObject function. To change the pen just selected to the current pen, the SelectObject function is used.

```
HPEN       hPen;

hPen=SelectObject(hdc,GetStockObject(WHITE_PEN));
```

The creation of customized pens is done a little differently. A custom pen can be created and selected with the CreatePen function in conjunction with the SelectObject function. The CreatePen function creates a logical pen with the syntax

CreatePen(nPenStyle,nWidth,rgbColor);

The parameter, *nPenStyle*, is a type *short* and can be specified by any of the values given earlier, for example, PS_SOLID. The value, *nWidth,* is also of type *short* and is described in logical units. The value, *rgbColor*, is a *DWORD* given in terms of a RGB color value, for example:

```
hPenRed=SelectObject(CreatePen(PS_SOLID,
                 2,RGB(255,0,0)));
```

In this case a pen will be created and selected for drawing solid lines, 2 pixels wide, in red. By carefully combining RGB values, a wide variety of colors can be obtained, for example:

RGB(0,0,0)   = a black pen
RGB(255,255,255)   = a white pen
RGB(255,0,0)   = a red pen
RGB(0,255,0)   = a green pen
RGB(0,0,255)   = a blue pen
RGB(255,0,255)   = a magenta pen
RGB(255,255,0)   = a yellow pen
RGB(0,255,255)   = a cyan pen

As mentioned, the RGB value is a *DWORD* that if specified as a hexadecimal value, would range from 0x00000000 to 0x00FFFFFF. For monochrome screens, hexadecimal values less than 800000H will default to a black pen, while larger values will default to white.

Once a pen is selected, only that pen can be used to draw within the device context. In order to use another pen, the first must be deselected. This is done by calling the DeleteObject function, for example:

```
DeleteObject(hPenRed);
```

Stock pens should not be deleted.

If multiple pens are desired in a program, they can all be created at the same time and selected individually. When the drawing is complete, the entire group can be deleted.

Using Brushes

Brushes are used to fill the closed figures created with GDI graphics functions. Brushes can be specified with several attributes, including colors, brush styles, and hatch styles. The default brush is a white brush (WHITE_BRUSH) filling the object with a solid pattern (BS_SOLID). "Solid" used in this sense refers to the fill pattern used by the brush, not the "purity" of the color. Other stock brush color choices include LTGRAY_BRUSH, GRAY_BRUSH, DKGRAY_BRUSH, BLACK_BRUSH, and HOLLOW_BRUSH or NULL_BRUSH. The colors of these stock brushes are achieved by dithering. Dithering produces shades of colors. On a monochrome screen, gray shades are obtained by using an 8×8 block of pixels, where the number of black and white pixels is varied. Varying the number of black and white dots creates the illusion of different shades. A large palette of colors can be obtained in a similar manner. Stock fill patterns include

BS_SOLID	Fill is color of brush
BS_HOLLOW (BS_NULL)	Color of brush ignored
BS_HATCHED	Hatch is color of brush
BS_PATTERN	Color of brush ignored
BS_INDEXED	

If cross-hatching is requested, it can be selected from the following group of hatch patterns:

HS_HORIZONTAL	-----
HS_VERTICAL	|||||
HS_FDIAGONAL	//////
HS_BDIAGONAL	\\\\\
HS_CROSS	+ + + + +
HS_DIAGCROSS	xxxxx

Brushes are referenced with the use of a handle of type *HBRUSH*. Stock brushes can be obtained with the GetStockObject function. To change the brush just selected to the current brush, the SelectObject function is used.

```
HBRUSH      hBrush;

hBrush=SelectObject(hdc,GetStockObject(LTGRAY_BRUSH));
```

The creation of customized brushes is a little different. A custom brush can be created and selected with the CreateSolidBrush or CreateHatch-Brush function used in conjunction with the SelectObject function. The function syntax is

```
hGBrush=SelectObject(hdc,CreateSolidBrush(RGB(0,225,0)));
                 (a green brush)

hRHBrush=SelectObject(hdc,CreateHatchBrush(HS_CROSS,
          RGB(225,0,0)));
                 (a red hatched brush)
```

RGB colors can be mixed in the following ways:

RGB(0,0,0)	= a black brush
RGB(255,255,255)	= a white brush
RGB(255,0,0)	= a red brush
RGB(0,255,0)	= a green brush
RGB(0,0,255)	= a blue brush
RGB(255,0,255)	= a magenta brush
RGB(255,255,0)	= a yellow brush
RGB(0,255,255)	= a cyan brush

As mentioned, the RGB value is a *DWORD* that if specified as a hexadecimal value, would range from 0x00000000 to 0x00FFFFFF. For monochrome screens, hexadecimal values less than 800000H will default to a black brush, while larger values will default to white.

Once a brush is selected, only that brush can be used to fill objects within the device context. In order to use another brush, the first must be deselected. This is done by calling the DeleteObject function, for example:

```
DeleteObject(hGBrush);
```

Stock brushes are not deleted.

If multiple brushes are desired in a program, they can all be created at the same time and selected individually. When the drawing is complete, the entire group of brushes can be deleted.

The Simple Bar Chart—Again

The bar chart shown earlier in the chapter lacked definition. The bars were merely outlines, drawn with a pen. (Actually, they were filled with a white brush.) Now, let's alter the basic code to produce several different brushes and fill each bar differently. Examine the code and notice how each brush was created, used, and deleted.

THE GDI3 MAKE FILE:

```
all : gdi3.exe

gdi3.obj: gdi3.c
    cl -c -AS -Gsw -Oas -Zpe gdi3.c

gdi3.exe: gdi3.obj gdi3.def gdi3.res
    link /NOD gdi3,,,libw slibcew, gdi3.def
```

THE GDI3.DEF DEFINITION FILE:

```
NAME        GDI3
DESCRIPTION 'Simplified Windows Platform'
EXETYPE     WINDOWS
STUB        'WINSTUB.EXE'
CODE        PRELOAD MOVEABLE DISCARDABLE
DATA        PRELOAD MOVEABLE MULTIPLE
HEAPSIZE    4096
STACKSIZE   9216
EXPORTS     WindowProc       @1
```

THE GDI3.C APPLICATION FILE:

```
/* Simplified Windows Platform (SWP)              */
/* (c) William H. Murray and Chris H. Pappas, 1989 */

#include <windows.h>

long FAR PASCAL WindowProc(HWND,unsigned,WORD,LONG);

char    szProgName[]="ProgName";

int PASCAL WinMain(hInst,hPreInst,lpszCmdLine,nCmdShow)
HANDLE hInst,hPreInst;
LPSTR  lpszCmdLine;
int    nCmdShow;
{
  HWND hwnd;
  MSG  msg;
  WNDCLASS wcSwp;
  if (!hPreInst)
  {
    wcSwp.lpszClassName=szProgName;
    wcSwp.hInstance     =hInst;
    wcSwp.lpfnWndProc   =WindowProc;
    wcSwp.hCursor       =LoadCursor(NULL,IDC_ARROW);
    wcSwp.hIcon         =LoadIcon(hInst,szProgName);
    wcSwp.lpszMenuName  =NULL;
    wcSwp.hbrBackground=GetStockObject(WHITE_BRUSH);
    wcSwp.style         =CS_HREDRAW¦CS_VREDRAW;
    wcSwp.cbClsExtra    =0;
```

```
      wcSwp.cbWndExtra    =0;
      if (!RegisterClass (&wcSwp))
        return FALSE;
   }
   hwnd=CreateWindow(szProgName,"GDI Graphics Primitives",
                     WS_OVERLAPPEDWINDOW,CW_USEDEFAULT,
                     CW_USEDEFAULT,CW_USEDEFAULT,
                     CW_USEDEFAULT,NULL,NULL,
                     hInst,NULL);
   ShowWindow(hwnd,nCmdShow);
   UpdateWindow(hwnd);
   while (GetMessage(&msg,NULL,NULL,NULL))
   {
     TranslateMessage(&msg);
     DispatchMessage(&msg);
   }
   return(msg.wParam);
}

long FAR PASCAL WindowProc(hwnd,messg,wParam,lParam)
HWND    hwnd;
unsigned messg;
WORD    wParam;
LONG    lParam;
{
   PAINTSTRUCT ps;
   HDC    hdc;
   HBRUSH hOrgBrush;
   HPEN   hOrgPen;
   HPEN   hPenRed=CreatePen(PS_SOLID,1,(RGB(255,0,0)));
   HPEN   hPenGreen=CreatePen(PS_SOLID,1,(RGB(0,255,0)));
   HPEN   hPenBlue=CreatePen(PS_SOLID,1,(RGB(0,0,255)));
   HBRUSH hBrushRed=CreateHatchBrush(HS_HORIZONTAL,RGB(255,0,0));
   HBRUSH hBrushGreen=CreateHatchBrush(HS_FDIAGONAL,RGB(0,255,0));
   HBRUSH hBrushBlue=CreateHatchBrush(HS_CROSS,RGB(0,0,255));

   switch (messg)
   {
     case WM_PAINT:
       hdc=BeginPaint(hwnd,&ps);

/*--------- your routines below ---------*/

       /* draw x & y coordinate axes */
       MoveTo(hdc,99,49);
       LineTo(hdc,99,350);
       LineTo(hdc,500,350);

       /* brush & pen color to fill first rectangle */
       hOrgBrush=SelectObject(hdc,hBrushRed);
       hOrgPen=SelectObject(hdc,hPenRed);
       Rectangle(hdc,100,350,200,200);

       /* brush & pen color to fill second rectangle */
       hOrgBrush=SelectObject(hdc,hBrushGreen);
       hOrgPen=SelectObject(hdc,hPenGreen);
       Rectangle(hdc,200,350,300,150);

       /* brush & pen color to fill third rectangle */
       hOrgBrush=SelectObject(hdc,hBrushBlue);
       hOrgPen=SelectObject(hdc,hPenBlue);
       Rectangle(hdc,300,350,400,250);
```

```
/* brush & pen color to fill fourth rectangle */
hOrgBrush=SelectObject(hdc,GetStockObject(BLACK_BRUSH));
hOrgPen=SelectObject(hdc,GetStockObject(BLACK_PEN));
Rectangle(hdc,400,350,500,75);

/* labels for each rectangle */
TextOut(hdc,135,300,"Red",3);
TextOut(hdc,225,300,"Green",5);
TextOut(hdc,330,300,"Blue",4);
TextOut(hdc,425,300,"Black",5);

/* restore original brush environment */
DeleteObject(hPenRed);
DeleteObject(hPenGreen);
DeleteObject(hPenBlue);
DeleteObject(hBrushRed);
DeleteObject(hBrushGreen);
DeleteObject(hBrushBlue);
/*--------- your routines above ---------*/

ValidateRect(hwnd,NULL);
EndPaint(hwnd,&ps);
break;
case WM_DESTROY:
PostQuitMessage(0);
break;
default:
return(DefWindowProc(hwnd,messg,wParam,lParam));
break;
}
return(0L);
}
```

Figure 10-9 shows the new and improved bar chart. You will have to admit it has a little more pizzazz.

Colors, Colors, Colors

So far, you have learned how to change the colors of pens and brushes. In this section you will also learn how to alter the background color of the window. The background color is set to white when the drawing window is created. In order to change the color this stock value will have to be replaced. The default text color is black. You will also learn how to alter the color of characters printed to the screen.

Setting Background Colors

The background color can be altered during a WM_CREATE message by obtaining the handle for the background brush with a call to the GetClass-

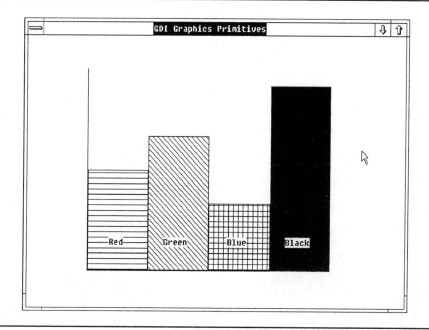

Figure 10-9.   Using colors and patterns in a bar chart

Word function. The handle is obtained by specifying the GCW_HBR-
BACKGROUND parameter.

```
GetClassWord(hwnd,GCW_HBRBACKGROUND);
```

The function returns a type *word,* giving the required handle. The
background brush can then be deleted by using the DeleteObject function.

```
DeleteObject(GetClassWord(hwnd,GCW_HBRBACKGROUND));
```

A new brush can replace the deleted background brush with a call to
the SetClassWord function

```
SetClassWord(hwnd,GCW_HBRBACKGROUND,hBrushBlue);
```

where *hBrushBlue* was a previously created brush.

By placing this code in WM_CREATE, the background will be colored,
once, at the beginning of the drawing session when the InvalidateRect
function is called.

Examine the next listing, which will draw several simple shapes to the screen against a blue background. In particular, notice how WM_CREATE is used to change the background color.

THE GDI4 MAKE FILE:

```
all : gdi4.exe

gdi4.obj: gdi4.c
    cl -c -AS -Gsw -Oas -Zpe gdi4.c

gdi4.exe: gdi4.obj gdi4.def gdi4.res
    link /NOD gdi4,,,libw slibcew, gdi4.def
```

THE GDI4.DEF DEFINITION FILE:

```
NAME        GDI4
DESCRIPTION 'Simplified Windows Platform'
EXETYPE     WINDOWS
STUB        'WINSTUB.EXE'
CODE        PRELOAD MOVEABLE DISCARDABLE
DATA        PRELOAD MOVEABLE MULTIPLE
HEAPSIZE    4096
STACKSIZE   9216
EXPORTS     WindowProc      @1
```

THE GDI4.C APPLICATION FILE:

```
/* Simplified Windows Platform (SWP)            */
/* (c) William H. Murray and Chris H. Pappas, 1989 */

#include <windows.h>

long FAR PASCAL WindowProc(HWND,unsigned,WORD,LONG);

char    szProgName[]="ProgName";

int PASCAL WinMain(hInst,hPreInst,lpszCmdLine,nCmdShow)
HANDLE hInst,hPreInst;
LPSTR  lpszCmdLine;
int    nCmdShow;
{
  HWND hwnd;
  MSG  msg;
  WNDCLASS wcSwp;
  if (!hPreInst)
  {
    wcSwp.lpszClassName=szProgName;
    wcSwp.hInstance     =hInst;
    wcSwp.lpfnWndProc   =WindowProc;
    wcSwp.hCursor       =LoadCursor(NULL,IDC_ARROW);
    wcSwp.hIcon         =LoadIcon(hInst,szProgName);
    wcSwp.lpszMenuName  =NULL;
    wcSwp.hbrBackground=GetStockObject(WHITE_BRUSH);
    wcSwp.style         =CS_HREDRAW|CS_VREDRAW;
    wcSwp.cbClsExtra    =0;
    wcSwp.cbWndExtra    =0;
    if (!RegisterClass (&wcSwp))
      return FALSE;
```

```
     }
   hwnd=CreateWindow(szProgName,"GDI Graphics Primitives",
                     WS_OVERLAPPEDWINDOW,CW_USEDEFAULT,
                     CW_USEDEFAULT,CW_USEDEFAULT,
                     CW_USEDEFAULT,NULL,NULL,
                     hInst,NULL);
   ShowWindow(hwnd,nCmdShow);
   UpdateWindow(hwnd);
   while (GetMessage(&msg,NULL,NULL,NULL))
   {
     TranslateMessage(&msg);
     DispatchMessage(&msg);
   }
   return(msg.wParam);
}

long FAR PASCAL WindowProc(hwnd,messg,wParam,lParam)
HWND    hwnd;
unsigned messg;
WORD    wParam;
LONG    lParam;
{
   PAINTSTRUCT ps;
   HDC    hdc;
   HBRUSH hOrgBrush;
   HBRUSH hBrushRed=CreateSolidBrush(RGB(255,0,0));
   HBRUSH hBrushGreen=CreateSolidBrush(RGB(0,255,0));
   HBRUSH hBrushBlue=CreateSolidBrush(RGB(0,0,255));

   switch (messg)
   {
     case WM_CREATE:
       /* color background */
       DeleteObject(GetClassWord(hwnd,GCW_HBRBACKGROUND));
       SetClassWord(hwnd,GCW_HBRBACKGROUND,hBrushBlue);
       InvalidateRect(hwnd,NULL,TRUE);
       UpdateWindow(hwnd);
       break;

     case WM_PAINT:
       hdc=BeginPaint(hwnd,&ps);

/*--------- your routines below ---------*/

       /* set background mode to transparent */
       SetBkMode(hdc,TRANSPARENT);

       TextOut(hdc,50,35,"Blue Background",15);

       /* brush color to fill circle */
       hOrgBrush=SelectObject(hdc,hBrushRed);
       /* draw a circle with ellipse function */
       Ellipse(hdc,220,100,420,300);
       TextOut(hdc,275,195,"red circle",10);

       /* brush color to fill rectangle */
       hOrgBrush=SelectObject(hdc,hBrushGreen);
       /* draw a rectangle */
       Rectangle(hdc,50,250,590,280);
       TextOut(hdc,260,255,"green rectangle",15);
```

```
              /* restore original brush environment */
              SelectObject(hdc,hOrgBrush);
              DeleteObject(hBrushRed);
              DeleteObject(hBrushGreen);
              DeleteObject(hBrushBlue);

/*--------- your routines above ---------*/

              ValidateRect(hwnd,NULL);
              EndPaint(hwnd,&ps);
              break;
           case WM_DESTROY:
              PostQuitMessage(0);
              break;
           default:
              return(DefWindowProc(hwnd,messg,wParam,lParam));
              break;
        }
     return(0L);
}
```

Figure 10-10 shows the objects. A variation on the listing will allow the same objects to be drawn with different line widths.

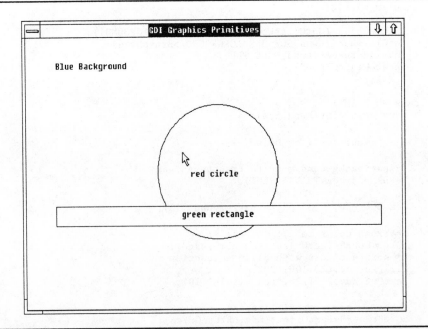

Figure 10-10.   Changing the background color

THE GDI5 MAKE FILE:

```
all : gdi5.exe

gdi5.obj: gdi5.c
    cl -c -AS -Gsw -Oas -Zpe gdi5.c

gdi5.exe: gdi5.obj gdi5.def gdi5.res
    link /NOD gdi5,,,libw slibcew, gdi5.def
```

THE GDI5.DEF DEFINITION FILE:

```
NAME        GDI5
DESCRIPTION 'Simplified Windows Platform'
EXETYPE     WINDOWS
STUB        'WINSTUB.EXE'
CODE        PRELOAD MOVEABLE DISCARDABLE
DATA        PRELOAD MOVEABLE MULTIPLE
HEAPSIZE    4096
STACKSIZE   9216
EXPORTS     WindowProc      @1
```

THE GDI5.C APPLICATION FILE:

```
/* Simplified Windows Platform (SWP)              */
/* (c) William H. Murray and Chris H. Pappas, 1989 */

#include <windows.h>

long FAR PASCAL WindowProc(HWND,unsigned,WORD,LONG);

char    szProgName[]="ProgName";

int PASCAL WinMain(hInst,hPreInst,lpszCmdLine,nCmdShow)
HANDLE hInst,hPreInst;
LPSTR  lpszCmdLine;
int    nCmdShow;
{
  HWND hwnd;
  MSG  msg;
  WNDCLASS wcSwp;
  if (!hPreInst)
  {
    wcSwp.lpszClassName=szProgName;
    wcSwp.hInstance     =hInst;
    wcSwp.lpfnWndProc   =WindowProc;
    wcSwp.hCursor       =LoadCursor(NULL,IDC_ARROW);
    wcSwp.hIcon         =LoadIcon(hInst,szProgName);
    wcSwp.lpszMenuName  =NULL;
    wcSwp.hbrBackground=GetStockObject(WHITE_BRUSH);
    wcSwp.style         =CS_HREDRAW|CS_VREDRAW;
    wcSwp.cbClsExtra    =0;
    wcSwp.cbWndExtra    =0;
    if (!RegisterClass (&wcSwp))
      return FALSE;
  }
  hwnd=CreateWindow(szProgName,"GDI Graphics Primitives",
                    WS_OVERLAPPEDWINDOW,CW_USEDEFAULT,
                    CW_USEDEFAULT,CW_USEDEFAULT,
                    CW_USEDEFAULT,NULL,NULL,
                    hInst,NULL);
```

```
  ShowWindow(hwnd,nCmdShow);
  UpdateWindow(hwnd);
  while (GetMessage(&msg,NULL,NULL,NULL))
  {
    TranslateMessage(&msg);
    DispatchMessage(&msg);
  }
  return(msg.wParam);
}


long FAR PASCAL WindowProc(hwnd,messg,wParam,lParam)
HWND    hwnd;
unsigned messg;
WORD    wParam;
LONG    lParam;
{
  PAINTSTRUCT ps;
  HDC  hdc;
  HPEN hOrgPen;
  HPEN hPenRed=CreatePen(0,2,RGB(255,0,0));
  HPEN hPenGreen=CreatePen(0,4,RGB(0,255,0));
  HPEN hPenBlue=CreatePen(0,20,RGB(0,0,255));

  switch (messg)
  {
    case WM_PAINT:
      hdc=BeginPaint(hwnd,&ps);

/*--------- your routines below ---------*/

      /* pen color to draw circle */
      hOrgPen=SelectObject(hdc,hPenRed);
      /* draw a circle with ellipse function */
      Ellipse(hdc,220,100,420,300);
      TextOut(hdc,275,195,"red circle",10);

      /* pen color to draw rectangle */
      hOrgPen=SelectObject(hdc,hPenGreen);
      /* draw a rectangle */
      Rectangle(hdc,50,250,590,280);
      TextOut(hdc,260,255,"green rectangle",15);

      /* pen color to draw wide line */
      hOrgPen=SelectObject(hdc,hPenBlue);
      /* draw a line */
      MoveTo(hdc,40,40);
      LineTo(hdc,500,60);
      TextOut(hdc,100,70,"a wide blue line",16);

      /* restore original brush environment */
      SelectObject(hdc,hOrgPen);
      DeleteObject(hPenRed);
      DeleteObject(hPenGreen);
      DeleteObject(hPenBlue);

/*--------- your routines above ---------*/

      ValidateRect(hwnd,NULL);
      EndPaint(hwnd,&ps);
```

```
      break;
    case WM_DESTROY:
      PostQuitMessage(0);
      break;
    default:
      return(DefWindowProc(hwnd,messg,wParam,lParam));
      break;
  }
  return(0L);
}
```

Figure 10-11 shows the modified objects and an additional thick blue line. Notice that the end points of this line are rounded. This is the default line-termination mode.

Setting Text Colors

The color and background of text sent to the graphics screen are very easy to alter. The color of text can be changed with the SetTextColor function, for example:

```
SetTextColor(hdc,RGB(255,0,255));
```

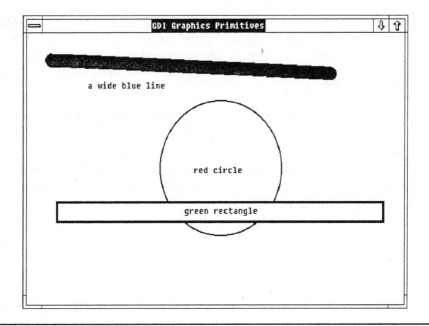

Figure 10-11.   Altering the line widths

This RGB value will set the text color to magenta. The background of each text color, by default, is based on the setting of the background mode and color. The background mode is either opaque or transparent. In the opaque mode (the default) the background color fills the space between the letters. This will be white unless the background color is changed. In transparent mode the background color is ignored and the space between characters is not filled. For labels within solidly filled objects you will probably choose a transparent mode. For labels within a hatch-filled object, the opaque mode will be your best selection. The background mode can be set with a call to the SetBkMode function.

```
SetBkMode(hdc,TRANSPARENT);
```

The background color can also be altered with a call to the SetBkColor function.

```
SetBkColor(hdc,RGB(0,255,255));
```

In this case the background color will be set to cyan.

Using the Proper Drawing Mode

The drawing mode selected determines how pens and brushes will be combined with objects already on the display screen. The drawing mode is selected with the SetROP2 function. The syntax is

```
SetROP2(hdc,nDrawMode);
```

where the function returns a type *short* and *nDrawMode* is also a type *short*. The value for *nDrawMode* can be any of the values shown in Table 10-3. The default value is R2_COPYPEN.

These modes are actually binary raster operation codes, or masks. The various options given in Table 10-3 are made from the Boolean functions such as AND, OR, XOR, and NOT.

Bitmaps

Bitmaps give the programmer the ability to copy, save, and replicate portions of the window. On a monochrome screen, for example, the information about which pixels are turned on and off is saved in memory as a bitmap. It can be played back at a later date to quickly duplicate the

Table 10-3. Available Drawing Modes

Value	Meaning
R2_BLACK	Pixel is black
R2_NOTMERGEPEN	Pixel is inverse of R2_MERGEOPEN color
R2_MASKNOTPEN	Pixel is a combination of display and inverse of pen color
R2_NOTCOPYPEN	Pixel is inverse of pen color
R2_MASKPENNOT	Pixel is combination of pen color and inverse of screen
R2_NOT	Pixel is inverse of display color
R2_XORPEN	Pixel colors in pen or display but not in both
R2_NOTMASKPEN	Pixel is inverse of R2_MASKPEN
R2_MASKPEN	Pixel colors are common to pen and display
R2_NOTXORPEN	Pixel is inverse of R2_XORPEN
R2_NOP	Pixel is unchanged
R2_MERGENOTPEN	Pixel is display color and inverse of pen color
R2_COPYPEN	Pixel is pen color
R2_MERGEPENNOT	Pixel is pen color and inverse display color merged
R2_MERGEPEN	Pixel is pen color and display color merged
R2_WHITE	Pixel is white

original screen. More uses for bitmaps will be examined in Chapter 13. However, before the end of this chapter, let us take a look at one bitmap function — BitBlt.

The BitBlt function was designed to move a bitmap from the source device context to the destination context. If the source and destination context are the same, the function can be used to replicate a pattern anywhere on the screen. The syntax is

```
BitBlt(hDestDC,x,y,nWidth,nHeight,
       hSrcDC,xSrc,ySrc,dwRop);
```

In the preceding function, *hDestDC* is the handle of the receiving device context, while *hSrcDC* is the handle of the device context that the bitmap will be copied from. The *x* and *y* values are of type *short* and specify the logical coordinates of the upper-left corner of the destination rectangle. The *nWidth* and *nHeight* values are of type *short* and specify the width and height of the destination rectangle and source bitmap. The *xSrc* and *ySrc* values are of type *short* and specify the logical X and Y coordinates of

Table 10-4.   Raster Operation Codes for BitBlt Function

Value	Description
SRCPAINT	Links destination and source bitmaps with ORs
SRCCOPY	Copies source to destination bitmap
SRCAND	Links destination and source bitmaps with ANDs
SRCINVERT	XORs destination and source bitmaps
SRCERASE	ANDs an inverted destination bitmap with source bitmap
NOTSRCCOPY	Copies inverted source bitmap to destination
NOTSRCERASE	Links source and destination with ANDs and then inverts them
MERGECOPY	ANDs the pattern and source bitmap
MERGEPAINT	ORs inverted source and destination bitmap
PATCOPY	Copies pattern to destination bitmap
PATPAINT	ORed inverted source with pattern bitmap
PATINVERT	ORed destination with pattern bitmap
DSTINVERT	Inverts destination bitmap
BLACKNESS	Makes output all black
WHITENESS	Makes output all white

the upper-left corner of the source bitmap. The *dwRop* value is of type DWORD. Table 10-4 shows possible values for *dwRop*.

As an example, here, the BitBlt function will be used to copy the bitmap pattern created with the Ellipse function. The function will be used to replicate the pattern throughout the screen.

```
THE GDI6 MAKE FILE:

all : gdi6.exe

gdi6.obj: gdi6.c
    cl -c -AS -Gsw -Oas -Zpe gdi6.c

gdi6.exe: gdi6.obj gdi6.def gdi6.res
    link /NOD gdi6,,,libw slibcew, gdi6.def


THE GDI6.DEF DEFINITION FILE:
```

```
NAME          GDI6
DESCRIPTION  'Simplified Windows Platform'
EXETYPE       WINDOWS
STUB         'WINSTUB.EXE'
CODE          PRELOAD MOVEABLE DISCARDABLE
DATA          PRELOAD MOVEABLE MULTIPLE
HEAPSIZE      4096
STACKSIZE     9216
EXPORTS       WindowProc        @1
```

THE GDI6.C APPLICATION FILE:

```c
/* Simplified Windows Platform (SWP)                */
/* (c) William H. Murray and Chris H. Pappas, 1989 */

#include <windows.h>

long FAR PASCAL WindowProc(HWND,unsigned,WORD,LONG);

char    szProgName[]="ProgName";

int PASCAL WinMain(hInst,hPreInst,lpszCmdLine,nCmdShow)
HANDLE hInst,hPreInst;
LPSTR  lpszCmdLine;
int    nCmdShow;
{
  HWND hwnd;
  MSG  msg;
  WNDCLASS wcSwp;
  if (!hPreInst)
  {
    wcSwp.lpszClassName=szProgName;
    wcSwp.hInstance     =hInst;
    wcSwp.lpfnWndProc   =WindowProc;
    wcSwp.hCursor       =LoadCursor(NULL,IDC_ARROW);
    wcSwp.hIcon         =LoadIcon(hInst,szProgName);
    wcSwp.lpszMenuName  =NULL;
    wcSwp.hbrBackground =GetStockObject(WHITE_BRUSH);
    wcSwp.style         =CS_HREDRAW|CS_VREDRAW;
    wcSwp.cbClsExtra    =0;
    wcSwp.cbWndExtra    =0;
    if (!RegisterClass (&wcSwp))
      return FALSE;
  }
  hwnd=CreateWindow(szProgName,"GDI Graphics Primitives",
                  WS_OVERLAPPEDWINDOW,CW_USEDEFAULT,
                  CW_USEDEFAULT,CW_USEDEFAULT,
                  CW_USEDEFAULT,NULL,NULL,
                  hInst,NULL);
  ShowWindow(hwnd,nCmdShow);
  UpdateWindow(hwnd);
  while (GetMessage(&msg,NULL,NULL,NULL))
  {
    TranslateMessage(&msg);
    DispatchMessage(&msg);
  }
```

```
      return(msg.wParam);
}

long FAR PASCAL WindowProc(hwnd,messg,wParam,lParam)
HWND    hwnd;
unsigned messg;
WORD    wParam;
LONG    lParam;
{
   PAINTSTRUCT ps;
   HDC     hdc;
   short   newx,newy;
   HBRUSH hOrgBrush;
   HBRUSH hMagentaBrush=CreateSolidBrush(RGB(255,0,255));

   switch (messg)
   {
     case WM_PAINT:
       hdc=BeginPaint(hwnd,&ps);

/*--------- your routines below ---------*/

       hOrgBrush=SelectObject(hdc,hMagentaBrush);

       /* draw a circle with ellipse function */
       Ellipse(hdc,20,10,70,60);

       /* now replicate the above bitmap many times */
       for(newy=10;newy<400;newy+=60)
       {
       for(newx=20;newx<600;newx+=60)
       BitBlt(hdc,newx,newy,50,50,hdc,20,10,SRCCOPY);
       }

       SelectObject(hdc,hOrgBrush);
       DeleteObject(hMagentaBrush);

/*--------- your routines above ---------*/

       ValidateRect(hwnd,NULL);
       EndPaint(hwnd,&ps);
       break;
     case WM_DESTROY:
       PostQuitMessage(0);
       break;
     default:
       return(DefWindowProc(hwnd,messg,wParam,lParam));
       break;
   }
   return(0L);
}
```

As you study the listing, notice that the bitmap pattern is always read from the same position. The parameters *newx* and *newy* specify the destination for the bitmap. Also notice that the source and destination device

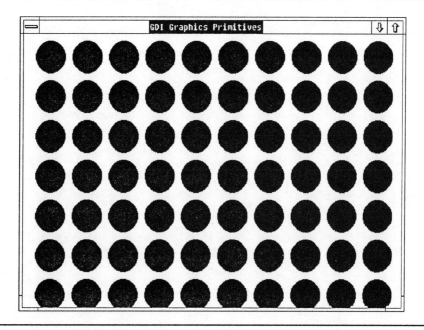

Figure 10-12. Using BitBlt to repeat a bitmap pattern

context handles are identical. Figure 10-12 shows the finished screen.

In the next chapter more sophisticated graphics programs will be developed using the graphics primitives illustrated in this chapter.

11

DEVELOPING PIE, BAR, AND LINE CHARTS

In the previous chapter you learned the fundamentals of programming with the graphics primitives, supplied by Microsoft, in the Windows environment. That and earlier chapters concentrated on individual graphics functions, icons, pointers, menus, and dialog boxes. In this chapter many of these individual concepts will be spliced together to yield professional-quality presentation graphics. You will also be introduced to a new Windows 3.0 programming feature—the Palette Manager.

The examples in this chapter are divided into three basic programs, for a pie chart, bar chart, and line chart. These charts, and the concepts they teach, form the basis of many business and scientific graphs. As you have moved from chapter to chapter you have learned how to refine features important for each of these graphs. By incorporating menus, dialog boxes, and pointers the programs will take on the "glitz" and "glitter" of commercial programs.

View the programs in this chapter as models you can develop further. They are complete and just waiting for your individual touch. Enter the code for each program, study what it can do, and then customize the code to suit your needs.

THE PALETTE MANAGER

Windows 3.0 provides the Palette Manager, which serves as a buffer between a user-developed application and an output device, such as a color monitor, printer, or plotter. The Palette Manager uses information contained in a program's logical palette and maps it to a system palette used by all Windows applications. When several logical palettes exist, the Palette Manager referees among them. The Palette Manager meets the request of the foreground window first, and then attempts to satisfy all subsequent windows.

In earlier programs colors were explicitly set with RGB values. Programs developed in that manner, while device-dependent, also work with earlier versions of Windows. The simplicity of this technique makes it useful for simple programs that do not require a great number of colors.

The Palette Manager was designed for color-intensive applications that are to be device-independent. The logical palette, created by your application and managed by the Palette Manager, can be accessed directly or indirectly. When using the direct method, the color is chosen by providing an index into the palette entries. When using the indirect method, a palette-relative RGB value is used. The palette-relative RGB specifications are very similar to the older explicit RGB values. Both methods will be examined in more detail in upcoming programs.

The Logical Palette Overhead

This section will examine the overhead necessary to create and utilize a logical palette within an application. There are five basic steps that must be accomplished in creating and using a logical palette.

1. Create a LOGPALETTE data structure.
2. Create the logical palette.
3. Select the palette into the device context.
4. Realize the palette (give the logical palette the requested colors).
5. Specify the palette colors (directly or indirectly).

Creating the LOGPALETTE Data Structure

Typically, an application will create a LOGPALETTE structure in the following manner:

```
#define PALETTESIZE 256
HANDLE  hPal;
NPLOGPALETTE pLogicalPal;
                   .

                   .

                   .
pLogicalPal=(NPLOGPALETTE) LocalAlloc(LMEM_FIXED,
            (sizeof(LOGPALETTE) +
            (sizeof(PALETTEENTRY)*(PALETTESIZE))));
pLogicalPal->palVersion=0x300;
pLogicalPal->palNumEntries=PALETTESIZE;
```

The various definitions used in the process are contained in the WIN-
DOWS.H header file. In this particular case, a PALETTESIZE of 256 is
defined, although larger sizes are permitted when the need arises. The
LOGPALETTE data structure contains the Windows version number, which
in this case is 0x300 (representing Windows version 3.00).

Creating the Logical Palette

The logical palette is created with the use of the CreatePalette function.

```
hPal=CreatePalette(pLogicalPal);
```

Selecting the Palette into the Device Context

The logical palette can be selected into the device context in the following
manner:

```
SelectPalette(hdc,hPal);
```

Note that only the SelectPalette function can be used to accomplish this
task.

Realizing the Palette

The selected palette must be realized before it can be used. The RealizePalette function is used here:

```
RealizePalette(hdc);
```

Specifying the Palette Colors

In an application containing many colors, the color magenta might be specified in the following manner:

```
/*MAGENTA*/
pLogPal->palPalEntry[6].peRed=0xFF;
pLogPal->palPalEntry[6].peGreen=0x00;
pLogPal->palPalEntry[6].peBlue=0xFF;
pLogPal->palPalEntry[6].peFlags=(BYTE) 0;
```

When using the direct method of specifying colors, an index into the logical palette can be used. PALETTEINDEX is a macro that accepts an index value. (Note that square brackets are not used here.)

```
colorshade=PALETTEINDEX(6);
```

The direct method of specifying colors allows the greatest control over the selected colors but becomes impractical when the number of colors is large. The indirect method of specifying colors eliminates this problem.

When using the indirect method a palette-relative RGB color reference is used instead of an index.

```
colorshade=PALETTERGB(0xFF,0x00,0xFF);
```

PALETTERGB, like PALETTEINDEX, is also a macro. PALETTERGB accepts three RGB values that specify the relative intensities of each of the primary colors. With this technique output devices supporting a system palette allow the Palette Manager to map colors from the logical palette. If the output device does not support a system palette, the color values specified in the palette-relative RGB will be used as explicit RGB colors.

THE PIE CHART

The pie chart is the easiest of the three examples to understand. This particular pie chart uses a dialog box for user input. Specifically, the dialog box prompts the user to enter up to ten numbers that define the size of each pie wedge. These integer numbers are then proportionally scaled to make up the 360-degree pie chart. Slices are colored sequentially. The sequence is defined by the programmer and contained in the global array lColor[]. Specifying colors in this manner uses the direct approach found in earlier Windows programs; the program will be device-dependent. This program also allows the user to enter a title for the pie chart, centered below the figure. You may wish to continue developing this example by adding a legend, label, or value for each pie slice.

If you follow the complete development cycle, you will have the following nine files on your diskette when the **MAKE** utility is finished: PIE11, PIE11.DEF, PIE11.H, PIE11.RC, PIE11.C, PIE11.CUR, PIE11.RES, PIE11.OBJ, and PIE11.EXE.

```
THE PIE11 MAKE FILE (PIE11):

all : piell.exe

piell.obj : piell.c piell.h
    cl -c -AS -FPi -Oas -Zpe piell.c

piell.res : piell.rc piell.cur
    RC -r piell.rc

piell.exe : piell.obj piell.def piell.res
    link /NOD piell,,,libw slibcew,piell
    rc piell.res
```

```
THE PIE11 DEFINITION FILE (PIE11.DEF):

;PIE11.DEF for C Compiling

NAME           piell
DESCRIPTION    'Pie Chart Program'
EXETYPE        WINDOWS
STUB           'WINSTUB.EXE'
CODE           PRELOAD MOVEABLE
DATA           PRELOAD MOVEABLE MULTIPLE
HEAPSIZE       4096
STACKSIZE      9216
EXPORTS        AboutDlgProc    @1
               PieDlgProc      @2
               WindowProc      @3
```

```
THE PIE11 HEADER FILE (PIE11.H):

#define IDM_ABOUT    40
#define IDM_INPUT    50
#define IDM_EXIT     70

#define DM_TITLE     280
#define DM_P1        281
#define DM_P2        282
#define DM_P3        283
#define DM_P4        284
#define DM_P5        285
#define DM_P6        286
#define DM_P7        287
#define DM_P8        288
#define DM_P9        289
#define DM_P10       290
```

```
THE PIE11 RESOURCE FILE (PIE11.RC):

#include "windows.h"
#include "pie11.h"

PieCursor CURSOR pie11.cur

PieMenu  MENU
BEGIN
  POPUP "Pie_Chart_Input"
  BEGIN
    MENUITEM "About...",      IDM_ABOUT
    MENUITEM "Input...",      IDM_INPUT
    MENUITEM "Exit",          IDM_EXIT
  END
END


AboutDlgBox DIALOG LOADONCALL MOVEABLE DISCARDABLE
        50,300,180,80
        STYLE WS_DLGFRAME|WS_POPUP
  BEGIN
    CONTROL "Interactive Pie Chart Program",-1,"static",
        SS_CENTER|WS_CHILD,2,60,176,10
    CONTROL "by William H. Murray & Chris H. Pappas",-1,
        "static",SS_CENTER|WS_CHILD,2,45,176,10
    CONTROL "OK",IDOK,"button",
        BS_PUSHBUTTON|WS_TABSTOP|WS_CHILD,75,10,32,14
  END


PieDlgBox DIALOG LOADONCALL MOVEABLE DISCARDABLE
        93,7,139,209
        CAPTION "Pie Chart Information"
        STYLE WS_BORDER|WS_CAPTION|WS_DLGFRAME|WS_POPUP
  BEGIN
    CONTROL "Pie Chart Title:",100,"button",
        BS_GROUPBOX|WS_TABSTOP|WS_CHILD,5,0,130,30
    CONTROL "Pie Chart Wedge Sizes",101,"button",
        BS_GROUPBOX|WS_TABSTOP|WS_CHILD,5,30,130,165
    CONTROL "Title: ",-1,"static",SS_LEFT|WS_CHILD,
        10,15,30,8
    CONTROL "",DM_TITLE,"edit",ES_LEFT|WS_BORDER|
        WS_TABSTOP|WS_CHILD,40,10,90,12
    CONTROL "Wedge #1: ",-1,"static",SS_LEFT|
        WS_CHILD,10,50,40,8
    CONTROL "Wedge #2: ",-1,"static",SS_LEFT|
        WS_CHILD,10,65,40,8
    CONTROL "Wedge #3: ",-1,"static",SS_LEFT|
        WS_CHILD,10,80,40,8
    CONTROL "Wedge #4: ",-1,"static",SS_LEFT|
        WS_CHILD,10,95,40,8
    CONTROL "Wedge #5: ",-1,"static",SS_LEFT|
        WS_CHILD,10,110,40,8
    CONTROL "Wedge #6: ",-1,"static",SS_LEFT|
        WS_CHILD,10,125,40,8
    CONTROL "Wedge #7: ",-1,"static",SS_LEFT|
        WS_CHILD,10,140,40,8
    CONTROL "Wedge #8: ",-1,"static",SS_LEFT|
        WS_CHILD,10,155,40,8
    CONTROL "Wedge #9: ",-1,"static",SS_LEFT|
        WS_CHILD,10,170,40,8
```

```
        CONTROL "Wedge #10:",-1,"static",SS_LEFT¦
            WS_CHILD,10,185,45,8
        CONTROL "10",DM_P1,"edit",ES_LEFT¦WS_BORDER¦
            WS_TABSTOP¦WS_CHILD,55,45,30,12
        CONTROL "20",DM_P2,"edit",ES_LEFT¦WS_BORDER¦
            WS_TABSTOP¦WS_CHILD,55,60,30,12
        CONTROL "30",DM_P3,"edit",ES_LEFT¦WS_BORDER¦
            WS_TABSTOP¦WS_CHILD,55,75,30,12
        CONTROL "40",DM_P4,"edit",ES_LEFT¦WS_BORDER¦WS_TABSTOP¦
            WS_CHILD,55,90,30,12
        CONTROL "0",DM_P5,"edit",ES_LEFT¦WS_BORDER¦WS_TABSTOP¦
            WS_CHILD,55,105,30,12
        CONTROL "0",DM_P6,"edit",ES_LEFT¦WS_BORDER¦WS_TABSTOP¦
            WS_CHILD,55,120,30,12
        CONTROL "0",DM_P7,"edit",ES_LEFT¦WS_BORDER¦WS_TABSTOP¦
            WS_CHILD,55,135,30,12
        CONTROL "0",DM_P8,"edit",ES_LEFT¦WS_BORDER¦WS_TABSTOP¦
            WS_CHILD,55,150,30,12
        CONTROL "0",DM_P9,"edit",ES_LEFT¦WS_BORDER¦WS_TABSTOP¦
            WS_CHILD,55,165,30,12
        CONTROL "0",DM_P10,"edit",ES_LEFT¦WS_BORDER¦WS_TABSTOP¦
            WS_CHILD,55,180,30,12
        CONTROL "OK",IDOK,"button",BS_PUSHBUTTON¦WS_TABSTOP¦
            WS_CHILD,20,195,24,14
        CONTROL "Cancel",IDCANCEL,"button",BS_PUSHBUTTON¦
            WS_TABSTOP¦WS_CHILD,90,195,34,14
    END


THE PIE11 APPLICATION FILE (PIE11.C):

/* Simplified Windows Platform (SWP)            */
/* (c) William H. Murray and Chris H. Pappas, 1989 */

#include <windows.h>
#include <string.h>
#include <math.h>
#include "pie11.h"

#define radius      180
#define maxnumwedge 10
#define pi          3.1415927

long FAR PASCAL WindowProc(HWND,unsigned,WORD,LONG);
BOOL FAR PASCAL AboutDlgProc(HWND,unsigned,WORD,LONG);
BOOL FAR PASCAL PieDlgProc(HWND,unsigned,WORD,LONG);

char szProgName[]="ProgName";
char szApplName[]="PieMenu";
char szCursorName[]="PieCursor";
char szTString[80]="(bar chart title area)";
unsigned int iWedgesize[maxnumwedge]={10,20,30,40};
long lColor[maxnumwedge]={0x0L,0xFFL,0xFF00L,0xFFFFL,
                          0xFF0000L,0xFF00FFL,0xFFFF00L,
                          0xFFFFFFL,0x8080L,0x808080L};

int PASCAL WinMain(hInst,hPreInst,lpszCmdLine,nCmdShow)
HANDLE hInst,hPreInst;
LPSTR  lpszCmdLine;
int    nCmdShow;
{
```

```
HWND hwnd;
MSG  msg;
WNDCLASS wcSwp;
if (!hPreInst)
{
  wcSwp.lpszClassName=szProgName;
  wcSwp.hInstance    =hInst;
  wcSwp.lpfnWndProc  =WindowProc;
  wcSwp.hCursor      =LoadCursor(hInst,szCursorName);
  wcSwp.hIcon        =LoadIcon(hInst,szProgName);
  wcSwp.lpszMenuName =szApplName;
  wcSwp.hbrBackground=GetStockObject(WHITE_BRUSH);
  wcSwp.style        =CS_HREDRAW|CS_VREDRAW;
  wcSwp.cbClsExtra   =0;
  wcSwp.cbWndExtra   =0;
  if (!RegisterClass (&wcSwp))
     return FALSE;
}
hwnd=CreateWindow(szProgName,"Pie Chart Program",
                  WS_OVERLAPPEDWINDOW,CW_USEDEFAULT,
                  CW_USEDEFAULT,CW_USEDEFAULT,
                  CW_USEDEFAULT,NULL,NULL,
                  hInst,NULL);
ShowWindow(hwnd,nCmdShow);
UpdateWindow(hwnd);
while (GetMessage(&msg,NULL,NULL,NULL))
{
  TranslateMessage(&msg);
  DispatchMessage(&msg);
}
return(msg.wParam);
}


BOOL FAR PASCAL AboutDlgProc(hdlg,messg,wParam,lParam)
HWND hdlg;
unsigned messg;
WORD wParam;
LONG lParam;
{
  switch (messg)
  {
    case WM_INITDIALOG:
      break;
    case WM_COMMAND:
      switch (wParam)
      {
        case IDOK:
          EndDialog(hdlg,TRUE);
          break;
        default:
          return FALSE;
      }
      break;
    default:
      return FALSE;
  }
  return TRUE;
}
```

```
BOOL FAR PASCAL PieDlgProc(hdlg,messg,wParam,lParam)
HWND hdlg;
unsigned messg;
WORD wParam;
LONG lParam;
{

switch (messg)
{
  case WM_INITDIALOG:
    return FALSE;
  case WM_COMMAND:
    switch (wParam)
    {
      case IDOK:
        GetDlgItemText(hdlg,DM_TITLE,szTString,80);
        iWedgesize[0]=GetDlgItemInt(hdlg,DM_P1,NULL,0);
        iWedgesize[1]=GetDlgItemInt(hdlg,DM_P2,NULL,0);
        iWedgesize[2]=GetDlgItemInt(hdlg,DM_P3,NULL,0);
        iWedgesize[3]=GetDlgItemInt(hdlg,DM_P4,NULL,0);
        iWedgesize[4]=GetDlgItemInt(hdlg,DM_P5,NULL,0);
        iWedgesize[5]=GetDlgItemInt(hdlg,DM_P6,NULL,0);
        iWedgesize[6]=GetDlgItemInt(hdlg,DM_P7,NULL,0);
        iWedgesize[7]=GetDlgItemInt(hdlg,DM_P8,NULL,0);
        iWedgesize[8]=GetDlgItemInt(hdlg,DM_P9,NULL,0);
        iWedgesize[9]=GetDlgItemInt(hdlg,DM_P10,NULL,0);
        EndDialog(hdlg,TRUE);
        break;
      case IDCANCEL:
        EndDialog(hdlg,FALSE);
        break;
      default:
        return FALSE;
    }
    break;

  default:
    return FALSE;
  }
  return TRUE;
}


long FAR PASCAL WindowProc(hwnd,messg,wParam,lParam)
HWND hwnd;
unsigned messg;
WORD wParam;
LONG lParam;
{
  HDC        hdc;
  HMENU      hMenu;
  PAINTSTRUCT ps;
  HBRUSH     hOrgBrush,hBrush;
  static FARPROC lpfnAboutDlgProc;
  static FARPROC lpfnPieDlgProc;
  static HWND hInst1,hInst2;
  static short xClientView,yClientView;

  unsigned int iTotalWedge[maxnumwedge+1];
```

```
   int           i,iNWedges;

iNWedges=0;
for (i=0;i<maxnumwedge;i++)
{
   if(iWedgesize[i]!=0) iNWedges++;
}

iTotalWedge[0]=0;
for (i=0;i<iNWedges;i++)
   iTotalWedge[i+1]=iTotalWedge[i]+iWedgesize[i];

switch (messg)
{
   case WM_SIZE:
     xClientView=LOWORD(lParam);
     yClientView=HIWORD(lParam);
     break;

   case WM_CREATE:
     hInst1=((LPCREATESTRUCT) lParam)->hInstance;
     hInst2=((LPCREATESTRUCT) lParam)->hInstance;
     lpfnAboutDlgProc=MakeProcInstance(AboutDlgProc,hInst1);
     lpfnPieDlgProc=MakeProcInstance(PieDlgProc,hInst2);
     break;

   case WM_COMMAND:
     switch (wParam)
     {
       case IDM_ABOUT:
         DialogBox(hInst1,"AboutDlgBox",hwnd,
                   lpfnAboutDlgProc);
         break;
       case IDM_INPUT:
         DialogBox(hInst2,"PieDlgBox",
                   hwnd,lpfnPieDlgProc);
         InvalidateRect(hwnd,NULL,TRUE);
         UpdateWindow(hwnd);
         break;
       case IDM_EXIT:
         SendMessage(hwnd,WM_CLOSE,0,0L);
         break;
       default:
         break;
     }
   break;

   case WM_PAINT:
     hdc=BeginPaint(hwnd,&ps);

/*--------- your routines below ---------*/

     TextOut(hdc,(310-(strlen(szTString)*8/2)),
             15,szTString,strlen(szTString));

     SetMapMode(hdc,MM_ISOTROPIC);
     SetWindowExt(hdc,500,500);
     SetViewportExt(hdc,xClientView,-yClientView);
     SetViewportOrg(hdc,xClientView/2,yClientView/2);
```

```
    for(i=0;i<iNWedges;i++)
    {
      hBrush=CreateSolidBrush(lColor[i]);
      SelectObject(hdc,hBrush);
      Pie(hdc,-200,200,200,-200,
          (short) (radius*cos(2*pi*iTotalWedge[i]/
          iTotalWedge[iNWedges])),
          (short) (radius*sin(2*pi*iTotalWedge[i]/
          iTotalWedge[iNWedges])),
          (short) (radius*cos(2*pi*iTotalWedge[i+1]/
          iTotalWedge[iNWedges])),
          (short) (radius*sin(2*pi*iTotalWedge[i+1]/
          iTotalWedge[iNWedges])));
    }

/*--------- your routines above ---------*/

    ValidateRect(hwnd,NULL);
    EndPaint(hwnd,&ps);
    break;

  case WM_DESTROY:
    PostQuitMessage(0);
    break;

  default:
    return(DefWindowProc(hwnd,messg,wParam,lParam));
  }
  return(0L);
}
```

The PIE11 and PIE11.DEF Files

As you can see from the PIE11 file listing, this program will use a pointer
(PIE11.CUR). You may use the SDKPAINT editor, as described in Chapter 6,
to create your own unique pointer or purchase the optional diskette and
take advantage of the ready-made art. This program also uses trigonometric
functions requiring the MATH.H header file. These functions require that
the program be compiled with the floating point option, /FPi. The
PIE11.DEF file varies only a little from previous .DEF files, in that it contains
three EXPORTS: AboutDlgProc, PieDiaProc, and WindowProc. You'll see
how those procedures are used when the main program is discussed a little
later.

The PIE11.H Header File

The PIE11.H header file contains identification information for various
menu and dialog items. Additionally, note that there are ten unique identification numbers that represent the ten values for wedge sizes input from
the dialog box by the user.

The PIE11.RC Resource File

The PIE11.RC resource file contains information for the pointer (PieCursor), menu (PieMenu), and two dialog boxes (AboutDlgBox and PieDlgBox). Figure 11-1 shows the About box and Figure 11-2 shows the data entry box. This file was created with the help of the Dialog Box Editor, discussed in Chapter 8. When using the Dialog Box Editor, you must have a fairly clear idea of how you want to represent various data fields, and so on. The various CONTROL values, which determine position and size of dialog box items, are calculated by the editor. If you are entering this program it would be easiest for you just to type in this resource file as it appears. As you scan the listing notice that some CONTROL statements begin with either text or a number in quotation marks. These numbers will appear in the entry fields of the final dialog box and serve as default values for the application program.

The PIE11.C Program

The PIE11.C program for this section allows the user to develop a pie chart with as many as ten slices. As mentioned, PIE11.C will allow the user to

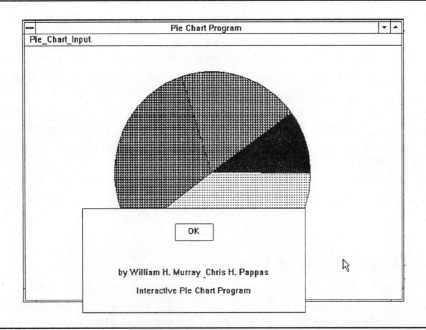

Figure 11-1. The pie chart About box

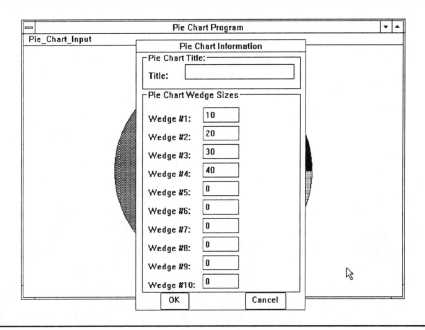

Figure 11-2.   The pie chart dialog box for data entry

input the data on pie slice sizes directly from a dialog box. Additionally, the user may enter the title of the pie chart. Don't let the size of this listing scare you; much of the code you see is the Windows platform developed in earlier chapters. New concepts will be divided into small pieces and discussed separately.

The first new and interesting piece of code occurs in the *case IDOK* statement under PieDlgProc. Upon selecting the data entry item (a dialog box) from the program menu the user is allowed to enter a pie chart title and the data for up to ten pie slices. This information is accepted when the OK push button is selected. The title is returned as a text string with the GetDlgItemText function. Numeric information is returned with the GetDlgItemInt function. This function, as you may recall, translates the numeric string information entered by the user into a short integer that can be a signed or unsigned number. Notice that this function requires four parameters. The handle and ID number are self-explanatory. The third parameter, which is NULL in this case, is used to flag a successful conversion. The fourth parameter is used to signal signed and unsigned numbers. In this case, a zero states that the dialog box is returning unsigned numbers. These numbers are saved in the global array *iWedgesize[]* for future use.

Except for gathering data, the real work in this program is done in the WindowProc procedure. Various pieces of information and data are sent as messages in the five *case* statements. Study the code and make sure you can find these statements: WM_SIZE, WM_CREATE, WM_COMMAND, WM_PAINT, and WM_DESTROY.

WM_SIZE is used in determining the size of the client or application window. Windows sends a message to WM_SIZE anytime the window is resized. For this example, the size will be returned in two variables, *xClientView* and *yClientView*. This information will be used by WM_PAINT to scale the pie chart to the window. It will also produce a miniature icon of the window when the minimum option is selected from the main menu.

During WM_CREATE the program's instance handle is obtained and saved as *hInst1* and *hInst2*. These values are used by the MakeProcInstance function to create a fixed portion of memory called the *instance thunk* for each dialog box procedure or function. This is necessary because each dialog box procedure is a far procedure. The address returned by Make-ProdInstance points to the instance thunk. Two are required in this case because two dialog box procedures are being used.

WM_COMMAND processes the messages required to open both dialog boxes. You will notice that WM_COMMAND contains three *case* statements. IDM_ABOUT is the ID for the About box procedure, while IDM_INPUT is the ID for the data entry dialog box.

WM_PAINT handles the actual drawing of the pie wedges to the screen. First, the pie chart title is printed to the screen using the coordinates for the default mapping mode. The title is centered using a simple approach that assumes a default character set eight pixels wide. If this is not satisfactory for your application another technique, presented in the last two programs in this chapter, includes the additional code developed in Chapter 9 for determining text size, and so forth.

Next, the mapping mode is changed to MM_ISOTROPIC. Recall from the previous chapter that the default drawing mode is MM_TEXT, which draws in pixel coordinates. Under MM_TEXT, point (0,0) is in the upper-left corner of the screen. MM_ISOTROPIC allows you to select the extent of both the X and Y axes. The mapping mode is changed by calling the function SetMapMode. When the function SetWindowExt is called with both parameters set to 500, the height and width of the client or application area are equal. These are logical sizes that Windows adjusts (scales) to fit the physical display device. The display size values are used by the SetViewportExt function. The negative sign for the Y coordinate specifies increasing Y values from the bottom of the screen. It should be no surprise that these are the values previously obtained under WM_SIZE. Additionally, for this example, let's center the pie chart on a traditional X-Y coordinate system, with the center of the chart at (0,0). The SetViewportOrg function will do this.

Before actually plotting the pie wedges, you must return to the beginning of the WindowProc procedure to understand how the pie wedges are scaled to fit a complete circle. There are several pieces of code that are very important.

```
 iNWedges=0;
for (i=0;i<maxnumwedge;i++)
   {
   if(iWedgesize[i]!=0) iNWedges++;
   }
```

This first nugget of code determines how many wedges have been requested. Since all of the wedges to be plotted will be greater than zero, the array *iWedgesize[]* can be scanned for the first zero value. For each non-zero value returned, *iNWedges* will be incremented. Thus, when you leave this routine, *iNWedges* will contain the number of wedges for this plot.

Next, a progressive total on wedge values will be returned to the *iTotalWedge[]* array. These values will help determine where one pie slice ends and the next begins. For example, if the user entered 10, 20, 30, and 40 for wedge sizes, *iTotalWedge[]* would contain the values 0, 10, 30, 60, and 100. Study the following code to make sure you understand how this was done.

```
 iTotalWedge[0]=0;
for (i=0;i<iNWedges;i++)
   iTotalWedge[i+1]=iTotalWedge[i]+iWedgesize[i];
```

The values contained in *iTotalWedge[]* are needed in order to calculate the beginning and ending angles for each pie wedge. You might recall from the previous chapter that the Pie function accepts nine parameters. The first parameter is the handle and the next four specify the coordinates of the bounding rectangle. In this case, for the mapping mode chosen, they are -200, 200, 200, and -200. The remaining four parameters are used to designate the starting X-Y pair and the ending X-Y pair for the pie arc. To calculate X values, the cosine function is used; to calculate Y values, the sine function is used. For example, the first X position is determined by multiplying the radius of the pie by the cosine of 2*pi*iTotalWedge[0]*. The 2*pi value is needed in the conversion of degrees to radians. The Y value is found with the sine function in the same way. Those two points serve as the starting coordinates for the first slice. The ending coordinates are found

with the same equations, but using the next value in *iTotalWedge[]*. In order
to scale each of these points to make all slices proportional and fit a
360-degree pie, each coordinate point is divided by the grand total of all
individual slices. This total is the last number contained in *iTotalWedge[]*.
Observe how this calculation is achieved in the next piece of code.

```
for(i=0;i<iNWedges;i++)
   {
   hBrush=CreateSolidBrush(lColor[i]);
   SelectObject(hdc,hBrush);
   Pie(hdc,-200,200,200,-200,
       (short) (radius*cos(2*pi*iTotalWedge[i]/
           iTotalWedge[iNWedges])),
       (short) (radius*sin(2*pi*iTotalWedge[i]/
           iTotalWedge[iNWedges])),
       (short) (radius*cos(2*pi*iTotalWedge[i+1]/
           iTotalWedge[iNWedges])),
       (short) (radius*sin(2*pi*iTotalWedge[i+1]/
           iTotalWedge[iNWedges])));
   }
```

A loop is repeated, to include drawing and filling all slices. This loop
will index through all *iNWedge* values. Since this program uses trigonometric functions, the MATH.H header file is included at the start of this
program. Figure 11-3 shows the default pie chart plot, while Figure 11-4
shows a unique application.

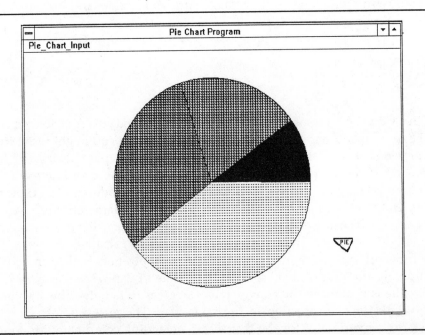

Figure 11-3.   The default pie chart

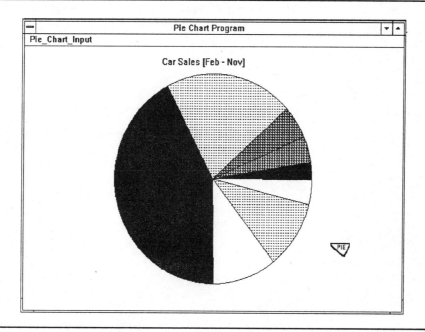

Figure 11-4. The custom pie chart of car sales

THE BAR CHART

The bar chart program closely parallels the pie chart program. It allows the user to enter up to ten bars via the dialog box. The bar widths are scaled so that the final figure will fill the entire horizontal axis. Thus, two bars or ten bars will produce the same size horizontal plot. The vertical heights of the bars are also scaled. The value for the largest bar is scaled to the maximum value of the Y axis, with all other values drawn in proportion to this bar. Automatic scaling allows for a wide range of data values, without the need for changing plotting ranges, and so on.

The bars are colored in a sequential manner, similar to the technique used for the pie chart. However, this program utilizes the power of the Palette Manager in controlling the logical palette. Since the Palette Manager is used, this program will be device-independent. Also note in the listing that this example uses the direct method of specifying palette colors with the help of the PALETTEINDEX macro.

This program also allows the user to input three labels. One label is used for the title, which is centered over the bar figure. The remaining two labels are for the vertical and horizontal axes. The vertical label is plotted vertically, from top to bottom.

You will have nine files on your diskette when the **MAKE** utility is finished: BAR16, BAR16.DEF, BAR16.H, BAR16.RC, BAR16.C, BAR16.CUR, BAR16.RES, BAR16.OBJ, and BAR16.EXE.

THE BAR11 MAKE FILE (BAR11):

```
all : bar11.exe

bar11.obj : bar11.c bar11.h
    cl -c -AS -FPi -Oas -Gsw -Zpe bar11.c

bar11.res : bar11.rc bar11.cur
    RC -r bar11.rc

bar11.exe : bar11.obj bar11.def bar11.res
    link /NOD bar11,,,libw slibcew,bar11
    rc bar11.res
```

THE BAR11 DEFINITION FILE (BAR11.DEF):

```
;BAR11.DEF for C Compiling

NAME            bar11
DESCRIPTION     'Bar Chart Program'
EXETYPE         WINDOWS
STUB            'WINSTUB.EXE'
CODE            PRELOAD MOVEABLE
DATA            PRELOAD MOVEABLE MULTIPLE
HEAPSIZE        4096
STACKSIZE       9216
EXPORTS         AboutDlgProc    @1
                BarDlgProc      @2
                WindowProc      @3
```

THE BAR11 HEADER FILE (BAR11.H):

```
#define IDM_ABOUT       40
#define IDM_INPUT       50
#define IDM_EXIT        70

#define DM_TITLE        280
#define DM_XLABEL       281
#define DM_YLABEL       282
#define DM_P1           283
#define DM_P2           284
#define DM_P3           285
#define DM_P4           286
#define DM_P5           287
#define DM_P6           288
#define DM_P7           289
#define DM_P8           290
#define DM_P9           291
#define DM_P10          292
```

```
THE BAR11 RESOURCE FILE (BAR11.RC):

#include "windows.h"
#include "bar11.h"

BarCursor CURSOR Bar11.cur

BarMenu  MENU
BEGIN
  POPUP "Bar_Chart_Input"
  BEGIN
    MENUITEM "About...",      IDM_ABOUT
    MENUITEM "Input...",      IDM_INPUT
    MENUITEM "Exit",          IDM_EXIT
  END
END

AboutDlgBox DIALOG LOADONCALL MOVEABLE DISCARDABLE
        50,300,180,80
        STYLE WS_DLGFRAME¦WS_POPUP
  BEGIN
    CONTROL "Interactive Bar Chart Program",-1,"static",
        SS_CENTER¦WS_CHILD,2,60,176,10
    CONTROL "by William H. Murray & Chris H. Pappas",-1,
        "static",SS_CENTER¦WS_CHILD,2,45,176,10
    CONTROL "OK",IDOK,"button",
        BS_PUSHBUTTON¦WS_TABSTOP¦WS_CHILD,75,10,32,14
  END


BarDlgBox DIALOG LOADONCALL MOVEABLE DISCARDABLE
        42,-10,223,209
        CAPTION "Bar Chart Information"
        STYLE WS_BORDER¦WS_CAPTION¦WS_DLGFRAME¦WS_POPUP
  BEGIN
    CONTROL "Bar Chart Title:",100,"button",
        BS_GROUPBOX¦WS_TABSTOP¦WS_CHILD,5,11,212,89
    CONTROL "Bar Chart Heights",101,"button",
        BS_GROUPBOX¦WS_TABSTOP¦WS_CHILD,5,105,212,90
    CONTROL "Title: ",-1,"static",SS_LEFT¦WS_CHILD,
        43,35,28,8
    CONTROL "",DM_TITLE,"edit",ES_LEFT¦WS_BORDER¦WS_TABSTOP¦
        WS_CHILD,75,30,137,12
    CONTROL "x-axis label:",-1,"static",SS_LEFT¦
        WS_CHILD,15,55,55,8
    CONTROL "",DM_XLABEL,"edit",ES_LEFT¦WS_BORDER¦WS_TABSTOP¦
        WS_CHILD,75,50,135,12
    CONTROL "y-axis label:",-1,"static",SS_LEFT¦
        WS_CHILD,15,75,60,8
    CONTROL "",DM_YLABEL,"edit",ES_LEFT¦WS_BORDER¦WS_TABSTOP¦
        WS_CHILD,75,70,135,12
    CONTROL "Bar #1: ",-1,"static",SS_LEFT¦
        WS_CHILD,45,125,40,8
    CONTROL "Bar #2: ",-1,"static",SS_LEFT¦
        WS_CHILD,45,140,40,8
    CONTROL "Bar #3: ",-1,"static",SS_LEFT¦
        WS_CHILD,45,155,40,8
    CONTROL "Bar #4: ",-1,"static",SS_LEFT¦
        WS_CHILD,45,170,40,8
```

```
      CONTROL "Bar #5: ",-1,"static",SS_LEFT|
          WS_CHILD,45,185,40,8
      CONTROL "Bar #6: ",-1,"static",SS_LEFT|
          WS_CHILD,130,125,40,8
      CONTROL "Bar #7: ",-1,"static",SS_LEFT|
          WS_CHILD,130,140,40,8
      CONTROL "Bar #8: ",-1,"static",SS_LEFT|
          WS_CHILD,130,155,40,8
      CONTROL "Bar #9: ",-1,"static",SS_LEFT|
          WS_CHILD,130,170,40,8
      CONTROL "Bar #10:",-1,"static",SS_LEFT|
          WS_CHILD,130,185,45,8
      CONTROL "10",DM_P1,"edit",ES_LEFT|WS_BORDER|WS_TABSTOP|
          WS_CHILD,90,120,30,12
      CONTROL "20",DM_P2,"edit",ES_LEFT|WS_BORDER|WS_TABSTOP|
          WS_CHILD,90,135,30,12
      CONTROL "30",DM_P3,"edit",ES_LEFT|WS_BORDER|WS_TABSTOP|
          WS_CHILD,90,150,30,12
      CONTROL "40",DM_P4,"edit",ES_LEFT|WS_BORDER|WS_TABSTOP|
          WS_CHILD,90,165,30,12
      CONTROL "0",DM_P5,"edit",ES_LEFT|WS_BORDER|WS_TABSTOP|
          WS_CHILD,90,180,30,12
      CONTROL "0",DM_P6,"edit",ES_LEFT|WS_BORDER|WS_TABSTOP|
          WS_CHILD,180,120,30,12
      CONTROL "0",DM_P7,"edit",ES_LEFT|WS_BORDER|WS_TABSTOP|
          WS_CHILD,180,135,30,12
      CONTROL "0",DM_P8,"edit",ES_LEFT|WS_BORDER|WS_TABSTOP|
          WS_CHILD,180,150,30,12
      CONTROL "0",DM_P9,"edit",ES_LEFT|WS_BORDER|WS_TABSTOP|
          WS_CHILD,180,165,30,12
      CONTROL "0",DM_P10,"edit",ES_LEFT|WS_BORDER|WS_TABSTOP|
          WS_CHILD,180,180,30,12
      CONTROL "OK",IDOK,"button",BS_PUSHBUTTON|WS_TABSTOP|
          WS_CHILD,54,195,24,14
      CONTROL "Cancel",IDCANCEL,"button",BS_PUSHBUTTON|
          WS_TABSTOP|WS_CHILD,124,195,34,14
    END
```

THE BAR11 APPLICATION FILE (BAR11.C):

```
/* Simplified Windows Platform (SWP)            */
/* (c) William H. Murray and Chris H. Pappas, 1989 */

#include <stdlib.h>
#include <string.h>
#include <windows.h>
#include "bar11.h"

#define maxnumbar 10
#define PALETTESIZE 256
HANDLE  hPal;
NPLOGPALETTE pLogPal;

long FAR PASCAL WindowProc(HWND,unsigned,WORD,LONG);
BOOL FAR PASCAL AboutDlgProc(HWND,unsigned,WORD,LONG);
BOOL FAR PASCAL BarDlgProc(HWND,unsigned,WORD,LONG);
```

```
char szProgName[]="ProgName";
char szApplName[]="BarMenu";
char szCursorName[]="BarCursor";
char szTString[80]="(bar chart title area)";
char szXString[80]="x-axis label";
char szYString[80]="y-axis label";
int  iBarSize[maxnumbar]={10,20,30,40};


int PASCAL WinMain(hInst,hPreInst,lpszCmdLine,nCmdShow)
HANDLE hInst,hPreInst;
LPSTR  lpszCmdLine;
int    nCmdShow;
{
  HWND hwnd;
  MSG  msg;
  WNDCLASS wcSwp;
  if (!hPreInst)
  {
    wcSwp.lpszClassName=szProgName;
    wcSwp.hInstance    =hInst;
    wcSwp.lpfnWndProc  =WindowProc;
    wcSwp.hCursor      =LoadCursor(hInst,szCursorName);
    wcSwp.hIcon        =LoadIcon(hInst,szProgName);
    wcSwp.lpszMenuName =szApplName;
    wcSwp.hbrBackground=GetStockObject(WHITE_BRUSH);
    wcSwp.style        =CS_HREDRAW|CS_VREDRAW;
    wcSwp.cbClsExtra   =0;
    wcSwp.cbWndExtra   =0;
    if (!RegisterClass (&wcSwp))
      return FALSE;
  }
  hwnd=CreateWindow(szProgName,"Bar Chart Program",
                    WS_OVERLAPPEDWINDOW,CW_USEDEFAULT,
                    CW_USEDEFAULT,CW_USEDEFAULT,
                    CW_USEDEFAULT,NULL,NULL,
                    hInst,NULL);
  ShowWindow(hwnd,nCmdShow);
  UpdateWindow(hwnd);
  while (GetMessage(&msg,NULL,NULL,NULL))
  {
    TranslateMessage(&msg);
    DispatchMessage(&msg);
  }
  return(msg.wParam);
}


BOOL FAR PASCAL AboutDlgProc(hdlg,messg,wParam,lParam)
HWND hdlg;
unsigned messg;
WORD wParam;
LONG lParam;
{
  switch (messg)
  {
    case WM_INITDIALOG:
      break;
```

```
      case WM_COMMAND:
        switch (wParam)
        {
          case IDOK:
            EndDialog(hdlg,TRUE);
            break;
          default:
            return FALSE;
        }
        break;
      default:
        return FALSE;
  }
  return TRUE;
}


BOOL FAR PASCAL BarDlgProc(hdlg,messg,wParam,lParam)
HWND hdlg;
unsigned messg;
WORD wParam;
LONG lParam;
{
  switch (messg)
  {
    case WM_INITDIALOG:
      return FALSE;
    case WM_COMMAND:
      switch (wParam)
      {
        case IDOK:
          GetDlgItemText(hdlg,DM_TITLE,szTString,80);
          GetDlgItemText(hdlg,DM_XLABEL,szXString,80);
          GetDlgItemText(hdlg,DM_YLABEL,szYString,80);
          iBarSize[0]=GetDlgItemInt(hdlg,DM_P1,NULL,0);
          iBarSize[1]=GetDlgItemInt(hdlg,DM_P2,NULL,0);
          iBarSize[2]=GetDlgItemInt(hdlg,DM_P3,NULL,0);
          iBarSize[3]=GetDlgItemInt(hdlg,DM_P4,NULL,0);
          iBarSize[4]=GetDlgItemInt(hdlg,DM_P5,NULL,0);
          iBarSize[5]=GetDlgItemInt(hdlg,DM_P6,NULL,0);
          iBarSize[6]=GetDlgItemInt(hdlg,DM_P7,NULL,0);
          iBarSize[7]=GetDlgItemInt(hdlg,DM_P8,NULL,0);
          iBarSize[8]=GetDlgItemInt(hdlg,DM_P9,NULL,0);
          iBarSize[9]=GetDlgItemInt(hdlg,DM_P10,NULL,0);
          EndDialog(hdlg,TRUE);
          break;
        case IDCANCEL:
          EndDialog(hdlg,FALSE);
          break;
        default:
          return FALSE;
      }
      break;

    default:
      return FALSE;
  }
  return TRUE;
}
```

```
long FAR PASCAL WindowProc(hwnd,messg,wParam,lParam)
HWND hwnd;
unsigned messg;
WORD wParam;
LONG lParam;
{
  HDC         hdc;
  PAINTSTRUCT ps;
  HFONT       hOFont,hNFont;
  HBRUSH      hOrgBrush,hBrush;
  static      FARPROC lpfnAboutDlgProc;
  static      FARPROC lpfnBarDlgProc;
  static      HWND hInst1,hInst2;
  static      short xClientView,yClientView;
  int         i,iNBars,iBarWidth,iBarMax;
  int         ilenMaxLabel;
  int         x1,x2,y1,y2;
  float       iBarSizeScaled[maxnumbar];
  char        sbuffer[10],*strptr;

  iNBars=0;
  for (i=0;i<maxnumbar;i++)
  {
    if(iBarSize[i]!=0) iNBars++;
  }

  iBarWidth=400/iNBars;

  /* Find bar in array with maximum height */
  iBarMax=iBarSize[0];
  for(i=0;i<iNBars;i++)
    if (iBarMax<iBarSize[i]) iBarMax=iBarSize[i];

  /* Convert maximum y value to a string */
  strptr=itoa(iBarMax,sbuffer,10);
  ilenMaxLabel=strlen(sbuffer);

  /* Scale bars in array.  Highest bar = 270 */
  for (i=0;i<iNBars;i++)
    iBarSizeScaled[i]=(float) iBarSize[i]*(270.0/iBarMax);

  switch (messg)
  {
    case WM_SIZE:
      xClientView=LOWORD(lParam);
      yClientView=HIWORD(lParam);
      break;

    case WM_CREATE:
      hInst1=((LPCREATESTRUCT) lParam)->hInstance;
      hInst2=((LPCREATESTRUCT) lParam)->hInstance;
      lpfnAboutDlgProc=MakeProcInstance(AboutDlgProc,hInst1);
      lpfnBarDlgProc=MakeProcInstance(BarDlgProc,hInst2);
      pLogPal=(NPLOGPALETTE) LocalAlloc(LMEM_FIXED,
              (sizeof(LOGPALETTE) +
              (sizeof(PALETTEENTRY)*(PALETTESIZE)))));
      pLogPal->palVersion=0x300;
      pLogPal->palNumEntries=PALETTESIZE;
```

```
        /*BLACK*/
        pLogPal->palPalEntry[0].peRed=0x00;
        pLogPal->palPalEntry[0].peGreen=0x00;
        pLogPal->palPalEntry[0].peBlue=0x00;
        pLogPal->palPalEntry[0].peFlags=(BYTE) 0;
        /*BLUE*/
        pLogPal->palPalEntry[1].peRed=0x00;
        pLogPal->palPalEntry[1].peGreen=0x00;
        pLogPal->palPalEntry[1].peBlue=0xFF;
        pLogPal->palPalEntry[1].peFlags=(BYTE) 0;
        /*RED*/
        pLogPal->palPalEntry[2].peRed=0xFF;
        pLogPal->palPalEntry[2].peGreen=0x00;
        pLogPal->palPalEntry[2].peBlue=0x00;
        pLogPal->palPalEntry[2].peFlags=(BYTE) 0;
        /*GREEN*/
        pLogPal->palPalEntry[3].peRed=0x00;
        pLogPal->palPalEntry[3].peGreen=0xFF;
        pLogPal->palPalEntry[3].peBlue=0x00;
        pLogPal->palPalEntry[3].peFlags=(BYTE) 0;
        /*CYAN*/
        pLogPal->palPalEntry[4].peRed=0x00;
        pLogPal->palPalEntry[4].peGreen=0xFF;
        pLogPal->palPalEntry[4].peBlue=0xFF;
        pLogPal->palPalEntry[4].peFlags=(BYTE) 0;
        /*YELLOW*/
        pLogPal->palPalEntry[5].peRed=0xFF;
        pLogPal->palPalEntry[5].peGreen=0xFF;
        pLogPal->palPalEntry[5].peBlue=0x00;
        pLogPal->palPalEntry[5].peFlags=(BYTE) 0;
        /*MAGENTA*/
        pLogPal->palPalEntry[6].peRed=0xFF;
        pLogPal->palPalEntry[6].peGreen=0x00;
        pLogPal->palPalEntry[6].peBlue=0xFF;
        pLogPal->palPalEntry[6].peFlags=(BYTE) 0;
        /*WHITE*/
        pLogPal->palPalEntry[7].peRed=0xFF;
        pLogPal->palPalEntry[7].peGreen=0xFF;
        pLogPal->palPalEntry[7].peBlue=0xFF;
        pLogPal->palPalEntry[7].peFlags=(BYTE) 0;
        /*MIX1*/
        pLogPal->palPalEntry[8].peRed=0x00;
        pLogPal->palPalEntry[8].peGreen=0x80;
        pLogPal->palPalEntry[8].peBlue=0x80;
        pLogPal->palPalEntry[8].peFlags=(BYTE) 0;
        /*MIX2*/
        pLogPal->palPalEntry[9].peRed=0x80;
        pLogPal->palPalEntry[9].peGreen=0x80;
        pLogPal->palPalEntry[9].peBlue=0x80;
        pLogPal->palPalEntry[9].peFlags=(BYTE) 0;

        hPal=CreatePalette(pLogPal) ;
        break;

    case WM_COMMAND:
      switch (wParam)
      {
        case IDM_ABOUT:
```

```
        DialogBox(hInst1,"AboutDlgBox",hwnd,
                lpfnAboutDlgProc);
          break;
        case IDM_INPUT:
          DialogBox(hInst2,"BarDlgBox",
                  hwnd,lpfnBarDlgProc);
          InvalidateRect(hwnd,NULL,TRUE);
          UpdateWindow(hwnd);
          break;
        case IDM_EXIT:
          SendMessage(hwnd,WM_CLOSE,0,0L);
          break;
        default:
          break;
      }
      break;

    case WM_PAINT:
      hdc=BeginPaint(hwnd,&ps);
      SelectPalette(hdc,hPal,1);
      RealizePalette(hdc);

/*--------- your routines below ---------*/

      /* Set View Port and Map Mode */
      SetMapMode(hdc,MM_ISOTROPIC);
      SetWindowExt(hdc,640,400);
      SetViewportExt(hdc,xClientView,yClientView);
      SetViewportOrg(hdc,0,0);

      /* Print Text to Screen */
      hNFont=CreateFont(12,12,0,0,FW_BOLD,
                        FALSE,FALSE,FALSE,OEM_CHARSET,
                        OUT_DEFAULT_PRECIS,
                        CLIP_DEFAULT_PRECIS,
                        DEFAULT_QUALITY,
                        VARIABLE_PITCH|FF_ROMAN,
                        "Roman");
      hOFont=SelectObject(hdc,hNFont);
      TextOut(hdc,(300-(strlen(szTString)*10/2)),
              15,szTString,strlen(szTString));
      TextOut(hdc,(300-(strlen(szXString)*10/2)),
              365,szXString,strlen(szXString));
      TextOut(hdc,(90-ilenMaxLabel*12),
              70,strptr,ilenMaxLabel);
      hNFont=CreateFont(12,12,900,900,FW_BOLD,
                        FALSE,FALSE,FALSE,
                        OEM_CHARSET,
                        OUT_DEFAULT_PRECIS,
                        CLIP_DEFAULT_PRECIS,
                        DEFAULT_QUALITY,
                        VARIABLE_PITCH|FF_ROMAN,
                        "Roman");
      hOFont=SelectObject(hdc,hNFont);
      TextOut(hdc,50,200+(strlen(szXString)*10/2),
              szYString,strlen(szYString));

      /* Draw Coordinate Axis */
```

```
      MoveTo(hdc,99,49);
      LineTo(hdc,99,350);
      LineTo(hdc,500,350);
      MoveTo(hdc,99,350);
      x1=100;
      y1=350;
      x2=x1+iBarWidth;

      /* Draw Each Bar */
      for(i=0;i<iNBars;i++)
      {
        hBrush=CreateSolidBrush(PALETTEINDEX(i));
        SelectObject(hdc,hBrush);
        y2=350-(int) iBarSizeScaled[i];
        Rectangle(hdc,x1,y1,x2,y2);
        x1=x2;
        x2+=iBarWidth;
      }
      SelectObject(hdc,hOFont);
      DeleteObject(hNFont);

/*--------- your routines above ---------*/

      ValidateRect(hwnd,NULL);
      EndPaint(hwnd,&ps);
      break;

    case WM_DESTROY:
      if (pLogPal->palNumEntries)
          DeleteObject(hPal);
      PostQuitMessage(0);
      break;

    default:
      return(DefWindowProc(hwnd,messg,wParam,lParam));
  }
  return(0L);
}
```

The BAR11 and BAR11.DEF Files

As you can see from the BAR11 file listing, this program will also use a pointer (BAR11.CUR). The SDKPAINT editor can be used to create a bar chart pointer, or you can purchase the optional diskette that contains the preceding program. A third option is, of course, to use the default pointer— the arrow. The program on the diskette uses a small bar graph for the pointer. The BAR11.DEF file is similar to the previous .DEF file, in that it contains three EXPORTS: AboutDlgProc, BarDlgProc, and WindowProc. You'll see how these procedures are utilized when the main program is discussed.

The BAR11.H Header File

The BAR11.H header file contains identification information for the menu and dialog items of the main program. Additionally, three ID values are associated with the title, X axis, and Y axis labels. This header file also contains ten unique identification numbers that represent the ten input values, for bar heights, entered from the dialog box by the user.

The BAR11.RC Resource File

The BAR11.RC resource file contains information for the pointer (Bar-Cursor), menu (BarMenu), and two dialog boxes (AboutDlgBox and BarDlgBox). The data entry box is shown in Figure 11-5. This file was created with the Dialog Box Editor. If you are entering this program, it will be easiest for you to just type in this resource file as it appears. It's long, so be careful as you type.

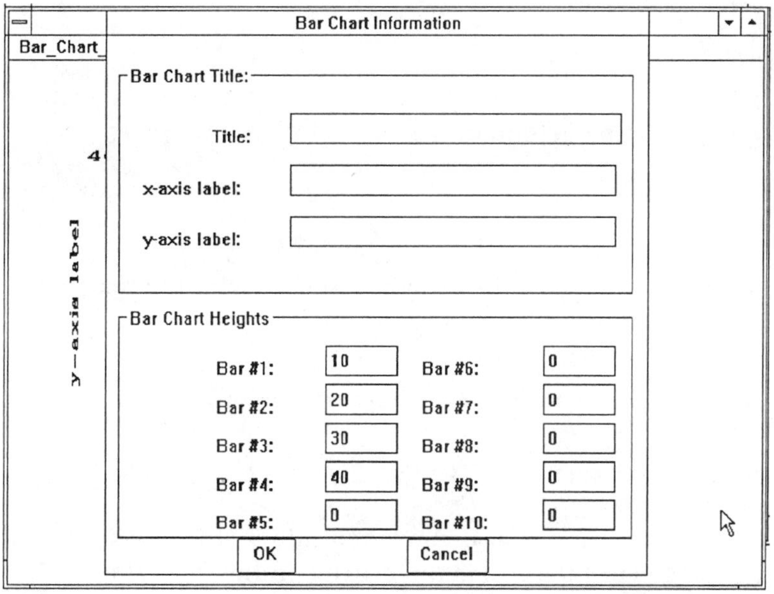

Figure 11-5.   The bar chart dialog box for data entry

The BAR11.C Program

The BAR11.C program for this section is very similar in design to the previous pie chart program. The data entered by the user in this program determines the height and number of bars to be plotted. The maximum is set to ten. The width and height of the bars are scaled to fit and fill the graph. Thus, a two-bar chart will have wider bars than one with five bars. The largest bar will be scaled to the chart's maximum height, with all other bars being sized proportionally. The user may enter a title, X axis, and Y axis labels for the bar chart. Since so many features of this program are similar to the pie chart example, let's concentrate on the major differences.

The data for the labels and height values is entered through the dialog box. This is passed to the global variables *iBarSize[], szTString, szXString,* and *szYString* in the normal manner.

Examine the code that starts in the WindowProc procedure. The global data array, *iBarSize[],* is examined for the first zero value. This value represents the end of data entry. By counting the number of non-zero entries, the number of bars (*iNBars*) can be determined.

```
iNBars=0;
for (i=0;i<maxnumbar;i++)
 {
 if(iBarSize[i]!=0) iNBars++;
 }
```

Since there are 400 data points available horizontally, the width of each bar (*iBarWidth*) can be determined by dividing 400 by *iNBars.*

```
BarWidth=400/iNBars;
```

The next step is to scan the array for the bar with the maximum height (*iBarMax*). This is done in a simple loop.

```
/* Find bar in array with maximum height */
iBarMax=iBarSize[0];
for(i=0;i<iNBars;i++)
  if (iBarMax<iBarSize[i]) iBarMax=iBarSize[i];
```

This maximum value is also converted into a string and pointed to by *strptr* in order to label the maximum Y value in the final plot.

```
/* Convert maximum y value to a string */
strptr=itoa(iBarMax,sbuffer,10);
ilenMaxLabel=strlen(sbuffer);
```

Knowing the height of the largest bar allows all other bar heights to be adjusted proportionally. These will be placed in a new array, *iBarSize-Scaled[]*. The maximum vertical height for bars is 270.

```
/* Scale bars in array.  Highest bar = 270 */
for (i=0;i<iNBars;i++)
  iBarSizeScaled[i]=(float) iBarSize[i]*(270.0/iBarMax);
```

Now skip down to the code contained under WM_PAINT. Notice that the MM_ISOTROPIC mapping mode is used in this example, too. This was done so that when the graph is minimized the icon produced will be a miniature bar graph.

The section of code devoted to printing labels actually creates two fonts. The first is a variable pitch Roman font for printing horizontal labels, while the second is the same font rotated 90 degrees, for plotting the vertical Y label. You might want to return to Chapter 9 for a review of how Create-Font utilizes its parameters.

Finally, the X-Y coordinate axes are drawn in black and the bars are plotted.

```
/* Draw Each Bar */
for(i=0;i<iNBars;i++)
  {
  hBrush=CreateSolidBrush(lColor[i]);
  SelectObject(hdc,hBrush);
  y2=350-(int) iBarSizeScaled[i];
  Rectangle(hdc,x1,y1,x2,y2);
  x1=x2;
  x2+=iBarWidth;
  }
```

Notice that the bars are drawn by subtracting the bar size from 350. This is required since the origin for the chart is in the upper-left corner of the window. The Rectangle function is used to draw each bar and fill it with the current color. For each pass through the loop, the *x1* value will be the *x2* value of the previous bar while *x2* will be incremented by the bar width, *iBarWidth*.

Figure 11-6 shows the default bar chart. Figure 11-7 shows a custom variation.

THE LINE CHART

The line chart program is a natural extension of the pie and bar chart programs. This program will allow the user to enter up to ten positive data

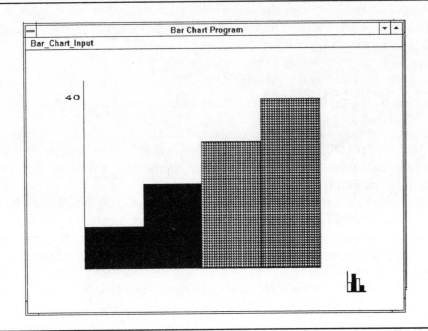

Figure 11-6.   The default bar chart

points (X-Y pairs) from a dialog box. The data is then scaled to the plot dimensions. The maximum Y value will be plotted at the top of the chart and the maximum X value at the extreme right of the chart. The maximum values for both X and Y are printed on their respective axes. The line chart program is the first program to provide tick marks on both the X and Y axes. Three labels can be added to this program, as was done in the bar chart program. At each data point pair, a small plus (+) symbol is drawn to represent the point. The LineTo function then draws a line between each of these symbols. You will notice when examining this listing that the program also utilizes the power of the Palette Manager. However, unlike the last example, this program uses the indirect method of specifying colors for the logical palette by using the PALETTERGB macro.

You may wish to change this program and permit the use of negative numbers. In that way, data could be plotted into all four quadrants.

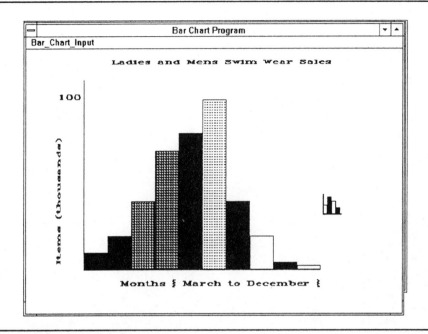

Figure 11-7.   A bar chart of swim wear sales

You will have nine files on your disk when the **MAKE** utility is finished: LINE11, LINE11.DEF, LINE11.H, LINE11.RC, LINE11.C, LINE11.CUR, LINE11.RES, LINE11.OBJ, and LINE11.EXE.

```
THE LINE11 MAKE FILE (LINE11):

all : line11.exe

line11.obj : line11.c line11.h
    cl -c -AS -FPi -Oas -Gsw -Zpe line11.c

line11.res : line11.rc line11.cur
    RC -r line11.cur

line11.exe : line11.obj line11.def line11.res
    link /NOD line11,,,libw slibcew, line11
    rc line11.res


THE LINE11 DEFINITION FILE (LINE11.DEF):

;LINE11.DEF for C Compiling
```

```
NAME            line11
DESCRIPTION     'Line Chart Program'
EXETYPE         WINDOWS
STUB            'WINSTUB.EXE'
CODE            PRELOAD MOVEABLE
DATA            PRELOAD MOVEABLE MULTIPLE
HEAPSIZE        4096
STACKSIZE       9216
EXPORTS         AboutDlgProc    @1
                LineDlgProc     @2
                WindowProc      @3
```

THE LINE11 HEADER FILE (LINE11.H):

```
#define IDM_ABOUT     40
#define IDM_INPUT     50
#define IDM_EXIT      70

#define DM_TITLE      280
#define DM_XLABEL     281
#define DM_YLABEL     282
#define DM_P0x        283
#define DM_P0y        284
#define DM_P1x        285
#define DM_P1y        286
#define DM_P2x        287
#define DM_P2y        288
#define DM_P3x        289
#define DM_P3y        290
#define DM_P4x        291
#define DM_P4y        292
#define DM_P5x        293
#define DM_P5y        294
#define DM_P6x        295
#define DM_P6y        296
#define DM_P7x        297
#define DM_P7y        298
#define DM_P8x        299
#define DM_P8y        300
#define DM_P9x        301
#define DM_P9y        302
```

THE LINE11 RESOURCE FILE (LINE11.RC):

```
#include "windows.h"
#include "line11.h"

LineCursor CURSOR Line11.cur

LineMenu  MENU
BEGIN
  POPUP "Line_Chart_Input"
  BEGIN
    MENUITEM "About...",       IDM_ABOUT
    MENUITEM "Input...",       IDM_INPUT
    MENUITEM "Exit",           IDM_EXIT
  END
END
```

```
AboutDlgBox DIALOG LOADONCALL MOVEABLE DISCARDABLE
        50,300,180,80
        STYLE WS_DLGFRAME|WS_POPUP
  BEGIN
    CONTROL "Interactive Line Chart Program",-1,"static",
        SS_CENTER|WS_CHILD,2,60,176,10
    CONTROL "by William H. Murray & Chris H. Pappas",-1,
        "static",SS_CENTER|WS_CHILD,2,45,176,10
    CONTROL "OK",IDOK,"button",
        BS_PUSHBUTTON|WS_TABSTOP|WS_CHILD,75,10,32,14
  END


LineDlgBox DIALOG LOADONCALL MOVEABLE DISCARDABLE 41,
        0,223,209
        CAPTION "Line Chart Information"
        STYLE WS_BORDER|WS_CAPTION|WS_DLGFRAME|WS_POPUP
  BEGIN
    CONTROL "Line Chart Title:",100,"button",
        BS_GROUPBOX|WS_TABSTOP|WS_CHILD,5,9,212,81
    CONTROL "Line Chart Heights",101,"button",
        BS_GROUPBOX|WS_TABSTOP|WS_CHILD,5,95,212,98
    CONTROL "Title: ",-1,"static",SS_LEFT|WS_CHILD,
        43,35,28,8
    CONTROL "",DM_TITLE,"edit",ES_LEFT|WS_BORDER|WS_TABSTOP|
        WS_CHILD,75,30,135,12
    CONTROL "x-axis label:",-1,"static",SS_LEFT|WS_CHILD,
        15,55,55,8
    CONTROL "",DM_XLABEL,"edit",ES_LEFT|WS_BORDER|WS_TABSTOP|
        WS_CHILD,75,50,135,12
    CONTROL "y-axis label:",-1,"static",SS_LEFT|WS_CHILD,
        15,75,60,8
    CONTROL "",DM_YLABEL,"edit",ES_LEFT|WS_BORDER|WS_TABSTOP|
        WS_CHILD,75,70,135,12
    CONTROL "x",140,"static",SS_LEFT|WS_CHILD,
        60,103,4,8
    CONTROL "y",141,"static",SS_LEFT|WS_CHILD,
        84,103,4,8
    CONTROL "x",142,"static",SS_LEFT|WS_CHILD,
        172,103,4,8
    CONTROL "y",143,"static",SS_LEFT|WS_CHILD,
        196,103,4,8
    CONTROL "Point #1: ",-1,"static",SS_LEFT|WS_CHILD,
        12,116,40,8
    CONTROL "Point #2: ",-1,"static",SS_LEFT|WS_CHILD,
        12,132,40,8
    CONTROL "Point #3: ",-1,"static",SS_LEFT|WS_CHILD,
        12,148,40,8
    CONTROL "Point #4: ",-1,"static",SS_LEFT|WS_CHILD,
        12,164,40,8
    CONTROL "Point #5: ",-1,"static",SS_LEFT|WS_CHILD,
        12,180,40,8
    CONTROL "Point #6: ",-1, "static",SS_LEFT|WS_CHILD,
        120,116,40,8
    CONTROL "Point #7: ",-1,"static",SS_LEFT|WS_CHILD,
        120,132,40,8
    CONTROL "Point #8: ",-1,"static",SS_LEFT|WS_CHILD,
        120,148,40,8
    CONTROL "Point #9: ",-1,"static",SS_LEFT|WS_CHILD,
        120,164,40,8
    CONTROL "Point #10:",-1,"static",SS_LEFT|WS_CHILD,
```

```
            120,180,45,8
        CONTROL "10",DM_P0x,"edit",ES_LEFT|WS_BORDER|WS_TABSTOP|
            WS_CHILD,52,112,20,12
        CONTROL "10",DM_P0y,"edit",ES_LEFT|WS_BORDER|WS_TABSTOP|
            WS_CHILD,80,112,20,12
        CONTROL "50",DM_P1x,"edit",ES_LEFT|WS_BORDER|WS_TABSTOP|
            WS_CHILD,52,128,20,12
        CONTROL "100",DM_P1y,"edit",ES_LEFT|WS_BORDER|WS_TABSTOP|
            WS_CHILD,80,128,20,12
        CONTROL "80",DM_P2x,"edit",ES_LEFT|WS_BORDER|WS_TABSTOP|
            WS_CHILD,52,144,20,12
        CONTROL "15",DM_P2y,"edit",ES_LEFT|WS_BORDER|WS_TABSTOP|
            WS_CHILD,80,144,20,12
        CONTROL "-1",DM_P3x,"edit",ES_LEFT|WS_BORDER|WS_TABSTOP|
            WS_CHILD,52,160,20,12
        CONTROL "-1",DM_P3y,"edit",ES_LEFT|WS_BORDER|WS_TABSTOP|
            WS_CHILD,80,160,20,12
        CONTROL "-1",DM_P4x,"edit",ES_LEFT|WS_BORDER|WS_TABSTOP|
            WS_CHILD,52,176,20,12
        CONTROL "-1",DM_P4y,"edit",ES_LEFT|WS_BORDER|WS_TABSTOP|
            WS_CHILD,80,176,20,12
        CONTROL "-1",DM_P5x,"edit",ES_LEFT|WS_BORDER|WS_TABSTOP|
            WS_CHILD,164,112,20,12
        CONTROL "-1",DM_P5y,"edit",ES_LEFT|WS_BORDER|WS_TABSTOP|
            WS_CHILD,192,112,20,12
        CONTROL "-1",DM_P6x,"edit",ES_LEFT|WS_BORDER|WS_TABSTOP|
            WS_CHILD,164,128,20,12
        CONTROL "-1",DM_P6y,"edit",ES_LEFT|WS_BORDER|WS_TABSTOP|
            WS_CHILD,192,128,19,12
        CONTROL "-1",DM_P7x,"edit",ES_LEFT|WS_BORDER|WS_TABSTOP|
            WS_CHILD,164,144,20,12
        CONTROL "-1",DM_P7y,"edit",ES_LEFT|WS_BORDER|WS_TABSTOP|
            WS_CHILD,192,144,20,12
        CONTROL "-1",DM_P8x,"edit",ES_LEFT|WS_BORDER|WS_TABSTOP|
            WS_CHILD,164,160,20,12
        CONTROL "-1",DM_P8y,"edit",ES_LEFT|WS_BORDER|WS_TABSTOP|
            WS_CHILD,192,160,20,12
        CONTROL "-1",DM_P9x,"edit",ES_LEFT|WS_BORDER|WS_TABSTOP|
            WS_CHILD,164,176,20,12
        CONTROL "-1",DM_P9y,"edit",ES_LEFT|WS_BORDER|WS_TABSTOP|
            WS_CHILD,192,176,20,12
        CONTROL "OK",1,"button",BS_PUSHBUTTON|WS_TABSTOP|
            WS_CHILD,54,195,24,14
        CONTROL "Cancel",2,"button",BS_PUSHBUTTON|WS_TABSTOP|
            WS_CHILD,124,195,34,14
    END


THE LINE11 APPLICATION FILE (LINE11.C):

/* Simplified Windows Platform (SWP)           */
/* (c) William H. Murray and Chris H. Pappas, 1989 */

#include <stdlib.h>
#include <string.h>
#include <windows.h>
#include "line11.h"

#define maxnumpts 10
#define PALETTESIZE 256
HANDLE  hPal;
```

```
NPLOGPALETTE pLogicalPal;

LONG FAR PASCAL WindowProc(HWND,unsigned,WORD,LONG);
BOOL FAR PASCAL AboutDlgProc(HWND,unsigned,WORD,LONG);
BOOL FAR PASCAL LineDlgProc(HWND,unsigned,WORD,LONG);

char szProgName[]="ProgName";
char szApplName[]="LineMenu";
char szCursorName[]="LineCursor";
char szTString[80]="(line chart title area)";
char szXString[80]="x-axis label";
char szYString[80]="y-axis label";
signed int iPtxSize[maxnumpts]={10,50,80,-1};
signed int iPtySize[maxnumpts]={10,100,15};


int PASCAL WinMain(hInst,hPreInst,lpszCmdLine,nCmdShow)
HANDLE hInst,hPreInst;
LPSTR  lpszCmdLine;
int    nCmdShow;
{
  HWND hwnd;
  MSG  msg;
  WNDCLASS wcSwp;
  if (!hPreInst)
  {
    wcSwp.lpszClassName=szProgName;
    wcSwp.hInstance    =hInst;
    wcSwp.lpfnWndProc  =WindowProc;
    wcSwp.hCursor      =LoadCursor(hInst,szCursorName);
    wcSwp.hIcon        =LoadIcon(hInst,szProgName);
    wcSwp.lpszMenuName =szApplName;
    wcSwp.hbrBackground=GetStockObject(WHITE_BRUSH);
    wcSwp.style        =CS_HREDRAW|CS_VREDRAW;
    wcSwp.cbClsExtra   =0;
    wcSwp.cbWndExtra   =0;
    if (!RegisterClass (&wcSwp))
      return FALSE;
  }
  hwnd=CreateWindow(szProgName,"Line Chart Program",
                    WS_OVERLAPPEDWINDOW,CW_USEDEFAULT,
                    CW_USEDEFAULT,CW_USEDEFAULT,
                    CW_USEDEFAULT,NULL,NULL,
                    hInst,NULL);
  ShowWindow(hwnd,nCmdShow);
  UpdateWindow(hwnd);
  while (GetMessage(&msg,NULL,NULL,NULL))
  {
    TranslateMessage(&msg);
    DispatchMessage(&msg);
  }
  return(msg.wParam);
}


BOOL FAR PASCAL AboutDlgProc(hdlg,messg,wParam,lParam)
HWND hdlg;
unsigned messg;
WORD wParam;
LONG lParam;
{
```

```
   switch (messg)
   {
     case WM_INITDIALOG:
       break;
     case WM_COMMAND:
       switch (wParam)
       {
         case IDOK:
           EndDialog(hdlg,TRUE);
           break;
         default:
           return FALSE;
       }
       break;
     default:
       return FALSE;
   }
   return TRUE;
}

BOOL FAR PASCAL LineDlgProc(hdlg,messg,wParam,lParam)
HWND hdlg;
unsigned messg;
WORD wParam;
LONG lParam;
{
   switch (messg)
   {
     case WM_INITDIALOG:
       return FALSE;
     case WM_COMMAND:
       switch (wParam)
       {
         case IDOK:
           GetDlgItemText(hdlg,DM_TITLE,szTString,80);
           GetDlgItemText(hdlg,DM_XLABEL,szXString,80);
           GetDlgItemText(hdlg,DM_YLABEL,szYString,80);
           iPtxSize[0]=GetDlgItemInt(hdlg,DM_P0x,NULL,1);
           iPtySize[0]=GetDlgItemInt(hdlg,DM_P0y,NULL,1);
           iPtxSize[1]=GetDlgItemInt(hdlg,DM_P1x,NULL,1);
           iPtySize[1]=GetDlgItemInt(hdlg,DM_P1y,NULL,1);
           iPtxSize[2]=GetDlgItemInt(hdlg,DM_P2x,NULL,1);
           iPtySize[2]=GetDlgItemInt(hdlg,DM_P2y,NULL,1);
           iPtxSize[3]=GetDlgItemInt(hdlg,DM_P3x,NULL,1);
           iPtySize[3]=GetDlgItemInt(hdlg,DM_P3y,NULL,1);
           iPtxSize[4]=GetDlgItemInt(hdlg,DM_P4x,NULL,1);
           iPtySize[4]=GetDlgItemInt(hdlg,DM_P4y,NULL,1);
           iPtxSize[5]=GetDlgItemInt(hdlg,DM_P5x,NULL,1);
           iPtySize[5]=GetDlgItemInt(hdlg,DM_P5y,NULL,1);
           iPtxSize[6]=GetDlgItemInt(hdlg,DM_P6x,NULL,1);
           iPtySize[6]=GetDlgItemInt(hdlg,DM_P6y,NULL,1);
           iPtxSize[7]=GetDlgItemInt(hdlg,DM_P7x,NULL,1);
           iPtySize[7]=GetDlgItemInt(hdlg,DM_P7y,NULL,1);
           iPtxSize[8]=GetDlgItemInt(hdlg,DM_P8x,NULL,1);
           iPtySize[8]=GetDlgItemInt(hdlg,DM_P8y,NULL,1);
           iPtxSize[9]=GetDlgItemInt(hdlg,DM_P9x,NULL,1);
           iPtySize[9]=GetDlgItemInt(hdlg,DM_P9y,NULL,1);
           EndDialog(hdlg,TRUE);
           break;
         case IDCANCEL:
           EndDialog(hdlg,FALSE);
```

```
            break;
          default:
            return FALSE;
        }
        break;

    default:
      return FALSE;
  }
  return TRUE;
}


long FAR PASCAL WindowProc(hwnd,messg,wParam,lParam)
HWND hwnd;
unsigned messg;
WORD wParam;
LONG lParam;
{
  HDC          hdc;
  PAINTSTRUCT  ps;
  HFONT        hOFont,hNFont;
  HPEN         hOrgPen;
  HPEN         hNewPen;
  static       FARPROC lpfnAboutDlgProc;
  static       FARPROC lpfnLineDlgProc;
  static       HWND hInst1,hInst2;
  static       short xClientView,yClientView;
  int          i,iNPts,iPtxMax,iPtyMax;
  int          ilenMaxYLabel,ilenMaxXLabel;
  int          x,y,xtic,ytic;
  float        iPtxScaled[maxnumpts];
  float        iPtyScaled[maxnumpts];
  char         sxbuffer[10],sybuffer[10],*strxptr,*stryptr;

  iNPts=0;
  /* Find Number of Points */
  for (i=0;i<maxnumpts;i++)
  {
    if (iPtxSize[i]>-1) iNPts++;
      else break;
  }

  iPtxMax=0;
  /* Find point in array with maximum X value */
  for (i=0;i<iNPts;i++)
    if(iPtxMax<iPtxSize[i]) iPtxMax=iPtxSize[i];

  /* Convert maximum x value to a string */
  strxptr=itoa(iPtxMax,sxbuffer,10);
  ilenMaxXLabel=strlen(sxbuffer);

  iPtyMax=0;
  /* Find point in array with maximum Y value */
  for (i=0;i<iNPts;i++)
    if(iPtyMax<iPtySize[i]) iPtyMax=iPtySize[i];

  /* Convert maximum y value to a string */
  stryptr=itoa(iPtyMax,sybuffer,10);
  ilenMaxYLabel=strlen(sybuffer);
```

```
/* Scale all X values in array.  Max X=400 */
for (i=0;i<iNPts;i++)
  iPtxScaled[i]=(float) iPtxSize[i]*400.0/iPtxMax;

/* Scale all Y values in array.  Max Y=300 */
for (i=0;i<iNPts;i++)
  iPtyScaled[i]=(float) iPtySize[i]*300.0/iPtyMax;

switch (messg)
{
  case WM_SIZE:
    xClientView=LOWORD(lParam);
    yClientView=HIWORD(lParam);
    break;

  case WM_CREATE:
    hInst1=((LPCREATESTRUCT) lParam)->hInstance;
    hInst2=((LPCREATESTRUCT) lParam)->hInstance;
    lpfnAboutDlgProc=MakeProcInstance(AboutDlgProc,hInst1);
    lpfnLineDlgProc=MakeProcInstance(LineDlgProc,hInst2);
    pLogicalPal=(NPLOGPALETTE) LocalAlloc(LMEM_FIXED,
                (sizeof(LOGPALETTE) +
                (sizeof(PALETTEENTRY)*(PALETTESIZE))));
    pLogicalPal->palVersion=0x300;
    pLogicalPal->palNumEntries=PALETTESIZE;

    /*BLUE*/
    pLogicalPal->palPalEntry[0].peRed=0x00;
    pLogicalPal->palPalEntry[0].peGreen=0x00;
    pLogicalPal->palPalEntry[0].peBlue=0xFF;
    pLogicalPal->palPalEntry[0].peFlags=(BYTE) 0;
    /*RED*/
    pLogicalPal->palPalEntry[1].peRed=0xFF;
    pLogicalPal->palPalEntry[1].peGreen=0x00;
    pLogicalPal->palPalEntry[1].peBlue=0x00;
    pLogicalPal->palPalEntry[1].peFlags=(BYTE) 0;
    /*YELLOW*/
    pLogicalPal->palPalEntry[2].peRed=0xFF;
    pLogicalPal->palPalEntry[2].peGreen=0xFF;
    pLogicalPal->palPalEntry[2].peBlue=0x00;
    pLogicalPal->palPalEntry[2].peFlags=(BYTE) 0;

    hPal=CreatePalette(pLogicalPal);
    break;

  case WM_COMMAND:
    switch (wParam)
    {
      case IDM_ABOUT:
        DialogBox(hInst1,"AboutDlgBox",hwnd,
                 lpfnAboutDlgProc);
        break;
      case IDM_INPUT:
        DialogBox(hInst2,"LineDlgBox",
                 hwnd,lpfnLineDlgProc);
        InvalidateRect(hwnd,NULL,TRUE);
        UpdateWindow(hwnd);
        break;
      case IDM_EXIT:
        SendMessage(hwnd,WM_CLOSE,0,0L);
        break;
```

```
           default:
              break;
           }
           break;

       case WM_PAINT:
           hdc=BeginPaint(hwnd,&ps);
           SelectPalette(hdc,hPal,1);
           RealizePalette(hdc);

/*--------- your routines below ---------*/

           /* Set View Port and Map Mode */
           SetMapMode(hdc,MM_ISOTROPIC);
           SetWindowExt(hdc,640,400);
           SetViewportExt(hdc,xClientView,yClientView);
           SetViewportOrg(hdc,0,0);

           /* Print Text to Screen */
           hNFont=CreateFont(12,12,0,0,FW_BOLD,
                              FALSE,FALSE,FALSE,OEM_CHARSET,
                              OUT_DEFAULT_PRECIS,
                              CLIP_DEFAULT_PRECIS,
                              DEFAULT_QUALITY,
                              VARIABLE_PITCH|FF_ROMAN,
                              "Roman");
           hOFont=SelectObject(hdc,hNFont);
           TextOut(hdc,(300-(strlen(szTString)*10/2)),
                   15,szTString,strlen(szTString));
           TextOut(hdc,(300-(strlen(szXString)*10/2)),
                   365,szXString,strlen(szXString));
           TextOut(hdc,(500-(ilenMaxXLabel*12/2)),
                   355,strxptr,ilenMaxXLabel);
           TextOut(hdc,(90-ilenMaxYLabel*12),
                   45,stryptr,ilenMaxYLabel);
           hNFont=CreateFont(12,12,900,900,FW_BOLD,
                              FALSE,FALSE,FALSE,
                              OEM_CHARSET,
                              OUT_DEFAULT_PRECIS,
                              CLIP_DEFAULT_PRECIS,
                              DEFAULT_QUALITY,
                              VARIABLE_PITCH|FF_ROMAN,
                              "Roman");
           hOFont=SelectObject(hdc,hNFont);
           TextOut(hdc,50,200+(strlen(szXString)*10/2),
                   szYString,strlen(szYString));

           /* Draw Coordinate Axis */
           hNewPen=CreatePen(PS_SOLID,1,
                              PALETTERGB(0x00,0x00,0xFF));
           hOrgPen=SelectObject(hdc,hNewPen);
           MoveTo(hdc,100,50);
           LineTo(hdc,100,350);
           LineTo(hdc,500,350);

           /* Draw X axis tic marks */
           xtic=140;
           for (i=0;i<10;i++)
           {
             ytic=350;
             MoveTo(hdc,xtic,ytic);
```

```
        ytic=347;
        LineTo(hdc,xtic,ytic);
        xtic+=40;
    }

    /* Draw Y axis tic marks */
    ytic=50;
    for (i=0;i<10;i++)
    {
        xtic=100;
        MoveTo(hdc,xtic,ytic);
        xtic=103;
        LineTo(hdc,xtic,ytic);
        ytic+=30;
    }

    /* Plot a + symbol for each point */
    hNewPen=CreatePen(PS_SOLID,1,
                        PALETTERGB(0xFF,0xFF,0x00));
    hOrgPen=SelectObject(hdc,hNewPen);
    for(i=0;i<iNPts;i++)
    {
        x=100+(int) iPtxScaled[i];
        y=350-(int) iPtyScaled[i];
        MoveTo(hdc,x-5,y);
        LineTo(hdc,x+5,y);
        MoveTo(hdc,x,y-5);
        LineTo(hdc,x,y+5);
    }

    /* Plot Lines between Points */
    hNewPen=CreatePen(PS_SOLID,1,
                        PALETTERGB(0xFF,0x00,0x00));
    hOrgPen=SelectObject(hdc,hNewPen);
    x=100+(int) iPtxScaled[0];
    y=350-(int) iPtyScaled[0];
    MoveTo(hdc,x,y);
    for(i=1;i<iNPts;i++)
    {
        x=100+(int) iPtxScaled[i];
        y=350-(int) iPtyScaled[i];
        LineTo(hdc,x,y);
    }

    SelectObject(hdc,hOFont);
    DeleteObject(hNFont);

/*--------- your routines above ---------*/

    ValidateRect(hwnd,NULL);
    EndPaint(hwnd,&ps);
    break;

case WM_DESTROY:
    if (pLogicalPal->palNumEntries)
        DeleteObject(hPal);
    PostQuitMessage(0);
    break;

default:
```

```
    return(DefWindowProc(hwnd,messg,wParam,lParam));
  }
  return(0L);
}
```

The LINE11 and LINE11.DEF Files

As you can see from the LINE11 file listing, this program will also use a pointer (LINE.CUR). Again, you will need to use the SDKPAINT editor to create your own pointer for this program as you did for the last two examples. The LINE11.DEF file is very similar to the previous .DEF file in that it contains three EXPORTS: AboutDlgProc, LineDlgProc, and WindowProc. When you study the main program listing you will see how these procedures are used.

The LINE11.H Header File

The LINE11.H header file contains identification information for the menu and dialog items of the main program. Notice in particular the need for ten identification values for X parameters (DM_P0x-DM_P9x) and ten identification values for Y parameters (DM_P0y-DM_P9y). Data points for the line chart program are entered as X-Y pairs from the dialog box.

The LINE11.RC Resource File

The LINE11.RC resource file contains information for the pointer (Line-Cursor), menu (LineMenu), and two dialog boxes (AboutDlgBox and LineDlgBox). This file was created with the Dialog Box Editor. If you are entering this program, it would be easiest for you to carefully type in this resource file as it appears here. As resource file listings get longer, additional care must be taken when typing. The data entry dialog box is shown in Figure 11-8.

The LINE11.C Program

The LINE11.C program for this section is very similar in design to the previous bar chart program. This program will allow the user to enter the same three labels (title, X-axis, and Y-axis) as the past program. Additionally, the dialog box will allow ten X-Y data pairs to be entered. The data points entered by the user will be scaled and plotted to the positive X and Y axes. The largest X point will be scaled to the maximum horizontal value,

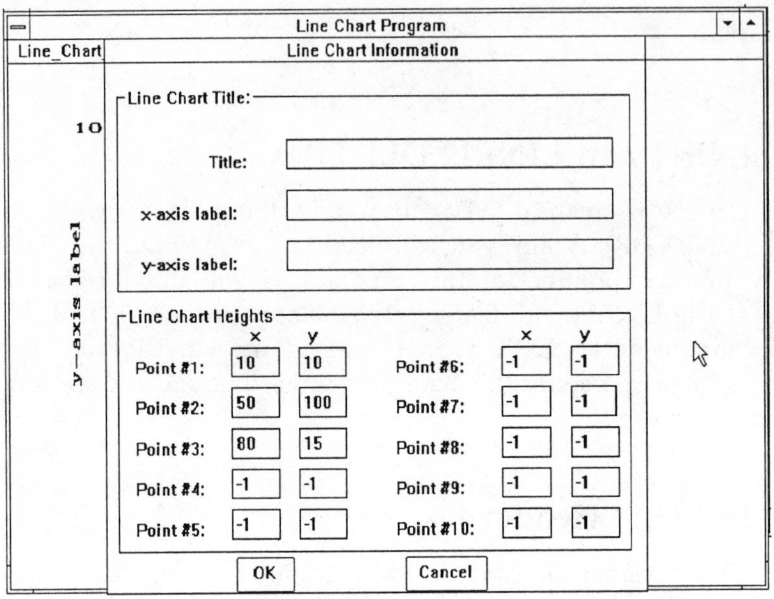

Figure 11-8.   The line chart dialog box for data entry

while the largest Y point will be scaled to the maximum vertical value on the screen. Many features of this program are similar to the pie and bar chart examples. The discussion will only concentrate on the new features this program utilizes.

In the first two examples of this chapter, the actual number of data entries was determined by scanning the data array until a zero was found. Since a zero X or Y value is permissible as a data point in this example, a different approach is used. The dialog box returns data points to two global arrays: *iPtxSize[]* and *iPtySize[]*. Since data is entered in pairs, it is only necessary to scan *iPtxSize[]* in order to determine the actual number of data points entered by the user. A loop is used to check each value and determine if the data value is zero or greater. A negative one (−1) is entered as the default value in the resource file. If the data is zero or greater, the variable *iNPts* is incremented. This solution is necessary because the function GetDlgItemInt returns a zero as a default value, whether data is properly converted or not. It is necessary to force the variable to a non-zero value outside the range of positive data points, thus the −1. Another approach could be used. The third parameter for GetDlgItemInt is a pointer to a flag of type *BOOL*. This flag can be used to signal an improper conversion. However, since this presented its own set of problems, it was decided to use the former technique; thus, the third parameter is set to NULL. Examine the code that starts directly under the beginning of the WindowProc procedure. The maximum X and Y values are needed for proper scaling of the data points. These values, *iPtxMax* and *iPtyMax*, are determined with the use of a loop. Each data array, *iPtxSize[]* or *iPtySize[]*, is scanned until the maximum value is found. It is this value that is returned to the two variables mentioned earlier.

The maximum X and Y values are important for another reason. They will be printed at the far end of both the X and Y axes. In order to do this they must also be converted to strings. This is accomplished, in both cases, with the familiar *itoa* function. The X-axis string will be pointed to by *strxptr* and the Y-axis string by *stryptr*. Additionally, the lengths of the strings are saved in two variables, *ilenMaxXLabel* and *ilenMaxYLabel*.

The values in each data array are then scaled to fit the graph. The scaling equation is similar to the routine used in both the pie and bar chart programs. The scaled points are saved in two new arrays, *iPtxScaled[]* and *iPtyScaled[]*.

Everything is ready for plotting titles, labels, marker symbols, and lines. Examine the code under WM_PAINT. The mapping mode and view port establish the same application screen as for the bar chart program. It should come as no surprise that the labels are plotted with the same fonts as well.

In this example, tick marks are added to both the vertical and horizontal axes. The tick marks are actually short line segments drawn with the MoveTo and LineTo functions on each axis, for example:

```
/* Draw X axis tic marks */
xtic=140;
for (i=0;i<10;i++)
  {
  ytic=350;
  MoveTo(hdc,xtic,ytic);
  ytic=347;
  LineTo(hdc,xtic,ytic);
  xtic+=40;
  }
```

This same approach can be used to form the small plus symbol (+) to be plotted at each X-Y data pair.

```
/* Plot a + symbol for each point */
for(i=0;i<iNPts;i++)
  {
  x=100+(int) iPtxScaled[i];
  y=350-(int) iPtyScaled[i];
  MoveTo(hdc,x-5,y);
  LineTo(hdc,x+5,y);
  MoveTo(hdc,x,y-5);
```

```
LineTo(hdc,x,y+5);
  }
```

Once the symbols are in place, lines are drawn between each point using MoveTo and LineTo. Note that the lines are drawn in red.

```
/* Plot Lines between Points */
x=100+(int) iPtxScaled[0];
y=350-(int) iPtyScaled[0];
MoveTo(hdc,x,y);
for(i=1;i<iNPts;i++)
  {
  x=100+(int) iPtxScaled[i];
  y=350-(int) iPtyScaled[i];
  LineTo(hdc,x,y);
  }
```

Figure 11-9 shows the default line chart produced by values contained in the resource file (LINE11.RC). Figure 11-10 shows how a line chart can be used to plot scientific data. Also examine Figure 11-11. Since Windows will

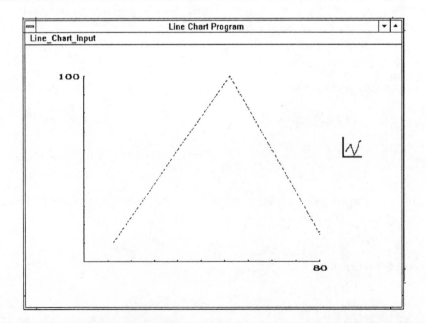

Figure 11-9.   The default line chart

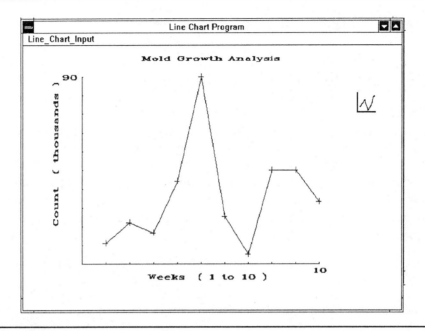

Figure 11-10.   A line chart showing a scientific data plot

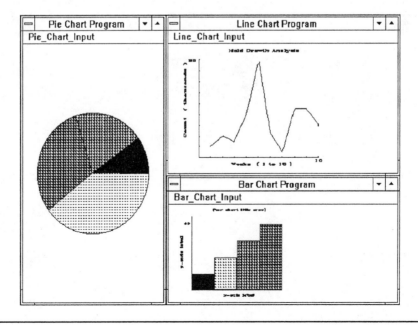

Figure 11-11.   Using the pie, bar, and line charts together for an added visual effect

allow several applications to run at the same time, you could plot and examine the same data with pie, bar, and line charts.

VARIATIONS ON THE BIG THREE

Where do you go from here? There are a lot of things you might consider to alter the three graphics programs in this chapter. The pie chart could be customized to give an exploded pie wedge for the largest slice. The bar chart could be made three-dimensional, producing a very nice effect. The line chart program could be changed to allow several lines to be plotted on the same chart. This could be achieved as easily as using one dialog box for each line desired. The world of presentation graphics is open to your imagination.

12

GRAPHICAL TECHNIQUES AND INTERACTIVE GRAPHICAL PROGRAMMING

Engineers, mathematicians, and scientists often express ideas and concepts in graphs and charts formed from user-entered data, just as business professionals do. This data can be plotted to the familiar pie, bar, and line charts developed in the previous chapter. But many times it is also necessary to generate data points from mathematical equations, and then to plot these points to the screen. This chapter will investigate techniques for drawing a sine wave, a damped sine wave, and a Fourier series wave form. You can then expand those concepts to include other engineering, mathematical, and scientific equations.

Even if you have no interest in plotting mathematical equations, there is interesting new information in this chapter. For example, it will show you how to use FloodFill to fill an irregular mathematical shape.

THE SINE WAVE

Trigonometry is a branch of mathematics that involves the study of triangles. In fact, the term literally means "triangle measurements." The sine function is one of the six fundamental trigonometric functions used in describing a triangle. None of this is of immediate importance, except for the fact that the majority of familiar electrical waves, such as common house current, radio waves, and so on, take the shape of a sine wave. As a result, this waveform is of interest to engineers, mathematicians, and scientists alike. The C library allows access to trigonometric functions such as sine, cosine, and tangent. This example uses the sine function to plot a sine wave in a window, from 0 to 360 degrees. The range of 0 to 360 degrees is one complete sine wave cycle. If radians are used, one complete cycle ranges from 0 to 2*pi radians. In most mathematical compiler libraries, the angle is expressed in radians. The sine function returns a real value of 0.0 when the angle is 0 degrees (0 radians). The maximum positive sine value (+1) occurs at 90 degrees (pi/2 radians). At 180 degrees (pi radians) the value is 0 again. Then at 270 degrees (3*pi/2 radians), the maximum negative value (−1) is produced. Finally, at 360 degrees (2*pi radians) the waveform has returned to 0.

THE SINE12 MAKE FILE:

```
all : sine12.exe

sine12.obj: sine12.c
    cl -c -AS -FPi -Gsw -Oas -Zpe sine12.c

sine12.exe: sine12.obj sine12.def sine12.res
    link /NOD sine12,,,libw slibcew,sine12.def
```

THE SINE12.DEF DEFINITION FILE:

```
NAME        SINE12
DESCRIPTION 'Simplified Windows Platform'
EXETYPE     WINDOWS
STUB        'WINSTUB.EXE'
CODE        PRELOAD MOVEABLE DISCARDABLE
DATA        PRELOAD MOVEABLE MULTIPLE
HEAPSIZE    4096
STACKSIZE   9216
EXPORTS     WindowProc       @1
```

THE SINE12.C APPLICATION FILE:

```
/* Simplified Windows Platform (SWP)                */
/* (c) William H. Murray and Chris H. Pappas, 1989 */

#include <windows.h>
#include <math.h>

#define pi 3.1415926535

long FAR PASCAL WindowProc(HWND,unsigned,WORD,LONG);

char    szProgName[]="ProgName";

int PASCAL WinMain(hInst,hPreInst,lpszCmdLine,nCmdShow)
HANDLE hInst,hPreInst;
LPSTR  lpszCmdLine;
int    nCmdShow;
{
  HWND hwnd;
```

```
   MSG  msg;
   WNDCLASS wcSwp;
   if (!hPreInst)
   {
     wcSwp.lpszClassName=szProgName;
     wcSwp.hInstance    =hInst;
     wcSwp.lpfnWndProc  =WindowProc;
     wcSwp.hCursor      =LoadCursor(NULL,IDC_ARROW);
     wcSwp.hIcon        =NULL;
     wcSwp.lpszMenuName =NULL;
     wcSwp.hbrBackground=GetStockObject(WHITE_BRUSH);
     wcSwp.style        =CS_HREDRAW|CS_VREDRAW;
     wcSwp.cbClsExtra   =0;
     wcSwp.cbWndExtra   =0;
     if (!RegisterClass (&wcSwp))
        return FALSE;
   }
   hwnd=CreateWindow(szProgName,"Sinewave",
                     WS_OVERLAPPEDWINDOW,CW_USEDEFAULT,
                     CW_USEDEFAULT,CW_USEDEFAULT,
                     CW_USEDEFAULT,NULL,NULL,
                     hInst,NULL);
   ShowWindow(hwnd,nCmdShow);
   UpdateWindow(hwnd);
   while (GetMessage(&msg,NULL,NULL,NULL))
   {
     TranslateMessage(&msg);
     DispatchMessage(&msg);
   }
   return(msg.wParam);
}

long FAR PASCAL WindowProc(hwnd,messg,wParam,lParam)
HWND   hwnd;
unsigned messg;
WORD   wParam;
LONG   lParam;
{
  PAINTSTRUCT ps;
  HDC hdc;
  double y;
  int i,x;

  switch (messg)
  {
    case WM_PAINT:
      hdc=BeginPaint(hwnd,&ps);

/*--------- your routines below ---------*/

      /* draw x & y coordinate axes */
      MoveTo(hdc,100,50);
      LineTo(hdc,100,350);
      MoveTo(hdc,100,200);
      LineTo(hdc,500,200);
      MoveTo(hdc,100,200);

      for (i=0;i<400;i++)
      {
        y=100.0*sin(pi*i*(360.0/400.0)/180.0);
        LineTo(hdc,i+100,(int) (200.0-y));
```

```
        }
/*--------- your routines above ---------*/

      ValidateRect(hwnd,NULL);
      EndPaint(hwnd,&ps);
      break;
    case WM_DESTROY:
      PostQuitMessage(0);
      break;
    default:
      return(DefWindowProc(hwnd,messg,wParam,lParam));
      break;
  }
  return(0L);
}
```

As you study the listing for this program, notice that there is an *#include* statement for the MATH.H header file. This will allow access to the necessary trigonometric function. The sine function returns real numbers, so provision has been made to access the coprocessor if it is available. Examine the **MAKE** file for this program and note that the -FPi option is being used during compile. Both of these options were discussed in Chapter 8.

This program is simple and makes exclusive use of the MoveTo and LineTo functions. Examine the following portion of code.

```
/*--------- your routines below ---------*/

      /* draw x & y coordinate axes */
      MoveTo(hdc,100,50);
      LineTo(hdc,100,350);
      MoveTo(hdc,100,200);
      LineTo(hdc,500,200);
      MoveTo(hdc,100,200);

      for (i=0;i<400;i++)
      {
        y=100.0*sin(pi*i*(360.0/400.0)/180.0);
        LineTo(hdc,i+100,(int) (200.0-y));
      }

/*--------- your routines above ---------*/
```

The X and Y axes are drawn using these functions. The actual sine wave is drawn by calculating the sine value for each angle, scaling the point, and drawing a line from the last point to the current point. These calculations are contained in a loop in which an index changes from 0 to 400. This range represents the number of pixels to be used in drawing the figure.

The variable i will be used to increment the waveform in the horizontal direction. Since i varies from 0 to 400, it will have to be scaled by (360/400) in order to produce angles in the range of 0 to 360 degrees. Since 2*pi radians equals 360 degrees, a little algebra yields

radians = (pi/180) * angle

You already know that the angle is expressed by

angle = i * (360/400)

thus

radians = pi * i (360/400) / 180

The LineTo function is now called. The horizontal points are offset, in the positive direction, by 100 pixels. The vertical points are subtracted from 200 to position them properly on the screen. Figure 12-1 shows the final result of this program. Try entering this program and altering the amplitude and frequency of the sine wave—you'll learn a lot in the process.

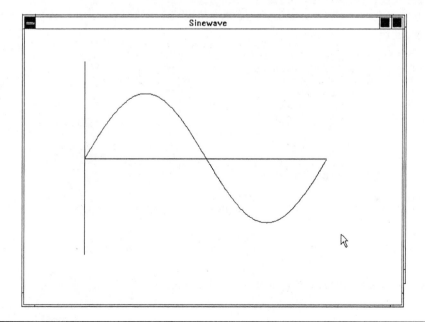

Figure 12-1. A simple sine wave

A DAMPED SINE WAVE

Have you ever been in a car with bad shock absorbers? One little bump sets the car bouncing. Believe it or not, a car with bad shocks produces a sine wave effect as it rolls down the road. Shock absorbers are added to damp the bounce and make it die out more quickly than it naturally would. Shock absorbers do not change the frequency of the bounce—only the amplitude. In electrical engineering there are electronic counterparts to the bouncing automobile. These oscillating waveforms can be damped with special electronic circuits. The degree of damping is often specified as *underdamped, overdamped,* or *critically damped.* Many times this damping is related to the natural number, ϵ, approximately 2.718. By raising ϵ to an exponential value varying from 0 to 4 in steps of 0.01, you can create an envelope about the sine wave. This is achieved by multiplying the sine value by the exponential value. This will produce a sine wave plot that will decrease exponentially over the length of the window.

THE DSINE12 MAKE FILE:

```
all : dsine12.exe

dsine12.obj: dsine12.c
    cl -c -AS -FPi -Gsw -Oas -Zpe dsine12.c

dsine12.exe: dsine12.obj dsine12.def dsine12.res
    link /NOD dsine12,,,libw slibcew, dsine12.def
```

THE DSINE12.DEF DEFINITION FILE:

```
NAME        DSINE12
DESCRIPTION 'Simplified Windows Platform'
EXETYPE     WINDOWS
STUB        'WINSTUB.EXE'
CODE        PRELOAD MOVEABLE DISCARDABLE
DATA        PRELOAD MOVEABLE MULTIPLE
HEAPSIZE    4096
STACKSIZE   9216
EXPORTS     WindowProc      @1
```

THE DSINE12.C APPLICATION FILE:

```
/* Simplified Windows Platform (SWP)            */
/* (c) William H. Murray and Chris H. Pappas, 1989 */

#include <windows.h>
#include <math.h>

#define pi 3.1415926535

long FAR PASCAL WindowProc(HWND,unsigned,WORD,LONG);

char    szProgName[]="ProgName";

int PASCAL WinMain(hInst,hPreInst,lpszCmdLine,nCmdShow)
HANDLE hInst,hPreInst;
LPSTR lpszCmdLine;
```

```
int    nCmdShow;
{
  HWND hwnd;
  MSG  msg;
  WNDCLASS wcSwp;
  if (!hPreInst)
  {
    wcSwp.lpszClassName=szProgName;
    wcSwp.hInstance    =hInst;
    wcSwp.lpfnWndProc  =WindowProc;
    wcSwp.hCursor      =LoadCursor(NULL,IDC_ARROW);
    wcSwp.hIcon        =NULL;
    wcSwp.lpszMenuName =NULL;
    wcSwp.hbrBackground=GetStockObject(WHITE_BRUSH);
    wcSwp.style        =CS_HREDRAW|CS_VREDRAW;
    wcSwp.cbClsExtra   =0;
    wcSwp.cbWndExtra   =0;
    if (!RegisterClass (&wcSwp))
      return FALSE;
  }
  hwnd=CreateWindow(szProgName,"Damped Sinewave",
                    WS_OVERLAPPEDWINDOW,CW_USEDEFAULT,
                    CW_USEDEFAULT,CW_USEDEFAULT,
                    CW_USEDEFAULT,NULL,NULL,
                    hInst,NULL);
  ShowWindow(hwnd,nCmdShow);
  UpdateWindow(hwnd);
  while (GetMessage(&msg,NULL,NULL,NULL))
  {
    TranslateMessage(&msg);
    DispatchMessage(&msg);
  }
  return(msg.wParam);
}

long FAR PASCAL WindowProc(hwnd,messg,wParam,lParam)
HWND    hwnd;
unsigned messg;
WORD    wParam;
LONG    lParam;
{
  PAINTSTRUCT ps;
  HDC hdc;
  HBRUSH hOrgBrush,hBrush;
  static short xClientView,yClientView;
  double y;
  int i,x;

  switch (messg)
  {
    case WM_SIZE:
      xClientView=LOWORD(lParam);
      yClientView=HIWORD(lParam);
      break;

    case WM_PAINT:
      hdc=BeginPaint(hwnd,&ps);

/*--------- your routines below ---------*/

      SetMapMode(hdc,MM_ISOTROPIC);
```

```
    SetWindowExt(hdc,400,400);
    SetViewportExt(hdc,xClientView,-yClientView);
    SetViewportOrg(hdc,100,220);

    /* draw x & y coordinate axes */
    MoveTo(hdc,0,150);
    LineTo(hdc,0,-150);
    MoveTo(hdc,0,0);
    LineTo(hdc,400,0);
    MoveTo(hdc,0,0);

    for (i=0;i<400;i++)
    {
       y=180.0*(exp(-i*0.01))*sin(pi*i*(1440.0/400.0)/180.0);
       LineTo(hdc,i,(int) y);
    }

    MoveTo(hdc,0,0);
    for (i=0;i<400;i++)
    {
       y=180.0*(exp(-i*0.01));
       LineTo(hdc,i,(int) y);
    }

    MoveTo(hdc,0,0);
    for (i=0;i<400;i++)
    {
       y=180.0*(exp(-i*0.01));
       LineTo(hdc,i,(int) -y);
    }

/*--------- your routines above ---------*/

    ValidateRect(hwnd,NULL);
    EndPaint(hwnd,&ps);
    break;
  case WM_DESTROY:
    PostQuitMessage(0);
    break;
  default:
    return(DefWindowProc(hwnd,messg,wParam,lParam));
    break;
  }
  return(0L);
}
```

This program, when compared to the first example, makes use of more sophisticated Windows features. Study the listing and notice the use of the WM_SIZE message. Whenever the window is resized, the returned values will be saved in *xClientView* and *yClientView*. This information allows you to scale the figure to the client window, even down to icon size. The Set-MapMode function is used to select the MM_ISOTROPIC mode. In the MM_ISOTROPIC mode, you may recall, the logical units are mapped to arbitrary units with equally scaled axes. Thus, one unit along the X axis is equivalent to one unit along the Y axis. The SetWindowExt function is responsible for stretching or compressing the logical coordinates in order to fit the actual device coordinates of the system. In this example, both the X and Y extents will be 400 logical units. Next, SetViewportExt is used to set the extents of the viewport specified by the device context. Notice that the *yClientView* is given as a negative. Thus, more positive values are at the top of the window and more negative values at the bottom. Finally, SetViewportOrg allows the origin to be specified for the mathematical plot. The previous example required offsetting the horizontal points by 100 and the vertical points by 200. With SetViewportOrg, the origin is set to 100,220 that will represent 0,0 for all points plotted on the graph, as shown in Figure 12-2. Thus, offsets will not be needed to correctly plot the points for the graph.

The effects of changing the viewport can immediately be noticed in the code that draws the coordinate axes.

```
/*--------- your routines below ---------*/
        SetMapMode(hdc,MM_ISOTROPIC);
        SetWindowExt(hdc,400,400);
        SetViewportExt(hdc,xClientView,-yClientView);
        SetViewportOrg(hdc,100,220);

        /* draw x & y coordinate axes */
        MoveTo(hdc,0,150);
        LineTo(hdc,0,-150);
        MoveTo(hdc,0,0);
        LineTo(hdc,400,0);
        MoveTo(hdc,0,0);

        for (i=0;i<400;i++)
        {
           y=180.0*(exp(-i*0.01))*sin(pi*i*(1440.0/400.0)/180.0);
           LineTo(hdc,i,(int) y);
        }

        MoveTo(hdc,0,0);
        for (i=0;i<400;i++)
        {
           y=180.0*(exp(-i*0.01));
           LineTo(hdc,i,(int) y);
        }

        MoveTo(hdc,0,0);
        for (i=0;i<400;i++)
        {
           y=180.0*(exp(-i*0.01));
           LineTo(hdc,i,(int) -y);
        }

/*--------- your routines above ---------*/
```

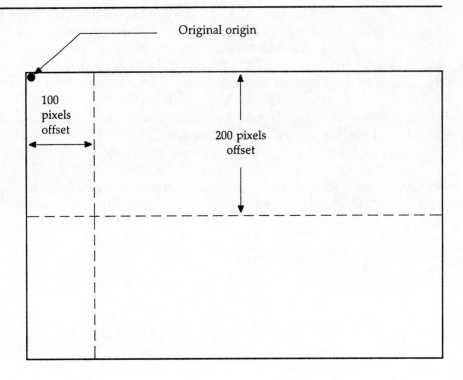

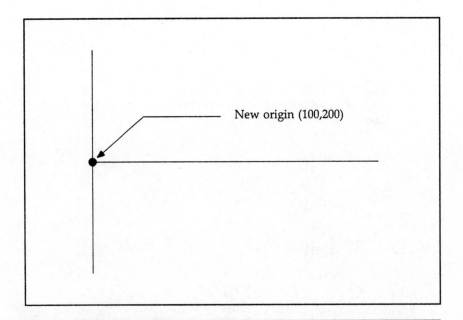

Figure 12-2. Changing the default coordinates

The loop from the first example is used here, with two changes. First, approximately four complete sine wave cycles are to be drawn to the screen. Hence, instead of 360, a value of 1440 is used in the equation. Second, the exponential function is multiplied by the sine function to yield the damped sine wave.

In order to make the final figure a little more interesting, the envelope is drawn by plotting the exponential function above and below the X axis. Figure 12-3 shows the resulting waveform.

What do you think—would this damped oscillation graph represent a good shock absorber for that '78 Ford?

A FOURIER SERIES

Another special application involves the fairly complicated calculation of a Fourier series. A French mathematician named Baron Jean Baptiste Joseph Fourier (1768–1830) observed that almost any periodic waveform can be constructed by simply adding the correct combinations of sine wave harmonics together. His results produce a wide variety of waveforms, from square to triangular. Electrical engineers are often interested in square

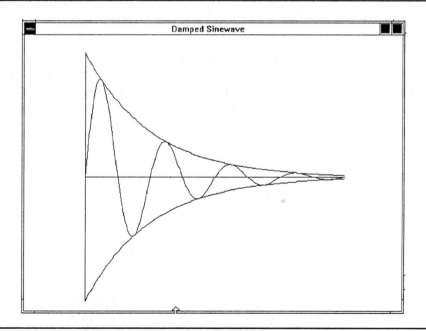

Figure 12-3. A damped sine wave and envelope

wave reproduction since square waves are made from a fundamental sine wave and its associated overtones. The quality of amplifiers and other communication devices depends on how well they can reproduce these signals. (For a more detailed treatment of the Fourier series, refer to college level physics or electrical engineering text books.) Fourier's formal equation is usually expressed as

$$y = A + A1(\sin \omega t) + A2(\sin 2\omega t) + A3(\sin 3\omega t) + A4(\sin 4\omega t) \ldots$$

Some waveforms only include odd or even harmonics, while for others all terms are included. And in some waveforms, the signs alternate between + and − for adjacent terms. This example constructs a square wave by adding the harmonic terms in a Fourier series together. The more terms that are used in the series, the more the final result will approach a precise square wave. For a square wave, the general Fourier series equation becomes this exact equation:

$$y = (\sin \omega t) + (1/3)(\sin 3\omega t) + (1/5)(\sin 5\omega t) + (1/7)(\sin 7\omega t) \ldots$$

You can see that only odd harmonics will contribute to the final result. Notice also, from the equation, that if only one harmonic is chosen, the result will be a sine wave. Also notice that each successive term uses a fractional multiplier−in other words, each successively higher harmonic affects the waveform less and less.

To fully appreciate what this program is about to accomplish, remember that each term in a Fourier series will be calculated separately by the program, with the sum of these individual terms being continuously updated. Therefore, if you ask for 1000 harmonics, 1000 separate sine values will be scaled, calculated, and added together to form a single point for the window. But this must be repeated for each point that is to be plotted on the screen. Therefore, 1000 calculations × 360 points = 360,000 calculations. How long would it take you to do that with a calculator? How long would it take a C program to make the same set of calculations? If it takes us 5 minutes to do 50 terms on a calculator, for 1000 terms it would take 100 minutes. One hundred minutes × 360 points = 36,000 minutes or 25 days (non-stop). There are really better things to do in life. How fast your program can calculate the points depends on two factors: the clock speed of the microprocessor and whether a coprocessor is present in your computer. If you are running this program on a 6 megahertz IBM AT (80286) without a math coprocessor, expect rather sluggish results. However, if you are running this on a 80286/80386 computer at clock rates above 18 megahertz with a coprocessor, you can expect the calculations to fly.

THE FOUR12 MAKE FILE:

```
all : four12.exe

four12.obj: four12.c
    cl -c -AS -FPi -Gsw -Oas -Zpe four12.c

four12.res: four12.rc
    rc -r four12.rc

four12.exe: four12.obj four12.def four12.res
    link /NOD four12,,,libw slibcew,four12.def
    rc four12.res
```

THE FOUR12 DEFINITION FILE:

```
NAME        FOUR12
DESCRIPTION 'Simplified Windows Platform'
EXETYPE     WINDOWS
STUB        'WINSTUB.EXE'
CODE        PRELOAD MOVEABLE DISCARDABLE
DATA        PRELOAD MOVEABLE MULTIPLE
HEAPSIZE    4096
STACKSIZE   9216
EXPORTS     WindowProc      @1
            FourierDlgProc  @2
```

THE FOUR12.RC RESOURCE FILE:

```
#include "windows.h"
#include "four12.h"

FourierMenu MENU
{
  POPUP "Fourier Data"
    {
      MENUITEM "Fourier Data...",    IDM_FOUR
      MENUITEM "Exit",               IDM_EXIT
    }
}

FourierData DIALOG LOADONCALL MOVEABLE DISCARDABLE
      74,21,142,70
      CAPTION "Fourier Data"
      STYLE WS_BORDER|WS_CAPTION|WS_DLGFRAME|WS_POPUP
{
  CONTROL "Title: ",-1, "static",SS_LEFT|WS_CHILD,6,5,28,8
  CONTROL "Title ",IDD_TITLE,"edit",ES_LEFT|WS_BORDER|WS_TABSTOP|
      WS_CHILD,33,1,106,12
  CONTROL "Number of terms: ",-1,"static",SS_LEFT|
      WS_CHILD,6,23,70,8
  CONTROL "1",IDD_TERMS,"edit",ES_LEFT|WS_BORDER|WS_TABSTOP|
      WS_CHILD,76,18,32,12
  CONTROL "Okay",IDOK,"button",BS_PUSHBUTTON|WS_TABSTOP|
      WS_CHILD,25,52,24,14
  CONTROL "Cancel",IDCANCEL,"button",BS_PUSHBUTTON|WS_TABSTOP|
      WS_CHILD,89,53,28,14
}
```

THE FOUR12.C APPLICATION FILE:

```c
/* Simplified Windows Platform (SWP)            */
/* (c) William H. Murray and Chris H. Pappas, 1989 */

#include <windows.h>
#include <string.h>
#include <math.h>
#include "four12.h"

long FAR PASCAL WindowProc(HWND,unsigned,WORD,LONG);

char szProgName[]="ProgName";
char szApplName[]="FourierMenu";
char mytitle[80]="Title";
int nterms=1;

int PASCAL WinMain(hInst,hPreInst,lpszCmdLine,nCmdShow)
HANDLE hInst,hPreInst;
LPSTR  lpszCmdLine;
int    nCmdShow;
{
  HWND hwnd;
  MSG  msg;
  WNDCLASS wcSwp;
  if (!hPreInst)
  {
    wcSwp.lpszClassName=szProgName;
    wcSwp.hInstance     =hInst;
    wcSwp.lpfnWndProc   =WindowProc;
    wcSwp.hCursor       =LoadCursor(NULL,IDC_ARROW);
    wcSwp.hIcon         =NULL;
    wcSwp.lpszMenuName  =NULL;
    wcSwp.hbrBackground=GetStockObject(WHITE_BRUSH);
    wcSwp.style         =CS_HREDRAW|CS_VREDRAW;
    wcSwp.cbClsExtra    =0;
    wcSwp.cbWndExtra    =0;
    if (!RegisterClass (&wcSwp))
      return FALSE;
  }
  hwnd=CreateWindow(szProgName,"Plotting A Fourier Series",
                    WS_OVERLAPPEDWINDOW,CW_USEDEFAULT,
                    CW_USEDEFAULT,CW_USEDEFAULT,
                    CW_USEDEFAULT,NULL,NULL,
                    hInst,NULL);
  ShowWindow(hwnd,nCmdShow);
  UpdateWindow(hwnd);
  while (GetMessage(&msg,NULL,NULL,NULL))
  {
    TranslateMessage(&msg);
    DispatchMessage(&msg);
  }
  return(msg.wParam);
}

BOOL FAR PASCAL FourierDlgProc(hdlg,messg,wParam,lParam)
HWND hdlg;
unsigned messg;
WORD wParam;
LONG lParam;
```

```
{
switch (messg)
  {
  case WM_INITDIALOG:
    return FALSE;
  case WM_COMMAND:
    switch (wParam)
    {
      case IDOK:
        GetDlgItemText(hdlg,IDD_TITLE,mytitle,80);
        nterms=GetDlgItemInt(hdlg,IDD_TERMS,NULL,0);
        EndDialog(hdlg,TRUE);
        break;
      case IDCANCEL:
        EndDialog(hdlg,FALSE);
        break;
      default:
        return FALSE;
    }
    break;
  default:
    return FALSE;
  }
return TRUE;
}

long FAR PASCAL WindowProc(hwnd,messg,wParam,lParam)
HWND    hwnd;
unsigned messg;
WORD    wParam;
LONG    lParam;
{
  PAINTSTRUCT ps;
  HDC  hdc;
  HBRUSH hOrgBrush;
  HBRUSH hMagentaBrush=CreateSolidBrush(RGB(255,0,255));
  static short xClientView,yClientView;
  static FARPROC lpfnFourierDlgProc;
  static HWND hInst;
  double y,yp;
  int i,j,ltitle;
  int angle;

  switch (messg)
  {
    case WM_SIZE:
      xClientView=LOWORD(lParam);
      yClientView=HIWORD(lParam);
      break;

    case WM_CREATE:
      hInst=((LPCREATESTRUCT) lParam)->hInstance;
      lpfnFourierDlgProc=MakeProcInstance(FourierDlgProc,hInst);
      break;

    case WM_COMMAND:
      switch (wParam)
      {
      case IDM_FOUR:
        DialogBox(hInst,"FourierData",hwnd,lpfnFourierDlgProc);
        InvalidateRect(hwnd,NULL,TRUE);
```

```
          UpdateWindow(hwnd);
          break;
        case IDM_EXIT:
          SendMessage(hwnd,WM_CLOSE,0,0L);
          break;
        default:
          break;
        }
        break;

    case WM_PAINT:
      hdc=BeginPaint(hwnd,&ps);

/*--------- your routines below ---------*/

      SetMapMode(hdc,MM_ISOTROPIC);
      SetWindowExt(hdc,400,400);
      SetViewportExt(hdc,xClientView,-yClientView);
      SetViewportOrg(hdc,100,220);

      hOrgBrush=SelectObject(hdc,hMagentaBrush);

      angle=0;
      yp=0.0;

      /* draw x & y coordinate axes */
      MoveTo(hdc,0,150);
      LineTo(hdc,0,-150);
      MoveTo(hdc,0,0);
      LineTo(hdc,400,0);
      MoveTo(hdc,0,0);

      for (i=0; i<=400; i++)              /* angle index    */
      {
        for (j=1; j<=nterms; j++)         /* harmonic index */
        {
          y=(150.0/((2.0*j)-1.0))*sin(((j*2.0)-1.0)*0.015708*angle);
          yp+=y;
        }
      LineTo(hdc,i,(int) yp);
      yp-=yp;
      angle++;
      }

      FloodFill(hdc,100,10,RGB(0,0,0));
      FloodFill(hdc,300,-10,RGB(0,0,0));

      ltitle=strlen(mytitle);
      TextOut(hdc,200-(ltitle*8/2),185,mytitle,ltitle);

      SelectObject(hdc,hOrgBrush);
      DeleteObject(hMagentaBrush);

/*--------- your routines above ---------*/

      ValidateRect(hwnd,NULL);
      EndPaint(hwnd,&ps);
      break;
    case WM_DESTROY:
      PostQuitMessage(0);
      break;
```

```
      default:
        return(DefWindowProc(hwnd,messg,wParam,lParam));
        break;
    }
  return(0L);
}
```

As you study the listing you will notice the inclusion of a rather simple dialog box. The purpose of the dialog box is to retrieve one value from the user—the number of harmonics the program will include in the plot.

The actual Fourier calculations are made within two loops.

```
for (i=0; i<=400; i++)                /* angle index     */
{
  for (j=1; j<=nterms; j++)           /* harmonic index */
  {
    y=(150.0/((2.0*j)-1.0))*sin(((j*2.0)-1.0)*0.015708*angle);
    yp+=y;
  }
LineTo(hdc,i,(int) yp);
yp-=yp;
angle++;
}

FloodFill(hdc,100,10,RGB(0,0,0));
FloodFill(hdc,300,-10,RGB(0,0,0));
```

The outer loop, using the i index, increments the horizontal plotting position across the window. This value represents the scaled angle for one complete cycle, as in the preceding examples. The inner loop, using the j index, calculates the appropriate number of Fourier values for each angle. For example, if i is pointing to a value representing 45 degrees, and the number of Fourier terms is 10, then ten calculations will be made in the inner loop for each i value. Since this deals with a simple series, those ten values are algebraically added to form the resulting point. Remember, if the number of Fourier terms is 1000, then 1000 values must be calculated and added together for each i value.

FloodFill is used to fill each portion of the resulting waveform. This function requires that X and Y values, within the region to be filled, be given when FloodFill is called. Also required is the specification of the bounding color. If there is just one tiny opening in the bounding color, expect exactly what you asked for—a *flood!* The whole screen will be filled with the specified color.

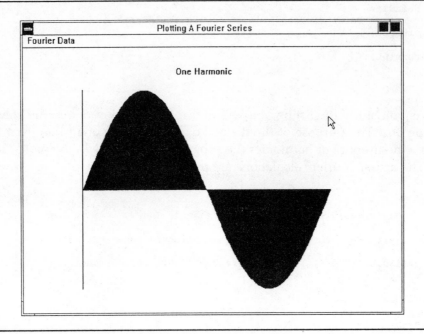

Figure 12-4. One harmonic from the Fourier series

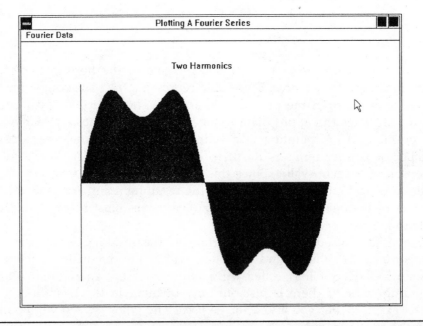

Figure 12-5. Two harmonics from the Fourier series

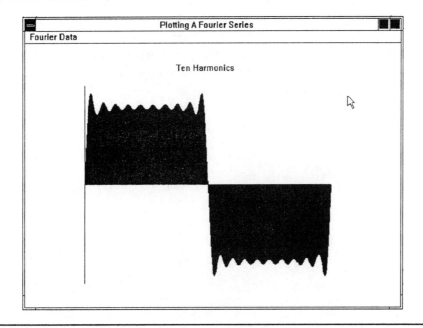

Figure 12-6.   Ten harmonics from the Fourier series

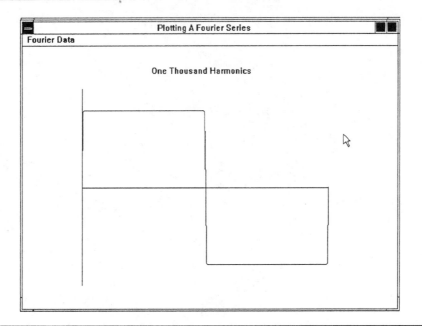

Figure 12-7.   One thousand harmonics from the Fourier series

Figure 12-4 is a sine wave produced by selecting one harmonic with the dialog box. Figures 12-5 and 12-6 show two and ten harmonic graphs, respectively. Finally, Figure 12-7 shows a graph using 1000 harmonics. How long did it take? You'll have to try it yourself to find out. Perhaps you would also like to alter these programs to utilize the Windows 3.0 Palette Manager discussed in Chapter 11.

13

FUN WITH GRAPHICAL
WINDOWS

The programs in this chapter represent a segment of Windows programs that are simply fun to use and experiment with. No book about Windows would be complete without a sketching program. This version, called Mouse-A-Sketch, allows you to apply your creative talents to the window canvas. Animation presents another interesting facet of graphics programming. Although one chapter cannot do justice to the topic of animation, three examples will be used to illustrate different animation techniques. The third animation example also includes an assembly language patch that will add the dimension of sound to your work.

MOUSE-A-SKETCH

The mouse will be used in the Mouse-A-Sketch program developed in this section to drag a "paintbrush" about on the screen. You'll be amazed by the bright colors of the VGA screen and equally impressed by the various sketching tricks you can perform with the mouse.

This program will allow you to select colors and pen widths from menus. You can then sketch to your heart's content by rolling the mouse around. Perhaps you will want to continue the development of this program by adding the ability to point to and click boxes and circles onto the screen.

If you complete the development cycle, you will have nine files when the **MAKE** utility is finished: SKETCH13, SKETCH13.DEF, SKETCH13.H, SKETCH13.RC, SKETCH13.C, SKETCH13.CUR, SKETCH13.RES, SKETCH-13.OBJ, and SKETCH13.EXE. Most of these files are similar to the Windows files of previous chapters.

THE SKETCH13 MAKE FILE:

```
all : sketch13.exe

sketch13.obj: sketch13.c sketch13.h
    cl -c -AS -Gsw -Oas -Zpe sketch13.c

sketch13.res: sketch13.rc sketch13.cur
    RC -r sketch13

sketch13.exe : sketch13.obj sketch13.def sketch13.res
    link /NOD sketch13,,,libw slibcew,sketch13
    rc sketch13.res
```

THE SKETCH13 DEFINITION FILE:

```
;SKETCH13.DEF for C Compiling

NAME            sketch13
DESCRIPTION     'Sketch Chart Program'
EXETYPE         WINDOWS
STUB            'WINSTUB.EXE'
CODE            PRELOAD MOVEABLE DISCARDABLE
DATA            PRELOAD MOVEABLE MULTIPLE
HEAPSIZE        4096
STACKSIZE       9216
EXPORTS         AboutDlgProc    @1
                WindowProc      @2
```

THE SKETCH13 HEADER FILE:

```
/* Header file for Sketch application */

#define IDM_ABOUT       100
#define IDM_CLEAR       101
#define IDM_EXIT        102

#define IDM_B1          301
#define IDM_B5          302
#define IDM_B10         303
#define IDM_B15         304
#define IDM_B20         305
#define IDM_B25         306
#define IDM_B30         307

#define IDM_BLACK       401
```

```
#define IDM_BLUE      402
#define IDM_RED       403
#define IDM_GREEN     404
#define IDM_CYAN      405
#define IDM_YELLOW    406
#define IDM_MAGENTA   407
#define IDM_WHITE     408


THE SKETCH13 RESOURCE FILE:

#include "windows.h"
#include "sketch13.h"

SketchCursor CURSOR Sketch13.cur

SketchMenu   MENU
BEGIN
  POPUP "Sketch_Info"
  BEGIN
    MENUITEM "&About...",        IDM_ABOUT
    MENUITEM "&Clear",           IDM_CLEAR
    MENUITEM "&Exit",            IDM_EXIT
  END
  POPUP "Color"
  BEGIN
    MENUITEM "&Black",           IDM_BLACK
    MENUITEM "&Blue",            IDM_BLUE
    MENUITEM "&Red",             IDM_RED
    MENUITEM "&Green",           IDM_GREEN
    MENUITEM "&Cyan",            IDM_CYAN
    MENUITEM "&Yellow",          IDM_YELLOW
    MENUITEM "&Magenta",         IDM_MAGENTA
    MENUITEM "&White",           IDM_WHITE
  END
  POPUP "Width"
  BEGIN
    MENUITEM "&1",               IDM_B1
    MENUITEM "&5",               IDM_B5
    MENUITEM "&10",              IDM_B10
    MENUITEM "&15",              IDM_B15
    MENUITEM "&20",              IDM_B20
    MENUITEM "&25",              IDM_B25
    MENUITEM "&30",              IDM_B30
  END
END


AboutDlgBox DIALOG LOADONCALL MOVEABLE DISCARDABLE
         50,300,180,80
         STYLE WS_DLGFRAME|WS_POPUP
  BEGIN
    CONTROL "Interactive Mouse Sketching Program",-1,"static",
        SS_CENTER|WS_CHILD,2,60,176,10
    CONTROL "by William H. Murray and Chris H. Pappas",-1,
        "static",SS_CENTER|WS_CHILD,2,45,176,10
    CONTROL "OK",IDOK,"button",
        BS_PUSHBUTTON|WS_TABSTOP|WS_CHILD,75,10,32,14
  END
```

THE SKETCH13 APPLICATION FILE:

```
/* Simplified Windows Platform (SWP)               */
/* (c) William H. Murray and Chris H. Pappas, 1989 */

#include <windows.h>
#include "sketch13.h"

#define PALETTESIZE 256
HANDLE  hPal;
NPLOGPALETTE pLogicalPal;

long FAR PASCAL WindowProc(HWND,unsigned,WORD,LONG);
BOOL FAR PASCAL AboutDlgProc(HWND,unsigned,WORD,LONG);

char szProgName[]="ProgName";
char szApplName[]="SketchMenu";
char szCursorName[]="SketchCursor";
BOOL bDrawtrail;
POINT omouselocation,nmouselocation;

int PASCAL WinMain(hInst,hPreInst,lpszCmdLine,nCmdShow)
HANDLE hInst,hPreInst;
LPSTR  lpszCmdLine;
int    nCmdShow;
{
  HWND hwnd;
  MSG  msg;
  WNDCLASS wcSwp;
  if (!hPreInst)
  {
    wcSwp.lpszClassName=szProgName;
    wcSwp.hInstance    =hInst;
    wcSwp.lpfnWndProc  =WindowProc;
    wcSwp.hCursor      =LoadCursor(hInst,szCursorName);
    wcSwp.hIcon        =LoadIcon(hInst,szProgName);
    wcSwp.lpszMenuName =szApplName;
    wcSwp.hbrBackground=GetStockObject(WHITE_BRUSH);
    wcSwp.style        =CS_HREDRAW|CS_VREDRAW;
    wcSwp.cbClsExtra   =0;
    wcSwp.cbWndExtra   =0;
    if (!RegisterClass (&wcSwp))
      return FALSE;
  }
  hwnd=CreateWindow(szProgName,"Mouse Sketching Program",
                    WS_OVERLAPPEDWINDOW,CW_USEDEFAULT,
                    CW_USEDEFAULT,CW_USEDEFAULT,
                    CW_USEDEFAULT,NULL,NULL,
                    hInst,NULL);
  ShowWindow(hwnd,nCmdShow);
  UpdateWindow(hwnd);
  while (GetMessage(&msg,NULL,NULL,NULL))
  {
    TranslateMessage(&msg);
    DispatchMessage(&msg);
  }
  return(msg.wParam);
}

BOOL FAR PASCAL AboutDlgProc(hdlg,messg,wParam,lParam)
HWND hdlg;
unsigned messg;
```

```
WORD wParam;
LONG lParam;
{
switch (messg)
  {
  case WM_INITDIALOG:
    break;
  case WM_COMMAND:
    switch (wParam)
    {
      case IDOK:
        EndDialog(hdlg,TRUE);
        break;
      default:
        return FALSE;
    }
    break;
  default:
    return FALSE;
  }
return TRUE;
}

long FAR PASCAL WindowProc(hwnd,messg,wParam,lParam)
HWND hwnd;
unsigned messg;
WORD wParam;
LONG lParam;
{
  PAINTSTRUCT ps;
  HDC        hdc;
  HPEN       hOrgPen;
  HPEN       hNewPen;
  static     FARPROC lpfnAboutDlgProc;
  static     HWND hInst;
  static     long colorshade=1;
  static     int penwidth=1;

  switch (messg)
  {

    case WM_CREATE:
      hInst=((LPCREATESTRUCT) lParam)->hInstance;
      lpfnAboutDlgProc=MakeProcInstance(AboutDlgProc,hInst);
      pLogicalPal=(NPLOGPALETTE) LocalAlloc(LMEM_FIXED,
                 (sizeof(LOGPALETTE) +
                 (sizeof(PALETTEENTRY)*(PALETTESIZE)))));
      pLogicalPal->palVersion=300;
      pLogicalPal->palNumEntries=PALETTESIZE;

      /*BLACK*/
      pLogicalPal->palPalEntry[0].peRed=0x00;
      pLogicalPal->palPalEntry[0].peGreen=0x00;
      pLogicalPal->palPalEntry[0].peBlue=0x00;
      pLogicalPal->palPalEntry[0].peFlags=(BYTE) 0;
      /*BLUE*/
      pLogicalPal->palPalEntry[1].peRed=0x00;
      pLogicalPal->palPalEntry[1].peGreen=0x00;
      pLogicalPal->palPalEntry[1].peBlue=0xFF;
      pLogicalPal->palPalEntry[1].peFlags=(BYTE) 0;
      /*RED*/
```

```
      pLogicalPal->palPalEntry[2].peRed=0xFF;
      pLogicalPal->palPalEntry[2].peGreen=0x00;
      pLogicalPal->palPalEntry[2].peBlue=0x00;
      pLogicalPal->palPalEntry[2].peFlags=(BYTE) 0;
      /*GREEN*/
      pLogicalPal->palPalEntry[3].peRed=0x00;
      pLogicalPal->palPalEntry[3].peGreen=0xFF;
      pLogicalPal->palPalEntry[3].peBlue=0x00;
      pLogicalPal->palPalEntry[3].peFlags=(BYTE) 0;
      /*CYAN*/
      pLogicalPal->palPalEntry[4].peRed=0x00;
      pLogicalPal->palPalEntry[4].peGreen=0xFF;
      pLogicalPal->palPalEntry[4].peBlue=0xFF;
      pLogicalPal->palPalEntry[4].peFlags=(BYTE) 0;
      /*YELLOW*/
      pLogicalPal->palPalEntry[5].peRed=0xFF;
      pLogicalPal->palPalEntry[5].peGreen=0xFF;
      pLogicalPal->palPalEntry[5].peBlue=0x00;
      pLogicalPal->palPalEntry[5].peFlags=(BYTE) 0;
      /*MAGENTA*/
      pLogicalPal->palPalEntry[6].peRed=0xFF;
      pLogicalPal->palPalEntry[6].peGreen=0x00;
      pLogicalPal->palPalEntry[6].peBlue=0xFF;
      pLogicalPal->palPalEntry[6].peFlags=(BYTE) 0;
      /*WHITE*/
      pLogicalPal->palPalEntry[7].peRed=0xFF;
      pLogicalPal->palPalEntry[7].peGreen=0xFF;
      pLogicalPal->palPalEntry[7].peBlue=0xFF;
      pLogicalPal->palPalEntry[7].peFlags=(BYTE) 0;
      /*CLEAR*/
      pLogicalPal->palPalEntry[8].peRed=0xFF;
      pLogicalPal->palPalEntry[8].peGreen=0xFF;
      pLogicalPal->palPalEntry[8].peBlue=0xFF;
      pLogicalPal->palPalEntry[8].peFlags=(BYTE) 0;

      hPal = CreatePalette ((LPSTR)pLogicalPal);
      break;

  case WM_COMMAND:
    switch (wParam)
    {
      case IDM_ABOUT:
        DialogBox(hInst,"AboutDlgBox",hwnd,lpfnAboutDlgProc);
        break;
      case IDM_CLEAR:
        colorshade=PALETTERGB(0xFF,0xFF,0xFF);
        InvalidateRect(hwnd,NULL,TRUE);
        break;
      case IDM_EXIT:
        SendMessage(hwnd,WM_CLOSE,0,0L);
        break;
      case IDM_BLACK:
        colorshade=PALETTERGB(0x00,0x00,0x00);
        break;
      case IDM_BLUE:
        colorshade=PALETTERGB(0x00,0x00,0xFF);
        break;
      case IDM_RED:
        colorshade=PALETTERGB(0xFF,0x00,0x00);
        break;
      case IDM_GREEN:
        colorshade=PALETTERGB(0x00,0xFF,0x00);
```

```
      break;
    case IDM_CYAN:
      colorshade=PALETTERGB(0x00,0xFF,0xFF);
      break;
    case IDM_YELLOW:
      colorshade=PALETTERGB(0xFF,0xFF,0x00);
      break;
    case IDM_MAGENTA:
      colorshade=PALETTERGB(0xFF,0x00,0xFF);
      break;
    case IDM_WHITE:
      colorshade=PALETTERGB(0xFF,0xFF,0xFF);
      break;
    case IDM_B1:
      penwidth=1;
      break;
    case IDM_B5:
      penwidth=5;
      break;
    case IDM_B10:
      penwidth=10;
      break;
    case IDM_B15:
      penwidth=15;
      break;
    case IDM_B20:
      penwidth=20;
      break;
    case IDM_B25:
      penwidth=25;
      break;
    case IDM_B30:
      penwidth=30;
      break;
    default:
      break;
  }
  break;

case WM_LBUTTONDOWN:
  omouselocation=nmouselocation=MAKEPOINT(lParam);
  SetCapture(hwnd);
  bDrawtrail=TRUE;
  break;

case WM_MOUSEMOVE:
  if (bDrawtrail)
  {
    omouselocation=nmouselocation;
    nmouselocation=MAKEPOINT(lParam);
    InvalidateRect(hwnd,NULL,FALSE);
    UpdateWindow(hwnd);
  }
  break;

case WM_LBUTTONUP:
  ReleaseCapture();
  bDrawtrail=FALSE;
  break;

case WM_PAINT:
```

```
        hdc=BeginPaint(hwnd,&ps);
        SelectPalette(hdc,hPal);
        RealizePalette(hdc);

/*--------- your routines below ---------*/

        hNewPen=CreatePen(PS_SOLID,penwidth,colorshade);
        hOrgPen=SelectObject(hdc,hNewPen);
        MoveTo(hdc,omouselocation.x,omouselocation.y);
        LineTo(hdc,nmouselocation.x,nmouselocation.y);
        SelectObject(hdc,hOrgPen);
        DeleteObject(hNewPen);

/*--------- your routines above ---------*/

        ValidateRect(hwnd,NULL);
        EndPaint(hwnd,&ps);
        break;

    case WM_DESTROY:
        if (pLogicalPal->palNumEntries)
          DeleteObject(hPal);
        PostQuitMessage(0);
        break;

    default:
        return(DefWindowProc(hwnd,messg,wParam,lParam));
    }
    return(0L);
}
```

The SKETCH13 Files

The SKETCH13 file listing is typical of all **MAKE** files developed to this point. The SKETCH13.DEF file is also similar to previous versions. It contains only two EXPORT statements—one for an About box and one for the graphics procedure.

The SKETCH13.H header file contains identification information for various menu and dialog items. You will notice three groups of menu identification numbers. One group represents the information obtained under the Sketch_Info menu. This menu contains an About box, and selections enabling you to clear the screen and make a quick exit from the program. The second menu, Color, allows the user to select from a palette of eight colors. The final menu, Width, allows the user to select one of seven pen widths, ranging from 1 to 30 pels.

The SKETCH13.RC resource file contains information for drawing the actual menu and dialog boxes to the window. The dialog box information in this file is returned by the Dialog Box Editor.

The C Code for SKETCH13

The C program uses various menu options that allow the user to select pen widths and palette colors. Most of the programming is traditional Windows program code. The main action takes place in several *case* statements in the WindowProc procedure.

As you will note, this program utilizes the Windows 3.0 Palette Manager. The logical palette is created with a WM_CREATE message. This code is similar to that developed and explained in Chapter 11. The various menu options are processed under WM_COMMAND. Additional *case* statements allow the variable *colorshade* to be set to the correct color value, corresponding to the correct menu selection. The *penwidth* variable is used to change the pen width of the drawing instrument. Both of these values are used by the CreatePen function to create a new pen width and color. The LineTo function uses the current *nmouselocation* information to complete a straight line from the point marked with the left mouse button to the current position. If that button is held down, this cycle is repeated on a continual basis, creating a smoothly flowing line as the mouse is moved. Since the line lengths will be short, curves and other shapes can be created.

When the left mouse button is pushed, WM_LBUTTONDOWN receives a message. The mouse coordinate information is passed through the variable *lparm*. This information then forms the coordinates for the MoveTo function. By pushing the left button, the user effectively moves the cursor to the current mouse position on the screen. The left button must be pushed to set the *bDrawtrail* flag to TRUE.

Now the user can move the mouse on the screen. WM_MOUSEMOVE intercepts the mouse move information, and if *bDrawtrail* is TRUE, it will record the mouse coordinates once again. If *bDrawtrail* is FALSE—that is, if the left mouse button wasn't pushed—no call will be made to invalidate the rectangle and hence update the window. However, if the flag is TRUE, both the InvalidateRect and UpdateWindow functions will be called. The mouse coordinates will be passed to the global variable *nmouselocation*. Finally, when the left button is released, WM_LBUTTONUP is used to intercept the message and set *bDrawtrail* to FALSE. With *bDrawtrail* set to FALSE, the mouse may be moved about on the screen without painting.

What kind of trouble can you get yourself into with a couple of cans of paint? Here you have the paint supplies—good luck in your painting under Windows.

Figures 13-1 and 13-2 show some attempts at being creative. Now you know why we write books instead of selling our art!

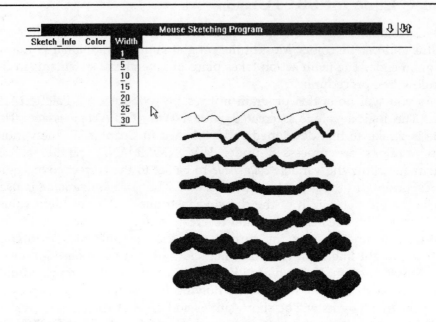

Figure 13-1.   Various pen widths for the Mouse-A-Sketch program

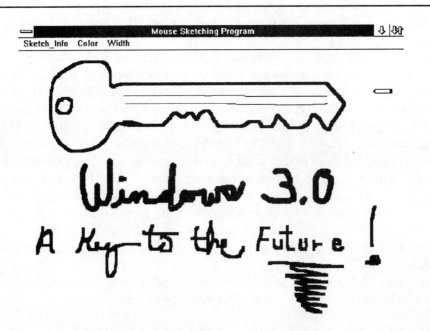

Figure 13-2.   Original drawing created with Mouse-A-Sketch

TRAIN PROGRAM 1

This first attempt at animation uses a very simple and popular animation technique: draw, erase, move, and redraw. First, a simple figure is drawn on the screen and allowed to remain there for a set time. In this case the outline of a train engine is used as the figure. Next, the figure is erased. This can be done by redrawing the figure in the background color, clearing a rectangular portion around the figure, or clearing the entire screen. In this example a small rectangular area surrounding the figure will be cleared. The coordinates for the figure are then shifted to the left or right by a small number of pixels, and the figure is redrawn. If the timing is right, you will get the sense of motion.

THE TRAN13A MAKE FILE:

```
all : tran13a.exe

tran13a.obj: tran13a.c
    cl -c -AS -Gsw -Oas -Zpe tran13a.c

tran13a.exe : tran13a.obj tran13a.def tran13a.res
    link /NOD tran13a,,,libw slibcew,tran13a.def
```

THE TRAN13A DEFINITION FILE:

```
;TRAN13A.DEF for C Compiling

NAME            TRAN13A
DESCRIPTION     'Train Program #1'
EXETYPE         WINDOWS
STUB            'WINSTUB.EXE'
CODE            PRELOAD MOVEABLE DISCARDABLE
DATA            PRELOAD MOVEABLE MULTIPLE
HEAPSIZE        4096
STACKSIZE       9216
EXPORTS         WindowProc    @1
```

THE TRAN13A APPLICATION FILE:

```
/* Simplified Windows Platform (SWP)              */
/* (c) William H. Murray and Chris H. Pappas, 1989 */

#include <windows.h>
#define SHAPESIZE 40

long FAR PASCAL WindowProc(HWND,unsigned,WORD,LONG);

char szProgName[]="Tran13a";

int PASCAL WinMain(hInst,hPreInst,lpszCmdLine,nCmdShow)
HANDLE hInst,hPreInst;
LPSTR  lpszCmdLine;
int    nCmdShow;
{
  HWND hwnd;
```

```
MSG   msg;
WNDCLASS wcSwp;
if (!hPreInst)
{
   wcSwp.lpszClassName=szProgName;
   wcSwp.hInstance    =hInst;
   wcSwp.lpfnWndProc  =WindowProc;
   wcSwp.hCursor      =LoadCursor(NULL,IDC_ARROW);
   wcSwp.hIcon        =NULL;
   wcSwp.lpszMenuName =NULL;
   wcSwp.hbrBackground=GetStockObject(WHITE_BRUSH);
   wcSwp.style        =CS_HREDRAW¦CS_VREDRAW;
   wcSwp.cbClsExtra   =0;
   wcSwp.cbWndExtra   =0;
   if (!RegisterClass (&wcSwp))
      return FALSE;
}
hwnd=CreateWindow(szProgName,"Shifting Train Program #1",
                  WS_OVERLAPPEDWINDOW,CW_USEDEFAULT,
                  CW_USEDEFAULT,CW_USEDEFAULT,
                  CW_USEDEFAULT,NULL,NULL,
                  hInst,NULL);

if (!SetTimer(hwnd,1,100,NULL))
   {
   MessageBox(hwnd,"Too many timers started!",
              szProgName,MB_OK);
   return FALSE;
   }

ShowWindow(hwnd,nCmdShow);
UpdateWindow(hwnd);
while (GetMessage(&msg,NULL,NULL,NULL))
{
   TranslateMessage(&msg);
   DispatchMessage(&msg);
}
   return(msg.wParam);
}

long FAR PASCAL WindowProc(hwnd,messg,wParam,lParam)
HWND    hwnd;
unsigned messg;
WORD    wParam;
LONG    lParam;
{
   HDC         hdc;
   PAINTSTRUCT ps;
   RECT        rShape;
   static short sStep,xClientview,yClientview,
                xCenterCoord,yCenterCoord;

   switch (messg)
   {

     case WM_SIZE:
       sStep=2;
       xCenterCoord=(xClientview=LOWORD(lParam))/2;
```

```
      yCenterCoord=(yClientview=HIWORD(lParam))/2;
      break;

   case WM_TIMER:
      GetClientRect(hwnd,&rShape);
      rShape.right=xCenterCoord+SHAPESIZE;
      rShape.bottom=yCenterCoord+SHAPESIZE;
      rShape.left=xCenterCoord;
      rShape.top=yCenterCoord;
      xCenterCoord+=sStep;
      if((xCenterCoord+SHAPESIZE>=xClientview)||
        (xCenterCoord<=0))
        sStep=-sStep;
      InvalidateRect(hwnd,&rShape,TRUE);
      break;

   case WM_PAINT:
      hdc=BeginPaint(hwnd,&ps);

/*--------- your routines below ---------*/

      /* Left Train Wheel */
      Ellipse(hdc,5+xCenterCoord,29+yCenterCoord,
              15+xCenterCoord,39+yCenterCoord);
      /* Right Train Wheel */
      Ellipse(hdc,25+xCenterCoord,29+yCenterCoord,
              35+xCenterCoord,39+yCenterCoord);
      /* Main Body of Train */
      Rectangle(hdc,2+xCenterCoord,19+yCenterCoord,
                37+xCenterCoord,29+yCenterCoord);
      /* Smoke Stack */
      Rectangle(hdc,17+xCenterCoord,0+yCenterCoord,
                23+xCenterCoord,19+yCenterCoord);

/*--------- your routines above ---------*/

      ValidateRect(hwnd,NULL);
      EndPaint(hwnd,&ps);
      break;

   case WM_DESTROY:
      KillTimer(hwnd,1);
      PostQuitMessage(0);
      break;

   default:
      return(DefWindowProc(hwnd,messg,wParam,lParam));
   }
 return(0L);
}
```

The amount of time the train remains on the screen is controlled by the SetTimer function in WinMain. When a timer event occurs, a WM_TIMER message is passed. This message is intercepted in the WindowProc procedure. In this example, a timer message is registered every 100 milliseconds (0.1 seconds).

A WM_SIZE message is used to determine the size of the current screen. From the information returned by *xClientView* and *yClientView*, the center coordinates are determined and saved in *xCenterCoord* and *yCenter-Coord*.

WM_TIMER establishes where the shape will be placed on the screen. First, the function GetClientRect copies the coordinates of the window's client area into a data structure pointed to by *rShape*. The coordinates specify the upper-left and lower-right corners of that area. The next four values establish the drawing area. SHAPESIZE was earlier defined to be 40 (pixels). Thus, the shape will initially be drawn on the screen with its top-left coordinates at *xCenterCoord* and *yCenterCoord*. The bottom-right values will be identical, except both will be offset by SHAPESIZE.

Each time a timer message is received, *xCenterCoord* is increased by *sStep*. Initially, this will shift the figure to the right by two pixels. A check is then made to see if the figure has bumped up against the right side of the window. If it has, the figure's motion is reversed by changing the step size to a negative value.

Finally, the rectangular area surrounding the figure is erased with a call to InvalidateRect. WM_PAINT automatically receives a message to update the window, and a new figure is drawn at the new coordinate positions. Thus, the little train moves back and forth across the screen.

The functions for drawing the train are contained under WM_PAINT. Two wheels are drawn with calls to the Ellipse function. The body of the engine, a small rectangle, is drawn with the Rectangle function. Finally, the engine's smokestack is drawn with another call to the Rectangle function.

The action of the little train is a bit jerky. Your eye can perceive the draw-clear-redraw action, which it interprets as a blinking or flashing action. Figure 13-3 shows the outline of the little engine. You were shown this technique so you could appreciate the way the next program works.

TRAIN PROGRAM 2

Smoother animation can be obtained by using a bitmap to reproduce the figure. In so doing, the constant draw-erase-redraw cycle can be eliminated, along with the annoying flicker.

Have you ever noticed how pointers and other icons seem to slide effortlessly across the screen as you move the mouse? This motion suggests that a bitmap can actually float over the drawing surface. Bitmaps were used in Chapter 6 to draw simple objects. In that chapter you learned how to create a bitmap, how to draw on the bitmap, and how to replicate that

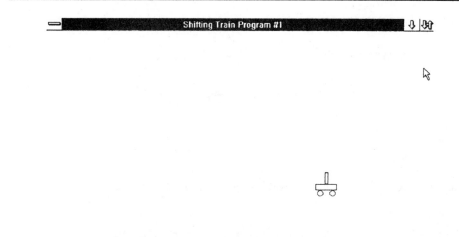

Figure 13-3.   A simple animated train engine

shape many times in the window. This chapter uses bitmaps again to aid in animation. This time a bitmap image of the train is created, and the BitBlt function is used to move it back and forth across the screen. The bitmap will erase its tracks as long as it contains a border surrounding the pattern that is the same color as the background.

THE TRAN13B MAKE FILE:

```
all: tran13b.exe

tran13b.obj: tran13b.c
    cl -c -AS -Gsw -Oas -Zpe tran13b.c

tran13b.exe: tran13b.obj tran13b.def tran13b.res
    link /NOD tran13b,,,libw slibcew,tran13b.def
```

THE TRAN13B DEFINITION FILE:

```
;TRAN13B.DEF for C Compiling

NAME            TRAN13B
DESCRIPTION     'Train Program #2'
EXETYPE         WINDOWS
STUB            'WINSTUB.EXE'
CODE            PRELOAD MOVEABLE DISCARDABLE
DATA            PRELOAD MOVEABLE MULTIPLE
HEAPSIZE        4096
```

```
STACKSIZE        9216
EXPORTS          WindowProc    @1
```

THE TRAN13B APPLICATION FILE:

```
/* Simplified Windows Platform (SWP)                 */
/* (c) William H. Murray and Chris H. Pappas, 1989 */

#include <windows.h>
#define BITMAPSIZE 40
#define PALETTESIZE 256
HANDLE  hPal;
NPLOGPALETTE pLogicalPal;

long FAR PASCAL WindowProc(HWND,unsigned,WORD,LONG);

char szProgName[]="Tran13B";

int PASCAL WinMain(hInst,hPreInst,lpszCmdLine,nCmdShow)
HANDLE hInst,hPreInst;
LPSTR  lpszCmdLine;
int    nCmdShow;
{
  HWND hwnd;
  MSG  msg;
  WNDCLASS wcSwp;
  if (!hPreInst)
  {
    wcSwp.lpszClassName=szProgName;
    wcSwp.hInstance     =hInst;
    wcSwp.lpfnWndProc   =WindowProc;
    wcSwp.hCursor       =LoadCursor(NULL,IDC_ARROW);
    wcSwp.hIcon         =NULL;
    wcSwp.lpszMenuName  =NULL;
    wcSwp.hbrBackground=GetStockObject(WHITE_BRUSH);
    wcSwp.style         =CS_HREDRAW!CS_VREDRAW;
    wcSwp.cbClsExtra    =0;
    wcSwp.cbWndExtra    =0;
    if (!RegisterClass (&wcSwp))
      return FALSE;
  }
  hwnd=CreateWindow(szProgName,"Shifting Train Program #2",
                    WS_OVERLAPPEDWINDOW,CW_USEDEFAULT,
                    CW_USEDEFAULT,CW_USEDEFAULT,
                    CW_USEDEFAULT,NULL,NULL,
                    hInst,NULL);

  if (!SetTimer(hwnd,1,100,NULL))
    {
    MessageBox(hwnd,"Too many timers started!",
               szProgName,MB_OK);
    return FALSE;
    }

  ShowWindow(hwnd,nCmdShow);
  UpdateWindow(hwnd);
  while (GetMessage(&msg,NULL,NULL,NULL))
  {
    TranslateMessage(&msg);
    DispatchMessage(&msg);
```

```
    }
  return(msg.wParam);
}

long FAR PASCAL WindowProc(hwnd,messg,wParam,lParam)
HWND    hwnd;
unsigned messg;
WORD    wParam;
LONG    lParam;
{
  static HANDLE hBitmap;
  static short StepSize,xClientview,yClientview,
                xCenterCoord,yCenterCoord;
  long          colorshade;
  HDC           hdc,hmdc;
  HBRUSH        hBrush;

  switch (messg)
  {
    case WM_CREATE:
      pLogicalPal=(NPLOGPALETTE) LocalAlloc(LMEM_FIXED,
                    (sizeof(LOGPALETTE) +
                    (sizeof(PALETTEENTRY)*(PALETTESIZE))));
      pLogicalPal->palVersion=300;
      pLogicalPal->palNumEntries=PALETTESIZE;

      /*BLACK*/
      pLogicalPal->palPalEntry[0].peRed=0x00;
      pLogicalPal->palPalEntry[0].peGreen=0x00;
      pLogicalPal->palPalEntry[0].peBlue=0x00;
      pLogicalPal->palPalEntry[0].peFlags=(BYTE) 0;
      /*BLUE*/
      pLogicalPal->palPalEntry[1].peRed=0x00;
      pLogicalPal->palPalEntry[1].peGreen=0x00;
      pLogicalPal->palPalEntry[1].peBlue=0xFF;
      pLogicalPal->palPalEntry[1].peFlags=(BYTE) 0;
      /*RED*/
      pLogicalPal->palPalEntry[2].peRed=0xFF;
      pLogicalPal->palPalEntry[2].peGreen=0x00;
      pLogicalPal->palPalEntry[2].peBlue=0x00;
      pLogicalPal->palPalEntry[2].peFlags=(BYTE) 0;

      hPal = CreatePalette ((LPSTR)pLogicalPal);
      break;

    case WM_SIZE:
      xCenterCoord=(xClientview=LOWORD(lParam))/2;
      yCenterCoord=(yClientview=HIWORD(lParam))/2;
      if (hBitmap)
        DeleteObject(hBitmap);
      StepSize=2;
      hdc=GetDC(hwnd);
      hmdc=CreateCompatibleDC(hdc);

      /* Create a bitmap */
      hBitmap=CreateCompatibleBitmap(hdc,
                                     BITMAPSIZE+StepSize,
                                     BITMAPSIZE);

      ReleaseDC(hwnd,hdc);
      SelectObject(hmdc,hBitmap);
```

```
        Rectangle(hmdc,-1,-1,BITMAPSIZE+StepSize+1,
                  BITMAPSIZE+1);

        SelectPalette(hmdc,hPal);
        RealizePalette(hmdc);

        /* Draw Train Wheels */
        colorshade=PALETTERGB(0x00,0x00,0xFF);
        hBrush=CreateSolidBrush(colorshade);
        SelectObject(hmdc,hBrush);
        /* Left Train Wheel */
        Ellipse(hmdc,5,29,15,39);
        /* Right Train Wheel */
        Ellipse(hmdc,25,29,35,39);

        /* Main Body of Train */
        colorshade=PALETTERGB(0xFF,0x00,0x00);
        hBrush=CreateSolidBrush(colorshade);
        SelectObject(hmdc,hBrush);
        Rectangle(hmdc,2,19,37,29);

        /* Smoke Stack */
        colorshade=PALETTERGB(0x00,0x00,0x00);
        hBrush=CreateSolidBrush(colorshade);
        SelectObject(hmdc,hBrush);
        Rectangle(hmdc,17,0,23,19);

        DeleteDC(hmdc);
        DeleteObject(hBrush);
        break;

     case WM_TIMER:
        if (!hBitmap)
       break;

        hdc=GetDC(hwnd);
        hmdc=CreateCompatibleDC(hdc);
        SelectObject(hmdc,hBitmap);
        BitBlt(hdc,xCenterCoord-BITMAPSIZE/2,
               yCenterCoord-BITMAPSIZE/2,BITMAPSIZE,
               BITMAPSIZE,hmdc,0,0,SRCCOPY);
        ReleaseDC(hwnd,hdc);
        DeleteDC(hmdc);
        xCenterCoord+=StepSize;
        if((xCenterCoord+BITMAPSIZE/2>=xClientview)||
          (xCenterCoord-BITMAPSIZE/2<=0))
          StepSize=-StepSize;
        break;

     case WM_DESTROY:
        if (hBitmap)
          DeleteObject(hBitmap);
        KillTimer(hwnd,1);
        if (pLogicalPal->palNumEntries)
          DeleteObject(hPal);
        PostQuitMessage(0);
        break;
```

```
    default:
      return(DefWindowProc(hwnd,messg,wParam,lParam));
  }
  return(0L);
}
```

The bitmap image is sized and initially drawn under WM_SIZE. WM_TIMER is used to move the bitmap across the screen. WM_PAINT is not needed in this program since the BitBlt function causes a transfer to take place each time a timer message is received.

WM_SIZE obtains the window's center coordinates just as it did in the first animation example. The CreateCompatibleDC function creates a *memory* device context that is compatible with the device specified by the handle *hdc*. This block of memory represents a display surface that can actually be drawn upon. The CreateCompatibleBitmap function is used to create a bitmap compatible with the device specified by the handle *hdc*. The bitmap created has the same number of color planes as the device.

Its horizontal dimension is given by the second parameter, while the vertical dimension is specified by the third parameter. For this example, BITMAPSIZE is defined as 40 pels. Thus, the horizontal dimension is 42 pels, while the vertical dimension is 40 pels. You might also note that the Rectangle function is used to specify an area that is one pel larger in each dimension; this gives the one-pel background border mentioned earlier.

Next, the train is drawn. This uses the same outline as for the first example, except this time the train is colored. This bitmap will produce a train with blue wheels, a red body, and a black smokestack, using a logical palette. Remember that the train is drawn in the memory device context.

WM_TIMER is responsible for drawing the bitmap with the BitBlt function. As a matter of fact, the BitBlt function will move the source bitmap specified by *hmdc* to the destination device given by *hdc*. The second and third parameters of this function specify the X and Y coordinates of the upper-left destination rectangle. The fourth and fifth parameters give the width and height of the destination rectangle and bitmap. The seventh and eighth parameters specify the upper-left coordinates of the source bitmap. The final parameter indicates the raster operation to be performed—in this case, SCRCOPY, which copies the source bitmap to the destination bitmap.

The bitmap is "moved" by changing the *xCenterCoord* value by *StepSize*, as in the previous example. Experiment with different bitmap shapes. Perhaps you might like to make a flying saucer that could fly in two dimensions instead of one. Figure 13-4 shows the bitmap engine. Unfortunately, animation can't be shown in the book.

This program still has a drawback, although it isn't too evident. Only a monocolored (white) background will work satisfactorily. This is because

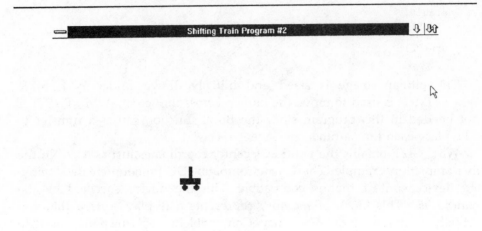

Figure 13-4. A streamlined animated train using a bitmap

the bitmap actually erases what is under it. If you had background scenery, it would be erased as the bitmap passed over. A more advanced technique would be to use additional child windows for the animation.

TRAIN PROGRAM 3

The final frontier of this simple animation work will be to add sound to the graphics. In this example, a collision noise will occur each time the train engine hits a window boundary.

Splicing a sound generator to a graphics routine does not seem like a difficult task—until you learn it will be done by adding a call to an external assembly language routine. As a matter of fact, this example is a prelude to what is coming in the next chapter.

```
THE TRAN13C MAKE FILE:

all: tran13c.exe

tran13c.obj: tran13c.c
    cl -c -AS -Gsw -Oas -Zpe tran13c.c

noise.obj: noise.asm
    masm noise;
```

```
transl3c.res: transl3c.rc
    rc -r transl3c.rc

tranl3c.exe: tranl3c.obj tranl3c.def tranl3c.res
    link /NOD tranl3c+noise,,,libw slibcew,tranl3c
    rc tranl3c.res
```

THE TRAN13C DEFINITION FILE:

```
;TRAN13C.DEF for C Compiling

NAME            TRAN13C
DESCRIPTION     'Train Program #3'
EXETYPE         WINDOWS
STUB            'WINSTUB.EXE'
CODE            PRELOAD MOVEABLE DISCARDABLE
DATA            PRELOAD MOVEABLE MULTIPLE
HEAPSIZE        4096
STACKSIZE       9216
EXPORTS         WindowProc     @1
                Noise          @2
```

THE TRAN13C ASSEMBLY LANGUAGE PATCH:

```
;Real Mode Assembly Language Programming Patch
;For execution on 80486/80286 machines

;An assembly language patch to provide access to the speaker
;port on IBM computers and compatibles

        PUBLIC    NOISE

        DOSSEG                  ;use Microsoft segment conventions
        .MODEL MEDIUM,PASCAL ;set model size & parameter pass
        .286                    ;80286 instructions

        .DATA
info dw    0                    ;temp storage

        .CODE
NOISE      PROC FAR      ;main procedure declaration
        cli         ;protect against interrupts
        mov  dx,0               ;initialize dx to zero
        in   al,61h             ;get speaker port info in al
        and  al,0FCh            ;mask it (keep all but lower two bits)
again: mov info,00h             ;place zero in scratch variable
        inc  dx                 ;increment dx
        cmp  dx,3h              ;have we repeated sound 2 times?
        je   endo               ;if yes, end program
doit: xor al,02h                ;xor lower two bits of al
        mov  cx,info            ;get current frequency from storage
        cmp  cx,300h            ;has it reached 768 hertz (approx.)
        je   again              ;if yes, let us repeat the sequence
        inc  info               ;if not, increase frequency by one
        out  61h,al             ;and output sound to the speaker
here: loop here                 ;the time delay
        jmp  doit               ;repeat?

endo:
        sti                     ;clear interrupt protection
        ret
NOISE endp                      ;end main procedure
        end                     ;end whole program
```

THE TRAN13C APPLICATION FILE:

```
/* Simplified Windows Platform (SWP)            */
/* (c) William H. Murray and Chris H. Pappas, 1989 */

#include <windows.h>
#define BITMAPSIZE 40
#define PALETTESIZE 256
HANDLE  hPal;
NPLOGPALETTE pLogicalPal;

long FAR PASCAL WindowProc(HWND,unsigned,WORD,LONG);
VOID FAR PASCAL Noise();

char szProgName[]="Tran13C";

int PASCAL WinMain(hInst,hPreInst,lpszCmdLine,nCmdShow)
HANDLE hInst,hPreInst;
LPSTR  lpszCmdLine;
int    nCmdShow;
{
  HWND hwnd;
  MSG  msg;
  WNDCLASS wcSwp;
  if (!hPreInst)
  {
    wcSwp.lpszClassName=szProgName;
    wcSwp.hInstance    =hInst;
    wcSwp.lpfnWndProc  =WindowProc;
    wcSwp.hCursor      =LoadCursor(NULL,IDC_ARROW);
    wcSwp.hIcon        =NULL;
    wcSwp.lpszMenuName =NULL;
    wcSwp.hbrBackground=GetStockObject(WHITE_BRUSH);
    wcSwp.style        =CS_HREDRAW|CS_VREDRAW;
    wcSwp.cbClsExtra   =0;
    wcSwp.cbWndExtra   =0;
    if (!RegisterClass (&wcSwp))
      return FALSE;
  }
  hwnd=CreateWindow(szProgName,"Shifting Train Program #3",
                    WS_OVERLAPPEDWINDOW,CW_USEDEFAULT,
                    CW_USEDEFAULT,CW_USEDEFAULT,
                    CW_USEDEFAULT,NULL,NULL,
                    hInst,NULL);

  if (!SetTimer(hwnd,1,100,NULL))
    {
    MessageBox(hwnd,"Too many timers started!",
               szProgName,MB_OK);
    return FALSE;
    }

  ShowWindow(hwnd,nCmdShow);
  UpdateWindow(hwnd);
  while (GetMessage(&msg,NULL,NULL,NULL))
  {
    TranslateMessage(&msg);
    DispatchMessage(&msg);
  }
  return(msg.wParam);
```

```
}

long FAR PASCAL WindowProc(hwnd,messg,wParam,lParam)
HWND    hwnd;
unsigned messg;
WORD    wParam;
LONG    lParam;
{
  static HANDLE hBitmap;
  static short StepSize,xClientview,yClientview,
               xCenterCoord,yCenterCoord;
  long          colorshade;
  HDC           hdc,hmdc;
  HBRUSH        hBrush;

  switch (messg)
  {
    case WM_CREATE:
      pLogicalPal=(NPLOGPALETTE) LocalAlloc(LMEM_FIXED,
                  (sizeof(LOGPALETTE) +
                  (sizeof(PALETTEENTRY)*(PALETTESIZE))));
      pLogicalPal->palVersion=300;
      pLogicalPal->palNumEntries=PALETTESIZE;

      /*BLACK*/
      pLogicalPal->palPalEntry[0].peRed=0x00;
      pLogicalPal->palPalEntry[0].peGreen=0x00;
      pLogicalPal->palPalEntry[0].peBlue=0x00;
      pLogicalPal->palPalEntry[0].peFlags=(BYTE) 0;
      /*BLUE*/
      pLogicalPal->palPalEntry[1].peRed=0x00;
      pLogicalPal->palPalEntry[1].peGreen=0x00;
      pLogicalPal->palPalEntry[1].peBlue=0xFF;
      pLogicalPal->palPalEntry[1].peFlags=(BYTE) 0;
      /*RED*/
      pLogicalPal->palPalEntry[2].peRed=0xFF;
      pLogicalPal->palPalEntry[2].peGreen=0x00;
      pLogicalPal->palPalEntry[2].peBlue=0x00;
      pLogicalPal->palPalEntry[2].peFlags=(BYTE) 0;

      hPal = CreatePalette ((LPSTR)pLogicalPal);
      break;

    case WM_SIZE:
      xCenterCoord=(xClientview=LOWORD(lParam))/2;
      yCenterCoord=(yClientview=HIWORD(lParam))/2;
      if (hBitmap)
        DeleteObject(hBitmap);
      StepSize=2;
      hdc=GetDC(hwnd);
      hmdc=CreateCompatibleDC(hdc);

      /* Create a bitmap */
      hBitmap=CreateCompatibleBitmap(hdc,
                                     BITMAPSIZE+StepSize,
                                     BITMAPSIZE);

      ReleaseDC(hwnd,hdc);
```

```
    SelectObject(hmdc,hBitmap);
    Rectangle(hmdc,-1,-1,BITMAPSIZE+StepSize+1,
            BITMAPSIZE+1);

    SelectPalette(hmdc,hPal);
    RealizePalette(hmdc);

    /* Draw Train Wheels */
    colorshade=PALETTERGB(0x00,0x00,0xFF);
    hBrush=CreateSolidBrush(colorshade);
    SelectObject(hmdc,hBrush);
    /* Left Train Wheel */
    Ellipse(hmdc,5,29,15,39);
    /* Right Train Wheel */
    Ellipse(hmdc,25,29,35,39);

    /* Main Body of Train */
    colorshade=PALETTERGB(0xFF,0x00,0x00);
    hBrush=CreateSolidBrush(colorshade);
    SelectObject(hmdc,hBrush);
    Rectangle(hmdc,2,19,37,29);

    /* Smoke Stack */
    colorshade=PALETTERGB(0x00,0x00,0x00);
    hBrush=CreateSolidBrush(colorshade);
    SelectObject(hmdc,hBrush);
    Rectangle(hmdc,17,0,23,19);

    DeleteDC(hmdc);
    DeleteObject(hBrush);
    break;

case WM_TIMER:
  if (!hBitmap)
 break;

  hdc=GetDC(hwnd);
  hmdc=CreateCompatibleDC(hdc);
  SelectObject(hmdc,hBitmap);
  BitBlt(hdc,xCenterCoord-BITMAPSIZE/2,
        yCenterCoord-BITMAPSIZE/2,BITMAPSIZE,
        BITMAPSIZE,hmdc,0,0,SRCCOPY);
  ReleaseDC(hwnd,hdc);
  DeleteDC(hmdc);
  xCenterCoord+=StepSize;
  if((xCenterCoord+BITMAPSIZE/2>=xClientview)||
    (xCenterCoord-BITMAPSIZE/2<=0))
  {
    StepSize=-StepSize;
    Noise();
  }
  break;

case WM_DESTROY:
  if (hBitmap)
    DeleteObject(hBitmap);
  KillTimer(hwnd,1);
  if (pLogicalPal->palNumEntries)
    DeleteObject(hPal);
  PostQuitMessage(0);
```

```
    break;

  default:
    return(DefWindowProc(hwnd,messg,wParam,lParam));
 }
 return(0L);
}
```

If you examine the **MAKE** file for this example, you will notice code for the assembly of a routine named NOISE. This routine is an assembly language routine that controls the speaker port of the computer. It can be found at the end of the listing. Windows jealously guards its control of hardware. You are on potentially shaky ground when you write routines, such as this one, that take control of hardware devices. This problem will be discussed further in the next chapter, but this particular routine should not cause any serious problems.

The .DEF file uses two EXPORTS: one to the WindowProc procedure and one to the external assembly language procedure NOISE. The IMPORT information is necessary for assembly language calls to computer ports under Windows 3.0. Again, there is more on this in the next chapter.

The C code for this example is identical to the last program, except for the addition of a call to NOISE. This occurs under WM_TIMER, just after the *StepSize* variable is negated after a collision with the wall. NOISE does not pass or receive any parameters. What could be simpler?

The assembly language code is fairly straightforward, too. The speaker port is port 97 (61 hexadecimal). The basic ploy in this routine is to turn the speaker on and off with a series of pulses. This can be done by setting bit 0 of the speaker port to zero in order to turn the speaker on. Next, an alternate group of ones and zeros is sent to bit 1, creating a sound. The pitch is controlled by the overall timing of the loop. The faster your computer runs, the higher the pitch. The value contained at the speaker port is obtained with the command

```
    in      al,61h
```

The 8-bit value returned to the *al* register is logically "ANDed" with 0FCh (11111100 binary). This effectively forces bits 0 and 1 to logical zero. The variable *info* will hold a number corresponding to a frequency; it is initialized to zero each time the outer loop is repeated. The outer loop will be repeated twice, causing a warbling sound. The inner loop exclusively ORs (xor) bit 1 of the *al* register with a 2 (10 binary). This will make the bit toggle to the opposite value each time the inner loop is circled—turning the speaker on and off. *Info* is incremented each time through the inner loop, until it reaches 768 (300 hexadecimal). This causes an increasing pitch in the inner loop.

You might experiment by changing various values in the assembly routine. If you change the 300h value to a higher number, the pitch will go higher and the sound will last longer. If you change the initial value placed in *info* to some value other than zero, the sound will start at that frequency.

The graphics routine is identical to the last example, as you might have noticed. The only change in the C code is a call to the assembly language routine.

EXPERIMENT AND HAVE FUN

The programming concepts presented in this chapter have been a combination of old and new ideas. By this time you should be quite comfortable working with the Windows platform, menus, dialog boxes, and so on. The new ideas involve integrating the mouse into the Windows environment, continued work with bitmaps as they apply to animation, and the patching of a simple assembly language program to your application code.

Experiment with and alter the code given in this chapter. Change the shape of the train engine or experiment with the sound generator. There is a lot to be learned. But above all, experiment and have fun!

14

THE ASSEMBLY LANGUAGE
CONNECTION

In the world of business, speed is often of the essence—hence, the success of the overnight delivery industry. But such service comes at a relatively high cost. Assembly language program interfaces are a similar case—sometimes necessary, but often with a high price tag.

In the last chapter, you were introduced to an assembly language patch for generating a sound from the speaker. This external assembly language procedure did not send or receive values from the host Windows program. It was simple, straightforward, and complete. Assembly language interfaces, such as that example, are usually easy to write and interface. But why assembly language when there is C?

Assembly language has two advantages that it offers to any programming environment: it is fast and it gives you the ability to perform feats that cannot be performed with high-level compilers. In this respect, assembly language code is closest to native machine code. For each assembly language mnemonic (instruction), such as *add,* there is an equivalent machine language instruction. This one-to-one relationship produces the fastest possible executable code. In the special feats category is assembly language's ability to control the hardware environment. Remember, if it can be done with the computer it can be done in assembly language. But herein is also the danger: you can perform tasks you are not supposed to be able to accomplish from within the Windows environment.

Windows jealously guards access to the computer hardware, such as the keyboard, monitor, and printer. In any multitasking operating system, such as Windows 3.0, allowing a program to access specific hardware devices can be very dangerous. Consider the problem that can occur if two programs want to receive keyboard input at the same time or send information to the printer. Which controls what any program will get at any given moment — the operating system or the environment shell? Windows is supposed to maintain control over the environment at all times. Thus, all hardware access by the programmer should be through "approved" Windows functions and routines.

Like the overnight delivery service, using assembly language to access hardware features comes with a high price tag and should only be used when necessary; however, there are times when more complicated alternatives such as software drivers are more than what's needed or just too difficult to create. The message we're trying to send is *use with caution.*

GETTING STARTED WITH ASSEMBLY LANGUAGE

If you have been programming in C for some time, you are probably familiar with assembly language. These two languages are closely related and in many situations can produce identical programming results. Many high-level programmers are introduced to assembly language when the need arises for a software solution between their high-level code and system hardware. Assembly language provides high-level compilers with features that might not have been included by the manufacturer. For example, IBM's first Pascal compiler for the IBM PC family did not provide a means of doing graphics. However, by providing an assembly language patch, graphics routines were developed and used by Pascal programmers. Assembly language also has a speed advantage. Good assembly language code is the fastest executing code you can write for a microprocessor.

If you are not familiar with assembly language programming or need to brush up on your skills, either *Assembly Language Programming Under OS/2* or *80386/80286 Assembly Language Programming*, both by William Murray and Chris Pappas and published by Osborne/McGraw-Hill, will be helpful.

The two examples in this chapter will continue to teach you how to call an assembly language patch from your Windows program. The first program sends a value from the Windows program to the assembly language program. The second example returns a value from the assembly language program, sending it back to the Windows program. Both examples use Microsoft's new method of passing values between programs. This technique is explained in both the Microsoft C and MASM documentation for parameter passing. Additionally, each program will teach you how to access the general purpose parallel port (LPT1) on the computer. Reading and writing to external hardware ports can be very useful in controlling hardware devices or accessing data from remote sources. You'll see in the two examples how to control a port from Windows.

The Parallel Port

The parallel port on most computers is a general purpose 8-bit output port capable of driving a wide range of printers, plotters, and other external devices. The parallel port shipped with all IBM PS/2 computers is different from the parallel ports of the earlier PC family. The new parallel port allows two basic modes of operation: *compatible mode* (compatible with the earlier parallel ports) and *extended mode.* In compatible mode the port functions like all earlier parallel ports. It is basically an output port capable of sending information from the computer to an external device. In extended mode the parallel port permits data to be sent or received through the port data bus. Thus, the port can be used for sending and receiving data. Figure 14-1 is a block diagram of the PS/2 parallel port.

The extended parallel port interface responds to two I/O classes of assembly code instructions: input (*in*) and output (*out*). When the controller is working in compatible mode, output instructions transfer data into two latches whose outputs are connected to the D-shell output connector on the back of the computer. Input instructions allow the computer to read back the contents of the two latches. A third input latch permits the PS/2 computer family to read the status of a number of pins on the D-shell connector. In extended mode the 8-bit data latch output is controlled by bit 5 of the parallel control port. Reading the 8-bit data bus, in the data address, is controlled by bit 5 of the parallel control port. It is this feature that permits external equipment to utilize the port in a truly bidirectional mode.

During POST initialization of PS/2 computers, which occurs at boot time, the parallel port is configured as an output port. Actually, the parallel port can be configured to three different address spaces. Address spaces are selected by running the system's setup routines and using the Programmable Option Select. This will perform an I/O write to port 258 (0102H). At this port address, bits 5 and 6 select the actual addresses. To obtain parallel 1

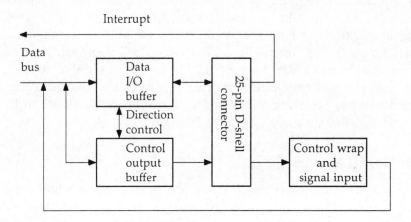

Figure 14-1.   A block diagram of the PS/2 parallel port

(LPT1), bit 5 is 0 and bit 6 is 0. To obtain parallel 2 (LPT2), bit 5 is 1 and bit 6 is 0. To obtain parallel 3 (LPT3), bit 5 is 0 and bit 6 is 1. Once the port is so configured, each of the preceding parallel options uses a unique set of addresses, as shown in Table 14-1.

When operating in extended mode, the extended option is selected with the Programmable Option Select. Again, this is usually done with the setup routines of the system by writing a 0 to bit 7 of the I/O address 258. Once this is done, the 8-bit parallel port becomes a bidirectional interface.

Table 14-1 gives the addresses of the data address port, status port, and parallel control port for each of three different configurations. Table 14-2 is a summary of the individual bits for LPT1. Additional information on each port is provided in the IBM Personal System/2 Model 60, 70, or 80 technical references.

Table 14-1.   Parallel Port Address Assignments

Number	Data Address	Status Address	Parallel Control Address
Parallel 1	03BCH	03BDH	03BEH
Parallel 2	0378H	0379H	037AH
Parallel 3	0278H	0279H	027AH

Table 14-2.   Bit Information for LPT1, the Parallel Port

	Bit 7	Bit 6	Bit 5	Bit 4	Bit 3	Bit 2	Bit1	Bit 0
Port 956	pin 9	pin 8	pin 7	pin 6	pin 5	pin 4	pin 3	pin 2
Pin Label	D7	D6	D5	D4	D3	D2	D1	D0
	Bit 7	Bit 6	Bit 5	Bit 4	Bit 3	Bit 2	Bit 1	Bit 0
Port 957	pin 11	pin 10	pin 12	pin 13	pin 15	X	X	X
Pin Label	busy	ackno	paper	select	error			
	Bit 7	Bit 6	Bit 5	Bit 4	Bit 3	Bit 2	Bit 1	Bit 0
Port 958	X	X	X	X	pin 17	pin 16	pin 14	pin 1
Pin Label					/sel	init	/atfd	/strob

/ indicates a complemented data line.

The data address port is an 8-bit data port. In compatible mode, data will be immediately written to the output pins when a write operation occurs. Likewise, a read operation from this port will produce the data that was last written (latched). In extended mode, data will only be written to the output pins if the direction bit was set to write (parallel control port) during a write operation. Also, if the direction is set to write, a subsequent read operation while in extended mode will produce the data that had been previously written to the output pins. However, if the direction of the parallel control port is set to read, the data from an external device is entered.

The status port is a read port for either the compatible or extended mode. As you can see in Table 14-3, this register supplies conventional printer status information to the microprocessor.

The parallel control port is a read/write port. This port allows you to control the operation of compatible and extended modes. A write operation to this port will latch data bits 0 to 5. Bit 5 corresponds to the compatible/extended mode option and is actually a write-only bit. Bits 0 to 4 accept information from the microprocessor to the printer and support conventional printer control information.

The output signals from the parallel port have sink currents of 20 mA and can source 0.55 mA. The high-level output voltage is 5.0 V, while the low-level output voltage is 0.5 V. Pins 1, 14, 16, and 17 are driven by open

Table 14-3.   Parallel Controller Registers and Ports

Data Address Port (Read/Write):

Bit	Description
0	Data, bit 0
1	Data, bit 1
2	Data, bit 2
3	Data, bit 3
4	Data, bit 4
5	Data, bit 5
6	Data, bit 6
7	Data, bit 7

Status Port (Read):

Bit	Description
0–1	(Reserved)
2	−IRQ status
3	−ERROR
4	Select
5	PE
6	−ACK
7	−BUSY

Parallel Control Port (Read/Write)

Bit	Description
0	STROBE
1	AUTO FD XT
2	−INIT
3	SLCT IN
4	IRQ EN
5	Direction
6–7	(Reserved)

---

collector outputs bootstrapped to +5 V through 4700 ohm resistors. Figure 14-2 is a drawing of the parallel port D-shell connector. Table 14-4 describes the pin assignment for this connector.

If all of this technical information is more than you ever wanted to know about the parallel port, be patient; the programming is fairly straightforward.

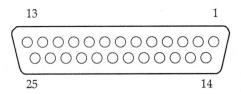

Figure 14-2.   A sketch of the D-shell connector

A SIMPLE LED TRAFFIC LIGHT

The light emitting diode (LED) traffic light hardware interface can be wired to any parallel port since it functions in only the conventional output mode.

Table 14-4.   Pin Assignments for Parallel Port Connector

Pin	Description
1	−STROBE
2	Data, bit 0
3	Data, bit 1
4	Data, bit 2
5	Data, bit 3
6	Data, bit 4
7	Data, bit 5
8	Data, bit 6
9	Data, bit 7
10	−ACK
11	BUSY
12	PE
13	SLCT
14	−AUTO FEED XT
15	−ERROR
16	−INIT
17	−SLCT IN
18−25	Ground

The previous section described the IBM parallel port's output as having sink currents of 20 mA and source currents of 0.55 mA. Since the output voltage from the port is TTL compatible (logic 1 is 5.0 V, while logic 0 is 0.5 V), the parallel port is capable of driving small LED lights directly.

If you are interested in wiring the three LED traffic lights to your parallel port, you will need only a few parts: a cable that will connect the parallel port to a prototyping board, some hookup wire, and three LED lights (red, green, and amber). For this example, a 25-pin D-shell connector was used to connect to the parallel port with a ribbon cable terminating in a 24-pin male dip header. Pin #13 was discarded from the D-shell connector. The prototyping board was simply the type that allows DIP chips to be easily inserted and removed. These parts can be found at basic electronic supply stores. If you purchase connectors that clamp over ribbon cable, no soldering will be necessary.

The voltages present at the parallel port are lower than that of a car battery and do not present a shock hazard. It is also just about impossible to do any damage to the computer even if wrong connections are made.

Warning: Remember, however, that you are making "live" connections to the computer. Be very careful not to connect the parallel port to any external device or outlet where unsafe voltages are present.

The Assembly Language Patch

The assembly language patch for this example is very simple.

```
;Real Mode Assembly Language Programming Patch
;For execution on 80486/80286 machines

;An assembly language patch to provide access to
;parallel printer port #956 (LPT1) on IBM computers

        PUBLIC    Traffic

        DOSSEG              ;use Microsoft segment conventions
        .MODEL    MEDIUM,PASCAL ;set model size & parameter pass
        .286                ;80286 instructions

        .CODE
Traffic PROC    FAR  litecontrol:WORD
        cli                 ;protect against interrupts

        mov   ax,litecontrol ;value being passed from C
        mov   dx,956        ;parallel printer port num
        out   dx,ax         ;send information

        sti                 ;clear interrupt protection
        ret                 ;return to calling program
```

```
Traffic endp          ;end main procedure
      end             ;end whole program
```

First, the model size and parameter passing type are set with the
.MODEL directive. In this case a MEDIUM model will be used and values
passed off the system stack in the PASCAL parameter passing convention.
The assembly language procedure is named Traffic and must be declared
PUBLIC in order for values to be shared between the Windows host (C)
and the assembly language patch (ASM). A value (*litecontrol:WORD*) will be
passed to this code from the Windows host program. The port number (956
decimal or 3BC hexadecimal) is moved to the *dx* register, and the value
from *litecontrol* is sent with the *out* mnemonic. The *cli* and *sti* mnemonics,
which surround this code, are used to prevent system interrupts while this
transmission is taking place. Since the parallel port is an 8-bit port, only the
contents of the *al* register are actually sent. By controlling the individual
bits, LEDs connected to the port's data lines can be turned on and off. The
LEDs for this example are wired to D0 (red) pin #2, D1 (amber) pin #3,
and D2 (green) pin #4 of the parallel port and the port's ground pin #18
through #25.

The Windows Code

The Windows program contains more or less traditional code, like what
you have seen in previous chapters. In order to make the example more
interesting, a traffic light will be drawn to the screen. The light on the
screen will sequence colors corresponding to the colors of the three LEDs
wired to the parallel port.

THE TLITE14 MAKE FILE:

```
ALL : tlite14.exe # ALL needed for C 6.0 up

tlite14.obj: tlite14.c
    cl -c -AS -Gsw -Oas -Zpe tlite14.c

traffic.obj: traffic.asm
    masm traffic;

tlite14.exe: tlite14.obj tlite14.def tlite14.res
    link /NOD tlite14+traffic,,,libw slibcew,tlite14.def
```

THE TLITE14.DEF DEFINITION FILE:

```
NAME        TLITE14
DESCRIPTION 'Simplified Windows Platform'
EXETYPE     WINDOWS
STUB        'WINSTUB.EXE'
CODE        PRELOAD MOVEABLE DISCARDABLE
```

```
DATA        PRELOAD MOVEABLE MULTIPLE
HEAPSIZE    4096
STACKSIZE   9216
EXPORTS     WindowProc        @1
            Traffic           @2
```

THE TLITE14.C APPLICATION FILE:

```
/* Simplified Windows Platform (SWP)              */
/* (c) William H. Murray and Chris H. Pappas, 1989 */

#include <windows.h>

long FAR PASCAL WindowProc(HWND,unsigned,WORD,LONG);
VOID FAR PASCAL Traffic(WORD litecontrol);

char    szProgName[]="ProgName";
int     litecontrol=3;

int PASCAL WinMain(hInst,hPreInst,lpszCmdLine,nCmdShow)
HANDLE hInst,hPreInst;
LPSTR  lpszCmdLine;
int    nCmdShow;
{
  HWND hwnd;
  MSG  msg;
  WNDCLASS wcSwp;
  if (!hPreInst)
  {
    wcSwp.lpszClassName=szProgName;
    wcSwp.hInstance     =hInst;
    wcSwp.lpfnWndProc   =WindowProc;
    wcSwp.hCursor       =LoadCursor(NULL,IDC_ARROW);
    wcSwp.hIcon         =NULL;
    wcSwp.lpszMenuName  =NULL;
    wcSwp.hbrBackground=GetStockObject(WHITE_BRUSH);
    wcSwp.style         =CS_HREDRAW|CS_VREDRAW;
    wcSwp.cbClsExtra    =0;
    wcSwp.cbWndExtra    =0;
    if (!RegisterClass (&wcSwp))
      return FALSE;
  }
  hwnd=CreateWindow(szProgName,"Traffic Light",
                    WS_OVERLAPPEDWINDOW,CW_USEDEFAULT,
                    CW_USEDEFAULT,CW_USEDEFAULT,
                    CW_USEDEFAULT,NULL,NULL,
                    hInst,NULL);

  if (!SetTimer(hwnd,1,3000,NULL))
    {
    MessageBox(hwnd,"Too many timers started!",
               szProgName,MB_OK);
    return FALSE;
    }

  ShowWindow(hwnd,nCmdShow);
  UpdateWindow(hwnd);
  while (GetMessage(&msg,NULL,NULL,NULL))
  {
    TranslateMessage(&msg);
    DispatchMessage(&msg);
```

```
    }
  return(msg.wParam);
}

long FAR PASCAL WindowProc(hwnd,messg,wParam,lParam)
HWND    hwnd;
unsigned messg;
WORD    wParam;
LONG    lParam;
{
  PAINTSTRUCT ps;
  HDC  hdc;
  HBRUSH hOrgBrush=CreateSolidBrush(RGB(255,255,255));
  HBRUSH hBrush;
  RECT    rect;
  rect.left=295;
  rect.top=155;
  rect.right=345;
  rect.bottom=305;

  switch (messg)
  {
    case WM_TIMER:
      if (litecontrol>2) litecontrol=0;
      litecontrol+=1;
      InvalidateRect(hwnd,&rect,1);
    break;

    case WM_PAINT:
      hdc=BeginPaint(hwnd,&ps);

/*--------- your routines below ---------*/

      /* draw traffic light outline */
      Rectangle(hdc,290,150,350,310);
      Ellipse(hdc,300,160,340,200);
      Ellipse(hdc,300,210,340,250);
      Ellipse(hdc,300,260,340,300);

      /* turn on red light */
      if (litecontrol==1)
        {
        hBrush=CreateSolidBrush(RGB(255,0,0));
        SelectObject(hdc,hBrush);
        Ellipse(hdc,300,160,340,200);
        SelectObject(hdc,hOrgBrush);
        Traffic(litecontrol);      /* turn on red LED */
        }

      /* turn on amber light */
      if (litecontrol==2)
        {
        hBrush=CreateSolidBrush(RGB(255,255,0));
        SelectObject(hdc,hBrush);
        Ellipse(hdc,300,210,340,250);
        SelectObject(hdc,hOrgBrush);
        Traffic(litecontrol);      /* turn on amber LED */
        }

      /* turn on green light */
      if (litecontrol==3)
```

```
      {
      hBrush=CreateSolidBrush(RGB(0,255,0));
      SelectObject(hdc,hBrush);
      Ellipse(hdc,300,260,340,300);
      SelectObject(hdc,hOrgBrush);
      Traffic(litecontrol+1);   /* turn on green LED */
      }

      SelectObject(hdc,hOrgBrush);
      DeleteObject(hBrush);

/*--------- your routines above ---------*/

      ValidateRect(hwnd,NULL);
      EndPaint(hwnd,&ps);
      break;
    case WM_DESTROY:
      KillTimer(hwnd,1);
      PostQuitMessage(0);
      break;
    default:
      return(DefWindowProc(hwnd,messg,wParam,lParam));
      break;
  }
  return(0L);
}
```

WM _ TIMER is used to sequence the lights. Each time a timer message is intercepted, the variable *litecontrol* is incremented. Actually, *litecontrol* can only take on the values 1, 2, and 3. Additionally, with each timer message, a call is made to the InvalidateRect function. This will force WM _ PAINT to redraw a portion of the screen, which in turn lights the correct lamp in the traffic light on the screen and the corresponding LED.

The traffic light outline is drawn with three circles that represent the red, amber, and green bulbs. For example, if *litecontrol* is a 1, the red lamp will be filled with red. The other lamps correspond to 2 and 3. For this program the timer was set to 3000 milliseconds; thus, each color will remain on the screen for three seconds.

If you study the program closely, you will notice that a call is made to the external procedure, Traffic, when any light on the screen is filled. For a red light, a 1 is sent to turn on bit 0 (0001) of the parallel port. An amber light requires a 2 since it is wired to bit 1 (0010), and a green light requires a 4 because it is wired to bit 3 (0100).

Once you have mastered this simple port control, you can write a Windows program that can light or sequence eight LEDs. Eight lights can be used because the parallel port is an 8-bit port, D0 to D7. Furthermore, if your interest is of a scientific nature, a digital-to-analog (DAC) converter could convert 8-bit digital information to a corresponding analog voltage.

INTERFACING DIGITAL SWITCHES

This hardware interface can only be used by computers with parallel ports capable of extended mode operation. Extended mode operation is available on most IBM PS/2 computers and some compatibles. If you are using an extended mode port, this program will teach you how to pass information from the assembly language program back to the host Windows program.

Since the parallel port can read information into the computer when working in extended mode, it provides a channel for data input. The eight lines can input binary data from 00000000_2 to 11111111_2. In the next example, eight simple switches are wired to the parallel port. It will then be possible to switch each of the data lines from logic 0 to logic 1. The results of various switch positions will be plotted on a simple graph.

Digital Input

The final program in this chapter illustrates digital input through the parallel port. The techniques shown in the following example could also be extended to allow the connection of an analog to digital converter (A/D). See *80386 Microprocessor Handbook* by Chris Pappas and William Murray (Berkeley, Ca.: Osborne/McGraw-Hill, 1988) for additional A/D details. A/D converters are used to convert analog voltages to digital signals that are compatible with the computer's data bus. Even if you are not interested in interfacing an analog-to-digital (A/D or ADC) converter to your computer, follow along during the explanation of the program's operation, and learn how to use this extended programming power.

Computers are digital devices that can be interfaced to external signals. If the signals are digital, with signal ranges between +5 V (logic 1) and 0 V (logic 0), they can usually be connected to the data bus of the computer by using a simple hardware interface. The wiring diagram for this example is shown in Figure 14-3. The switches in this example are not debounced, but that does not cause a problem in this setup. The data lines of the parallel port "float" high when they are not connected. This is why the switches must switch between +5 V and ground.

A Patch to Initialize the Parallel Port

The assembly language program consists of several major pieces of code. The procedure is named Diginput and must be declared PUBLIC. In this example a value (*digital:WORD*) will be passed from the assembly language patch back to the host Windows program. The first three blocks of code are

MSB

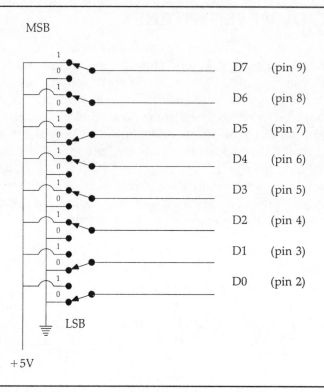

Figure 14-3.   Eight switches wired to the parallel port

required in order to initialize the parallel port to an input port. The decimal masks used here should be converted to their binary equivalents to determine which bits are being set and reset. Also note that several port lines must be complemented. (Remember, this program will only work with PS/2 or equivalent computers.)

```
;Real Mode Assembly Language Programming Patch
;For execution on 80486/80286 machines

;An assembly language patch to provide input from
;parallel printer port #956 (LPT1) on IBM
;PS/2 series computers with extended parallel ports

        PUBLIC      Diginput

        DOSSEG                  ;use Microsoft segment conventions
        .MODEL      MEDIUM,PASCAL ;set model size
        .286                    ;80286 instructions

        .CODE
Diginput PROC  FAR digital:WORD
        cli                     ;protect against interrupts
```

```
       mov   dx,148         ;set PS/2 port to SETUP mode
       in    al,dx
       and   al,127         ;mask data
       out   dx,al          ;return to same port

       mov   dx,258         ;enable PS/2 port for extended mode
       in    al,dx
       and   al,127         ;mask data
       out   dx,al          ;return to same port

       mov   dx,958         ;initialize port
       mov   al,32
       out   dx,al

       mov   dx,956         ;parallel printer port num
       in    al,dx          ;receive information
       mov   ah,0           ;keep & pass lower 8 bits
       mov   digital,ax     ;return value to C program

       sti                  ;clear interrupt protection
       ret                  ;return to calling program
Diginput ENDP              ;end main procedure
       END                  ;end whole program
```

Recall that the parallel port can be addressed through three internal ports. The parallel port (LPT1) has been assigned port numbers 956, 957, and 958 (decimal). Each port number controls different pins on the parallel port's 25-pin D-shell connector (see Table 14-2). For example, port 956 is wired in this manner:

	bit7	bit6	bit5	bit4	bit3	bit2	bit1	bit0
Port 956: Pin	pin 9	pin 8	pin 7	pin 6	pin 5	pin 4	pin 3	pin 2
Label:	D7	D6	D5	D4	D3	D2	D1	D0

Therefore, if you want to connect to the 8-bit data bus (D0 to D7), port 956 is the one that must be addressed. You'll see that block of code near the bottom of the program. The reading is taken from the port with an *in* mnemonic and the value is returned to the Windows program through the dummy variable, *digital*. The port only returns an 8-bit value, so the upper 8 bits of the *ax* register are forced to zero.

The C Windows Code

This program also uses WM_TIMER messages to pace the intercepted values from the assembly language patch.

THE SWITCH14 MAKE FILE:

```
ALL : switch14.exe # ALL needed for C 6.0 up

switch14.obj: switch14.c
    cl -c -AS -Gsw -Oas -Zpe switch14.c

diginput.obj: diginput.asm
    masm diginput;

switch14.exe: switch14.obj switch14.def switch14.res
    link /NOD switch14+diginput,,,libw slibcew,switch14.def
```

THE SWITCH14.DEF DEFINITION FILE:

```
NAME        SWITCH14
DESCRIPTION 'Simplified Windows Platform'
EXETYPE     WINDOWS
STUB        'WINSTUB.EXE'
CODE        PRELOAD MOVEABLE DISCARDABLE
DATA        PRELOAD MOVEABLE MULTIPLE
HEAPSIZE    4096
STACKSIZE   9216
EXPORTS     WindowProc      @1
            Diginput        @2
```

THE SWITCH14.C APPLICATION FILE:

```
/* Simplified Windows Platform (SWP)              */
/* (c) William H. Murray and Chris H. Pappas, 1989 */

#include <windows.h>
#include <stdlib.h>
#include <string.h>

long FAR PASCAL WindowProc(HWND,unsigned,WORD,LONG);
int  FAR PASCAL Diginput(VOID);

char    szProgName[]="ProgName";
char    szLabel[80]="Sampling Eight Digital Switches";
int     digital;
int     step=99;

int PASCAL WinMain(hInst,hPreInst,lpszCmdLine,nCmdShow)
HANDLE hInst,hPreInst;
LPSTR  lpszCmdLine;
int    nCmdShow;
{
  HWND hwnd;
  MSG  msg;
  WNDCLASS wcSwp;
  if (!hPreInst)
  {
    wcSwp.lpszClassName=szProgName;
    wcSwp.hInstance     =hInst;
    wcSwp.lpfnWndProc   =WindowProc;
    wcSwp.hCursor       =LoadCursor(NULL,IDC_ARROW);
    wcSwp.hIcon         =NULL;
    wcSwp.lpszMenuName  =NULL;
    wcSwp.hbrBackground=GetStockObject(WHITE_BRUSH);
    wcSwp.style         =CS_HREDRAW¦CS_VREDRAW;
```

```
    wcSwp.cbClsExtra    =0;
    wcSwp.cbWndExtra    =0;
    if (!RegisterClass (&wcSwp))
      return FALSE;
  }
  hwnd=CreateWindow(szProgName,"Digital Input from Switches",
                    WS_OVERLAPPEDWINDOW,CW_USEDEFAULT,
                    CW_USEDEFAULT,CW_USEDEFAULT,
                    CW_USEDEFAULT,NULL,NULL,
                    hInst,NULL);

  if (!SetTimer(hwnd,1,200,NULL))
    {
    MessageBox(hwnd,"Too many timers started!",
               szProgName,MB_OK);
    return FALSE;
    }

  ShowWindow(hwnd,nCmdShow);
  UpdateWindow(hwnd);
  while (GetMessage(&msg,NULL,NULL,NULL))
  {
    TranslateMessage(&msg);
    DispatchMessage(&msg);
  }
  return(msg.wParam);
}

long FAR PASCAL WindowProc(hwnd,messg,wParam,lParam)
HWND    hwnd;
unsigned messg;
WORD    wParam;
LONG    lParam;
{
  PAINTSTRUCT ps;
  HDC  hdc;

  switch (messg)
  {
    case WM_SIZE:
    step=99;
    break;

    case WM_TIMER:
    digital=Diginput();
    InvalidateRect(hwnd,NULL,0);
    break;

    case WM_PAINT:
      hdc=BeginPaint(hwnd,&ps);

/*--------- your routines below ---------*/

      MoveTo(hdc,99,49);
      LineTo(hdc,99,350);
      LineTo(hdc,500,350);
      MoveTo(hdc,99,350);

      SetPixel(hdc,step++,350-digital,RGB(0,0,255));

      TextOut(hdc,(300-(strlen(szLabel)*8/2)),
```

```
                365,szLabel,strlen(szLabel));
        if (step==500) KillTimer(hwnd,1);

/*--------- your routines above ---------*/

        ValidateRect(hwnd,NULL);
        EndPaint(hwnd,&ps);
        break;
      case WM_DESTROY:
        KillTimer(hwnd,1);
        PostQuitMessage(0);
        break;
      default:
        return(DefWindowProc(hwnd,messg,wParam,lParam));
        break;
  }
  return(0L);
}
```

Each time a WM_TIMER message is called, a new value is returned to the variable *digital* from the external procedure Diginput. This value is used to set the vertical (*y*) value in SetPixel. Thus, as *digital* changes, a graph will be drawn in the window. Up to 400 samples can be taken and plotted using conventional plotting techniques. Figure 14-4 is an example plot showing various values produced by the data switches.

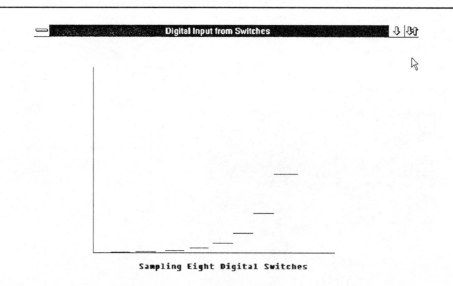

Figure 14-4.   Various switch positions for the eight switches connected to the parallel port

Getting information into the extended mode parallel port has proved to be rather simple. Now the concept could be extended a bit further. A solar cell and an A/D converter could also be wired as an input device to the parallel port. If a solar cell is connected, sunlight can be monitored over an extended period. Wouldn't this be useful information in the placement and design of a house?

MOVING FORWARD WITH ASSEMBLY LANGUAGE

As you have seen, small assembly language patches are very easy to make. Assembly language has the ability to make impossible C compiler and Windows tasks possible. Generally, interfacing with assembly language routines is simple and straightforward and offers no additional programming problems. Microsoft does warn that programs should not attempt to perform segment arithmetic, compare segment addresses, read or write past the ends of memory objects, or use code segment variables under the new rules for memory management.

15

INTRODUCTION TO THE OS/2 PRESENTATION MANAGER

There was once a boy who was given on his fourteenth birthday a key to his father's 1958 Buick. He couldn't drive at 14, but the key came to represent future freedom—it never left his possession. A year or two later his father sold the Buick and bought an Oldsmobile. Consequently, both father and son were extremely surprised when the 1958 Buick key unlocked the 1965 Oldsmobile. Although cars are basically the same in appearance and overall function, relatively few parts can be directly interchanged. In terms of driving, however, most cars behave the same way. The controls, such as the accelerator, brakes, and steering, are in the same places and function the same way on all cars.

Windows 3.0 and the OS/2 Presentation Manager are like two different makes of car. While their parts are not interchangeable, Microsoft has carefully crafted the function and placement of the controls to make the transition from one system to the other easier for you. And the message-based operating system is like the Buick key—common to Windows and Presentation Manager programming. When you understand how Windows programs work, you basically understand how Presentation Manager programs work. The Presentation Manager offers exciting new vistas of performance for OS/2 programmers.

This chapter discusses the characteristics of Windows programming under OS/2—in the Presentation Manager. As you read the descriptions of the Presentation Manager compare those concepts with what you have already learned about Microsoft Windows 3.0. By learning how to program under Microsoft Windows, you have prepared yourself for the Windows environment in the present as well as in the future. What you'll discover is that you already understand the fundamentals of window control—those fundamentals are directly interchangeable between Microsoft Windows 3.0 and Presentation Manager.

WHAT IS THE OS/2 PRESENTATION MANAGER?

The Microsoft OS/2 Presentation Manager, like Microsoft Windows 3.0, is designed to be an integral part of the operating system. Windows operates as a shell under DOS while the Presentation Manager operates as a shell over OS/2. The Presentation Manager interface is very similar to Windows and provides many of the well-known benefits associated with a windowed environment. These benefits include powerful window support, a consistent graphical user interface, and support for device-independent I/O devices. The Presentation Manager shell replaces the standard command-line C> or [C:] prompt of previous DOS and OS/2 versions with a window-based screen.

User Interface

The Presentation Manager addresses the ease-of-use problems associated with earlier DOS and OS/2 versions by combining a window environment with OS/2. Since the Presentation Manager presents a more intuitive graphical user interface, like Windows, novice users are able to learn application products more quickly. Thus, instead of complicated command-line statements the user can simply select an option from the window's screen. Figure 15-1 shows a typical Presentation Manager screen.

Real Versus Protected Mode Operation

The new generation of computers using the Intel 80486/80386/80286 microprocessors is capable of running in real or protected mode. In real mode they operate much like the Intel 8088-based IBM PC with the associated limit of 1 megabyte of memory, and can usually run only one program at a

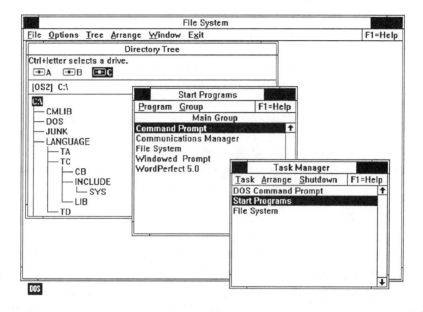

Figure 15-1.   A typical Presentation Manager screen

time. If they operate under DOS they are vulnerable to crashing when a program goes awry. When operating in protected mode under OS/2 Presentation Manager, the 80486/80386/80286-based computers do away with such restrictions.

OS/2's protected mode allows programs to grow larger than 640K, with applications taking advantage of up to 16 megabytes of physical memory and up to 1 gigabyte of virtual memory. OS/2's protected mode is much more robust than its real mode counterpart as a result of being able to perform multitasking.

With the OS/2 Presentation Manager, the multitasking capabilities of the 80486/80386/80286 are much easier to exploit than they are with multitasking Microsoft Windows 3.0 running under DOS. This is due to the tight integration of OS/2 and the windows environment that is provided by the underlying operating system kernel.

Using Overlapped Windows

There is no doubt the Presentation Manager will become the standard graphical user interface for OS/2. When operating in a Presentation Manager window, users will no longer have to learn about disk directories, file names, and other cryptic command-line arguments. Executing programs and managing the OS/2 file system with the Presentation Manager will become an intuitive and fast process—as it has for thousands of Windows users.

The Presentation Manager bears a strong resemblance to Microsoft Windows 3.0. In fact Windows 3.0 was updated to bring it into line with the Presentation Manager. For example, when Microsoft Windows was first developed it used titled windows, due to low resolution monitors and sluggish graphics algorithms. With the faster processors, streamlined algorithms, and enhanced displays, the Presentation Manager and Windows 3.0 now present multiple overlapped windows instead of titled windows.

Interfacing with the Keyboard

Although the Presentation Manager does have a keyboard interface it was really designed to be used with a mouse. However, there are times when keyboard entry is preferable. The keyboard interface now incorporates direct access to items in dialog boxes. For example, a user can now press ALT-F to quickly position the cursor in the file name field of the dialog box, in the same way the Windows applications in this book have.

Menu access has also been enhanced to allow the developer to define any letter in a menu command to execute the item. You are no longer limited to the first letter, as was the case in earlier versions of Microsoft Windows. This feature allows applications developers to provide meaningful command names, while still giving fast keyboard access to commands.

Interfacing with the Mouse

The Presentation Manager also uses an improved mouse interface to reduce accidental selections. For example, the earliest versions of Microsoft Windows required the user to first position the cursor over a menu bar item, click the mouse button to make the submenu visible, and then—while holding down the mouse button—drag the highlighted bar over the desired menu option. With the Presentation Manager, as with Windows 3.0, all you need do is click (then let go) on the menu bar to make the pop-up menu visible, and then click on the desired command within the given menu. No more dragging the highlighted bar.

Converting Windows Applications to the Presentation Manager

Although Microsoft Windows 3.0 and the OS/2 Presentation Manager appear to be similar, at present, programs written for Microsoft Windows need to be modified to work with the OS/2 Presentation Manager. This is because OS/2 restricts several operations in programs—for example, software interrupts such as the BIOS 10H interrupts used for screen control and direct hardware access through ports are generally not allowed. Programs written for DOS also have to be modified to work under OS/2.

Program changes go beyond simple substitutions of OS/2 functions for older DOS interrupts. Applications developers will also have to incorporate the new OS/2 Presentation Manager Windows application program interface (API), in order to standardize coding practices, improve error handling, and exploit new graphics capabilities. Chapters 16 and 17 are devoted to teaching you how to convert Windows application programs to Presentation Manager equivalents.

Presentation Manager Features

Some of the key features the OS/2 Presentation Manager provides include the ability to simultaneously view the output from multiple applications on the display and an expanded user interface to both OS/2 and application functions. It also incorporates a program interface that provides applications with additional capabilities, such as

- Windowing data onto the display screen

- Generating and displaying graphic and alphanumeric data on a range of output devices including display screens and various printers

- Presenting a consistent user interface across applications

- Handling input devices such as keyboard, mouse, and tablets

Much of this functionality is provided by new dynamic link libraries, called DLLs, which enhance the base operating system by providing a powerful and flexible graphical user interface. Dynamic link libraries contain predefined functions that are linked with an application program when it is loaded (dynamically), instead of when the .EXE file is generated (statically). This results in smaller, more efficient application program files.

The design of the Presentation Manager's graphics program interface (GPI) library is influenced strongly by the mainframe graphical display data manager (GDDM) system. Graphics application programs can easily incorporate Windows-style formatting by using the high-level API function calls to create a window, while incorporating dazzling, hardware-independent graphics with the GPI function calls.

And since all Presentation Manager applications are run under OS/2, they can naturally take advantage of OS/2's advanced features, such as multitasking, to access a full 16 megabytes of physical memory, and gigabytes of virtual memory, along with interprocess communication.

THE LOOK AND FEEL OF THE OS/2 KERNEL

The OS/2 kernel is the bare-bones, behind-the-scenes workhorse that performs many of the MS-DOS functions such as file I/O, along with protected mode multitasking and memory management. The Presentation Manager shell is the glitzy stage presentation that sells the tickets. You may recall that the first release of OS/2 (version 1.0) only included the kernel. The OS/2 kernel still provides a program selector that allows the user to select between several predefined text-based applications. Along with providing an 8086 compatibility mode, the Presentation Manager provides graphics applications with keyboard monitors, mouse interaction, and window management.

Both the OS/2 kernel and the Presentation Manager have their advantages and disadvantages. Most text-based applications written to run under the OS/2 kernel can be easily modified to run under the Presentation Manager's graphical interface. However, applications written to take advantage of the tremendously rich Presentation Manager graphics functions cannot be ported back to the kernel version.

A CLOSER LOOK AT THE PRESENTATION MANAGER

Understanding OS/2's Presentation Manager can best be accomplished by studying its various components. The most visible feature of the Presentation Manager is its graphical user interface. However this is just a small part of the complete system controlled by additional Presentation Manager applications, dynamic link libraries, and device drivers.

Dynamite — Using Dynamic Link Libraries

The largest portion of the Presentation Manager's operation is controlled by DLLs. This design concept allows Presentation Manager applications, along with the user interface code, to remain unchanged as the DLL capabilities are enhanced or modified.

There are basically three major libraries comprising the Presentation Manager: the VIO (advanced video input/output), the GPI, and the WIN (window management). These three systems support the user interface and applications development, which allows text applications designed for the OS/2 character mode to operate under the Presentation Manager windows system.

New DLLs can be easily added with the OS/2 facility that allows a parent process to provide alternate libraries for its child processes. Actually, when the Presentation Manager starts up, it installs replacement libraries for OS/2's kernel mode: VIO, KBD, and MOU calls. These replacements override the libraries used by standard OS/2 applications for text output, keyboard input, and mouse control. With the new libraries only in effect for those applications started under the Presentation Manager, other OS/2 applications remain unaffected and continue to use the standard libraries' system services.

These enhanced libraries not only add services for the Presentation Manager graphics interface, but also provide all the standard text-based services of the default VIO libraries. With these services mapped onto the graphics environment, many OS/2 text-mode applications can run without change in a Presentation Manager window. This allows text-mode applications to share processor time and display space with applications written expressly for the Presentation Manager environment. This is similar to the ability to run a DOS program under the Microsoft Windows environment.

The User Interface

When OS/2 is run in conjunction with the Presentation Manager, screen display is controlled by the Presentation Manager User Interface Shell, which replaces the simpler OS/2 kernel interface. The User Interface Shell, which became the default starting with Presentation Manager version 1.1, provides end users with six functions. Presentation Manager version 1.2 combines the functions of the Task Manager and Start-an-Application.

The Task Manager

This Presentation Manager graphics interface utility automatically adds each program as it is started to a current switch list. The switch list contains a list of all of the running programs currently available to the user, as shown in Figure 15-2.

For applications running under the Presentation Manager screen group, there is access to several sophisticated start-up facilities allowing them to register descriptive names on the Task Manager display. For example, in a multitasking environment in which several copies of a word processor such as WordPerfect could be running simultaneously, the word processor could dynamically modify the entry in the switch list from "WordPerfect" to "WordPerfect (Cover Letter)."

The switch list also includes applications running in screen groups outside the Presentation Manager, such as standard OS/2 character-mode programs. When the user selects a program from the switch list in the Task Manager window that program becomes the active application and receives keyboard input from the system. If the program is a Presentation Manager program its main application window is brought up to the top and made

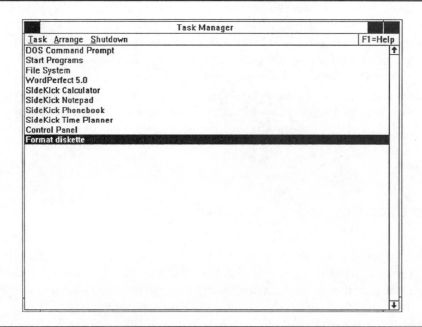

Figure 15-2.   Task Manager screen

completely visible to the user. If the application program is a character-mode application, the Presentation Manager screen group is moved to the background and the chosen application becomes the active and visible screen group.

Starting an Application   The Start-an-Application option presents the user with a list of all of the applications available and allows the user to select an application to start. A command-line option, similar to the OS/2 command line, can be used to start a program, as shown in Figure 15-3. Adding and deleting additional applications to the list is supported, along with the ability to update the application profile for each one.

Switching Applications   The user is presented with a list that includes both Presentation Manager and non-Presentation Manager OS/2 applications currently running. The user can select which application to work with next.

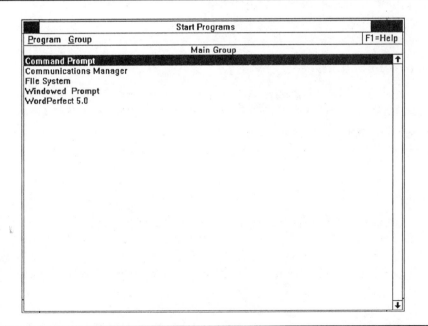

Figure 15-3.   Start Programs screen

The Position and Size of Application Windows

Each application running under the Presentation Manager uses one or more windows. Using the User Interface Shell, the user can define the location and size of the windows visible on the screen.

Printer Control

The User Interface Shell provides a menu giving the user control over the printing functions performed by the Presentation Manager.

OS/2 File Utilization

Similar in function to many of the disk organizer utilities available for DOS, the Presentation Manager filing system provides a graphic, tree-structured disk management tool. It allows the user to open any number of windows, each displaying a portion of a disk drive's directory.

Users can view files in different formats; they can copy, move, and rename files, print text files, organize directory setups, or format and label disks. By opening several directory windows at once, users can select and manipulate multiple files simultaneously and move them from one directory to another.

Control Functions

The User Interface Shell also provides the user with a reliable, easy-to-use method of selecting various Presentation Manager parameters. One example of this would be the selection of the screen background color, as illustrated in Figure 15-4.

Help Facility

Incorporated into the User Interface Shell is a context-sensitive help facility. Whenever a user of an OS/2 Presentation Manager application needs information on a current level of operation, pressing F1 at any time will display context-sensitive help for the current operation. If the user is not performing any particular operation when F1 is pressed, the help facility will supply a general application help screen with an index.

Additionally, a user can install two lines of help text within a program as part of a general system registration. This particular help then becomes available to the user directly from the system interface and allows the user

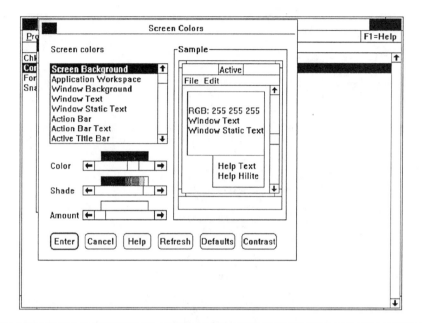

Figure 15-4.   Control box for screen colors

to learn a little about what the application does without actually having to run the program itself. A sample help screen is shown in Figure 15-5.

THE APPEARANCE OF THE DISPLAY SCREEN

The display screen's appearance varies with the combination of applications chosen to run. Basically, as each application is started by the user, it appears on the display screen. There are two classes of OS/2 applications: those that are supported by the Presentation Manager and those that are not.

Whenever an application that is supported by the Presentation Manager is started, the User Interface Shell menu remains on the display screen until the user removes it. For applications not supported by the Presentation Manager, the User Interface Shell disappears whenever the application is on the display screen.

Applications not supported by the Presentation Manager always take control of the entire display screen and cannot share the screen with other applications. They also cannot share the screen with the User Interface

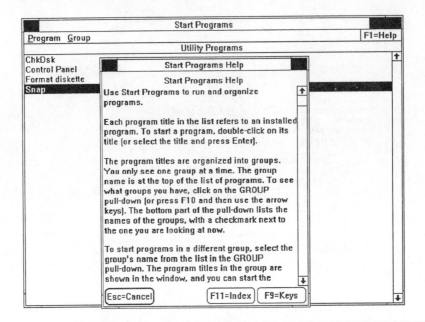

Figure 15-5.   Help screen

Shell. Therefore, non-Presentation Manager applications cannot be seen at all when the user is interacting with another application or with the User Interface Shell itself. Also, these applications cannot take advantage of the features of the Presentation Manager.

Applications written to take advantage of the Presentation Manager's special functions do not have to use the unique programming interfaces provided, but they do have to obey specific rules concerning use of the display screen and additional input devices. Such programs must use the Presentation Manager's programming interfaces and/or the basic OS/2 VIOxx, KBDxx, or MOUxx function calls.

The Presentation Manager screen group is composed of the User Interface Shell and all of the Presentation Manager-supported applications. Both have the ability to share the display screen simultaneously in overlapped windows. The term *window* is defined here as being a rectangular portion of the display screen used to display application data. This window may be as large as the display screen itself or may only partially fill the display. Any window overlapping another window will appear to cover the contents of the lower window, much as overlapping sheets of paper do.

Generally, an application will only have one window, although it may have several, supporting menus and dialog boxes, for example. There is also a hierarchy to window placement. Menus are always placed on top of and contained in the parent application window. Parent application windows are referred to as *top-level windows*. Any application may have one or more top-level windows.

A top-level window that is accepting input and output from the user is called the *active window*. An active top-level window can be distinguished from all other displayed windows by the fact that it lays on top of all other windows. Input then revolves around either the active window itself or the active window's menu or dialog box. Mouse input is generally directed toward the window under the current mouse pointer position. In this way, you can select a window to the active top-level position.

There are also input conditions interpreted by the User Interface Shell even when applications are not loaded. This input generally falls into the category of operations beyond the scope of any single application. An example of such input would be to allow the user to switch the active window by way of special key combinations or mouse selections.

The Pointer Image

The *pointer* is a small graphic arrow that moves around the screen in coordination with the mouse movements. However, its appearance can vary depending on the mouse's current function. For example, the pointer image has a certain shape when acting as the system pointer—this is the default arrow also common to Windows programs. Moving the pointer into an application window can redefine its image, as can moving the pointer between selectable and non-selectable items on the screen. The pointer image is automatically displayed on the screen for those systems that have a mouse and has top-level priority over any other screen image displayed.

Presentation Manager Window Features

The Presentation Manager's windows provide access to a number of optional features that occupy their borders. These are not merely smaller display areas within a larger one. In this fashion, these windows behave very much like Microsoft Windows windows. Each window on the display is surrounded by a border called a *frame window*. It is the frame window that provides users with access to several Presentation Manager functions:

- Borders
- Captions
- Maximize and minimize icons

- Menu bar
- Scroll bar
- System icon

As in Windows, the area in the center of any application window, which normally displays the main information for the application program, is called the *client area*. The client area is visible in the SideKick application shown in Figure 15-6.

Window Borders

The Presentation Manager defines a window border in one of four formats:

- A normal border, not selectable by the user
- A heavy border, selectable by the user for operations such as sizing a window
- A thin border, not selectable by the user
- No border at all

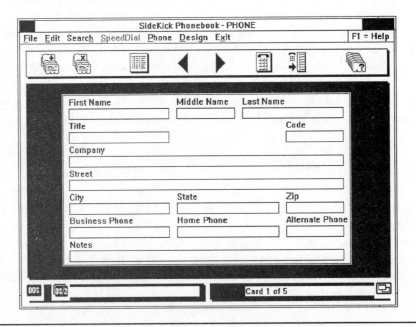

Figure 15-6.   Typical application for Presentation Manager

Captions

The *caption* is that portion of the window used to name the window. It is placed at the top of a window. When a caption is highlighted it indicates that the window is currently active and interacting with the user.

Maximize Icon

As in Windows, the maximize icon is an icon that the user can select in order to change the window to its maximum size, usually filling the entire display screen area.

Minimize Icon

Typically displayed at the bottom of the screen, the minimize icon allows the user to selectively reduce the window size to its minimum size.

Menu Bar

As in Windows, the menu bar is a horizontal bar at the top of a window. From here the end user makes selections that either send commands directly to the application or cause the selection and display of a pop-up menu. The pop-up menu may also contain dialog box options.

Scroll Bar

Each window may contain one or two optional scroll bars. The vertical scroll bar appears at the right edge of the window, and, if active, the horizontal scroll bar appears at the bottom of the window. The scroll bars are used to shift the window's display data up and down or left and right either under application or Presentation Manager control.

System Icon

The system icon allows the user to activate the system menu for the window. Standard system menu functions contain such commands as MOVE and SIZE.

PROGRAM INTERACTION WITH THE PRESENTATION MANAGER

The Presentation Manager, like Windows, provides two standard means by which an application program can interact with the user: menus and dialog boxes.

User Interaction with a Menu

Application programs that interact with menus do so by incorporating a menu bar within the associated window frame. The menu bar contains several key items. Once the user has selected a key item, the application program will display a pop-up menu. The menu contains those commands relating to the key item. For example, the user can select a drawing color or brush width. Once the user has made the selection, the application program removes the menu and executes the command.

User Interaction with a Dialog Box

An application program can also use dialog boxes to communicate with the user. Dialog boxes are usually selected from within a pop-up menu. Dialog

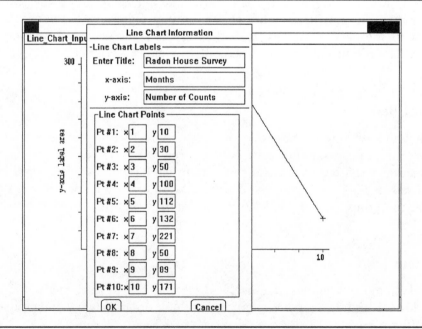

Figure 15-7.   Typical Presentation Manager dialog box

box items are followed by three dots to make them easy to recognize. Unlike a menu command selection, dialog boxes usually require more than a few quick keystrokes or mouse button clicks. Dialog boxes have the same function and appearance under the Presentation Manager as in Windows. A Presentation Manager dialog box is shown in Figure 15-7.

PRESENTATION MANAGER PROGRAMMING FUNCTIONS

The Presentation Manager provides applications programmers with a very rich and diverse application programming interface. Under certain circumstances, an application using the basic OS/2 KBD*xx*, VIO*xx*, and MOU*xx* functions may not have to be modified in order to be windowed when the Presentation Manager is present. However, by using the broad range of powerful functions provided by the API, programmers can enhance the functionality of an application while reducing the time and effort required to make the upgrade. The API can be broken down into the following six major functional groups:

- Application window control
- User Interface Shell access
- Input and message handling
- Alphanumeric output
- Graphics control
- Bitmap control

Controlling the Application Window

The Windows API provides an application program with total window control. With the Windows API, it can be determined in the application program how many windows it will use, their relative positions, sizes, and window frame form, what information will be displayed, and whether the window itself can be sized or moved.

Accessing the User Interface Shell

The User Interface Shell using the API allows an application to communicate with the user. User interaction occurs through screen displays using both menu bars and pop-up menus, with the application responding to various dialog box control functions. Control functions usually associated with an application's dialog box include message boxes, scroll bars, button presses, edit controls, static controls, and additional list boxes.

Handling Input with Messages

When using the input capabilities of the API, it can be determined in the application program what input it receives. Each application has its own input queue, with one or more Windows processing functions that control the input from the user via the keyboard or mouse.

Alphanumeric Output

Called the *advanced VIO*, the alphanumeric API permits an application to perform simple alphanumeric data output to a screen window or into bitmaps. It is an extension of the standard OS/2 VIO.

Graphics Control

An application can take advantage of the graphics program interface (GPI), and draw graphics data directly to a screen window, bitmap, or other device such as a printer or plotter. Objects that can be drawn include

- Lines
- Rectangles
- Ellipses
- Arcs
- Text strings
- Images
- Filled shapes

The GPI also allows an application to define color, area fill pattern, line style, and to select character fonts. By utilizing various transformations each of the graphics primitives can be modified. The graphics data can be controlled by the application program itself, or stored and modified by the Presentation Manager.

Bitmap Control

The use of bitmaps is also permitted under the Presentation Manager. A bitmap can be thought of as an image that is similar to the display screen window and, like a window, it can be drawn to, and can reside in main memory or be loaded to a particular device. A bitmap can be the source of information to be displayed on a screen. Bitmapping is most frequently used whenever rapid screen display changes are required, as in the case of menu displays or simple animation.

ADVANTAGES OF THE PRESENTATION MANAGER API

The Presentation Manager's API functions provide an extensive library of window management functions that support three major areas: window management, message management, and the user interface. Understanding the Presentation Manager window is critical to the proper design of an application that takes advantage of Presentation Manager services.

Basically, a window is a single unit of executable code to which messages can be sent. It is important to know that the window does not have to be associated with a visible portion of the display. To help distinguish between visible and non-visible windows, the Presentation Manager refers to the latter type as *object windows*. An object window can receive and send messages and perform internal processing, but it is not associated with a visible portion of the display screen. Each window created belongs to an application-selected window class, and all messages sent to windows of a particular class are handled by the same window procedure.

Managing the Window

The WIN library provides services that allow the user to create, display, enumerate, move, hide, and destroy windows, but does *not* provide services for drawing inside a window. Each window created in a Presentation Manager session has a window handle that serves as a unique address for the window so that messages can be sent to it. Windows are organized in a tree structure using the standard parent-child hierarchy.

Managing Messages

Message handling and processing lie at the heart of the Presentation Manager's design, as they did in Microsoft Windows. All application input, whether from the keyboard, mouse, system timer, or other applications, is received in the form of a message presented to an input queue. Under the Presentation Manager, *threads,* which are used for independently executing functions within an application, must explicitly create message queues to which their messages can be sent. They can specify the queue size required at creation. In a true multithread environment, an application can choose to have one thread create a message queue and then create new threads as necessary to process the messages the queue receives.

Additional services include functions that allow a Presentation Manager application to interact with the User Interface Shell, the graphics equivalent of the OS/2 Session Manager. A Presentation Manager application can add or delete itself from the list of available applications, modify which applications are listed, or activate another application by selecting it from the list. Both Presentation Manager and character-mode OS/2 applications can be entered onto the list and selected.

File Initialization

With the help of the User Interface Shell services, information can be retrieved from the Presentation Manager initialization file, called OS2.INI. OS2.INI contains modifiable initialization information used by both the Presentation Manager and applications developed under it.

Note: OS2.INI is not in standard ASCII file format. The contents of OS2.INI can only be modified under the management of Presentation Manager Control Panel.

THE VIO LIBRARY

Incorporated into the Presentation Manager is an alphanumeric presentation capability found in the VIO library. VIO library facilities use a cell-aligned format, which supports text-based output. In addition, the VIO library includes support for most of the standard VIO library functions OS/2 supplies. This enables programs that were not written for Presentation Manager to run in Presentation Manager windows without any additional modification.

The VIO library also supports concurrent loading of up to four character sets, with a variety of cell sizes. There is additional support for multiple language output, along with several date, number, and currency formats. For example, the Presentation Manager also supports code-page switching to foreign language symbol sets. For additional information on code-page switching see *Inside the Model 80,* by Chris Pappas and William Murray (Berkeley, Ca.: Osborne/McGraw-Hill, 1988).

THE GPI LIBRARY

The Presentation Manager's rich graphics program interface (GPI) incorporates many features found only on mainframe graphics systems. Applications written for the Presentation Manager have a larger set of graphics primitives than do those for equivalent Windows applications. Table 15-1 lists the Presentation Manager GPI functions. All GPI functions start with "Gpi." Compare the list to the Windows functions discussed in earlier chapters.

In addition to the basic drawing primitives such as lines and curved areas, the GPI supports complex arcs and curves like polyline and Bezier curves. All drawing functions work on the current-point/current-attribute concept and can be thought of as moving an imaginary pen around the display using previously defined parameters.

Additionally, areas of extreme complexity can be defined by drawing the outline with a combination of line and arc primitives, used in conjunction with the GpiBeginArea and GpiEndArea functions. These functions are capable of filling the defined area in a user-definable fill pattern, along with drawing an outline silhouette.

The GPI library provides excellent manipulation of character drawing by allowing the user to select the size, style, and angle of placement for character drawing.

By using the GPI library of digital-differential analyzer functions, known as DDA, which correspond to the standard line, arc, and spline drawing primitives, the Presentation Manager can generate and store a drawing without actually drawing it. Such a capability allows an application to analyze the drawing, possibly for proper placement of labeling information, perform the necessary formatting functions, and then rapidly execute the graphics.

Complex areas of the display can be defined with drawing primitives surrounded by calls to GpiBeginClipArea and GpiEndClipArea. In effect, this prevents any drawing primitive from displaying beyond the defined area.

Mouse-intensive applications that additionally incorporate complex graphics can work together very efficiently in the Presentation Manager environment. This is accomplished by allowing an application to store its

Table 15-1.   Popular Presentation Manager GPI Functions

GpiAssociate	GpiEndArea	GpiQueryAttrs
	GpiEndElement	
GpiBeginArea	GpiEndPath	GpiQueryBackColor
GpiBeginElement		
GpiBeginPath	GpiErase	GpiQueryBackMix
GpiBitBlt	GpiFillPath	GpiQueryBitmapBits
GpiBox	GpiFullArc	GpiQueryBitmapDimension
GpiCharString	GpiLabel	GpiQueryBitmapHandle
GpiCharStringAt		
GpiCharStringPos	GpiLine	GpiQueryBitmapParameters
GpiCharStringPosAt		
	GpiLoadBitmap	GpiQueryBoundaryData
GpiCloseFigure	GpiLoadFonts	
GpiCloseSegment		GpiQueryCharAngle
	GpiMarker	GpiQueryCharBox
GpiCombineRegion		GpiQueryCharDirection
	GpiModifyPath	GpiQueryCharMode
GpiComment		GpiQueryCharSet
	GpiMove	GpiQueryCharShear
GpiCreateBitmap		GpiQueryCharStringPos
	GpiOffsetClipRegion	GpiQueryCharStringPosAt
GpiCreateLogColorTable	GpiOffsetElementPointer	
	GpiOffsetRegion	GpiQueryClipBox
GpiCreateLogFont		GpiQueryClipRegion
	GpiOpenSegment	
GpiCreatePS		GpiQueryColor
	GpiPaintRegion	GpiQueryColorData
GpiCreateRegion		GpiQueryColorIndex
	GpiPartialArc	
GpiDeleteBitmap		GpiQueryCurrentPosition
	GpiPointArc	
GpiDeleteSegment		GpiQueryDefCharBox
GpiDeleteSegments	GpiPolyFillet	
GpiDeleteSetId	GpiPolyFilletSharp	GpiQueryDevice
	GpiPolyLine	GpiQueryDeviceBitmapFormats
GpiDestroyPS	GpiPolyMarker	
GpiDestroyRegion	GpiPolySpline	GpiQueryDrawControl
		GpiQueryDrawingMode
GpiDrawChain	GpiPop	
GpiDrawDynamics		GpiQueryEditMode
GpiDrawFrom	GpiQueryArcParams	
GpiDrawSegment		GpiQueryElement
	GpiQueryAttrMode	GpiQueryElementPointer
GpiElement		GpiQueryElementType

Table 15-1.   Popular Presentation Manager GPI Functions (*continued*)

GpiQueryFontFileDescriptions	GpiQueryStopDraw
GpiQueryFontMetrics	
GpiQueryFonts	GpiQueryTag
GpiQueryGraphicsField	GpiQueryTextBox
GpiQueryLineEnd	GpiQueryViewingLimits
GpiQueryLineJoin	GpiQueryViewingTransformMatrix
GpiQueryLineType	
GpiQueryLineWidth	GpiQueryWidthTable
GpiQueryLineWidthGeom	
	GpiRealizeColorTable
GpiQueryLogColorTable	
	GpiRectInRegion
GpiQueryMarker	
GpiQueryMarkerBox	GpiRectVisible
GpiQueryMarkerSet	
	GpiResetBoundaryData
GpiQueryMetaFileBits	
GpiQueryMetaFileLength	GpiResetPS
GpiQueryMix	GpiRestorePS
GpiQueryModelTransformMatrix	GpiSavePS
GpiQueryNearestColor	GpiSetArcParams
GpiQueryNumberSetIds	GpiSetAttrMode
GpiQueryPageViewport	GpiSetAttrs
GpiQueryPattern	GpiSetBackColor
	GpiSetBackMix
GpiQueryPatternRefPoint	
GpiQueryPatternSet	GpiSetBitmap
	GpiSetBitmapBits
GpiQueryPel	GpiSetBitmapDimension
	GpiSetBitmapId
GpiQueryPS	
	GpiSetCharAngle
GpiQueryRealColors	GpiSetCharBox
	GpiSetCharDirection
GpiQueryRegionBox	GpiSetCharMode
GpiQueryRegionRects	GpiSetCharSet
	GpiSetCharShear
GpiQueryRGBColor	
	GpiSetClipPath
GpiQuerySegmentAttrs	GpiSetClipRegion
GpiQuerySegmentNames	
GpiQuerySegmentPriority	GpiSetColor
GpiQuerySegmentTransformMatrix	
	GpiSetCp
GpiQuerySetIds	
	GpiSetCurrentPosition

Table 15-1.   Popular Presentation Manager GPI Functions (*continued*)

GpiSetDefaultViewMatrix	GpiSetPageViewport
GpiSetDrawControl	GpiSetPattern
	GpiSetPatternRefPoint
GpiSetDrawingMode	GpiSetPatternSet
GpiSetEditMode	GpiSetPel
GpiSetElementPointer	GpiSetPS
GpiSetElementPointerAtLabel	
	GpiSetRegion
GpiSetGraphicsField	
	GpiSetSegmentAttrs
GpiSetInitialSegmentAttrs	GpiSetSegmentPriority
GpiSetLineEnd	GpiSetSegmentTransformMatrix
GpiSetLineJoin	
GpiSetLineType	GpiSetStopDraw
GpiSetLineWidth	
GpiSetLineWidthGeom	GpiSetTag
GpiSetMarker	GpiSetViewingLimits
GpiSetMarkerBox	GpiSetViewingTransformMatrix
GpiSetMarkerSet	
	GpiStrokePath
GpiSetMetaFileBits	
	GpiUnloadFonts
GpiSetMix	
	GpiUnrealizeColorTable
GpiSetModelTransformMatrix	

drawings in one or more graphics segments, and then playing (not redrawing) those segments back to determine which primitives intersect with a given screen area.

Actually, the Presentation Manager provides two drawing modes: stored, just described, and draw and store. The latter also executes the graphics primitives to the screen or printed page.

Creating the Device Context and Presentation Space

Before an application can perform any drawing operations it must first create a device context, along with one or several presentation spaces.

Presentation spaces must be associated with a *device context*. A device context is a representation of the current attributes and the output state of a device. The Presentation Manager goes one step further with its presentation space. The relationship can be described this way: if the device context represents the current physical state of the output device and its device driver, the presentation space defines an application's view of a given device context. Therefore, all drawing modes, color selection, and coordinate references are considered attributes of the presentation space.

With correct code generation an application can examine a set of graphic drawing function calls and execute them in a user-definable presentation space, while mapping the final result to either a printer or plotter hardware device.

For those of you who have been writing window applications combined with graphics, you may be wondering what happens to a graphic image temporarily covered by a pop-up menu. The Presentation Manager can take care of the redraw by accessing the stored graphics data and repainting that portion of the image.

The attribute functions provided by the Presentation Manager drawing primitives provide an extremely rich and detailed fine-tuning capability. Attributes include color table definition, color selection, control over line style, width, pattern, scalable units, and multiple line-end types, such as beveled, mitered, and round.

Device Drivers

A device driver can be considered an automatic application that only communicates with the Presentation Manager kernel libraries. This interface provides a system connection with actual hardware devices, such as keyboards, mice, displays, printers, and plotters.

Device drivers interpret relatively low-level function calls (via the GPI library), such as a line draw primitive, and translate them into the appropriate command for the selected device.

PROGRAMMING CONSIDERATIONS UNDER THE PRESENTATION MANAGER

When designing graphics applications under the OS/2 Presentation Manager, a programmer must remember that Presentation Manager applications can be synchronously interrupted at any point and must be designed with this in mind. You might recall from earlier chapters that Windows is a nonpreemptive multitasking environment. In this environment a Windows application must yield control before Windows can assign control to another application. Under the Presentation Manager preemptive multitasking environment control decisions are made by the operating system exclusively.

By allowing an application to create and execute multiple threads, OS/2 has added a level of complexity to Presentation Manager software that does not exist under Microsoft Windows. For those of you new to the thread concept a good example of a thread can be found with a spreadsheet application. With threads the user would be allowed to continue cell data entry immediately after requesting an extremely complex spreadsheet recalculation. The recalculation command, or thread, is written to continue its function in the background, while the user, without pause, continues to add additional information.

To make matters even more interesting and complex, OS/2 provides interprocess and intraprocess communication via semaphores (the standard OS/2 synchronization method), queues (FIFO processing structure), and pipes (which allow two processes to communicate with each other). Working in conjunction with the shared memory capabilities of OS/2, along with highly modular application design, data can be transferred easily through the use of system services and Presentation Manager messages.

WHAT'S AROUND THE CORNER

A large amount of text has been devoted to explaining the details of the OS/2 Presentation Manager. You now know that the Presentation Manager will function in a manner similar to Windows, but with the extra bells and whistles of a true multitasking environment. You have also read, throughout this book, that by learning to program under Windows you will have an edge when switching over to the Presentation Manager programming. In the next chapter, you will learn how to take the basic Windows code that you have become familiar with, and compare it line by line with its Presentation Manager counterpart. You will see that the structure of the programs is basically the same.

16

WINDOWS VERSUS PRESENTATION MANAGER PROGRAMMING

Windows and the Presentation Manager are two separate and distinct products, yet they share a common look, feel, and message-based programming structure. As early as July 1989, Microsoft began hinting that unmodified Windows applications will be able to run under future versions of the Presentation Manager. How this might be accomplished has not been made clear, but aftermarket products might be employed to allow such compatibility. At present, however, for simple applications the conversion is fairly straightforward and does not offer the programmer any significant challenge.

Chapter 3 showed you how to establish a Windows platform from which most of your programming applications could be launched. Before attempting to show you how to convert a Windows application to an equivalent Presentation Manager application a similar platform needs to be established for the Presentation Manager. The first part of this chapter will be devoted to that task. The final portion of the chapter will illustrate two simple, and similar, programs—one for Windows and one for the Presentation Manager.

Presentation Manager graphics typically operate within a Presentation Manager window. Creating and manipulating Presentation Manager windows is an involved process, but is very similar to the process used by

Microsoft Windows. This section contains information on the minimum Presentation Manager window overhead required in order to execute simple graphics commands. This overhead is called a *PM window platform*. The Presentation Manager actually supports three types of presentation space (PS). The simplest presentation space to use is the *cached micro-PS*. It is also the most limited in terms of commands and devices. The other two types are the *micro-PS* and the *normal-PS*. This chapter uses the cached micro-PS. For more information on presentation spaces see *Presentation Manager Graphics: An Introduction* by Chris Pappas and William Murray (Berkeley, Ca.: Osborne/McGraw-Hill, 1989).

PRESENTATION MANAGER COORDINATES

At this point, you should be familiar with terms such as *screen coordinates* and *world coordinates*. For many graphics applications in the past, the coordinate origin was defined at the upper-left screen corner and was called a *screen* or *device coordinate system*. This allowed the screen surface to be represented as the first quadrant of a two-dimensional coordinate system, with positive X values increasing to the right and positive Y values increasing from top to bottom.

By default, the Presentation Manager's coordinate system has its origin at the lower-left corner of the display screen. Windows 3.0 defaults to the upper-left corner.

World coordinate definitions allow users to set any dimensions they choose without being hampered by the constraints of a particular output device. For example, architectural layouts might be specified in fractions of a foot, while other applications might define coordinate scales in terms of millimeters, kilometers, or light-years. Once the world coordinate definitions are given, the graphics system converts these coordinates to the appropriate device coordinates for display.

OS/2's Presentation Manager allows graphics applications to define picture points using any coordinate reference convenient for the user. The Presentation Manager itself will then perform any transformations necessary to convert user coordinates to screen values.

The Presentation Manager provides four levels of coordinate spaces: application convenient units, model space, page space, and device coordinates. For the work in this chapter, the Presentation Manager's default coordinate space, where the coordinate units of measurement are in pixels, will be used.

WINDOW COMMANDS FOR THE PRESENTATION MANAGER GRAPHICS PLATFORM

The previous chapter contained a table listing the most popular Presentation Manager graphics commands. However, in order to establish a PM window platform, several additional functions must be used. The graphics platform is established with the use of PM window functions. PM window functions start with "Win". This section will introduce you to a block of fundamental Presentation Manager window commands. Additional syntax and option information for each command can be obtained by using the Quick Help (QH) facility. The Quick Help facility is included with the Presentation Manager toolkit from Microsoft. The commands necessary for establishing the PM graphics platform are listed here, in alphabetical order:

WinBeginPaint
WinCreateMsgQueue
WinCreateStdWindow
WinDefWindowProc
WinDestroyMsgQueue
WinDestroyWindow
WinDispatchMsg
WinEndPaint

WinFillRect
WinGetMsg
WinInitialize
WinQueryWindowRect
WinRegisterClass
WinSetWindowPos
WinTerminate

These window commands are required to create a cached micro-PS environment from which the various graphics commands (listed in the previous chapter) can be executed under the Presentation Manager. They are accessed through the OS2.H header file, which in turn points to other Presentation Manager header files, such as OS2DEF.H. Let's look at each Win function, in the order that they are typically called from the graphics platform.

WinInitialize

The WinInitialize function is called before any other Presentation Manager function and returns a value called the *anchor block handle*. This value must be passed to other Presentation Manager functions that do not receive a handle parameter of any other handle type. The purpose of the function is to initialize an application thread for Presentation Manager system calls. If the thread cannot be initialized, a NULL is returned. This is typically the first function called. The usual syntax is hab = WinInitialize(0);

where *hab* is declared as a handle of type *HAB*. The C compiler treats this as a 32-bit far pointer.

WinCreateMsgQueue

The WinCreateMsgQueue function is responsible for creating a message queue for a thread. If successful, the queue handle is returned; otherwise a NULL value is returned. A value of 0 for the queue size will set the queue to the default size. Since most Presentation Manager functions pass information through the message queue, its creation is required for most programs. A message queue is required in the creation of a window, and a window is required in order to do graphics. Thus, a message queue is a necessary part of every program. The typical syntax is

hmq = WinCreateMsgQueue(hab,0);

where *hmq* is declared as a handle of type *HMQ*.

WinRegisterClass

The WinRegisterClass function registers a window class with the window manager. A TRUE is returned if the registration is successful, a FALSE if it is not. Registration is necessary if the class name is to be used to create windows of that class. *pszClassName* is a far pointer to the class name string. GraphicProc, the name of the procedure, points to the address of the window procedure being used. CS_SIZEREDRAW states the style of the window class. The final parameter gives the number of bytes to reserve (in words) when the window is created. The default value is accepted if 0 is entered. The syntax is

WinRegisterClass = (hab,pszClassName,GraphicProc,
                CS_SIZEREDRAW,0);

where the parameter *pszClassName* is declared as static *char* pszClassName[] = "FirstClass". GraphicProc is of type *MRESULT* EXPENTRY GraphicProc(HWND,USHORT,MPARAM,MPARAM).

WinCreateStdWindow

The WinCreateStdWindow function is responsible for creating and returning a standard class window. HWND_DESKTOP is the handle of the parent. If successful, a window frame handle is returned to *hfrm*. Otherwise, a NULL is returned. Although other techniques can be used to create a Presentation Manager window, WinCreateStdWindow is usually used.

The next two parameters, *flFrameStyle* and *flFrameFlags,* return the frame window style and window features. The style of a window is created by a combination of WS and FS frame styles. WS_VISIBLE makes the window visible. The absence of WS_VISIBLE will result in an invisible window. WS_VISIBLE obtains the size and position of your window from the shell. WinQueryTaskSizePos is used for this information. Various window features can be made up of the following FCF styles, ORed together:

FCF_TITLEBAR   FCF_MAXBUTTON
FCF_SYSMENU   FCF_MINMAX
FCF_MENU   FCF_VERTSCROLL
FCF_SIZEBORDER   FCF_HORZSCROLL
FCF_MINBUTTON

FCF_SIZEBORDER creates a sizing border around the window. FCF_TITLEBAR adds a title bar to your window. FCF_SYSMENU allows the use of a system menu. FCF_MINMAX creates a MIN/MAX box from which you can size your window. Additionally, you might want to use FCF_HORZSCROLL to create a horizontal scroll window, or use FCF_VERTSCROLL for a vertical scroll window. The actual numeric values associated with these identifiers, and others, can be found in the various OS2 and PM header files.

The next parameter, *pszClassName*, is a pointer to the class name specified earlier. The string printed by FCF_TITLEBAR is pointed to with the next parameter. In this case, the string "Cached-PS PM Graphics" will be printed in the title bar. The remaining four parameters represent the client style, module ID, resource ID, and the client handle, respectively. If FCF_MENU is not specified (this option won't be used for this platform) then the module ID and resource ID are ignored. The syntax used is

```
hfrm = WinCreateStdWindow(HWND_DESKTOP,flFrameStyle,
                    &flFrameFlags,pszClassName,
                    "Cached-PS PM Graphics",
                    0L,NULL,0,&hcnt);
```

WinSetWindowPos

This function allows the user to position and size the initial Presentation Manager application window.

> WinSetWindowPos(hwnd,hwndInsertBehind,
>   x,y,cx,cy,fs)

Here *hwnd* and *hwndInsertBehind* are handles to the window and the window placement order. *hwndInsertBehind* typically takes on one of the predefined values HWND_TOP, HWND_BOTTOM, or NULL. The points *x* and *y* are *short* values specifying the lower-left screen coordinate. The *short* values *cx* and *cy* specify the horizontal and vertical dimensions of the screen. The *ushort* value, FS, specifies window positioning values. The following values can be ORed together:

- SWP_SIZE (change window size)
- SWP_MOVE (change window position)
- SWP_ZORDER (change relative placement of window)
- SWP_SHOW (show the window)
- SWP_HIDE (hide the window)
- SWP_MINIMIZE (minimize the window)
- SWP_MAXIMIZE (maximize the window)

The syntax used in the platform is

> WinSetWindowPos(hfrm,NULL,10,10,610,470,SWP_SIZE¦
>   SWP_MOVE¦SWP_SHOW);

WinGetMsg

The WinGetMsg function waits for a queue message from the thread queue. The message is returned in *qmsg*. Most information passed by the user's program, in a window, is passed via the message queue. The last three parameters are for use with a window filter ID, the first filter message, and the last filter message. These parameters are not used in the initial window platform. The needed syntax is simply

> WinGetMsg(hab,&qmsg,NULL,0,0);

WinDispatchMsg

The WinDispatchMsg function dispatches the message pointed to by *qmsg* (see WinGetMsg). This function is similar to WinSendMsg. The syntax is

    WinDispatchMsg(hab,&qmsg);

Thus, WinGetMsg gets the message from the message queue and Win-DispatchMsg dispatches it to the specified window.

WinDestroyWindow

Once all the work is done within a window, the WinDestroyWindow function is called to destroy the window and any descendants. This implies that any other windows owned by the window handle are also destroyed. WinDestroyWindow returns TRUE if successful and FALSE if not. The syntax includes the handle returned by WinCreateStdWindow.

    WinDestroyWindow(hfrm);

WinDestroyMsgQueue

The WinDestroyMsgQueue function is used to close the given thread queue. A TRUE is returned if successful and a FALSE if not. The handle specified in the syntax is the handle returned by WinCreateMsgQueue.

    WinDestroyMsgQueue(hmq);

WinTerminate

The WinTerminate function terminates an application thread's use by the Presentation Manager. Note that the handle specified is the handle originally returned by WinInitialize. The syntax is

    WinTerminate(hab);

WinBeginPaint

In the initial applications, when WinGetMsg is called, a WM_PAINT message is returned for the window. These messages are returned only as often as the function WinGetMsg is called; they will not be placed in a queue.

The WM_PAINT message is processed by the WinBeginPaint function. WinBeginPaint returns the *hps* handle. The handle tells the procedure to redraw the contents of the window. The WinBeginPaint syntax is

    hps = WinBeginPaint(hwnd,NULL,NULL);

The first NULL parameter requires that a handle be obtained from the cached presentation space. If this is not the case, the window associated with *hwnd* is used.

WinQueryWindowRect

The WinQueryWindowRect function returns the window rectangle of the window in *rcl*. This information is for the WinFillRect function that follows. The rectangle returned is in window coordinates relative to the bottom-left corner of the screen, assuming the handle points to a top-level window. The syntax is

    WinQueryWindowRect(hwnd,&rcl);

WinFillRect

The WinFillRect function is one technique for painting the background of a window. GpiSetBackColor can also be used. This function uses the window coordinates returned by WinQueryWindowRect and a color specification. Microsoft specifies the color values with the names and values shown in Table 16-1.

The WinFillRect function is fast. For the initial platform, CLR_WHITE will be used. You may, of course, change this value to fit your own color preference. The syntax for WinFillRect is

    WinFillRect(hps,&rcl,CLR_WHITE);

WinEndPaint

In the graphics platform any graphics commands you wish to use are inserted between WinFillRect and WinEndPaint. The WinEndPaint function is used at the end of the WM_PAINT message. It is used to restore the presentation space to its original value. The handle specified was obtained from the WinBeginPaint function. The syntax is simple:

    WinEndPaint(hps);

Table 16-1.   Microsoft Presentation Manager Color Values

Name	Value
CLR_DEFAULT	−3L
CLR_WHITE	−2L
CLR_BLACK	−1L
CLR_BACKGROUND	0L
CLR_BLUE	1L
CLR_RED	2L
CLR_PINK	3L
CLR_GREEN	4L
CLR_CYAN	5L
CLR_YELLOW	6L
CLR_NEUTRAL	7L
CLR_DARKGRAY	8L
CLR_DARKBLUE	9L
CLR_DARKRED	10L
CLR_DARKPINK	11L
CLR_DARKGREEN	12L
CLR_DARKCYAN	13L
CLR_BROWN	14L
CLR_LIGHTGRAY	15L

WinDefWindowProc

The WinDefWindowProc function is the default function in the window switch statement. As such, it is passed *messg* and two parameters, *parm1* and *parm2*. The syntax for WinDefWindowProc is

    WinDefWindowProc(hwnd,messg,parm1,parm2);

THE PM GRAPHICS PLATFORM

The PM graphics platform will be formed by putting together the functions just discussed. This C program will be capable of establishing a Presentation Manager window for graphics work.

The window and graphics *#define* and *#include* files have been included at the top of the C program. By using *#define* INCL_PM, all Presentation Manager definitions will be included in your program code. Likewise, OS2.H is the main header file that will bring in all other Presentation

Manager header files. These include PMWIN.H, PMGPI.H, PMDEV.H, PMAVIO.H, PMSPL.H, and PMERRORS.H. All graphics routines will reside in a procedure named GraphicProc. If you compile and execute the Presentation Manager code in the next section, a single window will be created. Since no graphics commands have been included in the code the window will appear black with a white background. By altering the PM window platform code developed thus far, you will be able to produce a variety of window options such as scroll bars, title bars, and so on.

COMPARING THE WINDOWS AND THE PRESENTATION MANAGER PLATFORMS

The platform examples in this section produce code that is structurally similar. In fact, when you view the **MAKE** and .DEF files you may have a hard time telling which belong to Windows and which belong to the Presentation Manager. It is in the platform code proper that the obvious differences in code occur. Remember as you examine these programs that no menus or dialog boxes are used; thus no resource file is needed.

The MAKE Files

The Windows program code is named WNPLTFRM. You can see that the **MAKE** file has not changed from previous chapters. The Presentation Manager program code is named PMPLTFRM. The PM uses the standard system linker, LINK. Additionally, the OS2 library is specified.

```
The Windows MAKE file:

ALL : wnpltfrm.exe # ALL needed for C 6.0 up

wnpltfrm.obj: wnpltfrm.c
    cl -c -AS -Gsw -Oas -Zpe wnpltfrm.c

wnpltfrm.exe: wnpltfrm.obj wnpltfrm.def wnpltfrm.res
    link /NOD wnpltfrm,,,libw slibcew, wnpltfrm.def


The Presentation Manager MAKE file:

ALL : pmpltfrm.exe # ALL needed for C 6.0 up

pmpltfrm.obj : pmpltfrm.c
    cl -c -G2sw -Od -Zp -W2 -Lp pmpltfrm.c

pmpltfrm.exe : pmpltfrm.obj pmpltfrm.def
    link pmpltfrm, /align:16, NULL, OS2, pmpltfrm.def
```

The .DEF Files

The definition files for both platforms are similar. Notice that the Presentation Manager .DEF file includes PROTMODE, which specifies protected mode.

```
The Windows DEF file:

NAME        wnpltfrm
DESCRIPTION 'Simplified Windows Platform'
EXETYPE     WINDOWS
STUB        'WINSTUB.EXE'
CODE        PRELOAD MOVEABLE DISCARDABLE
DATA        PRELOAD MOVEABLE MULTIPLE
HEAPSIZE    4096
STACKSIZE   9216
EXPORTS     WindowProc     @1


The Presentation Manager DEF file:

NAME        pmpltfrm
DESCRIPTION 'Simplified PM Platform'
PROTMODE
STUB        'OS2STUB.EXE'
CODE        PRELOAD MOVEABLE DISCARDABLE
DATA        PRELOAD MOVEABLE MULTIPLE
HEAPSIZE    4096
STACKSIZE   9216
EXPORTS     GraphicProc    @1
```

The Platform Files

The greatest changes naturally occur in the C code. Windows code produces a program consistent with DOS's real mode environment, while Presentation Manager code runs in OS/2's protected mode.

```
The Windows Platform:

/* Simplified Windows Platform (SWP)             */
/* (c) William H. Murray and Chris H. Pappas, 1989 */

#include <windows.h>

long FAR PASCAL WindowProc(HWND,unsigned,WORD,LONG);

char szProgName[]="ProgName";

int PASCAL WinMain(hInst,hPreInst,lpszCmdLine,nCmdShow)
HANDLE hInst,hPreInst;
LPSTR  lpszCmdLine;
int    nCmdShow;
{
  HWND hwnd;
```

```
   MSG   msg;
   WNDCLASS wcSwp;
   if (!hPreInst)
   {
     wcSwp.lpszClassName=szProgName;
     wcSwp.hInstance    =hInst;
     wcSwp.lpfnWndProc  =WindowProc;
     wcSwp.hCursor       =LoadCursor(NULL,IDC_ARROW);
     wcSwp.hIcon        =NULL;
     wcSwp.lpszMenuName =NULL;
     wcSwp.hbrBackground=GetStockObject(WHITE_BRUSH);
     wcSwp.style         =CS_HREDRAW!CS_VREDRAW;
     wcSwp.cbClsExtra   =0;
     wcSwp.cbWndExtra   =0;
     if (!RegisterClass (&wcSwp))
       return FALSE;
   }
   hwnd=CreateWindow(szProgName,"Simplified Windows Platform",
                     WS_OVERLAPPEDWINDOW,CW_USEDEFAULT,
                     CW_USEDEFAULT,CW_USEDEFAULT,
                     CW_USEDEFAULT,NULL,NULL,
                     hInst,NULL);
   ShowWindow(hwnd,nCmdShow);
   UpdateWindow(hwnd);
   while (GetMessage(&msg,NULL,NULL,NULL))
   {
     TranslateMessage(&msg);
     DispatchMessage(&msg);
   }
   return(msg.wParam);
}

long FAR PASCAL WindowProc(hwnd,messg,wParam,lParam)
HWND    hwnd;
unsigned messg;
WORD    wParam;
LONG    lParam;
{
   PAINTSTRUCT ps;
   HDC  hdc;
   switch (messg)
   {
   case WM_PAINT:
     hdc=BeginPaint(hwnd,&ps);

/*--------- your routines below ---------*/



/*--------- your routines above ---------*/

     ValidateRect(hwnd,NULL);
     EndPaint(hwnd,&ps);
     break;
   case WM_DESTROY:
     PostQuitMessage(0);
     break;
   default:
     return(DefWindowProc(hwnd,messg,wParam,lParam));
     break;
```

```
     }
     return(0L);
}


The Presentation Manager Platform:

/* Simplified Windows Platform for PM Graphics      */
/* (c) William H. Murray and Chris H. Pappas, 1989 */

#define INCL_PM

#include <os2.h>

MRESULT EXPENTRY GraphicProc(HWND,USHORT,MPARAM,MPARAM);

main ()
  {
  static CHAR  pszClassName[]="FirstClass";
  HAB      hab;
  HMQ      hmq;
  HWND     hfrm,hcnt;
  QMSG     qmsg;
  ULONG flFrameFlags=FCF_SYSMENU|FCF_TITLEBAR|
                     FCF_SIZEBORDER|FCF_MINMAX;
  ULONG flFrameStyle=WS_VISIBLE;

  hab=WinInitialize(0);
  hmq=WinCreateMsgQueue(hab,0);
  WinRegisterClass(hab,pszClassName,GraphicProc,CS_SIZEREDRAW,0);
  hfrm=WinCreateStdWindow(HWND_DESKTOP,flFrameStyle,
                          &flFrameFlags,pszClassName,
                          "Cached-PS PM Graphics",
                          0L,NULL,0,&hcnt);
  WinSetWindowPos(hfrm,NULL,10,10,610,470,SWP_SIZE|
                  SWP_MOVE|SWP_SHOW);
  while (WinGetMsg(hab,&qmsg,NULL,0,0))
         WinDispatchMsg(hab,&qmsg);
  WinDestroyWindow(hfrm);
  WinDestroyMsgQueue(hmq);
  WinTerminate(hab);
  return 0;
  }

MRESULT EXPENTRY GraphicProc(hwnd,messg,parm1,parm2)
  HWND       hwnd;
  USHORT     messg;
  MPARAM     parm1,parm2;
  {
  HPS        hps;
  RECTL      rcl;

  switch (messg)
    {
    case WM_PAINT:
    hps=WinBeginPaint(hwnd,NULL,NULL);
    GpiErase(hps);
    WinQueryWindowRect(hwnd,&rcl);
    WinFillRect(hps,&rcl,CLR_WHITE);

/*--------- your routines below ----------*/
```

```
/*--------- your routines above ----------*/

    WinEndPaint(hps);
    break;

    default:
      return WinDefWindowProc(hwnd,messg,parml,parm2);
    }
  return 0;
  }
```

Compare the structure of both the Windows platform and the Presentation Manager platform. This is the code required to establish a graphics base in either operating system. Specific applications are built around this code and, of course, must use the specifications and functions of the particular environment.

The PM graphics platform that has been created produces a window like the one shown in Figure 16-1. This window is ready to accept most GPI graphics commands. The background color of the drawing area, as you recall, has been set to white. The default drawing color is black. With this platform, you are able to size, move, restore, and close the window with either keyboard or mouse commands.

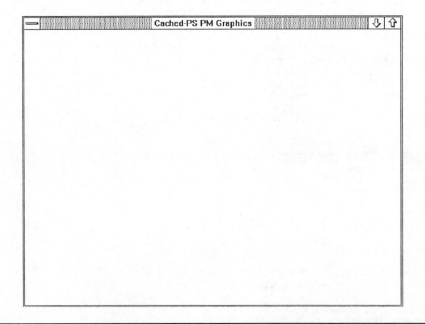

Figure 16-1.   The window created by the Presentation Manager platform code

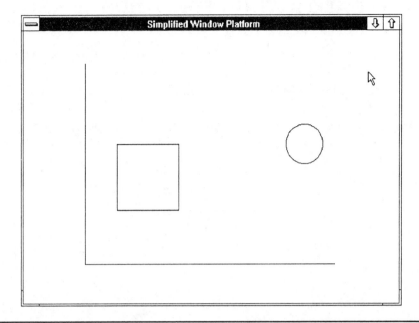

Figure 16-2.   Simple graphics shapes with the Windows 3.0 platform

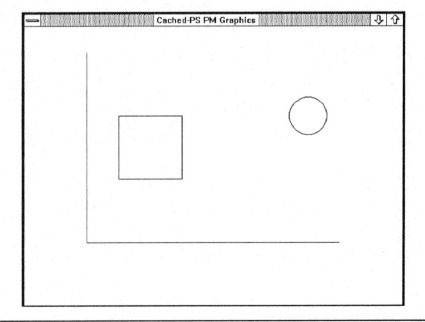

Figure 16-3.   Simple graphics shapes with the Presentation Manager platform

A SIMPLE APPLICATION FOR WINDOWS AND THE PRESENTATION MANAGER

As you saw in the previous section, both platforms have a portion of code that allows the insertion of graphics commands. For simple applications, you can use this boilerplate and insert the desired graphics commands. In the following example, code is given for both Windows and the Presentation Manager. This code will draw several graphics shapes in each application's window. Both windows produce equivalent results, as you can see from Figures 16-2 and 16-3.

GRAPHICS CODE FOR INSERTION INTO WINDOWS PLATFORM

```
/*--------- your routines below ---------*/

    /* draw separate line segments */
    MoveTo(hdc,99,49);
    LineTo(hdc,99,350);
    LineTo(hdc,500,350);
    MoveTo(hdc,99,350);

    /* draw a box with the Rectangle function */
    Rectangle(hdc,150,170,250,270);

    /* draw a circle */
    Ellipse(hdc,420,140,480,200);

/*--------- your routines above ---------*/
```

CODE FOR INSERTION INTO PRESENTATION MANAGER
PLATFORM

```
/*--------- your routines below ----------*/

    /* draw separate line segments */
    ptl.x=99;
    ptl.y=400;
    GpiMove(hps,&ptl);
    ptl.y=99;
    GpiLine(hps,&ptl);
    ptl.x=500;
    GpiLine(hps,&ptl);

    /* draw a box with the GpiBox function */
    ptl.x=150;
    ptl.y=200;
    GpiMove(hps,&ptl);
    ptl.x=250;
    ptl.y=300;
    GpiBox(hps,2L,&ptl,0L,0L);

    /* draw a circle */
    ptl.x=450;
    ptl.y=300;
    GpiMove(hps,&ptl);
```

```
GpiFullArc(hps,DRO_OUTLINE,1966080L);
```

```
/*--------- your routines above ----------*/
```

This example is, of course, intentionally simple in order to illustrate a point. The next chapter will examine several more complicated programs and try to determine tips, tricks, and techniques for easier conversions.

17

A FINAL WORD ON CONVERTING

In the last chapter you saw the similarities and differences between a Simplified Windows 3.0 Platform and a bare-bones Presentation Manager platform. You also learned how to develop **MAKE** files, definition files, and, of course, C application source code. With the development of the overhead behind you, it is now time to turn your attention to other programming details. Like the earlier Windows programs in this book, almost all Presentation Manager applications evolve from a basic platform (developed in Chapter 16).

This chapter will focus on menus, dialog boxes, and the resulting resource files. The main example used in this chapter is a Presentation Manager program that will create a bar chart similar to the Windows application developed in Chapter 11. No attempt has been made in this chapter to create code for a Windows application that parallels the Presentation Manager program presented here. However, if you compare the Windows bar chart program of Chapter 11 with the Presentation Manager example used here you will find that they are very similar and produce almost identical windows.

A MEETING OF THE MINDS

It has been said that the Presentation Manager is Windows done right. That may or may not be the case. Microsoft, as the developer of both products, has had the ability to control and mold both products to its needs. Windows was obviously their first attempt at a windows product. Microsoft learned a lot during the development of Windows. The Windows design team clearly set the stage for the Presentation Manager team in terms of "look and feel." But Windows 3.0 is a major revision that arrived after the introduction of the Presentation Manager version 1.1 and 1.2. In this sense, the Presentation Manager design team has had a major impact on Windows. Perhaps Windows programmers would rather say, "Windows 3.0 is the Presentation Manager done right." In either event, Microsoft and IBM have made it clear that they expect Windows to be used on machines with between 1 and 2MB of memory and OS/2 for systems with more memory.

The final result, regardless of which side you take, is a better product for the user and programmer. The meeting of the minds has produced software with overall application structures that are almost identical. The common thread between the products is a message system of passing information. It is only at the code level where major changes occur. These changes are primarily in function definitions.

When converting programs from Windows 3.0 to the Presentation Manager, what is actually converted is the program's *outline*. The form remains basically the same. It is up to the programmer to convert each function type and screen coordinate.

The features of Windows 3.0 are extremely impressive. Perhaps the only disappointment is the fact that the coordinate system was not brought in line with that of the Presentation Manager, which many find preferable. This means that bitmap files, icon files, and cursor files will have to be "flipped" when transporting them from Windows to the Presentation Manager. In simple cases, it will just be easier to re-create an icon or cursor for the new environment.

A PRESENTATION MANAGER BAR CHART

The following listing contains all of the files necessary to compile a bar chart program under the Presentation Manager, except for the icon and pointer files, which are not ASCII. Both the icon and pointer were created with the Presentation Manager icon editor. Like the Windows counterpart, the program will run without them, but icons and pointers do add flair to the final product.

THE PRESENTATION MANAGER MAKE FILE:

```
ALL : bar16.exe # ALL needed for C 6.0 up

bar16.obj: bar16.c bar16.h
    cl /c /Lp /Zp /Od /G2sw /W2 bar16.c

bar16.res: bar16.rc bar16.ico bar16.h bar16.ptr
    RC -r bar16

bar16.exe: bar16.obj bar16.def bar16.res
    link bar16, /align:16, NULL, OS2, bar16
    rc bar16.res
```

THE PRESENTATION MANAGER DEFINITION (DEF) FILE:

```
NAME        bar16
EXPORTS     About
EXPORTS     BarDiaProc
EXPORTS     GraphicProc
PROTMODE
HEAPSIZE    2048
STACKSIZE   9216
```

THE PRESENTATION MANAGER HEADER (H) FILE:

```
#define IDP_POINTER    2

#define ID_RESOURCE   10
#define ID_ABOUT      15
#define ID_OK         20
#define ID_CANCEL     25
#define ID_INPUT      30

#define IDM_ABOUT     40
#define IDM_INPUT     50
#define IDM_BARINPUT  60

#define DM_XAXIS      470
#define DM_YAXIS      475
#define DM_TITLE      480
#define DM_B1         481
#define DM_B2         482
#define DM_B3         483
#define DM_B4         484
#define DM_B5         485
#define DM_B6         486
#define DM_B7         487
#define DM_B8         488
#define DM_B9         489
#define DM_B10        490
```

THE PRESENTATION MANAGER RESOURCE (RES) FILE:

```
#include <os2.h>
#include "bar16.h"

POINTER ID_RESOURCE bar16.ico
POINTER IDP_POINTER bar16.ptr

MENU                     ID_RESOURCE
BEGIN
  SUBMENU "Bar_Chart_Input", IDM_BARINPUT
  BEGIN
    MENUITEM "About...",    IDM_ABOUT
    MENUITEM "Input",       IDM_INPUT
  END
END

DLGTEMPLATE              ID_ABOUT
BEGIN
  DIALOG "",ID_ABOUT,50,300,180,80,FS_DLGBORDER
  BEGIN
    CTEXT "Interactive Bar Chart Program",-1,2,60,176,10
    CTEXT "by William H. Murray & Chris H. Pappas",-1,2,
        45,176,10
    CONTROL "OK",ID_OK,75,10,32,14,WC_BUTTON,BS_PUSHBUTTON
        |BS_DEFAULT|WS_GROUP|WS_TABSTOP|WS_VISIBLE
  END
END

DLGTEMPLATE ID_INPUT LOADONCALL MOVEABLE DISCARDABLE
BEGIN
  DIALOG "Bar Chart Information",ID_INPUT,76,-10,176,236,
        FS_NOBYTEALIGN|FS_DLGBORDER|WS_VISIBLE|
        WS_CLIPSIBLINGS|WS_SAVEBITS,FCF_TITLEBAR
    BEGIN
      CONTROL "Bar Chart Title",257,-1,180,178,53,
          WC_STATIC,SS_GROUPBOX|WS_GROUP|WS_VISIBLE
      CONTROL "Bar Chart Bar Sizes",258,5,24,160,154,
          WC_STATIC,SS_GROUPBOX|WS_GROUP|WS_VISIBLE
      CONTROL "Enter Title:",260,3,214,50,8,WC_STATIC,
          SS_TEXT|DT_LEFT|DT_TOP|WS_GROUP|WS_VISIBLE
      CONTROL "     x-axis:",261,3,199,50,8,WC_STATIC,
          SS_TEXT|DT_LEFT|DT_TOP|WS_GROUP|WS_VISIBLE
      CONTROL "      y-axis:",262,3,185,50,8,WC_STATIC,
          SS_TEXT|DT_LEFT|DT_TOP|WS_GROUP|WS_VISIBLE
      CONTROL " Bar #1:",263,7,156,56,8,WC_STATIC,SS_TEXT|
          DT_LEFT|DT_TOP|WS_GROUP|WS_VISIBLE
      CONTROL " Bar #2:",264,7,142,56,8,WC_STATIC,SS_TEXT|
          DT_LEFT|DT_TOP|WS_GROUP|WS_VISIBLE
      CONTROL " Bar #3:",265,7,128,56,8,WC_STATIC,SS_TEXT|
          DT_LEFT|DT_TOP|WS_GROUP|WS_VISIBLE
      CONTROL " Bar #4:",266,7,114,56,8,WC_STATIC,SS_TEXT|
          DT_LEFT|DT_TOP|WS_GROUP|WS_VISIBLE
      CONTROL " Bar #5:",267,7,100,56,8,WC_STATIC,SS_TEXT|
          DT_LEFT|DT_TOP|WS_GROUP|WS_VISIBLE
      CONTROL " Bar #6:",268,7,86,56,8,WC_STATIC,SS_TEXT|
          DT_LEFT|DT_TOP|WS_GROUP|WS_VISIBLE
      CONTROL " Bar #7:",269,7,72,56,8,WC_STATIC,SS_TEXT|
```

```
                DT_LEFT|DT_TOP|WS_GROUP|WS_VISIBLE
        CONTROL " Bar #8:",270,7,58,56,8,WC_STATIC,SS_TEXT|
                DT_LEFT|DT_TOP|WS_GROUP|WS_VISIBLE
        CONTROL " Bar #9:",271,7,44,56,8,WC_STATIC,SS_TEXT|
                DT_LEFT|DT_TOP|WS_GROUP|WS_VISIBLE
        CONTROL "Bar #10:",272,7,30,56,8,WC_STATIC,SS_TEXT|
                DT_LEFT|DT_TOP|WS_GROUP|WS_VISIBLE
        CONTROL "Computer Sales",DM_TITLE,62,214,107,8,
                WC_ENTRYFIELD,ES_LEFT|ES_AUTOSCROLL|ES_MARGIN
                |WS_TABSTOP|WS_VISIBLE
        CONTROL "Models",DM_XAXIS,62,199,107,8,
                WC_ENTRYFIELD,ES_LEFT|ES_AUTOSCROLL|ES_MARGIN
                |WS_TABSTOP|WS_VISIBLE
        CONTROL "Number Sold",DM_YAXIS,62,185,107,8,
                WC_ENTRYFIELD,ES_LEFT|ES_AUTOSCROLL|ES_MARGIN
                |WS_TABSTOP|WS_VISIBLE
        CONTROL "40",DM_B1,81,156,56,8,WC_ENTRYFIELD,ES_LEFT
                |ES_AUTOSCROLL|ES_MARGIN|WS_TABSTOP|WS_VISIBLE
        CONTROL "30",DM_B2,81,142,56,8,WC_ENTRYFIELD,ES_LEFT
                |ES_AUTOSCROLL|ES_MARGIN|WS_TABSTOP|WS_VISIBLE
        CONTROL "10",DM_B3,81,128,56,8,WC_ENTRYFIELD,ES_LEFT
                |ES_AUTOSCROLL|ES_MARGIN|WS_TABSTOP|WS_VISIBLE
        CONTROL "0",DM_B4,81,114,56,8,WC_ENTRYFIELD,ES_LEFT
                |ES_AUTOSCROLL|ES_MARGIN|WS_TABSTOP|WS_VISIBLE
        CONTROL "0",DM_B5,81,100,56,8,WC_ENTRYFIELD,ES_LEFT
                |ES_AUTOSCROLL|ES_MARGIN|WS_TABSTOP|WS_VISIBLE
        CONTROL "0",DM_B6,81,86,56,8,WC_ENTRYFIELD,ES_LEFT
                |ES_AUTOSCROLL|ES_MARGIN|WS_TABSTOP|WS_VISIBLE
        CONTROL "0",DM_B7,81,72,56,8,WC_ENTRYFIELD,ES_LEFT
                |ES_AUTOSCROLL|ES_MARGIN|WS_TABSTOP|WS_VISIBLE
        CONTROL "0",DM_B8,81,58,56,8,WC_ENTRYFIELD,ES_LEFT
                |ES_AUTOSCROLL|ES_MARGIN|WS_TABSTOP|WS_VISIBLE
        CONTROL "0",DM_B9,81,44,56,8,WC_ENTRYFIELD,ES_LEFT
                |ES_AUTOSCROLL|ES_MARGIN|WS_TABSTOP|WS_VISIBLE
        CONTROL "0",DM_B10,81,30,56,8,WC_ENTRYFIELD,ES_LEFT
                |ES_AUTOSCROLL|ES_MARGIN|WS_TABSTOP|WS_VISIBLE
        CONTROL "OK",ID_OK,12,9,24,14,WC_BUTTON,BS_PUSHBUTTON
                |WS_TABSTOP|WS_VISIBLE
        CONTROL "Cancel",ID_CANCEL,111,9,40,14,WC_BUTTON,
                BS_PUSHBUTTON|WS_TABSTOP|WS_VISIBLE
    END
END


THE PRESENTATION MANAGER APPLICATION (C) FILE:

/* Cached-PS Window Platform for PM Graphics    */
/* (c) William H. Murray and Chris H. Pappas, 1989 */

#define INCL_PM

#include <os2.h>
#include <stddef.h>
#include <stdio.h>
#include <stdlib.h>
#include <string.h>
#include "bar16.h"
```

```
#define maxbars 10

long barsizeorg[maxbars]={40,30,10};
char title[80]="bar chart title area";
char xstring[80]="x-axis label area";
char ystring[80]="y-axis label area";

MRESULT EXPENTRY About(HWND,USHORT,MPARAM,MPARAM);
MRESULT EXPENTRY BarDiaProc(HWND,USHORT,MPARAM,MPARAM);
MRESULT EXPENTRY GraphicProc(HWND,USHORT,MPARAM,MPARAM);

main ()
  {
  static CHAR pszClassName[]="FirstClass";
  HAB     hab;
  HMQ     hmq;
  HWND    hfrm,hcnt;
  QMSG    qmsg;
  ULONG flFrameFlags=FCF_SYSMENU|FCF_TITLEBAR|
                     FCF_SIZEBORDER|FCF_MINMAX|
                     FCF_ICON|FCF_MENU;
  ULONG flFrameStyle=WS_VISIBLE;

  hab=WinInitialize(0);
  hmq=WinCreateMsgQueue(hab,0);
  WinRegisterClass(hab,pszClassName,GraphicProc,
                   CS_SIZEREDRAW,0);
  hfrm=WinCreateStdWindow(HWND_DESKTOP,flFrameStyle,
                          &flFrameFlags,pszClassName,
                          "Cached-PS PM Graphics",
                          0L,NULL,ID_RESOURCE,&hcnt);
  WinSetWindowPos(hfrm,NULL,10,10,610,470,SWP_SIZE|
                  SWP_MOVE|SWP_SHOW);
  while (WinGetMsg(hab,&qmsg,NULL,0,0))
    WinDispatchMsg(hab,&qmsg);
  WinDestroyWindow(hfrm);
  WinDestroyMsgQueue(hmq);
  WinTerminate(hab);
  return 0;
  }

MRESULT EXPENTRY About(hwnd,messg,parml,parm2)
  HWND    hwnd;
  USHORT messg;
  MPARAM parml,parm2;
  {
  switch (messg)
    {
    case WM_COMMAND:
      switch (LOUSHORT(parml))
      {
      case ID_OK:
        WinDismissDlg(hwnd, TRUE);
        return 0;
      }
      break;
    }
    return (WinDefDlgProc(hwnd,messg,parml,parm2));
```

```
}

MRESULT EXPENTRY BarDiaProc(hwnd,messg,parml,parm2)
   HWND   hwnd;
   USHORT messg;
   MPARAM parml;
   MPARAM parm2;
   {
   short B1,B2,B3,B4,B5,B6,B7,B8,B9,B10;
      switch (messg)
         {
         case WM_COMMAND:
            switch (LOUSHORT (parml))
               {
               case ID_OK:
                  WinQueryDlgItemText(hwnd,
                                          DM_TITLE,
                                          80,
                                          title);
                  WinQueryDlgItemText(hwnd,
                                          DM_XAXIS,
                                          80,
                                          xstring);
                  WinQueryDlgItemText(hwnd,
                                          DM_YAXIS,
                                          80,
                                          ystring);
                  WinQueryDlgItemShort(hwnd,
                                          DM_B1,
                                          &B1,
                                          0);
                  WinQueryDlgItemShort(hwnd,
                                          DM_B2,
                                          &B2,
                                          0);
                  WinQueryDlgItemShort(hwnd,
                                          DM_B3,
                                          &B3,
                                          0);
                  WinQueryDlgItemShort(hwnd,
                                          DM_B4,
                                          &B4,
                                          0);
                  WinQueryDlgItemShort(hwnd,
                                          DM_B5,
                                          &B5,
                                          0);
                  WinQueryDlgItemShort(hwnd,
                                          DM_B6,
                                          &B6,
                                          0);
                  WinQueryDlgItemShort(hwnd,
                                          DM_B7,
                                          &B7,
                                          0);
                  WinQueryDlgItemShort(hwnd,
                                          DM_B8,
                                          &B8,
```

```
                                      0);
            WinQueryDlgItemShort(hwnd,
                                 DM_B9,
                                 &B9,
                                 0);
            WinQueryDlgItemShort(hwnd,
                                 DM_B10,
                                 &B10,
                                 0);
            barsizeorg[0]=(long) B1;
            barsizeorg[1]=(long) B2;
            barsizeorg[2]=(long) B3;
            barsizeorg[3]=(long) B4;
            barsizeorg[4]=(long) B5;
            barsizeorg[5]=(long) B6;
            barsizeorg[6]=(long) B7;
            barsizeorg[7]=(long) B8;
            barsizeorg[8]=(long) B9;
            barsizeorg[9]=(long) B10;
            WinDismissDlg(hwnd, TRUE);
            return 0;

        case ID_CANCEL:
            WinDismissDlg(hwnd,TRUE);
            return 0;
        }
        break;
    }
    return WinDefDlgProc (hwnd,messg,parml,parm2);
}

MRESULT EXPENTRY GraphicProc(hwnd,messg,parml,parm2)
    HWND      hwnd;
    USHORT    messg;
    MPARAM    parml,parm2;
    {
    static    LONG      ColorDataInfo[]={CLR_NEUTRAL,
                                         RGB_BLACK,
                                         CLR_BACKGROUND,
                                         RGB_WHITE};

    static    HPOINTER barPtr;
    static    HWND     hmenu;
    static    HPS      hps;
    HDC       hdc;
    POINTL    ptl,ptli;
    GRADIENTL gradl;
    RECTL     rcl;
    int       i,nbars;
    unsigned  int lenxstring,lenystring,lentitle,lenmaxval;
    long      barwidth,barmax,newshade,newcolor,maxlabel;
    char      maxval[4];
    long      barsizescaled[maxbars];

    /* Length of various strings */
    lentitle=strlen(title);
    lenxstring=strlen(xstring);
    lenystring=strlen(ystring);
```

```
/* How many bars were actually entered? */
nbars=0;
for(i=0;i<maxbars;i++)
{
  if(barsizeorg[i]!=0) nbars++;
}

barwidth=400/nbars;

/* Find bar in array with maximum height. */
barmax=barsizeorg[0];
for (i=0;i<nbars;i++)
  if (barmax < barsizeorg[i]) barmax=barsizeorg[i];
maxlabel=barmax;

/* Convert maximum y value to a string */
itoa((int) maxlabel,maxval,10);
lenmaxval=strlen(maxval);

/* Scale all bars in array.  Bar with maximum height = 300 */
for (i=0;i<nbars;i++)
  barsizescaled[i]=barsizeorg[i]*300/barmax;

switch (messg)
  {
  case WM_CREATE:
    barPtr=WinLoadPointer(HWND_DESKTOP,NULL,IDP_POINTER);
    return 0;

  case WM_MOUSEMOVE:
    WinSetPointer(HWND_DESKTOP,barPtr);
    return 0;

  case WM_SIZE:
    if (hmenu==NULL)
      hmenu=WinWindowFromID(WinQueryWindow(hwnd,QW_PARENT,
                       FALSE),FID_MENU);
    return 0;

  case WM_COMMAND:
    {
    switch (COMMANDMSG(&messg)->cmd)
      {
      case IDM_ABOUT:
        if (WinDlgBox(HWND_DESKTOP,hwnd,About,
           NULL,ID_ABOUT,NULL))
           WinInvalidateRect(hwnd,NULL,FALSE);
      return 0;

      case IDM_INPUT:
        if (WinDlgBox(HWND_DESKTOP,hwnd,BarDiaProc,
           NULL,ID_INPUT,NULL))
           WinInvalidateRect(hwnd,NULL,FALSE);
      return 0;
      }
    }
    break;
```

```
       case WM_PAINT:
       hps=WinBeginPaint(hwnd,NULL,NULL);
       GpiCreateLogColorTable(hps,LCOL_RESET,
                              LCOLF_INDRGB,OL,4L,
                              ColorDataInfo);
       GpiErase(hps);

/*--------- your routines below ----------*/

       /* Draw X and Y coordinate axis */
       GpiSetColor(hps,CLR_BLACK);
       ptl.x=99;
       ptl.y=410;
       GpiMove(hps,&ptl);
       ptl.y=99;
       GpiLine(hps,&ptl);
       ptl.x=510;
       GpiLine(hps,&ptl);

       /* Draw Y axis tic marks */
       ptl.y=130;
       for (i=0;i<10;i++)
         {
         ptl.x=95;
         GpiMove(hps,&ptl);
         ptl.x=99;
         GpiLine(hps,&ptl);
         ptl.y+=30;
         }

       GpiSetCharMode(hps,CM_MODE3);

       /* Center and print bar chart title */
       ptl.y=410;
       ptl.x=300-((LONG) (lentitle/2)*6);
       GpiCharStringAt(hps,&ptl,(LONG) lentitle,title);

       /* Center and print horizontal axis label */
       ptl.y=50;
       ptl.x=300-((LONG) (lenxstring/2)*6);
       GpiCharStringAt(hps,&ptl,(LONG) lenxstring,xstring);

       /* Print vertical axis maximum value */
       ptl.y=400;
       ptl.x=70;
       GpiCharStringAt(hps,&ptl,(long) lenmaxval,maxval);

       /* Center and print vertical axis label */
       ptl.y=240-((LONG) (lenystring/2)*6);
       ptl.x=70;
       gradl.x=0;
       gradl.y=90;
       GpiSetCharAngle(hps,&gradl);
       GpiCharStringAt(hps,&ptl,(LONG) lenystring,ystring);

       /* Set initial values for plot */
       ptl.x=99;
       ptli.x=100;
       ptli.y=100;
       newshade=1;
```

```
       newcolor=1;

       /* Plot individual scaled bars */
       for (i=0;i<nbars;i++)
         {
         GpiSetColor(hps,newcolor);
         GpiSetPattern(hps,newshade);
         GpiMove(hps,&ptli);
         ptli.x=ptli.x+barwidth;
         ptl.y=barsizescaled[i]+100;
         ptl.x=ptl.x+barwidth;
         GpiBox(hps,3L,&ptl,0L,0L);
         newshade=newshade+1;
         newcolor=newcolor+1;
         }

/*--------- your routines above ----------*/

       WinEndPaint(hps);
       break;

       default:
         return WinDefWindowProc(hwnd,messg,parm1,parm2);
       }
       return 0;
  }
```

Before studying the header and resource files, let's look more closely at the application's source code (about the middle of the listing). Find the procedure named BarDiaProc. This is the Presentation Manager's equivalent to the BarDlgProc of the Windows program in Chapter 11. Both of these programs allow the user to enter up to ten bar values to be plotted on the chart. In Windows, the function GetDlgItemInt is used to retrieve integer information, while in the Presentation Manager the function WinQueryDlgItemShort is used. Again, other than changes in the specific commands or functions, the overall structure of obtaining dialog box information remains the same.

You may recall that the Windows 3.0 bar graph application uses the new Palette Manager to map logical palette information to a system palette. The Presentation Manager uses predefined colors from a table (see Chapter 16). Future versions of the Presentation Manager toolkit may contain a tool similar to the Windows 3.0 Palette Manager.

A Look at Header Files

There is really nothing new regarding header files. The following listing contains the header file from the Windows bar chart application (Chapter 11) and the Presentation Manager file. (It is repeated here for your convenience.)

THE WINDOWS HEADER (H) FILE:

```
#define IDM_ABOUT      40
#define IDM_INPUT      50
#define IDM_EXIT       70

#define DM_TITLE       280
#define DM_XLABEL      281
#define DM_YLABEL      282
#define DM_P1          283
#define DM_P2          284
#define DM_P3          285
#define DM_P4          286
#define DM_P5          287
#define DM_P6          288
#define DM_P7          289
#define DM_P8          290
#define DM_P9          291
#define DM_P10         292
```

THE PRESENTATION MANAGER HEADER (H) FILE:

```
#define IDP_POINTER    2

#define ID_RESOURCE    10
#define ID_ABOUT       15
#define ID_OK          20
#define ID_CANCEL      25
#define ID_INPUT       30

#define IDM_ABOUT      40
#define IDM_INPUT      50
#define IDM_BARINPUT   60

#define DM_XAXIS       470
#define DM_YAXIS       475
#define DM_TITLE       480
#define DM_B1          481
#define DM_B2          482
#define DM_B3          483
#define DM_B4          484
#define DM_B5          485
#define DM_B6          486
#define DM_B7          487
#define DM_B8          488
#define DM_B9          489
#define DM_B10         490
```

As you can see, this is standard C code. The only variation is in the number of defined values.

The Resource Files

Study the About listings for the Windows and Presentation Manager application in the next listing. Notice that the screen coordinates are identical.

THE WINDOWS RESOURCE (RC) FILE:

```
#include "windows.h"
#include "bar11.h"

BarCursor CURSOR Bar11.cur

BarMenu  MENU
BEGIN
  POPUP "Bar_Chart_Input"
  BEGIN
    MENUITEM "About...",        IDM_ABOUT
    MENUITEM "Input...",        IDM_INPUT
    MENUITEM "Exit",            IDM_EXIT
  END
END

AboutDlgBox DIALOG LOADONCALL MOVEABLE DISCARDABLE
        50,300,180,80
        STYLE WS_DLGFRAME|WS_POPUP
  BEGIN
    CONTROL "Interactive Bar Chart Program",-1,"static",
        SS_CENTER|WS_CHILD,2,60,176,10
    CONTROL "by William H. Murray & Chris H. Pappas",-1,
        "static",SS_CENTER|WS_CHILD,2,45,176,10
    CONTROL "OK",IDOK,"button",
        BS_PUSHBUTTON|WS_TABSTOP|WS_CHILD,75,10,32,14
  END

BarDlgBox DIALOG LOADONCALL MOVEABLE DISCARDABLE
        42,-10,223,209
        CAPTION "Bar Chart Information"
        STYLE WS_BORDER|WS_CAPTION|WS_DLGFRAME|WS_POPUP
  BEGIN
    CONTROL "Bar Chart Title:",100,"button",
        BS_GROUPBOX|WS_TABSTOP|WS_CHILD,5,11,212,89
    CONTROL "Bar Chart Heights",101,"button",
        BS_GROUPBOX|WS_TABSTOP|WS_CHILD,5,105,212,90
    CONTROL "Title: ",-1,"static",SS_LEFT|WS_CHILD,
        43,35,28,8
    CONTROL "",DM_TITLE,"edit",ES_LEFT|WS_BORDER|WS_TABSTOP|
        WS_CHILD,75,30,137,12
    CONTROL "x-axis label:",-1,"static",SS_LEFT|
        WS_CHILD,15,55,55,8
    CONTROL "",DM_XLABEL,"edit",ES_LEFT|WS_BORDER|WS_TABSTOP|
        WS_CHILD,75,50,135,12
    CONTROL "y-axis label:",-1,"static",SS_LEFT|
        WS_CHILD,15,75,60,8
    CONTROL "",DM_YLABEL,"edit",ES_LEFT|WS_BORDER|WS_TABSTOP|
        WS_CHILD,75,70,135,12
    CONTROL "Bar #1: ",-1,"static",SS_LEFT|
        WS_CHILD,45,125,40,8
    CONTROL "Bar #2: ",-1,"static",SS_LEFT|
        WS_CHILD,45,140,40,8
    CONTROL "Bar #3: ",-1,"static",SS_LEFT|
        WS_CHILD,45,155,40,8
    CONTROL "Bar #4: ",-1,"static",SS_LEFT|
        WS_CHILD,45,170,40,8
    CONTROL "Bar #5: ",-1,"static",SS_LEFT|
        WS_CHILD,45,185,40,8
    CONTROL "Bar #6: ",-1,"static",SS_LEFT|
```

```
                 WS_CHILD,130,125,40,8
     CONTROL "Bar #7: ",-1,"static",SS_LEFT|
         WS_CHILD,130,140,40,8
     CONTROL "Bar #8: ",-1,"static",SS_LEFT|
         WS_CHILD,130,155,40,8
     CONTROL "Bar #9: ",-1,"static",SS_LEFT|
         WS_CHILD,130,170,40,8
     CONTROL "Bar #10:",-1,"static",SS_LEFT|
         WS_CHILD,130,185,45,8
     CONTROL "10",DM_P1,"edit",ES_LEFT|WS_BORDER|WS_TABSTOP|
         WS_CHILD,90,120,30,12
     CONTROL "20",DM_P2,"edit",ES_LEFT|WS_BORDER|WS_TABSTOP|
         WS_CHILD,90,135,30,12
     CONTROL "30",DM_P3,"edit",ES_LEFT|WS_BORDER|WS_TABSTOP|
         WS_CHILD,90,150,30,12
     CONTROL "40",DM_P4,"edit",ES_LEFT|WS_BORDER|WS_TABSTOP|
         WS_CHILD,90,165,30,12
     CONTROL "0",DM_P5,"edit",ES_LEFT|WS_BORDER|WS_TABSTOP|
         WS_CHILD,90,180,30,12
     CONTROL "0",DM_P6,"edit",ES_LEFT|WS_BORDER|WS_TABSTOP|
         WS_CHILD,180,120,30,12
     CONTROL "0",DM_P7,"edit",ES_LEFT|WS_BORDER|WS_TABSTOP|
         WS_CHILD,180,135,30,12
     CONTROL "0",DM_P8,"edit",ES_LEFT|WS_BORDER|WS_TABSTOP|
         WS_CHILD,180,150,30,12
     CONTROL "0",DM_P9,"edit",ES_LEFT|WS_BORDER|WS_TABSTOP|
         WS_CHILD,180,165,30,12
     CONTROL "0",DM_P10,"edit",ES_LEFT|WS_BORDER|WS_TABSTOP|
         WS_CHILD,180,180,30,12
     CONTROL "OK",IDOK,"button",BS_PUSHBUTTON|WS_TABSTOP|
         WS_CHILD,54,195,24,14
     CONTROL "Cancel",IDCANCEL,"button",BS_PUSHBUTTON|
         WS_TABSTOP|WS_CHILD,124,195,34,14
   END


THE PRESENTATION MANAGER RESOURCE (RC) FILE:

#include <os2.h>
#include "bar16.h"

POINTER ID_RESOURCE bar16.ico
POINTER IDP_POINTER bar16.ptr

MENU                    ID_RESOURCE
BEGIN
  SUBMENU "Bar_Chart_Input", IDM_BARINPUT
  BEGIN
    MENUITEM "About...",      IDM_ABOUT
    MENUITEM "Input",         IDM_INPUT
  END
END

DLGTEMPLATE             ID_ABOUT
BEGIN
  DIALOG "",ID_ABOUT,50,300,180,80,FS_DLGBORDER
  BEGIN
    CTEXT "Interactive Bar Chart Program",-1,2,60,176,10
    CTEXT "by William H. Murray & Chris H. Pappas",-1,2,
       45,176,10
    CONTROL "OK",ID_OK,75,10,32,14,WC_BUTTON,BS_PUSHBUTTON
```

```
          ¦BS_DEFAULT¦WS_GROUP¦WS_TABSTOP¦WS_VISIBLE
    END
END

DLGTEMPLATE ID_INPUT LOADONCALL MOVEABLE DISCARDABLE
BEGIN
    DIALOG "Bar Chart Information",ID_INPUT,76,-10,176,236,
          FS_NOBYTEALIGN¦FS_DLGBORDER¦WS_VISIBLE¦
          WS_CLIPSIBLINGS¦WS_SAVEBITS,FCF_TITLEBAR
    BEGIN
      CONTROL "Bar Chart Title",257,-1,180,178,53,
          WC_STATIC,SS_GROUPBOX¦WS_GROUP¦WS_VISIBLE
      CONTROL "Bar Chart Bar Sizes",258,5,24,160,154,
          WC_STATIC,SS_GROUPBOX¦WS_GROUP¦WS_VISIBLE
      CONTROL "Enter Title:",260,3,214,50,8,WC_STATIC,
          SS_TEXT¦DT_LEFT¦DT_TOP¦WS_GROUP¦WS_VISIBLE
      CONTROL "      x-axis:",261,3,199,50,8,WC_STATIC,
          SS_TEXT¦DT_LEFT¦DT_TOP¦WS_GROUP¦WS_VISIBLE
      CONTROL "      y-axis:",262,3,185,50,8,WC_STATIC,
          SS_TEXT¦DT_LEFT¦DT_TOP¦WS_GROUP¦WS_VISIBLE
      CONTROL " Bar #1:",263,7,156,56,8,WC_STATIC,SS_TEXT¦
          DT_LEFT¦DT_TOP¦WS_GROUP¦WS_VISIBLE
      CONTROL " Bar #2:",264,7,142,56,8,WC_STATIC,SS_TEXT¦
          DT_LEFT¦DT_TOP¦WS_GROUP¦WS_VISIBLE
      CONTROL " Bar #3:",265,7,128,56,8,WC_STATIC,SS_TEXT¦
          DT_LEFT¦DT_TOP¦WS_GROUP¦WS_VISIBLE
      CONTROL " Bar #4:",266,7,114,56,8,WC_STATIC,SS_TEXT¦
          DT_LEFT¦DT_TOP¦WS_GROUP¦WS_VISIBLE
      CONTROL " Bar #5:",267,7,100,56,8,WC_STATIC,SS_TEXT¦
          DT_LEFT¦DT_TOP¦WS_GROUP¦WS_VISIBLE
      CONTROL " Bar #6:",268,7,86,56,8,WC_STATIC,SS_TEXT¦
          DT_LEFT¦DT_TOP¦WS_GROUP¦WS_VISIBLE
      CONTROL " Bar #7:",269,7,72,56,8,WC_STATIC,SS_TEXT¦
          DT_LEFT¦DT_TOP¦WS_GROUP¦WS_VISIBLE
      CONTROL " Bar #8:",270,7,58,56,8,WC_STATIC,SS_TEXT¦
          DT_LEFT¦DT_TOP¦WS_GROUP¦WS_VISIBLE
      CONTROL " Bar #9:",271,7,44,56,8,WC_STATIC,SS_TEXT¦
          DT_LEFT¦DT_TOP¦WS_GROUP¦WS_VISIBLE
      CONTROL "Bar #10:",272,7,30,56,8,WC_STATIC,SS_TEXT¦
          DT_LEFT¦DT_TOP¦WS_GROUP¦WS_VISIBLE
      CONTROL "Computer Sales",DM_TITLE,62,214,107,8,
          WC_ENTRYFIELD,ES_LEFT¦ES_AUTOSCROLL¦ES_MARGIN
          ¦WS_TABSTOP¦WS_VISIBLE
      CONTROL "Models",DM_XAXIS,62,199,107,8,
          WC_ENTRYFIELD,ES_LEFT¦ES_AUTOSCROLL¦ES_MARGIN
          ¦WS_TABSTOP¦WS_VISIBLE
      CONTROL "Number Sold",DM_YAXIS,62,185,107,8,
          WC_ENTRYFIELD,ES_LEFT¦ES_AUTOSCROLL¦ES_MARGIN
          ¦WS_TABSTOP¦WS_VISIBLE
      CONTROL "40",DM_B1,81,156,56,8,WC_ENTRYFIELD,ES_LEFT
          ¦ES_AUTOSCROLL¦ES_MARGIN¦WS_TABSTOP¦WS_VISIBLE
      CONTROL "30",DM_B2,81,142,56,8,WC_ENTRYFIELD,ES_LEFT
          ¦ES_AUTOSCROLL¦ES_MARGIN¦WS_TABSTOP¦WS_VISIBLE
      CONTROL "10",DM_B3,81,128,56,8,WC_ENTRYFIELD,ES_LEFT
          ¦ES_AUTOSCROLL¦ES_MARGIN¦WS_TABSTOP¦WS_VISIBLE
      CONTROL "0",DM_B4,81,114,56,8,WC_ENTRYFIELD,ES_LEFT
          ¦ES_AUTOSCROLL¦ES_MARGIN¦WS_TABSTOP¦WS_VISIBLE
      CONTROL "0",DM_B5,81,100,56,8,WC_ENTRYFIELD,ES_LEFT
          ¦ES_AUTOSCROLL¦ES_MARGIN¦WS_TABSTOP¦WS_VISIBLE
      CONTROL "0",DM_B6,81,86,56,8,WC_ENTRYFIELD,ES_LEFT
          ¦ES_AUTOSCROLL¦ES_MARGIN¦WS_TABSTOP¦WS_VISIBLE
```

```
    CONTROL "0",DM_B7,81,72,56,8,WC_ENTRYFIELD,ES_LEFT
        |ES_AUTOSCROLL|ES_MARGIN|WS_TABSTOP|WS_VISIBLE
    CONTROL "0",DM_B8,81,58,56,8,WC_ENTRYFIELD,ES_LEFT
        |ES_AUTOSCROLL|ES_MARGIN|WS_TABSTOP|WS_VISIBLE
    CONTROL "0",DM_B9,81,44,56,8,WC_ENTRYFIELD,ES_LEFT
        |ES_AUTOSCROLL|ES_MARGIN|WS_TABSTOP|WS_VISIBLE
    CONTROL "0",DM_B10,81,30,56,8,WC_ENTRYFIELD,ES_LEFT
        |ES_AUTOSCROLL|ES_MARGIN|WS_TABSTOP|WS_VISIBLE
    CONTROL "OK",ID_OK,12,9,24,14,WC_BUTTON,BS_PUSHBUTTON
        |WS_TABSTOP|WS_VISIBLE
    CONTROL "Cancel",ID_CANCEL,111,9,40,14,WC_BUTTON,
        BS_PUSHBUTTON|WS_TABSTOP|WS_VISIBLE
  END
END
```

Except for each product's unique definitions, the dialog box definitions are the same.

As you examine the bar chart input dialog boxes for each product, you will notice variations in screen values. This is due to the location of each input box on the screen, and is not a result of differences between the products.

Resource files, when carefully planned, should be fairly easy to convert from Windows to the Presentation Manager.

A FINAL WORD

If you are interested in a better overall understanding of the Presentation Manager code in this chapter, *Presentation Manager Graphics* by Chris Pappas and William Murray (Berkeley, Ca.: Osborne/McGraw-Hill, 1989) gives a more in-depth explanation. Additionally, if you are interested in a line-by-line analysis of a Windows and Presentation Manager application, see "Converting Windows Applications For Microsoft OS/2 Presentation Manager," by Michael Geary, *Microsoft Systems Journal*, January 1988. This article deals with an earlier Windows version, but the analysis is very well done.

There will come a day when an aftermarket company will produce software capable of converting Windows applications into Presentation Manager programs. Until then, file-by-file, function-by-function conversion is necessary. Fortunately, as you have seen, starting from scratch is not necessary because of the similarity of their message-based systems.

A

WINDOWS FUNCTIONS

This appendix contains an alphabetical list of functions from the Microsoft Windows application program interface (API). The documentation for each function contains the function prototype, a statement about the function's purpose, a brief description of the function's input parameters, and a description of any return values.

int AccessResource(hInstance,hResInfo)

Function

Opens the designated file and moves the file pointer to the beginning of the file. Supplies a DOS file handle to be used for file-read calls to load the resource.

Parameters

hInstance (HANDLE) specifies the instance of the module whose executable file owns the resource.

hResInfo (HANDLE) specifies the resource to be used.

Value Returned

A DOS file handle to the specified resource. Returns −1 when the resource cannot be found.

Notes

The file is opened for reading only. Applications must close the file after reading.

ATOM AddAtom(lpString)

Function

Adds the character string pointed to by *lpString* to the atom table, creating a new atom that identifies the string.

Parameters

lpString (LPSTR) points to a character string that will be added to the table.

Value Returned

Returned value defines the new atom. Returns NULL when unsuccessful.

Notes

Must be a NULL-terminated character string.

short AddFontResource(lpFilename)

Function

Will add the *lpFilename*-specified font to the list of available fonts, thereby making them available for the application to use.

Parameters

lpFilename (LPSTR) contains a character string that names the font resource file.

Value Returned

The return value contains the number of fonts loaded; otherwise, the function returns a 0.

Notes

Memory conservation can be accomplished by an application removing any unused font resources as soon as possible.

void AdjustWindowRect(lpRect,LStyle,bMenu)

Function

Calculates the necessary window size of the window based on the specified client window size.

Parameters

lpRect (LPRECT) points to a RECT structure containing the coordinates of the client window.

lStyle (long) defines the window styles of the window whose client rectangle is to be drawn.

bMenu (BOOL) indicates whether the window has a menu.

Value Returned
None.

void AnimatePalette(hDC,wStartIndex,wNumEntries, lpPaletteColors) [3.0 and later]

Function

Replaces an entry in a logical palette, causing Windows to immediately map the new entry into the system palette.

Parameters

hDC (HDC) specifies the device context.

sStartIndex (WORD) specifies the first entry in the palette that is to be animated.

wNumEntries (WORD) specifies the number of entries in the palette to be animated.

lpPaletteColors (LPSTR) points to an array of PALETTEENTRY structure to replace the palette entries pointed to by *wStartIndex* and *wNumEntries*.

Value Returned

None.

Notes

The function will only change entries with the PE_ANIMATE flag set in the corresponding PaletteEntry field of the LOGPALETTE data structure.

BOOL Arc(hDC,x1,y1,x2,y2,x3,y3,x4,y4)

Function

Draws an elliptical arc with the center of the arc bounded by the rectangle defined by *x1, y1,* and *x2, y2*. The arc begins at *x3, y3* and ends at *x4, y4*.

Parameters

hDC (HDC) identifies the device context.

x1 and *y1* (short) define the logical X and Y coordinates of the upper-left corner of the bounding rectangle.

x2 and *y2* (short) define the logical X and Y coordinates of the lower-right corner of the bounding rectangle.

x3 and *y3* (short) define the logical X and Y coordinates of the arc's starting point.

x4 and *y4* (short) define the logical X and Y coordinates of the arc's ending point.

Value Returned

A non-zero value is returned if the function is successful; otherwise, a zero is returned.

Notes

The width and height of the rectangle must not exceed 32,767 units.

HDC BeginPaint(hWnd,lpPaint)

Function

Gets the window ready for painting and using the *lpPaint* parameter, which points to a paint structure and fills the structure with information about the painting to be performed.

Parameters

hWnd (HWND) indicates the window to be repainted.

lpPaint (LPPAINTSTRUCT) points to a PAINTSTRUCT structure that will receive the painting parameters.

Value Returned

Returns the device context for the specified window.

Notes

BeginPaint must be called in response to a WM_PAINT message.

BOOL BitBlt(hDestDC,x,y,nWidth,nHeight,hScrDC, xSrc,ySrc,dwRop)

Function

Move a bitmap from the source device referenced by *hSrcDC* to some other device specified by *hDestDC*.

Parameters

hDestDc (HDC) identifies the device context that will receive the bitmap.

x and *y* (short) define the logical X and Y coordinates of the upper-left corner of the destination rectangle.

nWidth and *nHeight* (short) define the width and height (in logical units) of the destination rectangle and source bitmap.

xSrc and *ySrc* (short) define the logical X and Y coordinates of the upper-left corner of the source bitmap.

dwRop (DWORD) defines the raster operation to be executed. These operations define how the GDI (graphics device interface) blends colors in output operations involving brushes and source and destination bitmaps.

Raster Operation	Description
SRCPAINT	Using the Boolean OR, combines the destination and source bitmap pixels
SRCCOPY	Copies the source bitmap to the destination bitmap
SRCAND	Using the Boolean AND, combines the destination and source bitmap pixels
SRCINVERT	Using the Boolean XOR, combines the destination and source bitmap pixels
SRCERASE	Inverts the destination bitmap, combining the result with the source bitmap using the logical AND operation
NOTSRCCOPY	Copies an inverted source bitmap to the destination
NOTSRCERASE	Combines the destination and source bitmaps using the Boolean AND operation; then, inverts the result
MERGECOPY	Using a pattern, combines the source bitmap with the pattern using the Boolean AND operation
MERGEPAINT	Using the Boolean OR operation, combines the inverted source bitmap with the destination bitmap
PATCOPY	Copies the pattern to the destination bitmap
PATPAINT	Using the Boolean OR operation, combines an inverted source bitmap with the pattern. It then combines the result with the destination bitmap using the Boolean OR operation
PATINVERT	Using the Boolean OR operation, combines the destination bitmap with the pattern
DSTINVERT	Inverts the destination bitmap
BLACKNESS	Turns all output black
WHITENESS	Turns all output white

Value Returned

Returned value is non-zero for a successful draw; otherwise, a zero is returned.

Notes

The GDI will transform the *nWidth* and *nHeight* parameters. If the resulting values do not match between the destination display context and the source display context, the GDI will use the StretchBlt function to modify the source bitmap as necessary.

void BringWindowToTop(hWnd)

Function

Brings a pop-up or child window to the top of the stack of overlapping windows.

Parameters

hWnd (HWND) specifies the pop-up or child window to be brought to the top.

Value Returned

None.

Notes

The function is used to uncover a window that is obscured by any overlapping windows.

void CheckDlgButton(hDlg,nIDButton,wCheck)

Function

Places or removes a check mark from a button control, or changes the state of a three-state button.

Parameters

hDlg (HWND) specifies the dialog box containing the button.

nIDButton (int) defines the button control to be modified.

wCheck (WORD) defines the action to be performed. A non-zero value causes a check mark to be placed next to the button. A zero value removes the check mark. With a three-state button: 2 grays the button; 1 checks the button; 0 removes a check mark.

Value Returned

None.

Notes

The function sends a BM_SETCHECK message to the button control of the specified dialog box.

BOOL CheckMenuItem(hMenu,wIDCheckItem,wCheck)

Function

Using the pop-up menu pointed to by the *hMenu* parameter, this function either positions a check mark next to a menu item or removes the check mark from a previously selected menu item.

Parameters

hMenu (HMENU) identifies the pop-up menu.

wIDCheckItem (WORD) indicates which menu item is to be checked or unchecked.

wCheck (WORD) can be any combination of options combined using the logical OR operation. These include MF_CHECKED, MF_UNCHECKED, MF_BYPOSITION, or MF_BYCOMMAND. The *wCheck* parameter defines how to modify the menu item, along with a specification of how to locate the item.

Check Options	Description
MF _ CHECKED	Causes a check mark to be placed next to the selected menu item
MF _ UNCHECKED	Removes the check mark from a previously selected menu item
MF _ BYPOSITION	Uses the *wIDCheckItem* parameter and indicates that the position of the menu item has been given. The first menu item begins at position 0
MF _ BYCOMMAND	Causes the *wIDCheckItem* parameter to contain the menu item ID. MF _ BYCOMMAND is the default option

Value Returned

The return value indicates the previous state of the selected menu item (MF _ UNCHECKED or MF _ CHECKED).

Notes

Top-level menu items cannot be checked. The *wIDCheckItem* parameter can specify a menu or submenu item.

void CheckRadioButton(hDlg,nIDFirstButton, nIDLastButton,nIDCheckButton)

Function

This function will check the radio button identified by the *nIDCheckButton* parameter while simultaneously removing any previous check marks from all radio buttons referenced by the *nIDFirstButton* to the last radio button defined by *nIDLastButton*.

Parameters

hDlg (HWND) specifies the dialog box.

nIDFirstButton (int) is an integer value indicating the first radio button in the selected group.

nIDLastButton (int) is an integer value indicating the last radio button in the selected group.

nIDCheckButton (int) is an integer value indicating the radio button that is to be checked.

Value Returned

None.

Notes

The function sends a BM_SETCHECK message to the radio-button control referenced by the ID in a given dialog box.

BOOL Chord(hDC,x1,y1,x2,y2,x3,y3,x4,y4)

Function

Draws a chord using the selected pen, with a fill pattern based on the selected brush. A chord is defined as an area bounded by the intersection of an ellipse and a line segment.

Parameters

hDC (HDC) specifies the device context on which the chord will be drawn.

x1 (short) defines the upper-left corner X coordinate of the bounding rectangle.

y1 (short) defines the upper-left corner Y coordinate of the bounding rectangle.

x2 (short) defines the lower-right corner X coordinate of the bounding rectangle.

y2 (short) defines the lower-right corner Y coordinate of the bounding rectangle.

x3 (short) defines the X coordinate of one end of the line segment.

y3 (short) defines the Y coordinate of one end of the line segment.

x4 (short) defines the X coordinate of the opposite end of the line segment.

y4 (short) defines the Y coordinate of the opposite end of the line segment.

Value Returned

A non-zero value is returned if the arc is drawn. A zero value indicates that the arc was not drawn.

Notes

x1, *y1*, *x2*, and *y2* define the rectangle bounding the ellipse that is part of the chord. *x3*, *y3*, *x4*, and *y4* define the line that intercepts the ellipse.

HBITMAP
CreateBitmap(nWidth,nHeight,nPlanes,nBitCount,lpBits)

Function

Using the width, height, and bit pattern specified, the function creates a bitmap.

Parameters

nWidth (short) defines the width of the bitmap to be drawn, in pixels.

nHeight (short) defines the height of the bitmap to be created, in pixels.

nPlanes (BYTE) identifies the number of color planes to be used in the bitmap. The number of bits in each plane is calculated using the following formula:

$$nWidth \times nHeight \times nBitCount$$

lpBits (LPSTR) is a pointer parameter pointing to a short-integer array containing the initial bitmap bit values.

Value Returned

A successful return value identifies the bitmap created by the function. A NULL value indicates an unsuccessful attempt.

Notes

Using the SelectObject function, the created bitmap can be selected as the current bitmap for a memory display.

HBITMAP CreateBitmapIndirect(lpBitmap)

Function

Using the data structure pointed to by *lpBitmap*, the function creates a bitmap.

Parameters

lpBitmap (BITMAP FAR *) is a pointer to a BITMAP data structure containing the specifications for the bitmap.

Value Returned

A successful return value identifies the bitmap created by the function. A NULL value indicates an unsuccessful attempt.

Notes

The main difference between CreateBitmapIndirect and CreateBitmap is that the bitmap creation parameters are specified within a composite data structure rather than being passed separately.

HBRUSH CreateBrushIndirect(lpLogBrush)

Function

Use the data structure pointed to by *lpLogBrush* to create a logical brush. The LOGBRUSH data structure defines the intended brush's style, color, and pattern.

Parameters

lpLogBrush (LOGBRUSH FAR *) is a pointer to a LOGBRUSH data structure.

Value Returned

If successful, the value returned is to the created logical brush; otherwise, a NULL is returned.

Notes

A BS_INDEXED style will guarantee that the first eight indexed brushes will be unique for any selected device.

HWND CreateDialog(hInstance,lpTemplateName, hWndParent,lpDialogFunc)

Function

The *lpTemplateName* defines the size, style, and any controls associated with the modeless dialog box the function will create. The *hWndParent* parameter specifies the owner window of the dialog box, with *lpDialogFunc* pointing to the message processing function that will handle any messages received by the dialog box.

Parameters

hInstance (HANDLE) specifies the instance of the module whose executable file owns the resource.

lpTemplateName (LPSTR) is a pointer to a null-terminated character string naming the dialog box template.

hWndParent (HWND) is a handle to the window that owns the dialog box.

lpDialogFunc (FARPROC) is a procedure-instance address for the dialog function. The dialog function address must have been created by using the MakeProcInstance function. The callback function must use the Pascal calling convention and be declared FAR using the following form:

```
HWND FAR PASCAL DialogFunc(hWnd,wMsg,wParam, lParam)
HWND hwnd;          /* identifies message receiving
                       dialog box                   */
unsigned wMsg;      /* indicates the message number */
WORD wParam;        /* specifies 16 bits of additional
                       message-dependent information */
DWORD lParam;       /* specifies 32 bits of additional
                       message-dependent information */
```

Value Returned

A successful return contains a valid identifier to the dialog box. A −1 is returned if the function call was unsuccessful.

Notes

This function is used only if the dialog class is used for the dialog box. This is the default class used whenever no explicit class is given in the dialog box template. The function must not call *DefWindowProc*, but must process all unwanted messages internally by the dialog-class window function.

You should use the WS_VISIBLE style for the dialog box template if the dialog box should appear in the parent window during creation.

You should use the DestroyWindow function to delete a dialog box created by the CreateDialog function.

HWND
CreateDialogIndirect(hInstance,lpDialogTemplate, hWndParent,lpDialogFunc)

Function

The *lpDialogTemplate* data structure defines the size, style, and any controls associated with the modeless dialog box the function will create. The *hWndParent* parameter specifies the owner window of the dialog box, with *lpDialogFunc* pointing to the message processing function that will handle any messages received by the dialog box.

Parameters

hInstance (HANDLE) specifies the instance of the module whose executable file owns the resource.

lpDialogTemplate (LPSTR) is a pointer to a dialog box template structure.

hWndParent (HWND) is a handle to the window that owns the dialog box.

lpDialogFunc (FARPROC) is a procedure-instance address for the dialog function. The dialog function address must have been created by using the

MakeProcInstance function. The callback function must use the Pascal calling convention and declared FAR using the following form:

```
HWND FAR PASCAL DialogFunc(hWnd,wMsg,wParam,lParam)
HWND hwnd;       /* identifies the message receiving the
                    dialog box                     */
unsigned wMsg; /* indicates the message number  */
WORD wParam;    /* specifies 16 bits of additional
                    message-dependent information */
DWORD lParam;   /* specifies 32 bits of additional
                    message-dependent information */
```

Value Returned

A successful return contains a valid identifier to the dialog box. A −1 is returned if the function call was unsuccessful.

Notes

CreateDialogIndirect sends a WM_INITDIALOG message to the dialog function before displaying the dialog box, allowing the dialog function to initialize the dialog box controls.

This function is used only if the dialog class is used for the dialog box. This is the default class that is used whenever no explicit class is given in the dialog box template. The function must not call *DefWindowProc*, but must process all unwanted messages internally by the dialog-class window function.

You should use the WS_VISIBLE style for the dialog box template if the dialog box should appear in the parent window during creation.

You should use the DestroyWindow function to delete a dialog box created by the CreateDialog function.

HFONT
CreateFont(nHeight,nWidth,nEscapement,nOrientation, nWeight,cItalic,cUnderline, cStrikeOut,cCharSet, cOutputPrecision,cClipPrecision,cQuality, cPitchAndFamily,lpFacename)

Function

Creates a logical font that can be selected as the font for any device. The logical font that is created is based on the options that follow.

Parameters

nHeight (short) defines the logical font's height in one of three ways:

nHeight > 0	Transforms the height into device units and matches it with the cell height of the available fonts
nHeight = 0	Selects a reasonable default size
nHeight < 0	Transforms the height into device units and matches the absolute value against the character height of the available fonts

The font mapper follows these precedents for height comparisons:

- The font mapper first looks for the largest font that does not exceed the requested font size. If there is no such font available, then

- The font mapper looks for the smallest font available.

nWidth (short), using logical units, defines the average width of the characters in the font. When *nWidth* contains a zero value, the aspect ratio of the device will be matched with the digitization aspect ratio of the available fonts to select the best match.

nEscapement (short), using tenths of a degree increments, defines the angle of each line of text output in the specified font, relative to the bottom of the page.

nOrientation (short), using tenths of a degree increments, specifies the angle of each character's baseline relative to the bottom of the page.

nWeight (short) indicates the preferred weight of the font in the range of 0 to 1000. A value of 0 selects the default weight, with a value of roughly 450 defining a normal weight, and 750 representing bold.

cItalic (BYTE) indicates if the font is italic or not.

cUnderline (BYTE) indicates if the font is underlined or not.

cStrikeOut (BYTE) indicates if the characters in the font are struck out.

cCharSet (BYTE) indicates which character set is desired. Two values (ANSI_CHARSET and OEM_CHARSET) are predefined. Others may be purchased through specific font manufacturers.

cOutputPrecision (BYTE) indicates the preferred output precision. This specifies just how closely the output must match the requested font's characteristics. There are four choices:

    OUT_CHARACTER_PRECIS
    OUT_DEFAULT_PRECIS
    OUT_STRING_PRECIS
    OUT_STROKE_PRECIS

cClipPrecision (BYTE) indicates the preferred clipping precision. Clipping precision references just how each character that extends beyond the clipping region is to be "clipped." There are three choices:

    CLIP_CHARACTER_PRECIS
    CLIP_DEFAULT_PRECIS
    CLIP_STROKE_PRECIS

cQuality (BYTE) selects the preferred output quality. This parameter selects just how carefully the graphics device interface (GDI) must attempt to match the logical font with the actual physical fonts provided for the requested output device. There are three possible match conditions:

    DEFAULT_QUALITY
    DRAFT_QUALITY
    PROOF_QUALITY

cPitchAndFamily (BYTE) selects the pitch and family of the font. There are three pitch choices:

    DEFAULT_PITCH
    FIXED_PITCH
    VARIABLE_PITCH

There are six possible font families.

FF_DECORATIVE
FF_DONTCARE
FF_MODERN
FF_ROMAN
FF_SCRIPT
FF_SWISS

lpFacename (LPSTR) is a 30-character maximum null-terminated string that identifies the name of the font. If there is a question about the available typefaces, the EnumFonts function can be invoked to list the fonts.

Value Returned

A successful return contains a value identifying the created logical font. A NULL value indicates an unsuccessful creation.

Notes

It is important to understand that the CreateFont function does not create a new font. All it does is to match, as closely as possible based on the matching parameters specified, your preference with the actual physical fonts available.

HFONT CreateFontIndirect(lpLogFont)

Function

Creates a logical font based on the parameters specified in the *lpLogFont* data structure.

Parameters

lpLogFont (LOGFONT FAR *) is a pointer to a LOGFONT data structure defining the logical font's characteristics.

Value Returned

NULL is returned if the function was unsuccessful; otherwise, the value returned identifies the created logical font.

Notes

CreateFontIndirect is identical in purpose to CreateFont, with the exception that the "matching" parameters are stored in a data structure pointed to by *lpLogFont* rather than being explicitly declared. For a complete analysis of the various font-matching options, see the Parameters section of the Create-Font function.

HBRUSH CreateHatchBrush(nIndex,rgbColor)

Function

Creates a logical brush with the defined color and hatch pattern. Once created, the brush can then be selected as the current brush for any device.

Parameters

nIndex (short) selects one of the following hatch styles for the brush:

HS_BDIAGONAL	45-degree left-to-right cross-hatch (upward)
HS_CROSS	Horizontal and vertical cross-hatching
HS_DIAGCROSS	45-degree cross-hatch
HS_FDIAGONAL	45-degree left-to-right cross-hatching (downward)
HS_HORIZONTAL	Horizontal cross-hatching
HS_VERTICAL	Vertical cross-hatching

rgbColor (DWORD) selects an RGB color for the color of the hatch lines to be drawn.

Value Returned

The value returned identifies the logical brush that has been created. An unsuccessful attempt will return a NULL.

HMENU CreateMenu( )

Function

Creates a menu. While the created menu is initially empty, it can be filled by using the ChangeMenu function.

Parameters

No parameters are used.

Value Returned

Identifies the newly created menu. A NULL value indicates an unsuccessful attempt.

HPALETTE CreatePalette(lpLogPalette) [3.0 and later]

Function

Creates a logical color palette.

Parameters

lpLogPalette (PALETTE FAR *) is a pointer to a LOGPALETTE data structure.

Value Returned

Specifies a logical palette if the function was successful; otherwise, it is NULL.

HBRUSH CreatePatternBrush(hBitmap)

Function

Using the *hBitmap* parameter, creates a logical brush with the selected pattern.

Parameters

hBitmap (HBITMAP) points to a previously created bitmap, with a minimum sized pattern fill bitmap of 8 × 8.

Value Returned

Identifies either the created logical brush or a NULL for an unsuccessful attempt.

Notes

Once created, the brush pattern can be selected for any device that supports raster operations. Logical pattern brushes can be deleted with a call to DeleteObject without affecting the bitmap used to create the brush, thereby allowing the bitmap to be used to create other pattern brushes.

HPEN CreatePen(nPenStyle,nWidth,rgbColor)

Function

Creates a logical pen based on the style, width, and color selected.

Parameters

nPenStyle (short) selects the pen style from a list of six possibilities:

Constant	Pen Style
0	Solid
1	Dash
2	Dot
3	Dash-dot
4	Dash-dot-dot
5	NULL

nWidth (short) defines the pen's width in logical units.

rgbColor (DWORD) selects an RGB color for the pen.

Value Returned

Either identifies that the logical pen is successful or returns a NULL.

Notes

Any pen created with a physical width greater than 1 pixel will always have either a solid or null style.

HPEN CreatePenIndirect(lpLogPen)

Function

Creates a logical pen based on the parameters stored in the data structure pointed to by *lpLogPen*.

Parameters

lpLogPen (LOGPEN FAR *) is a pointer to a LOGPEN data structure.

Value Returned

Identifies either a valid logical pen or NULL for an unsuccessful attempt.

Notes

See the CreatePen function section for an explanation of the pen's possible appearances.

HRGN CreatePolygonRgn(lpPoints,nCount,nPolyFillMode)

Function

Creates a polygon region.

Parameters

lpPoints (LPPOINT) is a pointer to a POINT data structure that identifies the X and Y coordinates of one angle of the polygon.

nCount (short) identifies the number of elements in the array.

nPolyFillMode (short) selects either an ALTERNATE or WINDING polygon-filling mode.

Value Returned

Either identifies that the new region is successful or returns NULL.

HMENU CreatePopupMenu( ) [3.0 and later]

Function

Creates and returns a handle to an empty pop-up menu. Using the Insert-Menu and AppendMenu functions, an application can add items to the pop-up menu.

Parameters

It has no parameters.

Value Returned

Specifies the newly created menu if successful, NULL otherwise.

HRGN CreateRectRgn(x1,y1,x2,y2)

Function

Creates a rectangle.

Parameters

x1 (short) is the upper-left corner X coordinate.

y1 (short) is the upper-left corner Y coordinate.

x2 (short) is the lower-right corner X coordinate.

y2 (short) is the lower-right corner Y coordinate.

Value Returned

Returned value identifies the newly created rectangular region; otherwise, an unsuccessful attempt will return a NULL.

Notes

The width and height of the rectangle, defined by the absolute value of *x2−x1* and *y2−y1,* must not exceed 32,767.

HRGN CreateRectRgnIndirect(lpRect)

Function

Creates a rectangle. This function is identical to the CreateRectRgn function, except that its parameters are passed in a RECT data structure rather than being explicitly defined.

Parameters

lpRect (LPRECT) is a pointer to a RECT data structure containing the upper-left and lower-right limits for the rectangular region to be created.

Value Returned

Returned value identifies the newly created rectangular region; otherwise, an unsuccessful attempt will return a NULL.

Notes

The width and height of the rectangle must not exceed 32,767.

HRGN CreateRoundRectRgn(x1,y1,x2,y2,x3,y3) [3.0 and later]

Function

Creates a rounded rectangular region.

Parameters

x1 (int) identifies the logical X coordinate of the upper-left corner of the region.

y1 (int) identifies the logical Y coordinate of the upper-left corner of the region.

x2 (int) identifies the logical X coordinate of the lower-right corner of the region.

y2 (int) identifies the logical Y coordinate of the lower-right corner of the region.

x3 (int) identifies the width of the ellipse that will be used to draw the rounded corners.

y3 (int) identifies the height of the ellipse that will be used to draw the rounded corners.

Value Returned

A non-zero value indicates that the region was successfully drawn. A zero value indicates an unsuccessful draw.

HBRUSH CreateSolidBrush(rgbColor)

Function

Creates a logical brush using the selected color.

Parameters

rgbColor (DWORD) selects an RGB color for the brush.

Value Returned

If successful the return value identifies the newly created solid brush; otherwise, a NULL return indicates an unsuccessful creation attempt.

HWND CreateWindow(lpClassName,lpWindowName, dwStyle,x,y,nWidth,nHeight,hWndParent,hMenu, hInstance,lpParam)

Function

This frequently invoked Windows function creates either an overlapped, pop-up, or child window specifying the window's class, title, and style and can even set the window's initial position and size. If the window to be created has an owning parent or menu, this is also defined.

The function also sends the necessary messages, WM_CREATE, WM_GETMINMAXINFO, and WM_NCCREATE, to the window. If the WS_VISIBLE style option has been selected, all necessary window messages are sent to activate and visually display the window.

Parameters

lpClassName (LPSTR) points to a NULL-terminated character string naming the window's class.

lpWindowName (LPSTR) points to a NULL-terminated character string identifying the window by name.

x (int) defines the initial X coordinate position for the window.

Window Type	Description
Overlapped or Pop-Up	X coordinate of the window's upper-left corner in screen coordinates. If the value is CW_USEDEFAULT, Windows selects the default upper-left X coordinate
Child	X coordinate of the upper-left corner of the window in the client area of its parent window

y (int) defines the initial Y coordinate position for the window.

Window Type	Description
Overlapped or Pop-Up	Y coordinate of the window's upper-left corner in screen coordinates. If the value is CW_USEDEFAULT, Windows selects the default upper-left Y coordinate
Child	Y coordinate of the upper-left corner of the window in the client area of its parent window

nWidth (int) using device units, defines the width of the window.

Window Type	Description
Overlapped	Either the window's width in screen coordinates or CW_USEDEFAULT. If the latter, Windows selects the width and height for the window

nHeight (int), using device units, defines the height of the window.

Window Type	Description
Overlapped	Either the window's height in screen coordinates or CW_USEDEFAULT. If the latter, Windows ignores *nHeight*

hWndParent (HWND) specifies the parent window for the window that is about to be created. Overlapped windows must not have a parent (*hWndParent* must be NULL). A valid parent handle must be passed when creating a child window.

hMenu (HMENU), depending on the window's style, specifies a menu or a child-window identifier.

Window Type	Description
Overlapped or Pop-Up	Identifies the menu to be used with the window. A NULL value specifies the use of the class menu
Child	Contains a child-window identifier. This is determined by the application and is to be unique for all child windows of the same parent

hInstance (HANDLE) specifies the instance of the module to be identified with the window.

lpParam (LPSTR) is a pointer to the value passed to the window through the *lParam* parameter of the WM_CREATE message.

Value Returned

Either a valid new window identifier, if successful, or a NULL.

Notes

See Tables 2 through 9 in Chapter 4 for alphabetical listings of window control classes, window styles, and control styles.

HWND CreateWindowEX(dwExStyle,lpClassName, lpWindowName,dwStyle,x,y,nWidth,nHeight, hWndParent,hMenu,hInstance,lpParam) [3.0 and later]

Function

Creates an overlapped, pop-up, or child window with an extended style. Otherwise, the function is identical to the CreateWindow function.

Parameters

dwExStyle (DWORD) defines the extended style of the window being created. Can be set to WS_EXDLGMODALFRAME; this causes the window to be drawn with a modal dialog frame.

lpClassName (LPSTR) points to a null-terminated character string naming the window's class.

lpWindowName (LPSTR) points to a null-terminated character string identifying the window by name.

dwStyle (DWORD) specifies the style of window being created.

x (int) defines the initial X coordinate position for the window.

Window Type	Description
Overlapped or Pop-Up	X coordinate of the window's upper-left corner in screen coordinates. If the value is CW_USEDEFAULT, Windows selects the default upper-left X coordinate
Child	X coordinate of the upper-left corner of the window in the client area of its parent window

y (int) defines the initial Y coordinate position for the window.

Window Type	Description
Overlapped or Pop-Up	Y coordinate of the window's upper-left corner in screen coordinates. If the value is CW_USEDEFAULT, Windows selects the default upper-left Y coordinate
Child	Y coordinate of the upper-left corner of the window in the client area of its parent window

nWidth (int), using device units, defines the width of the window.

Window Type	Description
Overlapped	Either the window's width in screen coordinates or CW_USEDEFAULT. If the latter, Windows selects the width and height for the window

nHeight (int), using device units, defines the height of the window.

Window Type	Description
Overlapped	Either the window's height in screen coordinates or CW_USEDEFAULT. If the latter, Windows ignores *nHeight*

hWndParent (HWND) specifies the parent window for the window that is about to be created. Overlapped windows must not have a parent (*hWnd-Parent* must be NULL). A valid parent handle must be passed when creating a child window.

hMenu (HMENU), depending on the window's style, specifies a menu or a child-window identifier.

Window Type	Description
Overlapped or Pop-Up	Identifies the menu to be used with the window. A NULL value specifies the use of the class menu
Child	Contains a child window identifier. This is determined by the application and is to be unique for all child windows of the same parent

hInstance (HANDLE) specifies the instance of the module to be identified with the window.

lpParam (LPSTR) is a pointer to the value passed to the window through the *lParam* parameter of the WM_CREATE message.

Value Returned

A valid new window identifier if successful; otherwise, returns a NULL.

Notes

See the CreateWindow function for window control classes, window styles, and control styles.

BOOL DeleteDC(hDC)

Function

Deletes the designated device context.

Parameters

hDC (HDC) identifies the device context.

Value Returned

For a successful delete, a non-zero value is returned; otherwise, the return value is zero.

Notes

If the device context to be deleted is the last device context for a given device, the device is notified with all subsequent system storage resources used by the device being released.

BOOL DeleteMenu(hMenu,nPosition,wFlags) [3.0 and later]

Function

Deletes an item from the menu.

Parameters

hMenu (HMENU) specifies the menu to be changed.

nPosition (WORD) defines the menu item to be deleted.

wFlags (WORD) defines how the *nPosition* parameter is to be interpreted. The default is MF_BYCOMMAND, but it can also be set to MF_BYPOSITION.

Value Returned

TRUE if the function is successful, FALSE otherwise.

Notes

MF_POSITION specifies the position of the menu item, with the first item being numbered 0. However, if MF_BYCOMMAND is specified, *nPosition* specifies the ID of the existing menu item.

BOOL DeleteObject(hObject)

Function

Deletes a logical font, pen, brush, bitmap, or region from memory.

Parameters

hObject (HANDLE) represents a handle to the object (font, pen, brush, bitmap, or region).

Value Returned

A successful delete returns a non-zero value; otherwise, a zero is returned indicating that the handle was not valid.

Notes

To delete an object selected into a device context, the device context must be deleted first, followed by the deletion of the object itself.

BOOL DestroyMenu(hMenu)

Function

Destroys and frees any system memory associated with the menu pointed to by *hMenu*.

Parameters

hMenu (HMENU) defines the menu to be deleted.

Value Returned

A non-zero value is returned for a successful menu deletion; otherwise, a NULL is returned.

BOOL DestroyWindow(hWnd)

Function

Destroys the designated window. This complicated process of destroying a window involves possibly hiding or permanently closing the window. Also, messages are sent to the window to deactivate it or remove its input focus. Destroying the window additionally involves sending a message to flush the associated message queue. Messages sent include WM_DESTROY and WM_NCDESTROY.

Parameters

hWnd (HWND) indicates the window to be destroyed.

Value Returned

A non-zero value is returned for a successful menu deletion; otherwise a NULL is returned.

Notes

Should the parent window have any children, the associated child windows will be destroyed first, followed by the owning parent window.

DWORD DeviceCapabilities(lpDeviceName,lpPort,nIndex, lpOutput, lpDevMode)

Function

Retrieves the capabilities of the printer device driver.

Parameters

lpDeviceName (LPSTR) points to a null-terminated character string that contains the name of the printer device.

lpPort (LPSTR) points to a null-terminated character string that contains the name of the port to which the device is connected.

nIndex (WORD) defines the capabilities to query. It can be any one of the following values:

DC_FIELDS	Returns the *dmFields* of the printer driver's DEVMODE data structure
DC_PAPERS	Returns the list of supported paper sizes
DC_PAPERSIZE	Copies the dimensions of the supported paper sizes in tenths of a millimeter into an array of POINT structures
DC_MINEXTENT	Returns a POINT structure containing the minimum paper size that the *dmPaperLength* and *dmPaperWidth* fields of the device driver's DEVMODE data structure can specify
DC_MAXEXTENT	Returns a POINT structure containing the maximum paper size that the *dmPaperLength* and *dmPaperWidth* fields of the device driver's DEVMODE data structure can specify
DC_BINS	Returns the number of available bins
DC_BINNAMES	Copies a structure identical to that returned by the ENUMPAPERBINS escape
DC_DUPLEX	Retrieves the level of duplex supported
DC_SIZE	Retrieves the *dmSize* field of the printer driver's DEVMODE data structure
DC_EXTRA	Retrieves the number of bytes required for the device-specific portion of the DEVMODE data structure of the printer driver
DC_VERSION	Returns the version to which the driver conforms
DC_DRIVER	Retrieves the driver version number

lpOutput (LPSTR) points to an array of bytes.

lpDevMode (DEVMODE FAR *) is a pointer to a DEVMODE data structure.

Value Returned

Depends on the setting of the *nIndex* parameter.

int DialogBox(hInstance,lpTemplateName,hWndParent, lpDialogFunc)

Function

Creates a modal dialog box.

Parameters

hInstance (HANDLE) specifies the instance of the module whose executable file contains the dialog box template.

lpTemplateName (LPSTR) points to a null-terminated character string naming the dialog box template.

hWndParent (HWND) specifies the window that owns the dialog box.

lpDialogFunc (FARPROC) contains the current procedure-instance address of the dialog function. The callback function must use the Pascal calling convention and be declared FAR using the following form:

```
HWND FAR PASCAL DialogFunc(hWnd,wMsg,wParam,lParam)
HWND hwnd;     /* identifies the message receiving the
                  dialog box                        */
unsigned wMsg;/* indicates the message number */
WORD wParam;  /* specifies 16 bits of additional
                  message-dependent information */
DWORD lParam; /* specifies 32 bits of additional
                  message-dependent information */
```

Value Returned

Values returned by an application's dialog box are not processed by the application; instead they are processed by Windows. The return value is −1 if the function fails.

Notes

The size, style, and controls for the dialog box are referenced by the *lpTemplateName* parameter. Care should be taken since the DialogBox function first calls GetDC to obtain the display context. If the Windows display context cache has been filled by making calls to GetDC, DialogBox could accidentally access some other display context.

int DialogBoxIndirect(hInstance,hDTemplate, hWndParent,lpDialogFunc)

Function

Similar to the DialogBox function in that it will create a modal dialog box. However, instead of explicitly defining each parameter, the *hDTemplate* parameter points to a DLGTEMPLATE data structure containing the equivalent information.

Parameters

hInstance (HANDLE) specifies the instance of the module whose executable file contains the dialog box template.

hDTemplate (HANDLE) identifies a DLGTEMPLATE data structure.

hWndParent (HWND) specifies the window that owns the dialog box.

lpDialogFunc (FARPROC) contains the current procedure-instance address of the dialog function. The callback function must use the Pascal calling convention and be declared FAR using the following form:

```
HWND FAR PASCAL DialogFunc(hWnd,wMsg,wParam,lParam)
HWND hwnd;        /* identifies message receiving
                     dialog box              */
unsigned wMsg;  /* indicates the message number  */
WORD wParam;    /* specifies 16 bits of additional
                   message-dependent information */
DWORD lParam;   /* specifies 32 bits of additional
                   message-dependent information */
```

Value Returned

Values returned by an application's dialog box are not processed by the application; instead, they are processed by Windows. The return value is -1 if the function fails.

Notes

The size, style, and controls for the dialog box are referenced by the *lpTemplateName* parameter. Care should be taken since the DialogBox function first calls GetDC to obtain the display context. If the Windows display context cache has been filled by making calls to GetDC, DialogBox could accidentally access some other display context.

LONG DispatchMessage(lpMsg)

Function

Sends a message from the MSG data structure pointed to by *lpMsg*. The message is sent to the window function of the designated window.

Parameters

lpMsg (LPMSG) is an pointer to a MSG data structure. This structure contains message information from the Windows application queue.

Value Returned

The return value is determined by the window function. Generally, the returned value is not used; however, its meaning is dependent on the message that is actually being dispatched.

Notes

The MSG data structure must only contain valid message values.

BOOL DPtoLP(hDC,lpPoints,nCount)

Function

Will convert device points into logical points. The conversion that will be performed depends on the current mapping mode, along with the settings of the origins and extents for the selected device's window and viewport.

Parameters

hDC (HDC) specifies the device context.

lpPoints (LPPOINT) is a pointer to the array of POINTs.

nCount (short) defines the number of points in the POINT array.

Value Returned

A non-zero value is returned for a successful menu deletion; otherwise, a NULL is returned.

Notes

All of the points referenced in the POINTS array and pointed to by *lpPoints* will be mapped from the device coordinate system into the GDI's logical coordinate system.

BOOL DrawIcon(hDC,x,y,hIcon)

Function

Draws an icon on the selected device.

Parameters

hDC (HDC) represents the device context for a window.

x (int) defines the logical upper-left corner X coordinate of the icon.

y (int) defines the logical upper-left corner Y coordinate of the icon.

hIcon (HICON) specifies the icon to be drawn.

Value Returned

A non-zero value is returned for a successful menu deletion; otherwise, a NULL is returned.

Notes

Subject to the current mapping mode of the device context, the icon's upper-left corner will be placed at the location represented by the X and Y coordinates.

int DrawText(hDC,lpString,nCount,lpRect, wFormat)

Function

Draws formatted text within a rectangle. The text tabs are expanded as needed, as left, right, or center aligned, with each line of text broken as necessary to make certain that all lines fit within the defined area.

Parameters

hDC (HDC) specifies the device context.

lpString (LPSTR) is a pointer to the string to be drawn. However, if the *nCount* value is −1, the string pointed to must be null-terminated.

nCount (int) represents the number of bytes the string occupies. When *nCount* is −1, the DrawText function assumes *lpString* is null-terminated. Under these conditions the function automatically computes the character count.

lpRect (LPRECT) is a pointer to a RECT data structure containing the diagonal coordinates (logical units) for the rectangle the text must fit within.

wFormat (WORD) indicates the type of formatting to use. The values can be combined using the logical OR operation:

DrawText Formats	Description
DT_BOTTOM	Selects single-line, bottom-justified text
DT_CALCRECT	For single-line text the right side of the rectangle will be modified to contain the entire string. For multiple-line text the rectangle width remains as defined; however, the height of the rectangle is modified to accommodate the entire text. Both modes return the resulting height of the rectangle
DT_CENTER	Centers the text
DT_EXPANDTABS	Expands the tabs
DT_EXTERNALLEADING	Incorporates the font's external leading into the line height. Normally, this is not included
DT_LEFT	Aligns text flush left
DT_NOCLIP	Draws without clipping
DT_NOPREFIX	Ignores processing of prefix characters. When left on, the DrawText function uses the & character to indicate that the string should be underlined. && signals the printing of a single &
DT_RIGHT	Aligns text flush right
DT_SINGLELINE	Defines a single line, ignoring all carriage returns and linefeeds
DT_TABSTOP	Defines tab stops with the high byte of the *wFormat* parameter representing the number of characters for each tab stop
DT_TOP	Selects single-line top-justified text
DT_VCENTER	Selects vertically centered single-line text
DT_WORDBREAK	Activates word breaking. Allows text to be broken between lines to accommodate string length in respect to the rectangular perimeter

Value Returned

The returned value represents the height of the text.

Notes

DrawText uses the selected device context's font, text color, and background color for drawing the text. All formatting assumes multiple lines unless DT_SINGLELINE is specified.

BOOL Ellipse(hDC,x1,y1,x2,y2)

Function

Draws an ellipse.

Parameters

hDC (HDC) specifies the device context.

x1 (short) defines the upper-left corner X coordinate of the rectangle.

y1 (short) defines the upper-left corner Y coordinate of the bounding rectangle.

x2 (short) defines the lower-right corner X coordinate of the bounding rectangle.

y2 (short) defines the lower-right corner Y coordinate of the bounding rectangle.

Value Returned

A non-zero value indicates a successful ellipse creation; otherwise, a zero value indicates an unsuccessful attempt.

Notes

The width and height of the rectangle must not exceed 32,767 units.

BOOL
EnableMenuItem(hMenu,wIDEnableItem,wEnable)

Function

Enables, disables, or grays a menu item.

Parameters

hMenu (HMENU) identifies the menu.

wIDEnableItem (WORD) identifies the menu or pop-up menu item to be checked.

wEnable (WORD) specifies the action to take. The options can be logically ORed together:

Option	Description
MF_BYCOMMAND	Indicates that the *wIDEnableItem* parameter contains the menu item ID
MF_BYPOSITION	Indicates that the *wIDEnableItem* parameter contains the position of the menu item
MF-DISABLED	Disables the menu item
MF_ENABLED	Enables the menu item
MF_GRAYED	Grays the menu item

Value Returned

The returned value represents the previous state of the menu item.

Notes

The WM_SYSCOMMAND message can be used to enable or disable input to a menu bar.

void EndDialog(hDlg,nResult)

Function

Terminates a modal dialog box sending the result to the DialogBox function. However, the EndDialog function does not immediately terminate the dialog box. Initially, it sets the appropriate flag, which in turn directs the dialog box to terminate as soon as the dialog function is completed.

Parameters

hDlg (HWND) specifies the dialog box to be destroyed.

nResult (int) defines the value to be returned from the dialog box to the DialogBox function originally creating it.

Value Returned

None.

Notes

The dialog function can call the EndDialog function at any time.

void EndPaint(hWnd,lpPaint)

Function

Indicates that the painting for a given window is complete.

Parameters

hWnd (HWND) specifies the window that has been repainted.

lpPaint (LPPAINTSTRUCT) is a pointer to a PAINTSTRUCT containing the retrieved information given by the BeginPaint function call.

Value Returned

None.

Notes

A call to EndPaint must be made for each call to the BeginPaint function. While a call to BeginPaint can hide the caret, making a call to EndPaint will display the caret.

int FillRect(hDC,lpRect,hBrush)

Function

Using the specified brush, fills a rectangle.

Parameters

hDC (HDC) specifies the device context.

lpRect (LPRECT) is a pointer to a RECT structure containing the coordinates of the rectangle that will be filled with the specified brush.

hBrush (HBRUSH) selects the brush used to fill the rectangle.

Value Returned

The function returns an integer value that has no usage and is therefore ignored.

Notes

The rectangle cannot be filled unless a brush has been previously created by calling CreateSolidBrush, CreatePatternBrush, or CreateHatchBrush. The filled rectangle is brushed up to and including the upper border and left border. The bottom border and right border are left unpainted.

BOOL FillRgn(hDC,hRgn,hBrush)

Function

Paints a region using the selected brush pattern.

Parameters

hDC (HDC) specifies the device context.

hRgn (HRGN) marks the region to be filled using logical coordinates.

hBrush (HBRUSH) selects the brush to be used for filling the region.

Value Returned

A non-zero value indicates a successful outcome. A zero indicates an unsuccessful attempt.

BOOL FloodFill(hDC,x,y,rgbColor)

Function

Fills an area of the display surface bounded in the *rgbColor*. Painting begins at the X and Y coordinates specified.

Parameters

hDC (HDC) specifies the device context.

x (short) specifies the logical X coordinate of where the painting is to begin.

y (short) specifies the logical Y coordinate of where the painting is to begin.

rgbColor (DWORD) selects the RGB color value to be used to indicate the color of the border boundary.

Value Returned

A non-zero value means a successful fill; otherwise, a NULL is returned.

Notes

Not all device contexts support FloodFill.

int FrameRect(hDC,lpRect,hBrush)

Function

Using the specified brush, draws a border around the specified rectangle.

Parameters

hDC (HDC) specifies the device context.

lpRect (LPRECT) is a pointer to a RECT structure containing the coordinates of the rectangle that will be filled with the specified brush.

hBrush (HBRUSH) selects the brush used to fill the rectangle.

Value Returned

The function returns an integer value that has no usage and is therefore ignored.

Notes

The rectangle cannot be filled unless a brush has been previously created by calling CreateSolidBrush, CreatePatternBrush, or CreateHatchBrush. The frame border is always drawn one logical unit in width and height.

BOOL FrameRgn(hDC,hRgn,hBrush,nWidth,nHeight)

Function

Draws a border around the specified region using the selected brush, with the defined width and height.

Parameters

hDC (HDC) specifies the device context.

hRgn (HRGN) specifies the region to be enclosed with a border.

hBrush (HBRUSH) selects the brush used to fill the rectangle.

nWidth (short), using logical units, expresses the width of the border to be drawn in vertical brush strokes.

nHeight (short), using logical units, expresses the height of the border to be drawn in horizontal brush strokes.

Value Returned

A non-zero value indicates a successful attempt; otherwise, a zero is returned.

void FreeProcInstance(lpProc)

Function

Frees the specified function from the data segment in which it was bound.

Parameters

lpProc (FARPROC) is the procedure-instance address of the function about to be freed.

Value Returned

None.

Notes

lpProc must point to a function that was previously created using the MakeProcInstance function. An unrecoverable error condition can occur if an attempt is made to call the function after it has been freed.

long GetBitmapBits(hBitmap,dwCount,lpBits)

Function

Copies the specified bitmap into the buffer pointed to by *lpBits*.

Parameters

hBitmap (HBITMAP) specifies the bitmap to be copied.

dwCount (long) indicates the number of bytes to be copied.

lpBits (LPSTR) is a pointer to the buffer that is about to receive the bitmap array of short integers' copy.

Value Returned

The returned value indicates the actual number of bytes in the bitmap itself. A zero value indicates an error has occurred.

Notes

By calling the function GetObject, an accurate *dwCount* value can be obtained.

DWORD GetBitmapDimension(hBitmap)

Function

Returns the width and height of the specified bitmap.

Parameters

hBitmap (HBITMAP) specifies the bitmap.

Value Returned

Indicates the width and height of the bitmap as measured in tenths of a millimeter, with the high-order word representing the height and the low-order word indicating the width. If a previous call was not made to the SetBitmapDimension function, a zero value is returned.

Notes

The function assumes that a previous function call to SetBitmapDimension has been made.

DWORD GetBkColor(hDC)

Function

Returns the current background color of the specified device.

Parameters

hDC (HDC) specifies the device context.

Value Returned

Indicates the current RGB background color value.

short GetBkMode(hDC)

Function

Returns the background mode for the specified device.

Parameters

hDC (HDC) specifies the device context.

Value Returned

Indicates the current background mode (TRANSPARENT or OPAQUE).

Notes

The background mode is important because it is used with text, hatched brushes, and non-solid pen styles.

DWORD GetBrushOrg(hDC)

Function

Returns the current brush origin for the specified device context.

Parameters

hDC (HDC) specifies the device context.

Value Returned

Returns the origin of the current brush with the high-order word indicating the device unit's Y coordinate and the low-order word indicating the device unit's X coordinate.

Notes

The initial brush origin is always set at 0,0.

BOOL
GetCharWidth(hDC,wFirstChar,wLastChar,lpBuffer)

Function

Using the current font, returns the widths of individual characters in consecutive groups of characters.

Parameters

hDC (HDC) specifies the device context.

wFirstChar (WORD) using the current font, specifies the first character in a consecutive group of characters.

wLastChar (WORD) using the current font, specifies the last character in a consecutive group of characters.

lpBuffer (LPINT) is a pointer to the buffer that will receive the width of each character in a group of characters.

Value Returned

A non-zero value indicates a successful function call; otherwise, zero is returned.

Notes

Any character not defined for the current font will be given a default character width, which is usually based on a blank space character.

void GetClientRect(hWnd,lpRect)

Function

Copies the coordinates of a window's client area into the *lpRect* data structure.

Parameters

hWnd (HWND) specifies the window associated with the client area.

lpRect (LPRECT) is a pointer to a RECT structure.

Value Returned

None.

Notes

The returned coordinates represent the upper-left and lower-right corners of the client area. Client coordinates are relative to the window's upper-left corner, 0,0.

DWORD GetCurrentPosition(hDC)

Function

Retrieves the logical coordinates of the current position.

Parameters

hDC (HDC) specifies the device context.

Value Returned

Represents the current position, with the high-order word containing the Y coordinate and the low-order word containing the X coordinate.

DWORD GetCurrentTime( )

Function

Returns the current Windows time.

Parameters

No parameters are used.

Value Returned

The value returned indicates the current time in milliseconds.

void GetCursorPos(lpPoint)

Function

Returns the current cursor position using screen coordinates.

Parameters

lpPoint (LPPOINT) is a pointer to a POINT data structure receiving the cursor's screen coordinates.

Value Returned

None.

Notes

The current mapping mode of the window containing the cursor has no effect on the screen coordinates returned.

HDC GetDC(hWnd)

Function

Returns a handle to a display context for the client area of the specified window.

Parameters

hWnd (HWND) specifies the window whose display context is to be returned.

Value Returned

· Indicates the display context if it is a non-zero value. An unsuccessful call returns a NULL.

Notes

The returned value can be used for subsequent GDI function calls that draw in the client area.

LONG GetDCOrg(hDC)

Function

Returns the translation origin for the specified device context.

Parameters

hDC (HDC) specifies the device context.

Value Returned

Contains the final device coordinate translation origin, with the high-order word containing the Y coordinate and the low-order word containing the X coordinate.

Notes

The returned coordinates represent the offset used by Windows to translate device coordinates into client coordinates for any points in an application's window. This is relative to the physical origin of the display screen.

short GetDeviceCaps(hDC,nIndex)

Function

Returns device-specific information about the specified display device.

Parameters

hDC (HDC) specifies the device context.

nIndex (short) identifies the item to return.

Value Returned

Defines the value of the desired item.

Notes

nIndex defines the type of information to be returned as defined in Table A-1.

HWND GetDlgItem(hDlg,nIDDlgItem)

Function

Returns the handle of the control contained in the specified dialog box.

Parameters

hDlg (HWND) specifies the dialog box that contains the control.

nIDDlgItem (int) represents the integer ID of the item being retrieved.

Value Returned

Indicates the given control. If no control exists, as specified by *nIDDlgItem*, a NULL is returned.

Notes

The function can also be used with any parent-child window pair, not just dialog boxes.

unsigned GetDlgItemInt(hDlg,nIDDlgItem,lpTranslated,bSigned)

Function

Translates the text of a control of the specified dialog box (or parent-child window pair) into an integer value.

Table A-1.   Possible Values for *nIndex*

Index	Description
ASPECTX	Used for line drawing; represents the relative width of a device pixel
ASPECTY	Used for line drawing; represents the relative height of a device pixel
BITSPIXEL	Represents the number of adjacent color bits for each pixel
CLIPCAPS	A flag that indicates the device's clipping abilities. If 1, the device is capable of clipping to a rectangle; otherwise, it is 0
CURVECAPS	Bitmask representing the device's curve capabilities using the following definitions:

Bit Position	Definition
0	Device capable of circles
1	Device capable of pie wedges
2	Device capable of chord arcs
3	Device capable of ellipses
4	Device capable of wide borders
5	Device capable of styled borders
6	Device capable of borders that are wide and styled
7	Device capable of interiors

(**Note:** The high byte is 0.)

Index	Description
DRIVERVERSION	Returns the Version Number (100H)
HORZSIZE	Specifies the width of the physical display in millimeters
LINECAPS	Bitmask representing the device's line capabilities using the following definitions:

Bit Position	Definition
0	Reserved
1	Device capable of polyline
2	Reserved
3	Reserved
4	Device capable of wide lines
5	Device capable of styled lines
6	Device capable of lines that are wide and styled
7	Device capable of interiors

(**Note:** The high byte is 0.)

Table A-1.   Possible Values for *nIndex* (*continued*)

Index	Description
LOGPIXELSX	Specifies the number of pixels per logical inch along the display's width
LOGPIXELSY	Specifies the number of pixels per logical inch along the display's height
NUMBRUSHES	Specifies the number of device-specific brushes
NUMCOLORS	Specifies the number of entries in the device's color table
NUMFONTS	Specifies the number of device-specific fonts
NUMPENS	Specifies the number of device-specific pens
PDEVICESIZE	Specifies the size of the PDEVICE data structure
PLANES	Specifies the number of color planes
POLYGONALCAPS	Bitmask representing the device's polygonal capabilities using the following definitions:

Bit Position	Definition
0	Device capable of alternate fill polygons
1	Device capable of rectangles
2	Device capable of winding number fill polygons
3	Device capable of scanlines
4	Device capable of wide borders
5	Device capable of styled lines
6	Device capable of lines that are wide and styled
7	Device capable of interiors

(**Note:** The high byte is 0.)

RASTERCAPS	Value indicating the raster capabilities of the device using the following definitions:

Capability	Definition
RC_BANDING	Requires banding support
RC_BITBLT	Device capable of transferring bitmaps
RC_BITMAP64	Device capable of supporting bitmaps larger than 64K
RC_GDI20_OUTPUT	Device capable of supporting Windows 3.0 features
RC_SCALING	Device capable of scaling

Table A-1. Possible Values for *nIndex* (*continued*)

Index	Description
TECHNOLOGY	Specifies device technology using the following definitions:

Values	Definitions
0	Vector plotting device
1	Raster display device
2	Raster printer device
3	Raster camera device
4	Character stream (PLP) device
5	Metafile (VDM) device
6	Display file device

Index	Description
TEXTCAPS	Bitmap representing the device's text capabilities using the following definitions:

Bit Position	Definition
0	Device capable of character output precision
1	Device capable of stroked output precision
2	Device capable of stroke clip precision
3	Device capable of 90-degree character rotation
4	Device capable of character rotation
5	Device capable of scaling independent of X and Y
6	Device capable of doubled character scaling
7	Device capable of integer multiples for scaling
8	Device capable of multiples for exact scaling
9	Device capable of double-weight characters
10	Device capable of italicizing
11	Device capable of underlining
12	Device capable of strikeouts
13	Device capable of raster fonts
14	Device capable of vector fonts
15	Reserved; *must* be returned zero

Index	Description
VERTRES	Specifies the height of the display in raster lines
VERTSIZE	Specifies the height of the physical display in millimeters

Parameters

hDlg (HWND) specifies the dialog box that contains the control.

nIDDlgItem (int) represents the integer ID of the item being translated.

lpTranslated (BOOL FAR *) is a pointer to a Boolean variable receiving the translated flag.

bSigned (BOOL) identifies whether the retrieved value is signed.

Value Returned

Represents the translated value of the dialog box item text.

Notes

The function translates numeric characters into their equivalent signed or unsigned value. Translation skips over leading blanks and continues until either the end of the string is reached or a non-numeric character is encountered.

   If a minus sign is encountered, the value returned is a signed number; otherwise, it is unsigned. A value greater than 32,767 (signed) is returned as a zero. The same is true for an unsigned value greater than 65,635. The function sends a WM_GETTEXT message to the control.

int
GetDlgItemText(hDlg,nIDDlgItem,lpString,nMaxCount)

Function

Retrieves the text associated with the specified control into a string, returning the number of characters copied.

Parameters

hDlg (HWND) specifies the dialog box that contains the control.

nIDDlgItem (int) represents the integer ID of the item being translated.

lpString (LPSTR) is a pointer to the buffer receiving the copied text.

nMaxCount (int) represents the maximum number of characters (in bytes) to be copied to *lpString*. A string longer than the value specified will automatically be truncated.

Value Returned

Returns the actual number of characters copied. A zero value indicates no text was copied.

short GetMapMode(hDC)

Function

Returns the current mapping mode.

Parameters

hDC (HDC) specifies the device context.

Value Returned

Represents the current mapping mode.

BOOL GetMessage(lpMsg,hWnd,wMsgFilterMin, wMsgFilterMax)

Function

The function takes a message from the application's message queue and places it in the MSG data structure. Control is yielded if no messages are available.

Parameters

lpMsg (LPMSG) is a pointer to a MSG structure containing message information supplied by the Windows application queue.

hWnd (HWND) specifies the window whose messages are to be retrieved. If the parameter is NULL, the function will retrieve any message for the window that belongs to the calling application.

wMsgFilterMin (unsigned) is an integer value indicating the lowest message to be examined.

wMsgFilterMax (unsigned) is an integer value indicating the highest message to be examined.

Value Returned

A non-zero value indicates some message other than WM_QUIT was retrieved. A zero value indicates that the message retrieved was WM_QUIT.

Notes

Using the WM_KEYFIRST and WM_KEYLAST constants will retrieve only keyboard input-related messages. The WM_MOUSEFIRST and WM_MOUSELAST constants can filter out and retrieve only those mouse-related messages.

DWORD GetMessagePos( )

Function

Returns the screen coordinate mouse position after the last message was obtained by a call to GetMessage.

Parameters

The function has no parameters.

Value Returned

The low-order word contains the X coordinate, the high-order word the Y coordinate.

Notes

By making a call to the GetCursorPos function instead of GetMessagePos, an application can obtain the current position of the mouse instead of the time the last message occurred.

long GetMessageTime( )

Function

Returns the time of the last message retrieved by a call to the GetMessage function.

Parameters

The function has no parameters.

Value Returned

Represents the message time.

Notes

The returned value is a long integer expressing the elapsed time in milliseconds from the time the system was booted to the time the message was put into the application's message queue. By subtracting the time of a subsequent message from a previous message, an application can determine the delay time between messages. Care should be taken, however, as the count does not always increase. When the maximum value is reached for a long integer, the count will recycle to zero and begin again.

DWORD GetNearestColor(hDC,rgbColor)

Function

Returns the closest physical color to a specified logical color that the requested device can represent.

Parameters

hDC (HDC) specifies the device context.

rgbColor (DWORD) identifies an RGB color value specifying the color to be matched.

Value Returned

Represents the solid RGB color closest to the *rgbColor* request that the device is capable of producing.

DWORD GetNearestPaletteIndex(hPalette,rgbColor) [3.0 and later]

Function

Returns the index specifier of the entry in the logical palette that most closely matches an RGB color value.

Parameters

hPalette (HPALETTE) specifies the logical palette.

rgbColor (DWORD) identifies an RGB color value that specifies the color to be matched.

Value Returned

The logical-palette index that most nearly matches the RGB value.

short GetObject(hObject,nCount,lpObject)

Function

Assigns the logical data information defining a logical object to the buffer pointed to by *lpObject*.

Parameters

hObject (HANDLE) specifies a logical font, pen, brush, or bitmap.

nCount (short) represents the number of bytes to be copied to the buffer.

lpObject (LPSTR) is a pointer to a LOGFONT, LOGPEN, LOGBRUSH, or LOGBITMAP data structure that will receive the logical object information.

Value Returned

Specifies the number of bytes actually retrieved. If NULL, some error condition has occurred.

Notes

If the logical information being retrieved involves a bitmap, the function will only return the width, height, and color format bitmap information. To retrieve the actual bitmap, a call must be made to GetBitmapBits.

WORD GetPaletteEntries(hPalette,wStartIndex, wNumEntries,lpBuffer)

Function

Copies the RGB color values and flags contained in a range of entries in a logical palette to a buffer.

Parameters

hPalette (HPALETTE) specifies the logical palette.

wStartIndex (WORD) defines the first entry in the logical palette to be copied.

wNumEntries (WORD) defines the number of entries in the logical palette to be copied.

lpBuffer (LPSTR) is a pointer to a buffer to receive the palette entries.

Value Returned

The number of entries copied. It is zero if the function failed.

DWORD GetPixel(hDC,x,y,)

Function

The RGB color value of the point specified by *x* and *y* and within the clipping region is returned.

Parameters

hDC (HDC) specifies the device context.

x (short) defines the logical upper-left corner X coordinate of the point to be inspected.

y (short) defines the logical upper-left corner Y coordinate of the point to be inspected.

Value Returned

Contains the RGB color value of the point referenced. A -1 value indicates the point was not within the clipping region.

Notes

Not all device contexts support this function.

short GetPolyFillMode(hDC)

Function

Returns the current polygon filling mode (ALTERNATE or WINDING).

Parameters

hDC (HDC) specifies the device context.

Value Returned

ALTERNATE, for alternate polygon filling mode, or WINDING, for winding polygon filling mode.

short GetROP2(hDC)

Function

Returns the current drawing mode.

Parameters

hDC (HDC) specifies the device context.

Value Returned

Specifies the previous drawing mode.

Notes

The current drawing mode determines how the selected pen or interior color will be combined with the color already on the display.

int GetScrollPos(hWnd,nBar)

Function

Returns the current position of the specified scroll bar thumb.

Parameters

hWnd (HWND) identifies the window containing the standard scroll bar.

nBar (int) identifies the scroll bar to examine using one of the following values:

Value	Definition
SB_CTL	Returns the position of a scroll bar control, assuming that *hWnd* points to a window handle of a scroll bar control
SB_HORZ	Returns the position of a window's horizontal scroll bar
SB_VERT	Returns the position of a window's vertical scroll bar

Value Returned

Identifies the current position of the scroll bar thumb.

Notes

The returned value is a relative value depending on the current scrolling range. For example, a range of 0 to 50 would yield a mid-position value of 25.

void GetScrollRange(hWnd,nBar,lpMinPos,lpMaxPos)

Function

Returns the current minimum and maximum scroll bar positions for the defined scroll bar.

Parameters

hWnd (HWND) specifies the window that has a standard scroll bar or scroll bar control.

nBar (int) identifies the scroll bar to examine using one of the following values:

Value	Definition
SB_CTL	Returns the position of a scroll bar control, assuming that *hWnd* points to a window handle of a scroll bar control
SB_HORZ	Returns the position of a window's horizontal scroll bar
SB_VERT	Returns the position of a window's vertical scroll bar

lpMinPos (LPINT) is a pointer to an integer variable that will receive the scroll bar's minimum position value.

lpMaxPos (LPINT) is a pointer to an integer variable that will receive the scroll bar's maximum position value.

Value Returned

None.

Notes

The default range for a standard scroll bar is 0 to 100.

HANDLE GetStockObject(nIndex)

Function

Returns the handle to a predefined stock font, pen, or brush.

Parameters

nIndex (short) identifies the type of stock object to be returned.

Value	Definition
BLACK_BRUSH	Black brush
DKGRAY_BRUSH	Dark gray brush
GRAY_BRUSH	Gray brush
HOLLOW_BRUSH	Hollow brush
LTGRAY_BRUSH	Light gray brush
NULL_BRUSH	Null brush
WHITE_BRUSH	White brush
BLACK_PEN	Black pen
NULL_PEN	Null pen
WHITE_PEN	White pen
ANSI_FIXED_FONT	ANSI fixed system font
ANSI_VAR_FONT	ANSI proportional system font
DEVICE_DEFAULT_FONT	Device-dependent font
OEM_FIXED_FONT	OEM-supplied fixed font
SYSTEM_FONT	System-dependent fixed font

Value Returned

Identifies the selected logical object, or a NULL if the function call was unsuccessful.

Notes

DKGRAY_BRUSH, GRAY_BRUSH, and LTGRAY_BRUSH objects should not be used as background brushes for any window not using CS_HREDRAW and CS_VREDRAW styles. This can lead to misalignment of brush patterns when the window is sized or moved.

short GetStretchBltMode(hDC)

Function

Returns the current stretching mode.

Parameters

hDC (HDC) specifies the device context.

Value Returned

Can be WHITEONBLACK, BLACKONWHITE, or COLORONCOLOR.

Notes

Used in conjunction with StretchBlt, the stretching mode indicates how information is to be added or removed from bitmaps that are either compressed or stretched when drawn.

DWORD GetSysColor(nIndex)

Function

Returns the color value of the specified display object.

Parameters

nIndex (int) indicates the display object whose color is to be returned.

Value Returned

Represents the RGB color value of the selected object.

Notes

Monochrome displays usually interpret various colors as shades of gray.

int GetSystemMetrics(nIndex)

Function

Returns the system's metrics. The measurements represent the widths and heights of various display elements.

Parameters

nIndex (int) identifies the system measurement that is to be retrieved. (See Table A-2.)

Value Returned

Indicates the specified system metric.

Table A-2.   Possible System Metric Indexes

Index	Description
SM_CXSCREEN	Screen width
SM_CYSCREEN	Screen height
SM_CXFRAME	Width of sizeable window frame
SM_CXVSCROLL	Width of arrow bitmap on vertical scroll bar
SM_CYVSCROLL	Height of arrow bitmap on vertical scroll bar
SM_CXHSCROLL	Width of arrow bitmap on horizontal scroll bar
SM_CYHSCROLL	Height of arrow bitmap on horizontal scroll bar
SM_CYCAPTION	Height of caption
SM_CXBORDER	Width of non-sizeable window frame
SM_CYBORDER	Height of non-sizeable window frame
SM_CXDLGFRAME	Width of WS_DLGFRAME styled window
SM_CYDLGFRAME	Height of WS_DLGFRAME styled window
SM_CXHTHUMB	Width of horizontal scroll bar thumb
SM_CYVTHUMB	Height of horizontal scroll bar thumb
SM_CXICON	Icon width
SM_CYICON	Icon height
SM_CXCURSOR	Cursor width
SM_CYCURSOR	Cursor height
SM_CYMENU	Single-line menu bar height
SM_CXFULLSCREEN	Full-screen client area window width
SM_CYFULLSCREEN	Full-screen client area window height
SM_CYKANJIWINDOW	Kanji window height
SM_CXMINTRACK	Minimum window tracking width
SM_CYMINTRACK	Minimum window tracking height
SM_CXMIN	Window minimum width
SM_CYMIN	Window minimum height
SM_CXSIZE	Title bar bitmap width
SM_CYSIZE	Title bar bitmap height
SM_MOUSEPRESENT	Non-zero when mouse hardware is installed
SM_DEBUG	Non-zero for a Windows debugging version
SM_SWAPBUTTON	Non-zero when the left and right mouse buttons are swapped

Notes

The function can also indicate whether the Windows version being used is capable of debugging, if a mouse is present, and if so, if the left and right buttons have been swapped.

WORD GetTextAlign(hDC)

Function

Returns the status of the text-alignment flag.

Parameters

hDC (HDC) specifies the device context.

Value Returned

The returned value can be one or a combination of the following:

TA_BASELINE	Selects alignment along the X axis and the baseline of the selected font within the bounding rectangle
TA_BOTTOM	Selects alignment along the X axis and the bottom of the bounding rectangle
TA_CENTER	Selects alignment along the Y axis and the center of the bounding rectangle
TA_LEFT	Selects alignment along the Y axis and the left side of the bounding rectangle
TA_NOUPDATECP	Notes that the current position is not updated
TA_RIGHT	Selects alignment along the Y axis and the right side of the bounding rectangle
TA_TOP	Selects alignment along the X axis and the top of the bounding rectangle
TA_UPDATECP	Notes that the current position is updated

Notes

By using the logical AND operation, a particular flag's value can be checked. A zero value indicates that the flag was not set.

short GetTextCharExtra(hDC)

Function

Returns the current intercharacter spacing.

Parameters

hDC (HDC) specifies the device context.

Value Returned

Indicates the current intercharacter spacing.

Notes

The intercharacter spacing is defined in terms of logical units.

DWORD GetTextColor(hDC)

Function

Returns the current text color.

Parameters

hDC (HDC) specifies the device context.

Value Returned

Returns an RGB color value.

Notes

The returned color value indicates the color used for the foreground color of characters output by the call to the TextOut function.

DWORD GetTextExtent(hDC,lpString,nCount)

Function

Calculates the height and width of a line of text.

Parameters

hDC (HDC) specifies the device context.

lpString (LPSTR) is a pointer to a text string whose height and width are to be calculated.

nCount (short) indicates the number of characters in the text string.

Value Returned

Represents the height and width of the text string: the high-order word for the height, the low-order word for the width.

Notes

For those devices that use kerning for character placement, the sum of the extents of the individual characters may not equal the extent of the entire string.

short GetTextFace(hDC,nCount,lpFacename)

Function

Copies the typeface name of the desired font into a buffer.

Parameters

hDC (HDC) specifies the device context.

nCount (short) indicates the buffer size in bytes.

lpFacename (LPSTR) is a pointer to the buffer to receive the name of the typeface.

Value Returned

Either the number of bytes copied into the buffer, or a NULL for an unsuccessful attempt.

BOOL GetTextMetrics(hDC,lpMetrics)

Function

Places the metrics for the selected font into the TEXTMETRICS data structure pointed to by *lpMetrics*.

Parameters

hDC (HDC) specifies the device context.

lpMetrics (LPTEXTMETRIC) is a pointer to a TEXTMETRIC structure.

Value Returned

A non-zero value for a successful function call; otherwise NULL.

DWORD GetTickCount( )

Function

Returns the number of milliseconds that have elapsed since the system was started.

Parameters

The function has no parameters.

Value Returned

Indicates in milliseconds the amount of time that has elapsed since the system was started.

WORD GetVersion( )

Function

Returns the current Windows version number.

Parameters

The function has no parameters.

Value Returned

The high-order byte specifies the small revision number, for example, .01. The low-order byte identifies the large revision number, for example, 3.

DWORD GetViewportExt(hDC)

Function

Retrieves the X extent and Y extent of the selected device's context viewport.

Parameters

hDC (HDC) specifies the device context.

Value Returned

The X and Y extents are returned using device units. The high-order byte is used for the Y extent, and the low-order byte indicates the X extent.

DWORD GetViewportOrg(hDC)

Function

Returns the X coordinate and Y coordinate of the viewport origin associated with the specified context.

Parameters

hDC (HDC) specifies the device context.

Value Returned

Using device coordinates, the returned high-order byte contains the Y coordinate, and the low-order byte contains the X coordinate.

HDC GetWindowDC(hWnd)

Function

Returns the window's display context.

Parameters

hWnd (HWND) identifies the window to be used in determining the display context.

Value Returned

Either contains the display context for the specified window or, if unsuccessful, returns a NULL.

Notes

Display contexts are very important because they allow painting anywhere in a window. The painting includes title bars, menus, and scroll bars. The origin of the context is always the upper-left corner of the window, not the client area. Once painting beyond the client area is complete (which is not recommended), a call to *ReleaseDC* must be made releasing the display context.

BOOL GrayString(hDC,hBrush,lpOutputFunc,lpData, nCount,x,y,nWidth,nHeight)

Function

Draws grayed text at the X,Y coordinates specified.

Parameters

hDC (HDC) specifies the device context.

hBrush (HBRUSH) specifies the brush to be used for the graying.

lpOutputFunc (FARPROC) is the procedure-instance address of the application-dependent function that will actually draw the string. A NULL pointer indicates a call to the TextOut function.

lpData (DWORD) is a long pointer to the data to be passed to the output function. When NULL, *lpData* must contain a long pointer to a string.

nCount (int) defines the number of characters to be output. When zero, the function calculates the length of the string. When *nCount* contains −1 and the *lpOutputFunc* pointed to returns a zero value, *GrayString* will display the image without graying it.

x (int) indicates the logical X coordinate of the starting position of the rectangle enclosing the string.

y (int) indicates the logical Y coordinate of the starting position of the rectangle enclosing the string.

nWidth (int) is the logical unit width of the rectangle enclosing the string. When zero, the function calculates the width of the area and assumes that *lpData* points to a string.

nHeight (int) is the logical unit height of the rectangle enclosing the string. When zero, the function calculates the height of the area and assumes that *lpData* points to a string.

Value Returned

A non-zero value indicates a successful function call. A returned value of zero can mean one of two things: there was insufficient memory for creating the grayed bitmap, or either TextOut or the application-dependent output function returned a zero.

Notes

The callback function must use the Pascal calling convention and be de-clared FAR, using the following form:

```
BOOL FAR PASCAL OutputFunc(hDC,lpData,nCount)
HDC hDC;        /* identifies the memory device
                   context containing a bitmap
                   of nWidth and nHeight        */
DWORD lpData;  /* pointer to the character
                   string to be drawn           */
int nCount;    /* specifies the number of
                   characters to output          */
```

Note: The output function must draw the image relative to the 0,0 coordi-nates instead of the X,Y coordinates.

BYTE HIBYTE(nInteger)

Function

Returns the high-order byte of the integer specified.

Parameters

nInteger (int) indicates the integer value to be translated.

Value Returned

The high-order byte of the specified integer value.

BOOL HiliteMenuItem(hWnd,hMenu,wIDHiliteItem,wHilite)

Function

Emphasizes or de-emphasizes a top-level menu-bar item using highlighting.

Parameters

hWnd (HWND) specifies the window containing the menu.

hMenu (HMENU) specifies the top-level menu-bar item to be highlighted or unhighlighted.

wIDHiliteItem (WORD) is an integer value picking one of the menu items or indicating the offset of the menu item to be altered.

wHilite (WORD) can be one or a combination of the following:

MF _ BYCOMMAND	Causes *wIDHiliteItem* to be interpreted as the menu item ID. This is the default option
MF _ BYPOSITION	Causes *wIDHiliteItem* to be interpreted as a menu item offset
MF _ HILITE	Causes the selected item to be highlighted. If omitted, the item is de-emphasized
MF _ UNHILITE	De-emphasizes the selected item by removing the highlighting

Value Returned

A non-zero value indicates highlighting. A zero value indicates no highlighting.

Notes

MF _ HILITE and MF _ UNHILITE cannot be used with ChangeMenu.

WORD HIWORD(lInteger)

Function

Returns the high-order word from the long integer value passed.

Parameters

lInteger (long) identifies the long integer value to be translated.

Value Returned

Contains the high-order word of the specified long integer.

void InflateRect(lpRect,x,y)

Function

Enlarges or shrinks the height and width of the rectangle pointed to.

Parameters

lpRect (LPRECT) is a pointer to a RECT structure about to be modified.

x (int) defines the amount to enlarge or shrink the rectangle's width. Negative values shrink the width.

y (int) defines the amount to enlarge or shrink the rectangle's height. Negative values shrink the height.

Value Returned

None.

Notes

The coordinates of the rectangle must not be greater than 32,767 or less than $-32,768$ units.

BOOL InsertMenu(hMenu,nPosition,wFlags, wIDNewItem,lpNewItem) [3.0 and later]

Function

Inserts a new item at the position specified, moving other items down.

Parameters

hMenu (HMENU) specifies the menu to be changed.

nPosition (WORD) specifies the menu item ID if *wFlags* is set to MB_BY-COMMAND. If *wFlags* is set to MB_BYPOSITION, this parameter identifies the position of the existing menu item. The first item is numbered 0. A -1 value causes the new item to be inserted at the end of the list.

wFlags (WORD) defines how *nPosition* is to be interpreted.

wIDNewItem (WORD) defines either the command ID or the menu handle of the pop-up menu.

lpNewItem (LPSTR) defines the content of the new menu item.

Value Returned

TRUE if the function was successful, FALSE otherwise.

Notes

Whenever the menu changes, the application should call DrawMenuBar.

void InvalidateRect(hWnd,lpRect,bErase)

Function

Invalidates the client area within the specified rectangle by adding the rectangle to the window's update region.

Parameters

hWnd (HWND) specifies the window whose update region is about to be modified by the specified rectangle.

lpRect (LPRECT) is a pointer to a RECT structure containing coordinates of the rectangle to be used for adding to the update region. A NULL value will cause the entire client area to be added to the update region.

bErase (BOOL) indicates whether the background in the update region will be erased.

Value Returned

None.

Notes

If the update region is not empty and there are no other application queue messages for that window, Windows will send a WM_PAINT message.

void InvalidateRgn(hWnd,hRgn,bErase)

Function

Adds the current update region of the specified window to the given region in the client area, thereby invalidating it.

Parameters

hWnd (HWND) specifies the window whose update region is about to be changed.

hRgn (HRGN) specifies the region (in client area coordinates) that is to be added to the update region.

bErase (BOOL) defines whether the background within the update region is to be erased. A non-zero value erases the background. When it is zero, the background remains unchanged.

Value Returned

None.

Notes

When the update region is not empty and there are no application queue messages pending, Windows sends a WM_PAINT message.

void InvertRect(hDC,lpRect)

Function

Inverts the contents of the specified rectangle.

Parameters

hDC (HDC) specifies the device context.

lpRect (LPRECT) is a pointer to a RECT structure containing the logical coordinates of the rectangle to be inverted.

Value Returned

None.

Notes

On color monitors the color inversion depends on how colors are generated for the display. Monochrome monitors invert the image by making white pixels black and black pixels white. Two calls to the function will restore the original colors of the rectangle. A non-zero value indicates a successful inversion, zero unsuccessful.

BOOL InvertRgn(hDC,hRgn)

Function

Inverts the contents of the specified region.

Parameters

hDC (HDC) specifies the device context.

lpRgn (HRGN) contains the logical coordinates of the region to be inverted.

Value Returned

None.

Notes

On color monitors the color inversion depends on how colors are generated for the display. Monochrome monitors invert the image by making white pixels black and black pixels white. Two calls to the function will restore the original colors of the region. A non-zero value indicates a successful inversion, zero unsuccessful.

BOOL IsZoomed(hWnd)

Function

Identifies whether the specified window was maximized.

Parameters

hWnd (HWND) specifies the window.

Value Returned

A non-zero value indicates the window has been maximized. A zero value indicates that the window is either being displayed as an icon or is normal.

BOOL KillTimer(hWnd,nIDEvent)

Function

Kills the event timer with any pending WM_TIMER messages being removed from the associated message queue.

Parameters

hWnd (HWND) specifies the window linked to the specified timer event.

nIDEvent (short) identifies the timer event to be killed.

Value Returned

If the event was killed, the function returns a non-zero value. If the defined timer event cannot be located, the function returns a NULL.

Notes

The *nIDEvent* must be a valid identifier returned by a call to the function SetTimer.

void LineDDA(x1,y1,x2,y2,lpLineFunc,lpData)

Function

Calculates all of the points in a line defined by the X and Y coordinates.

Parameters

x1 (short) identifies the logical X coordinate of the starting point.

y1 (short) identifies the logical Y coordinate of the starting point.

x2 (short) identifies the logical X coordinate of the ending point.

y2 (short) identifies the logical Y coordinate of the ending point.

lpLineFunc (FARPROC) is the procedure-instance address of the application-defined function.

lpData (LPSTR) is a pointer to the application-defined data.

Value Returned

None.

Notes

The callback function must use the Pascal calling convention with the FAR option.

BOOL LineTo(hDC,x,y)

Function

Draws a line using the current pen from the current position up to, but not including, the point indicated by *x* and *y*. The current position is then set to *x,y*.

Parameters

hDC (HDC) specifies the device context.

x (short) defines the logical X coordinate of the ending point for the line.

y (short) defines the logical Y coordinate of the ending point for the line.

Value Returned

Non-zero for a successful line draw, zero otherwise.

HBITMAP LoadBitmap(hInstance,lpBitmapName)

Function

Loads the specified bitmap from the executable file identified by *hInstance*.

Parameters

hInstance (HANDLE) specifies the instance of the module whose executable file contains the bitmap to be loaded.

lpBitmapName (LPSTR) is a pointer to a null-terminated character string naming the bitmap.

Value Returned

Either specifies the selected bitmap or returns a NULL if the specified bitmap does not exist.

Notes

The function assumes that the bitmap is stored in a device-independent form.

HCURSOR LoadCursor(hInstance,lpCursorName)

Function

Loads the selected cursor from the executable file associated with the module pointed to by *hInstance*.

Parameters

hInstance (HANDLE) specifies the instance of the module whose executable file contains the cursor to be loaded. When the parameter is NULL, the function can be used to load a predefined Windows cursor, with *lpCursorName* being one of the following:

IDC _ ARROW	Selects the standard Windows arrow cursor
IDC _ CROSS	Selects the standard Windows crosshair cursor
IDC _ IBEAM	Selects the standard Windows I-beam text cursor
IDC _ ICON	Selects the standard Windows empty icon
IDC _ SIZE	Selects the standard Windows four-pointed arrow
IDC _ UPARROW	Selects the standard Windows vertical arrow cursor
IDC _ WAIT	Selects the standard Windows hourglass cursor

lpCursorName (LPSTR) is a pointer to a null-terminated character string naming the cursor.

Value Returned

Either specifies the selected cursor or returns a NULL if the specified cursor does not exist.

Notes

Using the low-order word of *lpCursorName*, the function can be used to load a cursor created by a call to the MakeIntResource function.

BYTE LOBYTE(nInteger)

Function

Returns the low-order byte of the short integer specified.

Parameters

nInteger (int) indicates the integer value to be translated.

Value Returned

The low-order byte of the specified integer value.

WORD LOWORD(lInteger)

Function

Returns the low-order word from the long integer value passed.

Parameters

lInteger (long) identifies the long integer value to be translated.

Value Returned

Contains the low-order word of the specified long integer.

BOOL LPtoDP(hDC,lpPoints,nCount)

Function

Converts logical points into device points.

Parameters

hDC (HDC) specifies the device context.

lpPoints (LPPOINT) is a pointer to an array of POINT data structures.

nCount (short) defines the number of points in the array of structures.

Value Returned

A non-zero value for a successful conversion, otherwise zero.

Notes

All of the points referenced in the POINTS array pointed to by *lpPoints* will be mapped from the device coordinate system into the GDI's logical coordinate system.

POINT MakePoint(lInteger)

Function

Converts a long value containing the X and Y coordinates of a particular point into a POINT structure.

Parameters

lInteger (LONG) is the long integer containing the points to be converted.

Value Returned

Identifies the POINT data structure created.

FARPROC MakeProcInstance(lpProc,hInstance)

Function

Creates the procedure-instance address.

Parameters

lpProc (FARPROC) is a procedure-instance address.

hInstance (HANDLE) specifies the instance associated with the specified data segment.

Value Returned

Either points to the function or contains a NULL if unsuccessful.

Notes

The created address points to prologue code that is actually executed before the function itself. This procedure allows the current instance of the function to access variables and data structures in that particular instance's data segment.

int max(value1,value2)

Function

Returns the larger of the two values specified.

Parameters

value1 (int) is the first integer value to be compared.

value2 (int) is the second integer value to be compared.

Value Returned

Identifies either *value1* or *value2*, whichever is larger.

BOOL MessageBeep(wType)

Function

Beeps the system speaker whenever a message box is displayed.

Parameters

wType (WORD) identifies an unsigned short-integer value that is identical to the value sent to the MessageBox function.

Value Returned

A non-zero value indicates a successful beep; otherwise, a zero is returned.

int MessageBox(hWndParent,lpText,lpCaption,wType)

Function

Creates and displays a window containing application-supplied messages, caption, icons, and push buttons.

Parameters

hWndParent (HWND) specifies the window that owns the message box.

lpText (LPSTR) is a pointer to the null-terminated message string that will be displayed.

lpCaption (LPSTR) is a pointer to a null-terminated string that will be used for the caption in the dialog box. When it is NULL the caption displayed will be "Error!"

wType (WORD) identifies the contents of the dialog box and can be any single value or logically ORed combination listed in Table A-3.

Value Returned

A zero return value indicates there is insufficient memory to create the message box. A successful creation will cause one of the following menu items to be returned by the dialog box:

IDABORT	Abort button was pressed
IDCANCEL	ESC key or cancel button was pressed. If the message box doesn't have a cancel button, pressing ESC will be ignored
IDIGNORE	The ignore button was pressed
IDNO	No button has been pressed
IDOK	OK button was pressed
IDRETRY	Retry button was pressed
IDYES	Yes button was pressed

Notes

Table A-3 contains an alphabetical list showing the possible contents of a dialog box.

Table A-3.   Dialog Box Contents

Indentifier	Description
MB_ABORTRETRYIGNORE	Indicates the message box has three buttons: ABORT, RETRY, and IGNORE
MB_APPLMODAL	Indicates the user must respond to the message box; this is the default (**Note:** This does not prevent the user from switching to other applications — see MB_SYSTEMMODAL.)
MB_DEFBUTTON1	Indicates the first button is the default
MB_DEFBUTTON2	Indicates the second button is the default
MB_DEFBUTTON3	Indicates the third button is the default
MB_ICONASTERISK	Means an asterisk icon will be displayed in the message box
MB_ICONEXCLAMATION	Means an exclamation point icon will be displayed in the message box
MB_ICONHAND	Means a hand icon will be displayed in the message box
MB_ICONQUESTION	Means a question mark icon will be displayed in the message box
MB_OK	Indicates the message box has one push button, labeled OK
MB_OKCANCEL	Indicates the message box has two push buttons, labeled OK and CANCEL
MB_RETRYCANCEL	Indicates the message box has two push buttons, labeled RETRY and CANCEL
MB_SYSTEMMODAL	Suspends all applications due to the seriousness of the event that is about to occur; the user must respond to the message box and cannot switch to other tasks
MB_YESNO	Indicates the message box has two buttons, labeled YES and NO
MB_YESNOCANCEL	Indicates the message box has three push buttons: YES, NO, and CANCEL

int min(value1,value2)

Function

Returns the lesser of two values.

Parameters

value1 (int) contains the first value to be compared.

value2 (int) contains the second value to be compared.

Value Returned

The smaller of the two values.

BOOL ModifyMenu(hMenu,nPosition,wFlags, wIDNewItem,lpNewItem) [3.0 and later]

Function

Changes an existing menu item at the position specified.

Parameters

hMenu (HMENU) specifies the menu to be changed.

nPosition (WORD) specifies the menu item ID if *wFlags* is set to MB_ BYCOMMAND. If *wFlags* is set to MB_BYPOSITION, this parameter iden-tifies the position of the existing menu item. The first item is numbered 0.

wFlags (WORD) defines how *nPosition* is to be interpreted.

wIDNewItem (WORD) defines either the command ID or the menu handle of the pop-up menu.

lpNewItem (LPSTR) defines the content of the new menu item.

Value Returned

TRUE if the function was successful, FALSE otherwise.

Notes

Whenever the menu changes, the application should call DrawMenuBar.

DWORD MoveTo(hDC,x,y)

Function

Moves the current position to the X and Y coordinates specified.

Parameters

hDC (HDC) specifies the device context.

x (short) identifies the logical X coordinate of the new location.

y (short) identifies the logical Y coordinate of the new location.

Value Returned

Contains the coordinates of the previous position. The high-order word contains the Y coordinate, the low-order word the X coordinate.

Notes

A call to MoveTo affects many other functions that use the current position.

void MoveWindow(hWnd,x,y,nWidth,nHeight,bRepaint)

Function

Sends a WM_SIZE message to the specified window.

Parameters

hWnd (HWND) specifies the child or pop-up window.

x (int) identifies the new X coordinate for the upper-left corner of the resized window.

y (int) identifies the new Y coordinate for the upper-left corner of the resized window.

nWidth (int) indicates the new width of the window.

nHeight (int) indicates the new height of the window.

bRepaint (BOOL) repaints the window when it is other than zero. When it is zero, the window is repainted after it has been moved.

Value Returned

None.

Notes

For child windows the new window coordinates are specified using client coordinates relative to the upper-left corner of the parent window's client area. Pop-up windows have their coordinates defined using screen coordinates relative to the upper-left corner of the screen.

void OffsetRect(lpRect,x,y)

Function

Using the signed X and Y offset values, the function moves the indicated rectangle.

Parameters

lpRect (LPRECT) is a pointer to a RECT structure that contains the rectangle about to be moved.

x (int) indicates how much to move the rectangle left (negative value) or right.

y (int) indicates how much to move the rectangle up (negative value) or down.

Value Returned

None.

Notes

The coordinates of the rectangle must not be greater than 32,767 or less than −32,768 units.

short OffsetRgn(hRgn,x,y)

Function

Using the signed X and Y offset values, the function moves the indicated region.

Parameters

hRgn (HRGN) identifies the region about to be moved.

x (int) indicates how much to move the region left (negative value) or right.

y (int) indicates how much to move the region up (negative value) or down.

Value Returned

Indicates the new region's type:

COMPLEXREGION	Identifies a region with overlapping borders
ERROR	Indicates that the region handle is not valid
NULLREGION	Indicates that the region is empty
SIMPLEREGION	Indicates that the region does not have any overlapping borders

Notes

The coordinates of the region must not be greater than 32,767 or less than −32,768 units.

DWORD OffsetViewportOrg(hDC,x,y)

Function

Modifies the specified viewport origin relative to the current values.

Parameters

hDC (HDC) specifies the device context.

x (short) indicates how many device units to add to the current origin's X coordinate.

y (short) indicates how many device units to add to the current origin's Y coordinate.

Value Returned

Contains the previous viewport origin expressed in device coordinates. The high-order word contains the Y coordinate, the low-order word the X coordinate.

Notes

The new viewport origin is calculated by adding the current origin to the X and Y values.

DWORD OffsetWindowOrg(hDC,X,Y)

Function

Modifies the specified window origin relative to the current values.

Parameters

hDC (HDC) specifies the device context.

x (short) indicates how many device units to add to the current origin's X coordinate.

y (short) indicates how many device units to add to the current origin's Y coordinate.

Value Returned

Contains the previous window origin expressed in device coordinates. The high-order word contains the Y coordinate, the low-order word the X coordinate.

Notes

The new window origin is calculated by adding the current origin to the X and Y values.

BOOL PaintRgn(hDC,hRgn)

Function

Paints the specified region with the selected brush.

Parameters

hDC (HDC) specifies the device context.

hRgn (HRGN) specifies the region to be filled.

Value Returned

Zero value for an unsuccessful paint. Non-zero value for a successful paint.

COLORREF PALETTEINDEX(nPaletteIndex) [3.0 and later]

Function

Accepts an index to a logical color palette entry and returns a palette entry specifier.

Parameters

nPaletteIndex (int) defines an index to the palette entry containing the color to be used for a graphics operation.

Value Returned

Returns the value of a logical palette index specifier.

BOOL PatBlt(hDC,x,y,nWidth,nHeight,dwRop)

Function

Creates a bit pattern on the indicated device context.

Parameters

hDC (HDC) specifies the device context.

x (short) identifies the logical X coordinate for the upper-left corner of the rectangle receiving the bit pattern.

y (short) identifies the logical Y coordinate for the upper-left corner of the rectangle receiving the bit pattern.

nWidth (short), using logical units, identifies the width of the rectangle receiving the bit pattern.

nHeight (short), using logical units, identifies the height of the rectangle receiving the bit pattern.

dwRop (DWORD) identifies the raster operation from the following list of codes:

PATCOPY	Copies the pattern to the destination bitmap
PATINVERT	Using the logical OR operation, combines the destination bitmap with the pattern
DSTINVERT	Inverts the destination bitmap
BLACKNESS	Turns all output black
WHITENESS	Turns all output white

Value Returned

Returns a non-zero value for a successful pattern draw, otherwise NULL.

Notes

The created device-dependent pattern is based on a combination of the selected brush and the pattern already on the device.

BOOL Pie(hDC,x1,y1,x2,y2,x3,y3,x4,y4)

Function

Draws a pie-shaped wedge using the selected pen. Then, fills the wedge with the selected brush. Drawing takes place in a counterclockwise direction.

Parameters

hDC (HDC) specifies the device context.

x1 (short) identifies the logical X coordinate of the upper-left corner of the bounding rectangle.

y1 (short) identifies the logical Y coordinate of the upper-left corner of the bounding rectangle.

x2 (short) identifies the logical X coordinate of the lower-right corner of the bounding rectangle.

y2 (short) identifies the logical Y coordinate of the lower-right corner of the bounding rectangle.

x3 (short) identifies the logical X coordinate of the starting point for the arc.

y3 (short) identifies the logical Y coordinate of the starting point for the arc.

x4 (short) identifies the logical X coordinate of the ending point for the arc.

y4 (short) identifies the logical Y coordinate of the ending point for the arc.

Value Returned

A non-zero value indicates the wedge was successfully drawn. A zero value indicates an unsuccessful draw.

Notes

The width and height of the rectangle specified must not exceed 32,767. Pie does not use the current position, nor does it update the current position after the wedge is drawn.

BOOL Polygon(hDC,lpPoints,nCount)

Function

Draws a polygon consisting of two or more points connected by lines.

Parameters

hDC (HDC) specifies the device context.

lpPoints (LPPOINT) is a pointer to an array of POINT structures containing the vertices of the polygon.

nCount (short) indicates the number of elements in the array.

Value Returned

A non-zero value indicates a successful draw; otherwise, the result is zero.

Notes

Polygon does not use the current position, nor does it update the current position after the polygon is drawn. The polygon is drawn using the current polygon filling mode. In ALTERNATE mode, the current pen is used to draw lines from the first point through subsequent points, with the interior filled using the current brush. While in WINDING mode, the current pen is used to draw a border that is computed using all of the points. The interior is also filled using the current brush.

BOOL Polyline(hDC,lpPoints,nCount)

Function

Draws a set of connected line segments.

Parameters

hDC (HDC) specifies the device context.

lpPoints (LPPOINT) is a pointer to an array of POINT structures containing the points to be connected.

nCount (short) indicates the number of elements in the array.

Value Returned

A non-zero value indicates a successful draw; otherwise, the result is zero.

Notes

Polyline does not use the current position, nor does it update the current position after the polyline is drawn.

BOOL PtInRect(lpRect,Point)

Function

Identifies whether the referenced point is inside the selected rectangle.

Parameters

lpRect (LPRECT) is a pointer to a RECT structure identifying the rectangle.

Point (POINT) is a pointer to a POINT structure indicating the point to be checked.

Value Returned

A non-zero value indicates that the point lies within the selected rectangle. A zero return value indicates that the point is not within the designated rectangle.

BOOL PtInRegion(hRgn,x,y)

Function

Using X and Y as point coordinates, indicates whether the point lies within the specified region.

Parameters

hRgn (HRGN) specifies the region that is to be examined.

x (short) indicates the logical X coordinate of the point to be checked.

y (short) indicates the logical Y coordinate of the point to be checked.

Value Returned

A non-zero value indicates the point lies within the selected region. A zero return value indicates the point is not within the designated region.

int RealizePalette(hDC) [3.0 and later]

Function

Maps to the system palette entries in the logical palette currently selected for a device context.

Parameters

hDC (HDC) specifies the device context.

Value Returned

The returned value identifies the number of entries changed in the system palette.

Notes

When RealizePalette is called, Windows guarantees that it will display all the colors it requests, up to the maximum number simultaneously available on the display, and displays additional colors by matching them to available colors.

BOOL Rectangle(hDC,x1,y1,x2,y2)

Function

Using the selected pen, draws a rectangle; then fills the interior with the selected pen.

Parameters

hDC (HDC) specifies the device context.

x1 (short) is the upper-left corner X coordinate.

y1 (short) is the upper-left corner Y coordinate.

x2 (short) is the lower-right corner X coordinate.

y2 (short) is the lower-right corner Y coordinate.

Value Returned

Returned value identifies the newly created rectangular region or an unsuccessful attempt returns a NULL.

Notes

The width and height of the rectangle, defined by the absolute value of $x2 - x1$ and $y2 - y1$, must not exceed 32,767.

int ReleaseDC(hWnd,hDC)

Function

Releases the device context, allowing it to be used by other applications.

Parameters

hWnd (HWND) is a handle to the window whose device context is about to be freed.

hDC (HDC) specifies the device context.

Value Returned

A non-zero value for a successful release; otherwise, a NULL is returned.

Notes

For every call that is made to GetWindowDC or GetDC retrieving a common device context, a call to ReleaseDC must be made.

BOOL RemoveMenu(hMenu,nPosition,wFlags) [3.0 and later]

Function

Deletes an item with an associated pop-up menu from the menu specified.

Parameters

hMenu (HMENU) specifies the menu to be changed.

nPosition (WORD) defines the position of the menu item to be removed. The first menu item is at position zero.

wFlags (WORD) must be set to zero.

Value Returned

TRUE for a successful deletion, otherwise FALSE.

Notes

Whenever a menu changes, the application should call DrawMenuBar.

BOOL RestoreDC(hDC,nSavedDC)

Function

Restores the device context specified.

Parameters

hDC (HDC) specifies the device context.

nSavedDC (short) identifies the device context that is to be restored. When the parameter is assigned a −1, the function will restore the most recently saved device context.

Value Returned

A non-zero value for a successful restore, zero otherwise.

Notes

The device context is restored by copying the information saved on the context stack by previous calls to the SaveDC function. Since the context stack can contain the state information for more than one device context, care must be taken when a call is made to RestoreDC. When the device context referenced by *nSavedDC* is not the top of the stack, the function will permanently delete the state information stored for all device contexts between the top and the *nSavedDC* context reference.

DWORD RGB(cRed,cGreen,cBlue)

Function

Selects an RGB color based on the supplied preferences combined with the color capabilities of the selected output device.

Parameters

cRed (BYTE) identifies the intensity for the red color.

cGreen (BYTE) identifies the intensity for the green color.

cBlue (BYTE) identifies the intensity for the blue color.

Value Returned

Indicates the RGB color that has been selected.

Notes

Each color field's intensity can be a value from 0 to 255 (inclusive). Three zero parameters select the color black. All three parameters being assigned 255 will select white.

BOOL RoundRect(hDC,x1,y1,x2,y2,x3,y3)

Function

Using the current pen, draws a rectangle with rounded corners. The interior of the rectangle is then painted using the selected brush.

Parameters

hDC (HDC) specifies the device context.

x1 (short) identifies the logical X coordinate of the upper-left corner of the rectangle.

y1 (short) identifies the logical Y coordinate of the upper-left corner of the rectangle.

x2 (short) identifies the logical X coordinate of the lower-right corner of the rectangle.

y2 (short) identifies the logical Y coordinate of the lower-right corner of the rectangle.

x3 (short) identifies the width of the ellipse that will be used to draw the rounded corners.

y3 (short) identifies the height of the ellipse that will be used to draw the rounded corners.

Value Returned

A non-zero value indicates the rectangle was successfully drawn. A zero value indicates an unsuccessful draw.

Notes

The width and height of the rectangle, defined by the absolute value of $x2-x1$ and $y2-y1$, must not exceed 32,767. RoundRect does not use the current position, nor does it update the current position after the rectangle is drawn.

short SaveDC(hDC)

Function

Saves the state of the current device context.

Parameters

hDC (HDC) specifies the device context.

Value Returned

Identifies the saved device context. A zero value indicates an error has occurred.

Notes

The saved device context state is pushed onto the device context stack and can be restored by invoking the RestoreDC function.

DWORD ScaleViewportExt(hDC,xnum,xdenom,ynum,ydenom)

Function

Modifies the viewport extents relative to their current values.

Parameters

hDC (HDC) specifies the device context.

xnum (short) identifies the value to use in multiplying the current X extent.

xdenom (short) identifies the value to use in dividing the current X extent.

ynum (short) identifies the value to use in multiplying the current Y extent.

ydenom (short) identifies the value to use in dividing the current Y extent.

Value Returned

The function returns the previous viewport extents using device units. The high-order word contains the old Y extent with the old X extent saved in the low-order word.

Notes

The new extents are calculated by multiplying the current values by the given numerators and then dividing them by the denominators.

DWORD
ScaleWindowExt(hDC,xnum,xdenom,ynum,ydenom)

Function

Modifies the window extents relative to their current values.

Parameters

hDC (HDC) specifies the device context.

xnum (short) identifies the value to use in multiplying the current X extent.

xdenom (short) identifies the value to use in dividing the current X extent.

ynum (short) identifies the value to use in multiplying the current Y extent.

ydenom (short) identifies the value to use in dividing the current Y extent.

Value Returned

The function returns the previous window extents using device units. The high-order word contains the old Y extent; the old X extent is saved in the low-order word.

Notes

The new extents are calculated by multiplying the current values by the given numerators and then dividing them by the denominators.

void ScreenToClient(hWnd,lpPoint)

Function

Converts the specified point from the screen coordinates of the display to client coordinates.

Parameters

hWnd (HWND) specifies the window whose client area will be used for the conversion.

lpPoint (LPPOINT) is a pointer to a POINT structure containing the screen coordinates that are to be converted.

Value Returned

None.

Notes

The translated coordinates are relative to the upper-left corner of the specified window's client area.

HANDLE SelectObject(hDC,hObject)

Function

Selects a logical object for the specified device context.

Parameters

hDC (HDC) specifies the device context.

hObject (HANDLE) specifies the logical object to be selected and may be any one of the following functions:

Object	Function Name
Bitmap	CreateBitmap
	CreateBitmapIndirect
	CreateCompatibleBitmap
Brush	CreateBrushIndirect
	CreateHatchBrush
	CreatePatternBrush
	CreateSolidBrush
Font	CreateFont
	CreateFontIndirect
Pen	CreatePen
	CreatePenIndirect
Region	CombineRgn
	CreateEllipticRgn
	CreateellipticRgnIndirect
	CreatePolyRgn
	CreateRectRgn
	CreateRectRgnIndirect

Value Returned

Identifies the object being replaced by *hObject* of the same type. Otherwise, if an error has occurred, a NULL is returned.

Notes

Selected objects become defaults used by many GDI functions that write text, draw lines, fill interiors, and clip output to selected devices. Device contexts can have up to five objects selected, with only one being used at a time. Each call to SelectObject causes the GDI to allocate space for that object in the data segment. DeleteObject should always be called whenever a selected object (font, pen, or brush) is no longer needed to conserve memory. Also, bitmaps can only be selected into one device context at a time.

HPALETTE SelectPalette(hDC,hPalette) [3.0 and later]

Function

Selects the logical palette specified by the *hPalette* parameter as the selected logical palette of the device context identified by *hDC*. The new palette replaces the previous palette.

Parameters

hDC (HDC) specifies the device context.

hPalette (HPALETTE) specifies the logical palette to be selected.

Value Returned

Returns the identifier of the logical palette being replaced by *hPalette*. Otherwise, a NULL is returned.

Notes

An application can select a logical palette for more than one device context.

long SendDlgItemMessage(hDlg,nIDDlgItem,wMsg, wParam,lParam)

Function

Sends a message to a dialog box's control.

Parameters

hDlg (HWND) specifies the dialog box that contains the control.

nIDDlgItem (int) identifies the dialog item that is to receive the message.

wMsg (unsigned) identifies the message value.

wParam (WORD) identifies any additional message information.

lParam (long) can be used for additional message information.

Value Returned

If the controller identified is invalid, the function returns a NULL. Otherwise, the return value represents the outcome of the function. A successful return value is generated by the control's window function.

Notes

Using SendDlgItemMessage is the same as obtaining a handle to the specified control and then calling SendMessage.

long SendMessage(hWnd,wMsg,wParam,lParam)

Function

Sends a message to single or multiple windows.

Parameters

hWnd (HWND) specifies the window that will be sent the message. If the parameter is FFFF (hexadecimal), the specified message will be sent to all pop-up windows currently in the system. The message is not sent to any child windows.

wMsg (unsigned) identifies the message value.

wParam (WORD) identifies any additional message information.

lParam (long) can be used for additional message information.

Value Returned

Depends on the message sent.

Notes

If the receiving window is part of the same application, the window function is called immediately. When the receiving window is part of some other task, Windows will switch to the task and then call the appropriate window function, sending the message. Note that the message is not placed in the destination task's application queue.

long SetBitmapBits(hBitmap,dwCount,lpBits)

Function

Sets the bits of a bitmap to the values specified.

Parameters

hBitmap (HBITMAP) specifies the bitmap to be set.

dwCount (DWORD) identifies the number of bytes in the bitmap.

lpBits (LPSTR) is a pointer to the array of short integers representing the bitmap bits.

Value Returned

Indicates the number of bytes used in setting the bitmap bits. A zero value indicates an error has occurred.

DWORD SetBitmapDimension(hBitmap,x,y)

Function

Specifies the width and height of a bitmap using 0.1 millimeter units.

Parameters

hBitmap (HANDLE) specifies the bitmap.

x (short) defines the width of the bitmap in 0.1 millimeter units.

y (short) defines the height of the bitmap in 0.1 millimeter units.

Value Returned

Returns the previous bitmap dimensions with the high-order word containing the previous height and the low-order word containing the previous width.

DWORD SetBkColor(hDC,rgbColor)

Function

Sets the current background color to the color specified. The function will choose the nearest logical color of the device if no direct match exists.

Parameters

hDC (HDC) specifies the device context.

rgbColor (DWORD) selects an RGB color for the new background color.

Value Returned

Contains the previous RGB background color. A return value of 80000000 (hexadecimal) indicates an error has occurred.

Notes

When the background mode is OPAQUE, the background color is used to fill the gaps between styled lines, hatched lines in brushes, and character cells. The graphics device interface (GDI) also uses the background color for converting bitmaps from color to monochrome or vice versa.

short SetBkMode(hDC,nBkMode)

Function

Sets the background mode.

Parameters

hDC (HDC) specifies the device context.

nBkMode (short) selects the background mode:

OPAQUE	Background color is used to fill the gaps between styled lines, hatched lines in brushes, and character cells
TRANSPARENT	Leaves the background unchanged

Value Returned

Returns the previous background mode (OPAQUE or TRANSPARENT).

Notes

The function tells the GDI whether to remove the existing background colors on the device surface before drawing text, hatched brushes, or any non-solid pen style.

DWORD SetBrushOrg(hDC,x,y)

Function

Sets the origin for all selected brushes into the specified device context.

Parameters

hDC (HDC) specifies the device context.

x (short) identifies the logical X coordinate of the new origin.

y (short) identifies the logical Y coordinate of the new origin.

Value Returned

Indicates the previous origin of the brush. The high-order word contains the Y coordinate, the low-order word the X coordinate.

Notes

The original brush origin is always set to the 0,0 coordinate.

HWND SetCapture(hWnd)

Function

Sends all mouse input to the window specified, regardless of the position of the mouse cursor.

Parameters

hWnd (HWND) specifies the window that is to receive all mouse input.

Value Returned

Indicates the previous window receiving the mouse input. A zero value indicates there is no such window.

HCURSOR SetCursor(hCursor)

Function

Sets the system cursor shape.

Parameters

hCursor (HCURSOR) specifies a previously loaded (LoadCursor) cursor resource.

Value Returned

Identifies the cursor resource defining the previous cursor shape. A zero value indicates that there was no previous shape.

Notes

The cursor shape should only be set when the cursor is in the client area or when it is capturing all mouse input.

void SetCursorPos(x,y)

Function

Sets the system cursor to the position specified.

Parameters

x (int) identifies the new screen X coordinate of the cursor.

y (int) identifies the new screen Y coordinate of the cursor.

Value Returned

None.

Notes

The cursor should only be moved when it is in the window's client area.

void SetDlgItemInt(hDlg,nIDDlgItem,wValue,bSigned)

Function

Sets the text of a control in the specified dialog box to the string represented by the integer value given by *wValue*.

Parameters

hDlg (HWND) specifies the dialog box containing the control.

nIDDlgItem (int) defines the control to be modified.

wValue (unsigned) indicates the value to be set.

bSigned (BOOL) indicates whether the integer value is signed.

Value Returned

None.

Notes

The function converts the *wValue* parameter to a string consisting of decimal digits. It then copies the string to the control. The function also sends a WM_SETTEXT message to the specified control.

void SetDlgItemText(hDlg,nIDDlgItem,lpString)

Function

Sets the text of a control in the dialog box.

Parameters

hDlg (HWND) specifies the dialog box containing the control.

nIDDlgItem (int) defines the control to be modified.

lpString (LPSTR) is a pointer to a null-terminated string that will be copied to the control.

Value Returned

None.

Notes

The function sends a WM_SETTEXT message to the specified control.

void SetDoubleClickTime(wCount)

Function

Sets the double-click time for the mouse.

Parameters

wCount (WORD) indicates the number of milliseconds that can occur between double mouse clicks.

Value Returned

None.

Notes

The *wCount* value specifies the maximum number of milliseconds that can occur between consecutive double mouse clicks. When *wCount* is set to zero, Windows uses a default of 500 milliseconds. Changing the double-click time affects the double-click time for all windows in the system.

short SetMapMode(hDC,nMapMode)

Function

Sets the mapping mode of the selected device context.

Parameters

hDC (HDC) specifies the device context.

nMapMode (short) selects one new mapping mode from the following:

MM_ANISOTROPIC	Maps logical units to arbitrary units with arbitrarily scaled axes
MM_HIENGLISH	Maps each logical unit to 0.001 inch
MM_HIMETRIC	Maps each logical unit to 0.01 millimeter
MM_ISOTROPIC	Maps logical units to arbitrary units with equally scaled axes
MM_LOMETRIC	Maps each logical unit to 0.1 millimeter
MM_LOENGLISH	Maps each logical unit to 0.01 inch
MM_TEXT	Maps each logical unit to 1 device pixel
MM_TWIPS	Maps each logical unit to 1/20 of a printer's point or approximately 1/1440 inch

Value Returned

Represents the previous mapping mode.

Notes

The mapping modes HIENGLISH, HIMETRIC, LOENGLISH, LOMETRIC, and TWIPS are used most frequently for applications drawing in physically meaningful units such as millimeters or inches. MM_TEXT mode permits the use of device-specific pixels whose size may vary from one device to another. MM_ISOTROPIC enables a 1:1 aspect ratio, which is most useful in maintaining the exact shape of an image. MM_ANISOTROPIC mode allows for independent adjustment of the X and Y coordinates.

WORD SetPaletteEntries(hPalette,wStartIndex, wNumEntries,lpColors) [3.0 and later]

Function

Sets RGB color values and flags in a range of entries in a logical palette.

Parameters

hPalette (HPALETTE) specifies the logical palette.

wStartIndex (WORD) identifies the first entry in the logical palette to be set.

wNumEntries (WORD) identifies the number of entries in the logical palette to be set.

lpColors (LPSTR) points to the first number of an array of PALETTEENTRY.

Value Returned

Indicates the number of entries set in the logical palette. A zero is returned if the function has failed.

Notes

When the logical palette is selected into a device context, the changes will not take effect until a call is made to RealizePalette.

DWORD SetPixel(hDC,x,y,rgbColor)

Function

Sets the color of the pixel indicated by *x* and *y*.

Parameters

hDC (HDC) specifies the device context.

x (short) specifies the logical X coordinate of the point to be set.

y (short) specifies the logical Y coordinate of the point to be set.

rgbColor (DWORD) indicates the RGB color to be used to paint the pixel.

Value Returned

Indicates the actual RGB color the pixel was painted. A −1 return value indicates an error condition. The color value returned could be different than the color specified if no direct match exists.

Notes

The point specified must be in the clipping region.

short SetPolyFillMode(hDC,nPolyFillMode)

Function

Sets the polygon fill mode.

Parameters

hDC (HDC) specifies the device context.

nPolyFillMode (short) selects the new filling mode. Can be either ALTERNATE or WINDING.

Value Returned

Indicates the previous filling mode. A NULL value indicates an error has occurred.

Notes

ALTERNATE and WINDING modes only differ for those polygons with overlapping complex forms. ALTERNATE mode fills every other enclosed region within the polygon; WINDING mode fills all regions.

void SetRect(lpRect,x1,y1,x2,y2)

Function

Creates a new rectangle by assigning the RECT data structure pointed to by *lpRect* to coordinates specified.

Parameters

lpRect (LPRECT) is a pointer to a RECT structure that will be assigned the new end points.

x1 (int) is the upper-left corner X coordinate.

y1 (int) is the upper-left corner Y coordinate.

x2 (int) is the lower-right corner X coordinate.

y2 (int) is the lower-right corner Y coordinate.

Value Returned

None.

Notes

The width and height of the rectangle, defined by the absolute value of $x2-x1$ and $y2-y1$, must not exceed 32,767.

void SetRectRgn(hRgn,x1,y1,x2,y2)

Function

Creates a rectangular region.

Parameters

hRgn (HANDLE) specifies the region.

x1 (short) is the upper-left corner X coordinate of the rectangular region.

y1 (short) is the upper-left corner Y coordinate of the rectangular region.

x2 (short) is the lower-right corner X coordinate of the rectangular region.

y2 (short) is the lower-right corner Y coordinate of the rectangular region.

Value Returned

None.

Notes

Unlike CreateRectRgn, SetRectRgn does not use the local memory manager. Instead, the function uses the space allocated for the region. *x1, y1, x2,* and *y2* indicate the minimum size of the allocated space.

short SetROP2(hDC,nDrawMode)

Function

Sets the current drawing mode.

Parameters

hDC (HDC) specifies the device context.

nDrawMode (short) selects from one of the following drawing modes:

R2_BLACK	The pixel is always black
R2_NOTIMERGEPEN	The pixel is the inverse of the R2_MERGEPEN color
R2_MASKNOTPEN	The pixel is a combination of the colors of the display and the inverse of the pen
R2_NOTCOPYPEN	The pixel is the inverse of the pen color
R2_MASKPENNOT	The pixel is a combination of the colors of the pen and the inverse of the display
R2_NOT	The pixel is the inverse of the display color
R2_XORPEN	The pixel is a combination of the colors in the pen and in the display
R2_NOTMASKPEN	The pixel is the inverse of the R2_MASKPEN color
R2_MASKPEN	The pixel is a combination of the colors in both the pen and the display
R2_NOTXORPEN	The pixel is the inverse of the R2_XORPEN color

R2_NOP	The pixel remains unchanged
R2_MERGENOTPEN	The pixel is a combination of the display color and the inverse of the pen color
R2_COPYPEN	The pixel is the pen color
R2_MERGEPENNOT	The pixel is a combination of the pen color and the inverse of the display color
R2_MERGEPEN	The pixel is a combination of the pen color and the display color
R2_WHITE	The pixel is always white

Value Returned

Specifies the previous drawing mode.

Notes

The drawing mode is for raster devices only and is not available on vector devices. The drawing modes represent the binary raster operations representing all of the possible binary Boolean functions AND, OR, and XOR as applied to two variables, along with the unary NOT operation.

int SetScrollPos(hWnd,nBar,nPos,bRedraw)

Function

Sets the current position of a scroll bar thumb.

Parameters

hWnd (HWND) specifies the window whose scroll bar will be set.

nBar (int) identifies which scroll bar thumb is to be set:

Value	Definition
SB_CTL	Sets the position of a scroll bar control, assuming that *hWnd* points to a window handle of a scroll bar control
SB_HORZ	Sets the position of a window's horizontal scroll bar
SB_VERT	Sets the position of a window's vertical scroll bar

nPos (int) identifies the new position within the valid scrolling range.

bRedraw (BOOL) indicates whether the scroll bar should be redrawn. A non-zero value indicates the scroll bar should be redrawn. If zero, it is not redrawn.

Value Returned

Indicates the previous position of the scroll bar thumb.

void SetScrollRange(hWnd,nBar,nMinPos, nMaxPos,bRedraw)

Function

Sets the minimum and maximum position values for the selected scroll bar.

Parameters

hWnd (HWND) specifies the window whose scroll bar will be set.

nBar (int) identifies which scroll bar thumb is to be set:

Value	Definition
SB_CTL	Sets the position of a scroll bar control, assuming that *hWnd* points to a window handle of a scroll bar control
SB_HORZ	Sets the position of a window's horizontal scroll bar
SB_VERT	Sets the position of a window's vertical scroll bar

nMinPos (int) sets the minimum scrolling position.

nMaxPos (int) sets the maximum scrolling position.

bRedraw (BOOL) indicates whether the scroll bar should be redrawn. A non-zero value indicates the scroll bar should be redrawn. If zero, it is not redrawn.

Value Returned

None.

Notes

If SetScrollRange is called right after SetScrollPos, *bRedraw* should be set to zero to prevent the scroll bar from being drawn twice.

short SetStretchBltMode(hDC,nStretchMode)

Function

Sets the stretching mode for the StretchBlt function.

Parameters

hDC (HDC) specifies the device context.

nStretchMode (short) selects one of the following stretching modes:

Value	Definition
BLACKONWHITE	Preserves the black pixels at the expense of white pixels by using the logical AND operation on the eliminated lines and those remaining
COLORONCOLOR	Deletes all eliminated lines without preserving the information
WHITEONBLACK	Preserves the white pixels at the expense of the black pixels by using the logical OR operation on the eliminated lines and those remaining

Value Returned

Indicates the previous stretching mode.

Notes

The function determines which scan lines or columns to eliminate when contracting a bitmap.

void SetSysColors(nChanges,lpSysColor,lpColorValues)

Function

Sets the system colors.

Parameters

nChanges (int) defines the number of system colors to be set.

lpSysColor (LPINT) is a pointer to an array of integers that specify the elements to be changed. The following is a list of valid system color indexes:

Value	Definition
COLOR_ACTIVEBORDER	Active window border index
COLOR_ACTIVECAPTION	Active window caption index
COLOR_APPWORKSPACE	MDI (multiple document interface) application background color index
COLOR_BACKGROUND	Desktop index
COLOR_CAPTIONTEXT	Text in caption, scroll bar arrow box, or size box index
COLOR_INACTIVEBORDER	Inactive window border index
COLOR_INACTIVECAPTION	Inactive window caption index
COLOR_MENU	Menu background index
COLOR_MENUTEXT	Text in menus index
COLOR_SCROLLBAR	Scroll bar gray area index
COLOR_WINDOW	Window background and thumb box index
COLOR_WINDOWFRAME	Window border and caption text background index
COLOR_WINDOWTEXT	Text in window index

Value Returned

None.

Notes

The function sends a WM_SYSCOLORCHANGE message to all windows, informing them of the color change(s). Windows is instructed to repaint the affected portions of all visible windows.

WORD SetTextAlign(hDC,wFlags)

Function

Sets the text alignment flag for the specified device context.

Parameters

hDC (HDC) specifies the device context.

wFlags (WORD) selects a mask affecting the horizontal and vertical alignment from the following list:

TA_BASELINE	Selects alignment along the X axis and the baseline of the selected font within the bounding rectangle
TA_BOTTOM	Selects alignment along the X axis and the bottom of the bounding rectangle
TA_CENTER	Selects alignment along the Y axis and the center of the bounding rectangle
TA_LEFT	Selects alignment along the Y axis and the left side of the bounding rectangle
TA_NOUPDATECP	Notes that the current position is not updated
TA_RIGHT	Selects alignment along the Y axis and the right side of the bounding rectangle
TA_TOP	Selects alignment along the X axis and the top of the bounding rectangle
TA_UPDATECP	Notes that the current position is updated

Value Returned

Indicates the alignment with the high-order word containing the vertical alignment and the low-order word containing the horizontal alignment.

Notes

Only one of the two flags that alter the current position can be chosen for the *wFlags* parameter.

short SetTextCharacterExtra(hDC,nCharExtra)

Function

Sets the amount of intercharacter spacing.

Parameters

hDC (HDC) specifies the device context.

nCharExtra (short) selects the amount of extra space to be added to each character.

Value Returned

Indicates the amount used for the previous intercharacter spacing.

Notes

When the current mapping mode is not set to MM_TEXT, the *nCharExtra* parameter is translated to the nearest pixel.

DWORD SetTextColor(hDC,rgbColor)

Function

Sets the text color.

Parameters

hDC (HDC) specifies the device context.

rgbColor (DWORD) selects an RGB color value to be used for text output.

Value Returned

Indicates the previous RGB color value used for text color.

Notes

SetBkColor is used to set the background color.

short SetTextJustification(hDC,nBreakExtra,nBreakCount)

Function

Justifies text using the *nBreakExtra* and *nBreakCount* parameters.

Parameters

hDC (HDC) specifies the device context.

nBreakExtra (short) selects the total amount of extra space to be added to the line of text.

nBreakCount (short) selects the number of break characters in the line.

Value Returned

Indicates the outcome of the function. A value of 1 indicates a successful call; otherwise, a zero value is returned.

Notes

The break character used to delimit words is the ASCII 32 or blank space character. By calling GetTextMetrics the current font's break character can be obtained.

WORD
SetTimer(hWnd,nIDEvent,wElapse,lpTimerFunc)

Function

Creates a system timer event.

Parameters

hWnd (HWND) specifies the window to be associated with the timer.

nIDEvent (short) specifies the timer event identifier.

wElapse (unsigned) identifies the elapsed time between timer events in milliseconds.

lpTimerFunc (FARPROC) is a procedure-instance address of the callback function to be notified when the timer event takes place.

Value Returned

An integer identifying the new timer event if *hWnd* was NULL. A non-zero value indicates the timer was created; otherwise, a zero is returned.

Notes

Since timers are limited global resources, it is important that the application check the value returned by SetTimer to verify a timer is actually available.

DWORD SetViewportExt(hDC,x,y)

Function

Sets the X and Y extents of the viewport of the selected device context.

Parameters

hDC (HDC) specifies the device context.

x (short), using device units, identifies the X extent of the viewport.

y (short), using device units, identifies the Y extent of the viewport.

Value Returned

Contains the previous viewport extents with the high-order word containing the previous Y extent and the low-order word containing the previous X extent. A NULL return value indicates an error has occurred.

Notes

When one of the mapping modes HIENGLISH, HIMETRIC, LOENGLISH, LOMETRIC, TEXT, or TWIPS is in effect, subsequent calls to SetWindowExt or SetViewportExt are ignored.

DWORD SetViewportOrg(hDC,x,y)

Function

Sets the viewport origin of the specified device context.

Parameters

hDC (HDC) specifies the device context.

x (short), using device units, indicates the X coordinate of the origin of the viewport.

y (short), using device units, indicates the Y coordinate of the origin of the viewport.

Value Returned

Contains the previous viewport origins with the high-order word containing the previous Y origin and the low-order word containing the previous X origin. A NULL return value indicates an error has occurred.

Notes

The viewport origin identifies the point in the device coordinate system that the GDI uses to map the window origin.

DWORD SetWindowExt(hDC,x,y)

Function

Sets the X and Y extents of the window of the selected device context.

Parameters

hDC (HDC) specifies the device context.

x (short), using device units, identifies the X extent of the window.

y (short), using device units, identifies the Y extent of the window.

Value Returned

Contains the previous window extents with the high-order word containing the previous Y extent and the low-order word containing the previous X extent. A NULL return value indicates an error has occurred.

Notes

When one of the mapping modes HIENGLISH, HIMETRIC, LOENGLISH, LOMETRIC, TEXT, or TWIPS is in effect, subsequent calls to SetWindowExt or SetViewportExt are ignored.

DWORD SetWindowOrg(hDC,x,y)

Function

Sets the window origin of the specified device context.

Parameters

hDC (HDC) specifies the device context.

x (short), using device units, indicates the X coordinate of the origin of the window.

y (short), using device units, indicates the Y coordinate of the origin of the window.

Value Returned

Contains the previous window origins with the high-order word containing the previous Y origin and the low-order word containing the previous X origin. A NULL return value indicates an error has occurred.

Notes

The window origin identifies the point in the device coordinate system that the GDI uses to map the window origin.

void SetWindowPos(hWnd,hWndInsertAfter,x,y,cx,cy,wFlags)

Function

Changes the size, position, and ordering of child, pop-up, and top-level windows.

Parameters

hWnd (HWND) specifies the window to be positioned.

hWndInsertAfter (HWND) specifies the window from the window manager's list that is to precede the positioned window.

x (int) identifies the X coordinate of the window's upper-left corner.

y (int) identifies the Y coordinate of the window's upper-left corner.

cx (int) specifies the new window's width.

cy (int) specifies the new window's height.

wFlags (WORD) can be any one of the following values:

SWP_DRAWFRAME	Draws a frame around the window
SWP_HIDEWINDOW	Hides the window
SWP_NOACTIVATE	Doesn't activate the window
SWP_NOMOVE	Ignores the *x* and *y* parameters and does not move the window
SWP_NOSIZE	Ignores the current *cx* and *cy* values and does not change the window's size
SWP_NOREDRAW	Doesn't redraw
SWP_NOZORDER	Ignores the *hWndInsertAfter* value, retaining the current ordering
SWP_SHOWWINDOW	Displays the specified window

Value Returned

None.

Notes

When SWP_NOZORDER is not specified, Windows will place the window in the position following the window specified by *hWndInsertAfter*.

void ShowScrollBar(hWnd,wBar,fShow)

Function

Hides or displays a scroll bar.

Parameters

hWnd (HWND) specifies the window containing the scroll bar.

wBar (WORD) identifies whether the scroll bar is a control or part of a window's non-client area. It can be any one of the following values:

SB_CTL	Sets the position of a scroll bar control, assuming that *hWnd* points to a window handle of a scroll bar control
SB_HORZ	Sets the position of a window's horizontal scroll bar
SB_VERT	Sets the position of a window's vertical scroll bar

fShow (BOOL) identifies whether or not Windows hides the scroll bar. If *fShow* has a zero value the scroll bar is hidden; otherwise, it is not hidden.

Value Returned

None.

Notes

ShowScrollBar does not destroy a scroll bar's position and range when it hides the scroll bar. A call to SetScrollBar will.

BOOL StretchBlt(hDestDC,x,y,nWidth,nHeight, hScrDC,xSrc,ySrc,nSrcWidth,nSrcHeight,dwRop)

Function

Moves a bitmap from a source rectangle to a destination rectangle.

Parameters

hDestDc (HDC) identifies the device context that will receive the bitmap.

x and *y* (short) define the logical X and Y coordinates of the upper-left corner of the destination rectangle.

nWidth and *nHeight* (short) define the width and height (in logical units) of the destination rectangle.

hSrcDC (HDC) specifies the device context that contains the source bitmap.

xSrc and *ySrc* (short) define the logical X and Y coordinates of the upper-left corner of the source rectangle.

nSrcWidth (short) specifies the logical unit width of the source rectangle.

nSrcHeight (short) specifies the logical unit height of the source rectangle.

dwRop (DWORD) defines the raster operation to be executed. These operations define how the GDI (graphics device interface) blends colors in output operations involving brushes and source and destination bitmaps.

Raster Operation	Description
SRCPAINT	Using the Boolean OR, combines the destination and source bitmap pixels
SRCCOPY	Copies the source bitmap to the destination bitmap
SRCAND	Using the Boolean AND, combines the destination and source bitmap pixels
SRCINVERT	Using the Boolean XOR, combines the destination and source bitmap pixels
SRCERASE	Inverts the destination bitmap, combining the result with the source bitmap using the logical AND operation
NOTSRCCOPY	Copies an inverted source bitmap to the destination
NOTSRCERASE	Combines the destination and source bitmaps using the Boolean AND operation; then, inverts the result
MERGECOPY	Using a pattern, combines the source bitmap with the pattern using the Boolean AND operation

Raster Operation	Description
MERGEPAINT	Using the Boolean OR operation, combines the inverted source bitmap with the destination bitmap
PATCOPY	Copies the pattern to the destination bitmap
PATPAINT	Using the Boolean OR operation, combines an inverted source bitmap with the pattern. It then combines the result with the destination bitmap using the Boolean OR operation
PATINVERT	Using the Boolean OR operation, combines the destination bitmap with the pattern
DSTINVERT	Inverts the destination bitmap
BLACKNESS	Turns all output black
WHITENESS	Turns all output white

Value Returned

Non-zero for a successful draw; otherwise, a zero is returned.

Notes

The function compresses or stretches the source bitmap in memory and then copies the result to the output device context.

BOOL TextOut(hDC,x,y,lpString,nCount)

Function

Writes a character string to the selected display.

Parameters

hDC (HDC) specifies the device context.

x (short) identifies the logical X coordinate of the string's starting point.

y (short) identifies the logical Y coordinate of the string's starting point.

lpString (LPSTR) is a pointer to a null-terminated string that is to be drawn.

nCount (short) identifies the number of characters in the string to be drawn.

Value Returned

A non-zero value indicates the string was successfully drawn; otherwise, a NULL is returned.

Notes

The current position is not used or updated by TextOut. All character origins are defined to be at the upper-left corner of the character position.

BOOL TrackPopupMenu(hMenu,wFlags,x,y,cx,hWnd) [3.0 and later]

Function

The function displays a "floating" pop-up menu.

Parameters

hMenu (HMENU) specifies the pop-up menu to be displayed.

wFlags (WORD) is not used and must be set to zero.

x (int) defines the horizontal position in screen coordinates of the left side of the menu on the screen.

y (int) defines the vertical position in screen coordinates of the top of the menu on the screen.

cx (int) defines the width in screen coordinates of the pop-up menu. A value of zero causes Windows to calculate the width based on the widest menu item.

hWnd (HWND) identifies the window that owns the pop-up menu.

Value Returned

TRUE for a successful call, otherwise FALSE.

int UpdateColors(hDC) [3.0 and later]

Function

The function updates the client area of the device context by matching the current colors in the client area to the system palette on a pixel-by-pixel basis.

Parameters

hDC (HDC) specifies the device context.

Value Returned

Return value is not used.

Notes

This function typically updates a client area faster than redrawing the area. This can result in the loss of some color information.

void UpdateWindow(hWnd)

Function

Updates the client area of the specified window by sending a WM_PAINT message.

Parameters

hWnd (HWND) is a handle to the window to be updated.

Value Returned

None.

Notes

The WM_PAINT message is sent directly to the window function of the selected window, bypassing the application queue.

void ValidateRect(hWnd,lpRect)

Function

Validates the client area within the given rectangle by removing the rectangle from the update region of the selected window.

Parameters

hWnd (HWND) is a handle to the window whose update region is about to be modified.

lpRect (LPRECT) is a pointer to a RECT structure containing the client coordinate rectangle to be removed from the update region.

Value Returned

None.

Notes

The function automatically validates the entire client area.

void ValidateRgn(hWnd,hRgn)

Function

Validates the client area within the given region by removing the region from the update region of the selected window.

Parameters

hWnd (HWND) is a handle to the window whose update region is about to be modified.

hRgn (HRGN) specifies the region that defines the area to be removed from the update region.

Value Returned

None.

Notes

The region coordinates are assumed to be in client coordinates.

void WaitMessage( )

Function

Yields control to all other applications when the current application has no other tasks to execute.

Parameters

The function has no parameters.

Value Returned

None.

BOOL WinHelp(hWnd,lpHelpFile,wCommand,dwData) [3.0 and later]

Function

Invokes the Windows help engine.

Parameters

hWnd (HWND) specifies the window requesting help.

lpHelpFile (LPSTR) is a pointer to a null-terminated string holding the directory path and/or name of the help file to be displayed.

wCommand (WORD) can be any one of the following values specifying the type of help requested:

Value	Meaning
HELP_CONTEXT	Displays help for a particular context identified by a 32-bit unsigned integer value specified in *dwData*
HELP_KEY	Displays help for a particular keyword identified by a string pointed to by *dwData*

Value	Meaning
HELP_LAST	Displays the last topic viewed by the user
HELP_QUIT	Terminates the help facility

dwData (DWORD) identifies the context or keyword of the help requested.

Value Returned

TRUE for a successful call; otherwise, FALSE.

Notes

All applications must make a call to WinHelp with *wCommand* set to HELP_QUIT before closing a window that has requested help.

TRADEMARKS

Ami®	Samna Corp.
AT®	International Business Machines Corp.
CodeView®	Microsoft Corp.
COMPAQ®	COMPAQ Computer Corp.
DESQview®	Quarterdeck Office Systems
Helvetica®	Linotype Co.
Inboard™ 386™/AT	Intel Corp.
LaserJet™	Hewlett-Packard Co.
Lotus®	Lotus Development Corp.
Microsoft®	Microsoft Corp.
MS-DOS®	Microsoft Corp.
Norton®	Peter Norton Computing, Inc.
OS/2™ (also Operating System/2™)	International Business Machines Corp.
Presentation Manager™	International Business Machines Corp.
Proprinter™	International Business Machines Corp.
PS/2® (also Personal System/2®)	International Business Machines Corp.
SideKick®	Borland International Inc.
Tektronix®	Tektronix
Times®	Linotype Co.
Turbo Pascal®	Borland International Inc.
WordPerfect®	WordPerfect Corp.
WordStar®	WordStar International Corp.

INDEX

The manuscript for this book was prepared and submitted to Osborne/McGraw-Hill in electronic form. The acquisitions editor for this project was Jeffrey Pepper, the technical reviewer was Jeff Hsu, and the project editor was Judith Brown.

Text design by Stefany Otis using Zapf for text body and display.

Cover art by Bay Graphics Design Associates. Color separation and cover supplier, Phoenix Color Corporation. Screens produced with InSet, from InSet Systems, Inc. Book printed and bound by R.R. Donnelley & Sons Company, Crawfordsville, Indiana.

DISKS AVAILABLE NOW

The *Windows Programming: An Introduction* supplementary disks (one set of three 5 1/4" disks) contain all the example templates used in this book and can save you hours of time and testing.

 You don't need to type in code —
all program code from the book is on these three disks and ready for immediate use.

 You don't need to debug your code —
all disk code is thoroughly tested and bug free.

With the *Windows Programming: An Introduction* supplementary disks, you can spend your valuable time perfecting your programming techniques instead of your typing skills.

 EASY INSTALLATION INSTRUCTIONS ARE PROVIDED!

Order Today!

$29.95 plus $2.00 shipping/handling for 5 1/4" disks (includes three disks)
$29.95 plus $2.00 shipping/handling for 3 1/2" disks (includes two disks)

Toll Free **800-227-0900** **Call**

(Monday-Friday 8:30 A.M. — 4:30 P.M. Pacific Standard Time)
Pay by check or money order, or use your American Express, VISA, or MasterCard.

Or fill out the coupon below, clip out and send to:
Osborne/McGraw-Hill, 2600 Tenth Street, Berkeley, CA, 94710, Attention: Supplementary Disk

- -

Please send me:

☐ Sets of *Windows Programming: An Introduction* supplementary disks — 5 1/4"
($29.95 for a set of three 5 1/4" disks plus $2.00 for postage and handling per set.) ISBN: 0-07-881581-9

☐ Copies of *Windows Programming: An Introduction* supplementary disks — 3 1/2"
($29.95 each plus $2.00 per disk package for postage and handling.) ISBN: 0-07-881582-7

Name: _____

Company: _____

Address: _____

City: _____ State: _____ ZIP: _____

Indicate method of payment.

☐ Check or Money Order # _____
(Please include shipping charge)

☐ VISA Card #   ☐ MasterCard #   ☐ American Express # _____

Expiration Date _____

 Signature _____

Allow 2 weeks for delivery — Prices subject to change without notice

This order subject to acceptance by McGraw-Hill — Offer good only in the U.S.A.